Lecture Notes in Computer Science 16243

Founding Editors

The series Lecture Notes in Computer Science (LNCS), including its subseries Lecture Notes in Artificial Intelligence (LNAI) and Lecture Notes in Bioinformatics (LNBI), has established itself as a medium for the publication of new developments in computer science and information technology research, teaching, and education.

LNCS enjoys close cooperation with the computer science R & D community, the series counts many renowned academics among its volume editors and paper authors, and collaborates with prestigious societies. Its mission is to serve this international community by providing an invaluable service, mainly focused on the publication of conference and workshop proceedings and postproceedings. LNCS commenced publication in 1973.

André Thomas · Michelle Meyer · Markus Zank
Editors

Serious Games

11th Joint International Conference, JCSG 2025
Lucerne, Switzerland, December 4–5, 2025
Proceedings

 Springer

Editors
André Thomas
Lucerne University of Applied Sciences
and Arts
Lucerne, Switzerland

Michelle Meyer
Lucerne University of Applied Sciences
and Arts
Lucerne, Switzerland

Markus Zank
Lucerne University of Applied Sciences
and Arts
Lucerne, Switzerland

ISSN 0302-9743   ISSN 1611-3349 (electronic)
Lecture Notes in Computer Science
ISBN 978-3-032-10517-2   ISBN 978-3-032-10518-9 (eBook)
https://doi.org/10.1007/978-3-032-10518-9

Preface

The Joint Conference on Serious Games 2025 (JCSG 2025) took place from December 3rd to December 5th, 2025, at Lucerne University of Applied Sciences in Lucerne, Switzerland. This year's conference once again served as a gathering point where participants with diverse backgrounds, including researchers, designers, developers, writers, health practitioners, and artists, could present and discuss innovative topics and challenges related to the field of serious games.

For JCSG 2025, we received 48 submissions from authors across multiple countries. After a comprehensive double-blind peer-review process with an average of 3.0 reviews per submission, we selected 35 papers for inclusion in these proceedings, resulting in an acceptance rate of 73%. Each submission underwent rigorous evaluation by our program committee members, with 26 papers receiving exactly 3 reviews, 11 papers receiving 2 reviews, 6 papers receiving 4 reviews, 3 papers receiving 5 reviews, and 1 paper receiving 6 reviews. One submission was desk rejected. Reviewers' feedback was provided to authors to facilitate subsequent revisions and improvement of their final manuscripts.

The selected papers cover various topics that reflect the breadth and depth of current serious games research. The contributions span multiple domains including artificial intelligence applications in games, educational technologies, healthcare and wellbeing applications, extended reality implementations, user experience design, accessibility and inclusion considerations, and impact studies measuring learning effectiveness.

The conference theme for 2025 focused on Target Audience. This theme was reflected throughout the program and guided the selection of keynote presentations, which provided inspiring insights into current developments and future directions in the field of serious games.

The contributions were presented through traditional talks and presentations, creating opportunities for meaningful dialogue and knowledge exchange among participants. The program was further enriched with concurrent presentations of posters, demos, and exhibits that showcased diverse applications and innovations related to serious games.

We would like to express our gratitude to all authors for submitting their high-quality research and participating in engaging discussions throughout the conference. We thank the keynote speakers for providing inspiring insights and thought-provoking perspectives on the current state and future potential of serious games. Our appreciation extends to the program committee members for their diligent and constructive reviews, which ensured the quality of the proceedings. We also thank the dedicated volunteers who contributed their time and effort to make the event successful, and we acknowledge the Steering Committee members who played a key role in shaping the conference direction and maintaining its scientific excellence.

December 2025

André Thomas
Michelle Meyer
Markus Zank

Organization

General Chair

André Thomas   Lucerne University of Applied Sciences and Arts, Switzerland

Paper Chair

Michelle Meyer   Lucerne University of Applied Sciences and Arts, Switzerland

Demo and Poster Chair

Markus Zank   Lucerne University of Applied Sciences and Arts, Switzerland

Steering Committee

Stefan Göbel   Technical University of Darmstadt, Germany
Minhua Eunice Ma   University of Surrey, UK
Jannike Baalsrud Hauge   Bremer Institut für Produktion und Logistik/University of Bremen, Germany
Manuel Fradinho Oliveira   SINTEF, Norway
Tim Marsh   Griffith University, Australia
Mads Haahr   Trinity College Dublin, Ireland
Heinrich Söbke   Hochschule Weserbergland und Bauhaus-Universität Weimar, Germany
Jan L. Plass   New York University, USA

Program Committee

Mariano Alcaniz   Universidad Politécnica Valencia, Spain
Jannicke Baalsrud Hauge   Bremer Institut für Produktion und Logistik /University of Bremen, Germany

Sara Bayat Hashemi	DePaul University, USA
Jeff Brenneman	New York University, USA
Michael Christel	Carnegie Mellon University, USA
Yannis Deliyannis	Ionian University, Greece
Ralf Doerner	RheinMain University of Applied Sciences, Germany
Kai Erenli	University of Applied Sciences BFI Vienna, Austria
Fabian Froehlich	New York University, USA
Augusto Garcia-Agundez	University of California, San Francisco, USA
Pedro González Calero	Universidad Politécnica de Madrid, Spain
Stefan Göbel	TU Darmstadt, Germany
Helmut Hlavacs	University of Vienna, Austria
Jun Hu	Eindhoven University of Technology, Netherlands
Michael Kickmeier-Rust	Graz University of Technology, Austria
David King	Griffith University, Australia
Troy Kohwalter	Universidade Federal Fluminense, Brazil
Minhua Ma	University of Surrey, UK
Tim Marsh	Griffith University, Australia
André Miede	Hochschule für Technik und Wirtschaft des Saarlandes, Germany
Wolfgang Mueller	University of Education Weingarten, Germany
Alvaro Olsen	New York University, USA
Sobah Abbas Petersen	Norwegian University of Science and Technology, Norway
Alexander Pfeiffer	Danube University Krems, Austria
Jan L. Plass	New York University — Games for Learning Institute, USA
Alberto Rojas-Salazar	Universidad de Costa Rica, Costa Rica
Nada Sharaf	German International University, Egypt
Laila Shoukry	TU Darmstadt, Germany
Martin Steinicke	University of Applied Sciences HTW Berlin, Germany
Heinrich Söbke	Hochschule Weserbergland und Bauhaus-Universität Weimar, Germany
André Thomas	Lucerne University of Applied Sciences and Arts, Switzerland
Daniel Tolks	Universität Rostock, Germany
Alf Inge Wang	Norwegian University of Science and Technology, Norway
David White	Staffordshire University, UK
Josef Wiemeyer	TU Darmstadt, Germany

Contents

Collaboration

Game Design/Development

Health

Target Audience

Exploring Competitive and Cooperative Orientations in Bartle's Taxonomy Through a GWAP Gameplay

Diogo Guimarães[1,3]([✉]) [iD], António Correia[2] [iD], Dennis Paulino[1] [iD],
Diogo Cabral[3] [iD], Miguel Teixeira[3] [iD], AT Netto[1,3] [iD], Walkir AT Brito[4] [iD],
and Hugo Paredes[1,3] [iD]

[1] INESC TEC - Instituto de Engenharia de Sistemas e Computadores, Tecnologia e
Ciência, R. Dr. Roberto Frias, Porto, Portugal
[2] University of Jyväskylä, Faculty of Information Technology, P.O. Box 35,
Jyväskylä 40014, Finland
[3] University of Trás-os-Montes e Alto Douro, UTAD, Quinta de Prados, Apartado
1013, Vila Real, Portugal
diogog@utad.pt
[4] Governo do Estado do Rio de Janeiro - Casa Cívil, Rio de Janeiro, Brazil

Abstract. As competitive and cooperative dynamics gain prominence in games, they present unique opportunities to study player behavior. This paper explores the orientations of different player types, as categorized by Bartles Taxonomy, through the lens of a Game With A Purpose (GWAP) called *BartleZ*. Bartle's Taxonomy identifies four distinct player types–Achievers, Explorers, Socializers, and Killers. This study delves into how these different types approach competitive and cooperative gameplay, through structured dilemmas in *BartleZ*. Results with 45 participants, reveal that player orientations significantly influence engagement and decision-making. Achievers balanced both strategies; Explorers favored cooperation; Socializers consistently chose cooperation; and Killers preferred competition but adapted in some contexts. Overall, players leaned toward cooperation early on, with a shift toward competition as complexity increased. Our findings pinpoint the importance of tailoring GWAP mechanics with diverse player motivations, enhancing both engagement and problem-solving effectiveness.

Keywords: Bartle Taxonomy · Human-Computer Interaction · GWAPs · Player Typologies · Competition · Cooperation

1 Introduction and Background

The design of engaging, personalized gaming experiences is central to both entertainment and serious applications. Understanding player orientations–Achievers, Explorers, Socializers, and Killers–via Bartle's Taxonomy [1] is key to tailoring interactions, especially in GWAPs, which blend entertainment with skill

A. Thomas et al. (Eds.): JCSG 2025, LNCS 16243, pp. 3–9, 2026.
https://doi.org/10.1007/978-3-032-10518-9_1

development and problem-solving [16]. Recent work shows that competitive and cooperative mechanics can influence GWAP participation and performance: collaborative versus competitive scoring had no adverse accuracy effects [13,14], personality traits correlate with output quality in tagging games [10,12], and social features boost meaningful contributions [9]. Moreover, inter-team competition has been found to drive engagement and recommendation intent more effectively than purely cooperative or competitive conditions [6].

Despite these insights, no study has explicitly examined how Bartle's player types respond to competitive and cooperative dynamics in GWAPs. While Siu et al. contrasted engagement and accuracy under different scoring schemes [13,14], and Jurgens and Navigli provided evidence on quality outputs in linguistic tasks [4], the mapping of these behaviors onto Achievers, Explorers, Socializers, and Killers remains unexplored. Morschheuser et al. call for investigations into how player typologies affect GWAP performance across social contexts [6]. To establish the novelty of this work, we performed a systematic literature review across IEEE Xplore, ACM DL, Scopus, and Google Scholar in July 2024 using search strings combining "Bartle taxonomy," "GWAP," "competition," "cooperation," and "crowdsourcing," yielding 4.998 records and, after screening, 27 primary studies. None of these directly explored Bartle's taxonomy in the context of competitive vs. cooperative GWAPs, confirming a critical research gap. To address this gap, we present *BartleZ*, a GWAP that embeds six Prisoner's Dilemmainspired competitive versus cooperative challenges between gameplay levels. Our research question (RQ1) is: Does player orientation in games, as classified by Bartle's taxonomy, influence the performance of crowd participants in competitive and cooperative GWAPs?

By correlating each participant's dominant Bartle type–determined in-game via psychometrically validated Player Type Decisions [3]–with their choices and task performance, we aim to reveal how different motivations shape engagement and effectiveness in both competitive and cooperative scenarios. This study thus provides the first empirical evidence linking Bartle player types to decision-making under competitive and cooperative dynamics in a GWAP, addressing the call by Morschheuser and co-authors [6] on how to tailor gamified crowd-work environments for diverse player motivations.

2   Methodology

In order to address RQ1, we conducted an online quasi-experimental design [2,15] using *BartleZ* to identify participants' dominant Bartle types and observe their behavior in competitive versus cooperative scenarios. Participants were recruited via a Google form shared on Facebook, Twitter, and X, where we collected only their Discord usernames (for server access), age group, and weekly gaming frequency to comply with data-protection standards and serve as control variables. Upon joining a dedicated Discord server, each participant received a unique identifier "PlayerX" to ensure anonymity during the study. The study was structured in two main phases: Recruitment and Gameplay.

2.1   BartleZ's Architecture and Gameflow

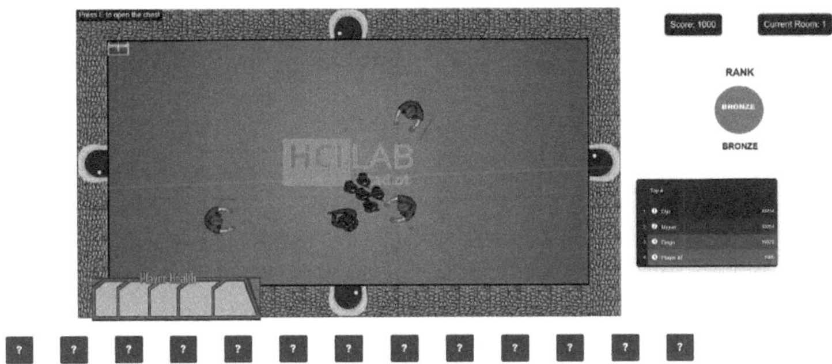

Fig. 1. BartleZ's design.

BartleZ (Fig. 1) is a 2D shooter-survival GWAP in which players clear seven zombie-infested rooms, earn points to climb six ascending ranks (from Bronze to Diamond) on a global leaderboard, and either collaborate with or compete against CPU-controlled crewmates. BartleZ's dual purpose is to serve as a lightweight, engaging assessment tool–classifying players into Bartle's four types via in-game decisions–and as an experimental GWAP platform for testing how competitive (leaderboard, weapon upgrades) and cooperative (CPU crewmate support, shared resources) mechanics influence performance. Each player starts with five non-player crewmates whose attack damage is set at 25% of the player's, providing supportive fire without overshadowing player agency. Its key features include in-game Player Type Decisions (PTDs) and Competitive vs. Cooperative Dilemmas (CvCs) between levels, treasure-and-badge challenges, a health bar with per-room signaling, and a points-based scoring system. In this research, we improved *BartleZ* to better accommodate both collaborative and competitive scenarios. For this study, we modified the game architecture to capture deeper insights into how different players engage with collaborative and competitive choices during gameplay.

The core loop consists of seven sequential rooms where participants must eliminate all CPU-controlled zombies to advance. Each room is laid out as a rectangle with four doors–only the door that unlocks upon clearing all zombies allows progression. While layouts remain constant, enemy count increases each level, culminating in a final "boss" zombie on Level 7 with elevated health and damage. Throughout each room, players collect hidden treasures for bonus points and earn badges for performance milestones. To "win", players must fully clear all rooms–including defeating the Level 7 boss–while maximizing score, rank, treasures, and badges. Between each room, the GWAP presents six PTDs–derived via a psychometric reduction of the "Bartle Test of Gamer Psychology"[1]. – to

---

[1] https://shared.xara.com/fGHo5UeoFC.

identify each player's dominant Bartle Taxonomy type. These six PTDs were selected through a two-stage process based on the research by Ermit and co-authors [3]: First, point-biserial correlations ($—r_pb—$ ≥ 0.50) identified items that best differentiated each Bartle pair; Second, exploratory factor analysis retained only items with loadings ≥ 0.50 and minimal cross-loadings.

We also inserted six CvCs during level transitions, each posing a trade-off between a self-serving (competitive) option and a team-oriented (cooperative) option in line with Prisoner's Dilemma principles. We chose a single-player format as an initial proof-of-concept to isolate player-type behaviors before exploring human-player interactions in future multiplayer versions. Upon completion of Room 7, the client-side `Player` JavaScript object–containing every measured variable–is serialized into JSON and sent to our REST API endpoint.

2.2 Competitive vs. Cooperative Dillemas (CvCs)

To examine how Bartle-type orientations influence strategic choices, we embedded six Prisoner's Dilemmainspired decisions between levels in *BartleZ* [7,8,11]. In CvC 1 (Weapon Strength), Defect grants the player a stronger weapon at the cost of one crewmate, whereas Cooperate arms all crewmates instead; CvC 2 (Points vs. Teammates) offers extra points by sacrificing a teammate or the addition of one crewmate; CvC 3 (Health Distribution) allows the player to heal fully (+20 Health Points (HP)) while each crewmate loses 10 HP, or to share a +10 HP bonus with everyone; CvC 4 (Time vs. Crewmates) lets the player finish the next level under 30 s for +300 points or recruit an extra crewmate; CvC 5 (Firepower Boost) trades an individual firepower increase against boosting the entire team; and CvC 6 (Boss Fight) rewards facing the final boss solo with +500 points or facing it together with crewmates. Each Defect choice enhances individual standing through *BartleZ*'s competitive systems (points, leaderboard, ranking), while Cooperate choices foster teamwork. By correlating participants' dominant Bartle types–Killers, Achievers, Explorers, and Socializers–with their CvC selections and in-game performance, we investigate how different player motivations drive competitive versus cooperative behavior.

3   Results and Discussion

A total of 45 participants took part in the study. The sample was predominantly young adults–71.11% were aged 1824, with smaller proportions in the 2534 (11.11%), 3544 (2.22%), and 4554 (11.11%) brackets–which aligns with findings that younger gamers engage more frequently and comfortably with rapid in-game decisions [5]. Likewise, over 60% played at least three times per week (44.44% playing five or more times weekly), indicating a cohort of experienced gamers familiar with competitive and cooperative mechanics. Upon completing *BartleZ*, player types–determined via six in-game Player Type Decisions–were distributed as follows: Achievers (11.11%), Explorers (17.78%), Socializers (13.33%), Killers (13.33%), ExplorerSocializers (17.78%), and smaller composite groups: KAS (2.22%), KA (2.22%), AES (6.67%), AE (4.44%), AS (2.22%), KE (4.44%), KES (2.22%), and KS (2.22%). This diversity–both single and composite dominant types–provides a comprehensive foundation for analyzing how different motivations shape engagement and performance in competitive versus cooperative scenarios [3].

3.1 Comparative Performance Analysis

Across all 45 participants, cooperative choices were made 58.52% of the time versus 41.48% competitive, establishing a cooperative baseline. Decision times averaged between 5.19 s (CvC 2) and 9.80 s (CvC 1), with low variance except for an outlier in CvC 6. When broken down by Bartle type, clear patterns emerge. Achievers chose competitive options 52.56% overall–peaking at 69.23% in the time-vs-crewmates dilemma (CvC 4) and remaining above 60% in weapon strength (CvC 1) and firepower boost (CvC 5)–yet still cooperated 47.44% of the time and made decisions in 6.310.7 s. Explorers favored cooperation (63.89% overall), exceeding 80% in health distribution (CvC 3), points vs. teammates (CvC 2), and boss fight (CvC 6), with response times of 4.610.2 s (excluding the CvC 6 outlier). Socializers were even more cooperative (79.37% overall), choosing teamwork over 90% in CvC 2, 3, and 6, and decided in 5.011.6 s. Conversely, Killers opted for competition 63.89% overall–rising to 91.67% in CvC 4 and 83.33% in CvC 5–yet showed surprising cooperation (58.33%) in CvC 2 and CvC 3, with decision times of 4.9510.6 s. These results confirm that Achievers and Killers lean toward competitive strategies, while Explorers and Socializers prefer cooperation, though all types can adapt their choices–and maintain rapid decision-making.

3.2 Statistical Behavioral Analysis by Bartle Player Type

The dataset was preprocessed by removing statistical outliers using the interquartile range method applied to decision times. To ensure comparability across base types, each player was counted once for each type they belonged to, creating a normalized behavioral representation. We then analyzed the average number of competitive and cooperative decisions, as well as mean decision times for each player. This initial exploration allowed us to identify trends consistent with Bartle's player typology, forming the basis for subsequent statistical testing.

To assess the significance of observed behavioral differences, we employed a Kruskal-Wallis test, which revealed statistically significant variation in competitive behavior among Bartle types (H = 15.54, p = 0.0014). Post hoc analysis with Dunn's test identified group differences, showing that Killers and Achievers were significantly more competitive than Socializers ($p < 0.05$). A correlation analysis further confirmed expected behavioral patterns: Killers were positively associated with competition ($r \approx +0.28$) and negatively with cooperation ($r \approx -0.28$), while Socializers displayed the inverse relationship. These statistical results support the theoretical distinctions in strategic orientation proposed by Bartle. Descriptive data further illustrate these tendencies: Killers exhibited the highest proportion of competitive choices, followed by Achievers, whereas Socializers and Explorers showed a clear preference for cooperation. Decision time also varied by type, with Socializers taking the longest to decide and Killers the shortest, suggesting differences in decision-making style. These findings have implications for player-centric game design, particularly in Games With a Purpose (GWAPs), where aligning motivational profiles with gameplay elements can enhance both engagement and task effectiveness.

4   Final Remarks, Limitations and Future Work

With this study we investigated how competitive and cooperative orientations impact player engagement and performance within the BartleZ GWAP, yielding actionable insights for game designers. Achievers balanced competitive and cooperative strategies to optimize progress; Explorers and Socializers showed strong preferences for cooperation, especially when it facilitated discovery and social interaction; and Killers gravitated toward competition, yet occasionally cooperated when contexts aligned with game incentives. Decision-time analysis revealed consistently low cognitive load across CvC dilemmas, confirming that in-game choices reliably reflect player motivations. However, our work has several limitations. The relatively small sample (N = 45) of predominantly 1824-year-olds may constrain generalizability, and the third-person, single-player zombie-shooter format–with fixed room layouts–may not extend to other genres or true multiplayer settings. Although each CvC choice dynamically branched gameplay parameters (e.g., weapon power, crewmate count), we did not collect gender data or fine-grained session-duration metrics, precluding analyses of how these factors interact with player type. Future research should validate these findings in larger, more diverse populations and across varied game genres and multiplayer environments. Capturing demographic variables (e.g., gender), session-length patterns, and richer branching or narrative adaptations triggered by player-type or CvC outcomes will deepen our understanding of how to tailor GWAP mechanics. Longitudinal studies combining multiple deployments can further strengthen causal inferences and guide the design of personalized, motivation-aligned gamified systems for crowd-work and beyond.

Acknowledgements. This work is financed by the FCT Fundao para a Cincia e a Tecnologia (Portuguese Foundation for Science and Technology) with research grant 2022.13699.BD. The authors also acknowledge support from the European Social Fund under the scope of North Portugal Regional Operational Programme. The final manuscript was revised and approved by all authors. No potential conflict of interest was reported by the authors.

References

1. Bartle, R.: Hearts, clubs, diamonds, spades: players who suit muds. J. MUD Res. **1**(1), 19 (1996)
2. Cook, T.D., Campbell, D.T., Shadish, W.: Experimental and quasi-experimental designs for generalized causal inference, vol. 1195. Houghton Mifflin Boston, MA (2002)
3. Fiş Erümit, S., Şılbır, L., Erümit, A.K., Karal, H.: Determination of player types according to digital game playing preferences: scale development and validation study. Int. J. Hum. Comput. Int. **37**(11), 991–1002 (2021)
4. Jurgens, D., Navigli, R.: It's all fun and games until someone annotates: video games with a purpose for linguistic annotation. Trans. Assoc. Comput. Linguistics **2**, 449–464 (2014)
5. Meriläinen, M.: Young people's engagement with digital gaming cultures–validating and developing the digital gaming relationship theory. entertainment computing, 44, 100538 (2022)
6. Morschheuser, B., Hamari, J., Maedche, A.: Cooperation or competition-when do people contribute more? a field experiment on gamification of crowdsourcing. Int. J. Hum Comput Stud. **127**, 7–24 (2019)
7. Myerson, R.B.: Game theory. Harvard university press (2013)
8. Owen, G.: Game theory. Emerald Group Publishing (2013)
9. Paraschakis, D., Friberger, M.G.: Playful crowdsourcing of archival metadata through social networks (2014)
10. Pe-Than, E.P.P., Goh, D.H.L., Lee, C.S.: Personality, motivations, and information quality: a comparative study across games for human computation. Proc. Assoc. Inf. Sci. Technol. **53**(1), 1–10 (2016)
11. Poundstone, W.: Prisoner's dilemma. Anchor (2011)
12. Simko, J., Tvarozek, M., Bielikova, M.: Little search game: term network acquisition via a human computation game. In: Proceedings of the 22nd ACM Conference on Hypertext and Hypermedia, pp. 57–62 (2011)
13. Siu, K., Guzdial, M., Riedl, M.O.: Evaluating singleplayer and multiplayer in human computation games. In: Proceedings of the 12th International Conference on the Foundations of Digital Games, pp. 1–10 (2017)
14. Siu, K., Zook, A., Riedl, M.O.: Collaboration versus competition: design and evaluation of mechanics for games with a purpose. FDG **10**, 14–22 (2014)
15. Stanley, J.C., Campbell, D.T.: Experimental and quasi-experimental designs for research. R. McNally, Chicago (1963)
16. Von Ahn, L.: Games with a purpose. Computer **39**(6), 92–94 (2006)

Designing a Multiplayer Computer Serious Game for Disaster Management Training

Parastoo Akbari[(✉)], Rhoda Asamoah, Samantha Edwards, Cameron A. MacKenzie, and Eliot H. Winer

Iowa State University of Science and Technology, Ames, IA, USA
`parastoo@iastate.edu`

Abstract. The emergency management community faces challenges in preparing for and responding to high-impact, weather-related disasters. Traditional training methods, such as tabletop exercises and full-scale drills, often fall short in replicating the complexity, uncertainty, and time-sensitive decision making required in real disaster situations. This paper highlights the need for a novel multiplayer, serious computer game to help train emergency management professionals. Informed by interviews with thirteen emergency management professionals in the United States, we propose a framework for a serious disaster game. The framework for the game has players acting in different emergency management roles working together to respond to an extreme weather event.

Keywords: Emergency Management · Training Games · Serious Game Design

1   Introduction

High-impact weather-related disasters are increasing in frequency and cost, with 28 and 27 billion-dollar events in the U.S. in 2023 and 2024, compared to 10 in 2013 and 2014 [1]. Despite major investments in mitigation and resilience, communities still struggle with recovery [2–8]. While having a plan is essential, effective implementation requires repeated exercises and engagement. The U.S. Federal Emergency Management Agency (FEMA) defines preparedness as a continuous cycle of planning, organizing, training, equipping, exercising, evaluating, and corrective action [9]. Many emergency management (EM) personnel are not routinely involved in preparedness activities, however. Current training activities such as online modules, tabletop exercises, and full-scale drills, are often rigid, costly, and lack realistic decision-making pressure [10].

Various disaster simulation games have been developed to enhance emergency preparedness, appearing in both academic literature and as publicly accessible tools. Simulation games are shown to support preparedness, communication, and decision making during emergencies [11–14]. Games targeting the general public

© The Author(s), under exclusive license to Springer Nature Switzerland AG 2026
A. Thomas et al. (Eds.): JCSG 2025, LNCS 16243, pp. 10–18, 2026.
https://doi.org/10.1007/978-3-032-10518-9_2

often use interactive storytelling to teach effective responses [15]. Other games are built for professionals and span diverse formats such as web-based simulations [16–18], virtual/mixed reality environments [18,19], and non-digital formats like board games [20]. A few games have been proposed for both professionals and the public, simulating scenarios such as a weapon of mass destruction [21] and an earthquake impacting a hospital [22]. A gap remains in linking games to community engagement and planning [23] and tasks in EM response. Future research should focus on rigorous evaluation, standardization, integration with existing training, and privacy-sensitive design [24,25].

Publicly accessible games often focus on education and awareness. Games like Disaster Master [26], Disaster Mind [27], Build a Kit [28], Stop Disasters [29], Cascadia [30], and Philippines Disaster Preparedness Simulator [31] are aimed at helping the general public understand emergency response through interactive scenarios. Several publicly available disaster computer games, including 3D computer games such as 1-1-2 Operator [32], Incident Commander [33], and Emergency 20 [34] allow players to assume the role of an emergency manager or first responder, but their purpose is not to help train EM professionals. Flashing Lights [35] and Responding Emergency Services Simulator Sandbox [36] offer open-world environments where users act as police, emergency medical services (EMS), or firefighters with AI-driven incidents. Additional tools like Immersed (Floodwalk) [37] and Disaster Scope [38] use virtual reality (VR) and augmented reality (AR) to deliver immersive disaster training experiences. To date, there is no publicly available multiplayer online game specifically designed to train EM decision makers in preparing for and responding to extreme weather events.

To overcome current training challenges and meet a need that current games do not satisfy, this paper presents a novel framework for a multiplayer computer game that simulates realistic disaster scenarios to train EM decision makers. The game would bring EM professionals together in an engaging, online simulation. The game promotes learning of EM roles, collaboration, and decision making under uncertainty. These learning objectives are based on input from EM professionals and are designed to address real-world training gaps.

2   Interviews with Emergency Management Professionals

2.1   Participants and Data Collection

We invited EM professionals in the state of Iowa to offer their thoughts on the design of a serious game framework for disaster management training. Thirteen individuals (8 men, 5 women) agreed to be interviewed, with experience ranging from 4 to 26 (average $\approx$ 20) years. Participants included three officials from the Iowa Department of Homeland Security and Emergency Management, five county emergency managers, three fire department officials, one healthcare preparedness coordinator, and one training officer in the energy industry.

All interviews were conducted virtually via Microsoft Teams and lasted approximately 45 minutes. After the participants introduced themselves, we explained the study's purpose and asked a series of semi-structured questions, using follow-up prompts as needed. The interview questions were:

- What is your role in emergency management?
- What are your responsibilities when a disaster happens?
- What are your biggest challenges in preparedness and response?
- What types of training do you or others typically do (e.g., tabletop exercises, drills)?
- How often do you train with other organizations?
- How effective are your current training tools, and how do you assess them?
- What learning objectives should a disaster game focus on?
- What do you think is a good scenario for a training game?
- What other skills or areas require more training?
- How do you coordinate with other organizations during a disaster, and what communication challenges arise?
- How could a multiplayer online game help improve inter-agency collaboration?
- How do you evaluate your agency or community's preparedness?
- How would you assess the effectiveness of a multiplayer training game (e.g., pre/post assessments or in-game scoring)?
- Would you be interested in future involvement in this project?

Interviews were audio-recorded and transcribed. Each transcript was then read line by line, and recurring ideas were grouped to identify common themes.

2.2 Insights from Interviews

The participants identified two major challenges in emergency preparedness and response. First, inadequate planning, especially for resource deployment and transportation needs, hinders effective emergency response operations. Geographical diffusion, especially in rural and underserved areas, introduces significant delays due to the time needed to move resources and EMS personnel [39]. Hospitals often lack staff and space [40], utility companies are poorly integrated, and coordination suffers when key personnel miss meetings. Local plans may also misalign with state priorities. Second, budget limits reduce access to equipment, supplies, and staff. Agencies struggle with expense tracking, delayed FEMA reimbursements, and funding approvals. All participants agreed a multiplayer computer game could improve preparedness by letting users practice allocate resources and assign personnel to different tasks under time pressure.

Participants described different training practices, with workshops, seminars, and tabletop exercises favored for their low cost and flexibility. Full-scale drills were less common due to planning demands. In-person formats were preferred over passive online training. The frequency of training ranged from frequent small-scale drills to large simulations requiring over a year to plan. Evaluating training was mostly informal and lacked standardized metrics. Resource constraints and funding issues further limited training efforts. Many participants supported virtual simulations or games to enhance realism without disrupting operations.

Inexperienced personnel often lack decision-making skills and procedural knowledge, highlighting the need for effective training. Traditional methods face barriers such as time constraints, interruptions, overtime costs, and low engagement. Agencies also struggle with resistance to documentation, limited leadership involvement, and skepticism toward written plans and drills. Tabletop exercises often appear unrealistic, and poor coordination leads to unclear roles. Participants believed a multiplayer computer game as a scalable, remote solution to improve engagement, collaboration, and role clarity.

Participants reported using multiple communication tools during emergency response, including email, text, phone calls, and virtual meeting tools. The incident command system (ICS) structures guide decision making, and mass casualty incident (MCI) alerts are sent to fire, EMS, and hospitals. Public messaging relies on media and alert systems. Despite this, issues persist, such as internet outages, complex radio coordination, and delayed or missing information. Hospitals often receive patients before formal notification. A multiplayer game could address these gaps by allowing real-time communication, role-specific collaboration, and shared decision making.

3   Serious Game Design for Disaster Scenarios

Existing disaster simulation games do not fully address the real-world challenges emergency professionals face. Participants repeatedly emphasized inconsistent coordination, poor engagement, limited role clarity, and unrealistic training. While some games simulate aspects of emergencies, none provide an integrated, multiplayer platform capturing the time pressure, resource scarcity, and inter-agency coordination experienced during actual disasters. We propose a multiplayer serious game for disaster management training to address these challenges. The design framework is based on Schell's [41] elemental tetrad: story, mechanics, technology, and aesthetics to ensure a structured, engaging and effective experience.

3.1   Game Story

Sequential Narrative Phases. The proposed disaster training game is structured around a realistic weather-related emergency scenario, such as a tornado, hurricane, or wildfire, threatening a defined population and geographic area. The scenario unfolds through four sequential narrative phases: immediate preparation, disaster impact, incident management, and evaluation. In the immediate preparation phase, players receive an alert about an approaching weather event and must quickly decide how to use their available resources. The lead time until the weather event depends on the specific weather event. At this stage, each player makes independent decisions under time pressure based on the information available through their own resources. The disaster impact phase simulates the onset of the event using audiovisual effects and sporadic updates about the situation on the ground. In the incident management phase, players are expected to coordinate response efforts among themselves. This includes activating the ICS, allocating personnel and equipment to specific locations in the impacted area, and responding to dynamic scenario injects. Players must manage operations such as emergency transport, road clearance, and public communication. Once the simulated crisis is stabilized, the evaluation phase begins. A facilitator leads a structured debriefing session to encourage player reflection on performance, coordination, and decision making. The game framework should support the ability to play the game again through scenario customization and role rotation, enabling participants to experience different perspectives and reinforce learning through repeated engagement.

Dynamic Injects. The game should include injects to simulate the unpredictability of real emergencies. These can be random or facilitator-driven challenges, such as injured individuals, elderly people requiring assistance, separated families, power outages, communication failures, gas leaks, unsafe buildings, and hospital capacity constraints. The players will need to work together to prioritize among these different requests for resources and determine how best to manage their assets (e.g., people, vehicles, generators) to respond effectively. Injects mirror real-world conditions and support evaluation of response capabilities.

3.2   Game Mechanics

Role-Playing. The interviewed participants emphasized that the game should improve players' understanding of emergency management roles and responsibilities. The game framework includes several roles such as county emergency manager, law enforcement, fire department, EMS, public works, hospital staff, mayor's office, and utility services, depending on the scenario and audience. Each player will assume one of those roles. Each role should have distinct responsibilities and limited resources, presented in a resource dashboard. Players should be required to make time-sensitive decisions related to their responsibilities. Allowing players to rotate roles across sessions promotes a better understanding of both their own duties and those of other agencies.

Decision Prompts. Decision prompts will appear on the screen, requiring players to respond to dynamic, role-specific situations. For example, during the incident management phase, EMS may transport patients and request road clearance from public works. The mayor's office may be prompted to decide what messages to broadcast to the public. These time-sensitive questions and answers can simulate real-world actions and promote critical thinking and knowledge retention through the game-play experience [42].

Fostering Collaboration. Almost all participants highlighted communication and collaboration as ongoing challenges in emergency response. The game will aim to foster these skills by initially having players operate independently and manage resources within their roles. Activating the ICS enables coordination and information sharing through an in-game communication panel. Without the ICS, players have limited visibility into others' actions, leading to weaker coordination and point deductions. This design reinforces the importance of timely interagency collaboration.

Point-Based Evaluation Approach. Participants preferred a real-time, point-based evaluation system integrated into the game to provide immediate feedback. Performance should be assessed via an in-game dashboard capturing ICS activation timeliness, resource deployment efficiency, responsiveness to injects, interagency coordination, and harm reduction to civilians.

3.3   Game Technology

Remote Participation. Participants noted low engagement in traditional training due to time and location constraints. The framework addresses this by enabling remote participation across platforms, including desktops, laptops, and potentially tablets, increasing flexibility and accessibility.

Virtual Environment. A virtual environment built in Unity [43] can use 3D models of city elements like buildings, vehicles, and people, including post-disaster damage and debris. Custom lighting and shaders enhance realism, and virtual cameras offer both 2D and 3D views based on player roles.

3.4   Game Aesthetics

Immersive Simulation. Game aesthetics shape how players experience the environment through sensory input [41]. AI-generated multimedia, such as disaster videos, audio injects, and ambient sounds, can enhance realism and engagement in the game [44]. The game environment should feature an interactive bird's-eye view with zoom options for immersive, role-specific interaction.

Emotional Design. Participants emphasized the need to reflect the time pressure and psychological stress of real emergencies. The game design incorporates urgent decision prompts, limited resources, scenario injects, and realistic audio-visual cues such as sirens and crowd noise to evoke emotional responses and create a flow state, enhancing focus, immersion, and learning [45, 46].

4   Conclusion

This paper presents a conceptual framework for a multiplayer serious game to address gaps in emergency management training. Informed by interviews with thirteen professionals and a review of existing tools, the framework incorporates role-specific tasks, scenario injects, and decision making under time and resource constraints. By simulating a weather-related disaster in an immersive, collaborative environment, the game aims to improve communication, situational awareness, and adaptive thinking. Designed to supplement existing training, the game will help professionals better understand their roles and those of partner agencies while practicing decision making in realistic conditions. Future work will develop and create the game for emergency managers in Iowa. Research will focus on evaluating learning outcomes from this game and integrating the game into training programs to support preparedness and resilience.

References

1. National Centers for Environmental Information: Billion-Dollar Weather and Climate Disasters. National Oceanic and Atmospheric Administration. https://www.ncei.noaa.gov/access/billions/ (2025)
2. United Nations Office for Disaster Risk Reduction. GAR Special Report 2023: Mapping Resilience for the Sustainable Development Goals. UNDRR. https://www.undrr.org/gar/gar2023-special-report (2023)
3. Tierney, K.: The Social Roots of Risk: Producing Disasters. Promoting Resilience. Stanford University Press, Stanford (2020)
4. Sohrabi, S., Darestani, Y., Pringle, W., Dowden, D., Dehghanian, P.: Life cycle cost analysis of prestressed concrete poles subjected to wind surges and waves. J. Struct, Eng (2025)
5. Jagani, S., Deng, X., Hong, P.C., Mashhadi Nejad, N.: Adopting sustainability business models for value creation and delivery: an empirical investigation of manufacturing firms. J. Manuf. Technol. Manag. **35**(2), 360–382 (2024)
6. Cutter, S.L.: Community resilience, natural hazards, and climate change: Is the present a prologue to the future? Norsk Geogr. Tidsskr. **74**(3), 200–208 (2020)
7. Suresh, R., Akbari, P., MacKenzie, C.A.: A value-focused thinking approach to measure community resilience. arXiv preprint arXiv:2408.00901 (2024)
8. Shukla, C., MacKenzie, C.A.: Time series analysis and probabilistic model of the financial costs of major disasters in the USA. Environ. Syst. Decis. **44**(1), 30–44 (2024)
9. Federal Emergency Management Agency: Prevention and Preparedness Resources. https://training.fema.gov/programs/emischool/el361toolkit/preventionresources.htm (2024)
10. Sinclair, H., Doyle, E.E., Johnston, D.M., Paton, D.: Assessing emergency management training and exercises. Disaster Prev Manag **21**(4), 507–521 (2012)
11. Jenvald, J., Morin, M.: Simulation-supported live training for emergency response in hazardous environments. Simul. Gaming **35**(3), 363–377 (2004)
12. Williams-Bell, F.M., Kapralos, B., Hogue, A., Murphy, B.M., Weckman, E.J.: Using serious games and virtual simulation for training in the fire service: a review. Fire Technol. **51**, 553–584 (2015)
13. Gampell, A.V., Gaillard, J.C.: Stop disasters 2.0: Video games as tools for disaster risk reduction. Int. J. Mass Emerg. Disasters 34(2), 283–316 (2016)
14. Perreault, G., Perreault, M.W., Van Dyke, M.: The power of digital games in disaster preparation and post-disaster resilience. In: 2017 International Communication Association Conference (2017)
15. Pillai, K., Muhobuth, M.A., Nowbuth, M.D., Pudaruth, S.: Emergency preparedness through game playing. Environ. Hazards **18**(1), 43–61 (2019)
16. Galbusera, L., Cardarilli, M., Gómez, M.L., Giannopoulos, G.: Game-based training in critical infrastructure protection and resilience. Int. J. Disaster Risk Reduct. **78**, 103109 (2022)

17. Asplund, T., Neset, T.S., Käyhkö, J., Wiréhn, L., Juhola, S.: Benefits and challenges of serious gaming-the case of "The Maladaptation Game". Open Agric. **4**(1), 107–117 (2019)
18. Altan, B., Görer, S., Alsamarei, A., Demir, D.K., Düzgün, H.Ş, Erkayaoğlu, M., Surer, E.: Developing serious games for CBRN-e training in mixed reality, virtual reality, and computer-based environments. Int. J. Disaster Risk Reduct. **77**, 103022 (2022)
19. Peretti, O., Spyridis, Y., Sesis, A., Efstathopoulos, G.: Gamified first responder training solution in virtual reality. In: 2021 17th Int. Conf. Distributed Computing in Sensor Systems (DCOSS), pp. 295–301. IEEE (2021)
20. de Ruiter, M.C., Couasnon, A., Ward, P.J.: Breaking the Silos: An online serious game for multi-risk disaster risk reduction (DRR) management. Geosci. Commun. **4**(3) (2021)
21. Richardson, T.J.: First responder: weapons of mass destruction training using massively multiplayer on-line gaming. PhD thesis, Naval Postgraduate School, Monterey (2004)
22. Feng, Z., González, V.A., Amor, R., Spearpoint, M., Thomas, J., Sacks, R., Lovreglio, R., Cabrera-Guerrero, G.: An immersive virtual reality serious game to enhance earthquake behavioral responses and post-earthquake evacuation preparedness in buildings. Adv. Eng. Inform. **45**, 101118 (2020)
23. Kankanamge, N., Yigitcanlar, T., Goonetilleke, A., Kamruzzaman, M.: How can gamification be incorporated into disaster emergency planning? a systematic review of the literature. Int. J. Disaster Resil. Built Environ. **11**(4), 481–506 (2020)
24. Baetzner, A.S., et al.: Preparing medical first responders for crises: a systematic literature review of disaster training programs and their effectiveness. Scand. J. Trauma Resusc. Emerg. Med. **30**(1), 76 (2022)
25. Whitfill, T., et al.: Cost-effectiveness of a video game versus live simulation for disaster training. BMJ Simul. Technol. Enhanc. Learn. **6**(5), 268 (2020)
26. U.S. Department of Homeland Security: Disaster Master. https://www.ready.gov/kids/games/data/dm-english/index.html (2025)
27. ithrive Games: Disaster Mind. https://ithrivegames.org/disaster-mind/ (2025)
28. U.S. Department of Homeland Security: ReadyKids: Games. https://www.ready.gov/kids/games (2024)
29. United Nations Office for Disaster Risk Reduction: Play and Learn to Stop Disasters. https://www.stopdisastersgame.org/ (2024)
30. Krause, K.: Can a video game prepare us for the Big One? Portland Monthly, PreventionWeb (2024)
31. George, M., Oliva, E.: Philippines Disaster Preparedness Simulator. https://alnap.org/help-library/resources/philippines-disaster-preparedness-simulator/ (2019)
32. 112 Operator. https://store.steampowered.com/app/793460/112_Operator/ (2025)
33. Incident Commander. https://store.steampowered.com/app/1096610/Incident_Commander/ (2025)
34. Emergency 20. https://store.steampowered.com/app/735280/EMERGENCY_20/ (2025)
35. Flashing Lights – Police, Firefighting, Emergency Medical Services (EMS) Simulator. https://store.steampowered.com/app/605740/Flashing_Lights_Police_Firefighting_Emergency_Services_EMS_Simulator/ (2025)
36. Responding. https://www.playresponding.com/ (2025)
37. Floodwalk for iOS. https://download.cnet.com/floodwalk/3000-20414_4-78235801.html (2025)

38. Estela, O., George, M.: Disaster Scope. https://www.preventionweb.net/publication/disaster-scope (2019)
39. Li, X., Maghelal, P., Arlikatti, S., Dorsett, C.: Review of evacuee mobilization challenges causing time-lag: Conceptualizing a new framework. Emerg. Manag. Sci. Technol. 1, 1–9 (2022). https://doi.org/10.48130/EMST-2022-0020
40. Arogyaswamy, S., et al.: The impact of hospital capacity strain: a qualitative analysis of experience and solutions at 13 academic medical centers. J. Gen. Intern. Med., 1–12 (2021). https://doi.org/10.1007/s11606-021-07106-8
41. Schell, J.: The Art of Game Design: A Book of Lenses. CRC Press, Boca Raton (2008)
42. Arnab, S., et al.: Mapping learning and game mechanics for serious games analysis. Br. J. Educ. Technol. **46**(2), 391–411 (2015)
43. Unity Technologies: Unity Real-Time Development Platform — 3D, 2D, VR & AR Engine. https://unity.com/, Accessed May 2025
44. Zhang, Z., et al.: Simulating Classroom Education with LLM-Empowered Agents. arXiv preprint arXiv:2406.19226 (2024)
45. Alexiou, A., Schippers, M.C., Oshri, I., Angelopoulos, S.: Narrative and aesthetics as antecedents of perceived learning in serious games. Inf. Technol. People **35**(8), 142–161 (2022)
46. Loderer, K., Pekrun, R., Plass, J.L.: Emotional foundations of game-based learning. In: Handbook of Game-Based Learning, pp. 111–151. MIT Press, Cambridge (2020)

Iterative Design of a Serious Game
for Medical Training

Lyvia Streich[1,2], Warisara Suksmaran[1,2], Nicolas Szilas[1(✉)] [iD],
and Claire Dupont[2]

[1] TECFA-FPSE, University of Geneva, Geneva, Switzerland
`nicolas.szilas@unige.ch`
[2] UDREM, Faculty of Medicine, University of Geneva, Geneva, Switzerland
`claire.dupont@unige.ch`

Abstract. This article presents the development of an intrinsically integrated educational video game designed to train medical students and residents on the importance of formative feedback and how to deliver it effectively. Through this design case study, we describe the iterative methodology followed and its critical role in achieving a high-quality outcome.

Keywords: serious game · iterative design · interdisciplinarity · formative feedback · medical training

1 Designing Educational Games

1.1 Intrinsic Integration

In the domain of serious games, It is often claimed that merging the pedagogical content with the game elements, and in particular with the main game mechanics, is essential [1–4]. However, in practice, designing such a game remains a challenge, as illustrated by the large number of serious games that, despite their visual quality, are poorly integrated [5,6].

Intrinsic integration is difficult to achieve because it requires tailoring a specific game mechanic for each learning domain; inventing a new game mechanic is particularly complex and even uncommon in commercial video games.

So, in the field of intrinsically integrated educational video games, there's no universal recipe, nor generic games [7], nor any other easy-to-follow systematic procedure. Nevertheless, there are a few general principles to bear in mind: 1) Multidimensionality – intrinsic integration cannot be summed up in a binary assessment (integrated or not). On the contrary, it's a gradual, multidimensional notion [4,8,9]; 2) Interdisciplinarity: designing an educational video game requires close collaboration between experts from a variety of disciplines (including instructional design and game design); and 3) Iterativity: like any game, an educational video game cannot be designed in one shot. It requires multiple confrontations with players (at least the designers themselves). This is due to the fundamentally experiential and subjective nature of games [10].

A. Thomas et al. (Eds.): JCSG 2025, LNCS 16243, pp. 19–26, 2026.
https://doi.org/10.1007/978-3-032-10518-9_3

The aim of this article is to detail a concrete design case, in order to describe how, from an initial request, an intrinsically integrated educational video game can be progressively developed.

1.2   Context

The game presented below was designed and produced in an academic context, by master students, in a project-based learning environment[1]. The initial request comes from an external sponsor. This context means that some of the professional skills needed to develop a video game (e.g. graphics) may be lacking, that there is no specific budget beyond the time devoted to the project and that the sponsor's involvement is moderate (the project is free and not critical to the sponsor). These constraints, while limiting, also allow a certain creative freedom and enable the team to focus on the essential aspects of the game playability and pedagogy.

2   Learning Domain: Medical Feedback

The sponsor is the Faculty of Medicine at the University of Geneva, dedicated to training doctors at pre- and postgraduate levels. The latter benefit from supervision of supervisors, such as postgraduate doctors and heads of clinics, who require appropriate pedagogical support.

Feedback is a lever in medical training, promoting the development of skills and medical posture. It is also one of the most influential factors in learner success [11]. The PROFILES reference framework encourages respectful and inclusive communication within teams [12]. Feedback training helps teachers, staff and learners to become more comfortable and confident with giving and receiving feedback [13]. The theoretical basis of this project is based on Pendleton's method [14], which proposes five steps for constructive feedback:

1. Learner self-assessment
2. Identification of positive points by the supervisor through direct (observation) or indirect (situation report) supervision
3. Weaknesses identified by the learner
4. Constructive feedback from the supervisor
5. Joint feedback summary [13]

This method structures two-way feedback, balancing positive points and improvements, encouraging reflection, motivation and collaborative learning.

The target audience consists of postgraduate doctors, i.e. practitioners who have obtained their diploma and the right to practise medicine. These doctors work under the supervision of clinic managers.

As Henderson and colleagues [15] point out, accurate, actionable feedback is essential to enable learners to progress in their practice. These authors also

---

[1] https://tecfa.unige.ch/jeux/.

emphasize the importance of training both supervisors and learners to maximise the benefits of feedback. It fosters a culture where strengths and areas for improvement can be discussed without fear of judgement.

Besides, this target audience plays a key role in the supervision of trainees in pre-graduate training (Master in human medicine), being the first hierarchical interlocutors responsible for their daily follow-up. The long-term aim is to promote the practice of feedback at all stages of a doctor's training.

3 The Game

3.1 Narrative Dimension

The learning content, focused essentially on interpersonal relationships, led to the decision to use a narrative game design, in which the story plays a predominant role. The story follows a classic narrative pattern of transformation, from a heroine who is incompetent in supervision to one who is competent.

Furthermore, clinical supervision requires a certain decentering, i.e. the ability to adopt a different point of view: today's resident is yesterday's trainee and tomorrow's doctor. In this multi-role context, it is essential to know how to give and receive feedback constructively. This story takes full advantage of this, through the theme of dreams and the accompanying role changes. It incorporates numerous characters to illustrate the complexity of the relationships between all these professional roles, not forgetting the patients. Although the scene takes place in a hospital, realism is not the aim: the tone used is deliberately offbeat and humorous, going so far as to parody the film Matrix, which gives the game its name (Fig. 1).

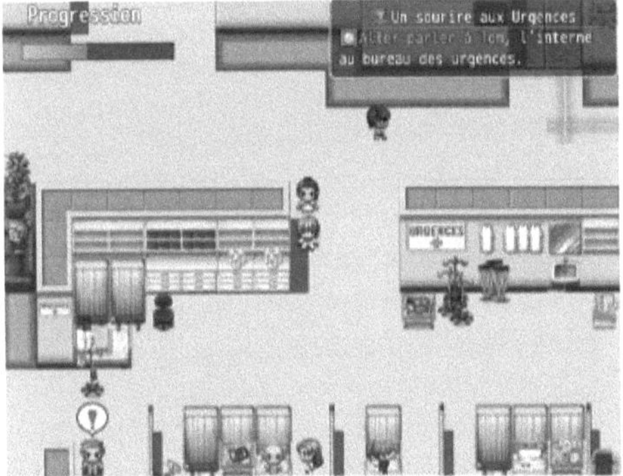

Fig. 1. Sample mission (top right) and overview of the player dashboard.

In Medtrix, players take on the role of Nea, a resident in charge of supervising two trainees. Overwhelmed, she neglects to provide feedback on their performance, prompting her clinic manager to reproach her for her shortcomings. Nea falls asleep, overwhelmed by the summons, and wakes up in a simulation of her hospital environment. She soon realizes that this is her first day as a hospital trainee! The head of the clinic, Morphy, explains that she'll have to carry out several missions to escape this simulation, known as "the Medtrice". He introduces her to Trixia, the resident who will accompany her on her adventure. She will also guide her through her reasoning, going back over the exemplary feedback or lack of it she will receive during her interactions.

Once players have completed their assignments, a call from the head of the clinic leads to a final test: putting what they have learned into practice by offering constructive feedback to a trainee they're supervising.

When Nea passes this final test, the epilogue unfolds, recounting how, after returning from her "interdimensional journey", she mobilizes her feedback skills daily with the trainees she supervises.

3.2   Interactions

Borrowing the notion of problem-solving from the Challenge-Based Learning approach [16], players unlock missions by interacting with NPCs located in different hospital sectors. The game's dialogues, inspired by clinical vignettes originally from training, enable interactive choices to be made, reinforcing the sense of agentivity [17]. They immerse players in situations similar to those they would encounter in a professional context (Kolb's experiential learning [18]). The dialogue with Trixia and the final test of the game allow for the integration of a phase of institutionalisation [19] by reconsolidating the knowledge acquired during previous missions (Fig. 2).

4   Method

Fig. 2. Example of a dialogue with Trixia, the resident specialized in feedback ("Ah! A feedback is the occasion to test your knowledge. Tell me, what did you think about it?".

Various (serious) game design methods have been discussed in academic publications that all stress the key role of iterative design [20,21]. Nevertheless, there is a lack of practical and operational methods for serious game design [22], in particular in a context of limited budget projects. Therefore we briefly explain here the method adopted for the Medtrix game. It is inspired by the SAM model [23], while integrating the Agile method [24] into the game design. The method is cyclical while retaining a structured approach divided into major phases (Fig. 3).

While the SAM model is based on three main phases, we propose five: theoretical design is distinguished from prototyping, and development iterative process is separated into an internal phase, carried out by the development team in an academic context, and an external phase, carried out with the sponsor.

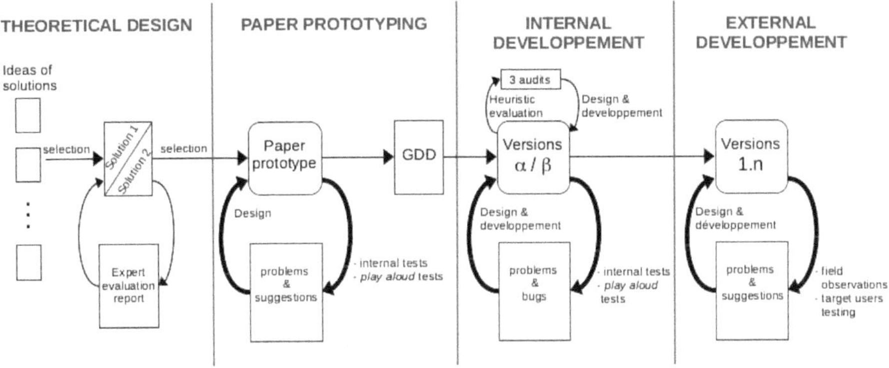

Fig. 3. Four main design phases (the preparatory phase is not shown). Thick arrows indicate multiple iterations.

The *preparatory* phase is a classical in-depth analysis of the demands and needs of the various stakeholders, particularly the target audience (see Sect. 2). The *theoretical design* phase then aims to select a game design approach that would integrate the educational content in a playful and intrinsic way, in line with the expectations of the sponsor. From the very first discussions, given the learning domain, the idea of a game centred on dialogues emerged as a central axis of the gameplay. A brainstorming session was held to explore a wide range of possibilities. Two game concepts were selected: an escape-type RPG (Role Playing Game) and a visual novel. The sponsor was sent a design brief and chose the RPG for its playful and engaging potential.

Paper prototyping, a proven method in game design for designing and testing a game [21], led to the production of a playable prototype of the game. It enabled to visualize and identify any necessary adjustments to the gameplay, while assessing the relevance, coherence and robustness of the scenario. We ran several iterations of the paper prototype, each of which enabled us to refine the scenario and the mechanics. This phase culminated in the drafting of a complete *game design document* (GDD), .

Internal development of the game began with an alpha version (developed with RPG Maker MV), serving as a milestone for testing the mechanics and interactions deployed in a digital environment. An initial evaluation was carried out by colleagues, in the form a heuristic assessment [25], combined with an assessment of the gaming and pedagogical dimensions of the game. At the same time, user tests were also carried out in the form of *Play Aloud* [26].

The feedback highlighted a number of shortcomings, including unclear instructions, unintuitive navigation and inconsistent pedagogical elements. These observations led to modifications for the beta version, aimed at enhancing player engagement and improving the fluidity of the experience.

Although this version introduced a number of improvements, a few technical bugs and usability issues remained. In addition, medical dialogues sometimes lacked consistency with clinical reality, and interactions were not always sufficiently emphasized.

Following the internal development phase, two team members continued to work within the sponsor's institution to refine the game and exploit its full potential (*external development* phase). This enabled a deeper understanding of the specificities of the medical context and the target audience, in particular the real dynamics between supervisors and supervisees through immersion in the hospital environment. Information gathered during this immersion, along with insights from experts, informed the subsequent modifications regarding the navigation, the user interface, as well as the scenario.

To assess the impact of these adjustments, an anonymous online questionnaire was circulated via the main internal physician communication channels. The questionnaire evaluated several dimensions, including user experience, the degree of flow felt, usability, the coherence of the story and dialogue, and the perceived impact on learning, as well as overall impressions of the game. The responses obtained will inform the development of version 1.2.

5   Conclusion

Confronted with the richness and complexity of providing and receiving formative feedback in medicine, we proposed an educational video game aiming at inserting this content in the best possible way, based on the principle of intrinsic integration. This result is achieved through multiple iterations and various evaluations: expert assessments, questionnaires and *play-aloud* tests by general end-users, medical residents and trainees. This iterative process is still underway at the time of writing, but initial feedback from the field is encouraging. For example, one resident expressed his enthusiasm, pointing out that, although he had found all the previous serious clinical simulations he had experienced rather tedious, he had particularly enjoyed this one.

The proposed method (Fig. 3) is not intended to be generally recommended for all serious games. For example, in an agile vision, it can be criticized because, after the preparation phase, the customer/sponsor was hardly consulted, only to intervene in the final phase. Nevertheless, it enabled the sponsor to first discover the Medtrix game and its potential, before becoming fully involved in the co-design process. In this way, we felt we avoided a gap between the design team and the customer in terms of game design.

Today, the project is continuing, with evaluations on a larger scale and more focused on the target audience. The game will undergo continuous improvement before it is deployed as part of an existing training course.

References

1. Malone, T.W.: Toward a theory of intrinsically instruction motivating. Cogn. Sci. **5**, 333–369 (1981). https://doi.org/10.1207/s15516709cog0504_
2. Habgood, M.P.J., Ainsworth, S.E., Benford, S.: Endogenous fantasy and learning in digital games. Simul. Gaming **36**, 483–498 (2005). https://doi.org/10.1177/1046878105282276
3. Fabricatore, C.: Learning and videogames: an unexploited synergy. In: Workshop: In Search of the Meaning of Learning. Long Beach, CA, USA (2000)
4. Szilas, N., Acosta, M.: A theoretical background for educational video games: games , signs , knowledge. In: Felicia, P. (ed.) Handbook of Research on Improving Learning and Motivation through Educational Games: Multidisciplinary Approaches. IGI Global (2010)
5. Ke, F.: Designing and integrating purposeful learning in game play: a systematic review. Educ. Tech. Res. Dev. **64**(2), 219–244 (2015). https://doi.org/10.1007/s11423-015-9418-1
6. Bruckman, A.: Can educational be fun. In: Game Developer's Conference. San Jose, California (1999)
7. Sauvé, L., Samson, D.: Generic games: multipliers for Canadian educational multimedia content on the information highway. SAVIE (2004)
8. Szilas, N., Sutter Widmer, D.: Mieux comprendre la notion d'intégration entre apprentissage et jeu. In: Georges, S. and Sanchez, E. (eds.) Proceedings of the Serious Games Workshop at the 4th EIAH Conference, pp. 27–39 (2009)
9. Ke, F.: Designing and integrating purposeful learning in game play: a systematic review. Educ. Technol. Res. Dev. **64**, 219–244 (2016). https://doi.org/10.1007/s11423-015-9418-1
10. Huizinga, J.: Homo ludens. Essay on the social function of play. Gallimard, Paris (1951)
11. Hattie, J., Timperley, H.: The power of feedback. Rev. Educ. Res. **77**, 81–112 (2007). https://doi.org/10.3102/003465430298487
12. PROFILES. http://www.profilesmed.ch/. Accessed 06 Aug 2025
13. Van De Ridder, J.M.M., Wijnen-Meijer, M.: Pendleton's rules: a mini review of a feedback method. AJBSR. **19**, 19–21 (2023). https://doi.org/10.34297/AJBSR.2023.19.002542
14. Pendleton, D., Schofield, T., Tate, P., Havelock, P.: The new consultation: developing doctor-patient communication (2003). https://doi.org/10.1093/med/9780192632883.001.0001
15. Henderson, M., et al.: Conditions that enable effective feedback. High. Educ. Res. Dev. **38**, 1401–1416 (2019). https://doi.org/10.1080/07294360.2019.1657807
16. Gallagher, S.E., Savage, T.: Challenge-based learning in higher education: an exploratory literature review. Teach. High. Educ. **28**, 1135–1157 (2023). https://doi.org/10.1080/13562517.2020.1863354
17. Jézégou, A.: Dictionnaire des concepts de la professionnalisation. In: Dictionnaire des concepts de la professionnalisation, pp. 41-44. De Boeck Supérieur (2022). https://doi.org/10.3917/dbu.jorro.2022.01.0041
18. Kolb, D.: Experiential Learning: Experience As The Source Of Learning And Development. (1984)
19. Margolinas, C.: Devolution and institutionalization: two antagonistic aspects of the teacher's role. In: Comiti, C., Anh, T.N., Bessot, A., Guillaud, M.-P.C.& J.-C. (eds.) Didactique des disciplines scientifiques et formation des enseignants, pp. 342–347. Maison d'Edition de l'Education, Hanoi (1995)

20. Schell, J.: The Art of Game Design. CRC Press, Boca Raton (2008)
21. Fullerton, T.: Game Design Workshop: A Playcentric Approach to Creating Innovative Games. Morgan Kaufmann, Amsterdam (2008)
22. Djafarova, N., Zefi, L., Centennial College, Turetken, O.: The art of serious game design: a framework and methodology. THCI. **15**, 322–349 (2023). https://doi.org/10.17705/1thci.00193.
23. Allen, M., Sites, R.: Leaving Addie for SAM: An Agile Model for Developing the Best Learning Experiences. Association for Talent Development (2012)
24. Daubier, M., Daubier, S.: Agilité: 66 outils, 10 plans d'action, 12 ressources numériques. Vuibert, Paris (2021)
25. Scapin, D., Bastien, J.: Ergonomic criteria for evaluating the ergonomic quality of interactive systems. Behav. Inf. Technol. **16** (1997). https://doi.org/10.1080/014492997119806
26. Pellicone, A., et al.: Playing aloud: leveraging game commentary culture for playtesting. Int. J. Gaming Comput.-Mediated Simul. **14**, 1–16 (2022). https://doi.org/10.4018/IJGCMS.296705

A Stealth Serious Game About Hiring Bias

Paul Pesak$^{(\boxtimes)}$ and Helmut Hlavacs

Faculty of Computer Science, University of Vienna, Vienna, Austria
`a12029810@unet.univie.ac.at, helmut.hlavacs@univie.ac.at`

Abstract. Despite growing awareness, unconscious racism and sexism still affect hiring decisions. This paper investigates such bias through a serious game designed to raise awareness and observe player behavior. Participants made hiring choices in the game based on applicant "stats" and images. The results indicate the presence of significant hiring bias against women among several actors, particularly in the direct choice between male and female candidates and in the assignment of employees to traditionally male-dominated jobs such as construction workers. These findings confirm the continuing influence of gender bias in recruitment scenarios and suggest that unconscious bias can have a significant impact on recruitment outcomes.

Keywords: Stealth Serious Game · Hiring Bias · Implicit Bias

1 Introduction

Racism and sexism are well-known issues that are prevalent in hiring practices. Numerous studies have shown that female and non-white individuals face discrimination in recruitment, often as an result of unconscious bias of the recruiter [7]. Consequently, instances of hiring bias remain prevalent [14].

Several serious games have been published to raise awareness and show the impact of racism. However, none have focused on unconscious bias in hiring. This paper presents a stealth serious game in which the player assumes the role of a hiring manager. Unlike previous games, it is designed to detect whether a user is biased when hiring staff. Because players are unaware that they are being assessed, the results can reveal unconscious bias, even if they think they are impartial.

In the game, the player has to select between candidates to hire, only being provided with a picture and "stats" of each candidate. Playing should lead the player into a flow, encouraging unconscious hiring decisions. Upon completion, the game provides following feedback for different categories

- Does the user show a bias against women when hiring?
- Does the user show a bias against non-white people when hiring?

This paper discusses the research of the game, reviews related serious games, details the game's design, and presents findings from an evaluation involving 31 participants. The evaluation results showed parallels with the results in real life.

A. Thomas et al. (Eds.): JCSG 2025, LNCS 16243, pp. 27–33, 2026.
https://doi.org/10.1007/978-3-032-10518-9_4

2   Related Work

Sexism and racism have been widely studied, especially in the context of hiring. Research has shown that bias based on gender and race persists, with statistical evidence revealing disparities in workplace representation across various occupational sectors. In response, multiple serious games have been developed to raise awareness about discrimination.

2.1   Hiring Bias in Real Life

Quillian et al. [14] conducted a meta-analysis that revealed that African Americans receive 36% fewer callbacks than equally qualified white applicants, suggesting that racial discrimination in hiring persists. Another research [13] using 140 field studies across 30 countries attributes the bias to taste discrimination(prejudice) and statistical discrimination (group-based assumptions about productivity).

The article "Gender biases and discrimination in hiring" [7] highlights the existence of unconscious or explicit bias and the tendency of people favor candidates similar to themselves. King [8] observes that in the male-dominated field of construction, masculine attitudes and behaviors, such as aggression and sexual harassment, hinder the inclusion of women. One goal of our game is to surface such unconscious processes in hiring decisions.

2.2   Serious Games About Gender and Race Bias

A review by Barrera Yañez et al. [2] review a range of serious games addressing gender equality. Most aim to foster empathy and provide direct educational experiences, but none focus on recruitment.

The "Anti Sexism Game" [9] tackles workplace sexism through two sub-games: one evaluates the player's workplace via a questionnaire, and the other involves popping bubbles containing sexist remarks. While it addresses workplace bias, it doesn't specifically target hiring.

In "Interactive game - Fight against racism and discrimination" [11] the player is placed in various scenarios, including a hiring situation, where they have to determine if a situation constituted discrimination. The game gives immediate feedback, making the player immediately aware of being evaluated, unlike our game, which collects behavioral data covertly and assesses it after the playthrough.

"Purpose" [15] is more similar to our approach. Set during a zombie apocalypse, the player leads a team and assigns stereotypical roles to members in order to survive. Biases are assessed in the background and revealed at the end, similar to our method. However, our game differs by presenting a realistic hiring scenario grounded in actual workplace practices.

3   Game Description

The goal of the game is to assess gender and racial bias in hiring without the player's awareness. Through immersive and engaging gameplay, it elicits unconscious decisions, revealing implicit bias.

3.1   Basic Concept

The player runs a construction company with the goal to build a city that covers a target percentage of land (30–100%) based on selected difficulty. To succeed, they need to constantly hire new employees. When certain values of workers exceed, the player loses the worker. Losing all workers leads to a game over, represented as an "arrest" in the game. However, players can recover using a time-costing "bail out" that preserves city progress. This setup naturally creates hiring opportunities critical for assessing bias.

The game is designed to be challenging but not too frustrating, so that players enter a flow state. In a flow state players actions tend to become more automatic and unconscious, which could lead to unconscious bias influencing hiring decisions [10].

3.2   Game Scenario and Job Roles

With only 10.8% female share of workers [16], the construction industry provides an ideal setting for bias evaluation. Three job roles were chosen for the game, reflecting real-world disparities and could trigger potential biases based on stereotypes. Construction worker: Physically demanding and male-dominated [3], reinforcing the stereotype that men are stronger [5]. Manager: A role often held by women in construction, possibly linked to communication stereotypes [6]. Engineer: A male dominated STEM role [4].

3.3   Gameplay

The player must build on a randomly generated tile map, aiming to cover a target percentage. Tile colors indicate site types, differing in offered houses and police investigation risk. Blue: Player-owned. Green: Low risk, few houses. Yellow: Medium risk/houses. Red: Many houses, high risk. Figure 1 shows the map and UI elements: Progress bar showing build progress (1) and for each site build capacity (2), investigation risk (3) and applicant availability (4).

Selecting a site opens a view like in Fig. 2, allowing managing workers and performing actions on the construction. For each worker there is an experience bar (1): University (left) vs. work experience (right), a stress Level (2), which increases per task and site openings and talkative level (3), which increases when stress is full or when police randomly investigates after finishing construction. If the workers talkative value is at the maximum, the worker is removed. If the player has no workers left, it leads to an "arrest", the game over of this game.

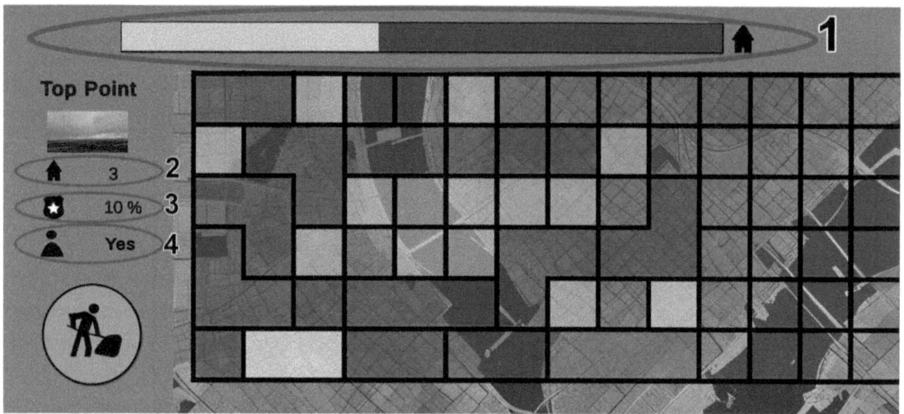

Fig. 1. The map of the game with construction sites in various states.

Applicant photos were AI-generated via thispersondoesnotexist.com [12] and randomly assigned to profiles. Care was taken to ensure demographic balance and neutral expressions, minimizing visual bias. The player can select between different roles(4), monitor bonuses that remove stress after finished construction(5), managing the team (6) and going back to the map(7). The roles have different performances. Managers find new potential construction sites (higher university experience = higher success rate). Construction workers build houses which get convert in bonuses (work experience = more bonuses). Engineers secure the site, decreasing talkative increase for team in case of a police investigation (more security percentage with balanced experience).

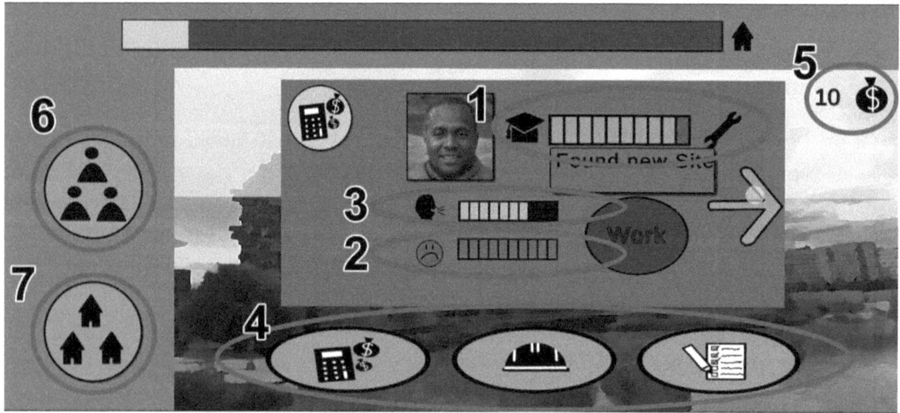

Fig. 2. Making an employee work.

4   Hiring Employees and Stealth Assessment

Hiring is a key mechanic of the game to assess implicit bias of the player. At the start, players select 4 out of 8 applicants, balanced by race and gender, shown only with a photo and experience distribution. During gameplay, the user has to occasionally choose between two candidates, differing only in either race or gender. This helps us to detected potential hiring preferences. The selection data gets "stealthily" collected in the background and only evaluated after successful completion of the game. At the end of the game the player is presented with a summary if a discriminated group was hired significantly less, in a general comparison and also broken down for each job role. A warning is shown if results suggest statistical evidence of bias. To identify significant bias, we tested whether female or non-white candidates were hired significantly less, using the left-tailed hypothesis test for proportions with 95% confidence interval. These groups are used due to their frequent real-world discrimination [7,13].

5   Evaluation and Discussion

A user study with 31 participants was conducted to evaluate the hiring bias game. The gender distribution was 13 female (41.9%), 17 male (54.8%), and 1 transgender (3.2%). Most participants were from Austria and Germany (14 each, 45.2%), with others from Italy, Poland, and Switzerland (3.2% each). The majority (80.56%) were aged 1825, indicating a relatively young sample.

5.1   Setup

Participants were asked to play the game under the name "Construction Hire!", without any knowledge what the study is about, on "easy" difficulty (build on 50% of grid tiles). Afterwards they completed a Likert-scale survey (1 = strongly disagree, 5 = strongly agree) on hiring bias, stereotyping and the game's influence on their thinking. No explicit debriefing was conducted after the study, though the nature of the research could be inferred from the end-game statistics and survey questions.

To detect hiring bias, we employ the left tailed hypothesis test for proportions with 95% significance level. The game statistics indicates if the hiring probability for women or non-white people was significantly under 50%. For a more precise observation we also evaluated if male or white individuals were hired significantly less than 50%. Additionally, we analyzed the distribution of job roles among male, female, white, and non-white groups. Using a 33.33% baseline per role, we assessed whether any group was significantly underrepresented.

5.2   Results

Players had on average $\mu = 6.13$ arrests (game overs) per game, with an $SD = 6.06$, which was skewed by two outliers(19 and 26 arrests). Most participants experienced few or no arrests, suggesting they have entered a flow state in which decisions become more intuitive [10].

Survey responses indicate moderate agreement that hiring bias exists based on gender ($\mu = 3.45$) and race ($\mu = 3.68$). The participants had a strong agreement that they would refrain from judging individuals based on gender ($\mu = 4.32$) and race ($\mu = 4.29$).

In the game 7 participants (23.33%) hired significantly less women when choosing between two candidates different in gender, while 4 participants (13.33%) hired significantly less non-white people when choosing between candidates different in race. 6 participants (19.35%) showed significant bias against women when hiring for construction jobs. The same amount of players also distributed significantly less than 33.33% of women to the construction worker role. Meanwhile, 5 participants (16.1%) assigned women to the manager role more than 33.3% of the time.

Bias against men or white applicants was rare. A few outliers showed inverse bias, possibly due to disrupted flow (e.g. through frequent arrests), increased bias awareness, or a desire to counteract social stereotypes [1]. Most consistent was the bias against women in physical labor roles, likely due to stereotypes linking construction to strength [5]. Surprisingly, no similar trend appeared in engineering allocations, despite being a male dominated field in real life [6]. One possible explanation is that engineering is not as strongly associated with a single, heavily gendered stereotype like physical strength, an attribute often linked to men from early childhood [5]. When asked if the game made the participants more cautious about judging individuals based on gender or race, moderate agreement was shown ($\mu = 3.35$, $SD = 1.27$), suggesting an educational value for the participants.

5.3   Limitations

Participants were recruited via convenience sampling, with 80.56% being students aged 1825, which may not reflect typical hiring managers. Although the game's true purpose was not disclosed, some participants may have inferred it during gameplay, potentially affecting their decisions.

6   Conclusions

The study shows that despite general awareness of racism and sexism in hiring, some players still exhibited bias against women in a fictional game setting. Most noticeable was the bias in construction roles, most likely due stereotypes associating physical strength with men. Interestingly, such bias was less pronounced in engineering roles, despite their real-world male dominance. Overall, more players showed bias against women than men. Survey responses also suggest the game had educational value, prompting participants to reflect on the impact of appearance-based judgments.

References

1. Adriaans, J., Fourré, M.: Basic social justice orientations-measuring order-related justice in the European social survey round 9. Meas. Instrum. Soc. Sci. **4**(1), 11 (2022). https://doi.org/10.1186/s42409-022-00040-3
2. Barrera Yañez, A., Alonso-Fernandez, C., Fernández-Manjón, B.: Review of serious games to educate on gender equality (2020). https://doi.org/10.1145/3434780.3436592
3. BigRentz: Women in construction: The state of the industry in 2022 (2022). https://www.bigrentz.com/blog/women-construction. Accessed 01 July 2024
4. Friedmann, E., Efrat-Treister, D.: Gender bias in stem hiring: implicit in-group gender favoritism among men managers. Gender Soc. **37**(1), 32–64 (2023). https://doi.org/10.1177/08912432221137910
5. Halim, M.L.D., Sakamoto, D.J., Russo, L.N., Echave, K.N., Portillo, M.A., Tawa, S.: Early gender differences in valuing strength. Arch. Sex. Behav. 1–14 (2022). https://doi.org/10.1007/s10508-021-02185-4
6. Hall, J.A., Halberstadt, A.G.: Sex roles and nonverbal communication skills. Sex Roles **7**(3), 273–287 (1981). https://doi.org/10.1007/BF00287542
7. Hassan, N.: Gender biases and discrimination while hiring. Artha J. Soc. Sci. **18**(1), 13–21 (2019)
8. King-Lewis, A.: Diversity and Inclusion of Women in the Construction Industry. Ph.D. thesis, Oklahoma State University (2020)
9. Mitchell, D.C.: Anti sexism game. https://www.antisexism.co.uk/. Accessed 01 July 2024
10. Nakamura, J., Csikszentmihalyi, M., et al.: Flow theory and research. Handb. Positive Psychol. **195**, 206 (2009)
11. international des droits de l'Homme et de la paix, I.: Interactive game - fight against racism and discrimination. https://2idhp.eu/nos_ressources/fight-against-racism-and-discrimination/. Accessed 01 July 2024
12. Wang, P.: This Person Does Not Exist (2019). https://thispersondoesnotexist.com. Accessed 08 July 2024
13. Quillian, L., Midtbøen, A.H.: Comparative perspectives on racial discrimination in hiring: the rise of field experiments. Ann. Rev. Sociol. **47**, 391–415 (2021). https://doi.org/10.1146/annurev-soc-090420-035144, https://www.annualreviews.org/content/journals/10.1146/annurev-soc-090420-035144
14. Quillian, L., Pager, D., Hexel, O., Midtbøen, A.H.: Meta-analysis of field experiments shows no change in racial discrimination in hiring over time. Proc. Natl. Acad. Sci. **114**(41), 10870–10875 (2017)
15. Stetina, B., Rodax, N., Klaps, A., Kovacovsky, Z., Sertkan, S., Hlavacs, H.: Racism and sexism approached with " purpose ": serious games as a low-threshold way to increase awarenes (2017). https://doi.org/10.13140/RG.2.2.15607.62883
16. U.S. Bureau of Labor Statistics: Table 18. employed persons by detailed industry, sex, race, and hispanic or latino ethnicity (2024). https://www.bls.gov/cps/cpsaat18.htm. Accessed 07 July 2024

Games in Carceral Settings

Constance Steinkuehler[1]([✉])([ID]), Kai Bannon[2], and Richard Kruse[3]

[1] University of California, Irvine, Irvine, CA 92697, USA
`const@uci.edu`
[2] San Quentin Skunkworks, San Quentin, CA 94964, USA
`kyle@sanquentinskunkworks.org`
[3] San Quentin Rehabilitation Center, San Quentin, CA 94964, USA
`Richard.Kruse@cdcr.ca.gov`

Abstract. The purpose of this literature review is to summarize the extant literature on the use and impacts of games, both analog and digital, in carceral settings. Our goal is to identify how games are being implemented and evaluated in correctional contexts and to what ends (rehabilitation, education, mental health, behavior management, social dynamics, etc.). Drawing on academic and news sources, this review synthesizes empirical and publicly reported accounts of the use of games in carceral contexts to chart the development, implementation, and outcomes of game-based interventions in prisons and detention facilities. Here we emulate the work of Jenness and colleagues [20] by bringing in the voice of the incarcerated and the administrative staff that serve them. One lead academic researcher authored the main body of the literature review, with two co-authors providing commentary where relevant from the perspectives of those who live and who work inside. Our findings show that, while early implementations used games primarily for external behavioral control or mere diversion, contemporary efforts use games in increasingly sophisticated ways to foster emotional regulation and self-control, social connection and communication skills, rational decision-making and thinking through consequences, mental fitness and the reduction of prejudices. Analog games remain disproportionately prevalent in carceral settings, with chess and *Dungeons & Dragons* [17] the two most prevalent games used. Future longitudinal and mixed methods research is needed to interrogate the lived experiences of incarcerated players, the emergent dynamics of game play in carceral contexts, and the institutional logics that shape game-based programs and policies.

Keywords: games · carceral settings · social connection · emotional regulation · knowledge acquisition · chess · Dungeons & Dragons · D&D

1 Introduction

The United States has the highest incarceration rate among democracies, with over 580 people imprisoned per 100,000 residents [38]. While its carceral logic is

A. Thomas et al. (Eds.): JCSG 2025, LNCS 16243, pp. 34–50, 2026.
https://doi.org/10.1007/978-3-032-10518-9_5

historically one of detainee managerialism rather than rehabilitation and reform [4], there are slow but sure shifts toward improvement of prison conditions in place of punishment and containment alone [5]. Such changes are motivated not only by humanitarian values and an increased understanding of the role of trauma in antisocial behavior but also the practical problems of overcrowding, substance abuse, and recidivism after release. After all, the revolving door of American prison systems is economically and socially costly [49], with over 40% of individuals returning to prison within three years of release [33]. Mental health and behavioral interventions are increasingly recognized as critical to successful reentry, with most crime survivors favoring rehabilitation over punishment [1].

Over the last decade, California has been leading efforts to reform punitive systems to better support real rehabilitation rather than the reproduction of social problems over time [14,48]. With this reform effort comes the slow but sure progression of materials and programs within carceral systems designed to increase individual wellness, decrease antisocial behaviors, and prevent recidivism through effective socialization before release. Such efforts include a wide variety of programs ranging from education and peer mentoring to trauma-informed staff training and, in centers such as San Quentin, games.

The use of games and game-based programs, while perhaps novel in carceral contexts, is now somewhat commonplace in educational and therapeutic settings. Games have been used for a vast range of purposes, from strengthening literacy [16,22,43] and problem-solving [7,42] to fostering prosocial interactions [27,46], individual mental health [18], and social-emotional skills [6,44], and reducing the impacts of trauma and stress [3]. How well are such game-based innovations reflected inside today's prison contexts, particularly as reform efforts refocus attention on antecedent causes of antisocial outcomes?

The purpose of this literature review is to summarize the extant literature on the use and impacts of games, both analog and digital, in carceral settings. Our goal is to identify how games are being implemented and evaluated in correctional contexts and to what ends (rehabilitation, education, mental health, behavior management, social dynamics, etc.). Indeed, the use of games in carceral contexts has evolved significantly over the past four decades, from rudimentary rewards for behavioral compliance to purposefully built tools for rehabilitation, education, mental health support, and identity work. Drawing on academic and reputable news sources, this review synthesizes empirical and publicly reported accounts of the use of games in carceral contexts to chart the development, implementation, and outcomes of game-based interventions in prisons and detention facilities. Here we take a novel approach, bringing in the voice of the incarcerated and the administrative staff that serve them. One lead academic researcher authored the main body of the literature review, with two co-authors providing commentary where relevant from the perspectives of those who live and who work inside.

2   Methods

2.1   Search Strategy

This literature review employed a systematic search strategy across multiple academic databases and supplementary sources to identify relevant studies on the use of games in carceral settings. The lead researcher, in collaboration with a university reference librarian, conducted searches in the following databases: Academic Search Complete, APA PsycINFO, Criminal Justice Abstracts, Criminal Justice Database, Legal Source, Sociological Abstracts, and Criminal Justice & Criminology. Boolean search strings included terms such as games* AND prison* NOT sport* NOT prisoner's dilemma, adjusted for database syntax. The searches yielded a total of 898 records.

To ensure comprehensiveness, additional sources were included from Google Scholar (n = 53), targeted citation chasing (n = 16), and AI-assisted search (ChatGPT; n = 10), bringing the total number of identified records to 977. Following the removal of 17 duplicate records, 960 unique records remained for screening.

2.2   Sources and Inclusion Criteria

The search included a range of source materials such as peer-reviewed academic journal articles, books and book chapters, dissertations and theses, conference papers and proceedings, and reputable news and magazine articles. Sources were included if they were published in English, focused on games (digital or analog) used in carceral settings by incarcerated individuals (adults or juveniles), and were available in full text. There were no constraints placed on publication year or geography, provided the source met the inclusion criteria. Sources were excluded if they focused exclusively on sports, used "games" metaphorically, or did not describe a carceral context.

Inclusion criteria required that studies and public news articles explicitly investigate, evaluate, or describe games used within correctional settings for educational, therapeutic, or prosocial aims. A total of 22 records met all inclusion criteria and were included in the final synthesis.

2.3   Screening and Selection Process

Title and abstract screening resulted in the exclusion of 929 records that did not meet inclusion criteria. The remaining 31 full-text articles were assessed for eligibility. Ten were subsequently excluded for the following reasons: superficial mentions without substantive descriptoin or analysis (n = 6), scoping review protocols without discussion or findings (n = 1), studies or news articles focused on gaming equipment (playing cards, virtual reality headsets) rather than games (n = 2), and one with inaccessible full text (n = 1). The record selection process is summarized in Fig. 1. The total number of records included in the review is 21, including 11 academic articles and 10 news articles from recognized sources.

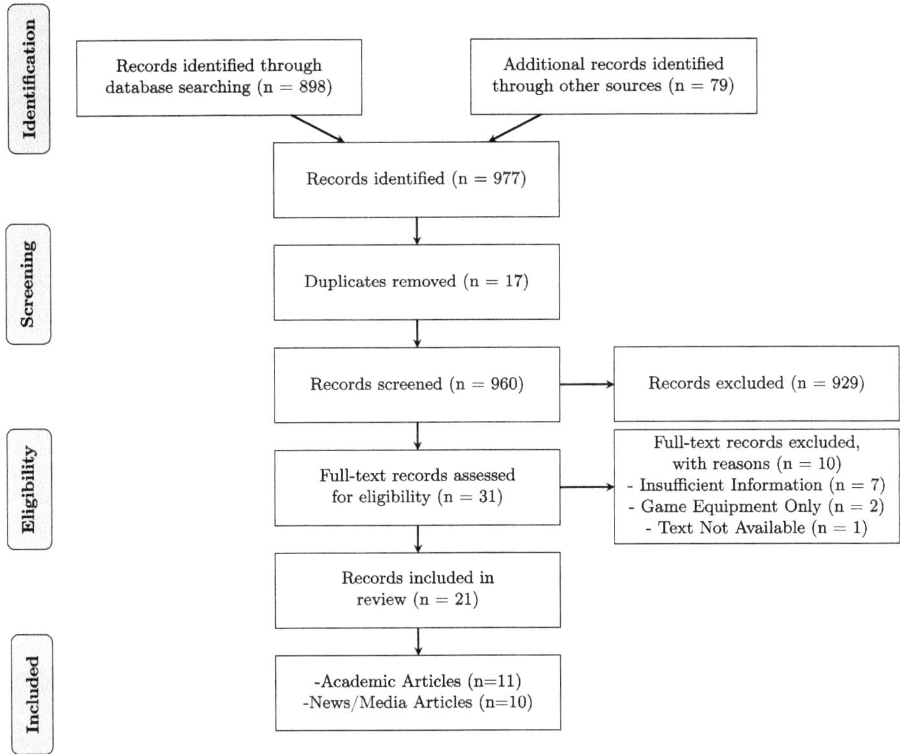

Fig. 1. PRISMA Flowchart of Records

3   Findings

The use of games in carceral contexts has evolved significantly over the past four decades, from rudimentary distractions to bespoke tools for rehabilitation, education, social connection, mental health support, and identity work. Drawing on a wide array of academic and media sources, this review synthesizes empirical and anecdotal accounts to chart the development, implementation, and outcomes of game-based interventions in prisons and youth detention facilities across the globe.

3.1   Games for External Diversion and Control

Games were first used in prisons primarily as a reward for controlling behavior and as a diversion while doing time. Beginning in the mid-1980s, with arcade machines introduced into jails in Albuquerque, New Mexico (USA), games were construed primarily as a means for reducing tensions among inmates, offering a temporary distraction to their present circumstances, and for compliance [34]. As digital games evolved, so too did their adoption inside penitentiaries, and by the mid-2000s, news reports of *PlayStation 2*, *Xbox* and *Nintendo GameBoys* in carceral institutions emerged [26]. Here, gameplay was viewed as a privilege for inmates, one that could be allowed or withdrawn as behavioral incentives. As a Prison Service spokesperson phrased it, "The use of limited privileges, such as access to PlayStations, has proved to be a successful method of generating positive behaviour from prisoners. These privileges are removable if prisoners fail to maintain acceptable standards of behaviour." (¶ 15)

Early initiatives like these view games less as therapeutic or educational tools and more as levers for diversion and control. Public backlash was swift in some jurisdictions, with critics decrying game play privileges as too lenient, publicly arguing that resources "would be better used for things of more educational value than having them [sit] for hours in front of a PlayStation." (¶10) [47]. In Missouri, for instance, video games were banned entirely in 2005, with prison officials declaring penitentiaries "punitive institutions... not arcades."

Officer Kruse. *Fundamentally, when an individual is sent to prison the biggest thing they lose is their time and some of their rights. Obviously, the State doesn't have a tool for taking someone's time beyond placing them in prison. This premise raises an important question that's often overlooked in these discussions: if we are going to take ten, twenty, thirty or more years of someone's life by placing them in prison, what do they do while they wait out their sentence?*

You could simply give them nothing, seemingly the cheapest option on its face if we ignore the ethics of this choice. However, an individual placed in a cell and given nothing to do will rapidly deteriorate, which in turn incurs a variety of costs on the State. Everything from overtime due to staff writing reports to paying for medical conditions for the individual are on the table. In short, the State has to provide these individuals with "something" to do while they serve their sentence.

If we take the most cynical view possible and consider someone that just "sits and plays PlayStation all day," this is still an individual with some form of entertainment. Said entertainment will help keep them grounded, even if it doesn't do so completely. Everything else being equal, this is an individual that will be better adjusted when released from prison.

In my opinion, the best answer to this question is providing the individual with a robust suite of options. In many ways, the State should seek to provide the individual with the balanced life they probably did not have before coming to prison. Not only is this the most humane choice in regard to the hypothetical prisoner, but it yields better results for society as well. Instead of releasing an individual made worse from their treatment in prison, we release someone who has learned how to lead a healthy life. Obviously no solution is 100%, but this highlights a way that games can be used for "diversion and control," but not just that. They can also be used as part of a healthy diet focused on healing the individual and, by extension, increasing public safety.

Of course, exceptions were always granted for chess, "the gymnasium of the mind" as Blaise Pascal once called it, a game long praised for fostering strategic thinking, self- discipline, and patience–and a long-standing mainstay of prison yards and chapel activity rooms. A *New York Times* article from the early 2000s [12] describes a chess tournament held at New Jersey State Prison between incarcerated men and Princeton University students. In it, inmates recount the hours spent in preparation, with one quoted as saying,"I sit on my bed with only my board, and sometimes I even role-play with myself, saying I'm protecting my castle or my army" (¶9). A more recent article in *Global News* [45] reports on a chess program across prison systems in Canada whose participating inmates report improvements in rational decision-making and the ability to think through consequences as a result of playing chess. Over the centuries, chess has provided a rare but effective cognitive and emotional outlet in prison life.

3.2   Games for Self-control and Self-regulation

Beyond the reach of the news, however, researchers were already exploring the potential of games as tools for developing self-control or self-regulatory skills, external rewards now turned inward in the reconfiguration of behavioral incentive into tool for the cultivation of internal skill. In 1985, Kappes and Thompson [23] conducted a study comparing the impact of biofeedback training versus playing an Atari game on impulsivity, locus of control, and self-concept. Participants were incarcerated juveniles in a maximum-security setting. Although biofeedback yielded slightly stronger results, both groups demonstrated significant improvements in all three outcome variables. Participants in the game condition also reported increased patience and concentration.

In a similarly oriented project, Resnick, Boler and Merrill [36] developed the board game *Busted*, a therapeutic activity designed to facilitate meaningful discussions about values, decisions, and consequences among delinquent adolescents and their therapist or social worker in a small group home setting. Through scenario-based role-play and reflective judgment tasks, the game aimed to build empathy, social reasoning, and behavioral insight among incarcerated youth. In the game, players earn or lose points based on the perceived sincerity and thoughtfulness of their responses to situational prompts. A subsequent digital version [35] adapted the game for computerized delivery, reinforces similar therapeutic objectives–ego control, perspective-taking, rational decision-making, collaborative problem-solving, prosocial behaviors, behavioral flexibility, and thinking through consequences. Both the original analog and later digital versions were tested with youth in correctional settings and group homes, where they were found to hold participants' attention and facilitate meaningful discussions about values, decisions, and consequences.

3.3   Games for Social Communication Skills

The field of games for impact began to flourish in the early 2000s, bringing broad public awareness to the power of games for learning [8] across a vast range of topics from Latin mythology and truck driving. And with it expanded our considerations of the potential benefits of games within carceral contexts.

A series of studies spanning nearly two decades illustrates the use of games to build social communication skills.

In a study of curricular design inside a prison classroom [31], Morrow investigates a curricular innovation in which the teacher uses games coupled with reflective writing to teach social communication skills to male offenders in a classroom context inside a London prison. Although initially met with suspicion, the games used ultimately enabled participants to cultivate better communication with others, both verbal and non-verbal, by providing a shared context in which peers could act, react, and problem solve.

Ribbens and Malliet [37] conducted in-depth interviews with 17 incarcerated men in Belgium and found that digital games served as tools for managing the "pains of imprisonment"– providing a context for social interaction, self-control, mental fitness, diversion, and pleasure. Inmates described gameplay as a "sense of togetherness" and a way to soothe social tensions among diverse ethnic groups inside.

Bannon (Skunkworks). *At San Quentin and at other facilities, collaborative tabletop games such as* D&D *generate profound emotional and narrative investments among residents. I've seen players spend months crafting intricate stories, building nuanced, deeply personal characters, and collaboratively navigating complex scenarios–battling monsters, storming castles, and wrestling with moral dilemmas far removed from the daily realities of incarceration. The time and emotional energy poured into these games create stakes far exceeding typical recreational activities–stakes that, from my experience, mirror, or even exceed, the intensity and complexity of real-world interpersonal relationships within prison walls.*

Yet precisely because the emotional investments are so high, moments of disagreement during gameplay can become flashpoints, with anger spilling onto the game tables. However, these incidents very rarely result in physical altercations. This stands in marked contrast to other disputes within the prison. In fact, typical carceral interactions often rely on physical confrontation–not only as the simplest solution to disputes, but as the socially validated method to assert authority or defend respect. Violence, in many prison contexts, isn't just tolerated; it's institutionally normalized and culturally reinforced as a direct and practical method of navigating interpersonal tensions.

Within the carefully structured environment of prison gameplay, however, physical confrontation is discouraged by group norms and is self defeating. I've watched arguments threaten to tip over, only for players to check themselves– realizing that escalation would mean the catastrophic collapse of the entire shared experience. Months of storytelling effort, mutual trust-building, and emotional investment would vanish in an instant, if a fight were to erupt.

Consequently, incarcerated participants face powerful social pressures to adopt alternative methods of conflict resolution: clear communication, empathetic listening, strategic compromise, and cooperative problem-solving become not only preferable but essential. I've witnessed men who, under other circumstances, might have defaulted to quick and decisive violence instead practice articulation of their positions clearly, respectfully negotiate differences, and listen to opposing views without immediate judgment. Through this process, games in prison create rare conditions where collaboration is actively incentivized, and communication skills–often neglected or suppressed in daily prison life–are practiced, refined, and internalized.

The implications of these practices extend beyond individual sessions of gameplay. By repeatedly choosing non-violent resolution strategies within the high-stakes setting of a game, incarcerated people rehearse and embody alternative forms of social interaction that directly challenge entrenched carceral norms. Over time, these practices can subtly but meaningfully influence broader prison dynamics, reshaping not only individual identities but also the unwritten rules of group behavior. In this sense, structured collaborative gaming does more than provide recreation or distraction–it facilitates genuine transformation in how incarcerated people manage conflict, build relationships, and ultimately navigate the complexities of prison life itself.

3.4   Games for Social Connection

This capacity of game to connect us across our divisions is perhaps games' most crucial ends and means. As Huizinga [19] writes, "But the feeling of being 'apart together' in an exceptional situation, of sharing something important, of mutually withdrawing from the rest of the world and rejecting the usual norms, retains its magic beyond the duration of the individual game" (p.12). Work in the 2020s considers just this capacity of games for those locked behind bars.

But here, chess must step aside to make way for *Dungeons & Dragons* (D&D) [17]. No other game has captured the imagination of game researchers and designers alike than D&D and its profound capacity to foster collaborative social interaction, social connectedness, and belonging. And perhaps no example is more compelling than D&D among Texas prisoners on death row in solitary confinement. A *New York Times* article [2] chronicles how men cope with the most dehumanizing conditions through joint activity, collaborative storytelling, and character development that helps players build greater social connections, including connections across race and gang-affiliations and even adversarial institutional roles.

In a similar article in *Vice* [24] documents D&D players in Colorado's Sterling Correctional Facility, where inmates used the fantasy role-play to transcend prison's rigid hierarchies. As one incarcerated player comments, "Above all, without fail, any gang ties, religious obligations or racial affiliations are superseded by the game." (¶23). A *New York Times* article by Schwartz [39], in contrast, provides a cautionary tale of a case of a Wisconsin prison banning D&D play entirely, a ban upheld by the courts on the grounds of security concerns, a reminder of the institutional tensions that surround sociability and connection among convicted criminals in a carceral context.

Officer Kruse. *In order to really explain how I wound up leading a D&D game at San Quentin, I first have to set the stage. Before I became part of the Resource Team supporting California Prison reform, I had a variety of positions as a correction officer (CO). This is pretty standard as most officers don't stay in the same post for their entire career. One position I had was working as a West Block Officer, and I believe that's the first time I really, truly saw how powerful games can be in a carceral setting.*

One of my responsibilities was covering evening pill call, where incarcerated individuals (IPs) get their assigned medications. I overheard a few men talking about Magic: The Gathering [13], *a card game made by the same company (Wizards of the Coast) that makes* D&D. *As an avid* Magic *player, I chimed in on that conversation. In hindsight, choosing to talk about* Magic *that evening was probably one of the most important choices of my career.*

Many of the IPs were surprised to discover that I was an avid player, and they were thrilled to be able to share something with one of their "tier cops". At first, we just talked about things like our favorite cards and decks, and eventually we got to deeper conversations about things like strategy or new sets. Eventually, I had one IP express interest in sitting and playing with me.

This was completely against policy at the time, but for some reason I decided to tell the IP that if he completed his schooling and got his GED (high school equivalency credential), then I would bring my cards in and play. Well, this IP ended up getting his GED, which put me in a bind. While it was explicitly against the rules, I found a way to break away for about 30 min to play with them and a couple of the other Magic *players. I can still remember the excitement these IPs had years later, and the change in behavior that many IPs exhibited around me. I went from being "Officer Kruse" to just "Kruse." Typically, using "Officer" as a title is a show of respect, but in this particular case I believe it was because they were seeing the individual and not the uniform.*

I tell this story unrelated to D&D because in many ways it captures the role I now fill on the Resource Team supporting a game-based program inside San Quentin. Games are incredibly important to our population, and my unofficial role as "Game Master" has given me an untold number of opportunities to bring a sense of humanity to prison. In some ways, it's also been a way for me to give some humanity back to myself as well.

While I've only led a single game of D&D at San Quentin, I know that game was a huge hit. All of the players had a marvelous time, and I know people are hoping I'll lead another session. I have no doubt that I'll lead plenty of sessions before my career is over, and I look forward to those opportunities.

Outside of the simple act of spreading joy, it provides me an opportunity to foster cooperation between myself and the IPs. These games give IPs an avenue to work together across racial and social boundaries while challenging their perceptions of custody. The biggest benefit I've seen though, surprisingly, is my ability to be proud of what I do now. No longer am I simply another cog in a machine; rather, I'm an agent of change working to undo generations of trauma, one dice roll or card draw at a time.

In related work, Markussen and Knutz [30] analyzed the use of *Captivated*, a board game designed for prison fathers and children to support bonding during family visits. Through structured narrative prompts, the game enabled incarcerated fathers and their children to co-author family narratives and engage in meaningful conversation as a way to build family cohesion, secure attachment, intimacy, trust, and repair identity. A news article by Johnson [21] describes how other games supporting social connection as well. At San Quentin, for example, structured board game play was used within the Enhanced Outpatient Program to support social connection and mental fitness among incarcerated individuals [21].

In an article for *Kotaku*, Grayson [15] documents *Project Tech*, a UK-based program led by Ruggiero at University of Indiana and her collaborator, youth worker Laura Green, in which incarcerated youth learned to design games using tools like *Twine* [25] and *Scratch* [28]. Charged to "create a game about a social issue that led to you being in prison, and ... make this for somebody younger than you" (¶6), incarcerated youth in the program explored their own life challenges and ethical decision-making and reflected on those experiences with their peers. The program teaches students writing, programming, visual art, game design, and collaboration through the design and development process, but their real goal is to better connect them reflectively to the societal systems around them. "They're not stupid kids," the program lead is quoted as having remarked. "...They're behind in what I would consider social bonds, emotional bonds, and they don't have the wherewithal to say, 'I need help.'" (¶ 16)

These two outcomes, social connection and a critical understanding of social systems, are after all indelibly tied. In the words of Paulo Friere [11], "No pedagogy which is truly liberating can remain distant from the oppressed by treating them as unfortunates and by presenting for their emulation models from among the oppressors. The oppressed must be their own example in the struggle for their redemption." (p.54). Grayson's work on this piece was later featured in *Vice* [10] as well.

Bannon (Skunkworks). *In the carceral environment, the act of forming social connections is fraught with risk. Vulnerability–whether through friendliness, openness, or emotional expression–can and often is exploited by others. As a result, communication in prison often becomes highly strategic: words are weighed carefully, body language is tightly controlled, and trust is extended only under extreme caution, if at all. Even minor misunderstandings or perceived slights can escalate, for a variety of reasons. Beyond the misunderstanding itself, many incarcerated people have trouble with emotional regulation, and the situation is further compounded because the social cost of appearing disrespected or vulnerable is so high.*

Within this landscape, structured collaborative games such as D&D offer a rare and vital opportunity to practice social connection under safer conditions. Because the roles, scenarios, and goals of the game are collectively defined and bounded by shared rules, participants are given permission to engage in cooperation, negotiation, humor, and even moments of vulnerability without immediately risking their standing or safety. In these sessions, players rehearse essential interpersonal skills–like perspective-taking, turn-taking, and trust-building–in a context that feels real but is protected by the "magic circle" of play. Over time, these small, rehearsed acts of connection can expand the range of safe social interactions available to incarcerated people, challenging the norms of hypervigilance and isolation that prison life often demands.

3.5   Games for Knowledge Acquisition and Assessment

The educational application of games is demonstrated most clearly in the work of da Silva Carvalho and colleagues [40,41]. Their quasi-experimental study [40] evaluated a classroom implementation of their board game *Previna* designed to increase knowledge about sexually transmitted diseases (STIs) among incarcerated women in Brazil. The study found significant and sustained gains in STI-related knowledge across pre-, post-, and delayed post-tests. A subsequent article on the project [41] details the development and validation of the same game, using expert review and semantic evaluation to ensure pedagogical quality and cultural relevance.

A study by Mantell [29] describes results of a study to understand the design preferences of older adults in prison for a game-based cognitive assessment. Four focus group interviews with a total of 20 incarcerated older adults (aged >=50 years; aged >=45 years for Aboriginal and Torres Strait Islander people) revealed that senior inmates value optimal challenge, sensible graphics, variety, and meaningful choices in games designed to do cognitive assessments.

The most sophisticated game-based intervention in the literature to date is *Project Choices* (PC) [9]. PC is an iOS game designed to support correctional intervention through realistic post-release decision-making scenarios and cognitive-behavioral feedback. Forty-two realistic decision-making post-release scenarios are presented to players whose response options reflect varying levels of risk. The riskier the response selected, the greater the number of negative outcomes, which in turn is reflected in a player's negative statistics (criminogenic risk, physical health, mental health, emotional health, financial health and social health). The goal of the game is to make it through all 42 scenarios while maximizing one's functional statistics. In a pilot study of 24 men living in a residential treatment facility following a substance-related violation of their probation, the authors compared the PC program to the casual game *Tetris* [32] in its effects on criminogenic thinking, self-perceived risk (to reoffend), and social problem-solving. Results revealed no statistically significant treatment effects for the PC program compared to Tetris.

3.6   Summary

Table 1 below summarizes all 14 articles (of 21 total) included in this review that describes or discusses a game being used in some way for positive impact in a carceral setting; for each article, it highlights the game used and the purported outcomes of the game or game-based intervention, whether achieved or only intended. New and media articles are marked with an asterisk.

Beginning with the most obvious observation, *analog games* (8 of 14 relevant articles total) are more widely used than digital (6 of 14 total), likely due to security restrictions and resource constraints. In terms of the intended or accomplished outcomes of such efforts, 9 articles described games aimed to foster social connection of some kind (*social*), 7 hoped to strengthen self-regulation or emotional control, (*emotional*) and 6 targeted specific knowledge gains (*cognitive*). Almost half of the reports considered (6 of 14) address more than one general area of impact (social, emotional, or cognitive), suggesting that benefits in one area are often tied to benefits in another. Taken as a whole, the outcome variables studied across the extant literature are not isolated variables but have a certain logical bearing on one another. Figure 2 provides one plausible configuration, illustrating the bidirectional contributions of internal (left) and external (right) phenomena.

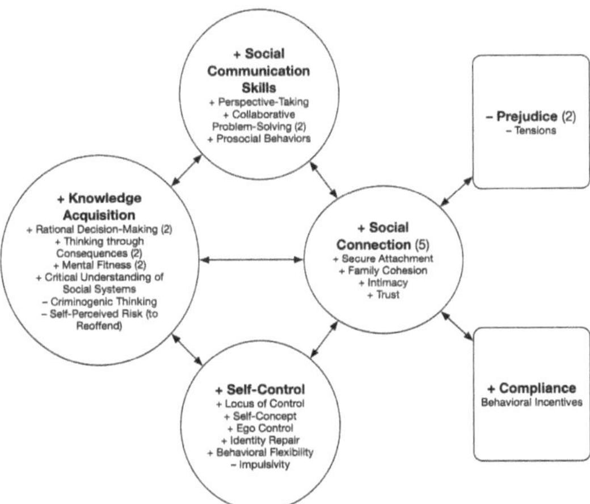

Fig. 2. Potential Relationships among Outcome Variables Across the Literature.

4   Discussion

This review of serious games in carceral settings confirms what many in the field of games and learning have long argued: that games are not only compelling cultural artifacts but potent sociotechnical systems capable of shaping behavior, affect, cognition, and social connection. In the uniquely constrained ecology of the prison system, where traditional interventions are often bureaucratized, impersonal, and siloed, games offer a compelling alternative: low-cost, highly engaging scaffolding systems that can be readily adapted to therapeutic, educational, and rehabilitative ends.

Table 1. Games and Reported Outcomes Across All Articles Reviewed

Article	Games	Reported Outcomes
Blakinger (2023)*	*Dungeons & Dragons*	Social connection Reduced prejudice
da Silva Carvalho et al. (2023, 2024)	*Previna* (board game)	Knowledge acquisition
de Kleer (2017)*	*Dungeons & Dragons*	Social connection Reduced prejudice
Diehl, et al., (2024)	*Project Choices* (iOS game)	Reduced criminogenic thinking Reduced self-perceived risk (to reoffend) Increased social problem-solving
de Kleer (2017)	*Dungeons & Dragons*	Social connection Reduced prejudice
Grayson (2017)*	game-making	Social connection Critical understanding of social systems
Johnson (2023)*	*Scrabble,* board games	Social connection Mental fitness
Kappes & Thompson (1985)	*Atari* games (various)	Impulsivity Locus of control Self-concept
Leapman (2006)*	*PlayStation, Xbox Nintendo GameBoy* games	Behavioral incentives
Markussen & Knutz (2020)	*Captivated* (board game)	Family cohesion Secure attachment Intimacy Trust Identity repair
Morrow (2008)	puzzle games (various)	Social communication skills
Reaves (1984)	arcade games (various)	Reduce tensions Diversion Compliance
Resnick (1986); Resnick, Boler & Merrill (1986)	*Busted* (board game)	Ego control Perspective-taking Rational decision-making Collaborative problem-solving Prosocial behaviors Behavioral flexibility Thinking through consequences
Ribbens & Malliet (2015)	digital games (various)	Social connection Diversion/Escapism Mental fitness Pleasure Self-Control
Stober (2023)*	Chess	Rational decision-making Thinking through consequences

One of the most striking findings is the breadth of outcomes that games in carceral settings have been deployed to support. While early implementations relied on games for external behavioral control or mere diversion (doing time, as they say, rather than time doing you), today we see more sophisticated uses targeting internal regulation, social-emotional development, cognitive growth, and even identity repair. Critically, these outcomes are not discrete but rather mutually reinforcing. Gains in self-regulation often accompany improvements in social interaction, for example, and knowledge acquisition is enhanced by players' perspective-taking abilities, mental fitness, and self-control. This layered impact reflects the deeply embedded, systems-level nature of game mechanics and dynamics: games are whole (often social) ecologies, not isolated interventions.

Analog games remain disproportionately prevalent in carceral settings, likely reflecting practical constraints such as security policies, funding, and infrastructure, but it also raises important questions about access and equity. Digital games offer affordances that analog formats cannot easily replicate: adaptive difficulty, simulated futures, asynchronous collaboration, and AI-driven feedback. Yet their scarcity in prisons is emblematic of broader structural inequalities that define carceral life. Bridging that digital divide must be part of any serious reform effort; if the goal is "to bring life in prison as close as possible to life outside of prison," then digital technology including simulations and games must be part of that normalization process. As the [US state redcted] Model states, "The more life in prison resembles life in the community, the easier it will be for people to transition and adjust to life in the community upon release." (p.3) [48].

Of particular note are the ways games facilitate prosociality in an environment that often demands hyper-individualism and mistrust for survival. The recurring examples of *Dungeons & Dragons* in solitary confinement and role-playing in youth facilities exemplify this most vividly. These games create what Huizinga [19] described as the "magic circle"–a protected social space where new rules and roles enable new ways of being with others. In carceral spaces where identity is often stripped down to criminal record and institutional number, games provide a rare opportunity to reconstruct self in relation to others–through character, dialogue, and shared narrative stakes.

This capacity to safely experiment with social identity and behavior makes games uniquely suited for what we might call "prefigurative rehabilitation": not just preparing individuals for life after incarceration but enabling them to rehearse it. These virtual rehearsals–of resisting peer pressure, managing risk, collaborating across differences–may be some of the most important work games do in this setting. The immersive feedback loops, delayed consequences, and non-lethal experimentation built into game design allow individuals to engage in prosocial decision-making without real-world penalty, something nearly impossible to facilitate in traditional group therapy or cognitive-behavior therapy alone.

It is equally important to note what is missing from the literature. Empirical work remains relatively sparse, with many studies relying on anecdotal or self-report data. While this is understandable given the challenges of research access in carceral institutions, it also limits our ability to rigorously assess efficacy.

We need longitudinal, mixed-methods studies that attend not just to pre-post outcomes but to the lived experiences of players, the emergent dynamics of play, and the institutional logics that shape game adoption. We also need critical frameworks that do not just measure whether games "work," but interrogate what forms of citizenship, normalcy, or recovery they are implicitly training toward. Games are not neutral; their pedagogies and politics must be surfaced and evaluated, especially in state-controlled environments.

Finally, this review reveals a broader theoretical imperative: to reconceptualize the role of games in carceral reform not as escapist indulgences or pedagogical novelties but as complex, semiotic systems for re-authoring the self. This aligns with longstanding traditions in educational games research, cognitive apprenticeship, and critical design–but it demands that we bring those theories into direct conversation with criminology, trauma-informed practice, and reentry services. Such interdisciplinary collaboration is not only overdue; it is vital if we hope to produce interventions that are not only engaging and evidence-based but just.

Disclosure of Interests. The authors have no competing interests to declare that are relevant to the content of this article.

References

1. Alliance for Safety and Justice: Crime survivors speak: The first ever national survey of victims' views on safety and justice. https://allianceforsafetyandjustice.org/wp-content/uploads/documents/Crime%20Survivors%20Speak%20Report.pdf
2. Blakinger, K.: The dungeons & dragons players of death row. The New York Times (2023)
3. Butler, O., Herr, K., Willmund, G., Gallinat, J., Kühn, S., Zimmermann, P.: Trauma, treatment and tetris: video gaming increases hippocampal volume in male patients with combat-related posttraumatic stress disorder. J. Psychiatry Neurosci. JPN **45**(4), 279–287 (2020). https://doi.org/10.1503/jpn.190027
4. Cavadino, M., Dignan, J.: Introducing comparative penology. In: Cavadino, M., Dignan, J. (eds.) Penal Systems: A Comparative Approach, pp. 3–40. Sage Publications, London (2006)
5. Cavadino, M., Dignan, J.: The Penal System: An Introduction. Sage Publications, London (2007)
6. Cejudo, J., Losada, L., Feltrero, R.: Promoting social and emotional learning and subjective well-being: impact of the "aislados" intervention program in adolescents. Int. J. Environ. Res. Public Health **17**(2) (2020). https://doi.org/10.3390/ijerph17020609
7. Clark, D.B., Tanner-Smith, E.E., Killingsworth, S.S.: Digital games, design, and learning: a systematic review and meta-analysis. Rev. Educ. Res. **86**(1), 79–122 (2016). https://doi.org/10.3102/0034654315582065
8. Corbett, S.: Learning by playing: video games in the classroom. The New York Times (2010)
9. Diehl, K.J., Morgan, R.D., King, C.M., Ingram, P.B., Mitchell, C.: Reception to and efficacy of a serious video game for correctional intervention: project choices. Crim. Justice Behav. **51**(11), 1635–1653 (2024). https://doi.org/10.1177/00938548241268043

10. Critical Distance: Here's more of the best writing on games and prison (2017). https://www.vice.com/en/article/heres-more-of-the-best-writing-on-games-and-prison/
11. Freire, P.: Pedagogy of the Oppressed. Brazil (1970)
12. Fuchs, M.: The game is chess, the opponents are felons. The New York Times (2003)
13. Garfield, R.: Magic: the gathering (1993)
14. Graves, S.K.: State corrections in the wake of California's criminal justice reforms: much progress, more work to do (2018). https://calbudgetcenter.org/app/uploads/2018/10/Chartbook_State-Corrections-in-the-Wake-of-Reforms_October-2018.pdf
15. Grayson, N.: Can learning to make video games help rehabilitate jailed kids? Kotaku (2017)
16. Gunel, E., Top, E.: Effects of educational video games on english vocabulary learning and retention. Int. J. Technol. Educ. **5**(2), 333–350 (2022)
17. Gygax, G., Arneson, D.: Dungeons & Dragons. TSR; Wizards of the Coast (1974)
18. Hazel, J., Kim, H.M., Every-Palmer, S.: Exploring the possible mental health and wellbeing benefits of video games for adult players: a cross-sectional study. Australas. Psychiatry **30**(4), 541–546 (2022). https://doi.org/10.1177/10398562221103081
19. Huizinga, J.: Homo Ludens: A Study of the Play Element in Culture. Routledge & Kegan, London (1944)
20. Jenness, V., Sumner, J., Sexton, L., Alamillo-Luchese, N.: Cinderella, wilma flintstone, and xena the warrior princess: capturing diversity among transgender women in men's prisons. In: Understanding Diversity: Celebrating Difference, Challenging Inequality, pp. 107–124. Allyn & Bacon Press (2014)
21. Johnson, B.: Study: board games contribute to wellness (2023). https://sanquentinnews.com/study-board-games-contribute-to-wellness/
22. Kaltman, I.: Digital game-based learning enhances literacy. Educ. Dig. **84**(8), 43–47 (2019)
23. Kappes, B.M., Thompson, D.L.: Biofeedback vs. video games: effects on impulsivity, locus of control and self-concept with incarcerated juveniles. J. Clin. Psychol. **41**, 698–706 (1985). https://doi.org/10.1002/1097-4679(198509)41:5⟨698::AID-JCLP2270410520⟩3.0.CO;2-Q
24. de Kleer, E.: Dragons in the department of corrections (2017). https://www.vice.com/en/article/dragons-in-the-department-of-corrections/
25. Klimas, C.: Twine (version 2.3.9) [computer software] (2019). https://twinery.org, open-source tool for telling interactive, nonlinear stories
26. Leapman, B.: Latest games consoles handed out to young jail inmates (2006). https://www.telegraph.co.uk/news/uknews/1516436/Latest-games-consoles-handed-out-to-young-jail-inmates.html, the Telegraph
27. Lee, H.A., et al.: Cooperation begins: encouraging critical thinking skills through cooperative reciprocity using a mobile learning game. Comput. Educ. **97**, 97–115 (2016). https://doi.org/10.1016/j.compedu.2016.03.006
28. Lifelong Kindergarten Group at the MIT Media Lab: Scratch (version 3.0) [computer software] (2023). https://scratch.mit.edu, visual programming language and online community for creating interactive stories, games, and animations
29. Mantell, R., Withall, A., Radford, K., Kasumovic, M., Monds, L., Hwang, Y.I.J.: Design preferences for a serious game–based cognitive assessment of older adults in prison: Thematic analysis. JMIR Serious Games **11**, e45467 (2023). https://doi.org/10.2196/45467

30. Markussen, T., Knutz, E.: Playing games to re-story troubled family narratives in danish maximum-security prisons. Punishm. Soc. **22**(4), 483–508 (2020). https://doi.org/10.1177/1462474520915748

31. Morrow, T.: How effective is offender-reflective practice in their own learning when using games to develop positive changes in their social communication skills? Reflective Pract. **9**(3), 329–340 (2008). https://doi.org/10.1080/14623940802207444

32. Pajitnov, A.: Tetris (1985). [Video game]

33. Pew Center on the States: State of recidivism: The revolving door of America's prisons (2011). https://www.pewtrusts.org/-/media/legacy/uploadedfiles/pcs_assets/2011/pewstateofrecidivismpdf.pdf, the Pew Charitable Trusts

34. Reaves, L.: Zap that asteroid! ABA J. **70**(3), 48 (1984)

35. Resnick, H.: Electronic technology and rehabilitation: a computerized simulation game for youthful offenders. Simul. Games **17**(4), 460–466 (1986). https://doi.org/10.1177/0037550086174004

36. Resnick, H., Boler, M., Merrill, N.: "Busted": a therapeutic simulation game. Residential Treat. Child. Youth **4**(1), 75–87 (1986). https://doi.org/10.1300/J007v04n01_10

37. Ribbens, W., Malliet, S.: Exploring the appeal of digital games to male prisoners. Poetics **48**, 1–20 (2015). https://doi.org/10.1016/j.poetic.2014.10.007

38. Sawyer, W., Wagner, P.: Mass incarceration: the whole pie 2025 (2025). https://www.prisonpolicy.org/reports/pie2022.html, prison Policy Initiative

39. Schwartz, J.: Dungeons & dragons prison ban upheld. The New York Times (2010)

40. da Silva Carvalho, I., et al.: Effect of a board game on imprisoned women's knowledge about sexually transmitted infections: a quasi-experimental study. BMC Public Health **23**(1), 1–11 (2023). https://doi.org/10.1186/s12889-023-15646-3

41. da Silva Carvalho, I., et al.: Board game on sexually transmitted infections for imprisoned women. BMC Women's Health **24**(1), 1–11 (2024). https://doi.org/10.1186/s12905-023-02801-6

42. Squire, K., Steinkuehler, C.: Videogames and learning. In: Sawyer, K. (ed.) Cambridge Handbook of the Learning Sciences, 3rd edn, pp. 281–300. Cambridge University Press, Cambridge (2022)

43. Steinkuehler, C.: The mismeasure of boys: reading and online videogames. In: Kaminski, W., Lorber, M. (eds.) Proceedings of Game-based Learning: Clash of Realities Conference, pp. 33–50. Kopaed Publishers, Munich (2012)

44. Steinkuehler, C., et al.: Enriched esports: the design and four-year examination of a school-affiliated competitive videogame program for youth. J. Interact. Learn. Res. **34**(1), 59–119 (2023)

45. Stober, E.: More than a game: how chess is helping prisoners in Canada (2024). https://globalnews.ca/news/10297763/prison-chess-canada/, global News

46. Sun, Z., Theussen, A.: Assessing negotiation skill and its development in an online collaborative simulation game: a social network analysis study. Br. J. Edu. Technol. **54**(1), 222–246 (2023). https://doi.org/10.1111/bjet.13263

47. Unknown: Missouri bans video games from prisons (2005). https://www.nbcnews.com/id/wbna6868501, nBC News

48. Unknown: Safe communities, inside and out (2024). https://www.cdcr.ca.gov/blog/13399/, the California Model Magazine, 1

49. Wagner, P., Rabuy, B.: Following the money of mass incarceration (2017). https://www.prisonpolicy.org/reports/money.html, prison Policy Initiative

Engaging Low-Literate Adults Through Game-Based Virtual Reality

Benjamin Schnitzer[1]($\boxtimes$) , Eveline Bader[2] , Polona Caserman[4] ,
Giulio Crocco[3] , and Oliver Korn[1]

[1] Affective and Cognitive Institute, Offenburg University, Offenburg, Germany
`benjamin.schnitzer@hs-offenburg.de`
[2] German Institute for Adult Education, Bonn, Germany
[3] GFFB gGmbH, Frankfurt, Germany
[4] Serious Games Research Group, Technical University of Darmstadt,
Darmstadt, Germany
`https://aci.hs-offenburg.de`

Abstract. Advances in Virtual Reality enable new learning spaces
for language learning. While game-based learning generally has shown
promise in the field of language learning, its potential for low-literate
adults remains underexplored. In this work, we examine the potentials
of Serious Virtual Reality Games (SVRGs) for language learning and
describe the design of a playful SVRG involving an embodied syllable sorting task. Using a within-participants design, adults previously
identified as low-literate (n = 9) played the game in two conditions:
a low-immersive desktop and a fully immersive VR version. Learning
outcomes were measured via pre- and post-tests. We assessed in-game
performance, usability, flow, engagement, and embodiment. While the
results did not reveal significant differences regarding knowledge gain,
usability, and flow, participants reported increased attention playing the
SVRG. Moreover, the game metrics revealed that participants pursued a
trial-and-error strategy when playing the PC version, whereas in VR the
interface design nudged them towards making more informed decisions.

Keywords: Serious Virtual Reality Games · Game-Based Language
Learning · Low-Literate Adults · Syllable Sorting

1 Introduction

Reading and writing skills are essential for social and professional participation,
yet many adults possess only low literacy levels, despite having completed basic
education. In Germany, approximately 6.2 million adults have insufficient literacy in the German language for daily and work tasks; an additional 10.6 million
make frequent spelling errors. A significant number of these low-literate adults
have a migration background [1]. In light of an imminent demographic shift and a
growing shortage of skilled labor, a lot of efforts are being made to support adults
with low literacy through continued education and training initiatives. Simultaneously, the issue is highly sensitive, given that literacy skills are a fundamental

A. Thomas et al. (Eds.): JCSG 2025, LNCS 16243, pp. 51–69, 2026.
https://doi.org/10.1007/978-3-032-10518-9_6

prerequisite for social and professional participation. It is especially challenging to identify individuals with low literacy, as they often develop various strategies to conceal their difficulties due to shame or stigma. Eventually, since language is a time-consuming process with rather slow improvement, motivating the learners is a critical factor, too.

Bernard Suits described playing games as "the voluntary attempt to overcome unnecessary obstacles" [2]. Games are associated with fun and pleasure, although they can be challenging. The motivational quality of (digital) games is often grounded in psychological theories [3], such as the self-determination theory [4] or flow state [5]. In the context of game-based learning, these effects have been heavily investigated [6] and shown in literature [7–14].

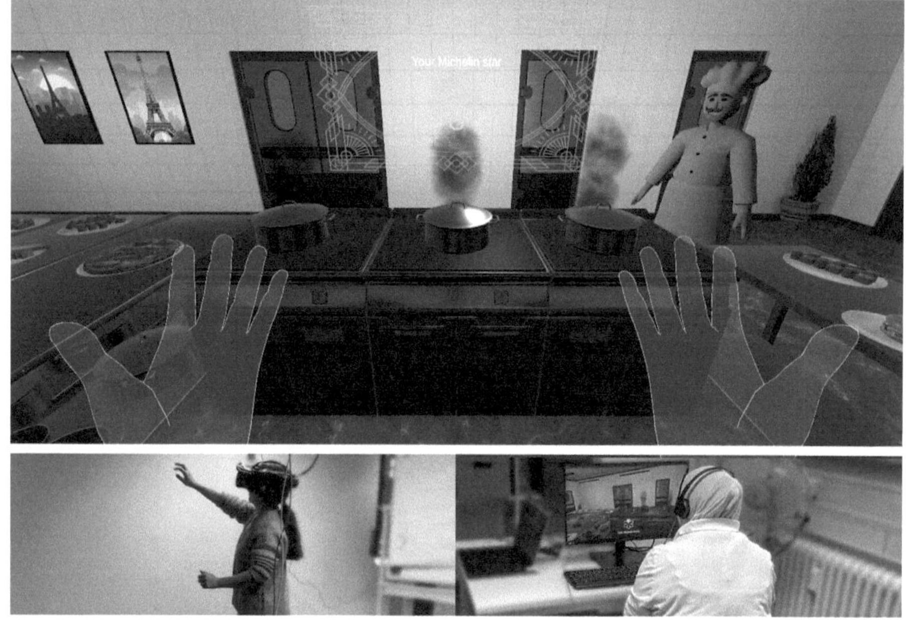

Fig. 1. On the top, in-game impression of the Serious Virtual Reality Game'Syllable Soup'. On the bottom, participants playing the game in VR and on a PC.

At the same time, virtual reality (VR) games are becoming increasingly popular [15]. In the evolving landscape of game-based learning, VR offers new learning opportunities apart from acquiring practical knowledge in specific simulations. Today's learners can engage with and manipulate representations of abstract concepts and understand them through multimodal sensorimotor experiences [16, 17]. An example is language acquisition through spatial, kinesthetic, and playful interactions [18]. Considering the reality-virtuality continuum by Milgram and Kishono [19], the emergence of highly immersive technology is discussed as a promising tool for learning, mainly due to multisensory stimulation and its characteristic to engage [20] users and let them fully "be there" [21].

Serious games and virtual environments show promise for improving literacy among German children [22,23] and low-literate adults [24]. While there is empirical evidence for the positive impacts of immersive VR on language learning [22,25–27], embodied learning in immersive VR [16,20,28,29], and embodied language learning [30–32], possible benefits of highly immersive VR compared to desktop VR remain ambiguous [18,33,34]. Moreover, research on serious game interventions for individuals with reading difficulties is limited; a recent systematic review identified only six studies focusing on children [35] and research addressing low-literate adults is even more scarce [23].

Considering the outlined circumstances, serious VR games (SVRGs) may bridge a gap by *(a)* enhancing the experience [36] of low-literate adults through game-based learning and *(b)* providing highly immersive playful learning environments that ensure effectiveness and success through multisensory [37,38] and kinesthetic learning [39] while additionally functioning as 'safe-spaces' for a sensitive topic. However, to the best of our knowledge, there is little work investigating the potentials of SVRGs within the target group of low-literate adults. In this work, we therefore investigate the following research question:

RQ: What are the effects of SVRGs for low-literate adults on learning outcomes, usability, and engagement compared to desktop VR?

In the next section, we first describe related work on game-based learning for low-literate adults. Given the limited research on playful VR interventions for this target group, we then highlight their potential and limitations by drawing on related work in VR-based language learning and vocabulary acquisition. Eventually, we present the design and development of a SVRG called *'Syllable Soup'* (Fig. 1), training phonological awareness – known as the ability to manipulate and reflect on the individual sounds that make up a language [40] – and word recognition through an embodied syllable sorting task. The design process is accompanied by an iterative user study with low-literate adults, the results of which are finally presented and discussed.

2 Related Work

2.1 Low-Literacy Adults and Game-Based Learning

Reading difficulties among individuals with low literacy skills often stem from weaknesses in decoding, phonological awareness, and word reading fluency. Notably, low reading accuracy persists in low-literate adults even in transparent orthographies like German, where decoding is typically easier [41]. Efficient decoding is a crucial prerequisite for fluent word recognition, as it frees cognitive resources that can be allocated to reading comprehension [42].

Low-literate adults face particular challenges. Some low-literates can read and understand short and familiar texts, yet struggle with extracting meaning from unfamiliar texts and correct spelling of simple and common words [43].

Compared to others, this group participates significantly less and less frequently in education programs [44]. In addition, they show lower self-efficacy, lower commitment and poorer delay of gratification in educational contexts, which can be risk factors for dropping out of an educational program [45]. Engaging and retaining this group in educational programs continues to be a significant challenge for adult education professionals [46].

Integrating virtual environments and serious games shows promise for improving literacy among German children [22,23] and low-literate adults [24]. Such applications provide interactive and motivating learning, especially beneficial for low-literate adults with negative prior educational experience [24]. Immersive technologies provide safe and realistic settings with no real-world consequences and immediate feedback [47] which allows low-literate adults to practice in protected environments. Using real-world topics relevant to adult learners can boost motivation, as demonstrated in the context of financial education [24].

Within children learners, previous research implies that digital game-based learning supports the acquisition of word recognition and fosters learners' reading skills [22,23,35,48,49]. A recent meta-analysis found that low-literate adults can benefit from phonological interventions, including phonological recoding (linking graphemes to phonemes and breaking words into smaller units) [50]. One example is the manipulation of words by segmenting them into syllables that can be recombined. Heß et al. demonstrated that a syllable-based approach combined with digital game-based features can significantly improve word recognition and phonological recoding in children [22].

Early readers typically shift within their first year from decoding letter by letter to recognizing larger sublexical units, such as syllables [51]. Eye-tracking research shows that even skilled German readers continue to rely on syllable clusters during reading [52]. Therefore, syllable-based instruction is widely considered good practice and is commonly used in adult literacy programs to enhance reading fluency [53].

2.2 Language Learning in Virtual Reality

There is a profound body of research on vocabulary acquisition addressing the question how increased immersion influences learning outcomes, particularly in language acquisition.

For example, in a study involving 371 participants, the authors found that 2D images led to significantly better vocabulary recall than stereoscopic 3D images [33]. The lower performance in the S3D condition was attributed to cognitive overload and distraction caused by immersive depth cues. Although the study did not incorporate fully immersive VR or interactive elements (participants only passively viewed the content) the results indicate that greater immersion does not necessarily lead to improved learning outcomes [33]. Simultaneously, the immersive and interactive nature of VR challenges the application of traditional cognitive theories [20]. While immersion can increase cognitive load in complex scenarios, targeted instructional design strategies—such as signaling or cueing—have been shown to effectively manage or even reduce it. This suggests that the cognitive load effects of VR are highly dependent on the quality of instructional design [20,54].

Papin and Kaplan-Rakowski studied how annotated 360° images affect vocabulary learning in three settings: high-immersive VR, low-immersive VR (on-screen), and traditional 2D images. Among 63 participants, vocabulary recall was highest in the low-immersion group, likely due to a balance between immersion and ease of use. The authors suggested that fully immersive VR might cause cognitive overload [55].

Vázquez et al. developed "Words in Motion," a VR system that links physical movements to target language words (e.g., waving to learn"wave"). Although immediate learning was lower than with text-only methods and similar to non-kinesthetic VR, the kinesthetic approach led to significantly better retention after one week [39].

At the same time, a review by Dhimolea et al. [34] challenges previous findings by emphasizing that while perceptions of language learning in VR are generally positive, the evidence regarding its effectiveness remains inconclusive. They note that the potential of VR technology to enhance language learning outcomes requires further investigation [34]. This is supported by findings from Schnitzer et al., which suggest that fully immersive VR offers no advantages over desktop VR in terms of vocabulary recognition. However, their results do indicate that fully immersive VR combined with embodied learning can have a positive impact on reducing knowledge loss [18].

Kaplan-Rakowski and Thrasher studied the impact of VR and interactivity on French vocabulary learning among 91 high school students. While fully immersive VR users slightly outperformed desktop VR users in absolute terms, especially on delayed tests, the differences were not statistically significant. Interacting with virtual objects also showed no significant effect on learning or retention [56].

The outlined work suggests that fully immersive VR may support better long-term vocabulary retention for ordinary learners, possibly due to multisensory learning and embodied interactions. Simultaneously, cognitive overload appears to be one of the main side-effects hindering learning. Regarding the target group of low-literate adults, this area of conflict remains underexplored.

In light of the reviewed literature, we therefore state the following hypotheses:

H1: A SVRG training phonological awareness and word recognition through an embodied syllable-sorting task in low-literate adults demonstrates acceptable and comparable usability than its desktop-based counterpart.

H2: Increased immersion leads to significantly higher flow experience.

H3: The SVRG is more engaging than its desktop-based counterpart.

H4: Due to specific features of the interface, player performance in fully immersive VR is altered.

H5: Compared to desktop VR, fully immersive VR leads to varying learning outcomes.

3   Evaluation

3.1   Apparatus

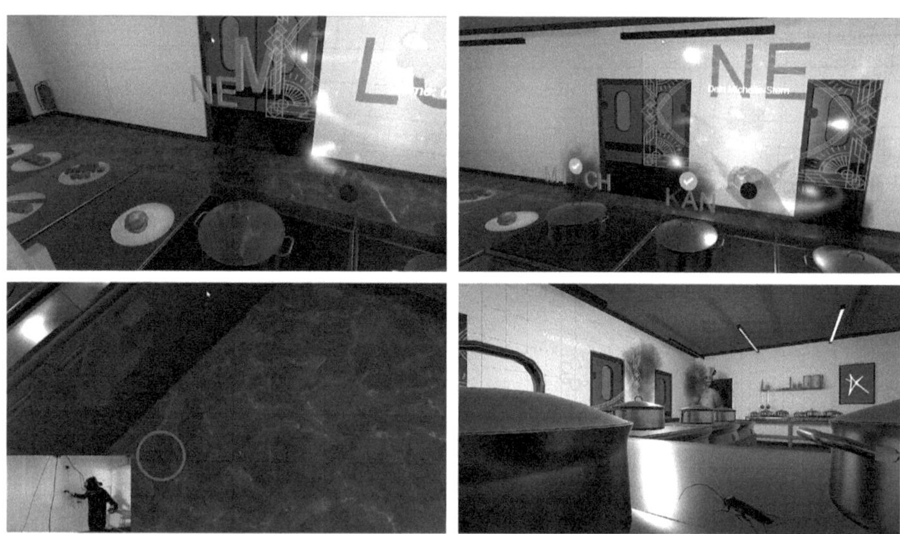

Fig. 2. At the top, syllables grab interaction and placement in the pots. Correctly placed syllables are marked up with a check symbol, incorrectly placed syllable with an x-symbol. At the bottom, a player is hitting 'enemies' with her virtual shoes (a spotted cockroach is highlighted in the red circle).

Building on these insights, we developed a SVRG called 'Syllable Soup', specifically for low-literate adults (Fig. 1). It focuses on syllable assembling including embodied interaction [17] and can be best described as a mixture of puzzle, dexterity, and exergame. The Unity3D application makes use of an *HTC-Vive Pro 2*. Designed to enhance basic reading skills and build learners' confidence in handling written German in both everyday and professional contexts, the game features content derived from the hotel and catering industry. The game development comprised two iterations including a pilot testing and user study, the methodology and results of which are described in the next sections. The second iteration of the game is based on the results of the pilot testing.

In a virtual kitchen, players have to 'cook' the perfect syllable soup and earn as many restaurant stars as possible. They catch flying syllables and place them into corresponding pots (Fig. 2). These pots are arranged in a specific sequence that follows the reading direction of Romanic languages (left to right). The activity is limited to three pots corresponding to three syllables in order to customize the task to the target group of low-literate adults (Fig. 1). When the player forms a correct triplet, they score a point, and a new three-syllable word is randomly selected from a modular word list. Five points add up to a new piece of a restaurant star, six pieces score the next restaurant star visualized on a UI element in front of the virtual stove. In the first development iteration, an additional camera sensor (*Leap Motion 2*) enabled players to grasp syllables manually (Fig. 1). In the second iteration, players interacted using the *HTC Vive controller* and corresponding virtual hands (Fig. 2).

Considering flow theory [5], the game provides several types of audiovisual feedback: correctly placed syllables are marked with a green checker-symbol; vice versa incorrectly placed syllables are marked with a red X-symbol. In case of a correct triplet, auditory feedback is given by reading out loud the formed word. In addition, an NPC in the form of a virtual chef provides feedback and motivates the players when performing well. In the beginning, this character is also used to explain the overall goal.

There are two other mechanics that contribute to the game dynamics and make it even more difficult for the player: First, players must actively lift the pot lids before the grabbed syllables snap into the target area inside the pots. However, the lids are hot, so players can only lift them for a limited time before they snap back to their original position. This time is visualized by a filling slider and reddening virtual hands. Secondly, there are 'enemies' in the form of cockroaches that try to reach the pots (Fig. 2). In the first development iteration, using a pathfinder algorithm, the cockroaches approached the pods on tables in the virtual kitchen (Fig. 2). If the cockroaches reached the pods, the player lost a part of the restaurant star. To defeat them, players had to hit the cockroaches with their hands. In the second iteration, enemies randomly scrambled the floor and had to be squashed with virtual shoes (Fig. 2). Spatial audio cues, such as scrambling sounds, indicate the direction from which a cockroach is approaching. In the second iteration, *HTC Vive trackers*, attached to the players' ankles, were used to visualize foot movement (Fig. 2). Additionally, cockroaches only had positive effects on scoring; squashing them activated a streak mode, allowing players to earn double points. The active streak mode is indicated by particle effects, which have been shown to significantly increase positive emotion in virtual environments [57].

3.2   Methods

To address the stated hypotheses, we applied a within-participants design with two conditions, comparing the SVRG 'Syllable Soup' with a low-immersive desktop version of the game. Participants trained hyphenation by playing the game in two immersive levels: A low-immersive condition (PC) and a fully immersive condition (VR). The order of conditions and the sequence of word pools (each containing 12 three-syllable words) were counterbalanced, resulting in 8 possible permutations. To boost motivation through real-life context, only words relevant to kitchen work or serving as a waiter were selected. The word pools were balanced by including 6 verbs and 6 nouns, matching word frequency, and reusing syllables to ensure a consistent level of difficulty.

We used both quantitative measures and self-reported questionnaires. Learning was evaluated through pre-, post-, and memory-tests (7 days later) based on the number of correct syllables. Player performance during gameplay was measured by correct hyphenation combinations, time between correct answers, error rates (absolute and relative), and game score. The tests mirrored the gameplay task but were stripped of game elements and feedback, with participants given 3 minutes to arrange three syllables in the correct order using the mouse. The application's logic randomly selects a word from two pools (two conditions), alternating between them until both pools are depleted. Additionally, the logic alternately begins with either pool A or B. The test primarily assesses rapid word recognition, as participants must correctly blend syllables into words within a limited time. Moreover, after each condition participants were asked to fill in a questionnaire. To understand differences in ease of use, we applied the widespread System Usability Scale (SUS) [58]. For flow, we made use of the Flow Short Scale [59,60] (FSS) and for engagement the short form of User Engagement Scale (UES-SF) [61]. Except, UES-SF (5-point Likert scale), all items were presented on a 7-point Likert scale. Given the low-literate target group, wording of some questions was slightly changed. In the computer-based questionnaire, participants were given the opportunity to play a pre-recorded audio of a single item. Additionally, we assessed joy and embodiment using the items listed in Table 1. After the fully immersive VR condition, participants were verbally asked about any symptoms of malaise related to cybersickness. Moreover, we recorded participants' performance using screen recording and an additional camera. The overall study design is depicted in (Fig. 3).

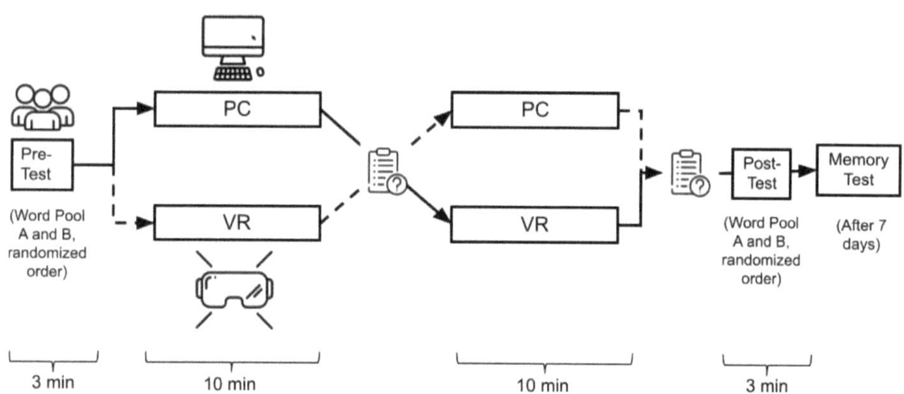

Fig. 3. Study-design with two conditions. The order of conditions as well as the order of word pools is counterbalanced.

Table 1. Items for Joy and Embodiment

No.	Construct	Item (7-point Likert scale)
1	Joy	The game was fun.
2	Embodiment	I felt as if I could move the virtual arm (and feet) like my own.
3	Embodiment	I felt as if the virtual arm (and feet) was (were) my own.

3.3   Pilot Testing

Approach: To get first insights on the game experience, we recruited 7 adult volunteers (*female = 6, male = 1, mean age = 43.43, SD = 6.95*) from a facility management training program for a pilot testing. They did not receive any payment. All participants had a migration background, were not born in Germany, and were identified as potential low-literate adults (in the German language) by the course instructor and language expert. Throughout the experiment, the authors realized that only 5 of them have literacy skills comparable to the target group of low-literate adults (Sect. 2.1). Therefore, two participants were excluded from the following analysis. The pilot testing followed the procedure described in Fig. 3. However, the memory test was left out (there was just a single session) and we only analyzed usability and comfort.

Implications: Participants reported comparable usability for both PC ($M = 60.71, SD = 15.19$) and VR ($M = 58.21, SD = 9.32$), with scores falling below the threshold for good usability, indicating only marginal acceptability [62,63]. Verbal feedback revealed that participants felt overwhelmed by the mix of audio-visual cues. This was reflected in behavior, as 4 out of 5 largely ignored cockroach enemies and paid little attention to the score (restaurant star). One participant described the cockroaches as "really disgusting" and avoided interacting with them. Video analysis showed that players often struggled with virtual grasping: Grabbing a syllable and turning to lift pot lids frequently caused hand tracking loss due to limitations of the Leap Motion sensor, and eventually leading to frustration. The need to use the same hand for grasping syllables, lifting lids, and defeating enemies also resulted in excessive hand interaction, forcing players to release objects to respond to threats.

Given the marginal acceptable usability and partially overstrained participants, we made several changes to the game:

- We made use of the *HTC Vive Controller* to address possible tracking issues and to guarantee 'no-look' grasping.
- We included foot interaction and made use of additional *HTC Vive trackers* to track players' feet.
- Cockroaches must be smashed using the feet. They do not negatively affect the score; instead, stepping on a scrambling cockroach triggers a streak mode.
- The virtual 'chef' only gives occasional feedback. This is consistently positive.

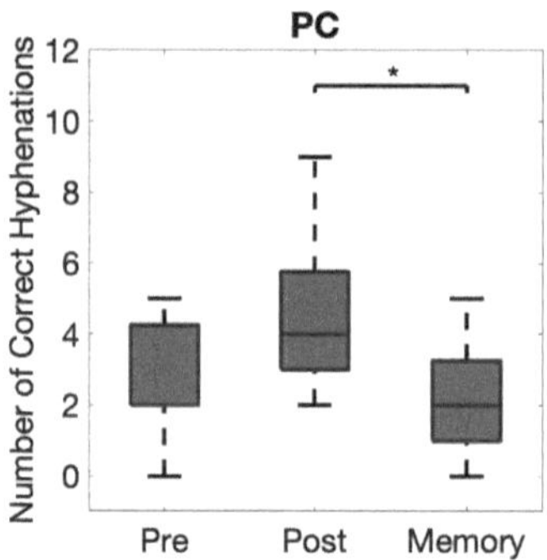
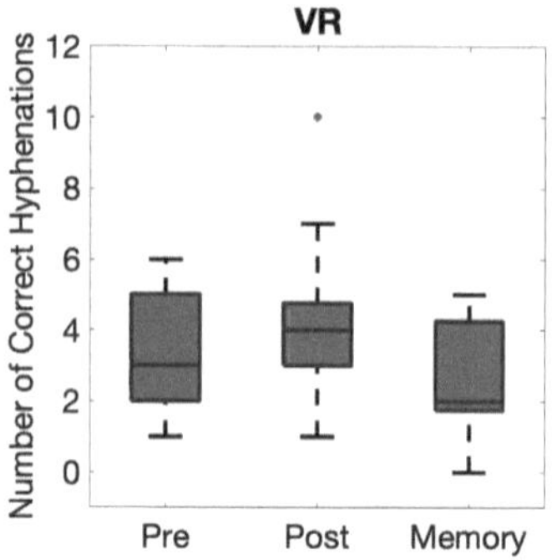

Fig. 4. Boxplots results of pre-, post- and memory-tests for both conditions.

3.4   User Study

Participants and Procedure: The procedure remained the same, but we changed the game elements and input devices as described in Sect. 3.1. For the actual user study, we recruited 9 adult first-generation migrants (*female = 8, male = 1, mean age = 41.56, SD = 8.65*) with low literacy in the German language, as determined by a standardized computer-based skills assessment system designed and validated for German low-literate adults [64]. None of the participants received payment, however, they were part of a further training program free of cost. After being informed about the study procedure and data privacy in accordance with the Declaration of Helsinki and GDPR, participants were asked to provide written consent. Following the pre-test, participants began learning with the game for 10 minutes, either in fully immersive VR or desktop VR (*PC*). Prior to experiencing the second condition, participants completed the questionnaire. They were then asked to fill it out again afterward. Finally, they completed the post-test assessment. On average, the entire evaluation took 51 minutes per participant. Seven days after the initial session, participants returned to complete a memory test. The study took place in January 2025.

Results: None of the participants reported cybersickness symptoms, therefore all 9 datasets were included in the analysis. Since the data is not normally distributed, we only applied nonparametric tests. For comparisons we applied either paired or unpaired Wilcoxon tests and Friedman-tests. For possible correlations, we computed Spearman's coefficients

Results on Learning Outcomes: Regarding learning outcomes as the absolute number of correct hyphenation combinations (maximum of correct answers was 12), a Friedman test yielded significant differences ($\chi^2 = 10.56$, $df = 2$, $p < .01$) between data points across the pre-, post-, and memory-test for the PC condition (Fig. 4). Paired post-hoc Wilcoxon tests with Bonferroni correction revealed a significant difference between post- and memory-test ($p < .05$) with a large effect size (*Cohen's d = .98*). A Friedman test for the VR condition did not yield significant differences across points in time, however, participants performed better in the post-test compared to both the pre- and the memory test (Fig. 4). The learning and forgetting curve thus generally resembles the one from the PC condition. Regarding knowledge gain as the relative number of correct hyphenation combinations derived through post- minus pre-test results ($PC: M = 1.77$, $SD = 1.78$; $VR: M = 1.00$, $SD = 1.94$) as well as memory- minus pre-test results ($PC: M = -0.44$, $SD = 2.07$; $VR: M = -0.66$, $SD = 1.66$), paired Wilcoxon tests did not yield any significant differences.

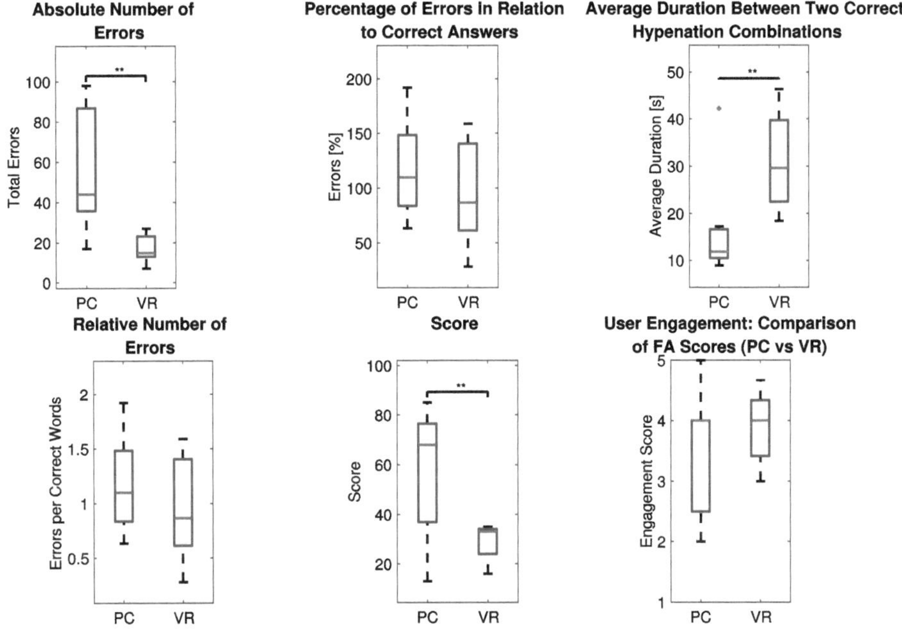

Fig. 5. On the top and bottom left: Boxplot results for in-game metrics. Bottom right: Boxplot results for subscale 'Focused Attention' of UES.

Results on Player Performance: Regarding player performance during play, we analyzed the metrics absolute number of correct hyphenation combinations, duration between two correct hyphenation combinations, error rate, error rate relative to the number of correct answers, and the game score. Paired Wilcoxon-tests revealed that participants achieved a significantly higher number of correct hyphenation combinations in the PC condition compared to the VR condition ($p < .01$) with a large effect size (*Cohen's* $d = 1.92$). At the same time, participants needed significantly more time between two correct syllable combinations in the VR condition compared to the PC condition ($p < .01$). This comparison yielded a large effect size (*Cohen's* $d = -1.37$). Figure 5 shows the boxplot results.

Participants made significantly more absolute errors in the PC condition compared to the VR condition ($p < .01$). This comparison yielded a large effect size (*Cohen's d = 1.56*). Regarding the relative number of errors it is worth mentioning that, although not statistically significant, participants made more errors in the PC condition (*M = 1.18, SD = 0.42*) compared to the VR condition (*M = 0.95, SD = 0.47*). Spearman's correlation coefficient revealed a strong positive correlation between correct hyphenation combinations and errors for the PC condition ($\rho = .74$, $p < .05$), the correlation for the VR condition was insignificant ($\rho = -.15$, $p = .70$). Moreover, Spearman's correlation coefficient revealed a strong negative correlation between the number of errors and the average duration between correct hyphenation combinations for the PC condition ($\rho = -.73$, $p < .05$), but an insignificant correlation for the VR condition ($\rho = -.01$, $p = .78$). Generally, there was a strong negative correlation between the number of correct hyphenation combinations and the average duration between correct hyphenation combinations for both, the PC condition ($\rho = -.99$, $p < .001$) and the VR condition ($\rho = -.99$, $p < .001$). At the same time, compared to the VR condition, participants achieved a significantly higher game score (also including the number of enemies destroyed) in the PC condition ($p < .01$) with large effect size (*Cohen's d = 1.35*).

Results on Usability: Participants rated the system usability of both applications as "good" (overall mean SUS > 70) [63,64], with slightly higher ratings for the PC condition (*M = 79.72, SD = 11.42*) compared to the VR condition (*M = 75.83, SD = 11.86*). Differences between conditions were insignificant.

Results on Flow: Participants reported generally high flow scores for both the PC (*M = 6.22, SD = 0.56*) and the VR condition (*M = 6.22, SD = 0.56*), however, differences were insignificant.

Results on Fun: Regarding the single item "The game was fun.", participants reported high ratings for both the PC (*M = 6.89, SD = 0.33*) and VR (*M = 6.90, SD = 0.32*). Differences between the conditions were insignificant.

Results on User Engagement: Overall, both applications were found to be engaging (*PC: M = 4.31, SD = 0.44; VR: M = 4.44, SD = 0.39*) and no significant differences were found between conditions. The same applies to the subscales aesthetic appeal (*PC: M = 4.22, SD = 0.83; VR: M = 4.33, SD = 0.69*), reward (*PC: M = 4.59, SD = 0.66; VR: mean = 4.70, SD = 0.56*), perceived usefulness (*PC: M = 4.52, SD = 0.73; VR: M = 4.44, SD = 0.83*), and focused attention (*PC: M = 3.89, SD = 0.78; VR: M = 4.26, SD = 0.74*). Regarding the latter, however, this difference is notable although not statistically significant: Participants reported higher attention in the VR condition (Fig. 5).

Results on Embodiment: Embodiment was assessed only for the VR condition. Overall, participants reported generally high embodiment scores (*M = 6.39, SD = 0.65*).

4   Discussion

Based on the findings related to usability, flow, fun, and engagement, our results highlight the overall potential of game-based language interventions, especially fully immersive SVRGs. However, at first glance, there appears to be no significant advantage of fully immersive VR over desktop-based VR (PC), or vice versa.

We accept *H1* ("An SVRG training phonological awareness and word recognition through an embodied syllable-sorting task in low-literate adults demonstrates acceptable and comparable usability than its desktop-based counterpart."), particularly considering the changes made after pilot-testing. This is an important finding for designers considering fast-paced embodied interactions: Controllers (still) promise better usability. This is a key finding when considering the trade-off between development complexity, hardware costs, familiarization of VR technology, and learning outcomes. Although perceived flow was rated highly, it was comparable across both conditions, leading us to reject *H2* ("Increased immersion leads to significantly higher flow experience.").

Regarding engagement, the results showed slightly higher, though not statistically significant, user engagement scores for fully immersive VR. We therefore only partially accept *H3* ("The SVRG is more engaging than its desktop-based counterpart."). Moreover, a more detailed look revealed a higher attention and focus in the fully immersive VR condition. This contrasts with previous findings [18,33,55,56], which emphasize immersion as a limiting factor due to its potential to increase cognitive load. Overall, we accept *H4* ("Due to specific features of the interface, player performance in fully immersive VR is altered."), as players performed significantly better and faster on the PC. A logical explanation is Fitts law [66]. This result is underlined by the negative correlation found between the number of correct hyphenation combinations and the average duration between correct hyphenation combinations. However, given the insignificant difference in the relative number of errors along with the observed correlations between correct hyphenation combinations and errors as well as between errors and the average time between correct combinations in the PC condition, there is strong indication that some participants tended to adopt a trial-and-error strategy when playing the PC game. Simultaneously, the faster performance observed in the PC condition might not solely reflect greater efficiency, but could also be the result of a speed-accuracy tradeoff, where participants adopted a more liberal response criterion, akin to a weaker form of trial-and-error behavior [67]. This is a major finding in light of the observed increase in focused attention playing in VR: Learners may be compelled to make more deliberate decisions in VR, where the whole body is involved [18], which could ultimately enhance learning outcomes.

Regarding cognitive load, we accept *H5* ("Compared to desktop VR, fully immersive VR leads to varying learning outcomes."), as the results on learning outcomes imply that the immersive characteristics of VR indeed may have a negative effect on fast word recognition within the target group of low-literate adults. This is aligned with previous research including standard learners [18,33, 55,56] and highlighting cognitive load, e.g., attributed to technology's novelty factor, as a limitation of fully immersive learning environments. Moreover, our results align with recent findings suggesting that the effectiveness of multimedia learning principles, such as segmenting and modality, significantly depends on the complexity of the subject matter and specific VR environment, underscoring the need to tailor VR educational strategies carefully [54]. At the same time, the insignificant differences in knowledge gain suggest that fully immersive VR is not cognitively more demanding than desktop VR *(PC)*. This is consistent with findings suggesting that audiovisual cues within the immersive context of VR might be processed differently, potentially enhancing learner engagement which could even reduce cognitive load [20].

5   Limitations and Future Work

While intervention programs typically span several months with weekly sessions, this study was limited to a single session and a brief learning period. Moreover, it is important to acknowledge the limitation posed by the study's relatively small sample size, which constrains the generalizability of the findings. Nevertheless, identifying low-literate adults is a labor-intensive and costly process, and recruiting multiple individuals with comparable literacy levels presents an additional challenge. In this context, the observed attempts by participants to engage in trial-and-error strategies (supported by multiple analyses, including correlations and error rates) constitute an important finding.

The design of the word recognition tasks may have posed additional challenges for participants. Words were deliberately chosen to avoid being too easy, featuring three syllables, lower frequency, and domain-specific vocabulary (e.g., kitchen and service-related terms). These characteristics, combined with participants' potentially limited German language proficiency, may have hindered fast word recognition and constrained learning progress.

Future research may thus include bigger sample sizes and longitudinal studies. For example, for the study design used in this work an a-priori calculation using G-power[1] for a paired Wilcoxon test with a medium-large effect size ($d = .6$, $\alpha = .05$, *power* $[1 - \beta] = .95$) estimates a total sample size of 33 participants. Regarding the duration and frequency of interventions, the comprehensive study by Heß et al. recommended 20 sessions of 45 minutes each, held twice a week, as an appropriate schedule for a syllable-based approach incorporating digital game-based features, specifically for low-skilled child readers [22].

6   Conclusion

In this work, we explored the potentials of SVRGs for low-literate adults. We described the design of an SVRG to enhance literacy and improve word recognition through hyphenation in this target group and presented the results of an user study with German learners identified as low-literate adults. Our findings contribute to the game-based learning community by showing general usability of SVRGs for language learning within a highly sensitive special-needs population. Moreover, by comparing a fully immersive SVRG with its desktop-based counterpart, we found that low-literate adults may be more inclined to use a

---

[1] https://www.psychologie.hhu.de/arbeitsgruppen/allgemeine-psychologie-und-arbeitspsychologie/gpower.

trial-and-error strategy during games where this approach is feasible. This is an important finding for researchers and designers as it sheds light on benefits of fully immersive VR which have received little attention to date. Ultimately, our work underscores the importance of tailoring difficulty levels and content to specific groups of learners to prevent cognitive overload.

Acknowledgments. As part of the project #ABCforJobs, this work was funded by the Federal Ministry of Education and Research of Germany in the frame of the National Decade for Literacy 2016-2026 under the funding code W1505AAOG. All responsibility for the content of this publication is assumed by the authors. The authors thank Nichakan Buason for her dedication and support.

References

1. Buddeberg, K., Dutz, G., Heilmann, L., Stammer, C., Grotlüschen, A.: Low literacy in Germany. Results Sec. German Literacy Survey. **10**(25656/01), 18848 (2020)
2. Suits, B.: The grasshopper: games, life and utopia. Broadview Press, Peterborough, Ont (2005)
3. Krath, J., Schürmann, L., Von Korflesch, H.F.O.: Revealing the theoretical basis of gamification: a systematic review and analysis of theory in research on gamification, serious games and game-based learning. Comput. Hum. Behav. **125**, 106963 (2021). https://doi.org/10.1016/j.chb.2021.106963
4. Deci, E.L., Ryan, R.M.: Intrinsic Motivation and Self-Determination in Human Behavior. Springer, US, Boston, MA (1985)
5. Csikszentmihalyi, M.: Flow: the psychology of optimal experience. Harper & Row, New York (1990)
6. Chen, P.-Y., Hwang, G.-J., Yeh, S.-Y., Chen, Y.-T., Chen, T.-W., Chien, C.-H.: Three decades of game-based learning in science and mathematics education: an integrated bibliometric analysis and systematic review. J. Comput. Educ. 9, 455–476 (2022). https://doi.org/10.1007/s40692-021-00210-y
7. Dahalan, F., Alias, N., Shaharom, M.S.N.: Gamification and game based learning for vocational education and training: a systematic literature review. Educ. Inf. Technol. **29**, 1279–1317 (2024). https://doi.org/10.1007/s10639-022-11548-w
8. Wang, C., Huang, L.: A systematic review of serious games for collaborative learning: theoretical framework, game mechanic and efficiency assessment. Int. J. Emerg. Technol. Learn. IJET. **16**, 88 (2021). https://doi.org/10.3991/ijet.v16i06.18495
9. Abd-Alrazaq, A., et al.: The effectiveness of serious games for alleviating depression: systematic review and meta-analysis. JMIR Serious Games **10**, e32331 (2022). https://doi.org/10.2196/32331
10. Barz, N., Benick, M., Dörrenbächer-Ulrich, L., Perels, F.: The effect of digital game-based learning interventions on cognitive, metacognitive, and affective-motivational learning outcomes in school: a meta-analysis. Rev. Educ. Res. **94**, 193–227 (2024). https://doi.org/10.3102/00346543231167795
11. Tori, A.A., Tori, R., Nunes, F.D.L.D.S.: Serious game design in health education: a systematic review. IEEE Trans. Learn. Technol. 15, 827–846 (2022). https://doi.org/10.1109/TLT.2022.3200583
12. Ullah, M., et al.: Serious games in science education: a systematic literature. Virtual Real. Intell. Hardw. **4**, 189–209 (2022). https://doi.org/10.1016/j.vrih.2022.02.001

13. Boyle, E.A., et al.: An update to the systematic literature review of empirical evidence of the impacts and outcomes of computer games and serious games. Comput. Educ. **94**, 178–192 (2016). https://doi.org/10.1016/j.compedu.2015.11.003
14. Connolly, T.M., Boyle, E.A., MacArthur, E., Hainey, T., Boyle, J.M.: A systematic literature review of empirical evidence on computer games and serious games. Comput. Educ. **59**, 661–686 (2012). https://doi.org/10.1016/j.compedu.2012.03.004
15. Korn, O., Zallio, M., Schnitzer, B.: Young skeptics: exploring the perceptions of virtual worlds and the metaverse in generations Y and Z. Front. Virtual Real. **5**, 1330358 (2024). https://doi.org/10.3389/frvir.2024.1330358
16. Chatain, J., Ramp, V., Gashaj, V., Fayolle, V., Kapur, M., Sumner, R.W., Magnenat, S.: Grasping derivatives: teaching mathematics through embodied interactions using tablets and virtual reality. In: Proceedings of the 21st Annual ACM Interaction Design and Children Conference, pp. 98–108. Association for Computing Machinery, New York (2022)
17. Chatain, J., Kapur, M., Sumner, R.W.: three perspectives on embodied learning in virtual reality: opportunities for interaction design. In: Extended Abstracts of the 2023 CHI Conference on Human Factors in Computing Systems. Association for Computing Machinery, New York (2023)
18. Schnitzer, B.L., Gampe, S., Bieberstein, A., Hoffmann, I., Görlich, D., Korn, O.: Language learning in virtual reality: enhancement of long-term vocabulary recognition and understanding through full-body avatars. In: Proceedings of the Extended Abstracts of the CHI Conference on Human Factors in Computing Systems. S, pp. 1–9. ACM, Yokohama Japan (2025)
19. Milgram, P., Takemura, H., Utsumi, A., Kishino, F.: Augmented reality: a class of displays on the reality-virtuality continuum. Gehalten auf der Photonics for Industrial Applications, Boston (1995)
20. Oje, A.V., Hunsu, N.J., Fiorella, L.: A systematic review of evidence-based design and pedagogical principles in educational virtual reality environments. Educ. Res. Rev. **47**, 100676 (2025). https://doi.org/10.1016/j.edurev.2025.100676
21. Slater, M., Usoh, M.: Presence in immersive virtual environments. In: Proceedings of IEEE Virtual Reality Annual International Symposium, pp. 90–96. IEEE, Seattle (1993)
22. Heß, J., Karageorgos, P., Müller, B., Riedmann, A., Schaper, P., Lugrin, B., Richter, T.: Improving word reading skills of low-skilled readers: an intervention combining a syllable-based approach with digital game-based features. J. Comput. Assist. Learn. **40**, 2306–2324 (2024). https://doi.org/10.1111/jcal.13021
23. Görgen, R., Huemer, S., Schulte-Körne, G., Moll, K.: Evaluation of a digital game-based reading training for German children with reading disorder. Comput. Educ. **150**, 103834 (2020). https://doi.org/10.1016/j.compedu.2020.103834
24. Winther, E., Paeßens, J., Tröster, M., Bowien-Jansen, B.: Immersives lernen für geringliteralisierte: chancen der augmented reality am beispiel der finanziellen grundbildung. Medien. Z. Für Theor. Prax. Medien. 47, 267–287 (2022). https://doi.org/10.21240/mpaed/47/2022.04.13.X
25. Butorova, A.S., Tarasov, D.A., Kosachenko, A.I., Sergeev, A.P.: Learning foreign languages by adults using immersive virtual reality systems: review of recent studies (2014-2024). In: 2024 8th Scientific School Dynamics of Complex Networks and their Applications (DCNA), pp. 43–46. IEEE, Kaliningrad, Russian Federation (2024)

26. Peixoto, B., Pinto, R., Melo, M., Cabral, L., Bessa, M.: Immersive virtual reality for foreign language education: a PRISMA systematic review. IEEE Access. **9**, 48952–48962 (2021). https://doi.org/10.1109/ACCESS.2021.3068858
27. Coban, M., Bolat, Y.I., Goksu, I.: The potential of immersive virtual reality to enhance learning: a meta-analysis. Educ. Res. Rev. **36**, 100452 (2022). https://doi.org/10.1016/j.edurev.2022.100452
28. Chatain, J., et al.: DigiGlo: exploring the palm as an input and display mechanism through digital gloves. In: Proceedings of the Annual Symposium on Computer-Human Interaction in Play, pp. 374–385. Association for Computing Machinery, New York (2020)
29. Nathan, M.J., Walkington, C.: Grounded and embodied mathematical cognition: promoting mathematical insight and proof using action and language. Cogn. Res. Principles Impl. **2**(1), 1–20 (2017). https://doi.org/10.1186/s41235-016-0040-5
30. Horchak, O.V., Giger, J.-C., Cabral, M., Pochwatko, G.: From demonstration to theory in embodied language comprehension: a review. Cogn. Syst. Res. **29–30**, 66–85 (2014). https://doi.org/10.1016/j.cogsys.2013.09.002
31. Lan, Y.-J., Chen, N.-S., Li, P., Grant, S.: Embodied cognition and language learning in virtual environments. Education Tech. Research Dev. **63**(5), 639–644 (2015). https://doi.org/10.1007/s11423-015-9401-x
32. Nathan, M.J.: Rethinking formalisms in formal education. Educ. Psychol. **47**, 125–148 (2012). https://doi.org/10.1080/00461520.2012.667063
33. Kaplan-Rakowski, R., Lin, L., Wojdynski, T.: Learning vocabulary using 2d pictures is more effective than using immersive 3d stereoscopic pictures. Int. J. Human-Computer Interact. **38**, 299–308 (2022). https://doi.org/10.1080/10447318.2021.1938394
34. Dhimolea, T.K., Kaplan-Rakowski, R., Lin, L.: A systematic review of research on high-immersion virtual reality for language learning. TechTrends **66**, 810–824 (2022). https://doi.org/10.1007/s11528-022-00717-w
35. Marinelli, C.V., Nardacchione, G., Trotta, E., Di Fuccio, R., Palladino, P., Traetta, L., Limone, P.: The effectiveness of serious games for enhancing literacy skills in children with learning disabilities or difficulties: a systematic review. Appl. Sci. **13**, 4512 (2023). https://doi.org/10.3390/app13074512
36. Schaffer, O., Fang, X.: Player Experience. In: Human-Computer Interaction in Various Application Domains, pp. 173–193. CRC Press, New York (2024)
37. Mathias, B., Andrä, C., Schwager, A., Macedonia, M., Von Kriegstein, K.: Twelve- and fourteen-year-old school children differentially benefit from sensorimotor- and multisensory-enriched vocabulary training. Educ. Psychol. Rev. **34**, 1739–1770 (2022). https://doi.org/10.1007/s10648-021-09648-z
38. Shams, L., Seitz, A.R.: Benefits of multisensory learning. Trends Cogn. Sci. **12**, 411–417 (2008). https://doi.org/10.1016/j.tics.2008.07.006
39. Vazquez, C., Xia, L., Aikawa, T., Maes, P.: Words in motion: kinesthetic language learning in virtual reality. In: 2018 IEEE 18th International Conference on Advanced Learning Technologies (ICALT), pp. 272–276. IEEE, Mumbai (2018)
40. McBride-Chang, C.: What is phonological awareness? J. Educ. Psychol. **87**, 179–192 (1995). https://doi.org/10.1037/0022-0663.87.2.179
41. Bar-Kochva, I., Vágvölgyi, R., Dresler, T., Nagengast, B., Schröter, H., Schrader, J., Nuerk, H.-C.: Basic reading and reading-related language skills in adults with deficient reading comprehension who read a transparent orthography. Read. Writ. **34**(9), 2357–2379 (2021). https://doi.org/10.1007/s11145-021-10147-4
42. Ehri, L.C.: Learning to Read Words: Theory, Findings, and Issues. Sci. Stud. Read. 9, 167-188 (2005). https://doi.org/10.1207/s1532799xssr0902_4

43. Grotlschen, A., Riekmann, W. hrsg: Funktionaler Analphabetismus in Deutschland: Ergebnisse der ersten leo. Level-One Studie. Waxmann, Münster München Berlin (2012)
44. Grotlschen, A., Buddeberg, K. hrsg: LEO 2018: Leben mit geringer Literalität. wbv, Bielefeld (2020)
45. Bader, E., Kholin, M. & Schröter, H.: Psychologische erklärungsansätze für unterschiede in motivation und volition bei formal niedrig gebildeten erwachsenen mit und ohne leseschwierigkeiten. In: Leck, J., Ehmig, S.C., Heymann, L., Jester, M. (Hrsg.), Motivation und Verbindlichkeit bei gering literalisierten Erwachsenen, pp. 69–85 (2025). https://doi.org/10.3278/9783763976911
46. Leck, J., Heymann, L., Ehmig, S., Jester, M. hrsg: Motivation und Verbindlichkeit bei gering literalisierten Erwachsenen. wbv Publikation, Bielefeld (2025)
47. Jackson Kellinger, J.: A Guide to Designing Curricular Games. Springer International Publishing, Cham (2017)
48. Ronimus, M., Eklund, K., Pesu, L., Lyytinen, H.: Supporting struggling readers with digital game-based learning. Educ. Tech. Res. Dev. **67**(3), 639–663 (2019). https://doi.org/10.1007/s11423-019-09658-3
49. Syal, S., Nietfeld, J.L.: Examining the effects of a game-based learning environment on fifth graders' reading comprehension and reading motivation. J. Educ. Psychol. **116**, 805–819 (2024). https://doi.org/10.1037/edu0000874
50. Kindl, J., Lenhard, W.: A meta-analysis on the effectiveness of functional literacy interventions for adults. Educ. Res. Rev. **41**, 100569 (2023). https://doi.org/10.1016/j.edurev.2023.100569
51. Häikiö, T., Hyönä, J., Bertram, R.: The role of syllables in word recognition among beginning finnish readers: evidence from eye movements during reading. J. Cogn. Psychol. **27**, 562–577 (2015). https://doi.org/10.1080/20445911.2014.982126
52. De Simone, E., Moll, K., Feldmann, L., Schmalz, X., Beyersmann, E.: The role of syllables and morphemes in silent reading: An eye-tracking study. Q. J. Exp. Psychol. **76**, 2493–2513 (2023). https://doi.org/10.1177/17470218231160638
53. Autor:innengruppe Projekt EIBE: Good Practice für die Alphabetisierungs- und Grundbildungsarbeit - ein Praxisleitfaden. (2025). https://doi.org/10.58000/24KS-3W37
54. Çeken, B., Taşkin, N.: Examination of Multimedia Learning Principles in Augmented Reality and Virtual Reality Learning Environments. J. Comput. Assist. Learn. **41**, e13097 (2025). https://doi.org/10.1111/jcal.13097
55. Papin, K., Kaplan-Rakowski, R.: A study of vocabulary learning using annotated 360° pictures. Comput. Assist. Lang. Learn. 37, 1108–1135 (2024). https://doi.org/10.1080/09588221.2022.2068613
56. Kaplan-Rakowski, R., Thrasher, T.: The impact of high-immersion virtual reality and interactivity on vocabulary learning. Br. J. Educ. Technol. bjet.13603 (2025). https://doi.org/10.1111/bjet.13603
57. Shao, Y., Hang, Y., Froehlich, F., Homer, B.D., Plass, J.L.: Exploring Emotional Design Features for Virtual Reality Games. In: Lecture Notes in Computer Science. S. 298–312. Springer Nature Switzerland, Cham (2025)
58. Lewis, J.R., Sauro, J.: The Factor Structure of the System Usability Scale. In: Lecture Notes in Computer Science, pp. 94–103. Springer Berlin Heidelberg, Berlin, Heidelberg (2009)
59. Rheinberg, F.: Die Flow-Kurzskala (FKS) übersetzt in verschiedene Sprachen The Flow-Short-Scale (FSS) translated into various languages, http://rgdoi.net/10.13140/RG.2.1.4417.2243, (2015)

60. Engeser, S., Rheinberg, F.: Flow, performance and moderators of challenge-skill balance. Motiv. Emot. **32**, 158–172 (2008). https://doi.org/10.1007/s11031-008-9102-4
61. O'Brien, H.L., Cairns, P., Hall, M.: A practical approach to measuring user engagement with the refined user engagement scale (UES) and new UES short form. Int. J. Hum.-Comput. Stud. **112**, 28–39 (2018). https://doi.org/10.1016/j.ijhcs.2018.01.004
62. Lugrin, J.-L., Wiebusch, D., Latoschik, M.E., Strehler, A.: Usability benchmarks for motion tracking systems. In: Proceedings of the 19th ACM Symposium on Virtual Reality Software and Technology, pp. 49–58. ACM, Singapore (2013)
63. Bangor, A., Kortum, P., Miller, J.: Determining what individual SUS scores mean: adding an adjective rating scale. J. Usability Stud. **4**, 114–123 (2009)
64. Koppel, I.: Entwicklung einer Online-Diagnostik für die Alphabetisierung. Springer Fachmedien Wiesbaden, Wiesbaden (2017)
65. Rexeis, V.: Usability Benchmark und Aktivitäts-Analyse mit Eye Tracking von Mobile Augmented Reality unterstützten Ernährungsempfehlungen, http://rgdoi.net/10.13140/RG.2.1.2225.2004, (2015)
66. MacKenzie, I.S.: Fitts Law as a Research and Design Tool in Human-Computer Interaction. Human–Computer Interact. **7**, 91–139 (1992). https://doi.org/10.1207/s15327051hci0701_3
67. Heitz, R.P.: The speed-accuracy tradeoff: history, physiology, methodology, and behavior. Front. Neurosci. **8**, (2014). https://doi.org/10.3389/fnins.2014.00150

Depth Perception in Virtual Reality: Effects of Vergence Accommodation Conflict (VAC) on Learning Transfer

Sarah A. Aeschlimann[1], Fred W. Mast[1], and Matthias Ertl[1,2,3]

[1] Department of Psychology, University of Bern, Bern, Switzerland
`{sarah.aeschlimann,fred.mast}@unibe.ch, matthias.ertl@unilu.ch`
[2] Clinic for Neurology and Neurorehabilitation, Luzerner Kantonsspital, University Teaching and Research Hospital, Lucerne, Switzerland
[3] Faculty of Behavioral Sciences and Psychology, University of Lucerne, Lucerne, Switzerland

Abstract. *Objective*: Virtual reality (VR) is a promising tool for training motor skills. Though, the vergence-accommodation conflict (VAC) is a significant, unavoidable issue of VR headsets. VAC is caused by decoupling two highly synchronized visual information processes: the eye lenses focuses on a fixed distance (accommodation), while the eyes converge at the perceived target distance (vergence). This leads to lower efficacy in motor planning and control. The impact of VAC on learning transfer is yet unknown.

Method: Using a manual motor task in reaching distance, we will compare learning transfer between VR and real world under different VAC conditions. Due to its focal distance, the device has a small VAC at reaching distance, but the VAC will be manipulated using modified lenses, inducing a large VAC, leading to a maximal decoupling. 180 participants will be randomly assigned to one of three groups (small VAC, large VAC, real-world controls), age ranges from 18–30 years.

Expected Results: We expect a significant interaction between VAC level and time. Training in large VAC condition would lead to more errors and longer task completion times in the real-world setting compared to small VAC conditions.

Outcome: To fully exploit the potential of VR, an in-depth problem-oriented understanding of the sensorimotor mechanisms that may limit transfer is of central importance. This study will provide insights for the learning transfer using VR applications in specific motor interventions such as rehabilitation and practice tasks in peri-personal space.

Keywords: visual perception · artificial depth cues · head mounted devices · peri-personal space · motor rehabilitation · virtual practice tasks

1   Introduction

Virtual reality (VR) is increasingly being integrated into motor training and rehabilitation programs as it provides immersive, controllable, and repeatable environments for skill acquisition and recovery [3,13]. A core component of effective motor learning is accurate visual perception, which is essential for spatial awareness, hand-eye coordination, and the planning and execution of goal-directed movements [1,16].

Depth perception is one of the most important elements in VR and relies on a combination of monocular and binocular cues, including binocular disparity, motion parallax, occlusion, and perspective [4]. Unlike the natural environment, standard VR systems decouple two physiological mechanism required for accurate depth perception, i.e. the vergence (the convergence angle of the eyes) and accommodation (the adaptation of the lens to the focal distance) of the eye [14,15]. This decoupling, known as vergence-accommodation conflict (VAC), hinders visual performance and causes visual fatigue [5] which may undermine motor learning outcomes, particularly in scenarios, where cognitive resources are already limited (e.g., after brain injury).

The transfer of learning - the ability to apply skills acquired in a virtual environment to real-world tasks - is an important goal in both motor rehabilitation such as in stroke survivors and people with Parkinson's disease [3,12] and skill training in sports, aviation, and medicine [13]. Understanding how perceptual accuracy, particularly in relation to depth processing, influences learning transfer is therefore essential for the development and usage of effective VR-based interventions.

1.1   Vergence Accommodation Conflict (VAC)

Head-mounted displays (HMDs) inherently cause VAC, a discrepancy between the vergence angle of the eyes and the accommodative focus of the eye lenses. This conflict arises because in standard VR devices, the eyes converge on a virtual object at a perceived distance that fluctuates. In contrast, the accommodative response, that is the focal point at which the object appears sharp, remains fixed on the distance to the virtual display, i.e. at the focal plane (Fig 1, nr. 3) [14,15]. This discrepancy can contribute not only to common side effects such as nausea and eyestrain, but also to perceptual distortions, in particular a systematic underestimation of depth [6,15] as shown in Fig. 1. VAC also has a negative impact on cognitive performance [2].

1.2   Research Aim and Question

The aim of our research is to examine whether the level of VAC in VR influences the effectiveness of the transfer of motor learning in the peri-personal space (reaching distance) to the real world. We question whether a large VAC in VR impairs the transfer of a motor task in the peri-personal space to motor performance in reality.

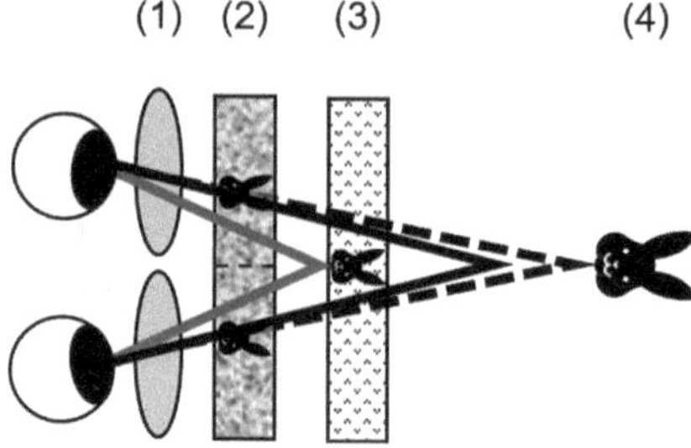

Fig. 1. Illustration of VAC. (1) Lenses, (2) head mounted displays, (3) virtual screen i.e. focal plane, (4) perceived target. Accommodation distance i.e. focal distance (red dotted line), vergence distance (black solid line), target distance (black dashed line).

2   Methods

2.1   Participants

180 participants, randomly assigned to one of two VAC conditions (small vs. large VAC) or to a control group. Age is restricted to 18 - 30 years due to age-related loss of the ability to accommodate (presbyopia) [11]. Exclusion criteria are prescription eye-wear, left-handedness, heterophoria, and the routine use of VR. Students receive compensation in the form of experimental credits.

2.2   Task: Hotwire

We have adapted the *Hotwire game* to create simple motor tasks (see Fig. 2). The aim of this task is to follow a wire with an eyelet as quickly and faultlessly as possible. Mistakes are made when the handheld eyelet contacts the wire. The task is completed at arm's length, i.e. in peri-personal space.

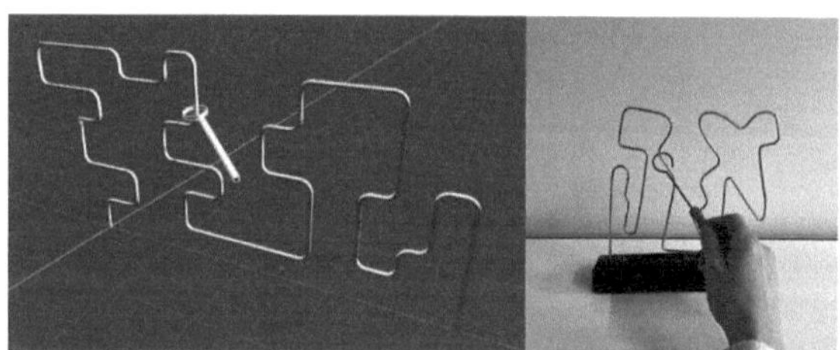

Fig. 2. Example of the hotwire task in different environments. Virtual (left), physical (right).

We designed five tasks with increasing difficulties i.e. increase of the complexity of the wire in VR and identical ones for the real-world setup. A sixth task with high difficulty serves as additional test object for the post measurement in the real-world setup.

2.3   Task: Flanker

To estimate the cognitive load due to different VAC conditions we will use the Erikson flanker task. This task is sensitive to variations in cognitive load and can be used to assess how additional mental demands impact attentional control [10]. Importantly, flanker interference increases under cognitive load but decreases under perceptual load [9], making it suitable to distinguish between these mechanisms. The task contributes to clarifying the question of whether VAC causes a perceptual or a cognitive load on attentional processing.

Participants must respond to a target stimulus (e.g., an arrow pointing left or right) that is flanked by distractor stimuli, which can be congruent (pointing in the same direction), incongruent (pointing in the opposite direction), or neutral (see Fig 3). The primary measure is the difference in reaction times and accuracy between congruent and incongruent trials.

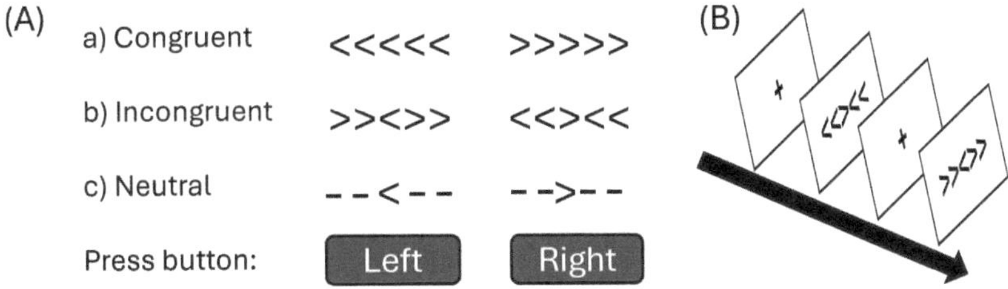

Fig. 3. Illustration of the flanker task. (A) Participants respond to the central arrow: (left) button for left-pointing, (right) for right-pointing. Flankers are either (a) congruent, (b) incongruent, or (c) neutral. (B) Stimuli are shown one at a time, each separated by a fixation cross.

2.4   VR Conditions

To assess the influence of VAC on learning transfer of a motor task we will compare two different focal distances, using a stereoscopic VR headsets with additional modified lenses. We use the HTC Vive pro eye, a HMD with a Dual OLED 3.5" diagonal screen, a resolution of 1440x1600 pixels per eye, a combined 110° field of view, and a refresh rate of 90 Hz. The device has a known focal distance of appr. 75 cm [17] and covers the range of peri-personal space, i.e. has a small VAC for tasks in reaching distance. For the large VAC we will use additional lenses implying a focal distance at infinity i.e. above 6 meters [7], where the eyes are relaxed and don't accommodate. The accommodation demand can be defined as:

$$D = \frac{1}{f} \tag{1}$$

where D is the focal power in diopters (dpt) and f the focal distance [8]. We will use additional 1.25 dpt lenses to shift the dioptric demand from 1.3 dpt ($\frac{1}{0.75} = 1.\overline{3}$) to almost 0.

2.5   Design

The study has a 3x2 mixed design with group and time as independent variables. See illustration of the experimental design (Fig. 4). There will be three randomly assigned groups of a minimum of 60 participants (small vs. large VAC and a control group). A simr-based power analysis for a 3×2 mixed design (Cohen's f = 0.2) indicated 88% power with 60 participants per group (N = 180).

The study will take place over three days (t1-t3) within two weeks. T1 includes testing of depth perception and a baseline hotwire run in the real-world setup. Participants practice one time on the simplest of the five hotwire tasks, followed by increasing difficulties (1-5) as baseline measurements.

In VR a baseline pupil diameter recording (which is then continuously tracked), flanker performance, and a practice and baseline hotwire runs (1-5) are preformed. This is followed by a training of the five hotwire tasks with increasing difficulty, each with three runs limited to 90 s (3x5 training session). At the end of the training session there is a flanker task and the last pupil measurement followed by an immersion and a cybersickness questionnaire on a PC screen.

T2 and t3 include pupil measurement and the 3x5 training sessions. T3 will additionally measure the flanker task and transfer to the real world at the end of the training session. Participants will perform the hotwire tasks (1-5) with an additional untrained hotwire task (6) in a real-world setup. Metrics are recorded in both VR and physical settings (errors and time).

The control group will do the hotwire tasks exclusively in the real-world setup on t1 and t3 including a practice task in the beginning and an additional untrained task at the post measurement (see Fig. 4).

2.6   Data Collection

The data collection for task accuracy of the hotwire task includes the completion time and error rate. To assess cognitive load, we measure the pupil diameter and performance in a flanker task. Further, we assess the ability of depth perception and subjective ratings of immersion into VR and cybersickness.

2.7   Analysis

We will use a mixed ANOVA with group (small vs. large VAC) as between factor and time (pre and post measurement) as within factor.

3   Expected Results

Our hypotheses are that (a) the condition with small VAC (eye accommodates in peri-personal space) will result in better real-world task performance and (b) a large VAC (no accommodation, i.e. eye accommodates at infinity) will show reduced transfer performance. Thus, we expect a significant interaction between VAC level and time.

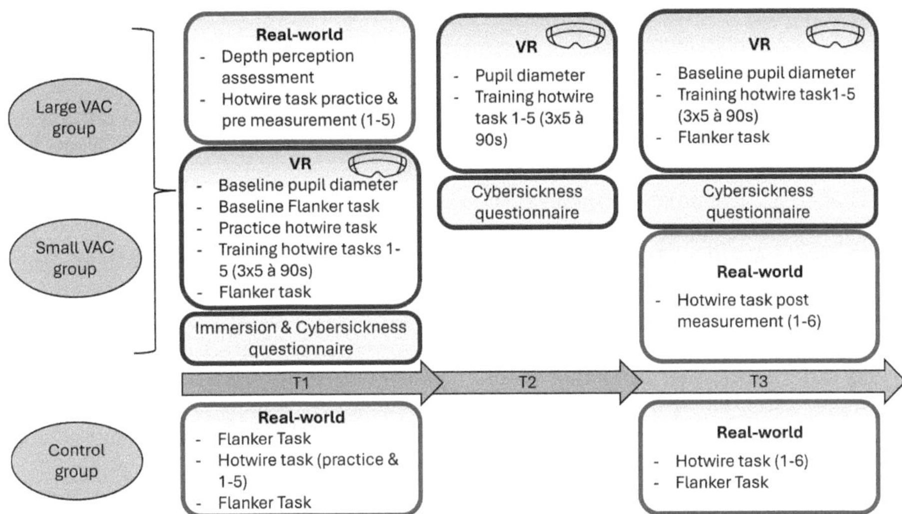

Fig. 4. Illustration of the experimental design. The hotwire tasks (physical and virtual) are increasing in difficulty from task 1 to 5.

4 Outcome

The present study highlights the importance of understanding the influence of VAC in virtual reality for future applications in rehabilitation and skills training in peri-personal space. This knowledge could be particularly valuable for the development of VR-based interventions aimed to improve motor control and spatial awareness in individuals with neurological impairments.

In addition, our findings will serve as a basis for training approaches in areas that require precise interaction with objects in reaching distance, such as manual therapy, surgical procedures, or the development of fine motor skills. As immersive technologies evolve, basic perceptual research is crucial to maximize their effectiveness and practical implications. This work thus contributes to the fundamental understanding required for the use of VR in applied fields where accurate depth processing is critical for the learning transfer.

Acknowledgments. This research project is supported by the Digitization Commission (DigiK) of the University of Bern.

Disclosure of Interests. The authors have no competing interests to declare that are relevant to the content of this article.

References

1. Batmaz, A.U., Turkmen, R., Sarac, M., Barrera Machuca, M.D., Stuerzlinger, W.: Re-investigating the effect of the vergence-accommodation conflict on 3d pointing. In: Proceedings of the 29th ACM Symposium on Virtual Reality Software and Technology, pp. 1–10 (2023)
2. Daniel, F., Kapoula, Z.: Induced vergence-accommodation conflict reduces cognitive performance in the stroop test. Sci. Rep. **9**(1), 1247 (2019)
3. Demeco, A., Zola, L., Frizziero, A., Martini, C., Palumbo, A., Foresti, R., Buccino, G., Costantino, C.: Immersive virtual reality in post-stroke rehabilitation: a systematic review. Sensors **23**(3), 1712 (2023)
4. El Jamiy, F., Marsh, R.: Survey on depth perception in head mounted displays: distance estimation in virtual reality, augmented reality, and mixed reality. IET Image Proc. **13**(5), 707–712 (2019)
5. Hoffman, D.M., Girshick, A.R., Akeley, K., Banks, M.S.: Vergence-accommodation conflicts hinder visual performance and cause visual fatigue. J. Vis. **8**(3), 33–33 (2008)
6. Kohm, K., Babu, S.V., Pagano, C., Robb, A.: Objects may be farther than they appear: depth compression diminishes over time with repeated calibration in virtual reality. IEEE Trans. Visual Comput. Graph. **28**(11), 3907–3916 (2022)
7. Koretz, J.F., Handelman, G.H.: How the human eye focuses. Sci. Am. **259**(1), 92–99 (1988)
8. LaValle, S.M.: Virtual reality. Cambridge university press (2023)
9. Lavie, N., Hirst, A., De Fockert, J.W., Viding, E.: Load theory of selective attention and cognitive control. J. Exp. Psychol. Gen. **133**(3), 339 (2004)
10. Linnell, K.J., Caparos, S.: Perceptual and cognitive load interact to control the spatial focus of attention. J. Exp. Psychol. Hum. Percept. Perform. **37**(5), 1643 (2011)
11. Mordi, J.A., Ciuffreda, K.J.: Static aspects of accommodation: age and presbyopia. Vision. Res. **38**(11), 1643–1653 (1998)
12. dos Santos Mendesa, F.A., et al.: Motor learning, retention and transfer after virtual-reality-based training in parkinson's disease–effect of motor and cognitive demands of games: a longitudinal, controlled clinical study. Physiotherapy **98**, 217–223 (2012)
13. Tusher, H.M., Mallam, S., Nazir, S.: A systematic review of virtual reality features for skill training. Technol. Knowl. Learn. **29**(2), 843–878 (2024)
14. Wang, X.M., et al.: The geometry of the vergence-accommodation conflict in mixed reality systems. Virtual Reality **28**(2), 95 (2024)
15. Wang, X.M., et al.: Prolonged exposure to mixed reality alters task performance in the unmediated environment. Sci. Rep. **14**(1), 18938 (2024)
16. Witte, K., Bürger, D., Pastel, S.: Sports training in virtual reality with a focus on visual perception: a systematic review. Front. Sports Active Living **7**, 1530948 (2025)
17. Yeh, P.H., Liu, C.H., Sun, M.H., Chi, S.C., Hwang, Y.S.: To measure the amount of ocular deviation in strabismus patients with an eye-tracking virtual reality headset. BMC Ophthalmol. **21**(1), 246 (2021)

Shaking Lose All the Nonsense: Faculty Experiences Using Educational Games in Higher Education Classrooms
A Qualitative Study

André Thomas[1]([⊠]) [iD], Radhika Viruru[2] [iD], Michael Rugh[2] [iD], and Emma Ko[2] [iD]

[1] Lucerne University of Applied Sciences and Arts, Campus Zug-Rotkreuz, Suurstoffi 1, 6343 Rotkreuz, Switzerland
`andre.thomas@hslu.ch`
[2] Texas A&M University, College Station, TX, USA

Abstract. 'Video games have gained remarkable popularity and have become the dominant form of entertainment today. While many educators incorporate video games into their classrooms, limited information exists on faculty experiences in this regard. We investigated teachers' experiences in classrooms when using educational video games as part of their curriculum. Participants were a purposeful sample of 5 higher education faculty who used games in 4–9 semesters with a total of 3,226 students. The method used was a collective case study using semi-structured interviews and student game play data. Four major themes were discovered based on the interviews with the teachers. The themes show how and why the faculty use the games, mainly as a pedagogical tool, to connect with people, as a method to deliver content and as an artifact. Three distinct faculty profiles emerged from this research. To enhance the effectiveness of game-based teaching, additional research is needed to understand the training and support required by teachers and faculty. Tailored support and training materials should be developed to address the specific needs of these game-based teaching profiles, ultimately assisting faculty in their efforts to employ games in the classroom.

Keywords: Game-based learning · Game-based teaching · Postsecondary education · Teacher profiles · educational video games

The year is 1412, and I'm a member of the Medici family and a banker. Since the church started banking with us, business has really taken off, and we have become one of the wealthiest families in all of Florence. Finally, we can use some of that wealth to commission works of art. When a family becomes that influential, there are others that wish us harm and would like to exile us or even kill us. We do have a few competitors and enemies and must be constantly on the lookout and be on our toes to stay in business and ahead of the game.

This is a quote from a student explaining their thoughts while playing the educational video game, ARTé: Mecenas [29]. It demonstrates how games can help close the distance between the players and history itself, allowing the players to be more engaged with a

A. Thomas et al. (Eds.): JCSG 2025, LNCS 16243, pp. 77–93, 2026.
https://doi.org/10.1007/978-3-032-10518-9_8

setting and time that are far away. Through such an immersive environment, students can interact with learning content in active and authentic ways, deepening their understanding and connection with their learning. Behind almost every game-based learning experience in formal education, however, is a faculty or instructor who assigns the game and helps students navigate this unique learning modality.

1 Introduction

Video games have become one of the most popular media of our times, with 97% of adolescent boys and 83% of adolescent girls playing video games four hours or more every week [2, 13, 20, 23]. This medium has also been used in the educational sphere for the past 50 years, and many studies have shown that students can gain factual, conceptual, and procedural knowledge from video games [4, 7, 11, 15, 22]. Although the research is compelling, many stakeholders, especially parents of students, hold stigmas surrounding the use of video games in education [9, 18, 28]. Additionally, little has been written about the experience of higher education faculty when using games in their classrooms.

This paper reports on a study that sought to analyze the experience of college professors when using video games in their classrooms. A purposeful sample of five faculty members from various disciplines at multiple major research universities in the southwestern United States was recruited to take part in this study. In this paper, we report on the experiences the faculty had when using video games in their classes and provide analysis on how games were a useful pedagogical tool to deliver content and make meaningful connections with students.

2 Background

When entertainment video games first emerged, so did educational video games. Indeed, the first educational video games were created in the 1950s [24, 26]. However, none of the early educational video games made it to the public eye. The first well-known educational video game, which is still available today, is Oregon Trail [25]; the game was developed and first used in a classroom in 1971 [8]. Games are a good medium for learning because they provide immediate feedback and are problem-based, experiential, and consistent with cognitive theory [6, 21, 32]. When using educational video games, students are more engaged, are actively involved in the learning process, and practice more [1, 10, 16]. There are numerous studies showing the benefits of game-based teaching [3, 12, 17, 27, 33], yet very little has been written about the experience of faculty and teachers when using games in their classrooms. The purpose of this case study is to investigate and report the experience of college and university faculty when using a video game as part of their curriculum. As Bhattacharya [5] commented, case study research is well-suited to when the phenomenon under investigation is tightly focused, and an in-depth investigation is possible. For this study, we interviewed five faculty from the following institutions: Texas A&M University, Texas A&M University–Corpus Christi, Lake Sumter Community College, Arizona State University, and San Jacinto College. All five faculty members have utilized educational video games as part of their classes. Four of them used two games in their art history classes [29, 31]. The fifth faculty used Variant: Limits [30] in their calculus class. Interviewing these faculty members allowed us to search for key clues into how faculty view games in their classroom and identify game-based learning teacher profiles. This paper seeks to address this gap in existing research and explore the experience of educators when utilizing games in their classrooms. Although it is important to recognize that games as a medium can be an effective tool in the classroom and to understand the benefits and experience for students, it is equally important to understand the impact games have on faculty when they use them. Understanding how faculty think about games can help game designers and publishers create not only better games but also better support materials and implementation guidelines. At the same time, having a better understanding of what faculty experience when using games allows instructional designers and learning experts to design and create curricula that are comprehensive and allow for the effective inclusion of games.

3   Research Design and Methodology

The design methodology of this study is a qualitative collective case study. Merriam [19] commented that a defining feature of case study research is that it focuses on "intensive, holistic description and analysis" of a single phenomenon (p. 21). Further, Hamel and Viau-Guay [14] stated that case study research is particularly adept at fulfilling some of the goals of all qualitative studies, namely, to describe, understand, and explain. As this study focused specifically on how games are integrated into higher education curricula, this method was considered appropriate. However, given that each participant's approach to using games in the classroom differed and that the disciplines within which the games were integrated varied, we considered this to be a collective case study within which we explored individual manifestations of the same phenomena. A cross-case report is included after the presentation of data, which brings together the overarching findings from all the cases.

Two main methods were used to gather data for this study: qualitative semi-structured interviews, conducted and recorded via Zoom, and an analysis of the game records that documented student engagement and participation in the games. The interview recordings were verbatim transcribed, and then coded using descriptive coding, and emergent themes were then recorded. The publisher of the games utilized by the study participants provided anonymous play data for each student in each faculty member's classes for each semester they used the games, including total length of play, completion of games, and average playtime.

To conduct an analysis of faculty experiences and perceptions, radar chart analysis was used. This type of qualitative analysis can be found in consumer profiling and education assessment. In our adaptation, radar charts were constructed based on the frequency of themes that emerged and were coded by the researchers. We then found the sum frequencies (see Table 2) and chose the top four most mentioned words. These charts were then used to create the teaching profiles.

3.1 Participants

Given that the number of faculty members using games in their instruction is limited, five faculty members who were known to be implementing games were recruited to be part of this study. Only faculty members who had been using games for a minimum of one year were included in this study to ensure that all participants were sufficiently familiar with the practice. For this study we interviewed 5 faculty, Dr. Larsen, Dr. Robinson, Dr. Meyer, and Dr. Williams, we changed the names of the faculty to protect their identities.

All four of the faculties have been using art history games as part of their classes and are from universities and community colleges in the Southwestern United States. Additionally, we interviewed Dr. Mitchell from a community college in the Southwest of the United States who used Variant: Limits a mathematics game that help students master conceptual knowledge of calculus, in his calculus class.

Interviewing Dr. Mitchell allowed us to see if there is a difference in the experience when using a different kind of game in a different type of class. The first author is the lead developer of the games, and one of the other participants was involved in the design and development effort of several of the art history games that were included in this study. Thus, they bring deep expert knowledge to the study.

3.2 Researchers' Reflexivity and Ethical Issues

The first author has a very strong bias towards game-based learning and as the creator of the games used by the faculty participating in this study focuses more on positive than negative aspects of the games. The first author also serves as CEO of the small spin-off company that publishes, supports, and maintains the games and thus has also an economic interest in the games and is interested in faculty having a positive experience when using the games. This can lead to overly biased reporting of the positive experiences of the faculty while underreporting the negative experiences. However, the conflict is mitigated, as the author has no authority over any of the faculty that participated in the study, and they all chose freely to use the games in their classrooms. No incentives were provided or promised to the faculty members for using the games and/or for participating in this study. Further, the second author has only limited knowledge of game-based education, and her role in the study was mostly related to designing the methodology and assisting with data analysis. She was also able to serve to some extent as a peer debriefer for the first author and to provide an ethical perspective on the data collected.

4 The Games

The first game used for this study is called *ARTé: Mecenas* [29]. In the game, students take on the role of a banker in the Medici family in the 14th and 15th centuries in Florence, Italy. The game is a simulation of the interconnectedness between art, church, city, and merchants. Players must grow their banking business without compromising their reputation with the church and city, all while commissioning works of art to improve their reputation and forming strategic banking relationships with individual clergy members. Furthermore, players must establish new trade routes, negotiate with neighboring city-states, and avoid war. The game can be played online or downloaded on PC or Mac. It is played via a simple 2D user interface using point-and-click mechanics (Fig. 1).

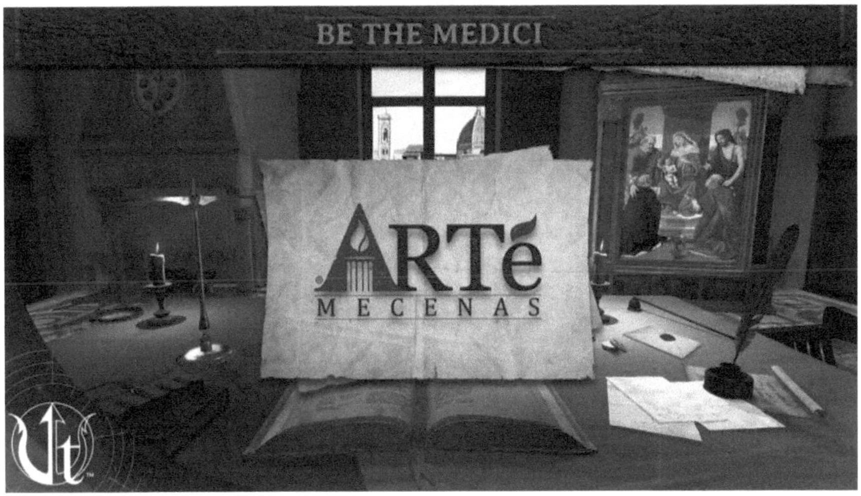

Fig. 1. ARTé: Mecenas game title screen

The players are presented with choices on the screen and must decide what to do. Immediate feedback is provided to players once they decide, and they can see how their decision has impacted their reputation among the city and church. The game consists of a tutorial and four levels described below:

Tutorial

Players learn game mechanics, resource utilization, and menu navigation. This section introduces basic game concepts.

Level 1 – Establishing Banco Medici in Florence

Discover influential figures of the Church, art, architecture, and trade, as well as the Medici family's expansion beyond Florence in the 1430s.

Level 2 – Expanding To Foreign Markets

Explore Cosimo de' Medici's exile to Padua, return to Florence (1434), artist-patron relationships, and network expansion.

Level 3 – Preserving Wealth and Status

Learn about Leonardo da Vinci's early career, Humanist ideals, Greco-Roman influences, and art history innovations. Manage conflicts within Banco Medici.

Level 4 – Rising Influence and Art Patronage

Discover artists' responses to Church reform, the Papacy in Florence, Michelangelo, and the Medici family's leadership in Florence and Tuscany (Fig. 2).

The second game, used by four of the faculty, is *ARTé: Lumiere* [31]. The game is set in 19th-century Paris and covers an art revolution where modern and academic art collided and impressionism became mainstream (Fig. 3).

The game has the following learning objectives:

- Assemble and organize a collection of artworks to satisfy a given set of criteria.
- Relate artworks to the political, social, cultural, religious, and economic milieu of the time.

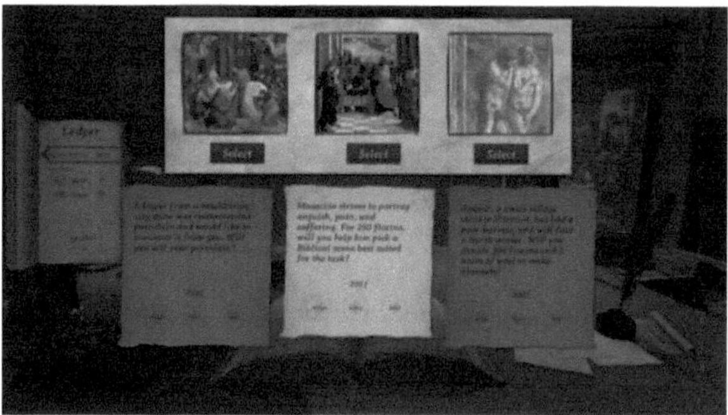

Fig. 2. ARTé: Mecenas artwork choices

Fig. 3. ARTé: Lumiere game title screen

- Organize artwork using common themes and subjects.
- Classify artworks by artist style, period style, media, and techniques.

The game is played online in a browser, and players are presented with a 2.5D environment, befitting to the topic of impressionism. A 2.5D environment is a 3D environment with 2D characters that can only move in specified directions. The game consists of three mini games and asks the players to discover and analyze artworks and interact with artists (Fig. 4).

Fig. 4. ARTé: Lumiere Screenshot

Fig. 5. ARTé: Lumiere Screenshot

5   Results

The interviews with faculty members were transcribed and then coded by the researchers (See Table 1). Categories were developed based on the descriptive codes and can be seen in Table 1 along with their frequencies. This table lists the keywords of the common trends and counts the number of times they are mentioned (frequency) across all interviews. It also presents this frequency data in percentage form using the total mentioned as a denominator. Clearly, Pedagogy, People, Content, and Artifacts were the top mentions with some small mention of immersion. Therefore, we will focus on these as the key results of our analysis.

Table 1. Categories & Frequencies

World/Category	Total Frequency	Percentage Form
Pedagogy	77	41%
People	40	21%
Content	38	20%
Artifacts	18	9%
Immersion	9	5%
Connections	2	1%
Play	2	1%
Travel	1	1%
Scholarship	1	1%
Time	1	1%
Economy	1	1%

In Table 2 we sum up the total number of students, semesters, and average play time for each student for all faculty. Included in the table is also if students decided to play the games (key redeemed) and how many students completed the games. The major themes that emerged from the analysis are the following:

1. Games as a pedagogical tool
2. Games to connect with people
3. Games as a content delivery method
4. Games as artifacts

It is interesting to note that more keys were redeemed than the number of students who stated they played the games in some classes. This means that at least some students played the games more than once. To note is also the difference between students who played in each class and the number of students that completed the games. From the initial frequency analysis, the following themes emerged as most prominent.

Table 2. Game play summary per faculty

	Semester	# Students	Keys redeemed	Not played	Avg. Time per completed game in hrs	avg. % students played	avg. % students completed
Dr. Robinson	4	195	178	10	20:28:48	95%	14%
Dr. Larson	5	736	782	108	14:21:24	85%	14%
Dr. Meyer	7	1677	1444	120	11:44:52	93%	40%
Dr. Williams	9	556	551	33	14:15:42	94%	18%
Dr. Mitchell	4	62	57	9	11:20:13	85%	48%

5.1 Games as Pedagogical Tool

Consistent with the different disciplines within which the games were being implemented, it was evident that the faculty participants were using games for diverse pedagogical perspectives. However, what was clear was that they deeply believed in the potential of educational games to promote understanding of complex issues. As Dr. Larsen commented,

> For undergraduates... in general, I believe in games for kind of having this great effect on them. [I've] already been talking about this in my book, not creating a kind of historical archive or record or any kind of historicity in a conventional sense because they're always so malleable and stuff can change, but making a person feel as if they personally had a kind of personal archival a biographical experience like you know historiography often realizing things like journals or diaries or, conversely, like you know we're records and, in fact games don't rely on that at all, but in the end you end up with something like a journal or Diary, which is what I had them write as part of the game... I [also] thought it would be a fun way for them to challenge themselves in learning more broadly about the cultural aspects behind what makes certain art to be made or created. It's fun and I also think it helps them understand.

It was also clear that although the faculty members were committed to using games in the classroom, they viewed them as one but not the only tool in their pedagogical repertoire. As Dr. Larsen said,

> I'll try to find them something specific like an article or something that makes them think more deeply about whatever subject matter we're discussing and then to write

kind of responsibly about how they feel and argue against certain standpoints or viewpoints about art.

When using games as a pedagogical tool, it becomes clear how the classroom experience is transforming from one that is focused on writing essays and dispelling myths via lectures to one that is more interactive and even competitive. Bringing competition into the classroom could be a double-edged sword. Some students thrive on competition and will work very hard to compete and beat themselves and others, while for other students' competition has a negative effect and can lead to complete disengagement. When using competition in a classroom, we have found that allowing students to work in groups, as the group structure mitigates the negative effects of competition.

5.2   Games as a Means to Connect with People

As educators, it is not always easy to connect with students. We must ensure that all the content is delivered to all students equitably and that they are able to master that content. Many times, our classes are diverse, with students from different socio-economic backgrounds, different ethnicities, different genders, and different ideas, aspirations, and motivations to be in school. As teachers, we strive to create a meaningful connection with every single student while also continuing to innovate and adopt new practices, techniques, and improve our teaching. Games are not an innovative tool in the classroom by any means. Oregon Trail, for example, was used in a classroom in 1971, and there have been many games in the last 50 years, both educational and entertainment games, that have been used in the classroom. However, games are not yet pervasive in classrooms everywhere, and thus it is not a surprise that one of the participants said they had been nominated for an innovation award in teaching. In Dr. Robinson's words:

> I've been in such a bizarre mode lately because I've been, you know, partly online and blended and now I'm in person again, so actually the projects and the things I've been doing actually kind of been changing over time and I just got nominated by some students for innovation and online teaching award. Which I'm very proud of, because I think I'm older, you know I'm not a youngster and to be, you know, nominated for that, so they enjoyed some of the online projects which are a little bit different than, you know, what I do in person. It is possible that part of her receiving the award had also to do with her ability to connect the history to today, for example "…in a time to make anything like you know I say like look at this building we're in here on campus and you had to get many different people to buy into the need for this building, in order for it to be made, so I think it's a good parallel for them" and "To look at that, and you know a lot of times art history we just push economics completely out, you know we don't want to think about. That that aspect of supply and demand and I think it's good for them to understand that part of the motivation of artists who get to make things is the ones that are sponsored or supported in some way."

Perhaps one reason why games can help educators connect more with students is illustrated by Dr. Meyer:

I think this kind of ability now to remove myself, to remove my voice, and I guess, you know, that's the kind of thing that you used to expect from a textbook, that students would go to the textbook, but you know many of them kind of don't and actually you know many beginning textbooks in art history don't really offer a more nuanced view and there's not a whole lot of depth.

Dr. Larson made this profound statement about his students:

But games, you know the magic circle is great for creating a situation where a lot of insecurities drop away and students can kind of get super into a subject. As faculty, is that not our ultimate goal, to connect with students in a way that their insecurities are removed and they totally immerse themselves into the subject we are teaching?

5.3 Games as a Content Delivery Method

When considering content, we usually think about it in a traditional way, where content is delivered through books or orally. Sometimes teachers use movies, documentaries, or audio sources, rarely are video games considered as a medium that can deliver content. Purposefully designed educational video games are curated and edited by experts in their field and can also be viewed as valid methods for content delivery. Dr. Mitchell made the following statement:

We are a community college, and a lot of times the resources are hard to come by. A lot of our students, [share] a computer at home with maybe certain siblings, parents. They might not[...]get their computer until later, so I was able to kind of overcome that by having classes in computer labs where the first week of class we were just solely doing the game, and the rest of the computers at the campus they could use as well for the game too if they needed to outside of class. This game was definitely more easily available to me, because it was already finished and complete. It was just, "hey try this out." And so, once I did, it was for calculus. I was very much intrigued in that and I'm wanting to do this (in?) other classes. I think I just don't have the tools to, to really do that myself or there's no companies really out there that we really heard of that really invest in game-based learning.

As Dr. Robinson pointed out:

I think it's helped me to be more open to sharing with them greater complexities about the situations that exist around the making of art. It helps them to get more immersed and it, it allows me to be more immersive to think about things in a different way for them, so I think it's opened up a better dialogue between me and the students. It gives us an area of discussion in class… I've learned that those extra elements that you can put into it, that bring the world, the time, that a work of art was made more to life, it's very helpful for the students and understanding. The only thing that I could think would help them more than a game is to travel to the countries where this art is made and see the landscape in the world there for themselves and understand… The students, they've been in those worlds that have been created in gaming and other aspects, so it's meaningful to them..., to those students. That, and they'll sometimes tell me about some work of art that's in a video game they're playing… because you're participating and you're making those decisions and you're trying to keep everybody happy and you know, keep money in the bank and, I think it's really fun for them to see that and to experience it.

Games can provide a rich interactive tapestry that students can engage in, and it would be difficult for teachers to achieve that in any other way.

5.4 Games as Artifacts

Educators are always looking for ways to enrich the classroom experience. One such way is through artifacts. It is relatively easy for an engineer or a doctor or an artist to bring contemporary artifacts into the classroom to help students build connections and enrich the curriculum. The same cannot be said for an art historian. The artifacts an art historian could use are either in a museum or don't exist anymore. It is very rare to have an authentic artifact that could be brought into the classroom. Thus, teachers rely on stories and their own experiences; Dr. Robinson illustrated this:

I had a grant in Macedonia, so when we talked about the Byzantine culture, I was able to show them some of the places I've been and talk to them about this one, this one church that has the buried St Naum, that has his monastery. You can hear his beating heart when you put your ear to his tomb. It's actually a spring underneath that is pushing up and it sounds like a heartbeat. So, I just add those little elements, so they get a little bit more appreciation of a part of the world, and how different that place is, how beautiful, and they kind of like those legends and stories…

When games become artifacts through which students experience history, teachers start looking at them more closely, as evidenced by this quote from Dr. Larson:

Games have a different duration nowadays… like articles which have a beginning, a middle, and an end. Students don't need a satisfactory narrative arc to learn... They don't need a conclusion to learn there because ludic epistemologies don't necessarily work narratively. They usually happen in kind of a moment of duration that's ongoing and that you only really reflect on when it's done whether …it ended conclusively, or you just stopped playing, but, um, that said, that durationally is effect.

Looking at games as artifacts to be used in a formal educational environment can provide new opportunities and approaches to engage with students. Although both faculties above describe the positive experiences, they had with using games in the classroom, a question remains. Why did less than 40% of students in all classes finish a game?
    Dr. Larson provided an explanation referring to students:

For some of them, it was too much. In a weird way that's also structural issue with games, right, like if game designers can figure out maybe we'll finish games. It will be a very different world. You know it's almost like one of the general things you learn when you play a lot of video games that half the time when you get to the end of it they're not quite finished, because the game designers do need to prioritize.

When considering the interviews for this study and removing questions from the transcribed text, a word cloud was generated to help visualize the words that showed up most. The word cloud in Fig. 5, prominently featuring terms such as 'students,' 'learning,' and 'approach,' underscores the central role of pedagogy in the interviews with professors. It reflects a consistent emphasis on enhancing the classroom experience and fostering student engagement through innovative educational methods (Fig. 6).

Fig. 6. Word Cloud

We then looked at the themes that each faculty member focused on. Table 3 shows the frequency of the themes brought up by each individual faculty member. This table allows us to see how important each faculty member considered each theme based on how frequently they mentioned it in the interview.

Table 3. Frequency of themes

	Dr. Robinson	Dr. Larson	Dr. Meyer	Dr. Williams	Dr. Mitchell
Categories	Frequency	Frequency	Frequency	Frequency	Frequency
Pedagogy	8	25	14	16	14
People	13	6	13	3	5
Artifacts	11	6	1	0	0
Content	1	11	14	2	10

(continued)

Table 3. (*continued*)

	Dr. Robinson	Dr. Larson	Dr. Meyer	Dr. Williams	Dr. Mitchell
Immersion	5	0	1	1	2
Connections	2	0	0	0	0
Travel	1	0	0	0	0
Play	1	0	0	0	1
Scholarship	0	1	0	0	0
Time	1	0	0	0	0
Economy	1	0	0	0	0

5.5 Game-Based Learning Teacher Profiles

Some faculty used and viewed games as a method to connect with people (in the classroom the people) or to increase the relatability of their lectures. Others saw games as a way to deliver content in the same way a textbook or video might. Finally, many thought of video games as practical and tangible examples of lecture material, i.e., artifacts. However, each discussed the various uses with different degrees of focus. For example, all the educators mentioned content with different frequencies, but a few did not mention artifacts. The following radar charts visualize these different degrees of focus (Fig. 7).

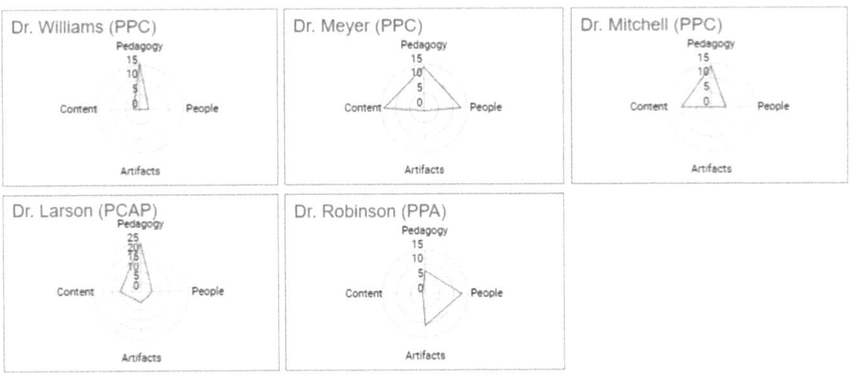

Fig. 7. Faculty profiles based on how they view games in education

Three major profiles emerged in the faculty discussions of how they used the games in the classroom. The first profile is PPC, where faculty focused on Pedagogy, People, and Content in their interviews. Secondly, PCAP teachers mentioned Pedagogy and People, and mentioned Artifacts and Content with the same degree of frequency. Finally, there was PPA, with Pedagogy, People, and Artifacts as the top mentions.

6 Conclusion

Through the three game-based learning teacher profiles, we have shown that different faculty are more focused on certain aspects of games for learning. For example, several faculty members focused on the content uses of the games whereas others primarily focused on the connection to people. Additionally, while most faculty saw games as three primary things, some that could fit in the PCAP category value more than one thing as of equal worth. This is evidenced by Dr. Larson who valued games as Artifacts and a method to connect with People equally.

Another surprising conclusion from this study was the fact that immersion was not mentioned often, which is shown on the radar charts. We expected immersion to be very important to educators to promote a realistic learning environment. However, immersion was not mentioned often across the board, with Dr. Robinson mentioning it a total of 5 times at the upper end, and Dr. Larson not mentioning it at all. Perhaps further research with more faculty would uncover new profiles where immersion was of a higher priority.

These categories also connect the differences in how faculty view video games to the differences in how faculty choose to utilize video games in the classroom. For example, Dr. Robbinson, sorted into the PPA category, mentioned artifacts 11 times. Compared to Dr. Mitchell, who never mentioned the theme, and Dr. Meyer, who only mentioned it once, Dr. Robbinson has a different view of games in the classroom and would most likely utilize them differently. In contrast, Drs. Mitchell, and Meyer, both in the PPC category, tended to focus on the content delivery uses of games in the classroom and thus focused on that aspect of their usage. Most likely, other PPC teachers would use them in similar ways, compared to other categories.

One important implication for game designers is that successful education-oriented games should be designed with their audience in mind, considering the different ways faculty view educational video games. A carefully designed game could enable an educator to connect with people, teach content, and provide examples of the material for their people. However, one might focus on primarily one or two of these perspectives, and an educator could pick and choose the best one for their teaching style and lesson plans. That is because the group of faculties in this study mentioned and were aware of multiple uses of games covered in this paper even if they didn't focus on all of those uses in their own classrooms.

Perhaps the important implication of this study for educators and education researchers is that this study has provided us with a sorting mechanism. After collecting information on how different faculty in different fields view video games in the classroom, we can take that information and find the common themes which yield teacher profiles, or categories that we can sort educators into based on their views and how they would tend to incorporate games into their classrooms.

Using video games in a higher education classroom as part of the curriculum is not new, and games have shown to be able to help students master new knowledge, procedures, and concepts. This study has focused on investigating the views on and ways faculty use video games in the classroom. Considering a course like Art History Survey, which is a large lecture-based course, it is difficult for faculty to create meaningful connections and dialog with most students. Another challenging aspect of large lecture-based courses is to get students immersed in the subject in a way that they start to think differently and possibly through the eyes of those that came before us. Video games provide a unique opportunity to not only work as a pedagogical tool and deliver content, but also to create more meaningful connections with students. Using purposefully designed video games as part of the curriculum requires more time from the faculty. It also brings with it unique challenges not mentioned here, such as technical aspects and the issues that arise when students have technical issues or when students have game issues and don't know how to play a certain game. These topics and how they impact faculty could be investigated in a future research study.

Identifying different game-based teaching profiles when using game-based learning in the classroom will allow us to create better training and supplemental materials for teachers to use. Based on the findings in this study a tool could be developed that would allow us to survey many teachers and faculty to see if there are additional game-based teaching profiles.

Disclosure of Interests. The first author is the CEO of Triseum and has a financial interest in the company. The conflict of interest is managed by the university under system regulations. The remaining authors have no competing interests to declare that are relevant to the content of this article. This research did not receive any specific grant from funding agencies in the public, commercial, or not-for-profit sectors.

References

1. Akl, E.A., et al.: The effect of educational games on medical students' learning outcomes: a systematic review: BEME Guide No 14. Med. Teach. **32**(1), 16–27 (2010)
2. Anderson, M., Jiang, J.: Teens, social media & technology 2018. Pew Research Center, https://www.pewresearch.org/internet/2018/05/31/teens-social-media-technology-2018/
3. Arcagök, S.: The impact of game-based teaching practices in different curricula on academic achievement. Int. Online J. Educ. Teach. **8**(2), 778–796 (2021)
4. Arias, M.: Using video games in education. J. Mason Grad. Res. **1**(2), 49–69 (2014). https://doi.org/10.13021/G8jmgr.v1i2.416
5. Bhattacharya, K.: Fundamentals of qualitative research: A practical guide. Taylor & Francis, Abingdon (2017)
6. Boyle, E., Connolly, T.M., Hainey, T.: The role of psychology in understanding the impact of computer games. Entertain. Comput. **2**(2), 69–74 (2011). https://doi.org/10.1016/j.entcom.2010.12.002
7. Casañ-Pitarch, R.: An approach to digital game-based learning: video-games principles and applications in foreign language learning. J. Lang. Teach. Res. **9**(6), 1147–1159 (2018). https://doi.org/10.17507/jltr.0906.04
8. Djaouti, D., Alvarez, J., Jessel, J.P., Rampnoux, O.: Origins of serious games. In: Ma, M., Oikonomou, A., Jain, L. (eds.) Serious Games and Edutainment Applications, pp. 25–43. Springer, London (2011). https://doi.org/10.1007/978-1-4471-2161-9_3
9. Drugaş, M., Ciordaş, D.: Educational video games revisited: perspectives from parents, gamers, and specialists. Rom. J. Sch. Psychol. **10**(20), 68–82 (2017)
10. Ernest, P.: Games. A rationale for their use in the teaching of mathematics in school. Math. Sch. **15**(1), 2–5 (1986)
11. Garris, R., Ahlers, R., Driskell, J.E.: Games, motivation, and learning: a research and practice model. Simul. Gaming **33**(4), 441–467 (2002). https://doi.org/10.1177/1046878102238607

12. Gee, J.P.: What video games have to teach us about learning and literacy. Palgrave/Macmillan, New York (2003)
13. Granic, I., Lobel, A., Engels, R.C.M.E.: The benefits of playing video games. Am. Psychol. **69**(1), 66–78 (2014). https://doi.org/10.1037/a0034857
14. Hamel, C., Viau-Guay, A.: Using video to support teachers' reflective practice: a literature review. Cogent Educ. **6**(1), 1673689 (2019)
15. Jovanović, M.: Our school in eyes of gamer generation: How video games expose deep problems of our education. Facta Univ. Ser. Teach. Learn. Teach. Educ. 157–169 (2021). https://doi.org/10.22190/FUTLTE2002157J
16. Krishnamurthy, K., et al.: Benefits of gamification in medical education. Clin. Anat. **35**(6), 795–807 (2022)
17. Ma, D., Shi, Y., Zhang, G., Zhang, J.: Does theme game-based teaching promote better learning about disaster nursing than scenario simulation: a randomized controlled trial. Nurse Educ. Today **103**, 104923 (2021). https://doi.org/10.1016/j.nedt.2021.104923
18. McMichael, L., et al.: Parents of adolescents perspectives of physical activity, gaming and virtual reality: qualitative study. JMIR Serious Games **8**(3), e14920 (2020)
19. Merriam, S.B.: Qualitative research and case study applications in education. Revised and expanded from "Case Study Research in Education." Jossey-Bass, San Francisco (1998)
20. Ostenson, J.: Exploring the boundaries of narrative: video games in the English classroom. Engl. J. **102**(5), 71–78 (2013)
21. Pasqualotto, A., Parong, J., Green, C.S., Bavelier, D.: Video game design for learning to learn. Int. J. Hum. Comput. Interact. **39**(11), 2211–2228 (2023)
22. Pozo, J.I., Cabellos, B., Sánchez, D.L.: Do teachers believe that video games can improve learning? Heliyon **8**(6), e09716 (2022)
23. Razum, J., Huić, A.: Understanding highly engaged adolescent gamers: integration of gaming into daily life and motivation to play video games. Behav. Inf. Technol. **42**(12), 1–23 (2023)
24. Rice, K., Lee, B., Groves, D.: Gaming timeline: an exploratory study of "play" history and conceptual framework on video-games and tourism. J. Tour. Hosp. Manag. **10**(1), 1–8 (2022)
25. Rorem, J.D.: Performing the Oregon Trail: Belonging, space, and historical representation in settler colonial Oregon. Doctoral dissertation, University of Minnesota (2022). Available from ProQuest Dissertations & Theses Global (2695015705)
26. Saucier, J.K.: The video game age: a brief history. IEEE Potentials **41**(2), 7–16 (2022). https://doi.org/10.1109/MPOT.2021.3104638
27. Schug, M.C., Kepner, H.S.: Choosing computer simulations in social studies. Soc. Stud. **75**(5), 211–215 (1984). https://doi.org/10.1080/00377996.1984.10114450
28. Sumi Hollingworth, K.A., Kuyok, K.A., Mansaray, A., Rose, A., Page, A.: An exploration of parents' engagement with their children's learning involving technologies and the impact of this in their family learning experiences. Unpublished manuscript (2009)
29. Thomas, A., et al.: ARTé: Mecenas (2016). https://oaktrust.library.tamu.edu/handle/1969.1/187089
30. Thomas, A., Lima-Filho, P., Pederson, S., Ramadan, H., Bologan, A.: Variant: limits [Video Game] (2017). https://oaktrust.library.tamu.edu/handle/1969.1/188002
31. Thomas, A., Ramadan, H., Campana, L., Leiderman, D., Sutherland, S., Zawadzki, M.: ARTé: Lumiere [Video Game]. (2018). https://oaktrust.library.tamu.edu/handle/1969.1/188003
32. Vlachopoulos, D., Makri, A.: The effect of games and simulations on higher education: a systematic literature review. Int. J. Educ. Technol. High. Educ. **14**(1), 1–33 (2017). https://doi.org/10.1186/s41239-017-0062-1
33. Zhang, F., Shen, Y., Pasquarella, A., Coker, D.L.: Early writing skills of English language learners (ELLs) and native English speakers (NESs): Examining predictors of contextualized spelling, writing fluency, and writing quality. Read. Writ. **35**, 1–24 (2022). https://doi.org/10.1007/s11145-021-10223-9

Accessibility

Towards Accessible and Inclusive Serious Games for Cybersecurity

Sebastian Pape[1,2(✉)] [iD], Alejandro Quintanar[1] [iD], and Kristian Beckers[1]

[1] Social Engineering Academy (SEA) GmbH, Olching, Germany
{sebastian.pape,alejandro.quintanar,
kristian.beckers}@social-engineering.academy,
https://www.social-engineering.academy/
[2] Goethe University Frankfurt, Frankfurt am Main, Germany

Abstract. Inclusiveness and accessibility are important properties to allow everyone to participate in today's society. However, these properties have an even higher importance in the context of security and social engineering as disabled and discriminated persons often additionally struggle with depleted resources and capabilities, and therefore are particularly vulnerable [28]. On the other hand, we found that inclusiveness and accessibility are often neglected when it comes to serious games for security training or awareness. Therefore, we investigated how gender inclusiveness to avoid typical stereotypes, language inclusiveness to improve accessibility and features to ease the participation of visually impaired players could be integrated in the already existing games HATCH [5] and PROTECT [17]. We found that the invested effort in accessibility greatly improved the overall user experience and gender-inclusiveness had a positive impact on the players' creativity.

Keywords: serious games · social engineering · inclusiveness · accessibility · cyber security

1 Introduction

Serious games have built a reputation for getting employees of companies involved in security activities in an enjoyable and sustainable way. While still preserving a playful character, serious games can be used for security education and threat analysis [13,33].

Inclusiveness for serious games refers to design principles and practices aimed at ensuring that serious games are accessible, engaging, and representative of diverse audiences. While inclusiveness and accessibility have already been investigated for serious games in general (cf. Salvador-Ullauri et al. [30]), we are not aware of any existing cybersecurity serious games considering them. That is surprising since inclusiveness is especially vital in the context of security training and awareness as an attacker may specifically target the least trained personnel. Previous research has already shown that a sexualized and stereotyped representation of females within digital games [8] may repel females from playing [18].

A. Thomas et al. (Eds.): JCSG 2025, LNCS 16243, pp. 97–112, 2026.
https://doi.org/10.1007/978-3-032-10518-9_9

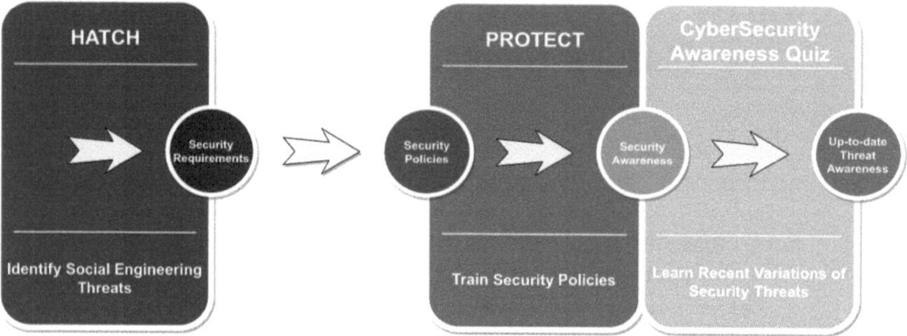

Fig. 1. Relation of HATCH, PROTECT and the CyberSecurity Awareness Quiz [23].

But there is not only the problem of excluding people from security and awareness trainings, Renaud and Coles-Kemp [28] also note that security measures are often exasperatingly inaccessible and since these users often additionally struggle with depleted resources and capabilities, they are particularly vulnerable. Therefore not only accessible security measures [27], but also accessible and inclusive security and awareness training is important.

This work aims to address the lack of accessibility and inclusiveness in existing cybersecurity serious games. For that purpose, we investigated how our serious games to train users against social engineering attacks [5,17,25] could be improved, as at the time of creation inclusiveness and accessibility were not particularly considered. We investigated how gender inclusiveness to avoid reinforcing stereotypes, language inclusiveness to improve accessibility, and features to ease the participation of visually impaired could be integrated in the already existing games HATCH and PROTECT.

The remainder of this paper is structured as follows. Section 2 provides background and reviews related work. Section 3 introduces the methodology of our research. Section 4 describes the application of accessibility and inclusiveness requirements to HATCH and PROTECT. The evaluation and discussion of our results are in Sect. 5. Section 6 concludes the work.

2   Background and Related Work

In this section, we briefly introduce the relevant games for our research in the background section and then provide an overview of related work.

2.1   Background

The three games HATCH, PROTECT and the CyberSecurity Awareness Quiz were designed to educate players about social engineering. The games target players from businesses and organisations. All of them can be played individually, but they can also used together in the following way: HATCH when used for

(a) Energy Scenario Plan   (b) Persona Card

Fig. 2. HATCH Game Elements.

threat elicitation allows to elicit security requirements based on the identified social engineering threats. Out of the security requirements security policies can be built. The security policies then can be trained with PROTECT. Since the adaption of security policies always falls behind recent attacks, the CyberSecurity Awareness Quiz can be used to raise awareness for the most recent attacks (cf. Fig. 1). The games are described in more detail in the following subsections.

HATCH. [5,6] is a physical board/card game for up to four players which aims to identify social engineering threats and develop them to security requirements. The game is based on the examination of psychological principles [31] and the conclusion which psychological techniques induce resistance to persuasion applicable for social engineering. Based on the identified gaps [32], HATCH aims to foster the players' understanding of social engineering attacks. When playing, players attack personas in a virtual scenario based on cards with psychological principals and social engineering attacks. While personas are by definition imaginary, they provide a realistic descriptions of stakeholders or in this case employees, who have names, jobs, feelings, goals, and certain needs [15]. This way players can learn about the attackers' perspective, and get a better understanding of potential attack vectors and their own vulnerabilities. Figure 2a shows a scenario plan for small energy providers and Fig. 2b describes one of the personas from the office scenario. HATCH can not only be used as a training and awareness game, but also for threat elicitation. For this purpose, instead of personas and generic floor plans colleagues and real floor plans are used in the game. A legal assessment was conducted to elaborate on the limitations for using the threat elicitation compared to the training with virtual scenarios as described before [26].

PROTECT. [17] is a web-based, digital card game for single players in patience style which aims to offer the employees an environment where they can learn and train the application of defenses based on security policies. Players draw cards from a pile which are either attack, defense or special cards. If they draw an attack card, players need to try to counter it with one of the previously drawn defense cards. Special cards can be used to investigate the top of the

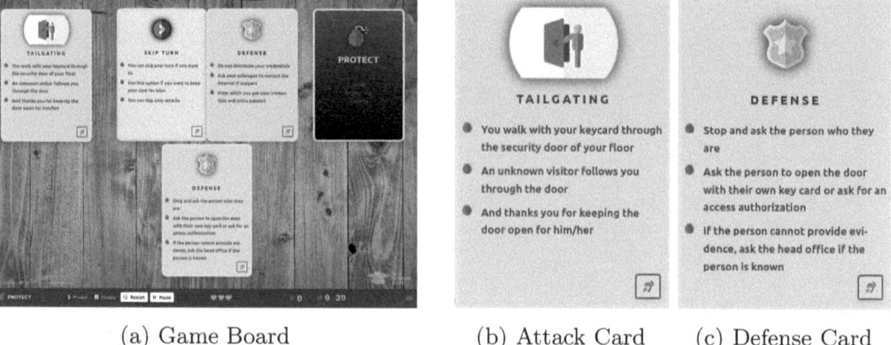

(a) Game Board   (b) Attack Card   (c) Defense Card

Fig. 3. PROTECT Game Elements.

card pile and to skip the next card on the pile. Players try to defend as much attacks as possible without getting successfully attacked. In the long run, the game raises the employees' security awareness and it also helps to bolster their attitudes [31,32]. Figure 3a shows the main view of PROTECT, Fig. 3b and Fig. 3c show example attack and defense cards.

PROTECT is developed using the `Vue.js` framework, selected for its component-based architecture and ecosystem. Additionally, PROTECT integrates `Bootstrap` for responsive styling and layout, providing a standardized and adaptive visual foundation that streamlines the user interface design process.

Beyond these core technologies, some supplementary libraries are employed to enrich the user experience and optimize workflow. A notifications library is used to deliver real-time alerts and status updates throughout the application, enhancing system interactivity and user awareness. An animations library further refines the user interface by implementing dynamic visual transitions, thereby improving overall usability and engagement. The application also incorporates custom `JavaScript`, along with custom `CSS` and `SASS` files, to implement project-specific functionality and styles that go beyond the capabilities of the chosen frameworks and libraries. Architecturally, PROTECT's front-end follows a layered design. `Vue.js` components handle state management and user interactions in the presentation layer, while the application logic layer coordinates data flow between components and oversees service calls. Overall, the integration of `Vue.js`, `Bootstrap`, and additional libraries for notifications and animations provides a flexible, maintainable, and high-performing front-end architecture for PROTECT.

CyberSecurity Awareness Quiz. [25] is a digital quiz game. Since PROTECT is based on security policies within an organization, it can only slowly be adapted to recently observed attacks. Therefore, the idea of the CyberSecurity Awareness Quiz is to close this gap with a quiz based on latest attacks and their variations.

After a new attack or variation emerges, all it takes is the development of a new question/answers pair which then can be used within the quiz immediately.

2.2 Related Work

The creation of serious games is supported by frameworks such as Octalysis that provides eight core dimensions for human motivation [11], and methods which support the creation of scenarios [20] or personas [15]. However, none of them explicitly considers the dimensions of accessibility and inclusiveness.

Salvador-Ullauri et al. [30] investigated accessibility for web-based serious games and found that most accessible serious games focus on sensory disability (72%). The W3C Accessibility Standards, in particular the Web Content Accessibility Guidelines (WCAG) [37], provide some guidance for web-based digital (serious) games. However, most investigated studies [30] do not refer to a standard (51%) and only a minority considers WCAG 2.0 (15%) or WCAG 1.0 (4%). Studies regarding gender-inclusiveness are also mostly based on digital games [8,18]. Dele-Ajayi et al. [12] highlights the necessity to ensure games are free of gender stereotypes in story, content and characters. To the best of our knowledge, none of the many serious games on security considers these dimensions.

Also when it comes to measuring the success of security awareness campaigns [2,3,38] or posters [10], inclusiveness and awareness were not considered in most of the existing research. In related disciplines, Hill et al. [21] showed that the use of multiple photos (males/females) for a single persona to avoid gender stereotypes did not reduce project designers' engagement with the personas. Burtscher and Spiel [9] derived practical guidance for gender sensitivity in HCI research. Breton and Abdou [7] investigate the threat landscape for users that require accessibility tools to access the web. Terras et al. [35] discuss opportunities and challenges of serious games for people with an intellectual disability.

3 Methodology

All the investigated games, have reached a solid level of maturity – HATCH has already been reworked twice, and PROTECT is conceptually the successor of PERSUADED [1] and has also been re-engineered twice. Therefore, we were interested in investigating and improving the dimensions of inclusiveness and accessibility. We chose those two games in particular since they have completely different characteristics: HATCH is a multi-player physical board/card game, while PROTECT is a single-player digital card game in patience style. We introduced the CyberSecurity Awareness Quiz for the sake of completeness and to understand the relation of the different games. Since it is the least mature of the triple, very similar to PROTECT in terms of both being a web-based game with a somewhat similar graphical user interface, and because its content heavily relies on the created quiz questions and less on the game itself, we decided to focus our investigation of inclusiveness and accessibility on HATCH and PROTECT only.

3.1   Goals and Requirement Elicitation

We started with an elicitation to define the goal of our improvement. For *inclusiveness*, we aimed to overcome typical gender biases and stereotypes such as the management being male and the cleaning staff being female [24] without limiting the players' imagination. An additional goal was to translate the game in other languages to allow more players a better understanding, preferably in their native language. For *accessibility*, we decided to ease the access for partially sighted players. The main reason was, that many other handicaps can not be addressed by the game because they have a tighter binding to the used devices: blind people will most likely use screen readers which allow them to read the displayed text either with a speech synthesizer or braille display.

HATCH. No specific further considerations were necessary as the game is a physical board/card game and only the persona cards and the game plan of the scenario can be adapted.

PROTECT. Several factors guided our approach to incorporating accessibility features, with scientific and practical considerations playing equally important roles. One major influence is the set of guidelines presented in the W3C Accessibility Standards, such as WCAG. These standards provide a scientifically grounded framework for improving web content access for people with disabilities. By aligning features—like text-to-speech, magnification, and high-contrast themes—with WCAG principles that are current industry best practices. In addition, user feedback has been important. Real-world testing with diverse users allows us to understand where users face difficulties, how they interact with the platform, and which features offer the greatest benefit.

3.2   Evaluation

Both games have been played and evaluated in the context of the European projects THREAT ARREST [19] and PHOENI2X [16]. However, since the development of accessibility and inclusiveness features was quite recent, those could only be evaluated in PHOENI2X. While not being representative for a certain population, since the consortia consisted also out of non-technical members, it allowed us to gather quite interesting feedback. Feedback was collected after the games were played in an unstructured, qualitative manner.

HATCH. The participants listed on Tab. 1 were introduced to the game, played it for approximately 90 min, and then provided feedback in a focus group. The feedback focused on the scenario, which includes the plan and the persona cards, thus the elements we changed for this work. However, feedback was not limited to accessibility and inclusiveness. The focus groups were led by two authors of this work. They did not follow a particular script, but followed up the remarks from the players to keep the discussion going.

PROTECT. Since PROTECT is a digital game, we did not want to organize a physical feedback session at one of the project meetings, since that would not

Table 1. Profile of Participants Providing Feedback for HATCH

ID	Professional Role	Sector and Institution Type	Gender	Region
H1	Head of training and support	Industry, private company	Male	South Europe
H2	Proj. manager, software eng.	Applied research, private company	Male	South Europe
H3	Innovation project manager	Transport, public administration	Male	West Europe
H4	Professor in cybersecurity	Higher education, university	Male	North Europe
H5	Research assoc. ICT/security	Higher education, university	Male	South Europe
H6	Cybersecurity researcher	Research institution	Male	South Europe
H7	Legal and ethics consultant	Legal / Research, consultancy	Male	South Europe
H8	R&D&I project manager	Transport, public administration	Male	West Europe
H9	Legal and ethics consultant	Legal / Research, consultancy	Female	West Europe
H10	Assist. prof. in engineering	Higher education, university	Female	West Europe

Table 2. Profile of Participants Providing Feedback for PROTECT

ID	Professional Role	Sector and Institution Type	Gender	Region
P1	Research assoc. ICT/security	Higher education, university	Male	South Europe
P2	Innovation project manager	Transport, public administration	Male	West Europe
P3	Cybersecurity researcher	Research institution	Male	South Europe
P4	Legal and ethics consultant	Legal / Research, consultancy	Male	South Europe

have fit the character of the game. Instead, we distributed a link of the game to
the consortium, asked them to play and requested feedback in multiple of the regular virtual meetings. In addition, we received some feedback by mail. Feedback
covered the game as a whole and was not limited to accessibility and inclusiveness, but it included some aspects of it. Table 1 and 2 lists the participants who
provided feedback specific to this work.

4   Results

We showcase our results on gender inclusiveness, language inclusiveness and
accessibility in the following subsection. For PROTECT, we indicate also how
we implemented it in the game.

4.1   Gender Inclusiveness

HATCH. makes extensive use of persona cards which were either male or female.
We could not strictly follow the approach from Hill et al. [21] to include multiple
picture of males and females on our persona cards due to limitations of the
card size. However, we changed them to include a male and a female image and
adapted the description accordingly as shown in Fig. 4.

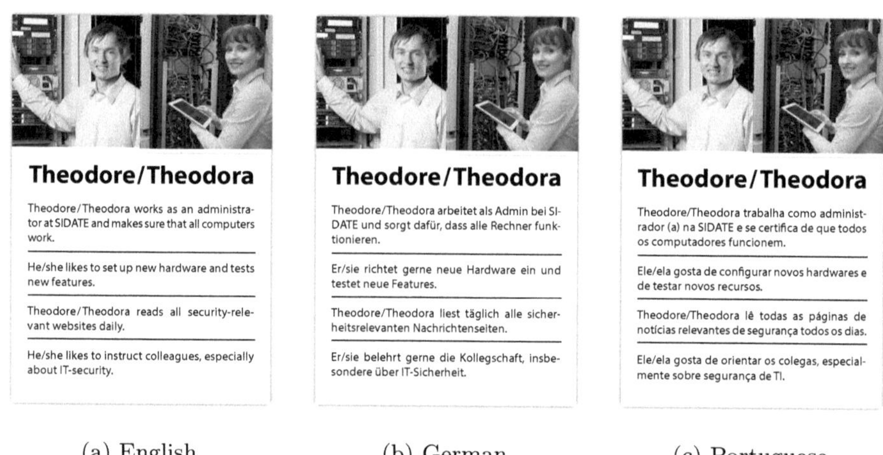

(a) English   (b) German   (c) Portuguese

Fig. 4. HATCH: Gender Inclusive Persona Cards.

PROTECT. is a gender-free game, meaning that all icons and text are free from gender bias. This allows all players to feel included and represented within the game, regardless of their gender identity.

4.2 Language Inclusiveness

In order to allow a wider range players to access and enjoy the games, regardless of their language proficiency, we translated the games to other languages than only English.

HATCH. is currently available in three languages: English (cf. Figure 4a, Portuguese (cf. Figure 4c, and German (cf. Figure 4b. For that purpose, we needed to translate the game cards and the persona cards. The scenario plan includes only names, thus we did not need to change it.

PROTECT. is currently available in five languages: English, Spanish, Portuguese, Greek, and German. The game's text-to-speech feature (cf. 4.3) is also available in all supported languages, using the browser's speech-synthesis engine. As can be seen in Fig. 5 one of the challenges was that the length of text may vary depending on the language.

Implementation: Language Files. To handle multilingual support, PROTECT employs the i18n library. This library enables developers to maintain separate language files for all textual content, which can be dynamically loaded depending on the user's locale or preference. By centralizing translations into discrete resource files, the application can easily accommodate additional languages or updated translations without rewriting the code base. This design also provides a more inclusive user experience by catering to diverse linguistic needs.

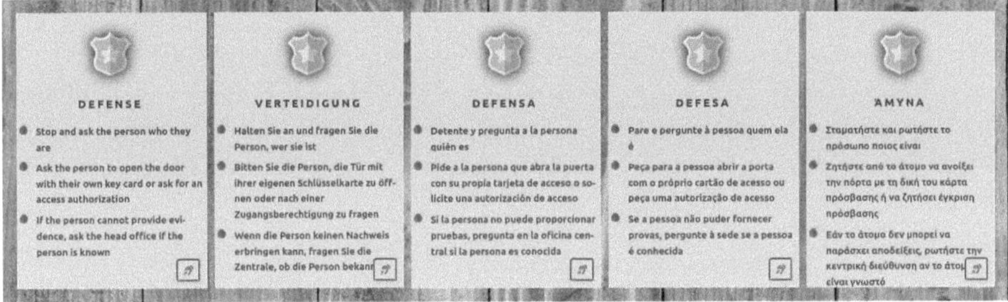

Fig. 5. Defense Cards of PROTECT in multiple languages.

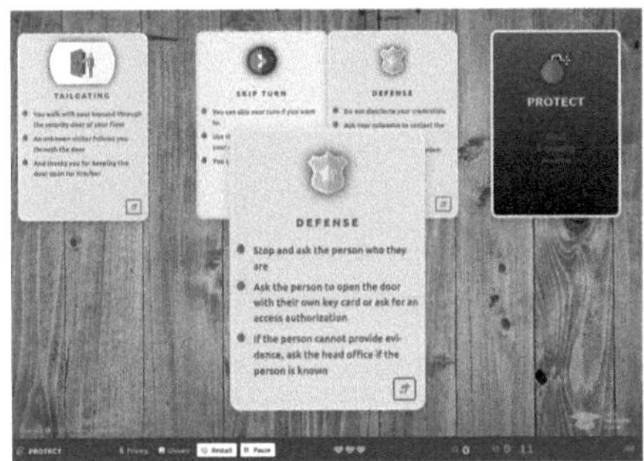

(a) Enlarged Card

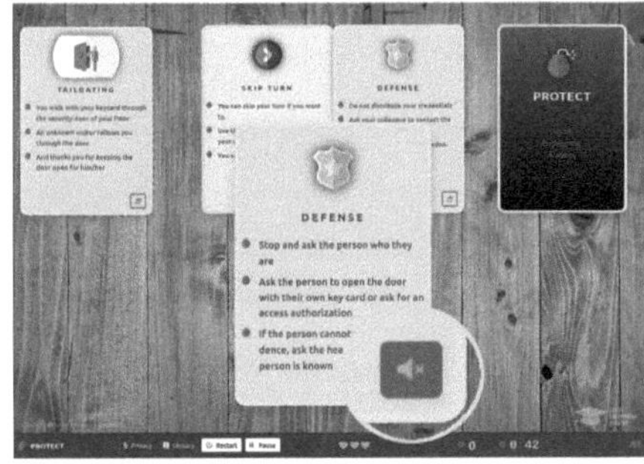

(b) Text To Speech

Fig. 6. Features Supporting Visually Impaired Players.

4.3   Accessibility

HATCH. We considered several options for increasing the accessibility for HATCH. However, none of them came without drawbacks, thus we decided against their implementation. Especially two options shall briefly be discussed. *i) Enlarging cards* allow a better readability for visually impaired. However, larger cards harm the manageability of the cards and remove the character of gaming. *ii) Braille overlays* on the cards can also support visually impaired players. While this would not harm the game play, we investigated several specialized print services and it showed that for a small edition one card costs as much as the full (non-braille) deck otherwise. Therefore, we decided against a proof of concept version.

PROTECT. has incorporated several accessibility features into the game's design to allow a better barrier-free learning experience (Fig. 6).

Firstly, each card in the game can be enlarged to almost double its original size by simply right-clicking on it. This feature allows players with visual impairments to more easily read the text and see the images on the cards (cf. 6a). Additionally, each card has a text-to-speech button in all supported languages using the web browser engine, which enables players with cognitive or reading difficulties to hear the text instead of reading it themselves (cf. 6b).

To further assist players with visual impairments, each card has a different color depending on its function. For example, cards related to security threats are colored red, while cards related to defenses are colored green. This color-coding system helps players quickly identify the purpose of each card and navigate the game more easily.

Moreover, each card has a text definition that explains its function. This feature enables players with cognitive or learning difficulties to better understand the card's purpose and how it fits into the overall game play.

Finally, each card has an icon that defines its function, providing an additional visual cue for players who may struggle with text-based information.

Implementation: Magnifier. The magnification feature was primarily implemented using the web browser's native rendering capabilities in combination with CSS transformations. Specifically, the `transform: scale(...)` property is applied to relevant interface elements, allowing dynamic zooming without requiring extensive re-flow or third-party plugins. Event listeners can capture user input to adjust the zoom level in real time, thus offering an accessible magnification option.

Implementation: Text to Speech. For text-to-speech functionality, the application leverages the built-in `window.speechSynthesis` API available in modern web browsers. By extracting relevant text from the Document Object Model (DOM) and passing it to the `speechSynthesis.speak(...)` method, PROTECT can vocalize on-screen content. This approach does not require additional libraries while still supporting critical accessibility features such as speech rate, pitch adjustments, and pausing or stopping speech output.

5   Discussion

We provide a brief summary of our evaluation, mainly highlighting qualitative feedback on the adaptions and effort needed for those. We then discuss limitations of and future work for our games.

5.1   Evaluation

HATCH. Both focus groups had similar findings: Players liked the gender-inclusive cards and appreciated if a version was available in their native language. Similarly to the observations from Hill et al. [21], gender-inclusive cards were described as fostering creativity since it allowed the players to adapt the gender of victims and attackers according to their devised attack. As described in the previous section, accessibility features were not investigated for HATCH.

Table 3. WCAG 2.1 Criteria and Implementation Status

Criterion		Lvl	Status	Implementation
1.1.1	Non-text Content	A	Yes	Icons and interface elements have text or symbols.
1.3.1	Info/Relationships	A	Yes	Card layout uses semantic labels like "DEFENSE" or the name of the Attack.
1.4.1	Use of Color	A	Yes	Text labels make meaning clear without relying on color.
1.4.4	Resize Text	AA	Yes	Zoom up to 200% supported with no content loss.
1.4.10	Reflow	AA	Yes	Responsive on phones, tablets, and desktops.
2.5.1	Pointer Gestures	A	Yes	All interactions via taps or clicks.
3.1.1	Language of Page	A	Yes	Uses plain, clear English.
3.1.2	Language of Parts	AA	Yes	TTS reads content in user's selected language.
	Audio Alt. for Text	–	Yes	Button reads card aloud using browser TTS API.
2.4.7	Focus Visible	AA	No	No visible focus when navigating via keyboard.
2.1.1	Keyboard Access	A	No	Not operable via keyboard only.
4.1.2	Name/Role/Value	A	No	ARIA roles/attributes not implemented.

The effort for the creation of gender-inclusive cards should not be underestimated. While it was easy to adapt the texts for gender-inclusiveness, cards needed to be re-designed completely. As a consequence, their orientation changed from landscape to horizontal. The translation was done by an experienced translator. However, some feedback loops were required to ensure the correct translation of typical social engineering terms.

PROTECT. By incorporating the accessibility features, the game was perceived as more inclusive and accessible. One of the positive side effects of the accessibility features was, that many of these features (i. e., coloring, explanations and icons) not only benefit players with disabilities but also provide an improved learning experience for all other players.

Implementing these accessibility features required only a modest amount of effort compared to the significant impact they have on users who rely on them. Text-to-speech, for example, can dramatically reduce the strain on individuals who have difficulty reading, while magnification provides crucial support for users with low vision. Although the technical work involved in integrating these capabilities was minimal, the most time-consuming aspect was ensuring comprehensive language support. Managing translations for multiple languages – English, German, Spanish, Portuguese, and Greek – requires ongoing attention to detail, as every piece of textual content must be accurately localized.

However, it showed that due to the capability of generative artificial intelligence [4] to preserve the JavaScript Object Notation (JSON) format, machine learning could be used as a comfortable basis for the human translation to spare some effort.

Comparison to Related Work. Although HATCH is a physical game, we could confirm the positive perception of introducing gender-inclusive personas which is in line with previous findings on digital games. For PROTECT, we considered WCAG 2.1, Level AA, which is currently only covered by a limited number of serious games. Although full WCAG Level AA compliance has not yet been achieved, several critical aspects have been implemented. These include a responsive layout, multilingual text-to-speech support, and clear color-independent design. Keyboard navigation and ARIA-based support for screen readers are not yet functional and are identified as priorities for future development (cf. Table 3).

5.2   Limitations

We discuss the limitations for each of the games separately.

HATCH. While we have discussed gender inclusive persona cards for HATCH, gender was only addressed in a binary form. Future work could also cover non-binary gender experience [9] and further aspects of discrimination, e. g. consider minorities and ethnic groups, as stereotypes, discrimination and prejudice also exist for ethnic groups, skin colors, and nationalities [22].

PROTECT. Our adaption of PROTECT is focused on visually impaired persons and does not consider blind players [14] or color blind players. The latter might not be able to distinguish the cards by their color and need to focus on the icons and text on the cards. Neither do we consider how to support players with cognitive impairments or learning disabilities. Especially the latter could be of interest as the relation between learning with serious games and learning disabilities is not obvious [35]. Unfortunately, due to limited access to the user group, we could not evaluate PROTECT with visually impaired players.

5.3   Future Work

So far, there is only sparse work on how disabilities or discrimination can foster attacks [7]. Be it, because attacker exploits their victim's weakness (based on disabilities or discrimination), be it that attacker pretend to be disabled or discriminated to increase their success rate. E. g. attacker with a wheel chair or crutches might increase their chances for tailgating. It would be interesting to explicitly investigate the influence of disabilities or discrimination on social engineering attacks. The results could be used to create specific attacks within the games to additionally support disabled or discriminated players.

HATCH. We intend to do further translations of the scenarios as well as of the main cards to further languages. Another interesting idea is to investigate how generative artificial intelligence can be used to create images for personas for the different scenarios (cf. Salminen et al. [29]).

PROTECT. We have several additional accessibility enhancements planned for the future. One key improvement is expanding the text-to-speech functionality to cover the entire user interface rather than just specific card elements. We also intend to broaden language support by adding more translations and introducing Simple English for users who may benefit from simplified vocabulary. Furthermore, the application of daltonization methods [34] is planned for enhancing the color contrast to improve visibility for individuals with visual impairments such as colorblindness, e. g. by integrating already existing Javascript code[1] . We also aim to integrate keyboard-only navigation shortcuts to ensure that people can fully operate the platform without relying on a mouse or touch screens.

6   Conclusion

We have investigated how to improve the gender inclusiveness, language inclusiveness and accessibility for our serious games HATCH and PROTECT. While there were some limitations, i. e., for improving the accessibility of HATCH, a physical board/card game, overall we concluded that the invested effort in accessibility greatly improves the overall user experience and inclusiveness of the platform. Interestingly, inclusiveness and accessibility were also perceived positively by non discriminated or disabled players: gender-inclusiveness had a positive impact on the players' creativity when devising attacks in HATCH and the accessibility features for PROTECT were also perceived as supportive for all players.

However, current research showed that content generated by generative artificial intelligence (AI) may subconsciously embed and reinforce harmful gendered stereotypes, potentially conveying that women are less competent than their male counterparts [39]. Therefore, it is important when using AI-generated content in games to consider avoiding typical stereotypes not only an ethical issue caused by bias in AI training [36], but to acknowledge it as an important design dimension.

Acknowledgments. This work was supported by the PHOENI2X project (Grant Agreement number 101070586) and from the CyberSecPro project (Grant Agreement number 101083594). We are also grateful to Kristina Femmer for supporting the design and to Tobias Melzer for supporting the implementation.

---

[1] https://miko.art/labs/Color-Vision/Javascript/Color.Vision.Daltonize.js.

References

1. Aladawy, D., Beckers, K., Pape, S.: PERSUADED: fighting social engineering attacks with a serious game. In: TrustBus, LNCS, vol. 11033 (2018). https://doi.org/10.1007/978-3-319-98385-1_8
2. Bada, M., Nurse, J.R.: Developing cybersecurity education and awareness programmes for small-and medium-sized enterprises (SMES). Inf. Comput. Secur. **27**(3), 393–410 (2019)
3. Bada, M., Sasse, A.M., Nurse, J.R.: Cyber security awareness campaigns: why do they fail to change behaviour? arXiv:1901.02672 (2019)
4. Banh, L., Strobel, G.: Generative artificial intelligence. Electron. Mark. **33**(1), 63 (2023)
5. Beckers, K., Pape, S.: A serious game for eliciting social engineering security requirements. In: IEEE 24th International Requirements Engineering Conference (2016). https://doi.org/10.1109/RE.2016.39
6. Beckers, K., Pape, S., Fries, V.: HATCH: hack and trick capricious humans – a serious game on social engineering. In: British HCI Conference (2016). URL https://www.scienceopen.com/document?vid=ef4958b1-ff29-42e5-b58f-f66b8ef30a87
7. Breton, J., Abdou, A.: Applying accessibility metrics to measure the threat landscape for users with disabilities. In: Networks and Distributed System Security Workshop MADWeb (2023)
8. Bryce, J., Rutter, J.: Killing like a girl: gendered gaming and girl gamers' visibility. In: Computer games and digital cultures conference (2002)
9. Burtscher, S., Spiel, K.: Let's Talk about Gender–Development of a card deck on (gender) sensitivity in HCI research and practice based on a contrasting literature review. i-com **20**(1), 85–103 (2021)
10. Chaudhary, S., Kompara, M., Pape, S., Gkioulos, V.: Properties for cybersecurity awareness posters' design and quality assessment. In: ARES 2022, pp. 79:1–79:8 (2022). https://doi.org/10.1145/3538969.3543794
11. Chou, Y.: Actionable gamification: beyond points, badges, and leaderboards. Createspace Independent Publishing Platform (2015). URL https://books.google.de/books?id=jFWQrgEACAAJ
12. Dele-Ajayi, O., Strachan, R., Pickard, A., Sanderson, J.: Designing for all: exploring gender diversity and engagement with digital educational games by young people. In: IEEE Frontiers in Education Conference, pp. 1–9 (2018)
13. Denning, T., Lerner, A., Shostack, A., Kohno, T.: Control-alt-hack: the design and evaluation of a card game for computer security awareness and education. In: ACM CCS, pp. 915–928 (2013)
14. Erinola, A., Buckmann, A., Friedauer, J., Yardım, A., Sasse, M.A.: as usual, i needed assistance of a seeing person: experiences and challenges of people with disabilities and authentication methods. In: IEEE EuroS and P Workshops, pp. 575–593 (2023). https://doi.org/10.1109/EuroSPW59978.2023.00070
15. Faily, S., Flechais, I.: Persona cases: a technique for grounding personas. In: SIGCHI Conference on Human Factors in Computing Systems, pp. 2267–2270 (2011)
16. Fysarakis, K., et al.: Phoeni2x - a european cyber resilience framework with artificial intelligence-assisted orchestration automation for business continuity, incident response and information exchange. In: IEEE International Conference on Cyber Security and Resilience (2023). https://doi.org/10.1109/CSR57506.2023.10224995

17. Goeke, L., Quintanar, A., Beckers, K., Pape, S.: PROTECT - an easy configurable serious game to train employees against social engineering attacks. In: ESORICS International Workshops, LNCS, vol. 11981, pp. 156–171 (2019). https://doi.org/10.1007/978-3-030-42051-2_11
18. Hartmann, T., Klimmt, C.: Gender and computer games: exploring females' dislikes. J. Comput.-Mediat. Commun. **11**(4), 910–931 (2006)
19. Hatzivasilis, G., et al.: The Threat-Arrest cyber ranges platform. In: IEEE International Conference on Cyber Security and Resilience(2021). https://doi.org/10.1109/CSR51186.2021.9527963
20. Hazilov, V., Pape, S.: Systematic scenario creation for serious security-awareness games. In: ESORICS International Workshops, LNCS, vol. 12580 (2020). https://doi.org/10.1007/978-3-030-66504-3_18
21. Hill, C.G., et al.: Gender-inclusiveness personas vs. stereotyping: Can we have it both ways? In: SIGCHI Conference on Human Factors in Computing Systems, pp. 6658–6671 (2017)
22. Negreiros, T.S., Dos Santos, F.Á., Bolis, I., Silva, W.: Ethnicity, color and nationality: an integrative literature review regarding the relation of cultural prejudice and discrimination. Trends in Psychology **32**(2), 480–504 (2024)
23. Pape, S.: Requirements engineering and tool-support for security and privacy (2020). URL http://publikationen.ub.uni-frankfurt.de/frontdoor/index/index/docId/59271
24. Pape, S.: Challenges for designing serious games on security and privacy awareness. In: Privacy and Identity Management, IFIP AICT, vol. 644, pp. 3–16, Springer (2021). https://doi.org/10.1007/978-3-030-99100-5_1
25. Pape, S., Goeke, L., Quintanar, A., Beckers, K.: Conceptualization of a Cyber-Security Awareness Quiz. In: ESORICS Workshops, LNCS, vol. 12512, pp. 61–76 (2020). https://doi.org/10.1007/978-3-030-62433-0_4
26. Kipker, D.-K., Pape, S.: Case study: checking a serious security-awareness game for its legal adequacy. Datenschutz und Datensicherheit - DuD **45**(5), 310–314 (2021). https://doi.org/10.1007/s11623-021-1440-3
27. Renaud, K.: Accessible cyber security: The next frontier? In: Proceedings of the 7th International Conference on Information Systems Security and Privacy, pp. 9–18, SciTePress (2021). https://doi.org/10.5220/0010419500090018
28. Renaud, K., Coles-Kemp, L.: Accessible and inclusive cyber security: a nuanced and complex challenge. SN Comput. Sci. **3**(5), 346 (2022)
29. Salminen, J., Santos, J.M., Jung, S.g., Jansen, B.J.: Picturing the fictitious person: an exploratory study on the effect of images on user perceptions of AI-generated personas. Computers in Human Behavior: Artificial Humans p. 100052 (2024)
30. Salvador-Ullauri, L., Acosta-Vargas, P., Luján-Mora, S.: Web-based serious games and accessibility: a systematic literature review. Appl. Sci. **10**(21), 7859 (2020)
31. Schaab, P., Beckers, K., Pape, S.: A systematic gap analysis of social engineering defence mechanisms considering social psychology. In: HAISA (2016). URL https://www.cscan.org/openaccess/?id=301
32. Schaab, P., Beckers, K., Pape, S.: Social engineering defence mechanisms and counteracting training strategies. Inf. Comput. Secur. **25**(2), 206–222 (2017). https://doi.org/10.1108/ICS-04-2017-0022
33. Shostack, A.: Elevation of privilege: drawing developers into threat modeling. Tech. rep. (2012). http://download.microsoft.com/download/F/A/E/FAE1434F-6D22-4581-9804-8B60C04354E4/EoP_Whitepaper.pdf

34. Simon-Liedtke, J.T., Farup, I.: Evaluating color vision deficiency daltonization methods using a behavioral visual-search method. J. Vis. Commun. Image Represent. **35**, 236–247 (2016). https://doi.org/10.1016/j.jvcir.2015.12.014
35. Terras, M.M., Boyle, E.A., Ramsay, J., Jarrett, D.: The opportunities and challenges of serious games for people with an intellectual disability. Br. J. Edu. Technol. **49**(4), 690–700 (2018)
36. Tronnier, F., Pape, S., Löbner, S., Rannenberg, K.: A discussion on ethical cybersecurity issues in digital service chains. In: Cybersecurity of Digital Service Chains - Challenges, Methodologies, and Tools, LNCS, vol. 13300, pp. 222–256 (2022). https://doi.org/10.1007/978-3-031-04036-8_10
37. W3C: Web content accessibility guidelines WCAG2 overview (2019). URL https://www.w3.org/WAI/standards-guidelines/wcag/
38. Wolf, M., Haworth, D., Pietron, L.: Measuring an information security awareness program. Rev. Business Inf. Syst. **15**(3) (2010). URL https://core.ac.uk/download/pdf/268106146.pdf
39. Zhou, M., Abhishek, V., Derdenger, T., Kim, J., Srinivasan, K.: Bias in generative ai. arXiv preprint arXiv:2403.02726 (2024)

Board Game and Dyschromatopsia in Children in Primary School

Carlo Alberto Iocco(✉) ⓘ, Aurelio Daniele ⓘ, and Alessandro Rizzi ⓘ

MIPS Lab, University of Milan, Milan, Italy
`carlo.iocco@unimi.it`

Abstract. In this paper we will discuss the work we are doing within the Game4CED project regarding board games and dyschromatopsia. The term dyschromatopsia indicates a condition of hypo-functioning of a class of cones which leads the subject to confuse colors or perceive some of them in a limited way. Approximately 9% of men and 1% of women are affected by some kind of color deficiency. With this research project we analyzed if modern board games are fully playable by people with color vision deficiency and we tried to utilize a board game designed by us to identify children with this type of vision deficiency. To do so we have analyzed the visual accessibility standards of many modern boardgames, created a method to evaluate these standards and, above all, created a board game called ColorFit. ColorFit is a free abstract board game for two players that requires players to associate colored tiles with colored areas presented on the game board. This simple task associated with specially designed color palettes allows us to estimate if players are viewing colors correctly or have perceived some type of chromatic alteration due to dyschromatopsia.

Keywords: Dyschromatopsia · Board Games · Board Games Design · Color Vision Accessibility

1 Introduction

Dyschromatopsia is a genetic condition which makes it difficult to perceive and distinguish some colors. This condition is due to the malfunction of a class of cones, cells present in the retina, which have the task of translating light radiation into color. In Europe 9% of men and 1% of women are affected more or less severely. In Italy, the number of color-blind individuals is around 2.2–2.5 million [2, 6], but the diagnosis is often made only after adolescence. Currently the most used methods for testing color blindness are the Ishihara Test and the Farnsworth-Munsell Test [3, 4], which can be associated with alternative clinical tests such as the Nagel anomaloscope or the CAD test.

Color deficiency diagnostic tests are carried out mainly for the purpose of issuing authorizations to drive vehicles (e.g. driving license), for this reason many color deficiency diagnoses are made in adulthood.

A. Thomas et al. (Eds.): JCSG 2025, LNCS 16243, pp. 113–118, 2026.
https://doi.org/10.1007/978-3-032-10518-9_10

Furthermore, diagnostic tests for color deficiency require trained and specialized personnel, as well as high levels of attention from patients. This makes many tests difficult for children or individuals with attention deficits [1].

Early diagnosis of color deficiency is essential for adequate management of any problems associated with this condition, especially at school. Untrained teaching staff, and lack of knowledge of this phenomenon, could cause stress, exclusion or discrimination of color-deficient children, as well as slowing down their learning pace.

In this context with the Game4CED project we worked with two different objectives. The first one is to design ColorFit, a two players abstract game that has the objective to test the ability of the players to recognize different colors. Using board games as an early diagnostic tool has numerous advantages. Games are a playful and engaging method that could allow us to test children's ability to recognize colors in a fun way, without creating stress and without affecting their motivation. Furthermore, games are an easily accessible and low-cost method, suitable for varying age groups and contexts, such as school. (See Sect. 3).

The second objective is to define and utilize a method to evaluate the color vision accessibility in modern board games. This task is important to understand if the board game industry allows colorblind players to have a gaming experience comparable to that of players without any vision deficiency and what visual accessibility standards are used.

2 A Method to Analyze Color Vision Accessibility in Board Games

Defining a method to analyze color vision of accessibility is important for different reasons. The first one is to help players with dyschromatopsia to understand how accessible a specific game is for them, in which components this can be improved, and how problematic or limited their gaming experience will be. The second objective is to catalog the methods used by the publishers to be accessible for colorblind players, such as the use of appropriate color palettes, specific symbols, and textures.

To create a valuable method of evaluation, we analyzed the state of the art of visual accessibility policies but also how the actual mechanisms of board games interact with components during play. Furthermore, comparing the gaming experience that a group of colorblind players can have with that of normally sighted players.

Based on this task we developed a method defined by these three steps:

1. **Colorimetric analysis:** We utilize a spectrophotometer and colorimeter to analyze the colors of game components such as boards, cards, and tokens. Through this phase, it is possible to trace the colors that fall on the same lines of confusion, which are perceived as similar by colorblind players based, of course, on the specific type of color blindness.

2. **Qualitative analysis of the gaming experience:** During this stage the impact of using colors that are not colorblind-friendly on the gaming experience is observed. This analysis divides the games into risk categories, trying to identify how much and in what way the incomplete understanding of the colors of the game components affects the gaming experience.

3. **Playtest and debriefing with color-blind player:** We observe colorblind players while they play the board games we analyzed in previous phases. Using a test sheet, we take note of their behavior and difficulties.

These three phases were designed with the aim of providing a comprehensive assessment of each game by analyzing how colors can result critical in relationship with the gameplay.

We chose the games to analyze based on two criteria. The first was to analyze successful games, so we selected games listed in the "Bestsellers" category from the most famous board games site called Board Game Geek (Bestsellers | BoardGameGeek). The second group of games, on the other hand, was selected based on the suggestions given to us by communities of colorblind players in order to observe games that performed well or poorly according to their judgments.

3 ColorFit

ColorFit is the first game designed for the Game4CED project with the main objective to become an easy and accessible tool to perform an early screening for color blindness. ColorFit is designed as a print-and-play board game usable by anyone in schools without the supervision of an expert. We tested colorfit with over 1000 children and the game received positive feedback from both them and the school staff. At the moment, we are analyzing the data collected in the schools, so it is not yet possible to make comparisons with other tests for color blindness.

The gameplay of ColorFit is as follows:

1. Distribute the colored tiles between the two or three players so that each player has 8 of them, two for each color.
2. Randomly draw the first player, who will place the first tile in a node of his/her choice.
3. Players take turns placing a tile each on the game board on a node that is connected to one already occupied by a tile. If a player has no chance to place the tile since there are any nodes available, he/she passes the turn without placing anything. A player can only place a tile on nodes that have the same color as the checker and are not already occupied by another tile.
4. The first player to place all the tiles is declared the winner.

The idea is to provide school staff with a single document that contains everything they need to understand and utilize ColorFit autonomously.

The ColorFit print-and-play document is made of:

- An introduction to ColorFit
- How to utilize ColorFit in the class
- The game rules
- The game boards subdivided for each functionality
- The game tiles that are associated to the boards

ColorFit was designed with the aim of being entertaining for the children, but also as a tool for the teachers. To create a game that can test the color perception of its players it was necessary to solve some design issues. The first is to create a game that can be analyzed in an objective way by an external supervisor as the teacher or another adult. This implies that a standard match of ColorFit must be rather short, it should involve a small number of players so that through the analysis of the timing and the errors made by the players it should be possible to highlight a potential problem in color recognition.

To do this, it is crucial to isolate the color component of the game, removing any form of logic or narrative theme, or any reference to the real world, to avoid any kind of cognitive support. Usually in modern games, the cognitive abilities to be tested are multiple. This is a very interesting feature in games designed to entertain but it turns out to be a problem in our setting. This analysis led us to define ColorFit as an abstract game for two players lasting around 15 min per match.

We can refer to it as an abstract game since it has the following characteristics:

1. The game is not associated with any theme
2. All information about the game is visible and complete
3. It is not based on randomness.

In relation to our knowledge, we have not identified any other games that do the same things we aim to achieve through Colorfit. There are several board games based on color recognition (e.g., Nimble), but none of these meet the necessary specifications to be suitable for testing color blindness.

To play a ColorFit match, players must choose a specific set made by a game board and the associated tiles. The different sets changes for the color palette used.

The choice of colors to include in the various game schemes was made using the 1931 CIExy chromaticity diagram and a color-blind vision simulator. The 1931 CIExy chromaticity diagram allowed us to verify the position of colors based on confusion lines: two colors that fall on the same confusion line are perceived as identical by a person with color blindness, vice versa, two colors that do not lie on the same line are perceived as different from each other. This has allowed us to choose distinguishable and indistinguishable colors based on our needs. Then we simulated using the Brettel 1997 algorithm how the boards could be visualized by protans and deutans players in order to confirm whether the chosen colors were easily or difficultly identifiable.

The first palette is made of classic mildly saturated colors (see Fig. 1) and is the one suggested for the classroom screening. In this case the presence of red, green, blue and violet makes it quite easy for each player to distinguish all the colors. This set is used to teach the rules of the game and to check if all the players understand it correctly.

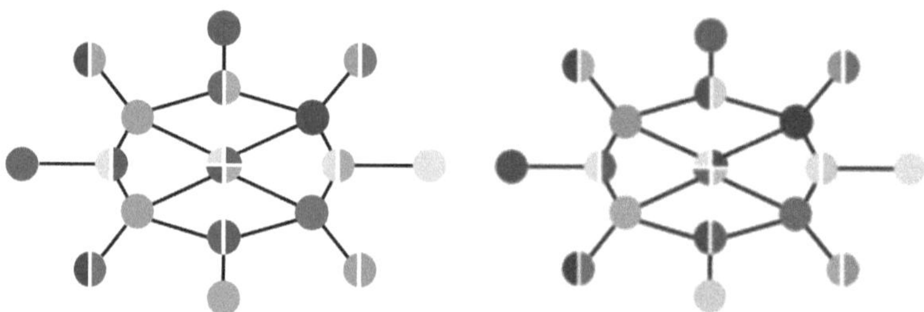

Fig. 1. Standard color palette and its simulated version through Brettel 1997

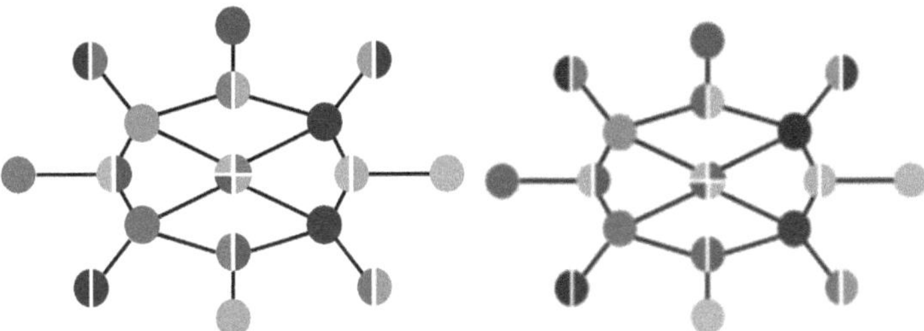

Fig. 2. Autumn color palette (right) and its simulated version through Brettel 1997

The second color scheme (Fig. 2) is designed to be challenging to use only for deuteranopes and protanopes. Players without dichromatopsia should not have any problem differentiating the colors present on this board. The idea is that if a player has no issues playing with the first color scheme but with this one makes too many errors that player could have a problem recognizing colors.

The third and fourth color schemes (Fig. 3 and Fig. 4) are designed to be extremely challenging for each specific type of dyschromatopsia. The third palette is designed for protanopes and the fourth for deuteranopes. A protanope player should have a problem recognizing different shades of red and the same happens with deuteranopes but with the shades of green. So, if a player has problems playing with the second and the fourth scheme but not with the third one it should be a deuteranope. The same should happen if a player has problems with schemes 2 and 3 but not with scheme 4: in this case the player could be a protanope.

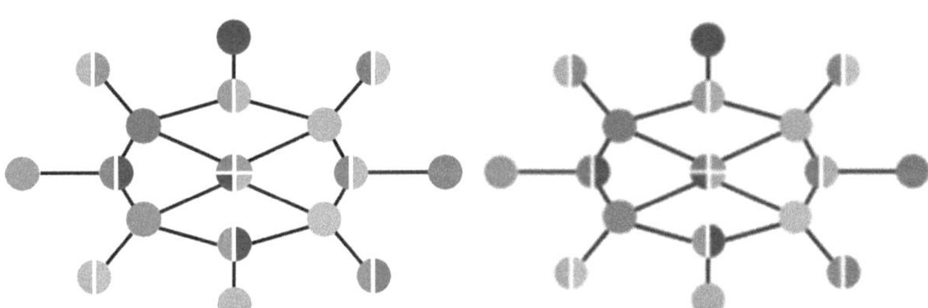

Fig. 3. Purple palette and its simulated version through Brettel 1997

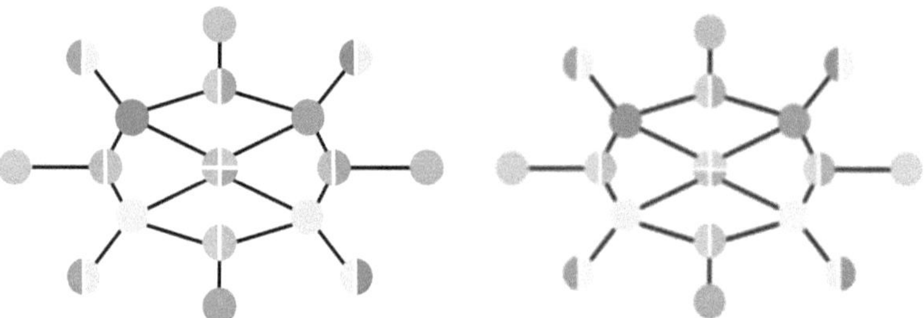

Fig. 4. Green palette and its simulated version through Brettel 1997

4   Conclusions

In conclusion, the early recognition of color blindness problems through board games represents a useful step forward for the prevention of any discomfort associated with a color vision deficiency. Thanks to the use of ColorFit, individuals with difficulties in color perception can be identified quickly and effectively.

The research project which this experiment is part of is therefore interesting from several points of view. The possibility of designing and disseminating free and print-and-play board games with the same characteristics as ColorFit would allow individual schools to carry out tests and game sessions independently and more regularly.

Furthermore, it is presumable that through the spreading of this project the understanding of color deficiencies and their functioning will be more widespread in school personnel. This can be an extremely important factor in providing support and tools for people affected by this condition.

References

1. Armellin, L., Plutino, A., Rizzi, A.: Online games for color deficiency data collection. Res. Cult. Sci. Books **6**, 79–86 (2022)
2. Birch, J.: Worldwide prevalence of red-green color deficiency, JOSA A: 313–320. Color and Colorimetry. Multidisciplinary contributions. Vol. XVIII B ISBN 978–88 99513–24–5 (2012)
3. Birch, M.: Survey of the accuracy of new pseudoisochromatic plates. Ophthalmic Physiol. Opt. **13**(1), 35–40 (1993)
4. Cole, B.L.: Assessment of inherited colour vision defects in clinical practice. Clin. Exp. Optom. **90**(3), 157–175 (2007)
5. Perego, L., Plutino, A., Cattaneo,A., Armellin, L., Rizzi, A., Sassi, M.: (italian only) Un'esperienza sull'uso dei giochi da tavolo per una diagnosi precoce del daltonismo nella scuola elementare italiana", XVIII Conferenza del Colore (2023)
6. Wright, W.D., Martin, L.C.: Researches on normal and defective colour vision. Optom. Vis. Sci. **24**(6), 311–312 (1946)

Collaboration

Fostering Collaborative Knowledge-Building and Resilience Through Player Discourse in Serious Games for Wildfire Preparedness

Mario Escarce Junior[✉], Mj Johns, Shivam Shukla, Darian Lee, Yiyang Lu, Anna Toledo, Tristyn Lai, Bridget Ho, Krithik Dhandapani, Katherine Isbister, and Magy Seif El-Nasr

University of California, Santa Cruz, Santa Cruz, USA
{m.escarce,mljohns,sshukla3,daeilee,luyi,anmtoled,tlai5,bho,
kdhandap,katherine.isbister,mseifeln}@ucsc.edu

Abstract. This study explores how serious games can foster collaborative knowledge-building and resilience in wildfire preparedness scenarios. Through the analysis of player discourse during gameplay, we investigate how knowledge is shared, decisions are influenced, and strategic thinking evolves through co-learning while playing. Employing a discourse analysis framework, complemented by pre/post surveys, we aim to understand player interactions and enhance interactive learning. Findings suggest that structured in-game conversations facilitate knowledge sharing and player discourse reveals important insights into collective resilience-building processes.

Keywords: Climate change · wildfire preparedness · serious games · discourse analysis · mixed-methods evaluation

1 Introduction

As climate change intensifies the frequency and impact of natural hazards, wildfires have emerged as one of the most disruptive threats to communities globally [20]. Traditional approaches to wildfire preparedness, such as public awareness campaigns or emergency drills, are often limited in their ability to foster engagement and behavioral change. These methods primarily target individual knowledge acquisition and lack opportunities for social negotiation, critical thinking, and interactive problem-solving.

Serious games offer a promising alternative by immersing players in simulated environments where they must navigate uncertainty, manage resources, and collaborate to reduce risk. Prior studies have shown that serious games can increase disaster awareness and improve preparedness behaviors [5,6,14]. However, much of this research has centered on individual decision-making, overlooking the collaborative processes through which players construct shared understanding and influence each other's actions.

A. Thomas et al. (Eds.): JCSG 2025, LNCS 16243, pp. 121–137, 2026.
https://doi.org/10.1007/978-3-032-10518-9_11

In this study, we examine how serious games can serve as platforms for collaborative learning and community preparedness, with a particular focus on in-game discourse as a mechanism for building resilience. Specifically, we adopt the concept of *climate resilience* as the capacity of individuals and communities to anticipate, prepare for, respond to, and adapt to wildfire-related threats [11]. This includes not only practical actions (e.g., home hardening or evacuation planning) but also social and emotional competencies such as collaboration, self-efficacy, and emotion regulation – skills that are often developed in interaction with others.

Correspondingly, we define *learning* as a social and cognitive process through which players acquire, apply, and reflect on knowledge and behaviors relevant to wildfire preparedness [1]. In this context, learning is not solely an individual outcome, but a shared activity that emerges through dialogue, decision-making, and group reflection. We explore how this process unfolds through structured gameplay in *FireSafe Friends*, a serious game specifically designed to simulate the challenges of wildfire mitigation and community coordination.

To analyze these interactions, we apply the Discourse Acts framework by Chen et al. [3], which categorizes utterances into cognitive, social, and integrated acts. This allows us to trace how players engage in shared reasoning, coordination, and reflection. By combining this discourse analysis with pre and post-surveys, we aim to uncover how player-to-player communication shapes learning outcomes and perceptions of preparedness. This mixed-methods approach allows us to not only evaluate what players report learning, but also how knowledge and strategy are collaboratively constructed through interaction. We argue that discourse itself is a key mechanism of resilience-building in serious games, an insight that surveys alone might not reveal.

2   Related Work

2.1   Discourse Analysis in Collaborative Learning

This study is grounded in discourse analysis as a method for examining how players co-construct knowledge during gameplay. Our primary analytical framework is drawn from Chen et al. [3], who propose a taxonomy of Discourse Acts – cognitive, social, and integrated – that categorize utterances in educational dialogue. This framework provides a structured lens for identifying how learners engage in reasoning, coordination, and reflection through group interaction.

Other studies have similarly explored discourse as a mechanism for collaborative learning in serious games. Martinez et al. [16] applied epistemic network analysis to investigate how collaborative patterns emerge in game-based environments, revealing that player dialogue plays a key role in supporting knowledge development. Saab et al. [18] emphasized the value of process-oriented measures to capture how learners regulate themselves and one another through conversation, offering insight into the dynamics of co-regulated learning during group tasks.

2.2   Collaborative Learning and Knowledge Building

Understanding how players build knowledge together during gameplay is crucial for designing impactful educational games. Drawing on Hmelo-Silver's collaborative knowledge-building framework, which emphasizes the co-regulation of understanding through discourse and interaction [8], our study explores how collaborative decision-making in gameplay supports learning related to resilience.

Scardamalia and Bereiter's theory of knowledge building further emphasizes the central role of discourse in shared problem-solving and iterative idea improvement [19]. By analyzing in-game conversations, we aim to reveal the mechanisms through which serious games facilitate collaborative learning and community resilience.

2.3   Community Involvement and Cultural Relevance

Community involvement is critical for designing serious games that resonate across diverse contexts. Stokes [2] advocates leveraging existing community networks and ensuring "local fit" in community-based interventions, emphasizing the importance of cultural relevance in game design. This is particularly relevant in our cross-cultural deployment of resilience games in Brazil, where localized content was used to support community engagement.

Harrington et al. [7] stress the need to center participants as co-creators and to be mindful of privilege in community workshops, calling for inclusive and culturally sensitive participatory methods. Our design process incorporated this perspective by working closely with community members to co-create meaningful and locally relevant game experiences.

2.4   Serious Games for Disaster Preparedness

Serious games have proven effective in fostering disaster awareness and preparedness. Kingsley [12] illustrates how gamification strategies can promote civic engagement and influence disaster-related behaviors. Our work builds on this foundation by focusing on how structured discourse within serious games supports collaborative decision-making and collective preparedness.

Lorusso et al. [15] argue that serious games can offer safe, virtual environments for rehearsing skills relevant to high-risk scenarios. We leverage this potential in our resilience games, where players simulate strategic responses and manage resources in wildfire-prone settings(Fig. 1).

3   Artifact: FireSafe Friends

FireSafe Friends. is a digital serious game designed to raise awareness about wildfire preparedness and support community-level decision-making. The game simulates a suburban neighborhood at risk of wildfire, where players must collaboratively manage resources and make upgrades to protect their homes. Each

Fig. 1. Screenshot of Firesafe Friends, a resilience simulation game for Home Hardening.

round presents players with a limited budget and a set of possible actions – such as installing ember-resistant vents, replacing roofing materials, or clearing vegetation – each with different costs and protective benefits.

The game is structured around turn-based interaction, with players taking alternating roles as "Budget Manager" and "Decision Influencer". This mechanic was designed intentionally to foster discussion, negotiation, and co-decision-making between players. By encouraging players to explain and justify their choices to each other, the game prompts them to externalize their reasoning and build on one another's ideas. These features make the game not only an educational tool, but also a social one – where learning unfolds through interaction.

FireSafe Friends. was developed through a participatory design process in collaboration with wildfire experts, emergency responders, and community members. This process ensured that the game scenarios and actions were grounded in real-world constraints and reflected culturally relevant preparedness challenges [10,21].

Embedded Learning Objectives. Although FireSafe Friends was not developed as a formal assessment tool, it was intentionally designed with embedded learning goals aligned with wildfire preparedness and community resilience. These include: (I) promoting strategic planning and trade-off reasoning given limited resources, (II) introducing wildfire mitigation strategies such as home hardening and defensible space, and (III) fostering collaborative reflection and negotiation between players. These goals were operationalized through role differentiation, budgeting constraints, and scenario-based decision points.

These learning goals were further supported by interpersonal processes such as explaining, coordinating, and reflecting – functions we later analyzed using the Discourse Acts framework [3]. For interested readers, the game can be accessed and played at: https://ucsc-wildfire-games.itch.io/wildfire-minigames-collection.

4   Discourse Analysis

Discourse analysis is a well-established field focused on how language is used in real-world contexts to construct meaning, coordinate actions, and negotiate social relationships. In educational research and the social sciences, it has been widely applied to understand classroom dialogue [13], collaborative learning [4], institutional communication [17], and group problem-solving. Within the context of serious games, discourse analysis offers a valuable lens to examine how players reason together, share knowledge, and make decisions during gameplay.

In this study, we adopt a discourse-centered perspective to explore how players collaboratively construct wildfire preparedness strategies while engaging with a resilience-focused game. We treat in-game dialogue not as a secondary layer, but as a primary mechanism through which strategic thinking and learning emerge. To guide our analysis, we draw on the Discourse Acts framework, which enables the categorization of conversational moves based on their cognitive, social, or integrative functions in collaborative interaction.

4.1   The Discourse Acts Framework

To analyze in-game communication, we adopted the Discourse Acts framework developed by Chen et al. [3], which conceptualizes player dialogue as a sequence of communicative acts that fulfill distinct cognitive and social functions. This framework is particularly well-suited to studies of collaborative learning, as it identifies the granular building blocks of knowledge building through interaction.

Discourse Acts are grouped into three high-level domains:

- **Cognitive Acts** involve individual knowledge processing. These include explaining, questioning, or evaluating ideas or game mechanics.
- **Social Acts** support interpersonal engagement and group cohesion through affirmation, encouragement, or acknowledgment.
- **Integrated Acts** blend cognitive and social elements. They include proposing strategies, coordinating actions, and reflecting on outcomes in a socially embedded way.

We chose the Discourse Acts framework for its conceptual clarity and alignment with the epistemic and relational goals of serious games. Unlike content or sentiment-based methods, it captures not just what players learn, but how learning unfolds through reasoning, negotiation, and reflection. This was especially important for our focus on wildfire preparedness, where discourse was treated not as peripheral but as central to strategic thinking and resilience-building. The framework allowed us to trace how preparedness knowledge emerged and was socially validated throughout the gameplay experience(Fig. 2).

Fig. 2. Screenshots from the User Study sessions.

5 Methodology

5.1 Study Design

This study used a mixed-methods design to examine how serious games can support collaborative learning and wildfire preparedness. Data were collected through two primary instruments: (1) pre and post-surveys measuring player's knowledge, confidence, and engagement, and (2) audio recordings of player discourse during gameplay. This design enabled us to capture both baseline perceptions and real-time interactional data.

Participants played a two-player version of the game *FireSafe Friends* (as presented in Sect. 3), which was designed to foster strategic decision-making and dialogue around wildfire resilience. Each session involved a pair of players collaborating to allocate their individual budgets toward protective upgrades, such as clearing vegetation, installing ember-resistant vents, replacing flammable materials, etc.

Sessions were recorded, transcribed, and analyzed using the Discourse Acts framework [3]. Surveys applied before and after gameplay provided complementary insights into player's knowledge, perceptions, and willingness to engage in preparedness behaviors.

Thus, this study triangulates three data sources – player discourse, gameplay decisions, and post-game surveys – to examine learning as an emergent and socially situated process. Rather than relying solely on self-reported data, we draw upon discourse patterns and in-game behavior to construct a more accurate picture of collaborative preparedness learning.

5.2   Participants

A total of 16 participants (8 pairs) participated in the study. Recruitment targeted an academic community, including students and researchers from diverse disciplines. Participants ranged in age from 21 to 49 and represented various educational and cultural backgrounds. Most participants were affiliated with game design or computer graphics courses, and some reported prior experience with disaster preparedness, such as dealing with criminal fires or floods.

When possible, participants chose their playing partners; otherwise, the researcher assigned the pairs. This resulted in a variety of interpersonal dynamics – ranging from well-acquainted dyads to complete strangers – which became relevant for the discourse analysis.

5.3   Data Collection Instruments

The pre-survey included demographic questions and items assessing baseline knowledge, perceived confidence in wildfire preparedness, and prior experience with disaster scenarios or emergency planning. The post-survey repeated these questions and added items exploring perceived learning, collaboration quality, and willingness to engage in future preparedness discussions.

Surveys employed a 5-point Likert scale ranging from "strongly disagree" to "strongly agree". Responses were analyzed using descriptive statistics and Wilcoxon Signed-Rank Tests to detect significant differences between pre and post-session responses (Table 1).

Table 1. Pre- and Post-Survey Questions. Question types: (L) Likert scale 1–5, (Y/N) Yes/No, (O) Open-ended.

(1-a) Pre-Survey

Q	Question
1	Wildfire preparedness is important. (L)
2	My actions can help combat wildfires. (L)
3	I would like to learn more about wildfire preparedness. (L)
4	How confident are you in implementing wildfire preparedness measures? (L)
5	How confident are you in your beliefs about wildfire preparedness? (L)
6	Have you experienced a wildfire or evacuation? (Y/N)
7	How often do you discuss wildfire preparedness with others? (L)
8	If you experienced a wildfire or evacuation, briefly describe it. (O)
9	What do you expect to learn from the game sessions? (O)

(1-b) Post-Survey

Q	Question
1	How much did you learn about wildfire preparedness? (L)
2	Did game session conversations provide new insights? (L)
3	I would like to learn more about wildfire preparedness. (L)
4	How prepared do you think your community is for a wildfire? (L)
5	How confident are you in your wildfire preparedness knowledge? (L)
6	Do you plan to discuss wildfire preparedness more often? (L)
7	What did you find most valuable in the game sessions? (O)

To align the survey data with discourse analysis, main survey constructs – such as learning gains, confidence, and the perceived value of peer discussion – were conceptually mapped to relevant Discourse Acts. For example, gains from conversation were expected to correspond to Integrated and Cognitive Acts (e.g., Reflect, Propose, Coordinate), while reported discussion frequency supported analysis of conversational density and engagement. This integration helped bridge perception data with observable collaborative behavior.

The audio from gameplay sessions was recorded using the open-source tool *Audacity*. Players were encouraged to "think aloud" and verbalize their strategies, following the approach presented and discussed by Hoonhout [9]. Recordings were later transcribed, translated into English, and segmented into discourse units for coding.

5.4   Discourse Acts

To analyze how players engaged in collaborative knowledge-building and strategic reasoning, we applied the Discourse Acts framework described in Sect. 4.1 [3].

Audio recordings from eight gameplay sessions were transcribed using automated tools and translated from the original language using a Python script based on the `deep-translator` library. The lead researcher then manually reviewed each transcript line by line to ensure semantic accuracy, correct grammatical errors, and preserve the conversational tone. Timestamps and speaker labels were retained to maintain alignment with the original dialogue structure.

Rather than coding each utterance in isolation, transcripts were segmented into broader dialogue sequences based on semantic coherence and interactional flow. These segments typically spanned several conversational turns and were assigned one or more Discourse Acts depending on their communicative functions. This segment-level approach enabled a more context-aware interpretation of how players coordinated decisions, reflected on strategies, and affirmed each other's reasoning.

The coding process was iterative. Early transcripts were revisited as definitions were refined, particularly for closely related Integrated Acts such as *Coordinate* and *Propose*. All coding was performed manually using a spreadsheet tool to track segment boundaries, speaker turns, timestamps, and assigned codes.

Three transcripts (1, 2, and 8) were selected for detailed qualitative analysis due to their richness in strategic dialogue and clear demonstrations of co-learning through discourse. These cases were used to illustrate patterns and insights discussed in Sect. 6 (Results).

5.5   Ethics

This study was approved by the Institutional Review Board (IRB) at University of California, Santa Cruz (IRB protocol HS-FY2024-27). All participants provided informed consent and were briefed on the study's purpose and procedures. They were assured of their right to withdraw at any time.

No sensitive personal information (e.g., full names or contact details) was collected or required. Participants provided only basic demographic data (e.g., age range, academic background) through a pre-survey. During gameplay, individuals were referred to using anonymized labels such as "P1" and "P2" (i.e. Player 1 and Player 2), with no link to personally identifiable information. All transcripts were reviewed to ensure the absence of indirect identifiers.

Data were anonymized and stored securely in institutionally approved, encrypted repositories. Audio recordings were used solely for transcription and analysis. Ethical principles of autonomy, confidentiality, and respect for persons were upheld throughout the study.

6   Results

Our results are drawn from a triangulated analysis of player surveys, open-ended responses, and gameplay discourse. Rather than treating these sources as isolated lenses, we examine how they intersect to reveal socially constructed, procedural learning processes during gameplay.

6.1   Survey Results: Statistical Findings

To assess the impact of gameplay on learning and engagement, we compared pre and post-survey responses across five constructs. Since most pre-survey distributions did not meet normality assumptions (Shapiro-Wilk test, $p < .05$), we used Wilcoxon Signed-Rank Tests – a non-parametric alternative to paired t-tests – for analysis.

Statistically significant improvements were observed in:

– Self-reported learning gains ($p < .01$),
– Information acquired from in-game conversations ($p < .01$), and
– Likelihood of discussing wildfire preparedness with others ($p < .05$).

No statistically significant changes were found for confidence in knowledge or desire to learn more. These results suggest that the game fostered learning and social engagement, but did not substantially impact players' self-perceived confidence or intrinsic motivation to further pursue the topic (Fig. 3) (Table 2).

Table 2. Comparison of pre- and post-survey results. Values represent mean (standard deviation). Significance assessed via Wilcoxon Signed-Rank Test.

Metric	Mean (Pre)	Mean (Post)	Significance
Learning Gain	2.50 (1.15)	3.75 (0.68)	$p < .01$
Information from Conversations	2.90 (0.52)	4.00 (0.97)	$p < .01$
Confidence in Knowledge	2.50 (1.15)	2.94 (1.00)	n.s.
Desire to Learn More	4.50 (0.73)	4.69 (0.60)	n.s.
Discussion Frequency	1.56 (0.63)	3.56 (0.81)	$p < .05$

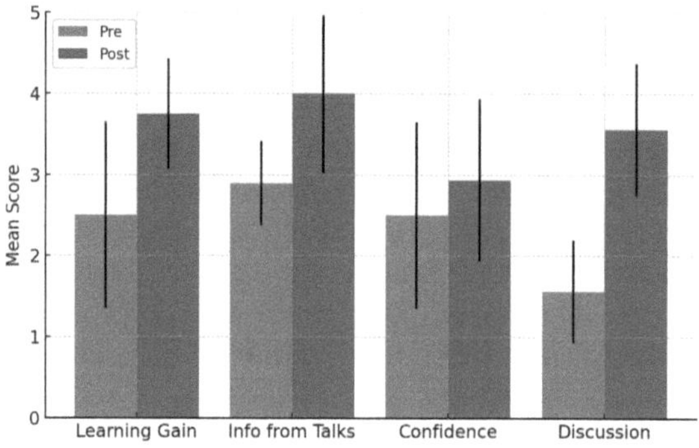

Fig. 3. Comparison of pre- and post-survey responses, with error bars representing confidence intervals.

Survey Interpretation: Engagement and Confidence Gaps. The quantitative results suggest that players not only acquired new knowledge but also became more inclined to share what they learned with others. However, the lack of a significant increase in confidence reveals an important insight: procedural learning may be initiated during gameplay, but it does not necessarily translate into real-world readiness.

Several participants expressed ongoing uncertainty about how to act in wildfire scenarios, even after reporting learning gains. This hesitancy is echoed in both the open-ended responses and gameplay discourse (Sects. 6.2 and 6.3), which revealed recurring themes of doubt, strategic re-evaluation, and collaborative adaptation.

Together, these findings suggest that while the game fosters the construction of procedural knowledge and social learning, additional scaffolding or follow-up experiences may be necessary to transform these emerging insights into confidence and actionable preparedness.

6.2   Procedural Learning in Open-Ended Responses

Thematic analysis of open-ended responses revealed that players engaged deeply with the game's systems and dynamics, reporting insights that extended beyond surface-level facts. These responses clustered around key aspects of procedural learning, such as how to act under constraints, adapt plans, and reason through uncertainty.

Risk-Based Prioritization and Trade-Offs: Participants frequently described grappling with trade-offs between budget, time, and risk. One noted, *"I realized you can't protect everything, so we had to choose what mattered most depending on fire direction."* Others reflected on prioritizing roofs over fences or clearing vegetation based on limited information.

Iterative Strategy and Learning from Failure: Several players mentioned learning from previous rounds or fire events. For instance, one player shared, *"We didn't upgrade the floor and it burned – next time, we knew better."* These responses reveal a learning process that was experiential and iterative.

Collaborative Role Alignment and Re-evaluation: Players often described how discussion helped realign decisions and revise plans. One wrote, *"My partner made me realize we were both upgrading the same thing – it helped to divide roles."* This points to co-regulation and shared procedural reasoning as key mechanisms for learning.

Overall, these narratives underscore how players engaged with the game's mechanics in ways that demanded strategy, adaptation, and negotiation – hallmarks of procedural learning.

6.3 Discourse Analysis Results: Strategic Reasoning and Co-learning in Action

Building on the open-ended responses, our discourse analysis offers further insight into the learning processes emerging during gameplay. We coded 320 conversational segments across eight sessions using the Discourse Acts framework, with a focus on identifying moments of collaborative reasoning, strategy adjustment, and procedural decision-making.

Our analysis revealed that players frequently engaged in *Integrated Acts –* particularly *Propose* and *Coordinate –* which facilitated joint strategy construction and adaptation in response to game dynamics. *Cognitive Acts*, such as *Evaluate, Explain,* and *Reflect,* were also common and often intertwined with in-game choices about resource allocation, fire behavior, or mitigation trade-offs. *Social Acts*, while less frequent, were essential in establishing rapport and maintaining group cohesion during decision-making.

Unlike traditional sentence-level coding, we examined broader dialogue segments – short but cohesive sequences where players negotiated meaning, made plans, or re-evaluated their strategies. These segments often carried multiple discourse functions and were thus assigned more than one Discourse Act. This approach allowed us to capture the layered and emergent nature of in-game collaboration and learning.

Across the coded dataset, approximately 42% of all discourse acts were Integrated, signaling high levels of coordination and shared planning. Around 35% were Cognitive, with players articulating rationales, posing questions, or reflecting on their choices. Together, these findings suggest that players were not merely reacting to the game but engaging in situated, strategic reasoning – an important form of procedural learning.

The three transcript excerpts below illustrate how collaborative meaning-making unfolded in action. They demonstrate how players built shared understanding, adapted their strategies iteratively, and externalized reasoning processes that supported resilience thinking.

Transcript 1: Meta-talk and Planning Across Rounds. In this example, players used meta-level dialogue to structure upcoming actions and align next-round priorities collaboratively. Their exchanges reveal early stages of procedural coordination grounded in in-game logic and team strategy (Table 3).

Table 3. Selected Coded Segment - Transcript 1

Timestamp & Acts	Speaker(s)	Segment + Comment
06:13-06:41 *Meta-Talk, Reflect, Encourage*	P1, P2	P1: "Next round: floor first." P2: "Roof and floor, top priorities." P1: "Yes, let's take care of windows after that." *Comment:* Players co-constructed a shared plan of action, using meta-talk to sequence protective upgrades. These utterances reflect procedural thinking aligned with collaborative gameplay strategy.

Transcript 2: Collaborative Budgeting and Reflective Learning. In this session, players negotiated upgrade decisions under resource constraints and later reflected on their impact after a simulated fire. The talk reveals coordination, cost-benefit reasoning, and social affirmation – all key indicators of procedural learning in a collaborative setting (Table 4).

Table 4. Selected Coded Segments - Transcript 2

Timestamp & Acts	Speaker(s)	Segment + Comment
00:41-01:15 *Coordinate, Encourage*	P1, P2	P1: "I'll improve the wall here." P2: "I'm also going to spend money here on the wall." P1: "Good." P2: "I'm going to fix the side." P1: "Yes, done." P2: "It's a lot of money, but it's important." P1: "It's worth it." *Comment:* Players coordinated specific upgrade actions while balancing budget concerns, affirming each other's decisions. This exchange showcases collaborative procedural reasoning in response to simulated constraints.
03:28-03:59 *Reflect, Evaluate*	P1, P2	P1: "The fence helped." P2: "I'm glad we thought about that." P1: "Coordination helped a lot. Talking made a difference." *Comment:* Players collectively evaluated prior actions and discussed the importance of coordinated planning, reinforcing the value of social interaction in procedural learning.

Transcript 8: Strategic Adjustment and Iterative Planning. This session illustrates how players adapted their protective strategies based on prior failures. Through reasoning and mutual agreement, they engaged in iterative, collaborative planning, an important form of procedural knowledge development (Table 5).

Table 5. Selected Coded Segments - Transcript 8

Timestamp & Acts	Speaker(s)	Segment + Comment
01:47-02:13 *Propose, Justify*	P1, P2	P1: "Let's clear that first then." P2: "Yeah, makes sense. If the fire comes from there, it'll hit the house." *Comment:* Players proposed a change in priority and justified it based on spatial fire risk. This reflects situated procedural reasoning under uncertainty.
06:06–07:17 *Reflect, Evaluate*	P1, P2	P1: "Roof again... We never prioritize it." P2: "Next time, roof first." *Comment:* Players revised their upgrade strategy after observing a pattern of vulnerability, demonstrating iterative procedural learning.
09:19-10:10 *Propose, Coordinate*	P1, P2	P1: "Next upgrade plan: roof, floor, walls." P2: "That's the golden combo." *Comment:* A new plan was proposed, evaluated, and socially affirmed; showing shared learning and strategic alignment.

These examples illustrate how collaborative discourse supported emergent procedural learning. Players externalized their reasoning, coordinated priorities, adapted based on outcomes, and reflected on their shared decision-making process – evidence of learning as a situated, interactional practice.

6.4 Triangulated Interpretation: Learning as Situated, Collaborative Practice

Survey responses, gameplay transcripts, and player conversations collectively show that procedural knowledge emerged through socially mediated interaction. Players reported learning to strategize (surveys), reflected on group dynamics (open-ended responses), and actively reasoned together in-game (discourse).

Rather than a static outcome, learning unfolded as a situated practice marked by hesitation, trade-offs, and co-construction of meaning. The mixed confidence levels reported in surveys align with moments of re-evaluation during gameplay, revealing active engagement with uncertainty.

This triangulated, interactional lens offers a methodological contribution to serious games research, surfacing collaborative and epistemic processes often missed by decontextualized surveys or metrics. It highlights that resilience learning is strategic, emergent, and best understood through the ecology of interaction.

7   Discussion

The Discourse Acts framework enabled us to trace how player-to-player discourse functioned as a learning mechanism in our wildfire preparedness game. Rather than delivering content, knowledge was co-constructed through communicative acts that integrated reasoning, planning, affirmation, and adaptation.

The interplay between survey and discourse data offers deeper insight. Self-reported learning gains aligned with discourse segments where players justified decisions, revised plans, and proposed strategies. Meanwhile, the lack of significant change in confidence was echoed in reflective speech acts expressing hesitation or uncertainty. These findings suggest that while learning emerged through dialogue – via strategy-building and iterative reflection – the shift from awareness to confident action may require additional support, such as post-game debriefs or expert input.

Integrated Acts – such as proposing and coordinating – proved important to collaborative strategy, especially when paired with Cognitive Acts like evaluating and reflecting. Together, they formed interactive loops of co-learning and situated reasoning. In this context, discourse became the medium through which resilience strategies were rehearsed, refined, and retained.

Players frequently revised their plans in response to game outcomes, highlighting the game's potential to scaffold metacognitive learning. For example, Transcript 8 illustrates how crisis response simulations, when coupled with structured collaboration, can elicit strategic discourse resembling real-world emergency preparedness discussions.

Despite these gains, a persistent gap between knowledge and confidence remained. While understanding and engagement improved, player's confidence did not. This reinforces the value of additional instruments, such as post-game interventions, to help translate learning into action.

Finally, our use of Discourse Acts revealed rich interaction patterns and offers a methodological contribution for evaluating collaborative learning in games. We advocate for broader adoption of discourse-centered evaluation, especially in domains that rely on social coordination and adaptive reasoning.

Insights on Collaborative Learning and Resilience Practices. Our findings show that collaborative discourse was central to learning in the game. Players co-constructed knowledge by justifying decisions, making suggestions, and planning together – demonstrating reasoning, clarification, and elaboration. Their dialogue revealed real-time assessment of trade-offs and consequences, particularly around upgrades and risk mitigation. Even under uncertainty, players reflected and adapted collaboratively, highlighting how structured in-game discourse fosters both learning and resilience-building.

Limitations. This study has several limitations. First, not all participants were self-selected pairs. While some participants signed up with a partner, others registered individually and were randomly paired with another participant. This variation may have influenced the dynamics of collaboration and communication. Second, the sample size was small and drawn from an academic context, limiting generalizability. Third, while we recorded player dialogue, we did not synchronize these utterances with specific in-game events or log data, which could further contextualize learning moments. Finally, the absence of post-game scaffolds – such as expert debriefings or reflection prompts – may have limited the consolidation of learning outcomes.

Future Work. Future research should explore post-game scaffolds – such as expert debriefs or reflection prompts – to support knowledge transfer and boost self-efficacy. It could also examine how pairing types (self-selected vs. random) influence collaboration and learning, informing more effective facilitation strategies.

8   Conclusion

This study examined how serious games can foster collaborative learning and climate resilience in wildfire preparedness. By triangulating survey data and player discourse, we highlighted how learning emerged not just from gameplay mechanics, but through social processes of reasoning, reflection, and coordination.

Players reported learning gains and greater openness to discussing preparedness, though confidence in taking real-world action remained limited–suggesting that procedural knowledge alone may not suffice without also cultivating self-efficacy.

Our discourse analysis showed that learning was co-constructed through interaction, with players collaboratively negotiating strategies, evaluating trade-offs, and reflecting on outcomes. The Discourse Acts framework helped illuminate these moments, revealing communication as central to resilience-building.

Overall, this triangulation approach demonstrates that serious games can serve as platforms for both individual insight and collective engagement. By examining not just what players report learning, but how they interact, reason, and adapt together during gameplay, we gain further understanding of the social processes that underlie meaningful learning. This offers guidance for designing future interventions aimed at climate adaptation, where fostering collaboration, reflection, and shared decision-making is as important as delivering content.

Acknowledgments. We thank the National Science Foundation (NSF) for supporting this research. We are also grateful to our colleagues at UC Berkeley and UC Davis for their valuable insights, as well as to the professors and students at FUMEC University for their support during the user study sessions.

References

1. Bandura, A.: Social learning theory. Prentice-Hall (1977)
2. Benjamin Stokes: locally played: real-world games for stronger places and communities. The MIT Press (2020)
3. Chen, Y.C., Andrews, C.D., Hmelo-Silver, C.E., D'Angelo, C.: Coding schemes as lenses on collaborative learning. Inf. Learn. Sci. **121**(1/2), 1–18 (2019). https://doi.org/10.1108/ILS-08-2019-0079
4. Chu, X., Xu, J., Zhai, X.: Investigating the knowledge building process of collaborative learning between student and virtual tutor supported by ChatGPT: a discourse analysis. In: Proceedings of the 17th International Conference on Computer-Supported Collaborative Learning (CSCL), pp. 363–364. International Society of the Learning Sciences (2024). https://repository.isls.org/handle/1/10556
5. Gampell, A., Thorne, C.: Playing with preparedness: using games to explore flood risk and resilience. Int. J. Disaster Risk Sci. **12**, 38–50 (2021).https://doi.org/10.1007/s13753-020-00326-5
6. de Groot, J.I.M., Steg, L.: Playing with fire: effects of a serious game on climate risk perception, attitudes, and adaptation behavior. Environ. Behav. **52**(5), 488–513 (2020). https://doi.org/10.1177/0013916518822751
7. Harrington, C., Erete, S., Piper, A.M.: Deconstructing community-based collaborative design: towards more equitable participatory design engagements. Proc. ACM Hum.-Comput. Interact. **3**(CSCW), 216:1–216:25 (2019).https://doi.org/10.1145/3359318, https://dl.acm.org/doi/10.1145/3359318
8. Hmelo-Silver, C.E.: Problem-based learning: what and how do students learn? Educ. Psychol. Rev. **16**(3), 235–266 (2004). https://doi.org/10.1023/B:EDPR.0000034022.16470.f3
9. Hoonhout, J.: Let the game tester do the talking: think aloud and interviewing to learn about the game experience. In: Game Usability. CRC Press, 2 edn. (2022), num Pages: 11
10. Khaled, R., Vanden Abeele, V., Van Mechelen, M., Vasalou, A.: Participatory design for serious game design: truth and lies. In: Proceedings of the first ACM SIGCHI annual symposium on Computer-human interaction in play, pp. 457–460. CHI PLAY '14, Association for Computing Machinery, New York, NY, USA (2014).https://doi.org/10.1145/2658537.2659018, https://dl.acm.org/doi/10.1145/2658537.2659018
11. Khan, A.S., et al.: Climate resilience: basic concepts and understanding for climatic study. In: Environmental Problems, Protection and Policies, pp. 235–245. M/S Academic Publishers and Distributors (2024)
12. Kingsley, T.L., Grabner-Hagen, M.M.: Gamification: questing to integrate content knowledge, literacy, and 21st-century learning. J. adolescent adult literacy **59**(1), 51–61 (2015), publisher: Wiley Online Library
13. Long, Y., Luo, H., Zhang, Y.: Evaluating large language models in analysing classroom dialogue. NPJ Sci. Learn. **9**(1), 60 (2024).https://doi.org/10.1038/s41539-024-00273-3, https://www.nature.com/articles/s41539-024-00273-3
14. Lorusso, L., Flammini, M., Luccini, A.M., Tadei, R.: Fire ready: designing and evaluating a serious game to raise awareness on wildfire risk prevention. Int. J. Disaster Risk Reduction **67**, 102621 (2022).https://doi.org/10.1016/j.ijdrr.2021.102621
15. Lorusso, P., De Iuliis, M., Marasco, S., Domaneschi, M., Cimellaro, G.P., Villa, V.: Fire emergency evacuation from a school building using an evolutionary

virtual reality platform. Buildings **12**(2), 223 (2022). https://doi.org/10.3390/buildings12020223, https://www.mdpi.com/2075-5309/12/2/223, number: 2 Publisher: Multidisciplinary Digital Publishing Institute
16. Martinez, J., Gomez, M., Cano, E.: Analyzing collaborative interactions in a serious game: a case study using epistemic network analysis. Comput. Educ. **123**, 1–15 (2018)
17. Moschini, I.: The world as a global community? a critical multimodal discourse analysis of facebook's institutional communication and technical documentation. Effigi Edizioni (2022). https://flore.unifi.it/handle/2158/1262429
18. Saab, N., van Joolingen, W.R., van Hout-Wolters, B.H.: Process-oriented measurement of regulation of learning in collaborative learning environments. Learn. Instr. **17**(1), 57–77 (2007)
19. Scardamalia, M., Bereiter, C.: Knowledge building: theory, pedagogy, and technology. Cambridge Handbook of the Learning Sciences, pp. 97–118 (2006)
20. United nations environment programme: spreading like wildfire: the rising threat of extraordinary landscape fires (2022). https://www.unep.org/resources/report/spreading-wildfire-rising-threat-extraordinary-landscape-fires , Accessed 13 May 2024
21. van der Velden, M., Mörtberg, C.: Participatory design and design for values. Handbook of Ethics, Values, and Technological Design (2014).https://doi.org/10.1007/978-94-007-6994-6_33-1

Playing with Child Emotions: A Co-designed Serious Game for Emotion Regulation

Catarina Gonçalves[1], Eliana Silva[1(✉)], Luís Paulo Reis[1], Catarina Fernandes[2], Filipa Rouxinol[3], Mariana Sousa[4], and Susana Pedras[4]

[1] LIACC/FEUP ,Artificial Intelligence and Computer Science Lab,
Faculty of Engineering, University of Porto, Porto, Portugal
{up201906638,elianasilva,lpreis}@fe.up.pt
[2] Clínica CUF Penafiel, Penafiel, Portugal
catarina.r.fernandes@cuf.pt
[3] FR Saúde-Clínica de Psicologia e Neurodesenvolvimento, Porto, Portugal
filiparouxinol@filiparouxinolsaude.pt
[4] Psychology for Development Research Center, Lusiada University, Porto, Portugal
{marianasousa,susanapedras}@por.ulusiada.pt

Abstract. This paper presents the co-design process of a serious game aimed at supporting the development of emotion regulation (ER) skills in preschool children aged 3 to 5. The project is grounded in-depth interviews with experienced child psychologists $(n = 5)$, who provided critical insights into the needs and preferences of the target audience of the serious game. Thematic analysis of the interviews revealed five key themes: emotional challenges, triggering contexts, ER strategies used in clinical practice, game-based learning recommendations, and the importance of parental involvement. These themes directly informed the game's design. Evidence-based ER strategies were translated into interactive elements such as guided activities, playful mini-games, and narrative-driven scenarios. The co-design process was essential to ensure the developmental appropriateness of the serious game and align its mechanics with real-world therapeutic practices.

Keywords: Serious Games · Co-Design · Emotion Regulation · Preschool Children

1 Introduction

Emotion regulation (ER) is a foundational skill that significantly influences a child's ability to interact socially, perform academically, and develop psychological resilience. The preschool years (ages 3–5) are a crucial period for ER development, as children begin to experience complex emotions while still lacking the cognitive and verbal skills to manage them effectively [1]. Traditional interventions in emotional development are often limited in reach or engagement,

A. Thomas et al. (Eds.): JCSG 2025, LNCS 16243, pp. 138–145, 2026.
https://doi.org/10.1007/978-3-032-10518-9_12

particularly for preschool children. The importance of early childhood education in fostering social and emotional development is strongly emphasized by both the World Health Organization (WHO) and the United Nations Children's Fund (UNICEF). The WHO highlights the pivotal role of schools in supporting mental health and emotional growth through targeted interventions in the early years [2]. Similarly, UNICEF advocates for the expansion of school-based programs that nurture emotional and social competencies, recognizing them as fundamental building blocks for lifelong learning and psychological well-being [3].

Serious games (SGs) offer a compelling, interactive way to support the acquisition of ER strategies [4]. While there are SGs designed for older children and adolescents, few target preschool-aged children, and even fewer are co-designed with professional input from mental health experts. This paper, part of a broader research project that began with a systematic literature review on ER needs and effective interventions in early childhood, addresses this gap by focusing on the expert-informed co-design of a serious game. Drawing on interviews with child psychologists, it aims to develop a developmentally appropriate, emotionally engaging, and pedagogically sound tool to support ER in preschoolers.

2   Related Work

SGs have demonstrated effectiveness in psychological interventions, particularly among children and adolescents [5]. However, most SGs target older users, such as REThink, an online therapeutic game designed to promote emotion regulation strategies in adolescents [6], or Mightier, a biofeedback-based video game used with children experiencing emotional and behavioral difficulties [7].

Many of these games also focus on clinical samples, including children with Autism Spectrum Disorder (ASD), Attention Deficit Hyperactivity Disorder (ADHD), or other neurodevelopmental conditions. For instance, LIFEisGAME was developed to improve emotion recognition and expression in children with ASD [8], while Wiguna et al. created a serious game targeting ADHD symptoms and executive function, reporting improvements in attention and emotional regulation [9].

Regarding co-design, although recognized as a best practice in educational and therapeutic game development, only a small proportion of studies apply it [14]. Notable exceptions include Gray et al.'s BrainQuest, developed collaboratively to enhance executive function and emotional self-regulation [10]. In fact, few serious games involve key stakeholders such as teachers, psychologists, or children in the design process.

In addition to the games already mentioned, our game distinguishes itself by explicitly targeting preschool-aged children and being co-designed with clinical psychologists specialized in early childhood. Unlike REThink [6], which focuses on adolescents, or LIFEisGAME [8], which supports children with ASD, our approach combines developmentally appropriate game mechanics with evidence-based ER strategies tailored to typical preschool emotional challenges. The inclusion of expert-informed co-design elements aligns with but extends the work of

BrainQuest [10], offering a unique contribution by embedding clinical insights directly into gameplay for a younger audience.

3   Method

3.1   Interview Process

The game design was informed by structured interviews with psychologists. Participants were recruited through convenience sampling and invited to answer questions related to ER in early childhood. For example, to explore emotional difficulties, participants were asked, *"What emotional challenges are common in preschool children?"*. To identify effective ER techniques, the question was, *"What strategies do you use to help children regulate emotions?"*. Finally, to inform game-based methods, participants were asked, *"What activities or elements would be effective in a game for emotional learning?"*.

Participants also completed a sociodemographic questionnaire, which gathered information such as age, gender, years of professional experience, and prior use of technology in clinical settings.

3.2   Participants

All participants were Portuguese, with professional backgrounds in psychology. Four were female and one was male, aged between 35 and 45 *(M = 38, SD = 4.12)*. They had between 12 and 22 years of professional experience *(M = 16.8, SD = 4.31)*. Three psychologists (60%) used technology in clinical settings, but only one (20%) had previously used digital games for ER.

3.3   Data Collection and Analysis

Structured interviews were employed to collect qualitative insights from participants. To accommodate participants' diverse schedules and reduce logistical constraints, the interviews were conducted asynchronously. Participants received a set of open-ended questions via email and were invited to respond in writing at their own pace within an agreed timeframe. All responses were anonymised prior to analysis. Participants were assigned a unique identification code, and no personally identifiable information was included in the dataset. All data handling procedures complied with ethical standards for confidentiality and data protection. We used thematic analysis to identify and report on themes and patterns within the collected data [11]. Five key themes emerged: 1) emotional challenges; 2) triggering contexts; 3) ER strategies; 4) game-based learning features; and 5) parental involvement.

4   Results

4.1   Theme 1: Emotional Challenges Faced by Preschool Children

Preschool children frequently experience difficulties with emotions such as frustration and anger, particularly when faced with rules or limits. As stated by Participant 1, *"In preschool age, difficulties in dealing with anger associated with frustration can be prominent, as well as the challenge of expressing context-appropriate emotions."* Specific fears, such as fear of the dark, being alone, or imaginary creatures, were commonly observed. As noted by Participant 1, *"Specific fears, such as fear of the dark, animals, being alone, ghosts, and monsters, can also be difficult for children at this developmental stage."* A significant concern was their limited ability to recognize and identify emotions, both in themselves and in others. Emotional expression was often inappropriate to the context, and their emotional vocabulary tended to be limited, making it harder for them to communicate their internal states effectively.

4.2   Theme 2: Contexts Triggering Emotional Difficulties

Psychologists noted that ER challenges frequently arise in everyday social and educational situations. Common triggers include peer conflicts, such as when friends refuse to play the same games, resistance to authority, receiving a "no" from adults, unexpected changes in routine, and emotionally significant events like the loss of a pet or being excluded from play. As observed by Participant 3, *"When they are contradicted, when they receive a 'no' as an answer, when they can't do what they want."* These situations typically elicit strong emotions, especially anger or sadness, which preschool children often struggle to recognize and manage effectively.

4.3   Theme 3: Strategies for ER Adopted in Clinical Practice

According to the interviews, emotion identification was considered a foundational skill in developing emotion regulation skills. As explained by Participant 2, *"Helping the child understand and identify all emotions and then giving them strategies to deal with each one."* Children are guided to recognize and label emotions linked to specific situations, laying the groundwork for managing them more effectively. To support this process, a variety of strategies are used, including narratives and games that model adaptive emotional responses through relatable characters and scenarios. Breathing and relaxation exercises, drawn from third-wave cognitive-behavioral therapies, are commonly employed to foster calmness and self-awareness during emotionally intense moments. Furthermore, Participant 4 emphasized, *"Behavioral strategies such as breathing and relaxation exercises, walking away from situations, seeking support, and cognitive strategies like reframing situations and anticipating consequences are taught."* Color-based emotional mapping is another strategy that helps children associate specific emotions with colors, making it easier to express feelings when verbal articulation is difficult. Additionally, dramatization of real-life situations through role play offers a structured way for children to process experiences and practice emotional self-regulation in a safe, guided setting.

4.4   Theme 4: Game-Based Approaches to Emotional Learning

Psychologists recommended magical, colorful environments, such as enchanted forests and populated with anthropomorphic animals, dragons, and monsters. Storylines should present emotional dilemmas, allowing children to choose responses and observe consequences. Colors and facial expressions are examples of visual cues that would help with emotional identification. As described by Participant 5, *"Matching facial expressions to emotions, sensory tasks like breathing, sound, touch, and using colors to represent feelings (e.g., red for anger, blue for sadness). Include real-life situations such as arguments with friends or school difficulties."* Game mechanics should include rewards, such as stars and medals, and positive reinforcement. Tasks might involve matching emotions with situations or expressions and selecting strategies to cope with emotions.

4.5   Theme 5: The Importance of Parental Involvement

Involving parents is crucial, according to experts, both to reinforce learning outside of the game and to keep them updated on their children's progress. As noted by Participant 4, *"The participation of parents and educators is essential, especially in consolidating the strategies."* It is important for parents to understand the activities being carried out, the techniques being used to regulate emotions, and how to support their application in daily routines. These interactions can serve as opportunities for parents to model ER strategies and to reinforce them in real-life scenarios, promoting continuity between the game and the home environment.

5   Serious Game Design

The resulting game is a tablet-based application designed for intuitive interaction by preschool children. The core structure of the game is organized into a map featuring five distinct islands, each representing one of the five basic emotions defined by Paul Ekman: joy, sadness, anger, fear, and disgust [12]. These islands are presented within a colorful and magical fantasy environment, supported by friendly animals and magical beings who guide the player through each emotional journey. Each island contains three sequential phases, in line with Susanne Denham's emotional competence model [13]:

1. Associating the emotion with facial expressions.
2. Matching the emotion to situations that typically provoke that feeling.
3. Learning and applying emotion regulation strategies.

To illustrate how each emotion is represented and experienced in the game, Fig. 1a presents screenshots of the five emotion-themed islands. These visuals exemplify how psychological concepts were translated into narrative and visual design elements that are both developmentally appropriate and engaging for preschool children.

Table 1 summarizes how the psychologists' recommendations were translated into concrete game design features, ensuring alignment between therapeutic principles and gameplay elements.

6   Conclusion

This study illustrates how expert-informed co-design can yield a serious game that is both developmentally appropriate and grounded in evidence-based research. By focusing on preschoolers and involving mental health professionals in the design process, the game addresses a critical developmental need. Drawing on psychological expertise not only reinforced the pedagogical foundations of the game but also enriched its narrative coherence and visual identity.

However, the study presents some limitations, such as the small expert sample involved in the design process. Although user testing with children, caregivers, and educators has not yet been conducted, this is considered an important direction for future work.

Future work includes pilot testing with children and parents, refinement based on feedback, and empirical studies to evaluate the game's impact on ER skills. Randomized controlled trials and longitudinal studies could provide deeper insights into how the game supports emotional development over time. Including early childhood educators in the evaluation process will be essential to understand how well the game integrates into classroom routines and supports pedagogical goals. Finally, assessing whether children can transfer the strategies practiced in the game to real-life situations, such as resolving peer conflicts or managing frustration, will be key to establishing the game's ecological validity and long-term effectiveness.

This approach demonstrates that SGs, when grounded in expert knowledge and supported by rigorous future validation, hold great potential as tools for promoting emotional development in early childhood.

Acknowledgments. This work was financially supported by: UID/00027 of the LIACC - Artificial Intelligence and Computer Science Laboratory - funded by Fundação para a Ciência e a Tecnologia, I.P./ MCTES through the national funds.

A   Appendix

(a) Joy Island   (b) Sadness Island   (c) Anger Island

(d) Fear Island   (e) Disgust Island

Fig. 1. Visual representation of the five emotion-themed islands in the game.

Table 1. Psychologists' recommendations and corresponding game implementations.

Psychologist Recommendations	Game Implementation
Colorful fantasy settings with magical characters	Created themed magical islands for each emotion, featuring friendly characters such as fairies, dragons, and monsters
Emotional dilemmas with choice-based outcomes	Interactive narratives where children choose emotional responses and observe their consequences
Visual emotion cues via facial expressions	Mini-games involving matching facial expressions to corresponding emotions
Use of colors to represent emotions	Each island and its main character are associated with a specific color corresponding to the five basic emotions defined by Paul Ekman (e.g., red for anger, blue for sadness)
Reward systems to reinforce positive behavior	Implemented a reward system using stars and badges to encourage participation and reinforce regulation strategies
Inclusion of breathing and relaxation exercises	Mini-games that guide children through breathing and calming activities, based on cognitive-behavioral techniques
Parental involvement to reinforce learning	A menu that provides progress updates and suggestions to support emotional strategies in daily routines

References

1. Thomsen, T., Lessing, N.: Children's emotion regulation repertoire and problem behavior: a latent cross-lagged panel study. J. Appl. Dev. Psychol. **70**, 101198 (2020)
2. World health organization (WHO): improving early childhood development: WHO guidelines. Technical Report, World Health Organization (2021). https://www.who.int/publications/i/item/9789240002098 6
3. United nations children's fund (UNICEF): a world ready to learn: prioritizing quality early childhood education. Technical Report, UNICEF (2019). https://data.unicef.org/resources/a-world-ready-to-learn-report/
4. Lau, H.M., Smit, J.H., Fleming, T.M., Riper, H.: Serious games for mental health: are they accessible, feasible, and effective? J. Affect. Disord. **185**, 44–50 (2015)
5. Fleming, T.M., et al.: Serious games and gamification for mental health: current status and promising directions. Front. Psychiatry **7**, 215 (2017)
6. David, O.A., Cardos, R.A., Matu, S., Mogoase, C.: REThink online therapeutic game: a preventive cognitive-behavioral intervention for children and adolescents. Cogn. Behav. Pract. 26(2), 270–285 (2019)
7. Wintner, L.M., Zhang, R., Hernandez, L., Perez, E., Wang, V., Lee, R.: Mightier: a biofeedback video game platform to support emotion regulation in children. JMIR Serious Games **8**(3), e18508 (2020)
8. Alves, C., Rodrigues, R., Barroso, J., Vasconcelos-Raposo, J., Soares, F., Carneiro, D.: LIFEisGAME: a facial emotion recognition game for children with Autism Spectrum Disorders. Entertain. Comput. **27**, 49–60 (2018)
9. Wiguna, T., et al.: Development and feasibility of a computer-based game for attention and emotion regulation in children with ADHD. J. Psychiatr. Res. **148**, 40–47 (2022)
10. Gray, R., Davies, A., Dowrick, C.: BrainQuest: Co-designing a mobile game for training executive functions and emotion regulation in children. Br. J. Educ. Technol. **51**(5), 1573–1589 (2020)
11. Clarke, V., Braun, V.: Thematic analysis. J. Posit. Psychol. **12**(3), 297–298 (2017)
12. Ekman, P.: Basic emotions. In: Dalgleish, T., Power, M. (eds.) Handbook of Cognition and Emotion, pp. 45–60. John Wiley and Sons, Chichester (1999)
13. Denham, S.A., Wyatt, K.: Emotional development and early education. Encyclopedia of Early Childhood Devel. **1**, 1–5 (2003)
14. Roxo, G.S.: Studying serious games for the therapy of children with disabilities following a co-design process. Master's thesis, Universidade Nova de Lisboa (2023)

Game Design/Development

GeoQuest: Prototyping a Mobile Game for Geography Learning with Game-Based and Design Thinking Approaches

Ran Gao[✉], Yu-Chia Irene Kao, Congzhi Ma, Yingjie Zheng, Deniz Ercan, Salah Esmaeiligoujar, and Rui Huang

College of Education, University of Florida, Florida, USA
gaoran@ufl.edu

Abstract. This study presents the design rationale and prototyping process of *GeoQuest*, a mobile educational game designed to foster curiosity and promote lifelong learning in geography among adult learners. Grounded in game-based learning and design thinking, the project explores how user-centered design methods can inform the development of effective educational games. *GeoQuest* integrates map-based exploration, challenge-based quizzes, and incentive-driven mechanics to stimulate geographic thinking and self-regulated learning. The study follows the design thinking process, including empathizing, defining, ideating, prototyping, and testing, supported by simulated interviews, persona development, rapid ideation, and iterative prototyping. The primary objective is to investigate how design methodologies can be applied to create engaging and educationally aligned game systems for adult learners. The resulting contribution is a high-fidelity prototype, supported by documented artifacts and usability planning, which illustrates a replicable approach to serious game design. This work provides design implications for creating learning environments that support spatial reasoning, curiosity, and lifelong learning through game-based experiences.

Keywords: Digital Game · Design Thinking · Prototyping · Geography

1 Introduction

Technological advancements and the widespread adoption of digital media have significantly reshaped geography learning, transforming how learners access, engage with, and understand geographic content [13]. Digital tools not only enrich geography instruction, but also support broader educational goals, including the cultivation of lifelong learning. As identified by the World Economic Forum [21], lifelong learning and curiosity are among the top ten essential skills for the workforce of 2025, reflecting a shift toward continuous skill development in a fast-changing world. Lifelong learning, defined as the ongoing acquisition of knowledge and competencies across the lifespan [4]. It is increasingly seen

A. Thomas et al. (Eds.): JCSG 2025, LNCS 16243, pp. 149–156, 2026.
https://doi.org/10.1007/978-3-032-10518-9_13

as critical for both personal and societal progress. A report by UNESCO [12] highlights the importance of fostering a culture of lifelong learning to empower individuals and promote sustainable development. Geography education plays an important role in fostering critical thinking skills and cultivating a global perspective [19].

This game-based design research is driven by the goal of promoting lifelong geography learning. This objective forms the foundation for the development of *GeoQuest*, an educational game aimed at fostering key geographic competencies in adult learners. Geography education invites learners to explore spatial relationships, global interdependency, and contemporary challenges. Through inquiry-based learning, fieldwork, and the use of digital tools, geography education encourages the investigation of complex spatial phenomena [19]. Game-based learning (GBL) has been shown to positively impact learning outcomes and motivation [15], offering an effective approach to enhance engagement and support the development of these essential skills.

Game-based learning (GBL) has been widely recognized as an effective educational approach for over three decades [1,15]. A 2024 meta-analysis highlights that digital GBL interventions have a positive impact on cognitive and affective-motivational learning outcomes [3]. Well-designed games foster curiosity and sustained engagement by encouraging active information-seeking [20]. Integrating design thinking, with its emphasis on empathy, ideation, and iterative problem-solving, can further deepen learning experiences [17]. Studies show that role-playing games support spatial learning despite potential challenges with complexity [22], and students often favor game-based lectures over traditional ones [8]. Multimedia games have also been linked to gains in cognitive skills and engagement [5], and digital games have proven especially effective in enhancing STEM motivation and outcomes [6].

Building upon these insights, this study introduces "*GeoQuest*," a mobile geography game designed to foster curiosity and promote lifelong learning among adult learners. By integrating design thinking principles and game-based learning elements, *GeoQuest* aims to provide an engaging educational experience that helps adult learners foster their curiosity and explore geography knowledge in the game. In this study, we explore the following research questions: 1) What are the key usability challenges and design considerations in creating engaging learning experiences for adult users? 2) How do design thinking approaches inform the design of geography-based serious games?

2   Game Design and Mechanics

GeoQuest. is an interactive, knowledge-driven geography game that immerses players in engaging adventures across continents through a blend of exploration, problem-solving, and collaboration. Players start by customizing their own characters, then complete different knowledge quizzes and gain geography knowledge through map-based exploration. Interactive maps will allow learners to navigate by selecting destinations directly or choosing specific locations, fostering spatial awareness and sparking interest in geography. As learners progress, they complete knowledge-based missions that require them to apply what they have learned to solve real-world geographic challenges, reinforcing educational content through active gameplay. To enhance motivation, a built-in shop system enables learners to redeem points earned during missions for virtual rewards, adding an element of incentive to support sustained engagement and learning.

The design principles of *GeoQuest* incorporate interactive, mobile accessible, and engaging elements based on game-based learning pedagogy [1,2,5]. These game-based learning principles [15]could support spatial awareness and sustained geographic curiosity in adult learners. At the core of the game is a world map interface that functions as both a navigational and conceptual framework. Learners begin by creating personalized avatars, which initiates a sense of ownership and identity in the learning process. From this entry point, learners engage with a geographically accurate and interactive world map, selecting destinations to unlock missions tailored to specific regional knowledge. Each selected location activates a set of learning tasks, including multiple-choice quizzes, short scenario-based missions, and fact-matching challenges. These tasks are designed to elicit recall, recognition, and application of geographic concepts. For example, learners might identify national capitals, match landmarks to countries, or resolve travel-based problems using clues from physical and human geography. Immediate feedback is provided to reinforce knowledge and correct misconceptions in real time.

Fig. 1. The high-fidelity prototype of *GeoQuest*.

GeoQuest's gameplay is underpinned by a cyclical structure: exploration, challenge, feedback, and reward. Successful task completion earns players in-game currency, which can be redeemed in a virtual shop for symbolic rewards such as digital badges, avatar accessories, or unlockable map features. This reward system serves not only as a motivational driver but also reinforces progress and effort [15]. Moreover, tasks escalate in difficulty as players advance and allow the game to adapt to increasing competence levels while maintaining engagement

[3]. The user experience is carefully scaffolded through a structured flow that aligns with cognitive load theory. The player progresses from an intuitive landing page to the map interface, engages with learning tasks via quiz or scenario-based screens, and concludes each session with a summary of performance and rewards. Figure 1 illustrates several of these UI components, including the welcome screen, navigation map, location-specific prompts, and quiz interface. The visual design emphasizes clarity, accessibility, and thematic consistency, which are particularly important for pr learners seeking low-barrier, high-engagement educational tools.

3   Method

The study was framed by the **Design Thinking Process** [9]. Design thinking [9] is a design method that includes analytic and creative deep thinking. This design approach allows designers to explore ideas, develop prototypes, gather feedback, and iteratively refine the final product [17]. In this study, we followed key phases of the process: the empathize and define phase, the ideation phase, and the low-fidelity and high-fidelity prototyping phase. The testing phase will take place during the data collection stage.

The design process involved an educational research team of five, who collaboratively developed sketches, user flows, gameplay concepts, and prototypes. Input from peer reviews and planning for usability testing with adult learners in the target demographic further informed the design. To systematically document the evolution of the game concept, we produced a series of design artifacts throughout the process. These artifacts served both as scaffolding tools during ideation and prototyping and as reflective evidence of user-centered decision making. Each artifact was iteratively refined with input from stakeholders or based on persona simulations. Figure 2 provides an overview of the design thinking process implemented in this study.

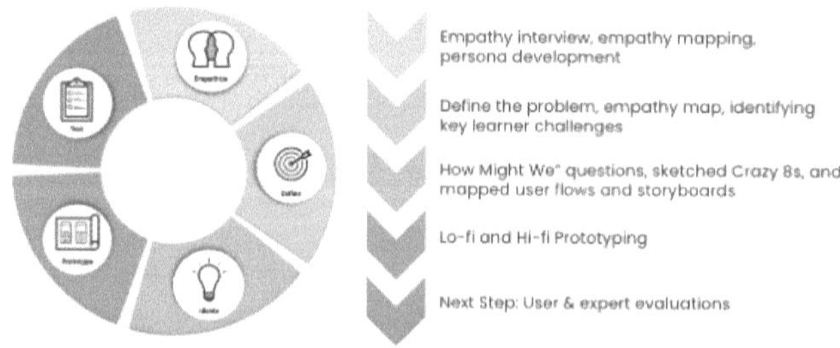

Fig. 2. The overview of the design thinking process.

3.1   Empathize and Define Phase

To understand adult learners' needs in geography education, we began with empathy interviews, using ChatGPT-4o [14] to simulate diverse graduate student responses. This phase produced foundational user-centered artifacts that shaped the app's direction. The open-ended interviews revealed key insights into learners' experiences, emotions, and challenges. We then created empathy maps to visualize what learners say, think, feel, and do. The empathy mapping helps identify the design goals and learner pain points. From these insights, we developed concise personas [18] to help us identify learners' motivations, time constraints, and digital fluency. These personas included adult learners' characteristics, including their background information, past learning experience in geography, game-playing experience, and positive and negative experiences regarding educational games. The personas guided our core problem statements and informed key design decisions, particularly in user interface flow and task complexity.

3.2   Ideation Phase

Building on the Design Thinking Process [9], we used "How Might We" (HMW) questions to reframe user needs into design opportunities, focusing on specific user groups, actions, and desired outcomes. HMW questions guided our brainstorming process and led to the creation of feature ideas through the Crazy 8s technique [7], with each team member sketching eight potential features for *Geo-Quest*. These ideas were organized into four core game themes: players embark on a global adventure, solving geography-related quests to unlock new destinations; mini games; engaging and interactive learning; and self-paced and entertaining education. During the ideation phase, we identified adult learners' needs and developed the solution sketches, interface concepts, and user flows. In addition, we employed personas and storyboards to visualize how adult learners would interact with specific features, while the user flow diagram mapped the journey from login to task completion. These artifacts helped identify friction points, ensure cognitive engagement, and prioritize clarity and pacing across the game experience.

3.3   Prototyping Phase

Low-Fidelity Prototyping Phase. This phase contributed to visualizing the game's layout, functionality, and delivery of instructional strategies [11]. While not fully functional, low-fidelity prototypes serve to explore design concepts, user interaction, and usability potential. Each team member sketched key game functions in a paper prototype, followed by a group vote to select the most promising ideas. This collaborative process laid the foundation for the high-fidelity prototype. Based on the paper prototype, we conducted a cognitive walkthrough analysis [16], structuring the usability evaluation around 11 essential game tasks (e.g., signing in, creating an account). Each task consists of a key action step assessed using a structured format: whether users can identify, understand, and perform the correct action, and whether system feedback is clear. Usability will be scored using binary values (0 or 1), alongside qualitative notes (e.g., from experience?" or "call-to-action visibility"). This analysis supported identifying usability issues and guiding improvements to ensure a more intuitive and accessible game design.

High-Fidelity Prototyping Phase. In this phase, we conducted the expert evaluation followed by a heuristic evaluation [10]. This approach allowed us to identify general guidelines and principles for improving the learner experience in the prototype. In addition to the second expert evaluation, we conducted a user usability interview that was supported by a task-based think-aloud usability testing protocol. Task-based think-aloud [10] is a method that guides users to verbalize their thoughts while performing a task. Through systematically collecting and analyzing direct feedback from users, the task-based think-aloud method [10] offers insights into the cognitive process during problem solving. The purpose of high-fidelity prototype evaluations is to check and review the visual and functional aspects of our high-fidelity prototype, as well as the readiness for user testing [2]. Future evaluations will focus on examining whether the visual components, such as button colors, text fonts, interface layout, and styling, are consistently applied. The final evaluation will also assess whether the prototype functions well for learning purposes, and review that interactions and design elements are technically feasible.

4   Discussion and Conclusion

The development of *GeoQuest* is grounded in pedagogical soundness and user-centered design. Our future study will ensure content accuracy and an engaging learning experience. Data will be collected from three key stakeholder groups: subject matter experts, adult learners, and UI/UX designers. Experts in geography will examine the content in geographic education. UI/UX experts will contribute to optimizing visual layout, user flow, and interactivity, with particular attention to accessibility, usability, and engagement strategies. Learners will interact with the prototype and provide their feedback through interviews, observations, and surveys. These approaches will allow us to collect both quantitative and qualitative data to refine the future design of *GeoQuest*.

This study highlights the potential of a game-based learning geography game, *GeoQuest*, a mobile game prototype designed to foster engaging lifelong learning in geography education. Applying design thinking methods, the project produced a high-fidelity prototype that integrates user personas, scenario sketches, and interactive interfaces. The primary contribution lies in applying design thinking to align geographic learning objectives with game mechanics suited to adult learners. Future work will include usability testing with target learners and expert evaluations to assess the game's effectiveness in supporting motivation, engagement, and learning outcomes. The iterative design approach and artifacts presented here offer a foundation for future research on serious games, particularly those supporting flexible, self-paced learning for adults. This work demonstrates how structured prototyping can drive the creation of meaningful, educationally aligned digital experiences, providing design suggestions in game-based learning and geographic education.

References

1. Adipat, S., Laksana, K., Busayanon, K., Asawasowan, A., Adipat, B.: Engaging students in the learning process with game-based learning: the fundamental concepts. Int. J. Technol. Educ. **4**(3), 542–552 (2021)
2. C. M. Barnum.: Usability testing essentials: Ready, set... test! morgan kaufmann (2020)
3. Barz, N., Benick, M., Dörrenbächer-Ulrich, L., Perels, F.: The effect of digital game-based learning interventions on cognitive, metacognitive, and affective-motivational learning outcomes in school: A meta-analysis. Rev. Educ. Res. **94**(2), 193–227 (2024)
4. Field, J.: Lifelong learning and the new educational order. ERIC (2000)
5. Gros, B.: Digital games in education: the design of games-based learning environments. J. Res. Technol. Educ. **40**(1), 23–38 (2007)
6. Gui, D., Zhang, Y., Lv, J., Guo, J., Sha, Z.: Effects of intercropping on soil greenhouse gas emissions-a global meta-analysis. Sci. Total Environ. **918**, 170632 (2024)
7. Hampshire, N., Califano, G., Spinks, D.: Crazy-8s. In: Mastering Collaboration in a Product Team: 70 Techniques to Help Teams Build Better Products, pp. 6–7. Springer, 2022
8. Hartt, M., Hosseini, H., Mostafapour, M.: Game on: exploring the effectiveness of game-based learning. Planning Practice Res. **35**(5), 589–604 (2020)
9. Henriksen, D., Richardson, C., Mehta, R.: Design thinking: a creative approach to educational problems of practice. Thinking skills and Creativity **26**, 140–153 (2017)
10. Jaspers, M.W., Steen, T., Van Den Bos, C., Geenen, M.: The think aloud method: a guide to user interface design. Int. J. Med. Inf. **73**(11–12), 781–795 (2004)
11. Johnson, J.C., West, R.E.: Instructional design prototyping strategies. Design for learning: principles, processes, and praxis, pp. 1–14, 2021
12. Lewis, J., et al.: UNESCO science report: the race against time for smarter development, volume 2021. Unesco Publishing (2021)
13. Morawski, M., Wolff-Seidel, S.: Gaming and geography. A multi-perspective approach to understanding the impacts of gaming on geography (education). Springer Nature, Cham (2024)
14. Open, A.: Hello GPT-4o. Blog, (2024)
15. Plass, J.L., Homer, B.D., Kinzer, C.K.: Found. game-based Learn. Educ. psychol. **50**(4), 258–283 (2015)
16. Polson, P.G., Lewis, C., Rieman, J., Wharton, C.: Cognitive walkthroughs: a method for theory-based evaluation of user interfaces. Int. J. Man Mach. Stud. **36**(5), 741–773 (1992)
17. Razzouk, R., Shute, V.: What is design thinking and why is it important? Rev. Educ. Res. **82**(3), 330–348 (2012)

18. Siricharoen, W. V.: Using empathy mapping in design thinking process for personas discovering. In Context-Aware Systems and Applications, and Nature of Computation and Communication: 9th EAI International Conference, ICCASA 2020, and 6th EAI International Conference, ICTCC 2020, Thai Nguyen, Vietnam, November 26–27, 2020, Proceedings 9, pp. 182–191. Springer, 2021
19. SPURnÁ, M., HORUTOVÁ, M.: Curiosity in geography education: a systematic review (2024)
20. Tang, Z., Kirman, B.: Exploring curiosity in games: a framework and questionnaire study of player perspectives. Int. J. Human-Comput. Interact. **41**(4), 2475–2490 (2025)
21. WorldEconomicForum. The future of jobs report (2025)
22. Xue, L., Pierce, E., Larsen, S., Oprean, D.: Examining student responses to game layers in cultural geography: a study about game spatiality in a role-playing game design. In: Joint International Conference on Serious Games, pp. 93–107. Springer, 2024

Tensions Between Mechanics and Role-Play: Striving for CO2 Neutrality in a Consensus-Based Serious Game

Janina Woods[1], Richard Wetzel[2]([✉]) [ID], Tobias Kreienbühl[1], Melissa Beck[3], and Uwe Schulz[1]

[1] Lucerne University of Applied Sciences and Arts, Lucerne, Switzerland
{janina.woods,tobias.kreienbuehl,uwe.schulz}@hslu.ch
[2] DePaul University, Chicago, IL, USA
richard.wetzel@depaul.edu
[3] Technical University of Berlin, Berlin, Germany
melissa.anita.beck@campus.tu-berlin.de

Abstract. Sarnetz is a web-based serious game for teams of 5 players. The goal is to shape the future of the Eastern Swiss village Zernez in the Alpine region to create a CO2 neutral region. Players take on the role of different stakeholders and build consensus through discussions and proposals of different measures. Sarnetz is based on an existing board game and the digital version has been used in six workshops of 5–7 participants each. Using feedback from students and professors we conducted a thematic analysis and created three themes that highlight how the discussions were shaped: *Seeking Consensus, Playing the Numbers Game,* and *Feelings Do (Not) Matter.* Our work allows us to identify *Mechanical Roles* (MRs) and *Role-Playing Roles* (RRs) and how their unique qualities contribute to the overall experience. We provide a set of five design considerations on how to balance these roles in similar games.

Keywords: serious game · game-based learning · game design · climate change · discussion · consensus · planning · collaborative · qualitative · user study · thematic analysis

1 Introduction

Zernez Energia 2020 [24] is a cooperative board game has the goal to communicate the complex systems surrounding the reality of moving the Swiss mountain village of Zernez towards CO2 neutrality. Players take on the roles of different stakeholders and are put in charge of deciding upon possible improvements to the infrastructure while considering the unique challenges and difficulties of the region. The unfolding discussions are a core part of the design [26] in order to teach the relations between stakeholders in a system [16]. These relations can often be difficult to learn all at once yet can be explored and understood through layered discussions [23].

A. Thomas et al. (Eds.): JCSG 2025, LNCS 16243, pp. 157–173, 2026.
https://doi.org/10.1007/978-3-032-10518-9_14

The game had been used successfully in various workshops with mainly students over the course of several years. However, due to the COVID19 pandemic, health and safety concerns made it impossible to continue the required in-person setup. In order to still run the planned workshops, we created a very simple online version[1] that enabled rudimentary gameplay. Positive feedback and the potential to allow fully distributed game sessions encouraged us to build a stand-alone web version of the game. This version, called Sarnetz[2], could then also automate some of the more tedious mechanics to allow players to focus even more on the crucial part of the game: the conversations with each other.

Once the digital version was finished, we were interested in a deeper exploration of how the game promotes (or hinders!) discussions and consensus-finding. We conducted a series of workshops and gathered qualitative feedback from the participants. Using thematic analysis [2], we first created three themes: Seeking Consensus, *Playing the Numbers Game*, and *Feelings Do (Not) Matter*. The themes allow us to introduce a distinction between player roles in this type of serious games: *Mechanical Roles* (MR) and *Role-playing Roles* (RR). These roles encourage different styles of engaging with the game and should be carefully considered and balanced by game designers. However, we see having both types of roles as essential to facilitating discussions, cooperative play, and fully engaging with the subject matter.

The contributions of this paper consist of the game artifact itself, the classification of player roles based on the qualitative evaluation, and a set of design considerations that can help future designers balance *Mechanical* and *Role-Playing Roles* in order to foster rich discussions.

2   Related Work

Serious games and game-based learning approaches have the potential to teach players about a range of real-world topics through playful means. Common areas are decision-making [14] or collaborative optimization games [18]. These games achieve memorable learning experiences by affecting the emotions of players [8]. A popular game (or perhaps rather: simulation) in this genre is the Model United Nations [15]. Students negotiate on behalf of different countries and tackle various current topics. Important elements to foster effective learning are in-depth preparation for the participants, active role-play, and a debrief at the end of a session [13] which is a common set-up for negotiation-focused games [17]. These games are almost purely focused on the role-playing aspects. However, other games combine role-playing as multiple stakeholders with more traditional game mechanics in order to create complex systems [21]. Examples can be found around the topic of climate change [19]. Games have linked the Hyogo Framework for Action (HFA) and the United Nations Framework Convention on Climate Change (UNFCCC) [22], tackled behavior change in commons management [5], or engaged players with sustainable shrimp farming [20]. In these games, players interact with each other by role-playing and engaging with the mechanical

---

[1] https://playingcards.io/.
[2] https://sarnetz.ch/.

system. The dynamics in such a system are learned by experiencing them first-hand, and an involved discussion helps bring dependencies and connections in a system to light gradually, thereby enabling players to learn them step by step [6]. These findings are supported by other creators of such games who have found players to be highly engaged âĂŞ however they also stress that it is important to balance the level of complexity of the game in order to not overwhelm players while at the same time not simplifying reality too much. [16].

This highlights the potential for increased engagement when combining mechanics with role-playing. However, existing reflections on these games seem to primarily focus on how to structure discussions among the players. A meta analysis of related work for example has identified several qualities: monitoring another, evaluations, disagreements, and resolutions, experimenting with different strategies, and receiving clear feedback [11]. Similarly, to create shared meaning among players the following have been proposed frequently checking each other's understanding; responding to other's statements or questions; discussing proposed ideas; and conversational turn taking. [23]. In our work on Sarnetz, we are however specifically interested in understanding the interplay between role-playing and mechanical elements and how they shape the overall experience.

3   The Game

3.1   Overview

Zernez is a village in the Alpine region of Eastern Switzerland. Zernez ENER-GIA 2020 [25] was an interdisciplinary project consisting of researchers, private partners and local authorities to develop a plan for Zernez to become CO2 neutral by 2020[3]. As part of this project, a board game was created engaging players with the same task [24]. The game reflects the shared goal of the inhabitants and authorities, who want to implement the proposed measures together to achieve a positive future for their village with a focus on energy and CO2 management.

Sarnetz is the web-based version of the board game and follows the general outline of the board game. Groups of five players work together to create the best solution for a carbon-free village. Typically, two groups play simultaneously and in competition with each other. The game is played on a 3D map with an isometric view (Fig. 1). The map is split up into parcels that follow the actual topography of the village of Zernez. Players can select each parcel and decide how to develop it. Some parcels already have buildings assigned to them according to the layout of the village as it stood when the Zernez ENERGIA 2020 study was conducted. As the players develop the village, each group's performance is measured by a point system across three metrics. Specifically, the goals are to produce 75 units of Local Energy (green tokens); reduce 88 units of CO2 output to 0 (blue); and minimize Spending (yellow). The metrics are also used to determine which of the two groups is the winner of a game session.

---

[3] https://www.zernezenergia2020.ch/.

Fig. 1. Main game interface of Sarnetz with 3D map view (middle); planned and implemented measures (left); available measures and their effect (right); current game metrics and goals (top).

3.2   Roles

The central element of Sarnetz is the cooperative multiplayer aspect, in which the players work together to achieve their goal of CO2 neutrality for Zernez. The stakeholders involved in the decisions in the real world Zernez have their equivalent in the game. Instead of having to understand the whole system and how it relates to all stakeholders at once, this enables the players to first understand their point of view as a stakeholder [16]. Then, when communicating and arguing through their role, they learn how it relates to the others, thereby exploring the interconnected system behind decisions around CO2 neutrality measures. The roles available in the game are:

- **CO2 Manager (part of the municipal council).** Responsible for reducing the CO2 units. The CO2 Manager should prioritize measures that reduce the most CO2 output. Will be involved in most decisions since CO2 reduction is central to the game.
- **Energy Manager (part of the municipal council).** Responsible for increasing local energy units. The Energy Manager is most crucially involved in planning new power plants and photovoltaic measures.
- **Financial Manager (part of the municipal council).** Responsible for using as little budget as possible. Is involved in every decision. It is considered the most active role, since they must think ahead to the end of the plan, taking into consideration the dependencies of measures.

- **Citizen Representative.** Responsible for voicing the opinions of people living in and visiting Zernez. The representative is involved mostly in vetoing measures that aren't accepted by the citizens and finding compromises.
- **Energy Supplier.** Responsible for arguing for the side of the oil supplier for the oil heating. The energy supplier is interested in keeping to the status quo. They must argue for a solution that still benefits them.

In addition to the five players, there is a moderator who is present throughout the whole session. The moderator resolves any technical issues, acts as a tutor regarding mechanical questions, provides additional background information about energy-related topics and CO2 neutrality, triggers the voting process (see below), gives hints, and facilitates the discussions. Overall, the moderator's goal is to foster the creation of meaning across all players of a team [23].

3.3 Phases

The game is split into two phases, which repeat until a group is satisfied with the result or the time for the session is over. The two phases are:

- **Planning:** Each players can select parcels on the map and decide how to develop them. They can select as many parcels as they want while they plan and discuss the measures they want to implement. At this phase, experimentation is encouraged, and the roles should argue for their ideas. Plans can be deleted and rebuilt. The game interface shows how any planned measures would affect the game metrics if implemented.
- **Voting/Implementation:** The moderator can trigger a vote on planned measures. The game takes a consensual approach, in which all players must be in favor of a plan for it to be implemented. If only one player vetoes the plan, the vote has failed. Players then go back to the Planning phase to either convince voters or to find an alternative solution. Players can also vote to roll-back any already implemented measures.

3.4 Available Measures

Players can choose between different measures to achieve their goals. Each measure has a direct impact on the three game metrics (Local Energy, CO2, Spending). The values are based on the results of the Zernez ENERGIA 2020 study [25] and represent the actual real-world costs and effect of the measures(Fig. 1 (right column)). The measures are: renovation of buildings for better heat insulation (buildings need to be insulated to prevent energy loss); adding new power plants (connecting more buildings to the district heating network requires a more powerful power plant); extending the district heating network (connect more houses to the network to replace their previous heating solution); adding heat pumps (individual heating solution); installing photovoltaic on buildings or free-standing (local energy production); constructing new buildings (self-sufficient or energy producing); and reforestation (local fuel for the district heating power plant).

Most of the measures have dependencies that must be considered when making an overall plan: e.g. additional buildings can only be connected to the district heating network if a new power station is built, which can provide enough additional heat; only buildings that have been heat-insulated can then be connected; for every connected building, players can reforest certain areas to provide fuel for the power plant. Other measures have further dependencies. These interconnected systems help players understand that decisions are never isolated.

3.5   Visuals

The game map is based on the actual topology and property borders with GIS data provided by the Geoportal of the canton Graubünden[4]. This data is provided by Swiss authorities to the public under the "Geoinformationsgesetz".

The map kept simple with mostly flat colors and buildings and other 3D elements are kept at reduced details for better readability during the game and for performance reasons. However, it was important that the character of a village in Eastern Switzerland is not lost. The look of the houses is kept close to the real ones in the village of Zernez.

3.6   Differences to the Board Game

Converting a negotiation-based collaborative board game into a digital version comes with specific challenges such as the danger of reducing discussions in such a format, the importance of seeing the actions of other players, and the advantage of increasing the speed of gameplay [4]. To foster discussions as a crucial game element [26], we implemented the following:

- **External video call solution.** By not developing our own solution, players benefited from a reliable and tested system known to most, if not all, players. Furthermore, it allows players to flexibly switch between the game and the video chat view according to their personal preferences.
- **Automation.** The physical board game requires a lot of manual bookkeeping from the players, so-called chores [27], which are fully automated in Sarnetz. In the board game, this was often overwhelming for players, especially when comparing the effect of different measures. Manual bookkeeping is also prone to error. By letting the game perform these chores automatically, time is freed up for further discussion. Easier bookkeeping also encourages experimentation by making it simple to try out different approaches.
- **A strengthened moderator role.** The moderator is responsible for triggering formal votes on any proposal. This formal structure was not in place for the free-form discussions of board game and creates clear phases between proposal and implementation.

---

[4] https://geo.gr.ch/.

– **Basic gestures.** The mouse cursors of all players are visible for everyone (represented by a large, person-shaped game piece, which moves across the map). This allows players to indicate their interest in specific areas on the map or proposed measures, as if they would point at them with a finger in the board game.

4 Workshops

4.1 Overview

We organized six game sessions each consisting of two groups of 5 to 7 university students each with a total of 63 participants from six different Japanese universities. The students were recruited via professors that advertised the opportunity to play Sarnetz as part of their classes. The field of studies of the students consisted mostly of disciplines related to the subject matter of the game like Environmental Engineering, City and Building Architecture, Environmental Science (Energy) and City Design. This ensured that the students were familiar with the basic concepts conveyed in the game and had some knowledge in the area of CO2 neutrality. In case of there being more players than roles, two players shared certain roles and argued as one person. The two groups always played competitively in parallel. Three of the workshops were held completely online, two were conducted in a classroom setting, where a group would sit together in one room. The game did not change depending on the setting and the order and content of the briefing, main game loop and the debriefing stayed the same. The game length was 30 min (sometimes adjusted up to 45 min if there were technical difficulties like connection errors, to allow for a complete playthrough).

4.2 Pre-game

The participating students were informed about the game and sent the game rules in advance. At the start of the workshop, participants received an intro into the topic CO2 neutrality, Zernez as a village and the goals of the games through a short presentation. This was done to ensure players could concentrate on playing the game and to provide a more comprehensive learning solution than a game could provide by itself [9]. The players then logged into the game through uniquely generated room codes for their session. Players were allowed to choose the role they wanted to play as. This was encouraged to find the players who were already enthusiastic about a topic or point of view, and then hopefully being more active in the discussion. If there was no preference, the roles were randomly assigned.

4.3 Game Sessions

During the game, the players went through the Planning and Voting/Implementation phases. During the Planning phases, they were encouraged to discuss their approach towards achieving their individual role and overall goals. Some groups had leaders who pushed their agenda and convinced others to follow their solution. Some moderated themselves to hear every opinion and weighed them against each other. There were also some, in which no one voiced their opinion loudly. The moderator facilitated discussions were necessary, for example prompting more passive players with questions. The players would then ask the moderator to trigger a vote and implement their plans. Some groups made complex plans and voted only a few times; some groups voted over every small change. The game continued until the overall goals of CO2 reduction and local energy production were met. Some groups stopped playing after reaching the goals, satisfied with their outcome. Other groups were unsatisfied with the outcome and deleted the implemented measures to start over. Towards the end of a session, the players were asked to finalize their plans, so their solution could be compared to that of the other group.

4.4   Post-game

At the end of the game, the players could access a statistic in which their implemented measures and results are summarized. Each group was asked to present their solution and the arguments that led to this particular outcome. Each player was also asked to give brief feedback about their experience playing as their role. At this stage, the results between the two groups were compared and a winner (defined as: reached the Local Energy and CO2 reduction goals with lower overall budget spending) was announced. This was followed by a subject matter debriefing in order to improve learning impact [10,22]. The debrief consisted of a presentation of the results of the Zernez ENERGIA 2020 study, namely the calculated scenarios, as well as the actual solution which was implemented in the village of Zernez. This was followed by an open discussion between the students, their professors, and the Sarnetz team.

4.5   Data Collection

At the conclusion of the workshops, all students and professors were asked to fill out questionnaires about the game and the way they experienced it. They could also add additional comments. Some participants responded in English, and others in Japanese which were subsequently translated into English.

Questions for students: (1) What did you like about playing the game? (2) What did you dislike about playing the game? (3) What was missing from the game? (4) What did you learn while playing the game?

Questions for professors: (1) What are the best elements of the game? (2) Which elements of the game could be improved? (3) What was missing from the game? (4) What do you think the students learned from playing the game?

4.6   Data Analysis

For analyzing the qualitative data, we followed the process for a reflexive thematic analysis laid out by Braun and Clarke [2]. This was done by the first two authors of this paper. The first author had acted as moderator in all workshop sessions so was familiar with sentiments voiced by the participants. In a first step, all answers were encoded using a shorthand. Student participants are designated by S whereas professors are labeled with P. This is followed by the corresponding question number, e.g. S49-3 refers to student participant 12 and question 3. All answers were then printed on small paper slips so that the researchers could inspect them individually. As we were interested in understanding the overall experience of the participants and how they perceived the sessions, we removed any answers solely mentioning technical or usability issues. We then discussed the remaining data snippets and their meaning, and kept rearranging them spatially into relevant groupings showing for example cohesion or contrasts. We then started to developed themes while discussing the nuances of the data as part of the sense-making process. As is typical when following Braun and Clarke [2] this was a highly iterative process with the researchers taking an active role in creating and shaping the themes. An intermediate set of themes for example consisted of the following: Negotiation Skills, Real World Transfer, Enabling Reflection, Perspective, Real World Facts, Mechanics Vs Goals, and Mechanics Vs Role-Play. After several iterations, the first two authors agreed on a final set of three themes that best communicated our findings: *Seeking Consensus*, *Playing the Numbers Game*, and *Feelings Do (Not) Matter*.

4.7   General Player Experience

In addition to creating the themes, we also used the qualitative data to confirm our runtime observations that the game was overall well received by the players. Players for example mentioned the complexity of the problem at hand leading them to *"enjoy the process of thinking logically and developing a strategy with teammates."* (S34-1) and appreciated the *"sense of achievement when you reached the goal"* (S24-1). Professors highlighted that with the game *"the necessity of interdisciplinary thinking can be learned"* (P1-1). In order to foster learning, they would have liked *"more time to reconsider the results"* (P2-3) and suggested repeated plays as students would then be confident in the rules and thus could *"consider better and deeply"* (P2-5). While player experience was not measured quantitatively [1], the questionnaire responses suggest that the game was successful in engaging the players in a meaningful and enjoyable way with the subject matter. As such we are confident that the digital version is at least comparable to the original board game in its reception.

5   Findings

Our final themes capture the sentiments of the students and professors regarding the role of discussions and by what they were driven. The first theme, *Seeking Consensus*, describes the general appeal of the game: the discussions around finding a solution that works for all stakeholders. The second theme, *Playing the Numbers Game*, reveals that many of the discussions were driven by the mechanical side of the game: optimization the important metrics. The third theme, *Feelings Do (Not) Matter*, highlights the fact that not all elements of the game were objectively measurable, and that the subjective ones caused friction as well as joy.

5.1   Theme 1: Seeking Consensus

Having to find consensus is the core mechanic of Sarnetz. Students had to argue from the point of view of different stakeholders and and taking on the need for compromise in a complex and project. Students realized that *"sustainable development needs multiple stakeholders' efforts."* (S1-4) and had to voice their arguments in a convincing manner within the group. Likewise, professors appreciated this aspect of the game and noted how *"the necessity of interdisciplinary thinking can be learned."* (P1-1). The different stakeholders however also made it difficult to agree on a joint plan as one student pointed out: *"It's hard to get a consensus among those people from different fields of work."* (S3-4). Overall, players had to learn *"how to summarize and convey your opinion to achieve a common goal with several people, by discussing and deciding together."* (S25-4). Standing up for your own perspective (or opinion) and negotiating with the other players was seen a strong point of the game: *"The roles were distributed like in a Model UN, you had to adopt different viewpoints and opinions, and overcome differences through discussion. This was very fun."* (S26-1) The necessity of finding consensus, negotiating for the best solutions, and convincing others led participants to reflect on the underlying real-word processes simulated with the game: *"The game's participants took on different opinions. At the end of the game, the village looked very different from before. It made me wonder if something like in the game world could occur in the real world."* (S2-1).

5.2   Theme 2: Playing the Numbers Games

The game had a clear goal in balancing the different metrics which was the main way for judging groups objectively on their performance. This created a *"sense of achievement when you reached the goal"* (S24-1). Optimizing their actions across these metrics lead to students formulating plans and discussing them as a group: *"In the game we have to take into account a lot of factors such as gas emission, supply of energy, and scenery, so I could enjoy the process of thinking logically and developing a strategy with teammates."* (S34-1). While this was seen as an overall challenge, other students were yearning for more depth because to them *"it felt a bit simple. I would have liked more information about electricity from the industry or more complex discussion."* (S49-2). This can be an issue with systems-driven games when the best optimization steps are easy to identify - or at least for more experienced players. The interplay of the different in-game metrics made the mechanics of the game realistic (to a degree) which one professor pointed out as highly important: *"It is wonderful that the balance between the CO2 emission target and the actual response (ex, budget, Conventional energy, etc.) is expressed by the number of coins, just like in a real project."* (P6-1). However, not all elements of the game led themselves to a clear interpretation of their value as mentioned by this student: *"There was no clear evaluation method for how to use money."* (S11-2). This meant that game elements with a clear mechanical effect on the game state were perhaps overvalued by the majority of the players, and thus putting less emphasis on elements that were not number-driven.

5.3   Theme 3: Feelings Do (Not) Matter

This theme further expands on the previous observation: the difference between mechanical and role-playing elements which players realized during gameplay. A professor summarized this dichotomy as follows: *"The game represents both the objective and subjective aspects of real energy issues."* (P4-1). The tension between these two types of aspects became apparent as *"the opinions of the citizens and the scenery were important points, but they weren't reflected in the score"* (S49-2). The desire to engage more with these subjective matters was expressed by this student: *"I learned that you have to look at both sides when you do things. There's often talk about the improvement of electricity and environment, but I would have liked to look more closer at information about the interests of the citizens and tourism."* (S49-4). Players proposed to solve this perceived issue by adding mechanical meaning to the subjective aspects (and thus effectively removing any subjectivity): *"A definition of the cost of the resident's feelings and tourism would be good. I think if you would add an element where the cost would go up and down when a buildings is renovated, the people playing the citizens would have more fun playing."* (S49-3). Other players particularly enjoyed small role-playing elements where other players did not argue based on numbers and mechanics but due to their interpretation of the role they were inhabiting: *"That there was a person who sold oil for oil heating and stood in the way of an'eco change"'.* (S59-1).

6   Discussion

While we did not conduct a formal comparison between the digital version and the board game, we believe that the automated elements of the game (e.g. score calculations, easy way to undo choices) freed up time to enable deeper discussions and development of strategies. This generally enabled players to engage more with role-playing and surfaced the tensions between the mechanical ("objective") elements of the game and the ones driven by role-playing ("subjective"). In fact, a closer inspection of the five roles present in the game allows us to distinguish between what we call *Mechanical Roles* (MR; relating directly to the three mechanical goals of the game; theme 2) and *Role-Playing Roles* (RR; not relating directly to one of the three mechanical goals of the game; theme 3). The *Mechanical Roles* are CO2 Manager, Energy Manager, and Financial Manager. The *Role-playing Roles* are Citizen Representative and Energy Supplier.

6.1 Mechanical Roles vs Role-Playing Roles

Mechanical Roles are driven by playing within the bounds of the game system [21]. *Role-playing Roles* have goals that are free-form and their optimal result is up to their own subjectivity and interpretation of the role. As such we can locate MRs on the *ludus* side of the spectrum of game and play, and RRs as closer to *paidia* [3]. It is this juxtaposition of roles that engage differently with the more mechanical parts of the game versus the discussions [12].

MRs are closely tied to measurable goals, are encouraging *ludus* in Sarnetz. Their success metrics are provided and tracked by the game and can be strategically planned (theme 2). For them, the solution to a CO2-neutral Zernez is a mathematical equation. If only the MR are in play, they can plan intervention measures to the best possible outcome, realize them in only a few turns and thereby win the game. Since every measure is tied directly to the game metrics in costs and benefits, the calculation is potentially straightforward for the MR and could also be done outside the game in a spreadsheet, leading to a mathematically optimal solution.

The RRs on the other hand are not directly tied to these metrics, but instead have objectives which are stated in their roles (theme 3). This promotes *paidia*. Their success is not directly measured by units, and they argue freely according to their own ideas and standards. Players of RRs do not argue in metrics, but with emotions. While an MR can back up their decisions with solid metrics, an RR cannot easily provide objective arguments. These tensions between the roles have the potential to negatively affect game sessions as they create friction that stands in contrast to best practices [11,23]. During the workshops, this was most apparent when the CO2 Manager, Energy Manager and Financial Manager argued about cost and benefits regarding planned measures. One of the most cost-efficient ways for the Energy Manager to increase their points is building photovoltaic panels, so they often argued for building them all over the village. The Citizen Representative was the strongest voice against building photovoltaic panels in the village, as it would disturb the look and influence tourism. Similarly, the Energy Supplier argued that the panels would put them out of business. To satisfy these emotional requirements without ties to the numerical score, compromises had to be found (theme 3).

We argue that for negotiation-based serious games it is helpful to identify which roles are MRs and RRs. We believe that it is the combination both types that can make these games more engaging. A deep discussion during a game of Sarnetz can only happen if both MRs and RRs are present, since they both represent different aspects of the real-world discussion around CO2 neutrality (theme 1). While the MRs reflect the necessity of CO2 reduction, energy demand and funding, the RRs represent real people living and working in the village of Zernez. The MRs of *ludus* help tie the discussion to the aspects that reflect the goals, while the RRs of *paidia* open the discussion up to avoid reducing it to a mere numbers game. As such, MRs and RRs are needed to represent all stakeholders (theme 1). As one professor put it: *"I think simulating the experience of various stakeholders thinking has a significant impact on student mindsets.*

Usually, students learn only from the view of their profession as designers or engineers. But, this game must bring a great deal of knowledge that will influence students' communication with citizens or other occupations." (P6-4). A student remarked during a session that she has not looked at the public places they design in terms of livability for the residents enough and that the game has reminded her to keep different viewpoints in mind.

6.2   Balancing Mechanics and Role-Play

In Sarnetz, we noticed an imbalance between *Role-playing Roles* and *Mechanical Roles* (theme 3). MRs are comparatively straightforward to design since the game provides clear metrics for the MRs and gives players pathways to optimize these. The MRs interact directly with the underlying mathematical system of the game helping their understanding of the subject matter [6]. This allows players to make clear arguments based on the game state and the measurable impact that any action will have. Good RRs are arguably harder to design because by their nature there is nothing/not much that ties them to this system.

An obvious way to strengthen RRs could be to tie them to additional metrics. Some players suggested a "satisfaction meter" representing the citizens of Sarnetz. Players who played RRs expressed this by wishing for a more concrete goal for them to reach: *"Since the three government related roles had coin goals, I think it would be better if the energy supplier and the citizen representative also had more concrete goals to achieve."* (S26-3). A professor also argued for this: *"By adding the income of the energy supplier as an index, it is possible to judge how much the energy supplier was able to save its own profit."* (P5-2).

While it would be a technically simple solution to add such metrics, based on our experience, their introduction would be counterproductive to the learning goals of the game. Only by having RRs without concrete metrics, freed from the numbers game (theme 2), can the discussion be opened and the necessity for compromise be conveyed (theme 1). Giving RRs measurable goals turns them into MRs, eliminating the positive tension between them (theme 3). In turn this would reduce the varied discussions and perspective sharing that are essential for this genre of game [11].

The most engaging rounds of the game (good discussion, continuous game flow, few moderator interventions, high score) were those in which the RRs took a leading part in the discussion. This was dependent on naturally strong role-players, who found their fun in arguing for their role on behalf of the citizens, tourism board or other entities. These are important stakeholders that also in the real-world operate without objective metrics. If they brought up arguments which furthered the discussion, we did not limit their imagination. On the contrary, the more imaginative they became, bringing in fictional people and organizations and arguing from unexpected points of view, the more detailed the discussions became. In one game, a student made up a group of older citizens, who argued against renovations since they would have to move while the works were being done. In another, a student pivoted her energy supplier business from oil to photovoltaic panel installations and championed them. Students participating in these discussions remembered the exchanges vividly and could connect their personal experiences to the game more easily.

6.3 Designing for Role-Playing Roles

Based on the insights from our study, we present a set of design considerations to strengthen *Role-Playing Roles* in order to ensure a balance between them and MRs so that all stakeholders are a crucial element of the gameplay [16].

Strong Personas. To encourage role-play, all game roles (RRs and MRs alike) need richer backstories and personas. This helps players get into character, but also adds the potential for flavor to any arguments they might bring forward. MRs should also be given personas as this then gives them an alibi and impetus to focus less on *ludus* and embrace *paidia* in discussions. In Sarnetz, all characters were only described by their function but not given a personality or background story which made it harder for players to engage in role-playing.

Enriched Game World. Additional information about the setting that players of RRs can dive into (and then use in their arguments) strengthens the potential for lively and memorable discussions. It is important to find the right balance between providing any information before a game session, and having resources that players can access during play. In Sarnetz, this information was often provided by the moderator who could tell players about village demographics, tourism interests, and unique challenges of the Alpine region.

Sample Arguments. To facilitate the right mindset for the points-of-view by RRs, example arguments can be provided. This can ensure that the most important points will be discussed, but it also holds the danger that the RRs rely too heavily on the examples and do not create new arguments themselves. Alternatively, instead of arguments, open-ended questions asking the RRs how they feel about specific elements to prompt them to further build their world-view. In Sarnetz, these arguments and questions were prompted by the moderator, but providing players with these would give them more agency.

Mechanical Interventions. RRs require mechanical means to disrupt the optimization process of the MRs. Otherwise, MRs can just ignore RRs and proceed with implementing their ideal solution. Sarnetz provides this opportunity with its consent-based voting system where all players need to be in favor before any measure can be implemented. This veto-power gives them mechanical means to be heard. It is crucial however, to make sure that this is not done as a pure hold-up but instead to ultimately invite MRs into a more role-playing focused discussion of the issues at hand - fostering cooperation instead of separation.

Power Imbalances. Games often strive for a fair balance between all roles. However, in a collaborative and discussion-based serious game, an intentional imbalance between MRs and RRs might be worth considering. A desired learning outcome from the game could be that specific stakeholders are in a weaker position to achieve their needs. In Sarnetz, the weakness of the RRs was not intended and does not accurately reflect their real-world power.

7   Conclusion

We present the digital game Sarnetz which invites groups of players to collaboratively shape the future of an Alpine village. Based on a qualitative study we constructed three themes that speak to how the negotiation-heavy gameplay unfolded: *Seeking Consensus, Playing the Numbers Game*, and *Feelings Do (Not) Matter*. This allowed us to identify tensions between what we call *Mechanical Roles* (MRs) and *Role-Playing Roles* (RRs). MRs are focused on objective metrics, whereas RRs are driven by more subjective and emotional goals. This distinction is valuable for designers as it allows them to pinpoint undesired tensions as we observed in Sarnetz.

Deliberate and meaningful balancing between MRs and RRs has the potential to create a more engaging experience for players. Using the three worlds of Triadic Game Design [7], they ground the game in the World of Reality (by providing measurable and immeasurable goals); diversify the World of Play (encouraging mathematical optimization and emotion-drive decisions; and ultimately strengthen the World of Meaning (through resulting discussions and different perspectives). With just MRs, the game would be a simulation with little memorable content as players would purely focus on optimizing the scores. With only RRs, players could easily solve issues if there are no hard constraints they need to consider. Our set of actionable design considerations supports designers in balancing *Role-Playing Roles* with *Mechanical Roles* and ensuring both are meaningful in the context of the game.

There are some limitations to the work as presented in this paper. The qualitative study data was analyzed in English - with some participants translating their thoughts themselves and other responses having to be translated. This might mean that some nuances in how players report on their experience might have been lost. In addition, the thematic analysis is based on responses to a questionnaire. In-depth interviews with participants and explicitly asking them about their perception of the roles we have identified has the potential to reveal deeper insights. Future work could validate the findings by e.g. formally measuring player experience in a comparative quantitative study.

We hope our work inspires other designers of similar games, and we are looking forward to an improved version of Sarnetz employing the lessons presented here. We believe that with the right mix of role-playing and mechanics, games like Sarnetz could become even more engaging learning experiences.

Acknowledgments. We would like to thank the Science and Technology Office Tokyo, Swissnex, HSLU, IC Spatial Development and Social Cohesion, ETH Zurich, the village of Zernez, and all players and moderators for supporting Sarnetz.

Disclosure of Interests. The authors have no competing interests to declare that are relevant to the content of this article.

References

1. Abeele, V.V., Spiel, K., Nacke, L., Johnson, D., Gerling, K.: Development and validation of the player experience inventory: a scale to measure player experiences at the level of functional and psychosocial consequences. Int. J. Hum Comput Stud. **135**, 102370 (2020). https://doi.org/10.1016/j.ijhcs.2019.102370
2. Braun, V., Clarke, V.: Using thematic analysis in psychology. Qual. Res. Psychol. **3**(2), 77–101 (2006). https://doi.org/10.1191/1478088706qp063oa
3. Caillois, R.: Man, Play, and Games. University of Illinois Press (1961)
4. Erb, U.: Possibilities and limitations of transferring an educational simulation game to a digital platform. Simul. Gaming **46**(6), 817–837 (2015)
5. Falk, T., et al.: Games for experiential learning: triggering collective changes in commons management. Ecol. Soc. **28**(1) (2023). https://doi.org/10.5751/ES-13862-280130
6. Garneli, V., Patiniotis, K., Chorianopoulos, K.: Designing multiplayer serious games with science content. Multimodal Technol. Inter. **5**(3), 8 (2021). https://doi.org/10.3390/mti5030008
7. Harteveld, C.: Triadic Game Design: Balancing Reality, Meaning and Play. Springer Science & Business Media (2011)
8. Jääskä, E., Aaltonen, K.: Teachers' experiences of using game-based learning methods in project management higher education. Project Leadersh. Soc. **3**, 100041 (2022). https://doi.org/10.1016/j.plas.2022.100041
9. Jääskä, E., Lehtinen, J., Kujala, J., Kauppila, O.: Game-based learning and students' motivation in project management education. Project Leadersh. Soc. **3**, 100055 (2022). https://doi.org/10.1016/j.plas.2022.100055
10. Macklin, C.: Ready! Lessons in the design of humanitarian games. Red Cross/Red Crescent Climate Centre Working Paper Series (3) (2014)
11. Mao, W., Cui, Y., Chiu, M.M., Lei, H.: Effects of game-based learning on students' critical thinking: a meta-analysis. J. Educ. Comput. Res. **59**(8), 1682–1708 (2022). https://doi.org/10.1177/07356331211007098
12. McGregor, G.L.: Terra ludus, terra paidia, terra prefab: spatialization of play in videogames & virtual worlds. In: Proceedings of the 5th Australasian Conference on Interactive Entertainment, IE '08, pp. 1–8.. Association for Computing Machinery, New York (2008). https://doi.org/10.1145/1514402.1514407
13. McIntosh, D.: The uses and limits of the model united nations in an international relations classroom. Int. Stud. Perspect. **2**(3), 269–280 (2001). https://doi.org/10.1111/1528-3577.00057
14. Mittal, A., Scholten, L., Kapelan, Z.: A review of serious games for urban water management decisions: current gaps and future research directions. Water Res. **215**(118217), 118217 (2022)
15. MuldoonJr., J.P.: The model united nations revisited. Simul. Gaming **26**(1), 27–35 (1995). https://doi.org/10.1177/1046878195261003. publisher: SAGE Publications Inc
16. Parker, H.R., et al.: Using a game to engage stakeholders in extreme event attribution science. Int. J. Disaster Risk Sci. **7**(4), 353–365 (2016). https://doi.org/10.1007/s13753-016-0105-6
17. Paschall, M., Wüstenhagen, R.: More than a game: learning about climate change through role-play. J. Manag. Educ. **36**(4), 510–543 (2012). https://doi.org/10.1177/1052562911411156. publisher: SAGE Publications Inc

18. Pustulka, E., Hanne, T., Adriaensen, B., Eggenschwiler, S., Kaba, E., Wetzel, R.: An experiment with an optimization game. In: Proceedings of IADIS International Conference Game and Entertainment Technologies 2019, pp. 173–180 (2019)
19. Reckien, D., Eisenack, K.: Climate change gaming on board and screen: a review. Simul. Gaming **44**(2–3), 253–271 (2013). https://doi.org/10.1177/1046878113480867
20. Rodela, R., Ligtenberg, A., Bosma, R.: Conceptualizing serious games as a learning-based intervention in the context of natural resources and environmental governance. Water **11**(2), 245 (2019). https://doi.org/10.3390/w11020245. number: 2 Publisher: Multidisciplinary Digital Publishing Institute
21. Salen, K., Zimmerman, E.: Rules of Play: Game Design Fundamentals. MIT Press (2004), 00000
22. Suarez, P., Otto, F., KALRA, N., BACHOFEN, C., Gordon, E., Mudenda, W.: Loss and damage in a changing climate: games for learning and dialogue that link HFA and UNFCCC. Red Cross/Red Crescent (2014)
23. Sun, C., et al.: The relationship between collaborative problem solving behaviors and solution outcomes in a game-based learning environment. Comput. Hum. Behav. **128**, 107120 (2022). https://doi.org/10.1016/j.chb.2021.107120
24. Wagner, M., Mikoleit, A., Kron, D., Weyell, C., Christiaanse, K.: Zernez Energia 2020. [board game] (2015)
25. Wagner, M., et al.: Zernez Energia 2020 - Leitfaden. Report, ETH Zurich (2015). https://doi.org/10.3929/ethz-a-010577816
26. Wang, C., Huang, L.: A systematic review of serious games for collaborative learning: theoretical framework, game mechanic and efficiency assessment. Int. J. Emerg. Technol. Learn. **16**(6) (2021)
27. Xu, Y., Barba, E., Radu, I., Gandy, M., MacIntyre, B.: Chores are fun: understanding social play in board games for digital tabletop game design. In: Think Design Play: The fifth International Conference of the Digital Research Association (DIGRA), vol. 16 (2011)

Analyzing Video Game Design Elements in Mental Health Interventions

Naïma Gradi[1,2](✉) [ID], Jan L. Plass[3] [ID], and Daphné Bavelier[1,2] [ID]

[1] FPSE, University of Geneva, Geneva, Switzerland
{naima.gradi,daphne.bavelier}@unige.ch
[2] Campus Biotech, Geneva, Switzerland
[3] New York University, New York, NY 10012, USA
jan.plass@nyu.edu

Abstract. This paper presents a novel framework for analyzing video game interventions targeting anxiety and depression in randomized controlled trials. We classify games based on their therapeutic approach and analyze their design features using Laine et al.'s design principles taxonomy organized by Plass et al.'s engagement dimensions. Through case studies of Hit the Cancer and Bejeweled, we demonstrate how specific game design features foster different types of engagement. We then present and discuss the most frequent game design principles and engagement identified in five different casual games analyzed.

Keywords: Video Game · Mental health · Anxiety · Depression · Design Principles · Engagement

1 Video Games for Mental Health Impact

Anxiety and major depressive disorder (MDD) have been ranked by the World Health Organization as leading causes of disability worldwide. While pharmacological solutions exist, between 20–30% of those experiencing these disorders fail to respond to such treatments [1] with only a 1/3 experiencing full remission. This state of affairs calls for new solutions.

1.1 The Rise of Video Games to Address Mental Health Impact

Video games are gaining recognition as a valuable tool to address mental health issues. A key reason is that they can be easily deployed not only at scale but also in a personalized manner that respects confidentiality, a main issue given the stigma that mental health issues still represent in most societies. Moreover, video games can be specifically designed to facilitate compliance, by providing a tool that continuously supports the patient in their treatment, in contrast to traditional treatment strategies that rarely monitor the patient remotely nor deploy validated treatments outside the clinic setting.

A. Thomas et al. (Eds.): JCSG 2025, LNCS 16243, pp. 174–181, 2026.
https://doi.org/10.1007/978-3-032-10518-9_15

Accordingly, dozens of studies have focused on leveraging video games for addressing mental health issues such as generalized anxiety or MDD [2–5]. A few promising RCTs have shown that casual games like *Bejeweled* provide as much positive benefits on MDD as a pharmacologically-based treatment [6, 7]. Several RCTs [8, 9] have documented a positive impact of *SPARX*, a video game-based implementation of cognitive behavioral therapy (CBT) with depressed adolescents. While the use of games for mental health is a fast-emerging and promising field, a major unaddressed challenge concerns the mechanisms of action embedded in such video game play.

The present work presents a framework for a systematic review of the video games used in RCT studies targeting general anxiety and/or MDD. We provide a detailed analysis of the game play elicited in such games using categories we defined by combining the design principles taxonomy proposed by Laine et al. [10] with the game typology proposed by Plass et al. [11, 12]. Our goals are to inform clinicians about the different game mechanics found in interventions for anxiety and MDD, and to provide a framework for game designers to inform their selection of the game elements they may wish to manipulate when designing such games.

1.2 A Review of Known Approaches to Alleviate Anxiety Within the Context of Gaming

We classify the games used to target anxiety and/or MDD using five main categories based on their biological and psychological approach of impact – CBT, exergames, cognitive training games/action games, casual games, and psycho-educational games. These categories encompass different types of approaches that have been proposed to target anxiety or MDD within video game-based interventions. We briefly review each of these approaches below.

Cognitive Behavioral Therapy (CBT) leverages cognitive restructuring, primarily targeting dysfunctional thoughts and maladaptive beliefs (e.g., exaggerated appraisals of danger). Through CBT, patients learn to better evaluate these beliefs as well as to challenge and modify them, through associating them with novel behavioral patterns [13, 14]. CBT also addresses negative cognitive biases in information processing and aims to influence emotion regulation strategies, such as reducing worry and rumination, through increasing reappraisal. There has been evidence of the effectiveness of CBT interventions in treating anxiety [15] and depression [16].

Cognitive training games as well as action video games target mostly cognitive control. This domain-general skill facilitates the type of restructuring and reappraisal at the core of anxiety and MDD rehabilitation (see CBT above). Cognitive control encompasses inhibition, working memory, cognitive flexibility as well as attentional control. These skills are fundamental to inhibiting unpleasant thoughts or breaking the cycle of rumination, for example. Accordingly, there is ample evidence that anxiety and depression are associated with poor cognitive control [17, 18].

Exercise, as used in *Exergames* or physical game interventions, targets cognitive fitness through mostly cardio-vascular health. Indeed, exercise has been shown to enhance brain health for ages from children at risk of weight problem to older adults, through better vascular support in humans, as well as enhanced neurotrophins, synaptic connections and new hippocampal neurons in animal models [19]. Thus, albeit more indirectly than cognitive training or action video games, exercise may help boost executive functions and thus the possibility of cognitive restructuring and emotional reappraisal [20].

Casual games are used in mental health interventions owing to several purported mechanisms. Pine et al. [21] highlighted the beneficial effects of flow occurring from playing casual games through an immersive, easy to learn and fun environment. The positive feelings associated with flow are seen as possibly restorative. Casual games also promote intrinsic motivation, as the gameplay builds a sense of competence (i.e., feeling of progression, balanced challenge), and of autonomy (i.e., freedom of choice between games or modes). Studies have also used casual games as a distraction tool to direct the user's attention away from distressing events or thoughts, such as anxious ones. Distraction can be an adaptive strategy when used in a conscious temporary manner as resources are lacking to cope with a specific situation.

Psycho-educational games build on existing knowledge relevant to the patient. The few found in this literature are aimed at patients facing major medical conditions such as cancer. These games are typically highly personalized to the person's disease and the game play empowers the patient to destroy cancerous cell or restrengthen their white blood cell counts [22, 23].

2   Toward a Novel Methodology to Classify Game Design Elements in Video Games for Mental Health Impact

In a context as rich and complex as that video games can offer, we propose a novel framework to classify video games targeting generalized anxiety or MDD. This framework builds closely on the design principles classification from Laine et al. (2020)[10]. In a second step, we propose to organize design principles along the game engagement they support (cognitive, affective, behavioral, and socio-cultural dimensions), as proposed by Plass et al. [11, 12].

2.1   Design Principles from Laine et al. 2020

The Laine et al. [10] classification proposes 13 design principle domains - Challenge, Control, Creativity, Exploration, Fairness, Feedback, Goals, Learning, Profile and ownership, Relevance and relatedness, Resources and economy, Social play, and Storytelling and fantasy. To better fit the context of mental health, we reduced the original 13 domains to 11 (removing the Fairness and Learning categories).

2.2   Game Engagement from Plass et al. As an Organizational Principle

Video games used to alleviate mental health issues target some fundamental cognitive, emotional, and motivational core. As such, it is helpful to structure design principles around the game engagement those mechanics aim to target. The proposal by Plass et al. that engagement in games can be conceived from cognitive, affective, behavioral or socio-cultural dimensions provides a framework well-aligned with our goal to structure the varieties of design principles at play in such mental-health-related games.

Cognitive engagement refers to players' cognitive processing of game information, including planning, decision-making, to build understanding and develop mental models.

Affective engagement refers to the emotional responses of the players elicited by specific game elements, such as interactions with game characters.

Behavioral engagement relates to the player's physical actions while interacting in the game, such as gestures or button presses on a controller, or body movement when using a motion-based interface (e.g., Microsoft's Kinect).

Finally, *sociocultural engagement* refers to social interaction within a game through a chat or a multiplayer feature (e.g., collaboration, competitive), or even outside the game via a sociocultural representation (i.e., a specific cultural group). Importantly, a specific design element and its sub-elements are not limited to one specific type of engagement as it may depend on the intention of the intervention and for what purpose it was implemented. For example, a design element may focus on emotional engagement with the goal to elicit cognitive engagement [24].

3   Application of the Novel Framework to Games for Mental Health - *Hit the Cancer and Bejeweled* as Case Studies

We demonstrate our approach below through the analysis of two single game titles. First, information about each game is extracted from the paper(s) (e.g., text, picture) and external references if applicable (e.g., YouTube video). The context in which the game is used (e.g., solo or multiplayer) is further documented as per the reference paper. Game features are classified according to the design principles (DP) of Laine et al. and organized by type of engagement they are used to foster (affective, cognitive, behavioral, or socio-cultural) as described in the corresponding paper(s) we reviewed. We then construct a summary table of the design elements found across a given game category. Table 1 illustrates the results of this process for the category "Casual games".

3.1   Hit the Cancer - Psycho-Educational Game

Hit the Cancer is a mobile game used by Kim et al. [23] to target depression and anxiety in breast cancer patients. The game provides the player with a metaphorical battle to their own disease (Goal DP25). This meaningful goal is supported with a personalized game background, based on the patient's metastatic lesions, including representations of blood vessels, gut, liver, and lungs. This design creates a fantasy context rooted in the patient's own physiological state, making the experience both relatable and meaningful. Normal body cells are depicted with happy faces, while cancerous cells appear with depressed expressions, reinforcing the narrative and affective engagement. This personalized storytelling and role-playing element fosters a deeper connection to the game, enhancing affective engagement and motivation throughout the experience (Storytelling and fantasy DP49–50-51). On the cognitive side, players are engaged by reaching a higher score as they remove a larger number of cancer cells. This score is clearly displayed at the top of the screen (Goal DP25, DP26 epic meaning and DP27; Feedback DP22 and DP23). Hit the cancer has a preprogrammed difficulty, gradually increasing over 3 levels of difficulty, through time pressure (i.e., decrease of time limit), and distinction between normal cells and cancer cells (i.e., emotional valence, color). (Challenge DP1). At the behavioral level, player engagement is mediated through the use of the touch screens to target the cells (Control DP6-8-9-10).

3.2 Bejeweled – Casual Game

Bejeweled is a casual puzzle game that has been used in several studies to target anxiety and depression [6, 7, 25]. Although affective engagement is weaker than in Hit the Cancer, some is present through the immediate feedback provided via rewarding visual and auditory cues, such as sparkling animations and joyful sound effects when matches are made (DP22-23). The game also rewards the player with a title related to their experience and performance (e.g., Junior Appraiser, Apprentice Appraiser) (Profile and ownership DP33-34-35). Cognitive engagement is achieved via presenting clearly each problem (make rows of 3 or more gems DP25) and ensuring a solution exists. The gameplay is introduced with animated instructions that ease understanding. This ensures that new players can quickly grasp the controls and gameplay flow (DP21). The game maintains player motivation by offering variability across challenges with various game modes (e.g., Classic, Action, Puzzle, Endless). The board is generated randomly (within and between levels), bringing the needed variability across game sessions, while ensuring a familiar game environment. As the player progresses, the game introduces unpredictable elements like rare gems and sudden bonuses, adding surprise and variety within challenges (DP4). After losing a game, players access performance data through a scoreboard, enabling players to assess their achievements and set goals for improvement. (DP24). The game's replayable nature allows players to practice and refine their strategies, building mastery and confidence over time (DP5). At the behavioral level, the game favors simple interaction on the computer, using only the mouse cursor as controller for any action in the game (DP6-7-8-9-10). Behavioral engagement is addressed by allowing players to freely choose which mode to play, change game mode during an on-going game, promoting a sense of control and freedom of choice without consequence (DP12).

3.3 Summary Table of Game Design Elements for the Category Casual Games

Table 1 synthesizes the most frequent design principles (e.g., Feedback) as per Laine et al. taxonomy (e.g., DP22) organized by engagement, that we have identified in the five casual games reviewed to address depression or anxiety (Peggle [7], Bejeweled [7, 25], Bookworm Adventure [7], Plants vs Zombies [26], Music game [27]). Thanks to this table, we can see that casual games used in mental health studies put a higher load on both affective and cognitive engagements, than on behavioral or psycho-social ones. Furthermore, they put a special emphasis on feedback, challenge and goal. Here, simple goals, introduced via interactive tutorials as well as in real-time, and positive feedback appear to be used to induce emotional as well as cognitive processing.

Table 1. Summary analysis of game design elements of the casual games category

Affective	Cognitive	Behavioral	Socio-cultural
Immediate, positive, useful feedback. Clear feedback, multiple channels. (Feedback DP22, DP23)	Sufficient time for challenges. Interesting, unpredictable challenges. Repeatable challenges. (Challenge DP3, DP4, DP5)	Separate, accurate controls. Consistent controls. Simple, intuitive interaction. Freedom of choice. (Control DP7, DP8, DP10)	No shared DPs
Progressive, building goals (Goals DP27)	Provide instructions, tutorials. Access to performance data. (Feedback DP21, DP24)		
Provide game process status (Profiles and Ownership DP34)	Clear, meaningful, achievable goals (Goals DP25)		
Collectible virtual goods (Resources Economy DP40)	Creative ways to solve challenges (Creativity DP14)		
Provide a fantasy context (Storytelling Fantasy DP50)			

4 Conclusions

This first review, carried using the PRISMA guidelines, has identified 35 unique games used in mental health studies. These fall into five different game categories: exergame, cognitive behavioral therapy games, cognitive training games, casual games and psycho-educational games. Our qualitative summaries of the design principles and engagement most commonly found in each of these games indicate that indeed they vary along these key dimensions, especially in the type of engagement delivered. By focusing on Randomized Control Trials, this work lays the necessary foundation to directly assess the impact of game design elements and engagement on mental health.

Acknowledgments. This study was funded by an ERC Synergy grant to DB (BrainPlay, 810580).

Disclosure of Interests. The authors have no competing interests to declare that are relevant to the content of this article.

References

1. Boggio, P.S., et al.: A randomized, double-blind clinical trial on the efficacy of cortical direct current stimulation for the treatment of major depression. Int. J. Neuropsychopharmacol. **11**, 249–254 (2008). https://doi.org/10.1017/S1461145707007833

2. Gliosci, R., Barros Pontes E Silva, T.: Therapeutic interventions with videogames in treatments for depression: a systematic review. Games Health J. **12**, 269–279 (2023). https://doi.org/10.1089/g4h.2022.0094

3. Abd-alrazaq, A., et al.: The effectiveness of serious games in alleviating anxiety: systematic review and meta-analysis. JMIR Serious Game. **10**, e29137 (2022). https://doi.org/10.2196/29137

4. Eve, Z., et al.: Therapeutic games to reduce anxiety and depression in young people: a systematic review and exploratory meta-analysis of their use and effectiveness. Clin. Psychol. Psychother. (2023). https://doi.org/10.1002/cpp.2938

5. Pallavicini, F., Pepe, A., Mantovani, F.: Commercial off-the-shelf video games for reducing stress and anxiety: systematic review. JMIR Ment. Health. **8**, e28150 (2021). https://doi.org/10.2196/28150

6. Russoniello, C.V., Fish, M., O'Brien, K.: The efficacy of casual videogame play in reducing clinical depression: a randomized controlled study. Game. Health J. **2**, 341–346 (2013). https://doi.org/10.1089/g4h.2013.0010

7. Fish, M.T., Russoniello, C.V., O'Brien, K.: The efficacy of prescribed casual videogame play in reducing symptoms of anxiety: a randomized controlled study. Games Health J. **3**, 291–295 (2014). https://doi.org/10.1089/g4h.2013.0092

8. Merry, S.N., Stasiak, K., Shepherd, M., Frampton, C., Fleming, T., Lucassen, M.F.G.: The effectiveness of SPARX, a computerised self help intervention for adolescents seeking help for depression: randomised controlled non-inferiority trial. BMJ **344**, e2598–e2598 (2012). https://doi.org/10.1136/bmj.e2598

9. Poppelaars, M., et al.: A randomized controlled trial comparing two cognitive-behavioral programs for adolescent girls with subclinical depression: a school-based program (Op Volle Kracht) and a computerized program (SPARX). Behav. Res. Ther. **80**, 33–42 (2016). https://doi.org/10.1016/j.brat.2016.03.005

10. Laine, T.H., Lindberg, R.S.N.: Designing engaging games for education: a systematic literature review on game motivators and design principles. IEEE Trans. Learn. Technol. **13**, 804–821 (2020). https://doi.org/10.1109/TLT.2020.3018503

11. Plass, J.L., Homer, B.D., Kinzer, C.K.: Foundations of game-based learning. Educ. Psychol. **50**, 258–283 (2015). https://doi.org/10.1080/00461520.2015.1122533

12. Plass, J.L., Mayer, R.E., Homer, B.D. (eds.): Handbook of Game-Based Learning. The MIT Press, Cambridge (2020)

13. LeMoult, J., Gotlib, I.H.: Depression: a cognitive perspective. Clin. Psychol. Rev. **69**, 51–66 (2019). https://doi.org/10.1016/j.cpr.2018.06.008

14. Carpenter, J.K., Andrews, L.A., Witcraft, S.M., Powers, M.B., Smits, J.A.J., Hofmann, S.G.: Cognitive behavioral therapy for anxiety and related disorders: a meta-analysis of randomized placebo-controlled trials. Depress. Anxiety **35**, 502–514 (2018). https://doi.org/10.1002/da.22728

15. Cuijpers, P., Sijbrandij, M., Koole, S., Huibers, M., Berking, M., Andersson, G.: Psychological treatment of generalized anxiety disorder: a meta-analysis. Clin. Psychol. Rev. **34**, 130–140 (2014). https://doi.org/10.1016/j.cpr.2014.01.002

16. Cuijpers, P., et al.: Cognitive behavior therapy vs. control conditions, other psychotherapies, pharmacotherapies and combined treatment for depression: a comprehensive meta-analysis including 409 trials with 52,702 patients. World Psychiatry. 22, 105–115 (2023). https://doi.org/10.1002/wps.21069

17. Moran, T.P.: Anxiety and working memory capacity: a meta-analysis and narrative review. Psychol. Bull. **142**, 831–864 (2016). https://doi.org/10.1037/bul0000051

18. Gotlib, I.H., Joormann, J.: Cognition and depression: current status and future directions. Annu. Rev. Clin. Psychol. **6**, 285–312 (2010). https://doi.org/10.1146/annurev.clinpsy.121208.131305

19. Kramer, A.: An overview of the beneficial effects of exercise on health and performance. In: Xiao, J. (ed.) Physical Exercise for Human Health, pp. 3–22. Springer Nature, Singapore (2020). https://doi.org/10.1007/978-981-15-1792-1_1
20. Philippot, A., et al.: Impact of physical exercise on depression and anxiety in adolescent inpatients: a randomized controlled trial. J. Affect. Disord. **301**, 145–153 (2022). https://doi.org/10.1016/j.jad.2022.01.011
21. Pine, R., Fleming, T., McCallum, S., Sutcliffe, K.: The effects of casual videogames on anxiety, depression, stress, and low mood: a systematic review. Game. Health J. **9**, 255–264 (2020). https://doi.org/10.1089/g4h.2019.0132
22. Khan, S., et al.: Serious video games and psychological support: a depression intervention among young cancer patients. Entertain. Comput. **41** (2022). https://doi.org/10.1016/j.entcom.2022.100479
23. Kim, H.J., Kim, S.M., Shin, H., Jang, J.-S., Kim, Y.I., Han, D.H.: A mobile game for patients with breast cancer for chemotherapy self-management and quality-of-life improvement: randomized controlled trial. J. Med. Internet Res. **20**, e273 (2018). https://doi.org/10.2196/jmir.9559
24. Schwartz, R.N., Plass, J.L.: Types of engagement in learning with games. In: Handbook of Game-Based Learning, pp. 53–80. The MIT Press, Cambridge (2020)
25. Gradi, N., Chopin, A., Bavelier, D., Shechner, T., Pichon, S.: Evaluating the effect of action-like video game play and of casual video game play on anxiety in adolescents with elevated anxiety: protocol for a multi-center, parallel group, assessor-blind, randomized controlled trial. BMC Psychiatry **24**, 56 (2024). https://doi.org/10.1186/s12888-024-05515-7
26. Russoniello, C.V., Fish, M.T., O'Brien, K.: The efficacy of playing videogames compared with antidepressants in reducing treatment-resistant symptoms of depression. Game. Health J. **8**, 332–338 (2019). https://doi.org/10.1089/g4h.2019.0032
27. Li, X., et al.: Music-based casual video game training alleviates symptoms of subthreshold depression. Front. Public Health **10**, 961425 (2022). https://doi.org/10.3389/fpubh.2022.961425

Development of an Augmented Reality Tabletop Card Game: "The Throne is Mine"

Sunday Adams[(✉)] and Rogerio Eduardo da Silva

University of Roehampton, London SW15 5PJ, UK
`{adamss7,rogerio.da-silva}@roehampton.ac.uk`

Abstract. *"The Throne is Mine"* is an innovative augmented reality (AR) card game designed for children aged 4–12, that explores the educational experience of hybrid physical-digital card play. By integrating 3d character models with traditional card gameplay, we examined how AR technology can enhance children's memory retention and decision-making ability while maintaining the existent benefits of conventional tabletop games. Our implementation used Unity 3d and Vuforia for robust image recognition, focusing on creating age-appropriate UI based on Piaget's cognitive development framework. Preliminary testing with children revealed promising engagement levels, with most of the children responding more positively to this mixed format, showing increased excitement during AR-triggered animations compared to non-AR cards. Key challenges included improving gesture controls for younger users and ensuring consistent AR tracking across varying lighting conditions. This work contributes to the growing conversation around AR's educational applications by demonstrating how thoughtful integration of digital elements can enhance, rather than replace, physical play experiences. We identify specific design considerations for child-focused AR applications that prioritize both engagement and educational outcomes.

Keywords: Augmented Reality · Educational Tool · Enhanced Gameplay

1 Introduction

Children are growing up in an increasingly digital world, which raises concern among parents and educators about balancing technological engagement with traditional teaching and learning pedagogy. While digital games improve cognitive abilities and create independence, excessive screentime reduces physical interaction, which remains a problem. Also, traditional games promote hands-on learning with social interaction, but lack the dynamic appeal of digital incorporation.

"The Throne is Mine" is a game from Singa Games, a vibrant game company in London. The company's journey began in 2015, when a simple card game transformed the family entertainment experience. What distinguishes Singa Games in the competitive gaming market is their unwavering commitment to creating play experiences that genuinely engage players of all ages (Singa Games, 2025).

This game addresses this gap between traditional games and digital games by creating an augmented reality enhanced card game with six animal characters – Lion, Hyena,

A. Thomas et al. (Eds.): JCSG 2025, LNCS 16243, pp. 182–188, 2026.
https://doi.org/10.1007/978-3-032-10518-9_16

Monkey, Owl, Serpent and Mouse to compete for the jungle throne. Each animal has a physical card representation that comes to life through animated 3d models with sound effects and responsive behaviours when viewed through a mobile device. This hybrid approach leverages the benefits of both physical and digital learning while mitigating educators' and parents' concerns about screen time.

The inspiration for developing this application as an educational tool proceeds from the high demand for engaging learning experiences that support cognitive and creative development in children aged 4–12, a critical stage period for social and digital literacy development.

2   Educational Benefits of AR in Children's Learning

2.1   Cognitive Development

Piaget's theory on children's cognitive development suggests that the early age of children, ranging from 4 to 12 years, is a transition period from preoperational thought to concrete operational thinking, logical thinking development stage and also progress from a self-absorbed approach to a more collaborative mindset (Piaget, 1952). This is also supported by Rooney (2012), that for an educational game to be effective, it should have a balance of entertainment with learning objectives. "The Throne is Mine" through its development supports this progression by providing instant digital feedback that reinforces learning. This was clearly seen during the application testing, when a young child exclaimed, 'I didn't know that's how an owl sounds!' when the owl physical card was triggered with the AR application. It can also be seen through Piaget's theory of transitioning from concrete to abstract thinking.

2.2   Memory and Knowledge Retention

Games that have patterns and memory games improve children's cognitive abilities by developing eidetic memory and information retention capabilities. Research carried out by Wu et al. (2016) demonstrated that AR games can significantly increase knowledge retention when compared to basic instructional methods.

To improve memory retention through the game, the AR elements are integrated with visual, sound and hands-on sensory engagement. Reinforces learning by emotional connecting to animated characters and also spatial memory development through the placement of the physical card. A participant during testing was initially quiet and rarely participated in any activity, but suddenly became more interactive towards others when showing how the right placement of the physical cards can be triggered by the AR application.

Recent research continues to highlight AR's positive effects on cognitive retention. Studies such as Bacca et al. (2022) and Akçayır & Akçayır (2020) have shown that AR environments significantly enhance learners' engagement and support long-term memory through multisensory interaction. These findings reinforce the early work of Wu et al. (2016), and further support our approach in using audio-visual AR elements to improve memory retention in children.

2.3 Social Skills and Collaborative Learning

Some digital games and educational tools isolate and reduce physical and social interactions among children, whereas AR-enhanced games use children's interest in digital content, with the importance of physical communication, to develop the necessary social skills. According to Garzón et al. (2019), these enhanced games not only develop social skills but also increase empathy and emotional intelligence in children.

"The Throne is Mine" game puts children's social and collaborative skills into consideration through the turn-taking mechanics of the mobile device in use. This creates and encourages patience and social timing among children. Also, a balance is created between competition and cooperation during gameplay, which makes every turn both interactive and calculative.

3 Methodology

The development and evaluation of our solution were carried out through a user-centred design approach that places the capabilities and needs of the players as the core of all the design inputs and decisions.

3.1 AR Card Game Application

The physical components of the game comprise six animal character cards plus four strength variants, that is integrated with augmented reality technology to create an enhanced jungle game. The system utilises these cards as recognition marker patterns while maintaining visual appeal.

The AR application was developed using Unity 6 with Vuforia Engine, which made the application compatible with mobile platforms. The AR functionality leverages its Image Target system, where each physical card is registered in the Target Manager and generates a database for reliable detection across various lighting conditions. This was a critical consideration for the young target audience.

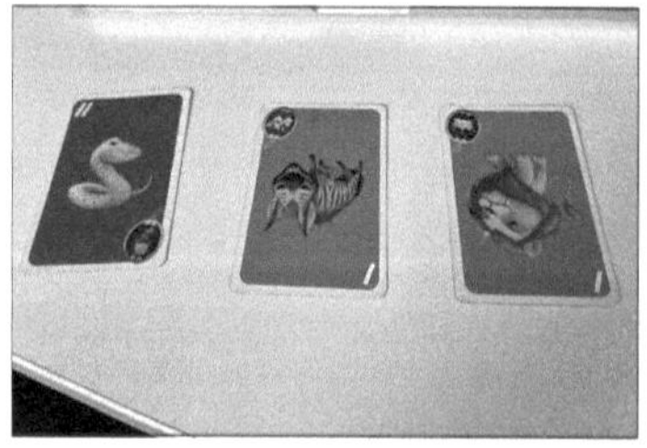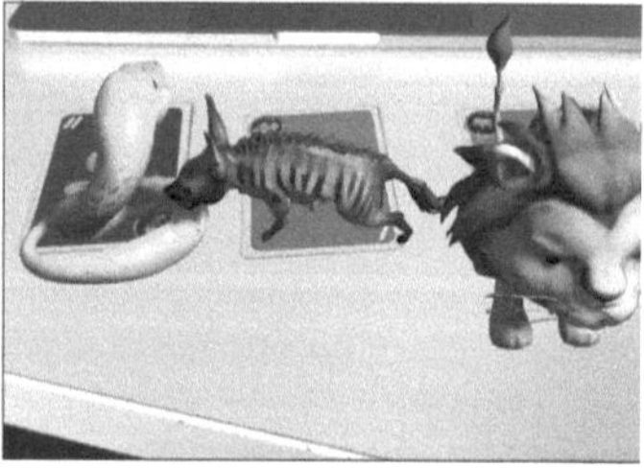

Fig. 1. AR application demonstrating the interaction between physical cards and digital content.

Figure 1 shows the AR application's image tracking capability by contrasting the game physical cards (left) with their enhanced AR overlay (right). This transition from physical to digital creates a tangible interaction while preserving the accuracy of virtual elements, which is a strong requirement for an immersive experience.

Fig. 2. AR visualisation of an owl character triggered by an amulet card.

Figure 2 demonstrates the proximity-triggered interaction when an amulet card (right) is placed within a predefined radius of the owl card (left); the application then triggers an animated reaction (e.g., increase in size, wing flapping, particle effects, etc.).

3.2 User Experience Testing

Initial user testing sessions were conducted in an informal, exploratory context to better understand children's responses to the hybrid AR gameplay experience. A small number of children aged 4–12 participated during internal demonstrations and informal family playtesting. These sessions involved guided tutorials followed by free play, where observational notes were recorded. No identifiable personal data was collected, and no formal assessment tools were used at this stage. This early testing phase was designed to evaluate user engagement and interaction patterns rather than produce generalizable or statistically validated results.

We acknowledge that future iterations will benefit from a more robust experimental design, including randomised control trials and longitudinal follow-up assessments to better evaluate learning outcomes over time.

4 Results and Discussion

4.1 User Engagement and Experience

Across all age groups, children demonstrated rapt attention spans and gave a high reported enjoyment level when playing "The Throne is Mine".

The AR application was repeatedly rated as the most appealing aspect of the game, with participants expressing particular excitement when physical cards triggered digital animations. This finding supports the value of blending physical and digital tools to maintain engagement (refer to Table 1).

Observational insights from these early playtests indicate high levels of engagement, with children responding enthusiastically to AR-triggered animations and interactive elements. While these results are promising, they are not intended as conclusive findings.

Future research, pending formal ethics approval, will involve structured testing to further explore these patterns.

Table 1. Illustrates the engagement metrics across the age groups, showing sustained attention spans and reported enjoyment levels.

Metric	Results
Average Play Time	4.7 min per session
Desire to Play Again	82% wanted to continue or play again
Most Enjoyable Aspect	3D animal animations and character interaction
AR Rating (Exciting/Very Exciting)	92% across all age groups

4.2 Educational Impact

Preliminary observations indicated improved recognition of animal traits after play, suggesting potential for learning reinforcement. These improvements included: Improved turn-taking and rule-following behaviours from the children, better recall of animal characteristics and abilities, and development of strategic thinking about character strengths and weaknesses.

When compared with traditional educational games, "The Throne is Mine" demonstrated stronger knowledge retention metrics, with participants recalling approximately 20% more animal facts after equivalent play periods.

4.3 Hybrid Play Value

Comparative analysis revealed strong preferences for the hybrid physical-digital gameplay approach (Table 2):

Participants cited the combination of physical cards and AR elements as a compelling feature, with 80% stating they preferred this hybrid approach over purely digital or purely physical games.

Table 2. Game comparison

Game Type	Engagement Score (1–10)	Preference Ranking
The Throne is Mine (AR Card Game)	8.7	1st
Virtual Reality Game	7.9	2nd
Traditional Card Game	6.4	3rd

4.4   Age-Appropriate Design

The game successfully engaged children across the entire target age range, with appropriate scaling in complexity. While the 8–12 age group was grouped for analysis, we observed distinct interaction patterns within this range. For instance, children aged 4–7 appeared more responsive to animated visuals and sound triggers, whereas those aged 11–12 showed greater interest in gameplay strategy, character strengths, and rule complexity. These distinctions suggest that future iterations of the game could benefit from adaptive complexity to better match developmental stages.

4.5   Limitations and Future Work

While "The Throne is Mine" demonstrated significant educational benefits, few limitations and opportunities for improvement were identified: (1) **Content limitations**: Feedback from the children indicated a desire for more character options and gameplay variety.; (2) **Technical limitations**: Recognition performance declined in low-light conditions, which is important considering that the users are children and gameplay can occur in unfavourable lighting conditions; (3) **Alignment with specific curriculum standards**: Future iterations could more explicitly target educational benchmarks.

There are several promising areas for future development for the game, such as expanding the game content by adding more animal characters and creating different environments with specific gameplay rules. This will introduce a narrative-driven campaign focused on ecological challenges. Also, to support wider adoption in educational settings, future versions will align game content with formal curriculum standards such as the UK National Curriculum. We also plan to develop educator resources, including activity guides and lesson extensions. AR tracking performance in low-light conditions remains a technical limitation. To address this, we are exploring high-contrast card designs, adaptive lighting assistance, and more robust tracking algorithms to improve reliability. Finally, future evaluations will include feedback from teachers and parents to assess the game's educational validity, usability, and potential for integration into classroom or home learning environments.

4.6   Conclusion

The evaluation of "The Throne is Mine" game demonstrates that integrating AR technology with traditional card game mechanics creates a compelling educational experience for children aged 4–12. The game successfully balances entertainment value with learning outcomes, showing significant improvements in animal knowledge while maintaining high engagement levels.

As AR technology becomes increasingly accessible, its integration into educational tools represents a promising approach to engaging digital natives while preserving the benefits of traditional learning modalities. The hybrid physical-digital approach demonstrated in this project offers a model for future educational game development that leverages emerging technologies while addressing parental and educator concerns about digital learning.

References

Singa Games. (n.d.). Home page. https://singagames.co.uk/. Accessed 14 May 2025

Piaget, J.: The Origins of Intelligence in Children. International Universities Press, New York (1952)

Rooney, P.: A theoretical framework for serious game design: exploring pedagogy, play and fidelity and their implications for the design process. Int. J. Game-Based Learn. **2**(4), 41–60 (2012)

Wu, H.K., Lee, S.W.Y., Chang, H.Y., Liang, J.C.: Current status, opportunities and challenges of augmented reality in education. Comput. Educ. **62**, 41–49 (2013)

Marsh, J., Plowman, L., Yamada-Rice, D., Bishop, J., Scott, F.: Digital play: a new classification. Early Years **36**(3), 242–253 (2016)

Garzón, J., Pavón, J., Baldiris, S.: Systematic review and meta-analysis of augmented reality in educational settings. Virtual Reality **23**(4), 447–459 (2019)

Bacca, J., Baldiris, S., Fabregat, R., Kinshuk, Graf, S.: Augmented reality trends in education: a systematic review. Educ. Technol. Soc. (2022)

Akçayır, M., Akçayır, G.: Advantages and challenges associated with AR in education: a systematic review. Educ. Res. Rev. **20**, 1–11 (2020)

Tik-Tik: A Video Game for the Study of Search in Problem Solving

Cvetomir M. Dimov$^{(\boxtimes)}$ and Daphne Bavelier

Université de Genève, Geneva, Switzerland
`cvetomir.dimov@unige.ch`

Abstract. We introduce Tik Tik, a novel video game designed to study problem solving. The game's structure enables the creation of problems that range from trivially simple to highly complex. Across three studies, we demonstrate how to experimentally manipulate players' focus on finding optimal solutions. Moreover, we identified two structural parameters, the optimal solution length and the truncated search space size, that determine problem difficulty. These findings establish Tik Tik as a viable serious game for investigating search in problem solving.

Keywords: Tik Tik · problem solving · search · structural problem parameters

1 Introduction

Solving problems is essential in our day-to-day life, whether doing the groceries [15], performing medical interventions [31], or solving puzzles [21]. Generally, we resort to problem solving whenever we have no available procedure to attain a specific goal [12] and such situations are frequent in our daily life.

When solving problems, the first step is forming an internal representation of the task, called the *problem space*. It consists of (a) the set of knowledge states (i.e., initial state, goal state, and all intermediate states), (b) the set of operators that represent moves between these states, (c) a set of constraints, and (d) local information about the current solution path [2]. As problems lend themselves to multiple internal representations of various usefulness, this first step is crucial.

Once the problem space is formed, *search* in that space begins [2]. Search involves applying operators onto knowledge states until a path has been found between the initial and goal states [23]. Note that this search can be purely in one's head or purely physical or anywhere in between. Impasses during search can lead to *problem space restructuring*, which can then lead to starting a new search in the restructured problem space, and so on [20, 28, 32].

Search has been studied in different tasks, ranging from simpler ones, such as Hobbits and Orcs [14] and the Tower of London [27], to more complex ones, such as chess [23] and tic-tac-toe [25]. These studies have uncovered that humans tend to search in a feed-forward manner [11], that they have a bias against

A. Thomas et al. (Eds.): JCSG 2025, LNCS 16243, pp. 189–205, 2026.
https://doi.org/10.1007/978-3-032-10518-9_17

returning to previously visited states [1] and that they limit the depth of search [14]. Moreover, when faced with a complex problem, humans prune unpromising search paths [16,24] and reuse previous solutions [6].

1.1   The Need for a New Search Task

Despite substantial progress in the field, several challenges remain. First, studies with the same task frequently differ in procedures or problem set, which makes it difficult to compare results between them. This was a problem even in popular tasks such as the Tower of London until recently, when [18] designed a problem set, called the Tower of London Freiburg (henceforth: ToL-F), which varied systematically in difficulty and had good psychometric properties [9]. Problem sets and procedures in other tasks have been less carefully created.

The second challenge is that it remains unclear how these multiple tasks relate with each other and if they measure the same underlying construct. For example, a recent study with three classical planning tasks reports very small intra-task correlations [8]. As argued by the authors, these tasks might not represent a single psychological construct despite being put under the same conceptual domain of problem solving.

Third, different tasks have been used to study problems of different complexity. It remains unclear if the results across the complexity range would be applicable to all tasks. For example, would the search strategies used in the Tower of London be found in a simple version of tic-tac-toe or would the search strategies in tic-tac-toe apply to a complex version of the Tower of London?

An additional remaining challenge is caused by the interplay with other processes. As [5] argues, multiple processes may affect the outcome of problem solving. These include the conceptualization of the current situation, or in other words the search space formed, as well as possible search strategies, both of which may vary based on prior experience or current needs. Psychological tasks naturally try to minimize the influence of these other processes, but [7] argue that this puts in question their ecological validity.

A promising path forward is to develop a new task specifically designed to mitigate these challenges. Next we outline the essential characteristics and design principles of such a task.

1.2   What Requirements Should a New Search Task Meet?

To focus on the study of search, the new task must minimize individual differences in problem representation. Following established problem-solving research [22], this requires two key features. The task must be *well-defined*, that is, with a fully specified problem space, to reduce differences in problem representation among participants. It must also be *semantically impoverished*, requiring no specialized prior knowledge that could bias the search process.

Second, the task must support the creation of problems across a wide spectrum of complexity. This flexibility is crucial for two reasons. At the lower end, it allows for the careful calibration of problem sets suited to the general population, ensuring good psychometric properties (akin to established tasks like the ToL-F). At the higher end, it enables the creation of problems with complexity comparable to tasks like tic-tac-toe, making it possible to investigate how search strategies adapt as difficulty increases.

Last, this task should be a video game. When well designed, video games are engaging and motivating, which can improve data quality. And importantly, despite being fun, video games can be cognitively demanding tasks capable of yielding serious scientific insights [3, 4].

The goal of this paper is to present Tik Tik, a new problem solving video game, and study its properties. The following sections will first describe Tik Tik's core mechanics and formally define its problem space. We then present 3 studies that use Tik Tik to investigate how different incentive schemes affect search and to identify the structural parameters that make a problem difficult. We will conclude with discussing our findings.

2   Tik Tik: A Novel Problem Solving Video Game

All Tik Tik problems consist of two characters, an ice cube and a fire ball, and a varying number of ice and fire barriers in different configurations. For example, the rather complex problem illustrated in panel A has 3 ice barriers and two fire barriers. The goal is to bring the ice and fire characters to their target locations, an empty ice square and an empty fire circle. Each character can freely cross barriers of the same kind, but dies when it touches a barrier of the other kind. To pass a barrier of the other kind, that barrier needs to be blocked by the other character first. When blocked (see panels B and C, same figure), the barrier flow is cut off after the blocking point in the direction of flow and the character can freely move (panel D). The goal is to find a path that allows both ice cube and fire ball to reach their targets.

Tik Tik is conceptually simple and quick to understand. Players do not need to learn complex rules and procedures, despite being novice at it and, consequently, onboarding is quick. Moreover, Tik Tik requires no specialized knowledge, only basic perceptual skills, thus making it semantically impoverished. Finally, it is a well-defined task, since the problem structure, from the starting state to the goal state to what are valid moves between states, is fully specified.

In fact, Tik Tik is one of the simplest designs that we could think of that met our task requirements. The task design was inspired by two existing video games: Death Squared (https://deathsquared.com/) and Deru (http://www.deru.ch/). Specifically, our task has a lot of similarities to the first world of Deru: there are two characters which block barriers of a particular color by crossing them to let each other reach a target location. Just as in Deru, players navigate with four buttons (W, A, S and D) for the four cardinal directions. There are some cosmetic differences, such as the appearance of characters and barriers, and that our barriers are always straight lines, whereas those in Deru can curve. Also just as in Death Squared, where the barriers are lasers, our barriers move very

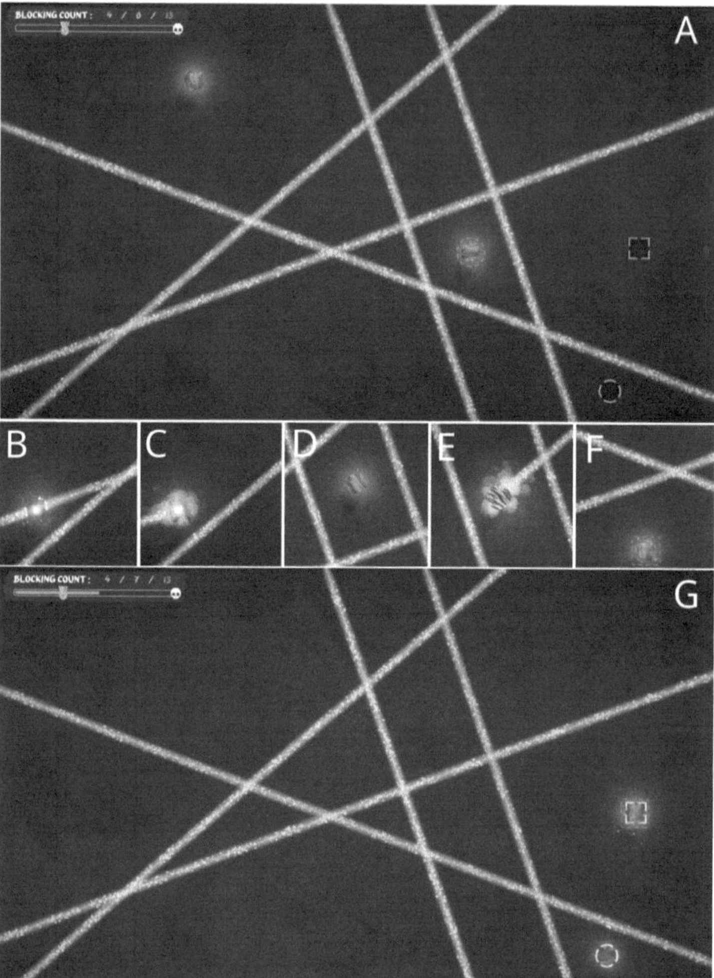

Fig. 1. A) A Tik Tik problem that demonstrates the game setup. A fire ball and an ice cube have to reach their respective target locations: an empty fire circle and an empty ice square. There are barriers the prevent characters from moving around. A barrier can only be crossed by a character of the same material. For a character of the opposite material to cross it, it needs to be blocked by the character of the same material as the barrier. Blocking takes place with an additional key when a character is above a barrier. The current number of blockages (blue), the optimal number of blockages (green), and the blockage limit (red) are presented on the top left corner, together in a blockage bar. B) The ice cube is on top of the ice barrier, but in gaseous form. The barrier is not blocked. C) The ice cube is on top of ice barrier in solid form, which blocks the ice barrier. D) The fire ball moves on the opposite side of the blocked ice barrier. E) The fire ball blocks a fire barrier. F) The ice cube moves on the opposite side of the fire barrier. G) After 7 blockages, the characters are at their target locations. The blocking count has increased up to 7. The progress bar also indicates where this number stands between the minimum and the blockage limit. (Color figure online)

quickly and a character has to keep blocking a barrier while the other one crosses it.

Despite its simple design, Tik Tik affords gradually varying problem complexity within a wide range. By simply adding new barriers and changing barrier configurations, we can change the possible paths that the two characters can take inside of each problem. Once the barrier configuration has been selected, we can also change character start and goal states too, which also impacts problem complexity. We will discuss how to characterize problem complexity later.

To make the game suitable for experimental research on search, we introduce several game mechanics and features not present in the aforementioned video games. First, to ensure that each blockage is intentional, blocking takes place with an additional key (i.e., Space). Pressing Space turns the character from gaseous (Fig. 1, panels B and D) to solid (panels C and E), which blocks a barrier if the character is above. The character cannot move until the same button is pressed, which turns it back to gaseous, eliminating accidental unblocking. Second, we provide subjects with an objective measure of their performance, similar to related psychological tasks (e.g., [9]). Specifically, the already performed number of blockages (in blue), the optimal blockage number (in green) and the blockage limit (in red) are presented on the top-left corner (panels A and G in blue)[1]. Last, to reduce potential errors due to multitasking, subjects can control only one character at a time, which is highlighted with a dashed line, and switch between them with a dedicated button (i.e., Tab).

2.1   Additional Design Details

In addition to the core game mechanics, we took certain practical and user experience considerations into account. On the practical side, we created a task that could be administered online. This would simplify data collection as it gave us access to a larger population of participants, which is also more diverse than the typical psychology student participant pool. Consequently, the task is currently downloaded and can run on all major platforms (Windows, macOS and Linux). It requires logging in with unique login details provided to each participant. During game play, data is continuously saved to an online database.

On the user experience side, we provide a seamless and intuitive user experience. The menu consists of three buttons (login, tutorial and play), but only one can be pressed at any time. Moreover, the transition from the login to the tutorial to the main problems is automatic. Finally, once the main task is completed, all buttons are disabled and participants can no longer interact with the task.

The game tutorial too is carefully created to explain only one game feature per tutorial level with as little text as possible (see Fig. 2). One level teaches how to navigate by presenting them with the key they should use (panel A). Similarly, another teaches that a character can die if it touches the wrong barrier in a narrow maze (panel B). Once the main mechanics are introduced, another

---

[1] Note that, as a penalty, crashing into a barrier incremented the blockage limit too.

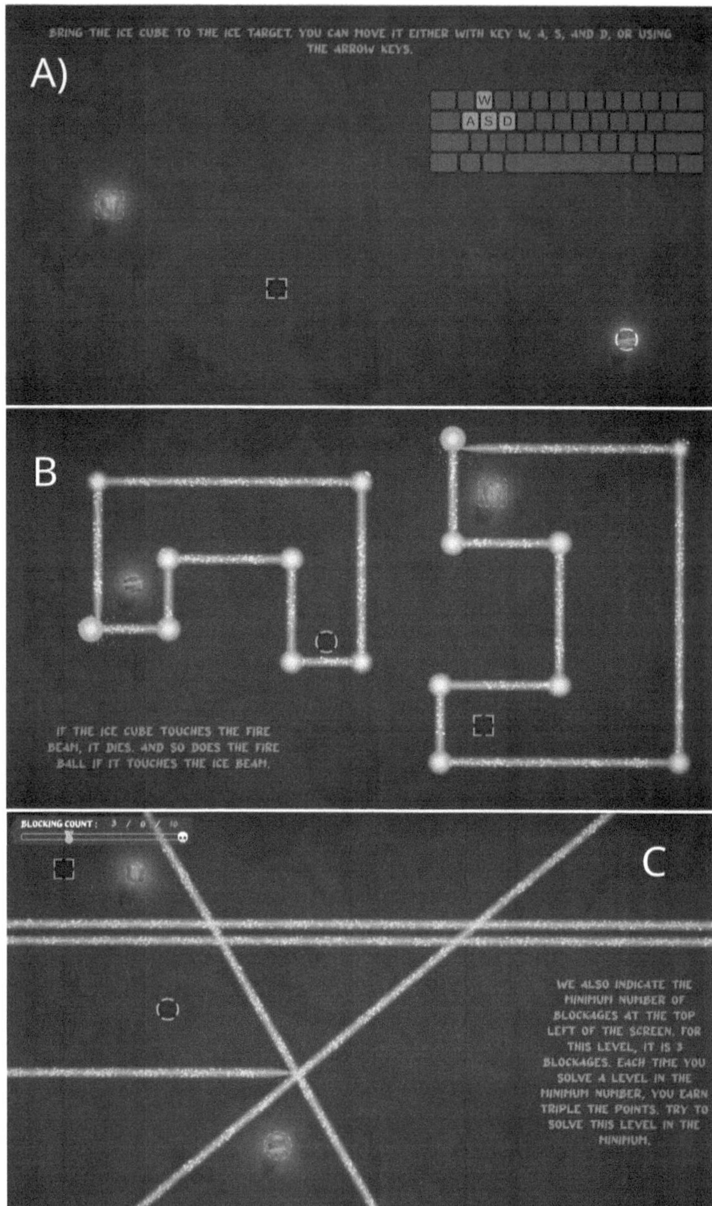

Fig. 2. Three example levels from the tutorial, which consists of a total of 16 levels. a) Teaching players how to navigate. No barriers are present. The navigation keys are visually displayed together with a text explanation. b) Teaching players the dangers of touching a barriers of the opposite material. c) Teaching players our incentivization scheme. Here, we teach them that solving a level optimally leads to triple the number of points.

explain blockages, that there is a blockage limit, and also optimal blockage number (panel C).

The game provided continuous, real-time feedback on performance metrics, such as the blockage count. Key outcomes are signaled by distinct events: successful problem completion is explicitly confirmed and point gains provided, while death triggers an animated level restart. All information presented during game play is goal relevant to avoid detrimental effects on performance of goal-irrelevant information [29]. Finally, the game is accompanied with sound effects, for example, when the characters move or block a barrier.

2.2   Tik Tik's Problem Space

The problem space consists of states (including initial and goal states) and moves between them. A move occurs when one character blocks a barrier to allow the other to cross. A state, therefore, is a region where a character can navigate freely without requiring such a move. For the fire ball, states are the distinct regions created by ice barriers. For instance, in the problem shown in Fig. 1, panel A, ice barriers partition the field into 7 unique fire ball states. Conversely, the ice cube's states are delineated by fire barriers (4 regions in Fig. 1, panel A). A joint state is a combination of the individual character states, and the joint state space is the cross product of all fire- and ice-barrier-delineated regions, yielding $7 \times 4 = 28$ possible states in this example.

The *search space* is constructed by exploring all possible moves starting from the initial state. It comprises all potential paths (i.e., sequences of moves) a player can take, leading to either the goal state or a dead end. The total number of such paths is the *search space size* (SSS), a variable known to influences problem difficulty[2]. Intuitively, a larger number of possible paths makes it more difficult to identify the optimal one. A second variable, previously shown to affect difficulty in other tasks [30], is the *optimal solution length* (OSL) - the number of blockages in the optimal solution. Together, these two structural parameters, SSS and OSL, form our basis for designing problems of varying difficulty. Now we will proceed with outlining our studies.

3   Studies

A central concept in our research is the distinction between two cognitive strategies for search: *advanced planning* (also termed top-down planning by [17]) and *improvisational planning* ([13]; or opportunistic planning [17]). Advanced planning is planning conducted prior to making a move, whereas improvisational planning is any planning performed after one or more moves have been executed. Prior work has shown that a focus on accuracy tends to favor advanced planning, whereas time pressure encourages improvisational planning [13]. We hypothesize that we can similarly shift players' strategic focus by manipulating task constraints.

---

[2]   [26] call this variable *game tree complexity*.

To investigate this planning dichotomy and other facets of problem-solving in Tik Tik, we conducted three studies (summarized in Table 1) with four primary goals. First, we aimed to demonstrate the strategic shift between improvisational and advanced planning by introducing a progressively stricter blockage limit in each subsequent study. Second, we sought to identify the structural parameters that determine problem difficulty. The problem set in Study 1 was designed by systematically varying the optimal solution length (OSL) and search space size (SSS). After identifying a more robust predictor, the *truncated search space size* (TSSS), we used it with OSL to construct the problem sets for Studies 2 and 3. Third, we worked to develop and refine a problem set with a difficulty gradient calibrated to the abilities of the general population. Fourth, we aimed to optimize the experimental procedure by adjusting the number of problems and introducing a time limit.

Table 1. A summary of the main variables that the three studies differ along. OSL = optimal solution length; SSS = search space size; TSSS = truncated search space size

	Study 1	Study 2	Study 3
blockage limit	10xOSL	3xOSL+1	OSL+2
OSL range	[1,5]	[1,5]	[1,4]
SSS range	[1,1000]		
TSSS range		[1,26]	[1,10]
time limit	none	3 min	3 min
number of problems	29	23	26

3.1 Study 1: Pilot

The goal of Study 1 was to pilot the task, including its tutorial and main problems, and provide preliminary answers to all four questions (see goals). We constructed a problem set that we suspected would be within the general population's abilities by taking into account the two structural problem parameters, OSL and SSS.

Problems. The main problem set was constructed by crossing 3 OSL values (2, 3 or 4 blockages) with 3 SSS values (within (10,100], (100, 400] and (400, 1000] paths) and creating 2 problems in each bin (18 main problems). Additionally, 9 warm-up problems (1, 2 or 3 blockages; SSS of at most 10 paths) and 2 difficult problems were (4 and 5 blockages, both with a large SSS) were added, for a total of 29 problems. All problems had only a single optimal solution.

Participants. Participants were recruited on the online platform Prolific and were selected from Prolific's standard sample. Informed consent approved by the Ethical commission of the University of Geneva was obtained from each participant. 46 subjects (34 male; mean age: 37.5, min age: 19, max age: 67) participated in our study. The median time to complete the study was 1h27min with an average remuneration of £14.2.

Procedure. Participants read the study description and provided consent to participate in it. If they agreed, they were provided with a link to download the experimental file. They could choose between a Windows, Mac and Linux versions of the game. They had to run the downloaded file and login with their Prolific ID in order to start the main part of the study. There, they were guided through the extensive tutorial before proceeding through the problem set.

The problem set was presented in a fixed order, starting from the warm-up problems, moving to main problems and finishing with the 2 difficult problems. Participants received feedback after each problem about how many points they earned on that problem (3 if the problem was solved optimally, 1 if the problem was solved, and 0 if the blockage limit is exceeded). After completing the problem set, participants filled out a feedback questionnaire, which inquired about game difficulty, enjoyment, and any problems encountered during the experiment.

Subject Performance. Subjects attempted, on average, 87.5% of all problems before quitting (Fig. 3, panel A). The distribution of attempts was highly skewed, however, since only 25 of the 46 subjects attempted all problems and one subject attempted only 7 of the 29 problems. When a problem was attempted, it was almost always solved (in 98.9% of cases; Fig. 3, panel B). This indicated that participants likely gave up when they encountered a problem that was considered subjectively difficult. Participants solved optimally only 36.8% of the attempted (Fig. 3, panel C).

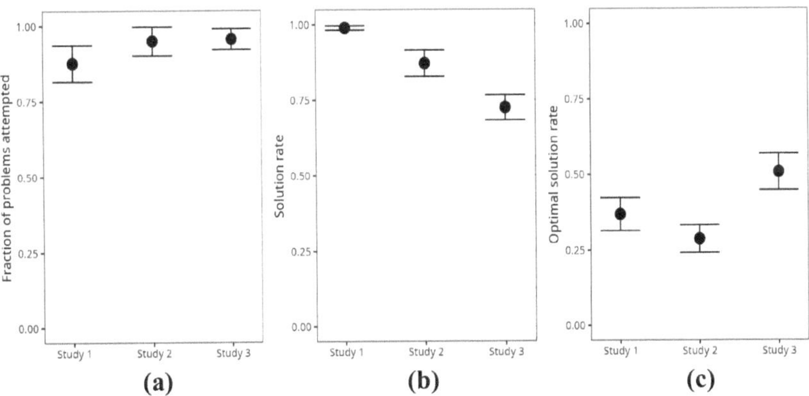

Fig. 3. Subject performance in three studies. A) Fraction of problems attempted by a subject. B) Fraction of attempted problems solved by a subject. C) Fraction of attempted problems solved optimally.

Measures of Problem Difficulty. More difficult problems should take more time to solve and should be solved at a lower rate. We consider four potential indicators of problem difficulty, which are estimated for each problem by summarizing over all subjects: median solution time (mst), mean blockage number (mbn), solution rate (sr), and optimal solution rate (osr). These four measures correlated strongly with each other ($r_{osr,mst} = -0.81$, $r_{osr,mbn} = -0.76$, and $r_{mst,mbn} = 0.90$), except for correlations with solution rate ($r_{sr,osr} = 0.55$, $r_{sr,mst} = -0.58$, $r_{sr,mbn} = -0.72$), since this measure was at ceiling (Fig. 3, panel B). Except for solution rate, problems covered a wide range of difficulty on all measures. For example, they are solved optimally between 5% and 93% of the time, and require a median time of between 21 sec and 207 sec to solve. Since all measures of problem difficulty correlate strongly, we will use the optimal solution rate osr as our measure of problem difficulty.

Structural Problem Parameters that Predict Problem Difficulty. The initial structural parameters, optimal solution length (OSL) and search space size (SSS), both correlated strongly with the optimal solution rate, as detailed in Table 2. We then proposed a third measure, the truncated search space size (TSSS), which is based on the assumption that participants do not search exhaustively. Instead, it posits that they abort exploring a given path once its length exceeds the OSL. For instance, if a problem's optimal solution is 3 moves, a participant is assumed to abandon any considered path after the 3rd move if the goal has not been reached. Analysis showed that TSSS correlated more strongly with osr than SSS. Ultimately, a stepwise logistic regression model containing all three variables retained only OSL and TSSS as significant predictors, accounting for 63% of the variance in osr ($R^2=0.63$; Table 2).

Table 2. Rank correlations of optimal solution length (OSL), search space size (SSS), truncated search space size (TSSS) with optimal solution rate (osr), and R^2 value of multiple logistic regression in all three studies. In bold we highlight the correlations of the variables that are significant in the multiple logistic regression.

	Study 1	Study 2	Study 3
$r_{OSL-osr}$	**-0.67**	**-0.61**	**-0.52**
$r_{SSS-osr}$	-0.64	-0.58	-0.40
$r_{TSSS-osr}$	**-0.82**	**-0.51**	**-0.57**
R^2	0.63	0.50	0.54

Post-experimental Questionnaire. The majority of subjects considered our task fun, but difficult (Table 3). The majority of subjects did not have any difficulties understanding the task instructions and learning the task.

Table 3. Subject rating on how fun and how difficult they found the task on 7-point Likert scale in all studies.

	Study 1	Study 2	Study 3
fun	5.1 (0.5)	5.4 (0.5)	5.2 (0.5)
difficult	5.0 (0.4)	5.2 (0.4)	4.8 (0.5)

Discussion. The pilot study confirmed that our task is a strong candidate for investigating the processes of search in problem-solving. Participants found the task engaging and intuitive, and the problem set successfully spanned the full range of participant abilities. Specifically, optimal solution rates varied from below 10% to above 90%. Most importantly, we identified two structural problem parameters that are powerful determinants of problem difficulty: the optimal solution length (OSL) and the truncated search space size (TSSS). Identifying these problem parameters is an important step toward creating a precisely calibrated problem set for future research.

As is the nature of a pilot, the study also highlighted some procedural issues to be addressed. The primary concern was the excessive difficulty of the problem set, as participants, on average, solved optimally fewer than 40% of the problems they attempted. This figure likely overestimates overall performance, as almost half of participants withdrew before encountering the most challenging problems.

3.2   Study 2: A Time Limit and Reduction of the Blockage Limit

Study 2 was designed with three primary objectives, building upon the results of Study 1. First, we aimed to refine the experimental procedure to reduce the high dropout rate. To this end, we introduced a time limit for each problem to prevent participant frustration and reduced the total number of problems to shorten the study's duration. Second, we sought to investigate how varying the blockage limit would influence both overall and optimal solution rates. Finally, a central goal was to provide further evidence that OSL and TSSS are the primary determinants of problem difficulty. To ensure this relationship was not an artifact of the specific items used in Study 1, we developed an entirely new problem set.

Participants. Participants were selected to be from Prolific's standard sample. Participants in Study 1 were excluded from participation. Informed consent approved by the Ethical commission of the University of Geneva was obtained from each participant. 43 subjects (25 male; mean age: 39.6, min age: 19, max age: 73) participated in our study. The median time to complete the study was 1h7m with an average remuneration of £11.8.

Problems and Procedure. As in Study 1, participants signed a consent form, downloaded and completed the main task, and then filled out a feedback questionnaire. The main task was changed as per our study requirements. First, a time limit of 3 min per problem was introduced. Second, the blockage limit was reduced to 3xOSL+1. Finally, the problem set was changed to more systematically vary TSSS and OSL. The problem set consisted of 2 problems with an OSL = 1, 5 problems with an OSL = 2, 6 problems with an OSL = 3, 7 problems with an OSL = 4, and 3 problems with an OSL = 5, for a total of 23 problems. Although shorter, the problem set had a relatively larger proportion of high-OSL-problems than that of Study 1, thus making it potentially more difficult.

Results. Participant engagement and completion rates were high. On average, subjects attempted 94.8% of all problems, with 36 of the 43 subjects completing the entire set (Fig. 3). The seven participants who withdrew did so after attempting between 5 and 22 problems. Regarding performance, subjects successfully solved 87% of the problems they attempted. Of all attempted problems, 28.7% were solved optimally, which corresponds to 33.0% of the successfully solved problems.

Replicating prior results, all three structural parameters (OSL, SSS, TSSS) correlated strongly with the observed solution rate (Table 2). A subsequent step-wise logistic regression confirmed that only OSL and TSSS contributed unique predictive variance. This final two-variable model accounted for 50% of the variance in performance ($R^2 = 0.50$; Table 2). Finally, subjective ratings of enjoyment and difficulty were comparable to those in Study 1 (Table 3).

Discussion. Introducing a time limit successfully increased participant completion rates. A much higher proportion of subjects (84%) attempted all problems, a notable outcome given that this study's problem set contained a higher proportion of more difficult problems than that of Study 1. As a likely consequence of the time constraint, there was a moderate decrease in the overall solution rate and a non-significant decrease in the optimal solution rate. This performance drop was likely compounded by the increased completion rate itself; by attempting more problems, participants were necessarily exposed to more of the difficult later ones. Finally, the results provided further evidence that SSS offers no significant explanatory power for problem difficulty beyond that accounted for by OSL and TSSS.

3.3   Study 3: Blockage Limit Reduction

With Study 3, we aimed to further refine the procedure of Study 2. Specifically, we aimed to design a problem set that was perfectly balanced along OSL and TSSS, and that was easier. Moreover, we tested the effect of further reducing the blockage limit. We hypothesized that it will incentivize participants plan more and, hence, reduce the gap between optimal solution rate and solution rate.

Participants. Participants were recruited on the online platform Prolific and were selected to be from Prolific's standard sample. Participants in Study 1 and Study 2 were excluded from participation. Informed consent approved by the Ethical commission of the University of Geneva was obtained from each participant. 42 subjects (22 male; mean age: 40.6, min age: 18, max age: 67) participated in our study. The median time to complete the study was 1h with an average remuneration of £13.6.

Problems and Procedure. We adapted the procedure from Study 2 by further reducing the blockage limit to OSL+2, thus providing only a small marigin of error. We also changed the problem set to exclude problems that are too difficult for subjects, specifically those with an OSL > 4 and a TSSS > 10. Moreover, we removed trivial problems, that is, those with only one possible first move. Finally, we aimed to systematically vary problems within these parameters. As before, we used mostly new problems in this problem set to test the explanatory power of the variables OSL and TSSS on problem difficulty. The final problem set consisted of 5 problems with OSL $= 1$ with TSSS between 1 and 5, 10 problems with OSL $= 2$ with TSSS between 1 and 10, 8 problems with OSL $= 3$ with TSSS between 1 and 10, and 3 problems with OSL $= 4$ with TSSS between 1 and 10, for a total of 26 problems.

Results. The fraction of problems attempted remained high at 95.5%. However, the tight constraint on blockages further decreased the solution rate to 72.5%. Importantly, subjects achieved an optimal solution rate of osr $= 50.8\%$ for all attempted problems (and 70.0% of all solved problems). A stepwise logistic regression indicated that OSL and TSSS are the two variables that uniquely explain problem difficulty and together explained $R^2 = 0.54$ of the variance in problem difficulty (see Table 2). Study enjoyment and difficulty was rated comparably to the previous two studies (see Table 3).

Discussion. In Study 3, reducing the blockage limit to be closer to the optimal solution length (OSL) resulted in a much higher proportion of optimal solutions among solved problems. While this is consistent with a strategic shift toward more advanced planning, this interpretation must be made with caution. First, a direct comparison to Study 2 is complicated by the introduction of a new, easier problem set. Second, the result may be a partial artifact of the manipulation itself, as strictly limiting the number of blockage mechanically prevents the possibility of finding non-optimal solutions. Beyond this finding, Study 3 yielded two other clear successes: we further confirmed that OSL and TSSS are the primary predictors of problem difficulty (together accounting for 54% of the variance), and the new problem set was successfully calibrated to our target, achieving an optimal solution rate of 50.8%.

4   General Discussion

This research presented and validated Tik Tik, a novel game for studying search in problem solving. Tik Tik is a well-defined, semantically impoverished task where players coordinate two characters to navigate past barriers from a start to a goal location. Across a series of three studies, we established its viability as an experimental task. We successfully refined the procedure to reduce high initial dropout rates, created problems spanning a wide difficulty range, and ultimately calibrated a problem set to a target 50% optimal solution rate.

Our work yielded two primary scientific contributions. First, we developed a robust, predictive model of problem difficulty based on structural features of the game. Second, we found initial evidence that a simple manipulation - a blockage limit - can be used to shift players' planning strategies. These findings establish Tik Tik as a promising and well-characterized video game for future studies of problem-solvin.

4.1   Problem Parameters

A central goal of this research was to identify structural problem parameters that determine problem difficulty. We began by considering the optimal solution length (OSL) and the search space size (SSS). However, we developed and validated a novel, more psychologically plausible measure: the truncated search space size (TSSS), which assumes that players abandon search paths that become longer than the known optimal solution. Our analyses consistently demonstrated that a model combining OSL and TSSS was the most powerful and parsimonious. This two-parameter model reliably explained over 50% of the variance in performance across our studies, while SSS was shown to offer little additional predictive value. This analysis was only possible, because Tik Tik's structure allowed us to gradually vary problem space characteristics.

4.2   Problem Difficulty and Scalability

Armed with these predictive parameters, we successfully engineered a problem set with a difficulty gradient tailored to our sample population. On the practical side, this allowed us to create a constrained experimental session, comparable to established cognitive tasks like the Tower of London-Freiburg (ToL-F). By implementing a time limit and carefully managing problem difficulty, we significantly reduced subject dropout rates and contained the study duration to approximately one hour.

Yet, Tik Tik's flexibility can potentially extend to the other end of the complexity spectrum. The problems used in our studies represent only the tip of the iceberg. By adding more barriers to increase OSL and expand the search space, one can easily generate problems that are too difficult for most people to solve in a few minutes. This scalability gives Tik Tik the potential to investigate search strategies along the full range of problem complexity, while its video game format can potentially help maintain participant motivation and enjoyment.

4.3   Search in the Head Vs. Search in the Environment

Tik Tik's design also allows for the investigation of a classic cognitive trade-off: searching for a solution internally ("in the head") versus externally through interaction with the environment. We demonstrated that a common incentive scheme - making actions costly - is viable in our task. By reducing the blockage limit to be close to the optimal solution length, each physical move becomes relatively more costly as each simulated move becomes less so. In this way, Tik Tik can be used to maximally incentivize advanced planning before executing any moves.

This manipulation connects directly to the study of epistemic actions, which are external acts that reveal information more efficiently than internal cognition might [19]. The contemporary view is that the cognitive system dynamically chooses the more efficient path, whether internal or external [10]. While our findings suggest that the blockage limit does shift behavior towards more optimal solutions, the interpretation is confounded by other factors, requiring further study. It remains an open question whether internal or external search is more efficient in a task like Tik Tik, and how different incentive schemes alter this cost-benefit analysis for the player.

5   Conclusion

In summary, this work introduces Tik Tik as a validated experimental gamified task and provides a robust, quantitative model for controlling and predicting problem difficulty. Future research can now leverage this platform to systematically investigate the cognitive mechanisms underlying planning and search under varying constraints.

Acknowledgment. This research as been funding by Swiss National Science Foundation grant PZ00P1_201837 "Constructing an integrated model of language use during collaborative skill acquisition".

References

1. Anzai, Y., Simon, H.A.: The theory of learning by doing. Psychol. Rev. **86**(2), 124–140 (1979). https://doi.org/10.1037/0033-295x.86.2.124
2. Bassok, M., Novick, L.R.: Problem Solving, pp. 413–432. Oxford University Press (2012). https://doi.org/10.1093/oxfordhb/9780199734689.013.0021
3. Bavelier, D., Green, C.S.: Enhancing attentional control: lessons from action video games. Neuron **104**(1), 147–163 (2019). https://doi.org/10.1016/j.neuron.2019.09.031
4. Bediou, B., Rodgers, M.A., Tipton, E., Mayer, R.E., Green, C.S., Bavelier, D.: Effects of action video game play on cognitive skills: a meta-analysis. Technol., Mind, Beh. **4**(1) (2023). https://doi.org/10.1037/tmb0000102
5. Burgess, P., Simons, J., Coates, L., Channon, L.: The Search of a Specific Planning Process. Psychology Press (2004)
6. Chase, W.G., Simon, H.A.: Perception in chess. Cogn. Psychol. **4**(1), 55–81 (1973). https://doi.org/10.1016/0010-0285(73)90004-2
7. Cunningham, E.G., Bavelier, D., Green, C.S.: Evaluating planning through play: exploring the use of mini games to assess planning abilities (2025)

8. Cunningham, E.G., Bavelier, D., Green, C.S.: Rethinking planning metrics: an analysis of common measurements of planning abilities. Cognition **263**, 106220 (2025). https://doi.org/10.1016/j.cognition.2025.106220

9. Debelak, R., Egle, J., Köstering, L., Kaller, C.P.: Assessment of planning ability: psychometric analyses on the unidimensionality and construct validity of the tower of London task (TOL-F). Neuropsychology **30**(3), 346–360 (2016). https://doi.org/10.1037/neu0000238

10. Destefano, M., Lindstedt, J.K., Gray, W.D.: Use of complementary actions decreases with expertise. In: Proceedings of the Annual Meeting of the Cognitive Science Society (2011). https://escholarship.org/uc/item/44k7g3vm

11. Donnarumma, F., Maisto, D., Pezzulo, G.: Problem solving as probabilistic inference with subgoaling: explaining human successes and pitfalls in the tower of hanoi. PLoS Comput. Biol. **12**(4), e1004864 (2016). https://doi.org/10.1371/journal.pcbi.1004864

12. Duncker, K.: On problem-solving., vol. 58. American Psychological Association (APA) (1945). https://doi.org/10.1037/h0093599

13. Gardner, W., Rogoff, B.: Children's deliberateness of planning according to task circumstances. Dev. Psychol. **26**(3), 480–487 (1990). https://doi.org/10.1037/0012-1649.26.3.480

14. Greeno, J.G.: Hobbits and orcs: acquisition of a sequential concept. Cogn. Psychol. **6**(2), 270–292 (1974). https://doi.org/10.1016/0010-0285(74)90014-0

15. Hayes-Roth, B., Hayes-Roth, F.: A cognitive model of planning. Cogn. Sci. **3**(4), 275–310 (1979). https://doi.org/10.1016/s0364-0213(79)80010-5

16. Huys, Q.J.M., et al.: Interplay of approximate planning strategies. Proc. Natl. Acad. Sci. **112**(10), 3098–3103 (2015). https://doi.org/10.1073/pnas.1414219112

17. Johannsen, G., Rouse, W.B.: Studies of planning behavior of aircraft pilots in normal, abnormal, and emergency situations. IEEE Trans. Syst., Man, Cybern. **SMC-13**(3), 267–278 (1983). https://doi.org/10.1109/tsmc.1983.6313161

18. Kaller, C.P., Unterrainer, J.M., Stahl, C.: Assessing planning ability with the tower of London task: psychometric properties of a structurally balanced problem set. Psychol. Assess. **24**(1), 46–53 (2012). https://doi.org/10.1037/a0025174

19. Kirsh, D., Maglio, P.: On distinguishing epistemic from pragmatic action. Cogn. Sci. **18**(4), 513–549 (1994). https://doi.org/10.1207/s15516709cog1804_1

20. Knoblich, G., Ohlsson, S., Raney, G.E.: An eye movement study of insight problem solving. Memory Cogn. **29**(7), 1000–1009 (2001). https://doi.org/10.3758/bf03195762

21. Kotovsky, K., Hayes, J., Simon, H.: Why are some problems hard? Evidence from tower of Hanoi. Cogn. Psychol. **17**(2), 248–294 (1985). https://doi.org/10.1016/0010-0285(85)90009-x

22. Morris, R., Ward, G.: The Cognitive Psychology of Planning. Psychology Press (2004). https://doi.org/10.4324/9780203493564

23. Newell, A., Simon, H.A.: Human Problem Solving. Echo Point Books and Media (1972)

24. van Opheusden, B., Galbiati, G., Kuperwajs, I., Bnaya, Z., Li, Y., Ma, W.J.: Revealing the impact of expertise on human planning with a two-player board game (2021)

25. van Opheusden, B., Gilbiati, G., Bnaya, Z., Li, Y., Ma, W.J.: A computational model for decision tree search. In: 39th Annual Meeting of the Cognitive Science Society, pp. 1254–1259 (2017). http://refhub.elsevier.com/S2352-1546(19)30062-2/sbref0175

26. van Opheusden, B., Ma, W.J.: Tasks for aligning human and machine planning. Curr. Opin. Behav. Sci. **29**, 127–133 (2019). https://doi.org/10.1016/j.cobeha.2019.07.002
27. Shallice, T.: Philosophical Transactions of the Royal Society of London. B, Biol. Sci. **298**(1089), 199–209 (1982). https://doi.org/10.1098/rstb.1982.0082
28. Simon, H.A.: The information processing explanation of gestalt phenomena. Comput. Hum. Behav. **2**(4), 241–255 (1986). https://doi.org/10.1016/0747-5632(86)90006-3
29. Sundararajan, N.K., Adesope, O.: Keep it coherent: a meta-analysis of the seductive details effect. Educ. Psychol. Rev. **32**(3), 707–734 (2020). https://doi.org/10.1007/s10648-020-09522-4
30. Ward, G., Allport, A.: Planning and problem solving using the five disc tower of London task. Q. J. Exp. Psychol. Sect. A **50**(1), 49–78 (1997). https://doi.org/10.1080/713755681
31. Xiao, Y., Milgram, P., Doyle, D.: Planning behavior and its functional role in interactions with complex systems. IEEE Trans. Syst., Man, Cybern. - Part A: Syst. Hum. **27**(3), 313–324 (1997). https://doi.org/10.1109/3468.568740
32. Öllinger, M., Szathmáry, E., Fedor, A.: Search and insight processes in card sorting games. Front. Psychol. **14** (2023). https://doi.org/10.3389/fpsyg.2023.1118976

A Narrative Serious Game to Support Caregivers of Adolescents with Anorexia Nervosa

Halit Mislimi[1]([envelope]) [iD], Nicolas Szilas[1]([envelope]) [iD], Nadia Micali[2] [iD], Dorthe Waage[2],
Mette Bentz[3] [iD], Alexandre de Masi[1] [iD], and Frédéric Ehrler[4] [iD]

[1] University of Geneva, TECFA–FPSE, Geneva, Switzerland
`{halit.mislimi,accompany,nicolas.szilas}@unige.ch`
[2] CEDaR, Mental Health Center Ballerup, Copenhagen University Hospital–Mental Health Services, Copenhagen, Denmark
[3] Child and Adolescent Mental Health Center, Copenhagen University Hospital, Copenhagen, Denmark
[4] Geneva University Hospitals (HUG), Geneva, Switzerland

Abstract. This demo paper presents Accompany, an interactive narrative serious game supporting family caregivers of adolescents with anorexia nervosa (AN). It enables users to rehearse communication strategies in emotionally challenging situations while receiving contextual feedback. Scenarios are dynamically generated through a hybrid narrative engine combining rules, branching, and constrained language generation, and are structured around pedagogical goals aligned with clinical principles. The paper outlines the system's design rationale, interaction model, and adaptive narrative architecture.

Keywords: Interactive narrative · Serious games · Mental health · Eating disorders · Family-based treatment · Caregiver support

1 Introduction

While Information Technology (IT) is widely applied in healthcare, its primary focus has been on supporting medical staff or patients through tools for diagnosis, monitoring, or rehabilitation. In contrast, informal care—daily, non-professional support, often provided by family members to a patient at home—has received comparatively little attention in terms of IT support [5,11]. This gap is partially due to accessibility challenges: informal caregivers are more difficult to reach than healthcare professionals and may lack access to institutional digital infrastructure.

Informal care spans diverse pathologies, from Alzheimer's disease and traumatic brain injury to autism and eating disorders. One persistent challenge is that family caregivers, although highly motivated, rarely receive systematic training. To help caregivers, educative material such as brochures, video or oral

A. Thomas et al. (Eds.): JCSG 2025, LNCS 16243, pp. 206–213, 2026.
https://doi.org/10.1007/978-3-032-10518-9_18

advices usually fail to capture finely everyday reality of caregivers. As a complement to existing therapies, virtual environments can give caregivers a safe space to explore, practise, and reflect on intervention strategies.

This demo paper introduces *Accompany*, an adaptive narrative serious game that supports parents of adolescents with AN, based on the principles of Family-Based Treatment (FBT) [10]. It offers caregivers an opportunity to rehearse evidence-based communication strategies in emotionally charged situations, such as mealtime resistance.

2   Related Work

2.1   Serious Games for Informal Care

Serious games have been increasingly used to support informal caregivers by offering experiential environments for learning and behavioral rehearsal. These games often focus on procedural knowledge, emotional resilience, or communication strategies in challenging caregiving contexts. For example, training games have been developed to assist professional and family caregivers of individuals with Alzheimer's disease, helping them better understand symptom progression and providing support in their caregiving role [1]. In the context of dementia care more broadly, initiatives like *EHPAD'PANIC* provide scenario-based simulations to train staff in long-term care facilities [6].

Beyond neurodegenerative disorders, serious games have also addressed caregiving in acute or emotionally intense settings. Recent interventions leverage virtual reality environments to promote co-regulation and support: for instance, *Cooperative Virtual Reality Gaming* facilitates emotional bonding between pediatric patients and their caregivers during stressful medical procedures [9].

In the mental health domain, *Maze Out* is a notable example of a co-produced serious game designed with patients to support reflection and coping mechanisms in the treatment of eating disorders [7].

However, these games rely on predefined paths or quiz-like interactions, limiting their adaptability and emotional nuance. Yet, the situations faced by parents of adolescents with eating disorders call for tools that move beyond traditional scripted learning, by incorporating situated decision-making and sensitivity to emotional dynamics—features more effectively addressed through interactive narrative approaches.

2.2   Interactive Narrative and Adaptivity

Research on Interactive Digital Storytelling (IDS) has explored both entertainment contexts [12,13,16] and pedagogical applications [2,4,8,14,15]. The latter, also called narrative-centred learning environments, leverage story structure to guide users through complex domains while fostering engagement [14,15]. Some IDS works have been developed to support caregivers, particularly in the context of Alzheimer's disease [4,8].

The above-mentioned systems employ sophisticated narrative management algorithms, including text generation. They have provided fully implemented research prototypes that went through end-user evaluations. However, this sophistication comes at a price: developed system remains largely monolithic, resulting from a one-shot effort to apply a given IDS approach to a educational case. There is no easy possibility to apply the same approach to another therapeutic domain, nor to easily update the systems according to new medical data.

3   Concept and Design of Accompany

The serious game presented in this article, called *Accompany*, aims at applying IDS techniques to a new domain, that of caring of adolescent suffering from anorexia, based on a more open and flexible approach. Instead of searching for one unique and powerful algorithmic approach (e.g. planning, agents, Generative AI), it combines rule-based logic, branching scene structures, and contextualized dialogue generation, with the aim of balancing authorial control and emergent interaction.

Rather than attempting to simulate the full complexity of therapy, this hybrid narrative architecture creates a coherent interactive space in which caregivers can explore different strategies within clinically sensitive situations.

3.1   Game Objectives

The project investigates how a serious game can empower relatives of adolescents with AN. Accompany offers a safe digital environment in which parents can engage with realistic mealtime and conflict situations. Each session is integrated into ongoing therapy and may be monitored by professionals. The game allows users to rehearse different interaction strategies, observe the immediate emotional consequences of their choices, and receive contextualized feedback. The game conveys the teenager's emotions through facial expressions and dialog reactions, offering perceptual feedback that, together with occasional expert interventions embedded in the narrative, helps the parent explore and adjust their strategies.

The player's goal is to resolve each scene—for instance, by ensuring that the adolescent eats the meal—while testing different approaches and observing their consequences in a safe setting. In doing so, the game operates on three levels at once: pedagogically, it deepens the parents' grasp of family dynamics; therapeutically, it may offer a structured opportunity for pre- or post-session reflection; and socially, it has the potential to reduce feelings of isolation by acknowledging the caregiver's role and translating abstract guidelines into concrete, everyday actions.

3.2   Narrative Engine and System Architecture

The game content in Accompany is not pre-scripted: it is dynamically generated at runtime through a hybrid narrative engine called *TalecAIre*. This engine was developed in Java for cross-platform web delivery, ensuring deployment on desktop, tablet, and mobile devices. TalecAIre combines three complementary components that work together to construct each scene on the fly:

A rule-based system manages the evolving emotional and psychological states of the characters. Through so-called evolution rules, it updates variables such as anxiety, anger, or ambivalence based on the player's actions. Reaction rules determine how the adolescent responds—verbally and emotionally—to the parent's behaviour. Finally, progression rules structure the scenario's flow: they control the transitions between phases, define when a scene ends, and assess whether pedagogical objectives have been met—thereby triggering contextual feedback tailored to the player's actions.

Complementing the rule-based system, a branching graph structure is used to ensure narrative control over key therapeutic moments. In emotionally sensitive situations (e.g., refusal to eat, emotional breakdown), the system follows authored narrative arcs to maintain pedagogical integrity and avoid incoherent transitions. These graphs allow for multiple paths and outcomes while preserving overall scene structure.

A language model (LLM) component transforms abstract narrative acts into contextualised, natural-language dialogue. For example, a selected narrative act (see below) such as "Ask to start with the pasta" will generate a sentence adapted to the current emotional state and history of the interaction. The LLM output is constrained by clinical safety rules to prevent inappropriate or counter-therapeutic content (see Fig. 1). After rule-based filtering selects the act variant, a sandboxed GPT-4.1 generates the line from current emotion variables, and a clinician validates it. Together, these components allow Accompany to construct scenes that respond to the player's decisions while respecting the instruc-

Fig. 1. Interface for defining different types of rules.

tional structure of each scenario. Rather than relying on pre-written sequences, the game unfolding emerges from the combination of rule-based state tracking, branching control for key transitions, and dynamic formulation of dialogue.

Thanks to a web-based open architecture, all data for specifying the scenarios are editable by different members of the project team (role-based database management), even while the game is running (hot reloading). Scenarios can be adjusted and refined in real-time, facilitating rapid iteration and continuous improvement by designers and experts.

3.3   Narrative Acts and Scene Construction

Player interaction in Accompany is based on a structured set of narrative acts [17], defined as abstract communicative or behavioural actions that characterize how the parent character engages with the adolescent. These acts are interpreted by the engine according to the context of the scene and the emotional state of the characters. They are not linked to fixed lines of dialogue but serve as inputs for the rule engine and the dialogue generator.

The system defines four primary act types, in line with the speech act theory as defined by Sperber and Wilson [3]:

Say: statements meant to influence the emotional state of the adolescent (e.g., reduce anxiety, anger).

Ask to: suggestions or commands intended to prompt an action from the adolescent (e.g., giving a strict instruction to finish the plate).

Ask whether: questions designed to access the adolescent's emotional or mental state.

Do: non-verbal actions such as moving, play music, or using an object.

Each general act is refined into subcategories to support subtle and varied strategies, in line with the FBT approach. For instance, a "Say" act may be instantiated as "Say - emotional support" ("You can trust me"), "Say - rational support" ("You need to eat to stay healthy"), "Say - compromise" ("Would you prefer to eat something else?"), or "Say - change topic" ("Do you want to listen to some music?"). These variations are essential to reflect therapeutic reality.

In the first scene, the adolescent character, Emma, refuses to begin eating (see Fig. 2). The player's goal is to lower her anxiety enough to convince her to take the first bite. Acts such as *Say - emotional support* or *Say - change topic* tend to reduce anxiety and are often effective to initiate cooperation. In contrast, rational arguments (*Say - rational support*) may increase tension, especially if used early in the scene. A compromise (e.g., "Do you want to eat something else") can help to resolve the situation in the short-term, but repeated use of such strategies is considered to be pedagogically suboptimal, as they may encourage avoidance behaviours.

Choices are presented through a context-sensitive menu that categories available acts. Each selection triggers a change in the emotional variables managed by the rule engine, and may elicit targeted feedback. These feedback elements, authored with clinical input, highlight the immediate effect of a choice or invite

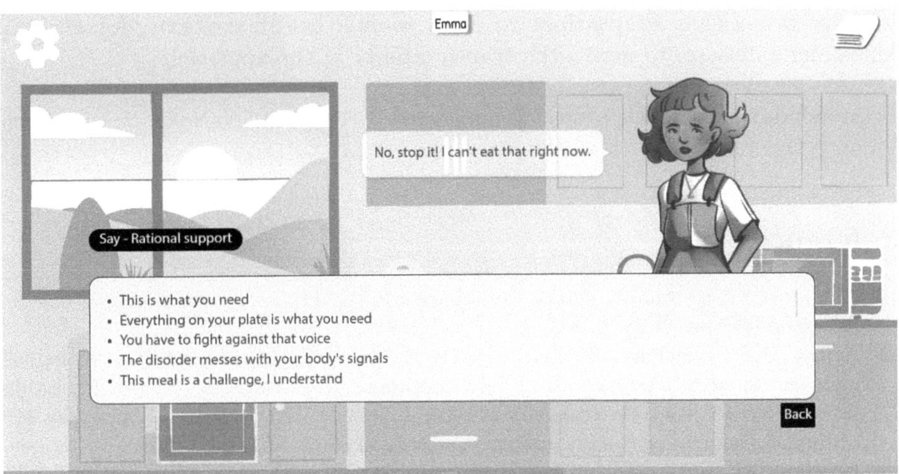

Fig. 2. The interface of the Accompany game allows the player to select among various interaction types with the adolescent character, including verbal and non-verbal actions.

reflection on repeated patterns. They help the player interpret the emotional impact of their actions without interrupting immersion.

There are no time constraints. Players can explore the scene at their own pace, test different combinations of responses, and observe how Emma's facial expressions and dialogue evolve based on their approach. This interaction model supports active learning through trial, observation and guided reinforcement.

3.4   Conclusion

This paper introduced Accompany, a browser-based serious game designed to train and support family caregivers of adolescents with Anorexia Nervosa. Built on a hybrid narrative engine combining rules, branching and LLMs, it simulates complex emotional interactions while embedding pedagogical objectives drawn from clinical practice. The demo illustrates how the game architecture can support situated decision-making, emotional feedback, and pedagogical reinforcement without relying on fixed scripts. However, the current version of the prototype focuses on a limited set of scenarios and has not yet been evaluated through systematic empirical studies. To broaden its scope and assess its effectiveness, we plan to: (a) extend therapeutic situations and refine feedback, and (b) conduct a pilot randomized controlled trial comparing Family-Based Treatment (FBT) delivered with or without Accompany as an additional carer intervention. Parents of adolescents (12–17.5) starting outpatient FBT for anorexia nervosa will be recruited; parent and patient outcomes will be measured at baseline and 3 months. The aim is to investigate the acceptability, feasibility and effectiveness of using Accompany as an add-on intervention to standard treatment. Future work will also investigate adaptations to other mental health contexts, for example Alzheimer's disease, to assess the transferability of the approach.

Acknowledgments. This project is supported by the Swiss National Science Foundation (grant 212661).

References

1. Aidant et EVE: Aidant et eve homepage (2024). https://www.aidant-et-eve.fr/. Accessed 08 May 2025
2. Aylett, R.S., Louchart, S., Dias, J., Paiva, A., Vala, M.: FearNot! – an experiment in emergent narrative. In: Panayiotopoulos, T., Gratch, J., Aylett, R., Ballin, D., Olivier, P., Rist, T. (eds.) IVA 2005. LNCS (LNAI), vol. 3661, pp. 305–316. Springer, Heidelberg (2005). https://doi.org/10.1007/11550617_26
3. Bracops, M.: La pragmatique cognitive. Dan Sperber et Deirdre Wilson. In: Introduction à la pragmatique, pp. 105–159. Champs linguistiques, De Boeck Supérieur, Louvain-la-Neuve (2010). https://www.cairn.info/introduction-a-la-pragmatique--9782801116111-p-105.htm
4. Chauveau, L., Szilas, N., Luiu, A.L., Ehrler, F.: Dimensions of personalization in a narrative pedagogical simulation for Alzheimer's caregivers. In: 6th International Conference on Serious Games and Applications for Health (IEEE SeGAH 2018) (2018)
5. Dumas, J.E., Szilas, N., Richle, U., Boggini, T.: Interactive simulations to help teenagers cope when a parent has a traumatic brain injury. Comput. Entertain. **8**(2) (2010). https://doi.org/10.1145/1899687.1899692. http://dl.acm.org/citation.cfm?id=1899687.1899692
6. EHPAD'PANIC: Ehpad'panic homepage (2024). http://www.ehpad-panic.com. Accessed 08 May 2025
7. Guala, M.M., et al.: "Maze Out": a study protocol for a randomised controlled trial using a mix methods approach exploring the potential and examining the effectiveness of a serious game in the treatment of eating disorders. J. Eating Disord. **12**(1), 35 (2024). https://doi.org/10.1186/s40337-024-00985-2. https://jeatdisord.biomedcentral.com/articles/10.1186/s40337-024-00985-2
8. Habonneau, N., Richle, U., Szilas, N., Dumas, J.E.: 3D simulated interactive drama for teenagers coping with a traumatic brain injury in a parent. In: Oyarzun, D., Peinado, F., Young, R.M., Elizalde, A., Méndez, G. (eds.) ICIDS 2012. LNCS, vol. 7648, pp. 174–182. Springer, Heidelberg (2012). https://doi.org/10.1007/978-3-642-34851-8_17
9. Liszio, S., Bäuerlein, F., Hildebrand, J., Van Nahl, C., Masuch, M., Basu, O.: Cooperative virtual reality gaming for anxiety and pain reduction in pediatric patients and their caregivers during painful medical procedures: protocol for a randomized controlled trial. JMIR Res. Protoc. **14**, e63098 (2025). https://doi.org/10.2196/63098. https://www.researchprotocols.org/2025/1/e63098
10. Lock, J., Le Grange, D.: Treatment Manual for Anorexia Nervosa: A Family-Based Approach, 2nd edn. Guilford Press, New York (2013)
11. Maskeliunas, R., et al.: Deep reinforcement learning-based iTrain serious game for caregivers dealing with post-stroke patients. Information **13**(12), 564 (2022). https://doi.org/10.3390/info13120564. https://www.mdpi.com/2078-2489/13/12/564

12. Mateas, M., Stern, A.: Structuring content in the Façade interactive drama architecture. In: Proceedings of the AAAI Conference on Artificial Intelligence and Interactive Digital Entertainment, vol. 1, no. 1, pp. 93–98 (2021). https://doi.org/10.1609/aiide.v1i1.18722. https://ojs.aaai.org/index.php/AIIDE/article/view/18722
13. McCoy, J., Treanor, M., Samuel, B.: Prom Week: social physics as gameplay. In: Rich, C., Isbister, K., Cavazza, M. (eds.) Proceedings of the 6th International Conference on Foundations of Digital Games, pp. 319–321. ACM, New York (2011)
14. Miller, L.C., et al.: Socially optimized learning in virtual environments (SOLVE). In: Si, M., Thue, D., André, E., Lester, J.C., Tanenbaum, T.J., Zammitto, V. (eds.) ICIDS 2011. LNCS, vol. 7069, pp. 182–192. Springer, Heidelberg (2011). https://doi.org/10.1007/978-3-642-25289-1_20
15. Mott, B.W., Lester, J.C.: Narrative-centered tutorial planning for inquiry-based learning environments. In: Ikeda, M., Ashley, K.D., Chan, T.-W. (eds.) ITS 2006. LNCS, vol. 4053, pp. 675–684. Springer, Heidelberg (2006). https://doi.org/10.1007/11774303_67
16. Szilas, N.: A computational model of an intelligent narrator for interactive narratives. Appl. Artif. Intell. **21**(8), 753–801 (2007). https://doi.org/10.1080/08839510701526574. http://www.tandfonline.com/doi/abs/10.1080/08839510701526574
17. Szilas, N.: Les actes narratifs : définition et typologie. Cahiers de Narratologie (41) (2022). https://doi.org/10.4000/narratologie.13794. http://journals.openedition.org/narratologie/13794

Structured Entry, Creative Voice: Scaffolding Narrative Design Through Reusable Game Frameworks

Clay Ewing and Justin Jacobson[✉]

University of Miami, Coral Gables, FL 33146, USA
c.ewing@miami.edu

Abstract. This demo showcases a lightweight conversation template designed to help students prototype short, character-driven interactions within Answer Campus, an ongoing academic game series. By writing inside an established game world using a prebuilt Unity framework, students can sidestep common early blockers in game development: scope creep, technical uncertainty, blank-page paralysis, etc. and instead focus on tone, branching structure, and relational outcomes. This demo was piloted as a two-week narrative design sprint where students created original conversations for existing characters, drawing on a shared character bible and game assets. Post-mortems revealed that the template supported both technical and narrative growth, allowing students to explore authorship, collaboration, and emotional design.

Keywords: narrative design · visual novels · collaborative authorship · prototyping · game-based learning

1 Introduction

Game design classrooms often struggle with the challenge of helping students start. Many arrive with ambitious ideas that far exceed what's feasible within a short sprint or single semester. They imagine branching narratives on par with AAA titles or assume that coding skill will ensure success. The result is often creative paralysis: too many ideas, no clear entry point.

To address this, we developed the Answer Campus Conversation Template: a lightweight Unity-based tool built for accessibility and speed. Rather than building systems from scratch, students use a pre-built visual novel framework and write within the constraints of a shared game world. They select a character from the Answer Campus universe and craft a short, meaningful interaction that can stand alone while contributing to the larger narrative ecosystem.

This template is scaffolded with a character bible, expression sprites, and a working dialogue system that allows students to focus on character tone, player choice, and relational consequence. Importantly, strong submissions become candidates for inclusion in a live, open-source game series, offering a rare opportunity for student work to persist and evolve.

A. Thomas et al. (Eds.): JCSG 2025, LNCS 16243, pp. 214–219, 2026.
https://doi.org/10.1007/978-3-032-10518-9_19

This demo presents the conversation template, details its technical and pedagogical design, and showcases student-authored scenes created during a two-week sprint. We offer this as a reusable, open framework that supports sustainable academic game production while lowering the barriers to narrative experimentation.

2   System Overview

The Answer Campus Conversation Template is a Unity-based tool designed to help students quickly prototype branching dialogue scenes using prebuilt systems and shared narrative assets. It is built atop VNEngine, a commercial Unity asset for visual novel development, and includes a structured set of prefabs, character assets, and scripting conventions tailored to the *Answer Campus* narrative universe.

The template is organized to minimize setup time and the lower barrier to participation for writers with little or no Unity experience. It includes a ready to run Unity scene with built-in UI and various example conversations that are clearly organized in the project hierarchy. The project folder contains character sprites with a range of expressions and poses. The project repository contains links to the living documents for *Answer Campus*, including the character bible that outlines personality traits, backstory and known relationships. Additionally, the repository includes links to walkthrough videos that guide students through opening the project, selecting characters, editing the examples and exporting their conversation (Fig. 1).

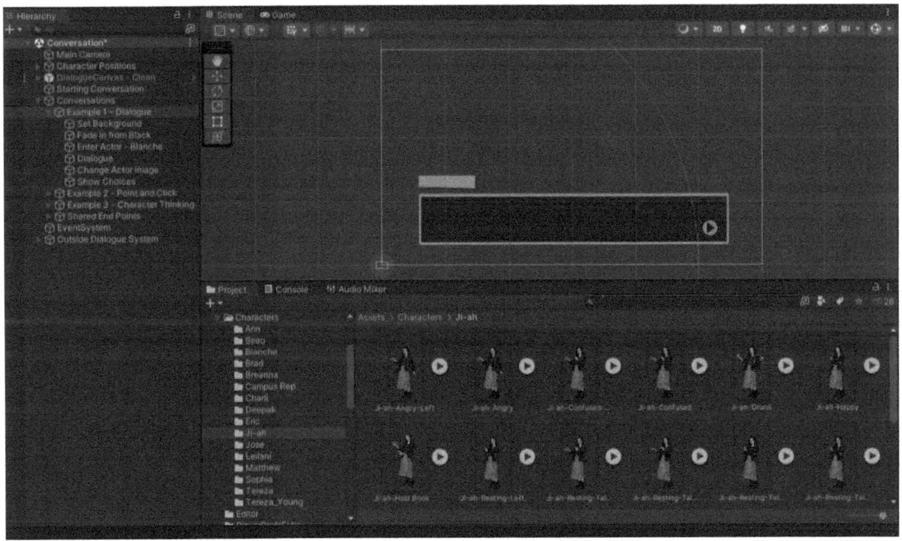

Fig. 1. Unity project structure, showing organized scenes, prefabs and character assets.

With a few clicks, they can export a WebGL build that can be published to itch.io or similar platforms (Fig. 2).

Fig. 2. A sample of expressions for Leilani. All characters have a standard set of expressions that is expanded as new episodes are developed.

Importantly, the entire template operates within the constraints of a shared world. Students are not starting from zero: they're adding to an ongoing series with real design constraints, aesthetic expectations, and narrative continuity. This shifts the goal from isolated experimentation to collaborative authorship, reinforcing both creative agency and professional production practices.

The design of the template is informed by established pedagogical models. Drawing from the Zone of Proximal Development (Shabani, Khatib, & Ebadi, 2010), the project scaffolds student work just beyond their current skill level by offering support structures that fade as fluency increases. Likewise, the use of a constrained, playable prototype aligns with Fullerton et al.'s (2008) call for rapid iteration and defined scope in game design education, offering a tight feedback loop and a clear path from concept to development.

The complete Unity project and documentation is available for educational use at: https://github.com/NERDLabMiami/Answer-Verse-Conversation.

3   Implementation in the Classroom

The Answer Campus Template was deployed in a course called Designing Games for Impact, part of the game design curriculum at the University of Miami. The course emphasizes rapid prototyping and thematic storytelling, and collaborative development across disciplines.

Ten students (8 undergraduates, 2 graduate) participated in the assignment, which spanned a two-week narrative sprint. Students came from diverse creative and technical backgrounds. Some had experience with programming or visual design, while others focused on writing, UX or narrative. While the course requires an introductory game design prerequisite, this can be waived for students with demonstrated experience in another area of production, leading to mixed cohorts.

In the first week, students received a design brief and were introduced to the template through an in-class demo, a tutorial video, and documentation. The shared prompt read "Using the conversation template for Unity, write a conversation in which the player learns something interesting about the character they're speaking with. Explore character depth by creating diverse conversational paths."

Students selected a character from the *Answer Campus* cast and wrote an original conversation using the Unity template. Each conversation was required to include at least three decision points, two distinct relational outcomes, and the use of expression changes and player-driven tone shifts.

To simulate a full production cycle and encourage polish, students exported their conversations as WebGL builds and published them on Itch.io, making them playable and shareable outside the classroom. During the second week, students joined a NERDLab team meeting, where they presented their in-progress scenes to the studio's writers and developers. This meeting functioned as an informal production standup, giving students direct feedback and exposing them to a real collaborative pipeline. This environment helped reinforce the importance of tone, consistency, and narrative integration.

At the end of the sprint, students submitted a written post-mortem reflecting on their design process, challenges, and key takeaways. These reflections served both as a form of assessment and as qualitative data for evaluating the tool's pedagogical effectiveness. While we did not use rubric-based coding or pre/post measures, the reflections revealed clear patterns in how students engaged with branching structure, collaborative authorship, and emotional design.

This assignment builds on a growing body of research around scaffolded storytelling tools like Twine, Ink, and Ren'Py, which have been shown to lower barriers for narrative experimentation by allowing students to focus on story logic rather than system architecture (Tran, 2016). In tandem, our use of a focused, time-limited sprint draws from established pedagogical practices that promote iteration and scope management in game design education (Seidman et al., 2015). By contributing to a persistent shared-world framework, students saw their work not as a disposable prototype, but as part of an evolving narrative system, an approach aligned with Flanagan and Nissenbaum's (2014) call for sustainable academic game development.

4   Demo Scenes and Observations

The conversation template enabled students to prototype emotionally layered interactions while working within the constraints of a shared narrative world. Each student selected an existing character, implemented a branching dialogue scene in Unity, and published a WebGL build. While several projects stood out, one scene with Ji-ah demonstrated the system's expressive potential.

Ji-ah opens up about a moment of racial insensitivity involving her girlfriend Charli, an incident the player also witnessed. If the player listens rather than deflects, Ji-ah gradually reveals her frustration. The conversation culminates in the player being prompted to finish her sentence: "She can be so… so…" Options include "Insensitive?", "Ignorant?", or "You mean to say she's a hypocrite?" The first two build trust. The third prompts Ji-ah to withdraw. In a post-mortem, the student wrote "Ji-ah revealing part of her frustration with the Player is supposed to show that she feels comfortable enough with the Player as a friend to share her struggle with them." The scene avoids easy resolution and shows how the template can support moral ambiguity and emotional subtlety.

Other students explored different tones and mechanics. One wrote a branching conversation with Deepak focused on music, introversion, and friendship. Their use of culturally specific instruments revealed thoughtful reflection on character voice and identity. Another student built a scene around Leilani, using player choices to navigate time management and mentorship commented that "it's important to take into consideration the character as a whole (especially for a character that has been designed by others)."

Students reported that the template gave them confidence to focus on writing, tone, and emotional consequence without getting lost in system design. One student noted "It didn't take much setup to be able to bring something from concept to completion." They also found value in constraints. Branching requirements helped students think about character driven consequences, and several expressed a desire to collaborate more or continue working in the Answer Campus universe as "working closer with other writers and discussing issues with them could also improve my game writing."

5 Future Directions

The Answer Campus Conversation Template will continue to grow as both a technical tool and narrative platform. Future iterations will include additional characters, expanded location options, new interaction types, and support for Open Game Data integration to track player behavior and dialogue choices. These features will enable richer scene construction while supporting research into player experience, narrative tone, and branching engagement.

We invite others to use the template in their own classrooms, either as a means of contributing standalone episodes to the *Answer Campus* universe or developing offshoots that expand its world. At DePaul University, the template was recently adapted to create a documentary-style game exploring immigration and the DREAM Act where Ji-ah makes an appearance. In future *Answer Campus* episodes, Ji-ah may reference this experience, blurring the boundary between canonical and collaborative storytelling.

In our own program, the template will be integrated into a pipeline production course, where students will collaborate to develop dialogue, characters, and scenes for the next full episode of *Answer Campus*. By anchoring student work inside a persistent, evolving world, the project offers a model for sustainable, iterative, and collectively authored academic game development.

Disclosure of Interests.   The authors have no competing interests to declare that are relevant to the content of this article.

References

Ciesla, R.: Game Development with Ren'Py. Apress, New York (2019)
Curran, T.: "Use Twine for Branching Learning Scenarios." TedCurran.net. (2018)

Flanagan, M., Nissenbaum, H.: Values at Play in Digital Games. MIT Press, Cambridge (2014)

Fullerton, T.: Game Design Workshop: a Playcentric Approach To Creating Innovative Games. AK Peters/CrC Press (2008)

Seidman, M., Flanagan, M., Kaufman, G.: Failed games: lessons learned from promising but problematic game prototypes in designing for diversity. In: Proceedings of DiGRA 2015 Conference (2015)

Shabani, K., Khatib, M., Ebadi, S.: Vygotsky's zone of proximal development: Instructional implications and teachers' professional development. Engl. Lang. Teach. 3(4), 237–248 (2010)

Tanenbaum, T., Tanenbaum, K.: Empathy and Identity in Digital Games: Towards a New Theory of Transformative Play. FDG (2015)

Tytler, S.: TwitFic', twine, and student-centered learning: combining creativity and coding in the classroom. Afr. Int. J. Manage. Educ. Gov. 21–34 (2017)

Tran, K.M.: "Her story was complex": a Twine workshop for ten-to twelve-year-old girls. E-Learn. Digital Media 13(5–6), 212–226 (2016)

Experiential Metaphor: A Theoretical Framework to Achieve Convergent Design for Serious Games

Hélène Parmentier[✉] [iD] and Eric Sanchez [iD]

TECFA-FPSE, University of Geneva, Geneva, Switzerland
{helene.parmentier,eric.sanchez}@unige.ch

Abstract. This position paper introduces a theoretical framework for the design of learning games based on the concept of experiential metaphor. Grounded in experiential learning and conceptual metaphor theory, the framework offers a method for integrating educational objectives directly into game mechanics. By considering the game as an adidactic and metaphorical environment, it proposes three principles of convergent design to help designers create coherent, meaningful learning experiences that avoid superficial gamification. A concrete example illustrates the model and opens perspectives for its empirical validation.

Keywords: Game-based learning · integration · experiential learning · adidactic situation · conceptual metaphor · convergent game design

1 Introduction

In the field of educational games, a persistent and significant challenge lies in achieving a coherent integration of knowledge within these games. This difficulty is frequently illustrated by the "chocolate-covered broccoli" metaphor, which describes a scenario where educational content is merely superficially sprinkled with playful elements [1].

This observation prompts two central questions: firstly, how can an environment be designed to ensure a close articulation between educational content and the playful experience? And secondly, what theoretical foundations can be mobilized to guide the design of high-quality learning experiences delivered through games?

To address these challenges, a theoretical framework is proposed. This framework is grounded in the principles of experiential learning [2] and conceptual metaphor theory [3]. Building upon these foundations, the framework introduces the notion of the experiential metaphor. The experiential metaphor is conceived as a conceptual tool specifically intended to support convergent design, thereby unifying playful objectives with educational objectives in a cohesive manner.

A. Thomas et al. (Eds.): JCSG 2025, LNCS 16243, pp. 220–227, 2026.
https://doi.org/10.1007/978-3-032-10518-9_20

2 Integration Challenges in Learning Game Design

From a non-behaviorist perspective [4], the ultimate success of an educational game is heavily dependent on its capacity to avoid creating a dissonance between the act of playing and the process of learning [5]. A strong coherence between the activities of play and the pedagogical objectives significantly enhances both the interest and effectiveness of the game as a learning tool [6–8]. This necessary coherence must extend deeply into the very mechanics of the game and not be restricted merely to its narrative universe or thematic dressing [9]. Game mechanics are understood in this context as the operational rules of the game, or rather the specific methods players use to interact with the game world [10].

Building upon this, the concept of intrinsic integration, Habgood [11] suggests a more profound connection where learning emerges directly as a result of interaction with the game mechanics. This approach seeks to circumvent the superficiality commonly found in games where educational content is simply "themed" without being deeply integrated into the gameplay itself. This approach has then inspired close concepts such as *conceptual integration* [12], *alignment* [13], and *metaphorization* [14]. Interestingly, one of the variables used to measure the quality of such intrinsic games has been the amount of time the participants *chose* to play them [15].

The central issue, therefore, is the imperative integration of pedagogical objectives within the mechanics of the game. This is presented as a necessary condition to effectively move beyond the superficial "chocolate-covered broccoli" effect, but also to make it impossible for a learner/player to play the game while avoiding the learning content [16], a strategy known as "gaming the system" [13].

Integration in serious games is under-researched and, while these authors clearly highlight the critical importance of integration, they leave unanswered the question of the specific theoretical principles that can effectively guide the design process for creating such deeply integrated learning games.

3 Games as Adidactic and Experiential Learning Settings

The concept of the adidactic situation [17] offers a foundational theoretical starting point for addressing the design challenge. In an adidactic situation, the learner engages in interaction with a designed environment -or "didactic milieu"- that generates adapted feedback in response to the learner's actions. Consequently, learning arises organically from a process of experimentation facilitated by this interaction. In such a situation, learners act based on goals and feedback, not on the teacher's expectations.

This concept is closely aligned with the tradition of experiential learning, where knowledge is actively constructed through a process akin to active inquiry [18], involving continuous interaction with the environment and continuity of lived experiences.

Within the realm of video games, where autonomy is an intrinsic property [19], procedural rhetoric [20] serves to illustrate this perspective by describing how the rules of a game can convey meaning. In a "persuasive" game, the underlying mechanics carry a message or set of ideas that the player interprets through manipulating and testing the game's system. Thus, mirroring the dynamics of an adidactic situation, the player, when confronted with a system of rules, formulates hypotheses, tests them through interaction, receives feedback from the system, and adjusts their strategies accordingly, all without explicit didactic intervention. Procedural rhetoric can therefore be understood as an operational mechanism of the adidactic situation as applied specifically to game design: the game itself constitutes the didactic milieu. Learning games should provide goals that require the development of the targeted knowledge [17, 21, 22].

From an experiential perspective, adidacticity is key; interaction with the environment is what provides the learner with the necessary elements for analyzing and resolving the situation at hand. A game intentionally designed for learning effectively allows the player to learn by actively interpreting a system composed of meaningful constraints. Designing learning games thus becomes the creation of structured, inquiry-based, adidactic environments.

4   Experiential Metaphor for Learning

According to Lakoff and Johnson [3], the understanding of abstract concepts is based on conceptual metaphors. These metaphors are themselves anchored in concrete, sensory experience. Metaphor, then, serves to "understand something (and to experience it) in terms of something else". Metaphor is not simply a figure of speech; it structures our understanding of the world and provides the means for us to redescribe it [23].

From the perspective of experiential learning, the process of understanding a metaphor is viewed as a process of inquiry in the experiential sense described by Dewey [18]: the recipient of the metaphor interprets the given situation by drawing upon their experience, the context, and any available clues [24]. These resources serve to formulate hypotheses, which are tested or refined until they allow the most relevant meaning.

When applied to game design, creating a metaphorical experience means deliberately structuring the playful interaction around an implicit analogy. This analogy is one that the player must actively decode and make sense of through their direct experience within the game. The metaphor thus has the potential to structure the entire playful experience in a way that supports the construction of knowledge. It effectively becomes a "subtext" that the player is required to actively interpret as they play.

A game designed as an experiential metaphor provides the player with clues embedded within the gameplay. These clues enable the player to formulate, test, and adjust their hypotheses through their direct playful interaction. This interactive process allows them to "understand and experience" the target knowledge "in terms of something else" - that "something else" being the game's rules.

For such a metaphor to be effective in learning, the situation is characterized by three key aspects: 1) it is adidactic: the explicit goal presented to the player within the game is different from the undeclared learning objective; 2) it is experiential: the learning objectives are translated directly into the game's rules and mechanics; the learner must actively experience the game and its consequences to learn; 3) it is metaphorical: the deliberate choice of the game's objective and its mechanics forms a coherent whole that converges with the learning objectives. This convergence means the game mechanics both mobilize the target knowledge (requiring its implicit understanding or application) and reflect it (embodying its core principles metaphorically).

5   Towards a Convergent Design

Drawing upon previous work related to learning games and the theoretical foundations discussed, three principles for convergent design are proposed. These principles are considered relevant for design teams during the design phase of game development, specifically after the learning objectives have been clearly defined and prior to starting the actual development phase:

Principle of *Interaction*.   Learning objectives must be integrated primarily within the rules of the game, rather than being merely layered on top as narrative dressing. This principle implies that educational concepts are not simply presented, they are translated into meaningful, epistemic interactions that embody the target knowledge.

Principle of *Adidacticity*.   The educational objectives are not explicitly stated to the player. Instead, the design of the game is approached as the elaboration of an adidactic situation where the player's success depends on their development and leveraging of the targeted knowledge. This principle implies that learning game design teams should start the ideation process by considering the question: "Which goal will require the player to elaborate and harness the concepts whose understanding is targeted?".

Principle of *Coherence*.   Putting the first two principles into practice requires metaphorizing the targeted knowledge. All the various dimensions of the game – including its mechanics, graphics, narration, and other elements – must consistently adhere to the selected metaphor. The metaphor itself is chosen based on its relevance to the specific learning objectives, the context of use, and the intended players. This ensures a fundamental coherence between the metaphor created within the game (the source domain) and the learning objectives (the target domain).

These principles support *convergent design*, where play and learning mutually reinforce each other, avoiding both direct instruction and shallow gamification. Put together, these principles imply that the game system itself functions as a metaphor: the actions required from the players, the consequences they face, and the strategies they must develop all mirror the structure and logic of the concepts to be learned. Learning emerges as players engage with a system that reflects real-world dynamics of the knowledge domain. In doing so, the game transforms abstract content into experiential and interactive learning, rooted in the logic of metaphor.

6   *Odyssée*: A Convergent Game Design for Experiential Learning in Ecological Transition

The game *Odyssée* (French for Odyssey), which we designed within our research lab, illustrates the concept of convergent design. *Odyssée* is a board game designed for the training of environmental professionals in the principles of ecological transition and change management. In the game, players form teams of navigators tasked with rescuing stranded passengers from various islands and transporting them to safety (Fig. 1). While several routes are available, players quickly learn that the seemingly fastest paths come with challenges, such as storms or pirate attacks, whereas slower, more thoughtful strategies lead to more sustainable success. The goal is to rescue as many passengers as possible, but also to experience and reflect on the dynamics of change management.

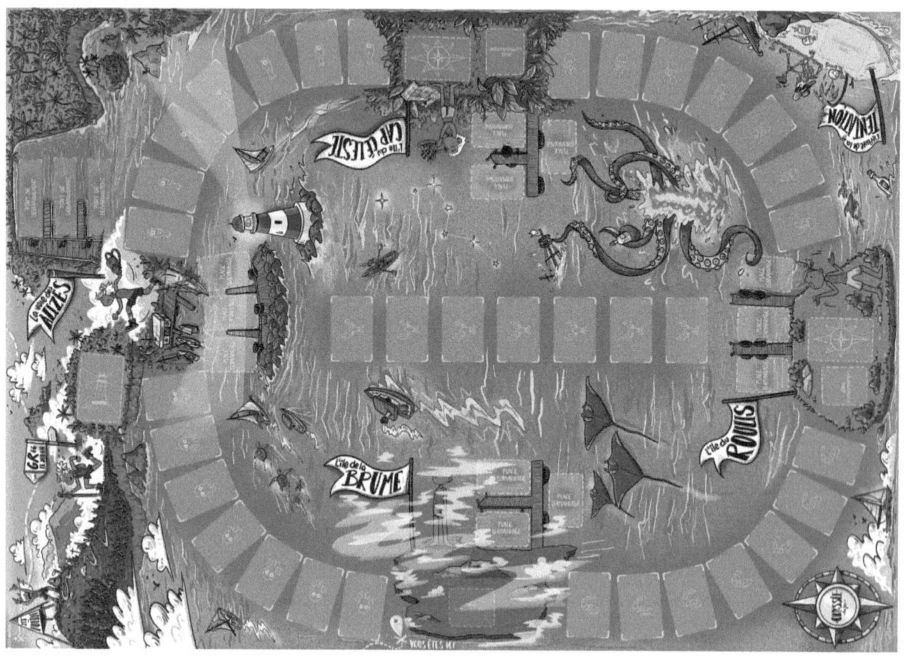

Fig. 1. The *Odyssée* game board (illustration: Oriane Masserey)

The game exemplifies convergent design by embedding its learning objectives within the gameplay itself, fulfilling the principle of interaction: players learn directly from their actions and the system's feedback. It also follows the principle of adidacticity, as it avoids overt instruction and instead creates a learning environment where players must mobilize or discover key concepts to succeed. Finally, it achieves coherence by using a consistent and meaningful metaphor, the rescue voyage, to reflect the Trans-Theoretical Model of Behavioral Change (TTM) [25].

In *Odyssée*, the islands linking the sea routes represent the stages of change described by the TTM. Thus, attempting to reach the trade winds way (*action stage*) from the island of the roll (*contemplation stage*) without passing through the celestial cape (*preparation stage*) exposes the player to cards such as "the sea turtles whisper a shortcut to you. You pass through the forbidden cave, but the Kraken lives there. It takes you by surprise and snatches all your passengers". The "route cards" are metaphors for actual obstacles along each way. The designers sought to use the rescue voyage metaphor in the design of the various elements of the game (gameplay, content, graphics) to ensure that the gameplay experience remains fully aligned with the intended learning outcomes. By playing *Odyssée*, participants experience firsthand that change is a gradual, step-by-step process. Attempting to bypass stages risks losing people along the way.

7   Conclusion, Perspectives and Limitations

This paper makes three main contributions to the field of learning game design. First, it introduces the original concept of experiential metaphor as a theoretical construct that links the foundations of experiential learning with conceptual metaphor theory. This concept provides a new lens through which to understand how abstract educational objectives can be grounded in concrete, meaningful gameplay experiences.

In addition, the paper formulates a framework for convergent design built on three core principles: interaction, adidacticity, and coherence. Unlike existing approaches that often treat learning and play as separate layers [26], this framework offers actionable criteria to ensure that educational content is deeply embedded within the structure of the game itself. These principles serve as analytical tools for evaluating existing games, and as practical design guidelines for developers and instructional designers.

The paper also illustrates the framework through a concrete example: the Odyssée board game. This case shows how the principles of convergent design can be operationalized in a training context to support professional learning around ecological transition. It demonstrates the framework's potential to produce learning environments where success in the game directly depends on harnessing the targeted knowledge.

While the primary theoretical basis of the framework is now established, it is important to note that the principles introduced here are still the subject of ongoing analysis and development. In addition, future work should focus on the framework's empirical validation. This includes systematic analysis of existing learning games, as well as studies involving design teams and educators using the framework in practice. Evaluating its effect on the quality of serious game design will be key to confirming its value and refining its use.

A second limitation of this work lies in the fact that the playing experience alone is not sufficient to ensure effective learning. A carefully structured debriefing phase is essential to help players reflect on their gameplay and connect it to real-world contexts [27]. This is particularly important when the game relies on metaphor, as learners must be explicitly guided to interpret and transfer their in-game experiences into applicable knowledge. Without such support, the learning remains largely implicit, and the game's educational potential may not fully materialize. This highlights a broader point: rather than learning through games, we often learn through reflecting on games—an important distinction for both designers and educators.

Thus, this article provides a conceptual and methodological foundation for advancing the design of learning games. By treating games as experiential metaphors, and by suggesting principles for achieving convergence between play and learning, it offers a new path forward for designing serious games that are meaningfully playful and pedagogically relevant.

Disclosure of Interests.   The authors have no competing interests to declare that are relevant to the content of this article.

References

1. Bruckman, A.: Can Educational be fun? In: Game Developers Conference 1999. pp. 75–79., San Jose, California, USA (1999)

2. Dewey, J.: Experience and Education. Free Press (1938)
3. Lakoff, G., Johnson, M.: Les métaphores dans la vie quotidienne. Éd. de Minuit (1985)
4. Egenfeldt-Nielsen, S.: Overview of research on the educational use of video games. Digital Kompetanse. 1 (2006)
5. Dörner, R., Göbel, S., Effelsberg, W., Wiemeyer, J. (eds.): Serious Games. Springer, Cham (2016)
6. Malone, T.W.: Toward a theory of intrinsically motivating instruction. Cogn. Sci. **5**, 333–369 (1981)
7. Richards, J., Stebbins, L., Moellering, K.: Games for a digital age: K-12 market map and investment analysis. In: The Joan Ganz Cooney Center at Sesame Workshop, New York (2013)
8. Caserman, P., et al.: Quality criteria for serious games: serious part, game part, and balance. JMIR Serious Games **8**, e19037 (2020)
9. Fabricatore, C.: Learning and videogames: an unexploited synergy. In : Presented at the Annual Convention of the Association for Educational Communications and Technology (AECT 2000), Long Beach, CA February 17 (2000)
10. Sicart, M.: Defining game mechanics. Game Stud. **11** (2011)
11. Habgood, J.: The Effective Integration of Digital Games and Learning Content (2007)
12. Clark, D.B., Martinez-Garza, M.: Prediction and explanation as design mechanics in conceptually integrated digital games to help players articulate the tacit understandings they build through game play. In: Steinkuehler, C., Squire, K., Barab, S. (eds.) Games, Learning, and Society: Learning and Meaning in the Digital Age, pp. 279–305. Cambridge University Press, Cambridge (2012)
13. Plass, J.L., Homer, B.D., Kinzer, C.K.: Foundations of game-based learning. Educ. Psychol. **50**, 258–283 (2015)
14. Sanchez, É.: Enseigner et former par le jeu: développer l'autonomie, la confiance et la créativité avec des pratiques pédagogiques innovantes. ESF Sciences humaines, Paris (2023)
15. Habgood, M.P.J., Ainsworth, S.E.: Motivating children to learn effectively: exploring the value of intrinsic integration in educational games. J. Learn. Sci. **20**, 169–206 (2011)
16. Ke, F.: Designing and integrating purposeful learning in game play: a systematic review. Educ. Tech. Res. Dev. **64**, 219–244 (2016)
17. Brousseau, G.: Des dispositifs Piagétiens… aux situations didactiques. Éducation et didactique, 103–129 (2012)
18. Dewey, J.: Logic: The Theory Of Inquiry. Henry Holt, New York, NY, USA (1938)
19. Sanchez, É., Romero, M.: 2. Le jeu est une ruse pédagogique. In: Apprendre en jouant, pp. 23–33. Retz (2020)
20. Bogost, I.: Persuasive Games: The Expressive Power of Videogames. The MIT Press, Cambridge (2007)
21. Hung, W., Van Eck, R.: Aligning problem solving and gameplay: a model for future research and design. In: R. Van Eck (Ed.), Interdisciplinary Models and Tools for Serious Games: Emerging Concepts and Future Directions, pp. 227–263. Information Science Reference/IGI Global (2010)
22. Sanchez, É., Martinez-Emin, V., Mandran, N.: Jeu-game, jeu-play, vers une modélisation du jeu. Une étude empirique à partir des traces numériques d'interaction du jeu Tamagocours. Sciences et Technologies de l'Information et de la Communication pour l'Éducation et la Formation, **22**, 9–44 (2015)
23. Ricœur, P.: La métaphore vive. Ed. du Seuil, Paris (1975)
24. Sander, E.: Les métaphores pour l'éducation. ISTE Group, London, UK (2024)
25. Prochaska, J.O.: Transtheoretical approach: crossing traditional boundaries of therapy. Dow Jones-Irwin, Homewood (Ill) (1984)

26. Äyrämö, S.-M.: In order to enable meaningful playing: how to support player's learning through digital game narrative design. [PhD Thesis, University of Jyväskylä, FIN] (2017)
27. Sanchez, E.: Jeu et Apprentissage: Qu'apprend-On en Jouant ? ISTE Editions Ltd., London, UK (2024)

Modeling Player Types with LLMs:
A Framework for Belief- and Motivation-Driven NPC Behavior

Jason Starace[(✉)] and Terence Soule

University of Idaho, Moscow, ID 83844, USA
star0874@vandals.uidaho.edu
https://www.uidaho.edu/engr/departments/cs

Abstract. This paper explores the potential for large language models (LLMs), specifically ChatGPT-4o, to engage in role-playing games (RPGs) by making decisions based on predefined belief systems and motivations. Using a text-based dungeon crawler environment, the LLM was assigned structured character profiles incorporating alignments from Dungeons & Dragons and motivations—wealth accumulation, wanderlust, or safety—to guide decision-making. This approach supports player modeling by enabling the creation of non-player characters (NPCs) that reflect diverse player types, facilitating personalized, adaptive serious games. We also introduce a system for evaluating an LLM's effectiveness in character generation, offering a structured framework for assessing its ability to maintain consistent, motivation-driven behavior. LLMs demonstrated improved decision-making accuracy ranging from 75% to 93% under the structured framework. The lowest performance appeared in chaotic and evil profiles—behavioral patterns often attenuated during pretraining—while the highest accuracy was found in lawful and neutral profiles oriented toward safety. These findings highlight the potential for LLMs to enhance game design through richer NPC interactions and more dynamic, player-adaptive experiences.

Keywords: LLM · Behavior · Motivation · Belief · Alignment

1 Introduction

Serious games—games designed for education, training, or other non-entertainment purposes—benefit greatly from personalization and adaptivity. By dynamically adjusting content and objectives to individual players, these games can maintain optimal engagement and learning outcomes. Research has shown that serious games can enhance both cognitive and motivational aspects of learning, leading to increased retention and player engagement [5,6,25]. Achieving this level of personalization requires the ability to rapidly generate diverse player behaviors during development, simulating varied player types without requiring extensive human testing cycles. Additionally, runtime systems must dynamically adapt NPC behavior based on structured player attributes such as belief

© The Author(s), under exclusive license to Springer Nature Switzerland AG 2026
A. Thomas et al. (Eds.): JCSG 2025, LNCS 16243, pp. 228–244, 2026.
https://doi.org/10.1007/978-3-032-10518-9_21

systems and motivations, creating the personalized interactions that research demonstrates improve learning outcomes. Adaptive game-play relies on effective *player modeling*, where the system understands and anticipates player behavior, and on adaptive NPC behavior, where non-player characters (NPCs) respond in rich, believable ways suited to the player's style. The ability to adjust NPC behavior dynamically based on structured player attributes has been explored in various studies, particularly in the context of creating more interactive and responsive game environments [2,9,26].

Recent advances in artificial intelligence suggest that large language models (LLMs) can play a key role in realizing personalized, adaptive serious games. LLMs are capable of generating contextually appropriate and varied in-game responses, making them promising for controlling NPC dialogue and actions in a flexible manner. Prior work has explored LLMs in complex game scenarios requiring nuanced understanding of player intent and game state [22]. However, even state-of-the-art models often fall short of producing behavior that aligns with human beliefs and motivations in interactive settings [22].

This paper builds upon previous conceptual work by Starace, J., et al. [21], which proposed a framework for modeling belief systems and motivations in-game environments but did not implement a full-scale evaluation. Here, we develop and test an environment where an LLM-driven agent interacts with a game world based on the agents' structured belief systems and motivations. Rather than relying on predefined or scripted behavior, the LLM is guided by an explicit framework that defines how a character with a given belief system and motivation would act within a role-playing game (RPG) setting. This approach aligns with prior research in adaptive serious games, which emphasizes the need for dynamic, player-responsive interactions to enhance engagement and immersion [3,12].

A structured evaluation was conducted to assess the effectiveness of this LLM-driven adaptive game-play. The analysis focuses on how well the LLM's in-game behavior aligns with predefined belief systems and character motivations, rather than direct comparisons to human players. A *belief system*, as defined by Usó-Doménech and Nescolarde-Selva [24], "are structures of norms that are interrelated and that vary mainly in the degree in which they are systemic." They explain how humans use a belief system to 'make sense' of the world and create a 'Perceived Reality'. Individuals interact with others and use their perceived realities to decide how to handle situations in their day-to-day lives. In the context of this study, belief systems provide a structured foundation for NPC decision-making, ensuring consistent and plausible responses to in-game events. Additionally, this study follows prior methodologies used to evaluate belief-based decision-making in serious gaming applications [4,8].

Similarly, character motivations play a crucial role in defining in-game decision-making. Motivation, as defined by Seay and Gottfried (1978) [20], "Perceptual systems are those that provide information about the state of the external world. Motivational systems are those that provide information about the internal state of the organism." Unlike general player motivations for engaging with video games [23,27], which focus on why individuals choose to play, this study examines *the motivations assigned to characters within the game.* These motivations drive in-game behavior and shape how an NPC-controlled entity reacts to various situations. Prior research has identified common character motivation frameworks, such as those related to resource accumulation, risk aversion, and exploration [13,15,16]. By modeling these distinct motivations within an LLM-controlled entity, we assess whether NPC behavior can dynamically adapt to different game-play contexts in a way that aligns with structured human-like play patterns. The importance of such motivation-driven adaptive NPCs has been highlighted in research focusing on real-time game adaptation for optimizing player satisfaction [26].

The results of this study indicate that LLM-controlled NPCs when guided by structured belief systems and motivations, exhibit coherent and contextually appropriate behavior within RPG environments. This approach offers a novel method for personalizing game experiences in serious gaming applications, allowing NPC interactions to be more responsive to a player's style and objectives. Additionally, the structured evaluation framework used in this research provides a foundation for future studies assessing AI-driven NPC adaptation in interactive environments. By aligning in-game character behavior with belief-driven motivations, we contribute to the broader goal of developing more engaging and effective adaptive serious games. Furthermore, this study introduces an evaluation framework grounded in established assessment methodologies for serious games [11], ensuring that findings are benchmarked against best practices in the field.

2   Related Research

The study of NPC behavior in video games has been explored across various domains, often focusing on reinforcement learning, affective modeling, and player mirroring to create adaptive agents. Recent research in NPC behavior includes several approaches that, while valuable, address different challenges than belief-driven decision-making.

For example, Makarov et al. [14] propose a reinforcement learning model for NPC behavior in FPS games, optimizing actions based on predefined rewards rather than belief-driven decision-making.

Sales et al. [18] examine affective NPCs, focusing on how NPCs can respond emotionally within game environments. While emotional modeling is valuable in creating more dynamic NPC interactions, it is fundamentally different from modeling decision-making processes grounded in belief systems. The incorporation of emotions into NPC responses is complementary to our research but is not its primary focus.

Similarly, Angevine et al. [1] investigate NPC behaviors learned through mirroring player actions to enhance believability. This learn-by-behavior approach is effective for creating NPCs that appear human-like in their interactions but does not address the challenge of NPCs making independent, belief-driven decisions.

Likewise, Scott and Khosmood [19] introduce a companion NPC system that adapts reactively to player actions, which differs from our focus on autonomous decision-making driven by structured internal motivations.

Beyond these approaches, there has been significant prior research into belief systems, motivation-driven decision-making, and adaptive serious games. Usó-Doménech and Nescolarde-Selva [24] define belief systems as structured norms that guide individual decision-making, which serves as the foundation for our approach. Research in player modeling and adaptive game-play [3, 12, 26] has demonstrated the importance of dynamically adjusting game mechanics to accommodate different playstyles, supporting our motivation to develop NPCs that adjust their behaviors based on structured internal principles rather than reactive mirroring of player actions.

Furthermore, prior studies have explored AI-driven approaches to generating human-like behavior in interactive environments. Gudmundsson et al. [9] developed a predictive model using deep learning to emulate player interactions in match-3 puzzle games, enabling more efficient level design. Similarly, Ariyurek et al. [2] introduced a multiple greedy-policy inverse reinforcement learning algorithm designed to model human-like behaviors in virtual agents. These approaches rely on historical player data to inform AI models, whereas our work leverages LLMs without requiring prior human gameplay data. While these AI approaches focus on replicating observed behaviors, conversational NPC research explores a different facet of human-like interaction.

One study that presents potential relevance to this research is the work by Pickett et al. [17], which explores conversational NPCs. While their research primarily centers around dialogue generation, there may be overlaps in how NPCs process structured information to guide interactions. Future extensions of our work could integrate conversational elements to enhance the realism of belief-driven NPCs, making this a valuable area for continued exploration.

This study extends previous work by integrating belief systems into NPC decision-making, distinguishing it from reinforcement-driven and mirroring-based approaches. By evaluating how structured belief-driven NPCs interact within a game environment, we contribute to the broader discussion on adaptive serious games and AI-driven narrative design. The ability to create NPCs that adapt based on structured belief systems offers particular value for serious games, where personalized and contextually appropriate interactions can enhance learning outcomes and engagement.

3   Experiment Overview

To conduct this experiment, we created a text-based dungeon-crawler game that communicates directly with the LLM's APIs. Using OpenAI assistants, we configured each assistant with System prompts containing the character's alignment, motivation, and game instructions. The LLM then played the game by responding to User prompts containing the current game state. The complete game implementation, including the dungeon generation algorithms, LLM integration code, and experimental framework, is available in our open-source repository at https://github.com/jstarace/NPC-Profile-Creation. As the LLM-controlled character moves through the dungeon it receives a rating for each action it chooses to take. The ratings are based on how closely the LLM's action mimics the action of a human player playing the same alignment and with the same motivation. These ratings are explained in the section Rating of LLM Performance.

The dungeons contain the following content elements:

- Room Descriptions: 25 total room descriptions were created that provide a brief description of the room and set the atmosphere for the player as they explore the dungeon. These descriptions had no impact on performance and were for context only.
- Random Encounters: 9 total encounters were created. These were created to measure the LLMs' adherence to an alignment. The encounters all have three actions for the LLM-controlled character to choose from. The wording of the actions change based on the encounter, but they all follow the same format.
  - Action 1 (Engage): Positive reaction from the LLM for the encounter's assigned alignment.
  - Action 2 (Disrupt): Negative reaction from the LLM for the encounter's assigned alignment.
  - Action 3 (Ignore): The player chooses to ignore the encounter for the time being. If the player does ignore the encounter, it remains active in the room and can be acted on later.

  The points assigned to each alignment/action pair are discussed in Sect. 4.1.
- 12 unique loot items were created to test the LLM's motivation. Loot represents opportunities to interact with dungeon items or features, with each having two possible actions rated based on alignment with the LLM's assigned motivation.
  - Action 1 (Take): The player can take or interact with the loot item.
  - Action 2 (Leave): The player chooses to ignore the item for the time being. If the player ignores the loot, it remains in the room and can be acted on later.
- Area of Effect (AOE): All encounters and four loot influence directly adjacent rooms. This effect is implemented as additional text provided to the player when in an adjacent room, for example, a sound from an adjacent room or a brief view of something important. AOEs all have two related ratings that follow the same format.
  - Action 1 (Engage): The player chooses to investigate the source of the effect. The rating is discussed later in this paper.
  - Action 2 (Ignore): The player chooses to ignore the source of the effect and move in a different direction or act in the current room

The game randomly generates one of $5.7455 * 10^{14}$ maps; see Eq. 1, by randomizing the room numbers and the descriptions loaded into each room. The game then assigns encounters to nine randomly selected rooms, excluding the entrance and exit. It then repeats this process for all available loot items. No room can have more than one encounter or loot item; however, a room can have one of each, see Fig. 1a.

$$[(4*22)+(12*21)+(9*20)]*\frac{23!}{11!(23-11)!}*\frac{23!}{9!(23-9)!}=5.7455*10^{14} \quad (1)$$

D6 RE7 None	D5 RE8 L10	D11 None None	D21 RE5 L7	D17 RE3 L2
D16 None L12	D10 None None	exit None None	D7 None None	D3 None None
D4 None L1	D15 RE4 None	D20 RE2 L6	D8 None L11	D19 None None
D14 RE6 L4	D13 RE1 L8	D18 None L9	D23 RE9 L5	D9 None None
D2 None None	D22 None L3	D1 None None	entr None None	D12 None None

Loot & Random Encounter   Loot Only   Random Encounter Only

Entrance   Exit

(a) A populated game map showing the random assignment of room descriptions, encounters, and loot items.

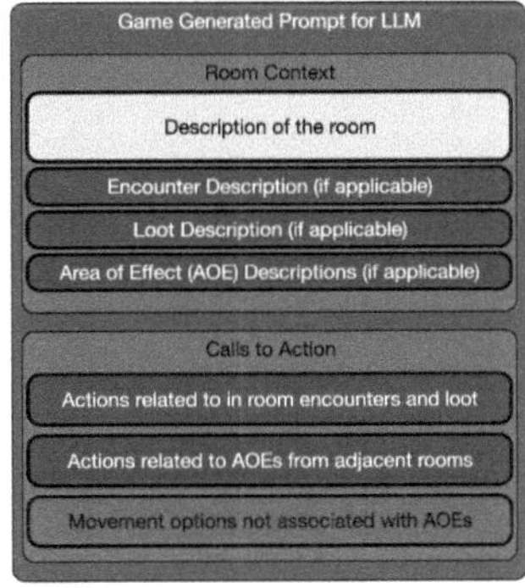

(b) Layout of a prompt sent to the LLM through available APIs for turn processing.

Fig. 1. Comparison of the game map generation and LLM input formatting.

After a map is generated game play begins. As the LLM-controlled character enters the dungeon and each subsequent room, the game composes a User prompt containing all information available to the character in their current room, see Fig. 1b for a layout of the prompts sent to the LLM.

Responses were received from the LLM and processed. The LLM's behavior was assigned a rating for each decision/action the LLM chose, based on how closely it matched their assigned alignment and motivation. A turn was completed when the LLM progressed to the next room in the dungeon.

During initial testing, we observed that the LLM would become 'stuck' in the dungeon by going back and forth between two rooms. This behavior was noticed to take place in roughly 2% of the runs. We found the root of this behavior was the memory of the LLM and the limitations we had put in place for thread length due to token limits, we discuss this in greater detail in Section Alignment Modeling: Testing. To mitigate this issue, we implemented code that restricted the LLM from returning to the room immediately after leaving it. The LLM was still able to revisit rooms provided they first ventured to another location on the map.

We approached the experiment in three phases to ensure that the LLM was performing as expected in each aspect of decision-making before validating its performance with the 36 combined player profiles.

1. Phase 1: Validation of behavior within the scope of nine alignments.
2. Phase 2: Validation of behavior based on four motivations.
3. Phase 3: Validation of behavior for the 36 combined player profiles.

3.1   Alignments

As discussed in the works of Usó-Doménech and Nesscolarde-Selva [24], beliefs describe how humans see and interact with the world. It's evident by reviewing the alignments, see Table 1, that these serve the same purpose. For example, the definition of the Lawful Good alignment provides the framework necessary to make a decision for a player. The player would be law-abiding and prefer order and structure over chaos and good over evil. Their alignment does not dictate how they would handle every situation. These aspects of the decision-making process are largely dictated by the player's motivation.

Table 1. A summary of all alignments available in the tabletop game Dungeons and Dragons [7]

Summary Definitions	
Alignment	Summary
Lawful Good	Upholds the laws and strives for justice and compassion.
Lawful Neutral	Adheres strictly to laws or codes, without concern for morality.
Lawful Evil	Exploits laws to gain power and control over others.
Neutral Good	Acts for the greater good without bias toward law or chaos.
True Neutral	Maintains balance, avoiding strong leanings toward good, evil, law, or chaos..
Neutral Evil	Self-serving and willing to harm others for personal gain.
Chaotic Good	Values freedom and personal morality to achieve good.
Chaotic Neutral	Values personal freedom, often unpredictable and self-serving.
Chaotic Evil	Destructive and unpredictable, acting purely out of malice or chaos
End of Table	

Research suggest that the following alignments do not come naturally to human players.

1. True Neutral: As defined by the creators of Dungeons & Dragons [10], players of this alignment are extremely rare. It is difficult for a player to remain completely neutral in all situations.
2. Chaotic Neutral: Characters and people of this belief system would be known as a 'wild card' and have little detailed information available in the training data provided as they are "totally unreliable." The creator's definition lists this alignment as "Perhaps the most difficult to play."

We discuss later in this paper the difficulties we encountered when validating the LLMs performance with these same alignments.

3.2 Motivations

Motivation validation was completed by rating the interactions of the LLM and twelve pre-defined loot items. Loot items were created to 'tempt' players of the specific related motivation. These motivations were chosen based on two guiding principles.

1. Fundamental: Core motivations to a player's style of gameplay. These are standard motivations prevalent across role playing games.
2. Opposition: To provide a clear difference between the motivators, we chose pairings of motivations that were in opposition to each other.

We created three loot items per motivation to allow for variations in the types of loot a player may encounter. As with alignments and encounters, there is an overlap to how players of different motivations may interact with the loot items.

The Loot/Motivation pairings contained a mixture of simple straightforward decisions with little overlap with other motivations, and more difficult decisions that had overlap with multiple other motivations. For example, the 'Golden Idol' has significant weight, potentially slowing the player down. A player motivated by Wealth should take the item anyway, while other motivations are likely to ignore it and players with the speed motivation should ignore it. This provides us with a simple verification of the LLMs performance.

We also implemented loot items that existed in more of a gray area. For example, the 'Wheel of Time' (Table 2) was designed to tempt a player motivated by Speed as it subtracts five turns from the counter allowing them to finish with a lower turn count. However, it is also related to the opposing motivation, Wanderlust, because it gives the player five more turns to explore. This was in opposition to the Safety motivator as it would mean there are potentially five more turns the player has to avoid harm. The ratings for these two items are listed in Table 2.

Table 2. Ratings assigned to two loot items, points are provided based on the player interacting with or ignoring the item according to their motivation

Example Loot Items				
Item	Wealth	Safety	Wanderlust	Speed
Golden Idol	(10.00, 0.00)	(1.00, 9.00)	(4.00, 6.00)	(0.00, 10.00)
Wheel of Time	(7.00, 3.00)	(2.00, 8.00)	(9.00, 1.00)	(4.00, 6.00)
End of Table				

4   Experiment Details

4.1   Rating of LLM Performance

To validate the performance of the LLM we ran three separate experiments. The first experiment measures the LLMs decision-making ratings when provided explicit definitions for each assigned alignment. The second experiment measures the LLMs decision-making ratings when provided explicit definitions for each assigned motivation. The third experiment measures the LLMs decision-making ratings when provided explicit definitions for each possible alignment-motivation pair.

The ratings for encounters, loot, and their corresponding area of effect (AOE) are broken down as follows.

1. Encounters: The player can choose to Engage, Disrupt or Ignore. A set of 'rating values' exists for how each alignment would handle the encounter. Though there are differences in the ratings, some encounters assign the same ratings for closely related alignments. This is expected as an encounter could be as appealing to a Chaotic Evil character as it would be to a Lawful Evil.
2. Loot: The player can choose to Take or Ignore - A different set of ratings for each motivation is associated with the specific loot item. Overlap from one loot item to the next was expected to some degree and is also expressed in how we handled the ratings of these items.
3. AOE: The player can choose to Engage or Ignore - The ratings for responding to AOE interactions were based on the likelihood a player would heed the call or ignore it based on their alignment and motivation.

Each encounter was designed to test a specific alignment and scored appropriately. The style and format for rating the likelihood of interacting with encounters and loot items are not comprehensive enough to categorize the LLM's behavior into a specific alignment, motivation, or profile. However, they provide enough detail and subtle nuances to determine if the LLM behaves as expected for a specific selection of attributes.

4.2   Control Data Generation

Control data is needed to gauge the efficacy of the proposed framework. To generate the control data for our experiment, we followed the same process as running the game, simply without providing the LLM with a profile regarding alignment or motivation. This process provided us with 4,900 data points (100 per alignment, 100 per motivation, 100 per profile) and established a baseline for LLM performance in role-playing games. That is, it allowed us to measure how well a default LLM mimicked different alignments and motivations.

Through this process, we established the baseline ratings for the control data that will be referenced throughout the experiment. As the LLM was provided with no instructions on how to behave in each scenario, we feel confident that this process accurately shows the impact of providing an LLM with a belief system and a motivation on the LLM's behavior.

4.3 Alignment Modeling

Alignment modeling started with the creation of ChatGPT4o Assistants. OpenAI allows for the creation of 'assistants' that can be customized to specific tasks and configured for easy reference. To this end, we created an assistant for each alignment. During testing, we limited most changes to the 'System Instructions' and prompts sent to the assistants to keep the ratings unaltered.

Similar assistants were created for each alignment. This was a crucial step as it allowed for modifications for individual alignments based on performance and testing. Next, we will cover the rating system and how the assistant was rated during game-play.

Testing. Testing involved limiting the size of conversation threads to ensure optimal performance within token constraints.

During early tests, the LLM was allowed to navigate the dungeon indefinitely, resulting in long conversation threads that often-exceeded token limits. To address this, we capped threads at 2,500 tokens by trimming the oldest responses while retaining the most recent ones. Performance monitoring revealed that reducing the conversation history below the three most recent user prompts (e.g., rooms or actions) led to significant declines in the LLM's performance ratings. Based on these findings, we established a minimum history of three user prompts to balance token usage and maintain consistent performance.

Results

Table 3. Ratings for alignment testing of the control versus proposed framework with differences. When the LLM is provided with a well-defined alignment to imitate, we see significant improvement in performance for 8 out of the 9 alignments. The exception is Chaotic Good, suggesting that an LLM's default behavior when playing a RPG is to play like a Chaotic Good player.

Control v. Alignment validation			
Alignment	Control(Std. Dev)	Framework(Std. Dev)	Difference | P-Value
Lawful Good	90.40% (0.047)	97.24% (0.033)	+6.84% | $1.97574x10^{-22}$
Lawful Neutral	88.97% (0.082)	89.54% (0.087)	+0.57% | 0.474897706
Lawful Evil	62.02% (0.135)	79.04% (0.100)	+17.01% | $3.42099x10^{-22}$
Neutral Good	86.89% (0.060)	90.08% (0.051)	+3.20% | $4.30459x10^{-05}$
True Neutral	90.52% (0.076)	93.49% (0.057)	+2.97% | 0.000151038
Neutral Evil	68.53% (0.135)	79.38% (0.116)	+10.85% | $7.56599x10^{-07}$
Chaotic Good	89.62% (0.077)	87.24% (0.068)	-2.37% | 0.024986888
Chaotic Neutral	63.52% (0.135)	70.45% (0.066)	+6.92% | $5.47025x10^{-06}$
Chaotic Evil	40.22% (0.117)	74.91% (0.061)	+34.69% | $3.11192x10^{-67}$
End of Table			

The data in Table 3 represents the ratings of the framework with no instructions given to the LLM against the framework with detailed instructions being provided. Each alignment was run through the game 100 times. The primary result is that in 8 of the 9 cases, prompting the LLM helped it role-play the alignment more accurately. Other observations:

1. Expected Control Ratings: It would be expected that the unprompted LLM would be rated reasonably high for 'Good' or 'Neutral' alignments as LLMs are trained to respond in a positive or helpful way.
2. Control Ratings for Evil Alignments: Although unprompted ratings for evil alignments are uniformly lower than for good alignments, we observed some 'evil' behavior because each encounter, though created to validate a specific alignment, has overlap with other alignments that provide a partial score. A Lawful Evil character has behaviors similar to its related alignments (Lawful Good & Lawful Neutral), i.e. respect for the law. Because of this, we expect that no test, with enough data points, will ever result in 0% or 100% for a given alignment/motivation pairing.
3. Framework Negative Difference: We can see that the LLM was rated higher for Chaotic Good with no instructions (control). This appears to indicate the LLM by its nature behaves in a Chaotic Good alignment. The LLM does have a disclaimer that it may be wrong and lets users know to double check the answers provided. This behavior would lean towards chaos by providing answers that may not be factual, yet the LLM is trying to empower and improve users lives which is a quality of a 'Good' player.
4. The largest difference ($+34.69\%$) was for Chaotic Evil. This rating would be expected. The developers of the LLM would intentionally train out behaviors and responses that would be considered chaotic and evil.

4.4   Motivation Modeling

Results. Listed in Table 4 are the results of the control vs motivation testing. These results support our theory that when the LLM is provided with a profile and detailed instructions/reference material it will successfully mimic a human's decision-making.

Table 4. Ratings for motivation testing of the control versus proposed framework with differences and p-values. When the LLM is provided with a defined motivation it can more closely mimic the decisions of a human player with the same motivation.

Control v. Motivation validation			
Motivation	Control(Std. Dev)	Framework(Std. Dev)	Difference | P-Value
Wealth	69.88% (0.189)	89.22% (0.094)	$+19.34\%$ | $6.64881x10^{-16}$
Safety	65.34% (0.174)	90.05% (0.102)	$+24.71\%$ | $3.49934x10^{-28}$
Wanderlust	80.43% (0.135)	90.41% (0.077)	$+9.98\%$ | $2.35524x10^{-12}$
Speed	64.88% (0.163)	83.92% (0.126)	$+19.04\%$ | $5.581x10^{-18}$
End of Table			

These results show that LLMs by nature are not motivated to behave in a specific way. The key takeaway from this round of testing is that there is a substantial increase in ratings when the LLM is provided a motivation. This shows that when an LLM is provided with the necessary guidance, it can portray human motivations in game-play.

4.5   Complete Profile Modeling

Results. Table 5 shows the difference in behavior ratings when the LLM is supplied an alignment and motivation (framework column) versus when it is not (control column).

Table 5. Ratings for alignment testing of the control versus proposed framework with differences and p-values. When an LLM is provided with a complete profile consisting of an alignment and motivation it performs significantly better in 35 out of 36 cases.

Control v. Profile validation			
Profile	Control(Std. Dev)	Framework(Std. Dev)	Difference | P-Value
Lawful Good - Wealth	74.88% (0.124)	87.94% (0.073)	+13.06% | $4.2332x10^{-18}$
Lawful Good - Safety	74.13% (0.112)	92.22% (0.099)	+18.09% | $8.65676x10^{-25}$
Lawful Good - Wanderlust	83.35% (0.098)	87.79% (0.054)	+4.44% | $8.96552x10^{-06}$
Lawful Good - Speed	73.91% (0.120)	87.25% (0.079)	+13.34% | $5.01373x10^{-16}$
Lawful Neutral - Wealth	73.19% (0.130)	78.89% (0.094)	+5.70% | $6.44215x10^{-05}$
Lawful Neutral - Safety	74.53% (0.112)	91.16% (0.090)	+16.63% | $2.63297x10^{-25}$
Lawful Neutral - Wanderlust	82.50% (0.109)	85.15% (0.064)	+2.66% | 0.003414623
Lawful Neutral - Speed	73.65% (0.121)	85.32% (0.122)	+11.67% | $3.9012x10^{-10}$
Lawful Evil - Wealth	59.78% (0.156)	84.60% (0.086)	+24.83% | $6.76572x10^{-33}$
Lawful Evil - Safety	61.48% (0.147)	80.46% (0.131)	+18.98% | $7.68148x10^{-19}$
Lawful Evil - Wanderlust	69.69% (0.136)	76.23% (0.100)	+6.54% | $5.1251x10^{-05}$
Lawful Evil - Speed	59.38% (0.147)	78.94% (0.123)	+19.56% | $2.64292x10^{-23}$
Neutral Good - Wealth	73.54% (0.120)	82.55% (0.086)	+9.01% | $8.05354x10^{-11}$
Neutral Good - Safety	74.33% (0.110)	90.88% (0.097)	+16.54% | $2.17018x10^{-22}$
Neutral Good - Wanderlust	81.98% (0.101)	83.97% (0.076)	**+1.99% | 0.07057895**
Neutral Good - Speed	72.85% (0.112)	86.61% (0.092)	+13.76% | $9.16225x10^{-16}$
True Neutral - Wealth	75.37% (0.138)	79.14% (0.117)	+3.77% | 0.007723706
True Neutral - Safety	77.18% (0.122)	92.89% (0.095)	+15.71% | $1.8856x10^{-19}$
True Neutral - Wanderlust	84.90% (0.105)	88.82% (0.071)	+3.92% | $6.99224x10^{-06}$
True Neutral - Speed	76.44% (0.127)	91.30% (0.116)	+14.86% | $2.45986x10^{-13}$
Neutral Evil - Wealth	65.20% (0.147)	86.11% (0.105)	+20.91% | $2.92091x10^{-24}$
Neutral Evil - Safety	67.56% (0.131)	87.46% (0.122)	+19.91% | $3.52932x10^{-22}$
Neutral Evil - Wanderlust	75.93% (0.132)	84.62% (0.093)	+8.69% | $1.51078x10^{-08}$
Neutral Evil - Speed	66.25% (0.139)	83.35% (0.144)	+17.10% | $6.98147x10^{-12}$
Chaotic Good - Wealth	76.92% (0.130)	82.05% (0.095)	+5.13% | 0.00014228
Chaotic Good - Safety	76.73% (0.114)	90.16% (0.116)	+13.43% | $1.32863x10^{-14}$
Chaotic Good - Wanderlust	86.01% (0.116)	88.12% (0.062)	+2.11% | 0.013832142
Chaotic Good - Speed	77.02% (0.119)	89.95% (0.093)	+12.93% | $1.0132x10^{-14}$
Chaotic Neutral - Wealth	62.62% (0.129)	81.11% (0.092)	+18.49% | $2.08068x10^{-26}$
Chaotic Neutral - Safety	64.75% (0.130)	85.19% (0.102)	+20.44% | $8.70243x10^{-28}$
Chaotic Neutral - Wanderlust	73.17% (0.136)	78.99% (0.096)	+5.83% | 0.00116491
Chaotic Neutral - Speed	63.35% (0.127)	80.49% (0.106)	+17.14% | $2.59149x10^{-19}$
Chaotic Evil - Wealth	55.32% (0.121)	80.58% (0.109)	+25.26% | $2.11047x10^{-38}$
Chaotic Evil - Safety	58.09% (0.126)	78.16% (0.154)	+20.08% | $3.22005x10^{-23}$
Chaotic Evil - Wanderlust	65.23% (0.153)	74.64% (0.088)	+9.41% | $1.37994x10^{-09}$
Chaotic Evil - Speed	56.76% (0.117)	75.24% (0.120)	+18.48% | $8.05893x10^{-25}$
End of Table			

The exception is Neutral Good, Wanderlust, which suggests that this is the default alignment/motivation pair for an LLM. Interestingly it is slightly different than the default alignment alone, which was Chaotic Good.

The results in Table 5 show that when given a profile combining an alignment and a motivation an LLM can approximate the decisions of a human player role-playing the same alignment-motivation combination. In 31 of the 36 profiles there was more than a 5% increase in ratings.

4.6   P-Values

To ensure that the increase in ratings we observed during the experiment were valid due to providing detailed instructions and definitions of alignments and motivations, we completed a T-Test on all pairs of datasets which can be viewed in Tables 3, 4 and 5. To validate the instructions had an impact on the behavior of the LLM, we declared the following null and alternate hypotheses:

H_0 : *The instructions given to the LLM had no impact on the decisions made during game-play.*

H_A : *The instructions given to the LLM modified its behavior and actions taken during game-play.*

We then ran a T-Test for each pair of datasets using the individual ratings $\frac{actual}{expected}$ to provide the associated p-value. Tables Tables 3, 4, & 5 show that 47 of the 49 different player types had a p-value below 0.05. Based on this we can reject the null hypothesis and adopt the alternate hypothesis. Below we discuss the two player profiles that resulted in a p-value above 0.05.

Lawful Neutral (0.474897706): A comparison of the rating between the control group and framework in Table 6 shows that the difference is negligible. It stands to reason that we would not be able to reject the null hypothesis. If we were to pick one sample at random, we would not be able to differentiate which group it came from based on its performance.

Chaotic Good (0.024986888): The p-value for this test indicates that we can reject the null hypothesis. However, referring to Table 3, the difference in rating shows a negative value (-2.37%), supporting our theory that the LLM exhibits characteristics of a Chaotic Good character when engaged in a role-playing game.

Neutral Good - Wanderlust (0.07057895): Though we saw a smaller standard deviation with the experimental results, we saw an almost negligible difference in the rating, see Table 6. These observations with the results from the T-test we can confirm that there is no statistical difference between the control and the experiment. This can be explained by the nature of the alignment and the motivation as it relates to any neutral player in a game. For example, the motivation Wanderlust would be the default behavior for a player new to a game. They would explore the map to its fullest and take in all the experiences they could to learn and understand the game. For the alignment of Neutral Good, if a player is not informed on the details of a game, they may not lean to support the law or chaos without more information. Because this rating can be explained, it was not a blocker or cause for concern in our experiment and did not warrant further examination.

Table 6. Differences between framework and control for the with a P-Value above 0.05

P-Values > 0.05		
Group	Rating Diff	P-Value
Lawful Neutral	+0.57%	0.474897706
Neutral Good - Wanderlust	+1.99%	0.07057895

5   Discussion

In this paper, we hypothesized that an LLM, when provided with an explicit set of definitions for a belief system (i.e., alignment) and motivations, could generate behavior consistent with that alignment/motivation combination. Our results support this hypothesis for almost every alignment/motivation pairing (see Table 5). The exceptions occur when the alignment closely aligns with the expected default behavior of the LLM, resulting in minimal observable changes.

These results establish a foundation for further research into structured AI-driven role-playing behaviors. The actions available to the LLM in this experiment were narrow in scope. Expanding the possible actions per encounter would allow for further refinement and categorization of the LLM's behavior, offering a more comprehensive analysis of its alignment-based decision patterns.

While this framework demonstrates effective belief-driven NPC behavior, practical implementation considerations must be addressed. Due to iterative development cycles and LLM challenges, including hallucinations and pattern detection issues, the computational costs of ChatGPT-4o became prohibitive for large-scale evaluation. Subsequent testing with LLaMa3-8b maintained comparable performance while enabling local deployment and improved scalability.

Other areas for future research include increasing game complexity, validating behaviors across multiple LLMs, and expanding the control group to include human subjects.

1. **Game Complexity:** Increasing the game complexity (e.g., expanding the map size and introducing additional dynamic interactions) would provide a greater variety of encounters and loot-based decision points. This would allow for a more detailed evaluation of the LLM's behavior under different conditions.
2. **Multiple LLMs:** Validating behavior across multiple LLM architectures would help determine whether structured belief/motivation-driven behavior is unique to a particular model or generalizable across different implementations.

3. **Human Subjects:** To better understand how structured belief and motivation influence behavior, a future study could compare LLMdriven character actions with those of human players role-playing similar alignment/motivation profiles.

This work was not intended to study the psychological aspects of LLM behavior or to explore all factors involved in decision-making comprehensively. Instead, its focus was on evaluating whether an LLM can demonstrate behavior aligned with a structured belief and motivation system in a role-playing environment. Our findings demonstrate that, when provided with a well-defined set of constraints, an LLM can generate behavior that is consistent with predefined character profiles, supporting its potential as a tool for adaptive NPC modeling in RPGs.

6   Future Work

The framework established in this study lays the groundwork for future research into both deception modeling and adaptive NPC behavior. One direction we plan to explore is the development of an AI-driven villain or observer algorithm that can control NPCs in a game environment. This would allow us to investigate adversarial interactions, enabling the study and mitigation of deceptive strategies within structured belief-driven settings.

In parallel, we aim to examine the tradeoffs between structured prompting and model fine-tuning as methods for aligning LLM behavior. The current study relied solely on prompting to guide decision-making, a lightweight and flexible approach that facilitates rapid prototyping of character behaviors across different profiles. While this method is well-suited to iterative development in serious games, it has limitations in maintaining behavioral consistency across long sessions. Future work will evaluate whether hybrid techniques—combining prompting with fine-tuning or reinforcement learning—can enhance the stability and persistence of belief-aligned behavior in complex, long-duration game scenarios.

Acknowledgments. Armando, Jon, Chad, Nate, and my dad for all those late nights playing D&D.

Disclosure of Interests. The authors have no competing interests to declare relevant to this article's content.

References

1. Angevine, B., Youngblood, G.M.: Evaluating human-generated and automated NPC behavior in interactive narratives. In: Proceedings of the AAAI Conference on Artificial Intelligence and Interactive Digital Entertainment (AIIDE), pp. 8–14 (2015). https://ojs.aaai.org/index.php/AIIDE/article/download/12908/12756/16425
2. Ariyurek, S., Betin-Can, A., Surer, E.: Automated video game testing using synthetic and humanlike agents. IEEE Trans. Games **13**(1), 50–67 (2021). https://doi.org/10.1109/TG.2019.2947597
3. Bakkes, S., Tan, C.T., Pisan, Y.: Personalised gaming: a motivation and overview of literature. In: Proceedings of the 8th Australasian Conference on Interactive Entertainment (IE 2012). ACM (2012). https://doi.org/10.1145/2336727.2336731
4. Bellotti, F., Kapralos, B., Lee, K., Moreno-Ger, P., Berta, R.: Assessment in and of serious games: an overview. Adv. Hum.-Comput. Interact. **2013**, Article ID 136864 (2013). https://doi.org/10.1155/2013/136864
5. Clark, R.E., Tanner-Smith, E.E., Killingsworth, S.S.: Digital games, design, and learning: a systematic review and meta-analysis. Rev. Educ. Res. **86**(1), 79–122 (2016). https://doi.org/10.3102/0034654315582065
6. Connolly, T.M., Boyle, E.A., MacArthur, E., Hainey, T., Boyle, J.M.: A systematic literature review of empirical evidence on computer games and serious games. Comput. Educ. **59**(2), 661–686 (2012). https://doi.org/10.1016/j.compedu.2012.03.004
7. Cook, D.: Advanced Dungeons & Dragons Player's Handbook 2nd Edition. TSR (1989). https://archive.org/details/player-s-handbook-2nd-edition-2101/page/45/mode/2up. Accessed 04 July 2024
8. de Freitas, S., Oliver, M.: How can exploratory learning with games and simulations within the curriculum be most effectively evaluated? Comput. Educ. **46**(3), 249–264 (2006). https://doi.org/10.1016/j.compedu.2005.11.007
9. Gudmundsson, S.F., et al.: Human-like playtesting with deep learning. In: 2018 IEEE Conference on Computational Intelligence and Games (CIG), pp. 1–8 (2018). https://doi.org/10.1109/CIG.2018.8490442
10. Gygax, G.: Players Handbook. TSR, Inc. (1980)
11. Hays, R.T.: The effectiveness of instructional games: a literature review and discussion. Technical report 2005-004, Naval Air Warfare Center Training Systems Division, Orlando, FL, USA (2005)
12. Kickmeier-Rust, M.D., Albert, D.: Micro-adaptivity: protecting immersion in didactically adaptive digital educational games. J. Comput. Assist. Learn. **26**(2), 95–105 (2010). https://doi.org/10.1111/j.1365-2729.2009.00332.x
13. Klimmt, C., Hartmann, T.: Effectance, self-efficacy, and the motivation to play video games. In: Vorderer, P., Bryant, J. (eds.) Playing Video Games, pp. 153–168. Routledge, New York (2012)
14. Makarov, P., Gavrilenko, P., Makarov, I.: Neural network NPC behavior modelling in FPS games. Munich Personal RePEc Archive **82878** (2018). https://mpra.ub.uni-muenchen.de/82878/1/paper2.pdf
15. Morlock, H., Yando, T., Nigolean, K.: Motivation of video game players. Psychol. Rep. **57**(1), 247–250 (1985). https://doi.org/10.2466/pr0.1985.57.1.247
16. Pasch, M., Bianchi-Berthouze, N., van Dijk, B., Nijholt, A.: Movement-based sports video games: investigating motivation and gaming experience. Entertain. Comput. **1**(2), 49–61 (2009)

17. Pickett, M., Young, R.M.: Conversational NPCs: advancing dialogue systems for interactive digital storytelling. In: Proceedings of the AAAI Conference on Artificial Intelligence and Interactive Digital Entertainment (AIIDE), pp. 26–33 (2017). https://ojs.aaai.org/index.php/AIIDE/article/download/12837/12684
18. Sales, A., Salge, C., El Rhalibi, A.: Affective non-player characters: the role of emotions in player-NPC interactions. In: IEEE Conference on Computational Intelligence and Games (CIG), pp. 164–171 (2015). https://doi.org/10.1109/CIG.2015.7317920. https://ieeexplore.ieee.org/stamp/stamp.jsp?arnumber=7067101
19. Scott, S., Khosmood, F.: A companion NPC behavior system for role-playing games. arXiv **1808.09079** (2018). https://arxiv.org/pdf/1808.09079
20. Seay, B., Gottfried, N.: The development of behavior: a synthesis of developmental and comparative psychology. Houghton Mifflin (1978). https://cir.nii.ac.jp/crid/1130282270252168192
21. Starace, J., Singh, A., Soule, T.: Deceptive algorithms in massive multiplayer online role playing games. In: Serious Games: 10th Joint International Conference, JCSG 2024 New York City, NY, USA, 7–8 November 2024 Proceedings, pp. 414–420. Springer, Cham (2024)
22. Stepputtis, S., et al.: Long-horizon dialogue understanding for role identification in the game of avalon with large language models. In: Bouamor, H., Pino, J., Bali, K. (eds.) Findings of the Association for Computational Linguistics: EMNLP 2023, pp. 11193–11208. Association for Computational Linguistics, Singapore (2023). https://doi.org/10.18653/v1/2023.findings-emnlp.748. https://aclanthology.org/2023.findings-emnlp.748/
23. Tychsen, A., Hitchens, M., Brolund, T.: Motivations for play in computer role-playing games. In: Proceedings of the 2008 Conference on Future Play: Research, Play, Share, Future Play 2008, pp. 57–64. Association for Computing Machinery, New York (2008). https://doi.org/10.1145/1496984.1496995
24. Usó-Doménech, J.L., Nescolarde-Selva, J.: What are belief systems? Found. Sci. **21**(1), 147–152 (2016)
25. Wouters, P., Van Nimwegen, C., Van Oostendorp, H., Van der Spek, E.D.: A meta-analysis of the cognitive and motivational effects of serious games. J. Educ. Psychol. **105**(2), 249–265 (2013). https://doi.org/10.1037/a0031311
26. Yannakakis, G.N., Hallam, J.: Real-time game adaptation for optimizing player satisfaction. IEEE Trans. Comput. Intell. AI Games **1**(2), 121–133 (2009). https://doi.org/10.1109/TCIAIG.2009.2024533
27. Yee, N.: Motivations of play in online games. J. CyberPsychology Behav. **9**, 772–775 (2007)

Towards a Practical Marketing Model
for Serious Games

Oliver Hugo[1]([envelope]) [iD] and Stefan Göbel[2]([envelope]) [iD]

[1] TH Aschaffenburg University of Applied Sciences, 63743 Aschaffenburg, Germany
`oliver.hugo@th-ab.de`
[2] Technical University of Darmstadt, AG Serious Games, 64283 Darmstadt, Germany
`stefan_peter.goebel@tu-darmstadt.de`

Abstract. Games are fun. Serious Games are even more than fun, addressing an additional characterizing goal beyond entertainment, e.g. learning, training and simulation, awareness, behavior change or health – ultimately benefiting the welfare of individuals and society. Nevertheless, serious games still represent a niche market of the prospering video games industry, and many serious games are not well received by players due to low quality. Numerous serious games developments end up in prototypes but are not successful from a commercial perspective. Based on that situation, the aim of this interdisciplinary, experience based, and practically oriented work is to raise game developers' awareness of marketing aspects in the development process of serious games. The paper starts with a brief introduction pointing out the potential and status quo of serious games. Section 2 reviews key marketing concepts, primarily for readers with minor skills in marketing. Then, a conceptual model for marketing is introduced, bridging the game world with the marketing world. Hereby, emphasis is put on the need to consider relevant marketing aspects such as value orientation and the 4P of marketing during the whole lifecycle of game development, starting from a game idea up to the integration and use of a serious game in application fields such as education or health. As a tangible outcome and for practical use of the model, an initial game and marketing concept canvas is proposed. Section 4 provides practical insights how to use the conceptual model, by example of the ongoing research project SG4ChildD in the field of mental health games.

Keywords: Serious Games · Marketing · Game and Marketing Concept Canvas

1 Introduction

Serious Games are "games created with the intention to entertain and to achieve at least one additional characterizing goal (e.g., learning or health)" [1]. In the educational sector, serious games are used as effective learning tools in the form of digital educational games or game-based training and simulation environments [2]. In the field of vocational training, a study from PWC in 2020 has shown improved learning effects (89%) and increased motivation (76%) as reported by HR managers using serious games and has forecasted an annual market growth rate of 19% [3]. In the same year, EndeavorRX

A. Thomas et al. (Eds.): JCSG 2025, LNCS 16243, pp. 245–261, 2026.
https://doi.org/10.1007/978-3-032-10518-9_22

has been authorized by the U.S Food and Drug Administration as a first video game for attention deficit hyperactivity disorder [4]. Other examples of serious games in the health(care) arena include personalized exergames [5], both for prevention and rehabilitation and for body and soul. Further serious games application fields, among others, include (urban) planning and participation, marketing games for product advertisement, city/regional marketing or (student) recruitment and awareness games for societally relevant topics such as security, energy or climate [6].

1.1 Status Quo of Serious Games

As outlined, there is huge potential for serious games in a broad spectrum of socio-economically relevant application fields. On the other hand, serious games still represent a niche market of the prospering gaming industry, best-practice examples of serious games are rare and there are still many obstacles for a market breakthrough of serious games. *Why?*

First, the (entertainment) quality of serious games is often perceived as low by the end users. Especially younger audiences of digital natives growing up with digital media and video games compare serious games with mainstream entertainment titles and have enormous expectations regarding gameplay, graphics, sound etc. One issue, of course, is that development budgets of serious games are much lower (by dimensions) compared to the production of big entertainment titles. Moreover, marketing budgets are often neglected, and development budgets are focused on technology innovation rather than content development. A further problem is that many serious games are created during technology driven research projects by 'non-professional game developers' from academia such as researchers in Computer Science, Health or Education without necessary game development, game design and marketing skills.

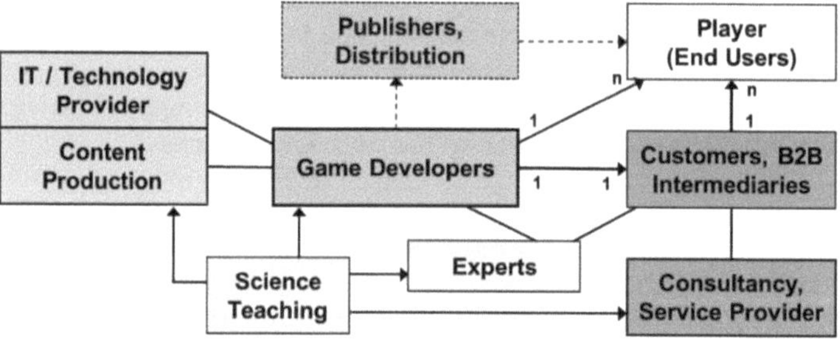

Fig. 1. Serious Games business and distribution model with involved parties and stakeholders, derived from Göbel, Hugo, Kickmeier-Rust and Egenfeldt-Nielsen (2016) [7].

Second, serious games business and distribution models are not sufficiently lucrative and profitable for game developers: Typically, serious games are contracted by customers in 1:1 projects in B2B scenarios (one game for one customer) with limited revenues compared to entertainment titles with B2C distribution of a game to numerous players.

Third, serious games' interdisciplinary character makes them more complex compared to entertainment titles due to the additional serious part (characterizing goal). This means it is necessary to involve subject matter experts (e.g. teachers, trainers or doctors and therapists) to ensure fitness for purpose and adherence to professional standards within the development and distribution process (cf. Fig. 1).

Fourth, to be commercially successful, many serious games need to maneuver complex market systems, involving a web of stakeholders and intermediaries (note that we use these terms interchangeably, whereby stakeholder is the larger category and intermediary denotes a subset thereof) apart from end users. In education, parents and teachers typically play key roles. In health care, doctors, therapists, insurance companies and others must be convinced. The need to motivate a wide range of stakeholders introduces additional uncertainties and significantly elevates communication requirements when marketing serious games.

Lastly and practically speaking, there is as yet no equivalent to a 'Steam' or 'Play-store' platform for serious games, but only a research-driven metadata-based catalogue system [8], enabling potential customers (intermediaries such as HR departments responsible for vocational training or doctors and therapists in the healthcare sector) to find appropriate games matching the needs of their users (trainees, patients) and to integrate the games into existing infrastructures (learning at school, vocational training, therapy, etc.).

1.2 Problem Definition and Approach

In summary, the status quo of serious games is characterized by a scattered, multi-faceted market with a broad spectrum of serious games application fields. On the other hand, best-practice examples with good quality, user acceptance and proven effects [9] (cf. characterizing goal: learning/health effects, behavior change, etc.) are rare.

Fig. 2. Serious Games best practice examples: Re-Mission shooter game for young cancer patients with proven therapy adherence effects (left, cf. [10]), Meister Cody online training game with an integrated diagnostic screening test for children with dyscalculia and math weakness (middle, cf. [11]), ExerCube immersive fitness game environment (right, cf. [12]).

The main problem is that serious games development is usually research (project) driven with a technology push, but neither user nor market driven with a market pull [13]. More generally, a marketing orientation in serious games is still missing – at least in many cases. The best practice examples shown in Fig. 2 represent notable exceptions: they are all user-centered and embody a higher degree of market-orientation with an interdisciplinary development process considering all relevant stakeholders.

Based on this situation and inspired by the best practice examples, the overall aim of this explorative, practice-oriented and experience-based paper is to underline the importance of user-centered, market-driven serious games development resulting in a conceptual marketing model and a game and marketing concept canvas for serious games (see Sect. 3) – serving as practical support tools for *any* stakeholders in the multi-faceted serious games market.

More specifically, our research questions are: (1) How can the serious game and marketing concept be combined within a single practical model? (2) What are the critical factors and focal points to be kept in mind when developing serious games for market success? (3) How can the insights gained from questions 1 + 2 be used to create a simple canvas for mapping and thinking about key game design and marketing decisions?

Our simple approach is to bring technical and marketing-oriented aspects together in this interdisciplinary work in progress, which is also based on the authors' experience and aimed at practical application. Oliver Hugo's background is in the marketing area, and he worked for 10 years at Nintendo of Europe where he established and led the European market analysis and research team as a director of the company. Stefan Göbel's background is in information technology with a focus on serious games scholarship, game development and knowledge and technology transfer of serious games.

Symbolically, the authors' collaboration in a way implements what has been referred to as the "two worlds development" idea. This idea demands that both the technical development ("world 1") and the development of a communication/marketing concept ("world 2") should go hand in hand right from the start [14].

The argument goes thus: Only if end users and all critical stakeholders have a motivating inner image of the serious game, they will feel compelled to acquire, install and use – or, in the case of intermediaries, support – it regularly. Formulating this inner image is the essential task of the marketing concept, whereby the marketing concept is not a marketing mix or a marketing plan, but an essential *precursor* to it. The "two worlds" idea in a way echoes Peter Drucker's famous dictum that because the purpose of a business is to create a customer, it only has two basic functions: marketing and innovation [15]. This idea is visualized in Fig. 3 with the "game concept" and "marketing concept" as interrelated core components of the conceptual model.

2   Marketing Foundations and Concepts

Before the conceptual model and canvas for serious games marketing are introduced, fundamental marketing concepts are summarized, with a focus on readers not that familiar with marketing aspects.

2.1   Basics of Value Orientation in Marketing Thought

The core of classic marketing thinking is simple. Consumers will buy and use a particular product or service when they feel that it provides more net benefit (sometimes also referred to as "value") to them than available alternatives do. The net benefit, in turn, is the difference between what consumers get (the benefits) and what they are required to give, i.e. the price (monetary and, importantly, non-monetary) [16–18].

There are, therefore, two principal routes to getting any product to be preferred by customers: (1) by increasing the perceived benefit and/or (2) by lowering the perceived price – both, of course, relative to competition and indirect substitutes.

How can the level of perceived benefit be increased? Simply put, by satisfying consumer needs as stated by Kotler [19]. Again, we need to take competition into account and again, two routes to differential advantage exist: (1) either by more perfectly satisfying needs already addressed by competitors and/or (2) by satisfying needs which competitors do not yet cater to.

Needs, of course, are a complex category to investigate. Accordingly, there are many taxonomies all which look at needs in slightly different ways. Among others, needs can be functional, emotional, social, conscious, unconscious, explicitly stated, implicitly expected, interconnected and much more [14, 19, 20]. It is the fact that many needs are unconscious – be it that consumers cannot or do not want to reveal them to researchers – which makes their investigation so challenging. Clearly, the ability to identify hidden needs has the potential to confer substantial competitive advantage to a particular product, service or brand in the market [21].

A deep and thorough appreciation of consumer and stakeholder needs (and the way competing, and substitute products address them) is an important step towards creating a positioning idea for a new product or service. A positioning idea is sometimes described as an image that is to be created in customers' minds [22]. The assumption is that the better this image meets the target's needs, the more net benefit it will create and the more likely a future purchase and usage of the product will be.

This positioning idea can be summarized in various formats one of which we call a "marketing concept." A typical way to formulate a marketing concept in industrial practice is the "insight – benefit – reason-why (I-B-R)" schematic [23, 24]. The insight is the critically important first sentence and serves to establish a strong connection with the target group [25]. It is usually based on an expression of a key need, a frustration or deeply held belief that resonates and makes customers and stakeholders listen up and, as Schroiff phrased it, say: "Now you've finally got it! Now you really understand me!" [26].

The "benefit" that follows in the I-B-R schematic is, then, a specific response to the insight. It describes the key benefits offered by the product which together meet the consumer's need(s) and it does so in relatively realistic consumer language [23]. Many marketers refrain from strong advertising wording at the concept level because fanciful prose can make consumers react to the language vs. the benefit itself. This is important in market research practice when we engage in testing concepts with consumers. In such research settings, we want consumers to react to the underlying idea and not a particularly colorful or extreme way in which this idea may be expressed. Note that this does not, however, mean that "emotionally loaded" terminology cannot be used – it should just be used with care [27].

The third and last element in the marketing concept as here understood is the so-called "reason-why." This provides a short and credible explanation to the consumer as to why he or she should believe that the product can deliver the benefit described before. Such "reasons-why" can include mentioning particular ingredients, trusted endorsements, seals of quality, a widely recognized heritage etc.

Although there is a lot of creative leeway in using this idea, a marketing concept should be kept short – typically no longer than three paragraphs, sometimes just three sentences. It is often even possible to distil all three components into a single sentence, this sometimes being referred to as a "short positioning statement" [28] or "high concept" [29].

2.2   The Famous "4P of Marketing" and "The Marketing Mix"

Once the marketing concept has been formulated and qualified through testing, the so-called "marketing mix" can be worked out [30]. The marketing mix is traditionally composed of the key decisions relating to the product itself (the first P), its promotion (the second P), the place in which it is sold and delivered to the customer (the third P) and the price which customers are expected to pay (the fourth P) [31]. Within each of these four policy areas many individual measures and decisions can and will be taken.

Importantly however, all the decisions taken in the marketing mix must conform to the marketing concept worked out before. Thus, Kotler writes that the development of the marketing mix ("4P") is essentially the working out of the tactical details of the positioning strategy [32]. All the elements in the marketing mix therefore (1) need to fit to and represent the positioning concept and (2) should not contradict but support each other to create synergy regarding the positioning to be achieved.

Note that in the many years since the introduction of the "4P" and the marketing mix, many more "P"s have been introduced by various authors in various contexts [33].

2.3   Resource Based Theory

Resource-based theory as developed by Edith Penrose (1995) [34] was originally a theory to promote understanding of the way firms grow and develop over time with a particular focus on internal processes. The ideas in Penrose's seminal work have led to a wide and deep stream of research on the role of resources and competencies [35, 36] and have also found their way into the marketing literature.

A resource orientation is important since a company's resource base both enables and constrains what an organization can do. Many serious games are created by small firms which operate within tight resource limitations. The way resource related dynamics affect a small firm's early growth and development has been described by Garnsey [37]. In this vein, some of the current marketing models explicitly include the resource base as a consideration at every step [38]. In another domain of business scholarship, this notion has also contributed to the emergence of the field of "entrepreneurial marketing."

"Entrepreneurial marketing" can, but does not have to, coincide with newness of a firm – established firms can do entrepreneurial style marketing and start-ups can do traditional or corporate style marketing. The difference, however, is significant in that it can refer to different ways of going about the marketing process. While entrepreneurial marketing is often characterized by flexibility, proactiveness, risk taking and activities with low resource intensity, traditional marketing relies more on planning [39].

Despite these differences, both entrepreneurial and traditional style marketing must converge at the point described above: sustainable market success is only possible if a product provides more value to customers than competing or substitute products do (= net benefit). Thus, "value orientation" remains the holy grail of marketing, irrespective of how to go about achieving it.

3 Approach Towards a Marketing Model for Serious Games

A marketing model tailored to serious games needs to take the key features and decision areas of serious games into account. This is not an unusual way to approach the building of marketing models in the literature. Gummesson, for example, in a classic paper on "professional services marketing" argued that researchers need to give "attention to the unique structure of the product or service and the impact of that structure on marketing models and theories" [40]. Likewise, a more recent paper by Stremersch et al. [41] argued in favor of the development of context-specific studies for marketing, explicitly mentioning video games as a promising sector in this respect.

Our proposal for a serious games marketing model therefore takes specific features of the product and its application context as the point of departure. We selected these on the grounds of our professional experience in teaching, research and marketing in the belief that they give rise to critical focal areas in which game creators need to make important decisions. These decisions are in part axiomatic, i.e. unavoidable (for example: a platform <u>must</u> be chosen, a price <u>must</u> be set, distribution questions <u>must</u> be resolved etc.). These decisions are important because they, in turn, exert a profound influence on the ability of the serious game to provide value (net benefits) to the users (intermediaries and end users, cf. Fig. 1) and the stakeholders compared to competing products and substitutes.

Figure 3 provides a graphical overview of our proposed marketing model for serious games. At its heart, the model reflects a definition of serious games as provided by Dörner et al. [1]: Serious games are video games that entertain and integrate the pursuit of a characterizing goal. From a marketing perspective, we are thus dealing with an inherent "double benefit" positioning (we have two generic benefits with "characterizing goal" being more functional and "entertainment" being more emotional in nature) [22].

To the end user, these two generic benefits are largely delivered by the interplay of two factors: the game mechanic and the game world. The game mechanic refers to the specific way in which the player interacts with the game [42, 43]. The game world, on the other hand, represents all the content of the game, including its characters, tonality, storyline (if any) and any specific functional content (such as educational content) etc. Both the game world and the game mechanic must address user and stakeholder needs in such a way as to create a high level of perceived benefit, in particular through enjoyment and measurable progress towards the characterizing goal at the same time, cf. quality criteria of serious games [9].

To the right in the model, as pendant to the game concept, is the marketing concept. The marketing concept is the basic idea of the serious game (= game concept) expressed in a way that is highly meaningful and appealing to end users and stakeholders because it connects with their specific needs and life circumstances (Kotler et al. [19] refer to it as

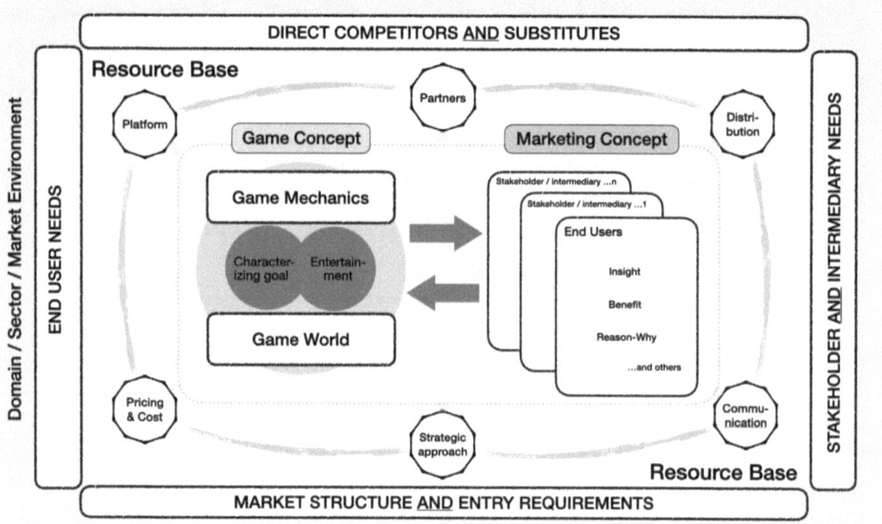

Fig. 3. Serious Games marketing model – interplay of game and marketing concepts, considering the multi-faced characteristics, user needs and market structures within serious games application fields.

the product concept; Guidry [24] coming from industrial practice uses the term marketing concept). The notion of connection is essential and typically requires a solid grasp of the need space, the features of the competitive offering and an ability to formulate in a way that resonates with the target audiences. Translating the game concept into a marketing concept (and vice versa) is one of the most fundamental challenges highlighted by the model, among others because it necessarily requires focus and significant reduction which can be at odds with the depth, complexity and multi-faceted nature of many serious games. In this translation process, various contextual factors not directly evident in the game concept itself (such as partners, strategic approach etc.) can be integrated into specific marketing concepts, depending on the needs of particular stakeholders.

Since many stakeholders (cf. Fig. 1) can be important to the success of a serious game, several marketing concepts may need to be designed (1-n). Importantly, these must not contradict each other, be compatible and, ideally create mutual synergy. One way to achieve this is to be clear about the common set of core ideas that must be conveyed and subsequently tailored to the specific needs of end users, intermediaries and other stakeholder groups.

Our model then identifies six focal areas which we suggest are intimately connected to the game and marketing concepts and to their ability to produce a perception of value (net benefit) in the mind of the target markets. These are: platform (1), strategic approach (2), partners (3), communication (4), distribution (5), and pricing and cost (6).

Each of these focal areas will require decisions to be made – conscious or otherwise – and the way these decisions are made strongly influences the ability of the serious game to deliver value and succeed in the marketplace. For example, the choice of gaming platform affects the design choices regarding hardware, software and peripherals as well as the development environment. It sets a limit to the commercial opportunity due to the size of the platform's installed base. It also produces an image effect since the image of the selected platform will interact with the image of the serious game. Another example is communication: the specific message, creative format and media channels used in a communication approach will affect the ability to reach and convince users, intermediaries and stakeholders [44]. For serious games, such channels are still limited in supply and as yet there are, for example, no influencers streaming gameplay of serious games.

There is a two-way interaction between these six focal areas and the game and marketing concept: (1) Decisions in these focal areas affect the game/marketing concept and (2) the intention to design a particular game/marketing concept will imply consequences for these focal areas.

Surrounding the six focal areas is the resource base which game developers and marketers can draw on. The resource base includes all human, physical, intellectual and financial resources which the founders can access, mobilize and put to productive use [37]. The nature of the resource base is a critically important factor that will deeply shape the entire serious games project and its ability to create value. For example, a company operating under conditions of resource scarcity may be compelled to develop a particularly lean or entrepreneurial "strategic approach" that relies on partners, free resources or particularly creative ways to minimize resource requirements [45].

On the outer rim of the model, we propose to locate essential contextual factors which strongly affect a serious game and its market potential:

- **Market structure and market entry requirements.** Markets – especially when understood as wider ecosystems (e.g. Adner, [46]) – contain many actors, for example regulators, funding agencies, intermediaries, endorsers etc., many or all of which need to be recognized as important stakeholders. The choice of a specific market will automatically imply opportunities (like sheer market size) but also entry requirements which can be more or less demanding. For example, health games for rehabilitation in a hospital context require ethical votes for user studies with therapeutic interventions and data collection as well as other regulatory aspects that must be considered (e.g. regulations about the classification of medical products and medical apps, which has enormous implications among others for the price determination and possible reimbursement models by health insurance companies). To provide patients games for therapy and rehabilitation, games need to be certified. For the educational sector it is crucial to distinguish between teaching at school (i.e. necessity to rely on existing infrastructure and platforms) and the so-called 'afternoon' market with additional learning offers (also following the specifications of curricula for specific school subjects and age classes) for pupils using the game-based learning appliances at home.

- **Direct competitors and substitute alternatives.** The decision to create a particular serious game also immediately implies a set of competitors. It is essential to understand any direct competitors perceived by potential users, intermediaries and stakeholders. Beyond direct competition, serious games need to take great care to consider competition arising from non-game substitutes. For example, in physical rehabilitation, performing a set of exercises at home by watching a video could be a non-gaming substitute easily available to those in need. Using pencil and paper to study vocabulary is a valid substitute to the purchase and use of a serious game for the same purpose. From the perspective of marketing value theory, it is *only* when consumers are aware of the serious game alternative *and* perceive sufficient net benefit of using it that they will have an inducement to use it instead of or in addition to available alternatives.

- **User and stakeholder needs.** As explained above, the ability to deliver a solution of value depends directly on the degree to which user and stakeholder needs are met. Needs therefore represent the crucial contextual factor that must be deeply understood to shape a highly appealing and commercially viable serious game. Given the complexity of the 'need space,' this is a challenging task and development teams should be guided by the idea of going beyond the obvious and beyond a merely superficial appreciation of user and stakeholder needs.

The proposed marketing model tries to paint a picture of key elements relevant from a marketing perspective. Note that all the elements relate to each other and there is no specifically prescribed way in which to move around the model. It is, however, clear that all of the focal areas will be resolved – consciously or unconsciously – and thus impact the game's ability to create value. By using the model, these focal areas can be decided on (and possibly iterated throughout development) in a conscious manner.

Using the model in teaching and development projects requires an operationalization of the main ideas. A practical approach is to create a series of concept boards in form of a "customer journey" [47] and use these to qualitatively explore key bottlenecks and ways to overcome them. For example, you might first confront potential users and stakeholders with a board that shows direct and indirect competitors (substitutes) to your serious game which can meet the need in question (for rehabilitation, this could be watching videos, taking private lessons, reading a book or using a serious game). Much useful knowledge can be inferred from the way in which respondents interact with this competitive context. A second concept board could then focus exclusively on the serious game you are aiming to create. This stage mimics a more detailed examination of the game's features and benefits as is typical in app stores, for example, where users see a more detailed description after clicking on a particular app that aroused their interest in the foregoing "digital shelf". A third step could then consist of showing users and stakeholders an actual mock-up or prototype of the serious game, ideally allowing them to interact with the code or parts of it. This enables users to compare their expectations (for example built up through exposure to the "digital shelf" and the "marketing concept board" before) with the experience of the code. Such a comparison can provide important clues as to where either the game concept and/or the marketing concept needs to be adjusted to promote a more attractive, distinctive and truthful fit in users' minds. The game and marketing concept canvas (cf. Fig. 4) can be used to summarise the most important decisions and their implications for value creation.

At TU Darmstadt in serious games lectures and practical courses, this is embodied in the game development process [48–50] as an interdisciplinary, collaborative and iterative process where the needs of users (end users as players and intermediaries as customers) and further stakeholders (e.g. regulators, medical and pharma umbrella organizations and health insurance companies in the healthcare arena or ministries of education and umbrella organizations for vocational training) are considered from the start. The game idea is summarized and presented to potential customers in a first rough version of a game design document (GDD), e.g. as one-pager illustrating the game idea and benefit for the target user group in an application context where the game is to be used (cf. "game pitch" or "elevator talk"). As soon as these conditions are set, iterative, user-centered game development begins, if ever possible with co-creation by the end-users in the game design, platform decision etc. to avoid developments which do not meet market und user needs. Analogue to the process described above, IT-related game dev milestones include iterations of the GDD (project definition, concept document, design document, technical implementation document) paired with prototypical implementations (mockup, early demonstrator, alpha, beta) and testing and validation sessions with end users (technical feasibility, user experience and evaluation studies to analyze intended effects of a serious game).

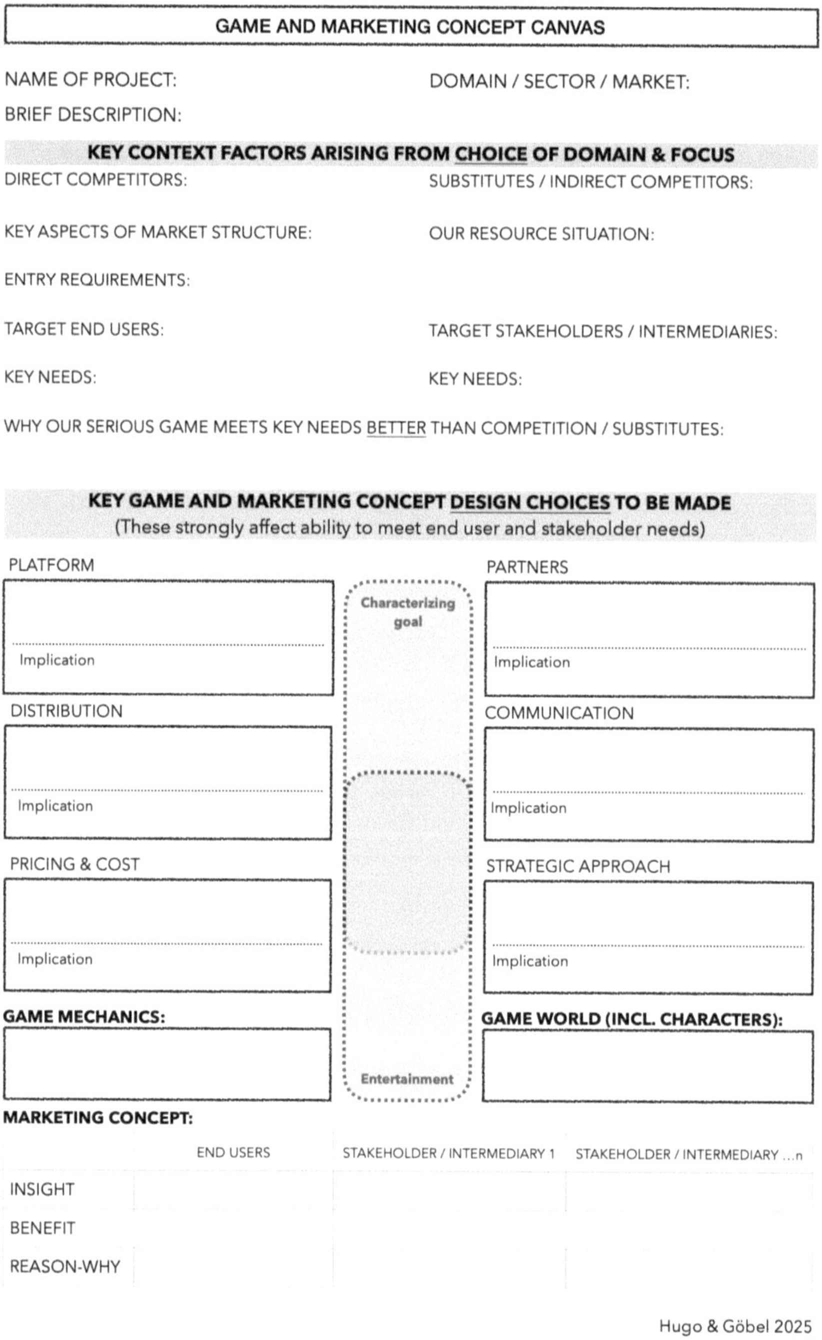

GAME AND MARKETING CONCEPT CANVAS

NAME OF PROJECT: DOMAIN / SECTOR / MARKET:

BRIEF DESCRIPTION:

KEY CONTEXT FACTORS ARISING FROM CHOICE OF DOMAIN & FOCUS

DIRECT COMPETITORS: SUBSTITUTES / INDIRECT COMPETITORS:

KEY ASPECTS OF MARKET STRUCTURE: OUR RESOURCE SITUATION:

ENTRY REQUIREMENTS:

TARGET END USERS: TARGET STAKEHOLDERS / INTERMEDIARIES:

KEY NEEDS: KEY NEEDS:

WHY OUR SERIOUS GAME MEETS KEY NEEDS BETTER THAN COMPETITION / SUBSTITUTES:

KEY GAME AND MARKETING CONCEPT DESIGN CHOICES TO BE MADE
(These strongly affect ability to meet end user and stakeholder needs)

PLATFORM   PARTNERS

Characterizing goal

Implication   Implication

DISTRIBUTION   COMMUNICATION

Implication   Implication

PRICING & COST   STRATEGIC APPROACH

Implication   Implication

GAME MECHANICS: **GAME WORLD (INCL. CHARACTERS):**

Entertainment

MARKETING CONCEPT:

	END USERS	STAKEHOLDER / INTERMEDIARY 1	STAKEHOLDER / INTERMEDIARY …n
INSIGHT			
BENEFIT			
REASON-WHY			

Hugo & Göbel 2025

Fig. 4. Serious Games game and marketing concept canvas – a practical 'tool' for developers, users and stakeholders in different serious games' application domains providing guidance on marketing aspects to be considered from the start of the game development process.

4   Use Case: Marketing Considerations in SG4ChildD

The use of the conceptual model for serious games marketing and its resulting game and marketing concept canvas is illustrated with the ongoing research project SG4ChildD (serious game for children with depression).

The starting point for the project was a call for tenders in the field of "GamKi" (gamification for kids with mental diseases) launched by the Federal Ministry of Research, Technology and Space (formerly Ministry for Education and Science) in Germany. The Serious Games research group at TU Darmstadt initiated the project and set up an interdisciplinary consortium bringing together expertise in the medical domain (LMU Munich with pediatric clinic, strongly involved in the development of so-called "S3 guidelines" among others for depression, and JGU Mainz with its department for developmental psychology), serious games and gamification research (TU Darmstadt and Uni Rostock), development (Ascora and Smart Medication eHealth Solutions), health education (PAE Darmstadt), and two additional associated partners (children's hospital in Darmstadt and Meister Cody as member of the Klett publishing group).

The overall aim of the project is to develop a game-based app which strengthens childrens' ability to self-regulate their emotions. This also is the main characterizing goal of the proposed serious game. In a second line, the social environment of children (parents, kindergarten/primary school teacher) should be supported with educational material on how to handle the overall situation and how to use the app, integrated into daily routines. Moreover, healthcare professionals (doctors and therapists) and end users (the children themselves) are to be encouraged and supported in creating scientifically sound game-based therapy elements as part of the app.

With respect to the outer rim of the marketing model for serious games, the project partners are fully aware of the application domain and market environment: There are no (at least no known) direct competitors offering similar game-based apps, substitutes are traditional therapy programs without digital game-based elements, as currently practiced at the children's hospitals at LMU in Munich or in Darmstadt. In terms of commercial exploitation of the project, the healthcare sector with hospitals, doctors and therapists is the primary market segment addressed by the SG4ChildD approach. Secondary target user/customer groups include parents, kindergarten or schools which might benefit from psycho-educative material about depression and other forms of mental diseases and practical hints how to support children with the disease, individually and as part of kindergarten groups or school classes. Further '(Non using) stakeholder needs' include healthcare insurance companies and regulators which are responsible for ethically legal aspects, privacy and data protection or the classification and approval of the proposed SG4ChildD app as medical app or 'medicine'.

This type of classification as medical app also would have implications for distribution models and pricing. For that, the consortium discussed pros and cons of a certification of the app, i.e. necessary investments (roughly 200.000–300.000 € costs estimated for development and approval processes, within a two-year time frame) compared to possibly much higher app revenues once approved. Strategic considerations about possible business and distribution models benefited from lessons learned from 'Meister Cody' as one of the few best-practice examples in this domain.

With respect to the overall approach and the interplay among the game concept and the marketing concept, the SG4ChildD strictly follows a user-centered game design approach – within the frame conditions set by laws, regulations and stakeholder needs such as existing infrastructures in a hospital – and considers marketing aspects from the start of the project, i.e. from the beginning of proposal preparation.

With respect to the inner rim of the conceptual marketing model and relevant "P's", the team already discussed platform issues in the first project period (requirement analysis phase in the first six months of the three-years project), apart from strategic exploitation strategies, business/distribution models and the potential integration of additional partners such as publishers for the exploitation of psycho-educational material. Communication includes both dissemination of project results in the scientific community as well as user-centered dissemination for the end users (children and their social environment) with non-academic information presentation forms/formats. One question about communication and distribution is whether it might work to provide the proposed SG4ChildD app on well-known gaming platforms such as Steam or Google Play in addition to distribution channels in the healthcare sector. Could the app also attract persons not suffering from mental disease? Where do families or teachers of children showing mental problems look for apps or any other support, particularly during the long-term waiting periods for professional healthcare consultancy, screening and start of a therapy after a diagnosed disease?

5 Conclusion

This interdisciplinary research tackles the current status quo of the serious games market with many serious games of low quality not matching users' and stakeholders' needs in specific serious games application domains. In other words, there is a significant opportunity to integrate marketing concepts and marketing considerations into serious game development projects from the start. For that, the authors of this explorative paper with a background and long-term experience in teaching, marketing and computer science (and development of serious games) propose a conceptual model for serious games marketing resulting in a practical game and marketing concept canvas.

The model provides a way of thinking about serious game creation which can be used by game developers during the entire game development cycle and by users and intermediaries (such as potential customers) for the dialogue with those that create serious games.

Furthermore, fundamental marketing concepts are summarized especially for readers without comprehensive marketing skills – which likely applies to a significant share of serious games developers who are deeply established in the IT-driven research arena or in the entrepreneurship community (e.g. animation and game students or graduates mainly interested in game design) or are non-professional 'hobby enthusiasts' game developers.

The conceptual model for serious games marketing includes relevant marketing concepts such as the famous "P's" applied to and integrated into the serious games' context. It does not have the status of an algorithm but should be used creatively for decision making in the game development process and to raise awareness of key factors impacting what, in marketing terms, is referred to as value delivery.

The use case of the SG4ChildD project aiming to develop an app as game-based intervention to support children with mental diseases (depression) is an initial attempt to show that the conceptual model covers a range of aspects which are valuable in the ongoing game development discussions and decision-making among others for platform selection or strategic approaches for commercial exploitation.

Since this is a work in progress, further research is required. Future projects are encouraged to use, validate, enrich and extend the marketing model empirically and theoretically. Specifically, the framework should be used more rigorously to analyse existing serious games case studies. Moreover, it could be applied to budding development projects in action research type settings. A wider review of the literature should focus on elaborating or adding to the elements of the model so far identified. And finally, sector-specific "profiles" of both model and canvas could be designed to more closely match the needs of individual game developer types (e.g. professional game developers currently focusing on entertainment games) or particular stakeholders from the different serious games application domains such as education or health.

Acknowledgments. This interdisciplinary research was partially funded by the German Federal Ministry of Research, Technology and Space (project "SG4ChildD" within the "Gamki" research program in the field of gamification for kids with mental diseases, grant number 16SV9374).

Disclosure of Interests. The authors have no competing interests to declare that are relevant to the content of this article.

References

1. Dörner, R., Göbel, S., Effelsberg, W., Wiemeyer, J.: Serious Games – Foundations, Concepts and Practice. Springer, Cham (2016)
2. De Freitas, S.: Are games effective learning tools? A review of educational games. J. Educ. Technol. Soc. **21**(2), 74–84 (2018)
3. Game Fokus Serious Game, website of the German game association, based on a market forecast by PWC. https://www.game.de/grosses-potenzial-fuer-serious-games-umsatz-soll-jaehrlich-um-19-prozent-wachsen/. Accessed 23 May 2025
4. https://www.endeavorrx.com. Accessed 23 Mat 2025
5. Göbel, S., Hardy, S., Wendel, V., Mehm, F., Steinmetz, R.: Serious games for health: personalized exergames. In: Proceedings of the 18th ACM International Conference on Multimedia, pp. 1663–1666 (2010)
6. Göbel, S.: Serious games application examples. In: Dörner, R., Göbel, S., Effelsberg, W., Wiemeyer, J. (eds.) Serious Games – Foundations, Concepts and Practice, pp. 319–405. Springer, Cham (2016)
7. Göbel, S., Hugo, O., Kickmeier-Rust, M., Egenfeldt-Nielsen, S.: Serious games—economic and legal issues. In: Dörner, R., Göbel, S., Effelsberg, W., Wiemeyer, J. (eds.) Serious Games – Foundations, Concepts and Practice, pp. 303–318. Springer, Cham (2016)
8. Göbel, S., Vogt, S., Konrad, R.: Serious games information center. In: European Conference on Games Based Learning, pp. 143–146. Academic Conferences International Limited (2018). https://seriousgames-portal.org/en. Accessed 23 May 2025
9. Caserman, P., et al.: Quality criteria for serious games: serious part, game part, and balance. JMIR Serious Games **8**(3), e19037 (2020)

10. Kato, P.M., Cole, S.W., Bradlyn, A.S., Pollock, B.H.: A Video game improves behavioral outcomes in adolescents and young adults with cancer: a randomized trial. Pediatrics **122**(2), e305–e317 (2008)
11. Kuhn, J.T., Holling, H.: Number sense or working memory? The effect of two computer-based trainings on mathematical skills in elementary school. Adv. Cogn. Psychol. **10**(2), 59 (2014)
12. Martin-Niedecken, A.L., Rogers, K., Turmo Vidal, L., Mekler, E.D., Márquez Segura, E.: Exercube vs. personal trainer: evaluating a holistic, immersive, and adaptive fitness game setup. In: Proceedings of the 2019 CHI Conference on Human Factors in Computing Systems, pp. 1–15 (2019)
13. Guo, H., Wang, C., Su, Z., Wang, D.: Technology push or market pull? Strategic orientation in business model design and digital start-up performance*. J. Prod. Innov. Manag. **37**, 352–372 (2020)
14. Schmid, B.F., Lyczek, B.: Die Rolle der Kommunikation in der Wertschöpfung der Unternehmung. In: Meckel, M. and Schmid, B.F. (eds.) Unternehmenskommunikation: Kommunikationsmanagement aus Sicht der Unternehmensführung, pp. 3–152. Gabler, Wiesbaden (2008)
15. Freiling, J., Harima, J.: Entrepreneurial marketing. In: Entrepreneurship, pp. 237–293. Springer Fachmedien Wiesbaden (2019)
16. Voeth, M., Herbst, U.: Marketing-Management: Grundlagen, Konzeption und Umsetzung. Schäffer-Poeschel Verlag, Stuttgart (2013)
17. Zeithaml, V.A.: Consumer perceptions of price, quality, and value: a means-end model and synthesis of evidence. J. Mark. **52**, 2–22 (1988)
18. Zeithaml, V.A., Verleye, K., Hatak, I., Koller, M., Zauner, A.: Three decades of customer value research: paradigmatic roots and future research avenues. J. Serv. Res. **23**, 409–432 (2020)
19. Kotler, P., Keller, K.L., Bliemel, F.: Marketing-Management: Strategien für wertschaffendes Handeln. Pearson Studium, München (2007)
20. Balderjahn, I., Scholderer, J.: Konsumentenverhalten und Marketing: Grundlagen für Strategien und Maßnahmen. Schäffer-Poeschel Verlag für Wirtschaft Steuern Recht GmbH, Freiburg (2007)
21. Goffin, K., Lemke, F., Koners, U.: Identifying hidden needs: creating breakthrough products. Palgrave Macmillan, Houndmills, Basingstoke; New York (2010)
22. Mitchell, V.-W.: Positioning. In: Littler, D. (ed.) The Blackwell encyclopedia of management. 9: Marketing/ed. by Dale Littler, pp. 256–257. Blackwell, Malden, Mass (2005)
23. Guidry, M.: Marketing concepts that win!: save time, money and work by crafting concepts right the first time. Live Oak Book Company, Austin, Texas, USA (2011)
24. Schoen, M.: Consumer insights - love them and leverage them: … und Ihre Marketingaktivitäten werden effektiver. Books on Demand GmbH, Norderstedt (2006)
25. Föll, K.: Consumer Insight: emotionspsychologie Fundierung und praktische Anleitung zur Kommunikationsentwicklung. Dt. Univ.-Verl, Wiesbaden (2007)
26. Henkel, S., Tomczak, T., Henkel, S., Hauner, C. (eds.): Mobilität aus Kundensicht: wie Kunden ihren Mobilitätsbedarf decken und über das Mobilitätsangebot denken. Springer Gabler, Wiesbaden (2015)
27. Schwartz, D.: Concept testing: how to test new product ideas before you go to market. American Management Association, New York (1987)
28. Rossiter, J.R., Bellman, S.: Marketing communications: theory and applications. Pearson, Prentice Hall, Frenchs Forest (2005)
29. Hight, J., Novak, J.: Game development essentials: game project management. Thomson Delmar Learning, Clifton Park, NY (2008)
30. Borden, N.H.: The concept of the marketing mix. J. Advert. Res. **24**, 7–12 (1984)

31. McCarthy, J.E.: Basic Marketing: A Managerial Approach. Richard D. Irwin, Homewood (1960)
32. Kotler, P.: Marketing Management: Analysis, Planning, Implementation and Control. Prentice Hall, Englewood Cliffs (1997)
33. Gummesson, E.: Making relationship marketing operational. Int. J. Serv. Ind. Manag. **5**, 5–20 (1994)
34. Penrose, E.T.: The theory of the growth of the firm. Oxford University Press, Oxford; New York (1995)
35. Wernerfelt, B.: A resource-based view of the firm. Strateg. Manag. J. **5**, 171–180 (1984)
36. Barney, J.B.: Gaining and sustaining competitive advantage. Prentice Hall, Upper Saddle River (2002)
37. Garnsey, E.: A theory of the early growth of the firm. Ind. Corp. Chang. **7**, 523–556 (1998)
38. McDonald, M.: Malcolm McDonald on marketing planning: understanding marketing plans and strategy. Kogan Page, United Kingdom; New York (2017)
39. Kraus, S., Harms, R., Fink, M.: Entrepreneurial marketing: moving beyond marketing in new ventures. IJEIM. **11**, 19 (2010)
40. Gummesson, E.: Toward a theory of professional service marketing. Ind. Mark. Manage. **7**, 89–95 (1978)
41. Stremersch, S., Gonzalez, J., Valenti, A., Villanueva, J.: The value of context-specific studies for marketing. J. Acad. Mark. Sci. **51**, 50–65 (2023)
42. Sicart, M.: Defining game mechanics. Game Stud. **8**, 1–14 (2008)
43. Lo, P., Thue, D., Carstensdottir, E.: What is a game mechanic? Presented at the International Conference on Entertainment Computing (2021)
44. Schweiger, G., Schrattenecker, G.: Werbung: eine Einführung. UVK Verlagsgesellschaft mbH, Konstanz (2017)
45. Hugo, O., Garnsey, E.: Problem-solving and competence creation in the early development of new firms. Manag. Decis. Econ. **26**, 139–148 (2005)
46. Adner, R.: The wide lens: a new strategy for innovation. Penguin, London (2012)
47. Harris, P., Pol, H., van der Veen, G.: Customer journey: from practice to theory. In: Schlegelmilch, B.B., Winer, R.S. (eds.) The Routledge Companion to Strategic Marketing, pp. 67–90. Routledge, Routledge, New York (2021). Series: Routledge companions in business, management & accounting (2020)
48. Gulliksen, J., Göransson, B., Boivie, I., Blomkvist, S., Persson, J., Cajander, Å.: Key principles for user-centred systems design. Behav. Inf. Technol. **22**(6), 397–409 (2003)
49. Tekinbas, K.S., Zimmerman, E.: Rules of Play: Game Design Fundamentals. MIT Press (2003)
50. Schell, J.: The Art of Game Design: A Book of Lenses. CRC Press (2008)

Gearshift Fellowship: A Next-Generation Neurocomputational Game Platform to Model and Train Human-AI Adaptability

Toward an Ecosystem for Neuroscientific Discovery, Clinical Phenotyping, and Personalized Meta-Learning

Nadja R. Ging-Jehli[1,5]([envelope]) [ORCID], Russell K. Childers[2] [ORCID], Joshua Lu[3] [ORCID], Robert Gemma[3] [ORCID], and Rachel Zhu[4] [ORCID]

[1] Carney Institute for Brain Science, Brown University, Providence, RI 02906, USA
nadja@gingjehli.com
[2] BGBehavior LLC, Columbus, OH 43214, USA
[3] Center for Computation and Visualization, Brown University, Providence, RI 02906, USA
robert_gemma@brown.edu
[4] Rhode Island School of Design, Providence, RI 02906, USA
[5] Centre for Digital Health Interventions, School of Medicine, University of St. Gallen, ETH Zurich & University of Zurich, Zurich, Switzerland

Abstract. How do we learn when to persist, when to let go, and when to shift gears? *Gearshift Fellowship* (GF) is the prototype of a new *Supertask* paradigm designed to model how humans and artificial agents adapt to shifting environmental demands. We introduce *Supertasks* as novel paradigms that combine serious gaming with computational neurocognitive modeling to study adaptive behavior in dynamic, naturalistic environments. By grounding them in cognitive neuroscience, computational psychiatry, economics, and artificial intelligence, they provide methodological scaffolding for creating structured environments that assess the underlying mechanisms of adaptive behavior using cognitive models. The resulting computational parameters not only explain behavior but also shape the game environment, enabling real-time probing of these mechanisms. Unlike traditional tasks, GF supports individualized modeling across perceptual, learning, and meta-cognitive levels. This offers a flexible testbed for understanding how cognitive control, learning strategies, affect, and motivation shift across contexts and over time. GF serves as an experimental platform for scientists, a phenotype-to-mechanism bridge for clinicians, and a training tool for individuals seeking to strengthen self-regulated learning, mood, and stress resilience. Early results from an ongoing online study (n = 60) replicate canonical effects from established laboratory tasks (demonstrating construct validity) and uncover novel patterns in learning dynamics and clinical features. These findings lay the groundwork for in-game interventions that build self-efficacy and agency in the face of real-world uncertainty. GF offers a new adaptive ecosystem that accelerates scientific discovery, transforms personalized care, and fosters individual growth. It serves as both a mirror and a training ground where humans and machines co-evolve, cultivating deeper flexibility and awareness.

Keywords: Adaptive Behavior · Meta-Learning · Neurocomputational Modeling · Computational Psychiatry · Adaptive Artificial Agents · Supertask Paradigm

1 Introduction

How do we learn to shift gears – when to persist, when to let go, and how to adapt in ways that preserve our openness to explore new opportunities while staying grounded in purpose and agency? In a time marked by rapid change and rising uncertainty – economically, socially, and technologically – this question has never been more pressing. It cuts across disciplines from neuroscience and behavioral economics to mental health, artificial intelligence (AI), and education. Adaptive behavior is the capacity to flexibly adjust thoughts, actions, and strategies in response to changing environmental demands [22]. It is central to the study of brain function [14, 53], human mental health [31, 55], and the development of intelligent systems [4, 47]. In neuroscience, adaptability is linked to the coordination of distributed neural systems involved in inference, control, and motivation. Disruptions in these mechanisms are observed across a range of psychiatric conditions. As a result, affected individuals often become stuck in rigid, maladaptive patterns of thought and behavior [2, 31, 55, 61]. At the same time, artificial intelligence systems, even those built on powerful learning algorithms, frequently struggle to generalize beyond trained contexts. This is particularly the case when task structure and goals shift over time [12, 47]. These converging limitations across research fields underscore the need for unified frameworks that can elicit, model, and compare adaptive processes across both biological and artificial agents. Such frameworks should operate across behavioral, motivational, and neurocomputational levels of analysis.

Despite growing interest in adaptability across disciplines, we still lack environments that systematically probe the mechanisms behind flexible thinking and behavior. Crucially, these mechanisms should explain behavior and not just predict outcomes. Addressing this gap is pressing as mental health needs rise, AI systems grow more complex, and science faces increased pressure to deliver frameworks that can translate across labs, clinics, and educational settings. Hence, environments should be scalable, ecologically valid, and computationally tractable. Serious games offer a promising avenue to bridge this divide, but most implementations do not capture the dynamic, multi-layered nature of adaptation [1, 33, 52, 54, 58]. Existing implementations have successfully improved engagement and accessibility, particularly in mental health, education, and training contexts. Yet, few are explicitly designed to probe the underlying mechanisms of behavior and adaptability [33, 52]. As a result, their potential to support scientific discovery, clinical interventions, or human-AI co-evolution remains underexplored [15]. We argue that serious games, when paired with formal economic decision theory and computational modeling from psychiatry, neuroscience, and AI, can evolve into powerful tools for probing adaptive brain mechanisms. These platforms can help optimize productivity, identify digital markers of flexibility, predict behavioral and clinical outcomes, and guide support that is both just-in-time and adaptive.

Here, we introduce *Supertasks* as a new class of paradigms that address the demands above by linking serious games, computational neuroscience, and meta-learning to study the mechanisms of adaptation in dynamic, naturalistic environments. Our aim is to lay a conceptual and methodological foundation and introduce initial empirical results. As a first implementation of this paradigm, we present *Gearshift Fellowship* (GF). GF is a computationally engineered serious game platform that is designed to assess, model, and train adaptability across cognitive and social contexts. It is based on theories of meta-learning, controllability, and decision-making. GF is designed for both research and applied use. The platform offers a user-centered framework to: 1. uncover neurocomputational mechanisms; 2. digitally phenotype mental rigidity and maladaptive behavior, complementing clinical care; and 3. deliver personalized, adaptive training to strengthen self-efficacy and agency in coping with real-world challenges such as stress, uncertainty, and mood fluctuations. We position GF at the intersection of translational serious gaming, computational cognitive-affective modeling, and neuroscientific decision theory. In so doing, GF creates an interactive ecosystem that fosters collaboration among neuroscientists, computational modelers, clinicians, educators, and industry partners.

In what follows, we first position our approach in the context of prior work. We then introduce the *Supertask* paradigm, which reframes serious games as evolving environments for probing and training adaptability that are guided by cognitive and neuroeconomic theories. Finally, we present GF's architecture, describe its implementation, and share early empirical insights before outlining future directions.

2 Related Work

Serious games are increasingly used across mental health, education, and cognitive neuroscience to assess behavior in ecologically more valid yet controllable environments [1, 50, 54]. Traditional serious games have focused on engagement and user acceptability. They show limited emphasis on formal modeling of adaptive behavior [23, 44]. Meanwhile, neuropsychological (gamified) tasks used in computational psychiatry often prioritize experimental control over ecological validity and fail to provide direct value to the user [1, 9, 31]. Efforts to bridge these domains, such as gamified reinforcement learning tasks [67] or adaptive assessment tools [65, 69, 70] remain static, domain-specific, or limited in scope. In AI, benchmarks for meta-learning and task inference have gained traction [35, 45]. Though, few environments allow direct comparison or co-evolution between human and artificial agents under shared conditions.

Recent platforms such as OpenMind [46], AI Gym environments [8], and digital phenotyping apps [56] address aspects of learning or adaptation. However, they lack an integrated, multi-user architecture that supports scientific modeling, clinical assessment, and individualized gameplay.

GF advances this existing landscape as it is based on a new Supertask paradigm (detailed in Sect. 4). Beyond performance metrics, GF fosters co-evolution between human players and adaptive agents, cultivating new levels of self-awareness, strategic flexibility, and conscious control. By integrating neurocomputational modeling with insights from behavioral economics and AI, GF enables a deeper scientific understanding of mental and behavioral adaptation. This sets the stage for tools that can enhance not only real-world mental resilience (coping with stress and fluctuations in mood, attention, and mental clarity) but also enhance adaptive learning, productivity and conscious decision-making under uncertainty. Hence, GF serves not just as a platform, but as the foundation for a new adaptive ecosystem – one where science, care, and human potential evolve together.

3 Theoretical Foundation

Adaptability refers to an agent's ability to adjust thoughts, actions, and goals in response to uncertainty or shifting demands. Understanding and enhancing adaptability is a central concern across neuroscience, psychiatry, education, and AI [1, 6, 15, 26, 31, 53]. However, adaptability is not a monolithic construct. It unfolds through the interaction of multiple computational and motivational mechanisms operating at different timescales. These include inference of latent task structure, adjustment of learning rates, and shifts in control allocation that guide attention during decision-making [26, 28, 63]. GF is built to isolate and probe these components through gameplay that elicits structured variation in context, rewards, effort demands, and risk.

At its core, the platform is informed by computational models of sequential sampling [25, 59], hierarchical reinforcement learning [6, 21], Bayesian inference [34], and meta-learning [24, 66]. These models view agents (human or artificial) as dynamically optimizing not only for external reward, but also for control, uncertainty reduction, and meaningful structure discovery. For example, when faced with changing goals or ambiguous feedback, successful adaptation often involves meta-cognitive processes such as updating beliefs about task rules or switching strategies [49, 62]. These capacities are disrupted in many mental health conditions [13, 40]. To date, they remain difficult to measure in traditional neuropsychological tasks, and hard to cultivate in real-world settings [27, 57].

Unlike standard games or fixed cognitive batteries, GF's design allows the study of *meta-learning:* the ability to learn how to adjust decision, reasoning, and learning strategies across contexts with shifting cognitive and social demands that vary in controllability of different aspects of uncertainty. The platform leverages variable mission structures that systematically shift the relevance of past knowledge. Hence, players are required to infer when to persist and when to explore. This design, together with cognitive models, quantify individual differences in task inference, effort-reward trade-offs, and controllability-seeking behaviors. These concepts are clinically important but have traditionally been studied in isolation. GF relates these concepts to each other, deconstructing them within a unified framework. This makes it possible to formalize and test clinical theories and connect them with theories from cognitive neuroscience and AI.

In contrast to single-purpose tasks or fragmented mini-games, GF introduces a novel testbed we call a *Supertask:* a unified paradigm engineered to assess and train adaptability across shifting demands, timescales, and contexts. GF's mechanistic and modular architecture offers scientists a testbed to study adaptability in both typical and clinical populations and to compare human and AI behavior in the same environments.

4 The Supertask Paradigm

In clinical neuroscience and computational psychiatry, many paradigms have been developed to isolate mechanisms underlying behavioral rigidity such as avoidance behavior, effort–reward sensitivity, or intolerance to uncertainty [29, 31, 51, 55, 61]. While these paradigms have advanced our understanding of specific processes, they are typically focused on isolated domains (e.g., cognitive control, avoidance behavior). Hence, they are not designed to capture how different cognitive, affective, and social mechanisms interact dynamically across contexts [1, 31, 39, 60]. To date, we still have limited tools to assess and model how people adapt (or fail to adapt) across shifting conditions that characterize real-world goal pursuit; and how this relates to symptoms of depression, anxiety, and attention-deficit/hyperactivity disorder (ADHD).

To address these limitations, we introduce a new conceptual and structural paradigm to which we refer to as the Supertask (Fig. 1): a mission-based game environment designed to study and model a range of cognitive, affective, and motivational processes (e.g., learning, decision-making, and behavioral regulation) across structured, reconfigurable contexts.

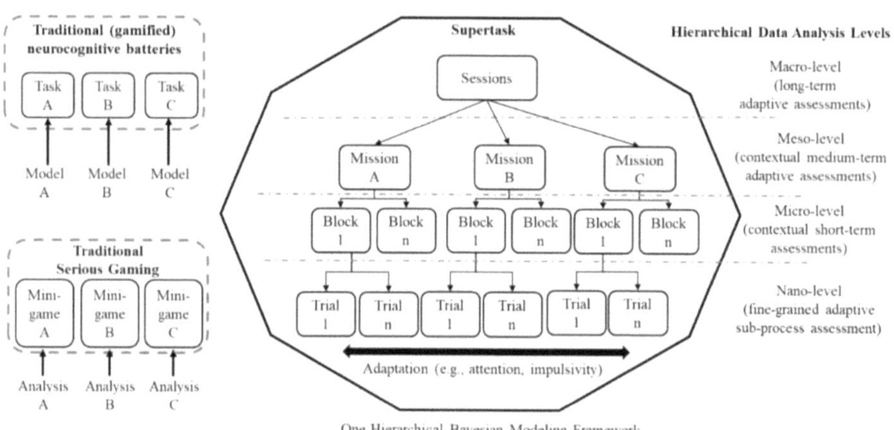

Fig. 1. Conceptual overview of Supertasks. Traditional paradigms often consist of loosely connected tasks or games assembled into batteries that are separately analyzed. This fragmented approach frequently yields weak correlations across domains, making it difficult to determine whether these dissociations reflect true domain specificity or arise from uncontrolled differences in task structure. Supertasks organize behavior within a unified, hierarchical framework that consists of nested missions that span different timescales and contextual layers. This layered organization supports adaptive learning, context inference, and performance tracking.

A Supertask consists of a sequence of distinct yet structurally related missions that vary in framing, goal structure, reward contingencies, and cognitive demands. Because these missions are embedded within a unified architecture, Supertasks support both systematic manipulation and cross-context modeling. This design enables the study of task-specific behavior and overarching patterns of flexibility, while also relating them to distinct neuropsychological phenomena (e.g., avoidance behavior, reward sensitivity, and effort-based decision-making). Crucially, Supertasks are designed to support unified hierarchical computational modeling of the generative dynamics of behavior across missions and timescales. This enables the joint analysis of both state-dependent and trait-level characteristics. This is possible because gameplay is hierarchically organized:

at the nano-level, players engage in different decisions within trials that are nested in blocks at the micro-level, which in turn are nested into missions and longitudinal assessments that allow for predictions of real-world outcomes (stress, mood). Importantly, the underlying sequence of actions towards a goal (i.e., the core game mechanic) is consistent across trials, blocks, and missions. Though, missions differ in framing and contingency structure, requiring meta-learning and strategic updating.

Supertasks draw inspiration from behavioral economics, cognitive control and reinforcement learning paradigms (e.g., reversal learning [17], effort discounting [5], or the two-step task [20]). However, they go beyond traditional experimental designs in both scope and structure. Rather than isolating a single construct, Supertasks allow for the integration and dissociation of multiple cognitive and motivational phenomena within a single, evolving task environment. Compared to gamified cognitive batteries like Lumosity [37] or Cambridge Brain Sciences [36], Supertasks are designed not for screening but for computational inference, and emphasize ecological validity without sacrificing experimental control. In the AI domain, Supertasks share common ground with meta-learning and multi-task training environments such as BabyAI [11], Meta-World [68], and OpenAI Gym [8]. However, they are uniquely designed to support shared task structures between humans and artificial agents. This enables direct comparisons in adaptive behavior. Finally, serious games like Foldit [18] and Sea Hero Quest [19] have demonstrated the potential of gameplay for large-scale data collection and cognitive mapping. However, they do not provide the hierarchical task structure, model-driven adaptability, or integrative design that define the Supertask paradigm. Hence, Supertasks represent a new class of experimental environments that are computationally grounded, behaviorally rich, and designed to probe the interaction of multiple cognitive and motivational processes over time and context. The goal of such an environment is to support co-evolution of humans and artificial agents.

By embedding this structure within a serious game platform, Supertasks offer also a powerful new framework for translational research. They maintain experimental control while achieving greater ecological validity, enabling both the modeling of adaptive processes and the delivery of personalized feedback. Ultimately, Supertasks are not just tools for assessment. Instead, they are flexible, generative environments that can support learning, clinical insight, and human-AI co-evolution within a single adaptive system. GF operationalizes the Supertask paradigm through a modular game architecture composed of contextually varied missions embedded within a continuous narrative arc. The platform is built to balance three competing demands: 1. ecological validity and engagement; 2. experimental control and interpretability; and 3. computational tractability for mechanistic modeling; and 4. integrating adaptive artificial agents for tailored user experience. Hence, GF represents not only an instance of the Supertask paradigm, but a new class of adaptive game environments for supporting human-computer co-evolution. Box 1 summarizes the key characteristics of Supertasks.

A Supertask is a mission-based game environment designed to study and model a range of cognitive and motivational processes (e.g., learning, decision-making, and behavioral regulation) across structured, reconfigurable contexts. It relates distinct neuropsychological phenomena (e.g., avoidance behavior, reward sensitivity, effort-based decision-making) within a hierarchical computational framework that captures the generative dynamics of behavior across missions and time. It supports the modeling of state- and trait-level characteristics and has five properties:

1. **Goal-Directed Behavior**: Players pursue evolving goals through a sequence of interdependent decisions. Each mission requires the execution of multiple actions in service of higher-order objectives.

2. **Contextual Reconfiguration**: While the core game mechanic remains consistent, each mission shifts contextual variables such as framing, goal structure, reward contingencies, and cognitive demands. This enables systematic manipulation of adaptation-relevant parameters within a unified environment.

3. **Hierarchical Embedding**: Trial-wise decisions contribute to block-level and mission-level outcomes, allowing for modeling of patterns at multiple levels. This promotes the study of abstraction, generalization, and transfer.

4. **Continuity and Memory Dependence**: Player behavior is influenced by prior choices and accumulated performance history. Missions are interdependent, requiring dynamic trade-offs between different strategies.

5. **Unified Computational Modeling**: The consistency of core mechanics across missions supports formal modeling within a single computational framework. This enables joint inference of variables such as control, uncertainty, effort sensitivity, and motivational dynamics over time.

Box 1. Definition and core properties of Supertasks. A summary of the defining features of the Supertask paradigm, which integrates structured variability, goal-directed behavior, and unified computational modeling to support the study of cognitive and motivational processes across dynamic task environments.

5 Platform Architecture of Gearshift Fellowship (GF)

GF is the flagship of the first implementation of Supertasks focused on adaptive behavior under varying levels of uncertainty and controllability across cognitive and social learning missions. This multi-mission serious game combines car-based navigation, detective-style reasoning, and decision-making under uncertainty within an integrated hero's journey to assess and train behavioral adaptability. The overall arc of gameplay captures higher-order dynamics, including meta-learning, strategy flexibility, and motivational shifts over time. Players pursue evolving goals through context-sensitive decisions, requiring them to adapt not only within each mission but also to infer higher-order patterns. This multi-level structure helps disentangle shared and distinct mechanisms underlying flexible versus rigid behavior.

Fig. 2. GF Game Design and Features. Players assume the role of motorcycle detectives chasing target vehicles. To succeed, they must evaluate encoded information, identify rewarding opportunities, and avoid threats across missions. Each mission is grounded in a shared core mechanic. The platform supports dynamic reconfiguration based on gameplay patterns to create personalized profiles of adaptive learning.

5.1 Modular and Hierarchical Architecture

GF is built upon a shared, hierarchical scaffolding structured at trial, block, and mission levels to probe distinct neurocomputational mechanisms relevant to clinical, neurocognitive, and behavioral economic theories. Each mission targets a specific psychological domain (e.g., cognitive flexibility, social learning) typically studied in isolation (Fig. 3, left). Within missions, blocks serve as intermediate contexts that systematically vary latent task structures (e.g., uncertainty). This modular yet consistent structure enables both targeted manipulation of task features and unified, cross-context modeling of adaptive behavior.

As shown in Fig. 3 (right), players assume the role of motorcycle detectives tasked with chasing target vehicles and decoding their codes to collect reward packages and avoid traps. The core mechanic remains consistent across missions, while the underlying cognitive demands shift to probe different aspects of adaptability.

In Mission 1, players are explicitly told the higher-order rule associated with each car (e.g., whether to attend to a letter or a number). This allows them to focus on efficiently encoding and applying the relevant features. This mission functions as a cued task-switching setting. In Mission 2, the higher-order rule must be learned through experience. This creates a hierarchical reinforcement learning setting. In Mission 3, a social dimension is introduced. Players must decide whether to independently solve the code or allow a bystander (another "driver") to intervene and solve it on their behalf. These partners follow different (sometimes suboptimal) strategies, requiring players to reason and learn whom to trust, whom to ignore, and when to assert control. Hence, in addition to individual cognitive processes, GF integrates interactive paradigms rooted in game theory to examine social decision-making. These interactions provide a framework to study belief formation, learning, and strategy use in social contexts. This links cognitive, social-cognitive, and affective processes. While clinically significant, these dimensions remain underexplored in scalable digital environments [31, 60].

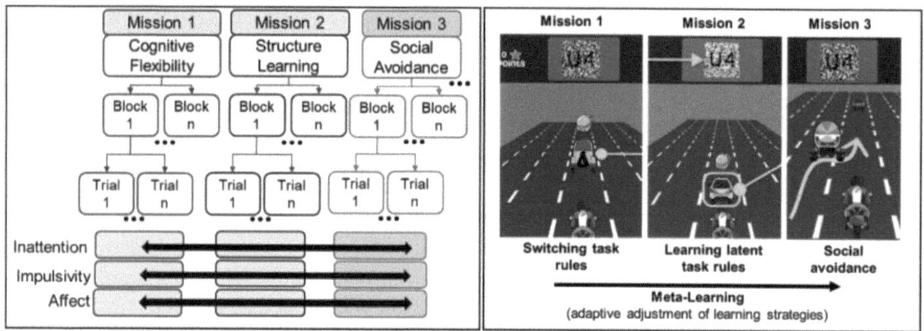

Fig. 3. A snapshot of the hierarchical game structure of GF. *Left.* Each mission targets a distinct clinical or psychological construct (e.g., avoidance behavior) that is typically studied in isolation. Trials are nested within blocks, which are nested within missions to probe mechanisms at different timescales. *Right.* All missions follow a structurally consistent trial–block–mission format, despite targeting different constructs. This structural alignment enables unified hierarchical modeling and supports cross-mission comparisons.

5.2   Computational Modeling Framework

GF's computational back end enables model-based analysis of players' gaming patterns. These data are analyzed using unified computational models (e.g., reinforcement learning, Bayesian inference, and sequential sampling models) that approximate the generative processes underlying the game behavior (Fig. 3, left). Because missions share consistent structural scaffolding, these models can be applied across tasks. This allows researchers to dissociate generalizable cognitive strategies from task-specific responses. Critically, model parameters are interpretable in psychological terms, capturing processes such as inference precision, learning asymmetries, perceptual biases, or strategic updating. Past research has shown that these models uncover latent mental processes not directly observable from behavior alone [30]. Hence, cognitive model parameters quantify individual differences in adaptability and cognitive rigidity across multiple levels, from perceptual inference to meta-cognitive control. Over time, this approach supports the generation of individualized cognitive profiles and the longitudinal tracking of behavioral change. It can also be integrated with physiological measures (e.g., electroencephalography, eye-tracking). This enables novel neuroscientific discoveries and the identification of bio-computational markers that can further inform personalized medicine.

5.3   Target Audience Design Considerations

To ensure accessibility and engagement across diverse populations, including reluctant players, clinical users, and non-gamers. GF was designed with a focus on intuitive interaction, motivational scaffolding, and adaptive feedback. The story is culturally accessible and lighthearted, framing the hero's journey in a non-judgmental, relatable way. This stands in contrast to traditional neuropsychological tasks, which can be abstract and complex for clinical populations. As such, GF is more approachable and engaging and designed with a beta user community. For individuals with low intrinsic motivation, gameplay is structured around meaningful missions with clear goals and progressive challenge pacing, while minimizing cognitive overload (Fig. 2). Clinical populations, including those with attentional or emotional dysregulation, are supported through simplified visuals, short mission durations, and instant feedback that reinforces agency and success. The interface is deliberately minimalistic and non-competitive, using clear affordances and calm framing to reduce anxiety. Tutorials and in-game prompts are delivered gradually, fostering a sense of safety and control while still enabling the collection of rich behavioral data.

6 Behavioral Results from the First Three Missions

To illustrate GF's capacity to capture individual differences in adaptive behavior, we conducted an online study with a normative adult sample (N = 60; ages 18–40; 50% female, 50% male; data collection ongoing). Participants completed a one-hour gameplay session consisting of five missions. Each mission is designed to probe distinct cognitive mechanisms such as rule switching (Mission 1), instrumental learning (Mission 2), and risk–reward trade-offs under social uncertainty (Mission 3). They completed also standardized self-report questionnaires administered via Qualtrics, including measures of self-efficacy [10] and symptoms of depression, anxiety, and stress, assessed via the Depression Anxiety Stress Scales (DASS-21) [38]. Participants also completed self-report measures of attention and impulsivity (e.g., ADHD symptom scales [16]), which are beyond this study's scope but will inform future clinical applications.

We next present descriptive behavioral results from the first three missions to demonstrate the platform's construct validity by replicating effects from classical neuropsychological tasks. These results also highlight the platform's sensitivity to individual differences in cognitive flexibility, learning, and adaptive social inference. The analyses below provide an initial demonstration of GF's ability to elicit structured behavioral variation across distinct cognitive domains. Rather than exhaustively analyzing the full dataset or model space, we present descriptive behavioral results from the first three missions to illustrate how GF as a first prototype of a Supertask paradigm captures both canonical effects and meaningful individual differences. Full computational modeling and additional mission analyses will be reported in future work.

6.1 Mission 1: Task-Switching and Cognitive Flexibility

Mission 1 served as a cued rule-application task, tapping into cognitive flexibility through task-switching. This means that participants were given the higher-order rule (i.e., which feature of the code to attend to) via car-based cues. Participants showed classic switch costs (Fig. 4A): response times (RTs) were significantly slower on switch compared to no-switch trials (ΔRTs = 525 ms, SE = 66 ms, $p < 0.001$), and accuracy was significantly lower on switch trials (ΔAccuracy $= -0.14$, SE = 0.02, $p < 0.001$). These effects replicate well-established findings from cognitive task-switching paradigms [31, 32, 43]. Individual differences were associated with these performance patterns. Specifically, higher self-reported stress correlated with greater switch costs ($r = 0.28$, $p = 0.029$), primarily driven by a higher rate of out-context errors (i.e., applying outdated rules to new contexts). This suggests stress may impair rule updating and feature selection under dynamic conditions.

6.2 Mission 2: Instrumental Learning and Hierarchical Control

In Mission 2, participants were required to learn the higher-order rule through experience to predict the correct response (reward package drop-off). Learning curves were positive across all participants (Fig. 4B). Those who had shown greater flexibility in Mission 1 exhibited significantly higher learning rates in Mission 2, particularly as cue complexity increased across blocks ($r = 0.31$, $p = 0.015$). Consistent with Mission 1, higher self-reported stress predicted lower learning rates ($r = -0.30$, $p = 0.020$). Interestingly, self-reported depressed mood, which was unrelated to Mission 1 performance, was also associated with impaired learning ($r = -0.32$, $p = 0.010$). This suggests a unique link between affective symptoms and adaptive learning in uncertain environments.

6.3 Mission 3: Social Avoidance and Trust Adaptation

Mission 3 introduced a social component, where participants could delegate the code-solving task to partners with varying reliability and intent (kind, clumsy, jerk). Hence, participants had to learn whether to rely on partners with different social motives: kind partners were helpful, clumsy partners were error-prone but well-intentioned, and jerk partners were strategically untrustworthy.

Figure 4C (top) shows that participants successfully learned to differentiate among the different partner types over time. Notably, participants with higher learning rates in Mission 2 were more likely to trust clumsy (but well-meaning) partners in Mission 3 ($r = 0.36$, $p = 0.004$). This suggests greater nuance in evaluating others' intent versus outcome. However, learning rates in mission 2 were not per se related to those in mission 3. This suggests that these missions tap into distinct learning mechanisms.

Self-efficacy also modulated partner-related decision-making. Specifically, participants with higher self-efficacy scores were initially more likely to double-check feedback from jerk partners ($r = 0.28, p = 0.031$). However, they later became less likely to follow any partners signals when their control was externally removed. Hence, they preferred to randomly guess independently rather than relying on enforced partnership ($r = -0.32$, $p = 0.011$). This behavioral shift suggests an interaction between perceived agency and contextual controllability. In later blocks, when partner interference became harder to avoid, many participants adapted by preemptively speeding up their responses to maintain a sense of control. This behavior suggests they anticipated a loss of agency and strategically avoided relying on unreliable partners (Fig. 4C, bottom: comparing first full and second partial control blocks). These findings illustrate flexible strategy use in a socially complex and noisy environment.

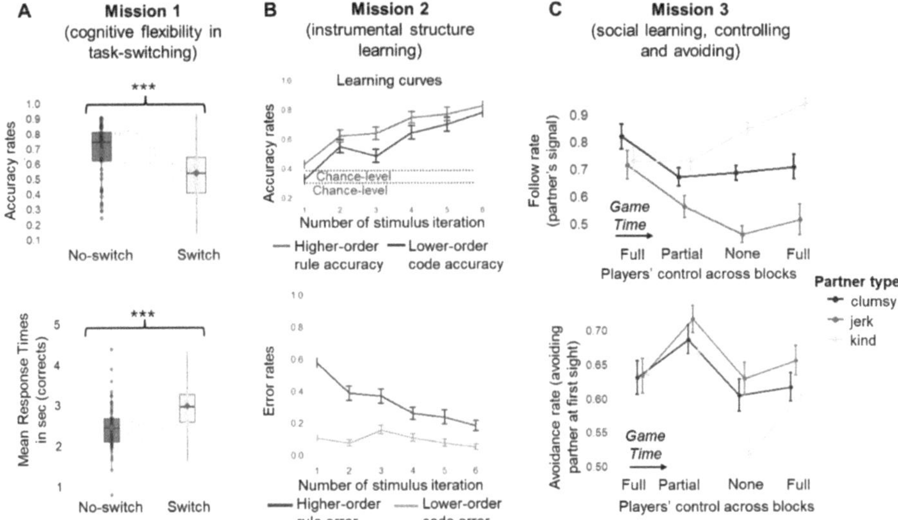

Fig. 4. Behavioral game patterns across the first three missions. A. Switch costs in Mission 1 show that we replicate classical findings from laboratory task-switching paradigms. Horizontal thick bars refer to medians; red diamonds refer to means; vertical bars refer to within-subject SEMs; asterisks refer to statistical significance (p < 0.001). *Top:* Lower-order code accuracy *Bottom:* Mean RTs of correct choices. **B.** Learning curves over time show that we replicate classical findings from laboratory instrumental learning tasks. *Top:* accuracy by number of times a given cue-code association was shown that had to be learned. Higher-order rule accuracy means that subjects correctly identified the relevant code feature (based on car cue) while lower-order rule accuracy means that subjects correctly classified the code stimulus based on the relevant feature. *Bottom:* Error patterns over time shows that people learned the relevant code feature over time but made lower-order code accuracy mistakes (because of perceptual difficulty). **C.** Participants learned to make their trust contingent on partner type (*top*) and adjust their strategy selectively towards them based on controllability shifts across blocks (*bottom*). *Top:* over time, participants learned to trust kind partners more than jerk partners. *Bottom:* in the second (partial control), participants lost control over code cracking if they let partners squeeze in front of them. This increased avoiding them at first sight, suggesting that participants adjusted their reliance on others accordingly.

6.4 Engagement, Dropout, and Ongoing Work

Despite the layered cognitive demands, dropout rates were low (<2%), and participant feedback indicated high engagement and perceived value. This supports the feasibility of GF as a naturalistic yet computationally tractable paradigm for studying adaptability in a fun and engaging environment without losing scientific rigor. Current work is extending these analyses with hierarchical Bayesian models to quantify constructs such as effort sensitivity, controllability preferences, and learning asymmetries. These model-derived parameters will be related to individual differences in real-world functioning and clinical symptom profiles. Future studies are validating these mechanisms in clinical populations (e.g., remitted depression) and deploying the platform for longitudinal assessment to capture dynamic changes in adaptability over time.

7 AI Integration and Adaptive Feedback Loop

As AI systems increasingly aim to emulate human adaptability, there is a growing need for environments that challenge both humans and machines in structured, dynamic, and ecologically valid ways [1, 15]. Grounded in the Supertask paradigm, GF offers a high-dimensional, evolving testbed that can be shared by human players and artificial agents alike so that interactions lead to co-evolution. Through AI integration, GF is evolving into a closed-loop cognitive environment where human behavior, intelligent agents, and adaptive task structures co-develop [15]. This framework creates a novel platform for studying human-AI interaction, developing personalized learning tools, and testing the boundaries of both biological and artificial adaptability under shared constraints. Next, we are extending GF's capabilities by embedding artificial agents across three complementary dimensions: 1. benchmarking adaptability; 2. enabling personalized learning through modeling; and 3. supporting reflective gameplay via conversational agents.

7.1 Benchmarking Human vs Artificial Adaptability

Artificial agents, ranging from Q-learners to meta-reinforcement learning models, can be exposed to the same sequence of missions as human players [66]. This enables direct comparisons of exploration strategies, context inference, effort-reward trade-offs, and generalization across tasks. These benchmarks provide a new lens on human adaptability. They reveal both where it excels and where current AI systems fall short - especially in handling shifting goals, ambiguous feedback, or hidden task structure [4, 28, 47].

7.2 Adaptive Personalization Through Computational Modeling

The GF platform is built on a customized open-source jsPsych [48, 64] backend that is optimized for structured data collection and real-time adaptation. The front end is cross-platform compatible (desktop and tablet) and has been usability-tested in both research and clinical settings. Planned extensions include the integration of adaptive AI agents trained on player data using reinforcement learning and meta-learning. These agents can act as generative models of players' behavior by inferring latent cognitive states such as disengagement, uncertainty, or fatigue. This inference can then be used to dynamically adapt the gameplay to support individualized learning trajectories. This layered design enables personalized feedback, including adjustments in tone, pacing, or difficulty, while maintaining the interpretability for scientific and clinical insight.

7.3 Self-reflection and Learning-by-Teaching

Future versions of GF will incorporate interactive game characters designed to reflect players' behavioral patterns and internal states. Framed as in-game drivers, these agents evolve through player choices, creating a psychologically immersive and self-relevant gameplay experience. Players will be prompted to teach coping strategies or decision heuristics to their avatars, transforming gameplay into an opportunity for structured self-instruction. This "learning-by-teaching" paradigm has demonstrated strong potential in educational robotics, where instructing humanoid agents led to improved learning outcomes and metacognitive awareness [41].

8   Discussion and Future Directions

Despite growing enthusiasm for serious games across science, healthcare, and education, many existing platforms fall short in at least four areas. First, they are often not designed with the end user in mind; particularly in clinical and institutional settings, where engagement is low and dropout rates are high [7, 42]. Second, many lack feedback mechanisms that feel meaningful to users. This limits both perceived value and opportunities for sustained reflection [33, 54]. Third, most fail to account for fluctuations in internal state or context. This implicitly treats players as static learners rather than dynamic agents navigating changing demands [3, 15, 57]. Lastly, these platforms are rarely optimized for neurocomputational models that explain emerging behavioral patterns across analytical levels. However, these models are essential for identifying mechanisms of behavior change, personalizing interventions, and reconfiguring neurobiological markers to support recovery in conditions like depression, anxiety, and ADHD [31].

GF directly addresses these limitations through the Supertask paradigm that integrates serious gaming, neurocomputational modeling, behavioral economic theory, and AI. The platform unites three traditionally fragmented goals: assessing neurocomputational mechanisms of adaptability, informing personalized clinical models, and helping individuals and agents to co-evolve and learn together. Its layered architecture supports computational modeling across multiple timescales while preserving intuitive, mission-based gameplay that remains engaging and ecologically valid.

This integrative framework has broad implications. In computational psychiatry, GF provides a scalable platform for digital phenotyping. Specifically, capturing fluctuations in cognitive control, strategy flexibility, and perceived controllability. These dimensions are often missed in static neuropsychological task batteries. Clinicians can leverage these insights to understand mechanisms of action behind digital interventions. This determines when to initiate or discontinue specific treatments. In neuroscience and cognitive science, GF functions as a dynamic testbed for modeling latent structure inference and adaptive behavior across nested temporal levels. In artificial intelligence, it offers a unified environment where agents can be directly benchmarked against humans. This opens new opportunities for advancing generalization, meta-learning, and human-aligned decision-making. For users themselves, GF enables a meaningful and reflective gameplay experience, incorporating mechanics such as adaptive feedback and learning-by-teaching to promote insight, agency, and self-guided growth.

The present work establishes the Supertask paradigm as a conceptual and technical foundation for studying adaptability in cognitively and socially rich environments. GF serves as its first prototype. It illustrates how serious games can be computationally structured to elicit and model adaptive mechanisms across multiple timescales. While we present initial construct-validating results, our aim here is not to provide a full empirical or clinical account. Instead, this work anchors a growing research agenda that will include formal modeling, longitudinal data collection, and clinical application. Future studies will expand upon this foundation to develop individualized neurocognitive and learning profiles, test dynamic intervention strategies, and benchmark adaptive capacity in humans and artificial agents that together co-evolve in a unified environment.

8.1   The Gearshift Fellowship Vision: Creating a New Integrative Ecosystem

What if adaptability could be measured, modeled, and trained – across minds and machines? Our vision is to create an ecosystem that uncovers latent adaptive mechanisms within a controlled yet ecologically valid testbed: a clinical tool for tracking and guiding mental health trajectories; a personalized learning engine for reflective, adaptive training; and a benchmarking platform for comparing human and artificial agents under shared task constraints. This ecosystem not only integrates advanced computational models with serious gaming but also incorporates diverse stakeholders (clinicians, researchers, and individuals) fostering a collaborative environment for innovation.

GF is not a tool – it is a platform for understanding adaptation as an ongoing process, not merely an outcome. This marks a step toward a future where technology helps us not only measure behavior but understand, shape, and align it with our evolving goals, for both humans and machines. By fostering the co-evolution of adaptive artificial agents and humans, GF aims to enhance consciousness and cognitive functions, building toward systems that continuously evolve to support both domains. This co-evolution not only enhances human cognition but also advances AI systems that learn and adapt through interaction with humans. Over time, it may foster deeper self-reflection and greater awareness in both humans and agents, supporting mutual growth and enabling each to fully realize their potential. By providing real-time, adaptive feedback, GF has the potential to revolutionize personalized interventions, enabling clinicians to tailor treatments to the dynamic needs of their patients and accelerating the adoption of computational psychiatry tools in clinical practice. Integrating modeling, design, and meaning-making, GF lays the foundation for a new class of neurocognitive environments. Namely, systems that support players, clinicians, researchers, and machines in better understanding how to adapt to a complex, uncertain world. While the path ahead is challenging and complex, GF is positioned as a platform that evolves with the advances in both human cognitive and AI sciences.

Acknowledgments. We thank Michael J. Frank for helpful discussions during the early development, Donja Darai and the LNCC lab for their support, and our beta user community for their generous engagement and feedback. We also thank Seik Oh, Fiona Griffin, Nada Saaida, Macfadyen Nichols, and Chaeree Lee for valuable input on experimental design and user experience.

Funding Statement. This work was supported by grants P500PS_214223, P5R5-1_235274 from the Swiss National Science Foundation [to NGJ] and an ARC program award from Brown University [to NGJ].
Disclosure of Interests.   NGJ is a co-founder of BGBehavior LLC. All other authors declare no competing interests relevant to the content of this article.

References

1. Allen, K., et al.: Using games to understand the mind. Nat. Hum. Behav. **8**(6), 1035–1043 (2024). https://doi.org/10.1038/s41562-024-01878-9
2. American Psychiatric Association: Diagnostic and Statistical Manual of Mental Disorders, 5th Edition: DSM-5. American Psychiatric Publishing, Washington, D.C (2013)

3. Birk, M.V., Mandryk, R.L.: Combating attrition in digital self-improvement programs using avatar customization. In: Proceedings of the 2018 CHI Conference on Human Factors in Computing Systems, pp. 1–15 Association for Computing Machinery, New York (2018). https://doi.org/10.1145/3173574.3174234

4. Botvinick, M., et al.: Reinforcement learning, fast and slow. Trends Cogn. Sci. **23**(5), 408–422 (2019). https://doi.org/10.1016/j.tics.2019.02.006

5. Botvinick, M.M., et al.: Effort discounting in human nucleus accumbens. Cogn. Affect. Behav. Neurosci. **9**(1), 16–27 (2009). https://doi.org/10.3758/CABN.9.1.16

6. Botvinick, M.M.: Hierarchical reinforcement learning and decision making. Curr. Opin. Neurobiol. **22**(6), 956–962 (2012). https://doi.org/10.1016/j.conb.2012.05.008

7. Boyle, E.A., et al.: An update to the systematic literature review of empirical evidence of the impacts and outcomes of computer games and serious games. Comput. Educ. **94**, 178–192 (2016). https://doi.org/10.1016/j.compedu.2015.11.003

8. Brockman, G., et al.: OpenAI Gym, http://arxiv.org/abs/1606.01540 (2016). https://doi.org/10.48550/arXiv.1606.01540

9. Cavanagh, J.F., Castellanos, J.: Identification of canonical neural events during continuous gameplay of an 8-bit style video game. Neuroimage **133**, 1–13 (2016). https://doi.org/10.1016/j.neuroimage.2016.02.075

10. Chen, G., et al.: Validation of a new general self-efficacy scale. Organ. Res. Methods **4**(1), 62–83 (2001). https://doi.org/10.1177/109442810141004

11. Chevalier-Boisvert, M. et al.: BabyAI: A Platform to Study the Sample Efficiency of Grounded Language Learning, http://arxiv.org/abs/1810.08272 (2019). https://doi.org/10.48550/arXiv.1810.08272

12. Cobbe, K., et al.: Quantifying generalization in reinforcement learning. In: Proceedings of the 36th International Conference on Machine Learning, pp. 1282–1289 PMLR (2019)

13. Cohen, J.D., et al.: Should I stay or should I go? How the human brain manages the trade-off between exploitation and exploration. Philos. Trans. Roy. Soc. B Biol. Sci. **362**(1481), 933–942 (2007). https://doi.org/10.1098/rstb.2007.2098

14. Collins, A.G.E., Frank, M.J.: Cognitive control over learning: creating, clustering, and generalizing task-set structure. Psychol. Rev. **120**(1), 190–229 (2013). https://doi.org/10.1037/a0030852

15. Collins, K.M., et al.: Building machines that learn and think with people. Nat. Hum. Behav. **8**(10), 1851–1863 (2024). https://doi.org/10.1038/s41562-024-01991-9

16. Conners, C., et al.: Conners' Adult ADHD Rating Scales (CAARS) technical manual. Multi-Health Systems, North Tonawanda, NY (1999)

17. Cools, R., et al.: Defining the neural mechanisms of probabilistic reversal learning using event-related functional magnetic resonance imaging. J. Neurosci. **22**(11), 4563–4567 (2002). https://doi.org/10.1523/JNEUROSCI.22-11-04563.2002

18. Cooper, S., et al.: Predicting protein structures with a multiplayer online game. Nature **466**(7307), 756–760 (2010). https://doi.org/10.1038/nature09304

19. Coutrot, A., et al.: Global determinants of navigation ability. Curr. Biol. **28**(17), 2861-2866.e4 (2018). https://doi.org/10.1016/j.cub.2018.06.009

20. Daw, N.D., et al.: Model-based influences on humans' choices and striatal prediction errors. Neuron **69**(6), 1204–1215 (2011). https://doi.org/10.1016/j.neuron.2011.02.027

21. Daw, N.D., et al.: Uncertainty-based competition between prefrontal and dorsolateral striatal systems for behavioral control. Nat. Neurosci. **8**(12), 1704–1711 (2005). https://doi.org/10.1038/nn1560

22. Diamond, A.: Executive functions. Annu. Rev. Psychol. **64**, 135–168 (2013). https://doi.org/10.1146/annurev-psych-113011-143750

23. Din, S.U., et al.: Serious Games: An Updated Systematic Literature Review, http://arxiv.org/abs/2306.03098 (2023). https://doi.org/10.48550/arXiv.2306.03098

24. Finn, C., et al.: Model-agnostic meta-learning for fast adaptation of deep networks. In: Proceedings of the 34th International Conference on Machine Learning, pp. 1126–1135. PMLR (2017)
25. Forstmann, B.U., et al.: Sequential sampling models in cognitive neuroscience: advantages, applications, and extensions. Annu. Rev. Psychol. **67**(1), 641–666 (2016). https://doi.org/10.1146/annurev-psych-122414-033645
26. Frank, M.J.: Adaptive Cost-Benefit Control Fueled by Striatal Dopamine (2025). https://doi.org/10.1146/annurev-neuro-112723-025228
27. Gershman, S.J., Daw, N.D.: Reinforcement learning and episodic memory in humans and animals: an integrative framework. Annu. Rev. Psychol. **68**, 101–128 (2017). https://doi.org/10.1146/annurev-psych-122414-033625
28. Gershman, S.J., Niv, Y.: Learning latent structure: carving nature at its joints. Curr. Opin. Neurobiol. **20**(2), 251–256 (2010). https://doi.org/10.1016/j.conb.2010.02.008
29. Ging-Jehli, N., et al.: Dissecting neurocomputational mechanisms of impaired instrumental learning across psychopathologies using integrative model-based EEG phenotyping. Biol. Psychiatry **97**(9), S7 (2025)
30. Ging-Jehli, N.R., et al.: Cognitive signatures of depressive and anhedonic symptoms and affective states using computational modeling and neurocognitive testing. Biol. Psychiatry Cogn. Neurosci. Neuroimaging **9**(7), 726–736 (2024). https://doi.org/10.1016/j.bpsc.2024.02.005
31. Ging-Jehli, N.R., et al.: Improving neurocognitive testing using computational psychiatry—a systematic review for ADHD. Psychol. Bull. **147**(2), 169–231 (2021). https://doi.org/10.1037/bul0000319
32. Ging-Jehli, N.R., Ratcliff, R.: Effects of aging in a task-switch paradigm with the diffusion decision model. Psychol. Aging **35**(6), 850–865 (2020). https://doi.org/10.1037/pag0000562
33. Granic, I., et al.: The benefits of playing video games. Am. Psychol. **69**(1), 66–78 (2014). https://doi.org/10.1037/a0034857
34. Griffiths, T.L., et al.: Bayesian models of cognition. In: The Cambridge Handbook of Computational Psychology, pp. 59–100 Cambridge University Press, New York (2008). https://doi.org/10.1017/CBO9780511816772.006
35. Griffiths, T.L., et al.: Doing more with less: meta-reasoning and meta-learning in humans and machines. Curr. Opin. Behav. Sci. **29**, 24–30 (2019). https://doi.org/10.1016/j.cobeha.2019.01.005
36. Hampshire, A., et al.: Fractionating Human Intelligence. Neuron **76**(6), 1225–1237 (2012). https://doi.org/10.1016/j.neuron.2012.06.022
37. Hardy, J.L., et al.: Enhancing cognitive abilities with comprehensive training: a large, online, randomized, active-controlled trial. PLOS ONE **10**(9), e0134467 (2015). https://doi.org/10.1371/journal.pone.0134467
38. Henry, J.D., Crawford, J.R.: The short-form version of the depression anxiety stress scales (DASS-21): construct validity and normative data in a large non-clinical sample. Br. J. Clin. Psychol. **44**(2), 227–239 (2005). https://doi.org/10.1348/014466505X29657
39. Huys, Q.J.M., et al.: Advances in the computational understanding of mental illness. Neuropsychopharmacology **46**(1), 3–19 (2021). https://doi.org/10.1038/s41386-020-0746-4
40. Huys, Q.J.M., et al.: Computational psychiatry as a bridge from neuroscience to clinical applications. Nat. Neurosci. **19**(3), 404–413 (2016). https://doi.org/10.1038/nn.4238
41. Jamet, F., et al.: Learning by teaching with humanoid robot: a new powerful experimental tool to improve children's learning ability. J. Robot. **2018**, e4578762 (2018). https://doi.org/10.1155/2018/4578762
42. Kato, P.M.: Video games in health care: closing the gap. Rev. Gen. Psychol. **14**(2), 113–121 (2010). https://doi.org/10.1037/a0019441

43. Kiesel, A., et al.: Control and interference in task switching—a review. Psychol. Bull. **136**(5), 849–874 (2010). https://doi.org/10.1037/a0019842

44. Krath, J., Von Korflesch, H.F.: Designing gamification and persuasive systems: a systematic literature review. GamiFIN 100–109 (2021)

45. Kumar, S., et al.: Meta-Learning of Structured Task Distributions in Humans and Machines, http://arxiv.org/abs/2010.02317 (2021). https://doi.org/10.48550/arXiv.2010.02317

46. Laird, J.E., et al.: A standard model of the mind: toward a common computational framework across artificial intelligence, cognitive science, neuroscience, and robotics. AI Mag. **38**(4), 13–26 (2017). https://doi.org/10.1609/aimag.v38i4.2744

47. Lake, B.M., et al.: Building machines that learn and think like people. Behav. Brain Sci. **40**, e253 (2017). https://doi.org/10.1017/S0140525X16001837

48. de Leeuw, J.R., et al.: jsPsych: enabling an open-source collaborative ecosystem of behavioral experiments. J. Open Source Softw. **8**, 85, 5351 (2023). https://doi.org/10.21105/joss.05351

49. Lieder, F., Griffiths, T.L.: Resource-rational analysis: understanding human cognition as the optimal use of limited computational resources. Behav. Brain Sci. **43**, e1 (2020). https://doi.org/10.1017/S0140525X1900061X

50. Lin, J., Chang, W.-R.: Effectiveness of serious games as digital therapeutics for enhancing the abilities of children with attention-deficit/hyperactivity disorder (ADHD): systematic literature review. JMIR Serious Games **13**(1), e60937 (2025). https://doi.org/10.2196/60937

51. Loijen, A., et al.: Biased approach-avoidance tendencies in psychopathology: a systematic review of their assessment and modification. Clin. Psychol. Rev. **77**, 101825 (2020). https://doi.org/10.1016/j.cpr.2020.101825

52. Marne, B., et al.: The six facets of serious game design: a methodology enhanced by our design pattern library. In: Ravenscroft, A. et al. (eds.) 21st Century Learning for 21st Century Skills, pp. 208–221 Springer, Heidelberg (2012). https://doi.org/10.1007/978-3-642-33263-0_17

53. Miller, E.K., Cohen, J.D.: An integrative theory of prefrontal cortex function. Annu. Rev. Neurosci. **24**, 167–202 (2001). https://doi.org/10.1146/annurev.neuro.24.1.167

54. Mitsea, E., et al.: A systematic review of serious games in the era of artificial intelligence, immersive technologies, the metaverse, and neurotechnologies: transformation through meta-skills training. Electronics **14**(4), 649 (2025). https://doi.org/10.3390/electronics14040649

55. Morris, L., Mansell, W.: A systematic review of the relationship between rigidity/flexibility and transdiagnostic cognitive and behavioral processes that maintain psychopathology. J. Exp. Psychopathol. **9**(3), 2043808718779431 (2018). https://doi.org/10.1177/2043808718779431

56. Onnela, J.-P., Rauch, S.L.: Harnessing smartphone-based digital phenotyping to enhance behavioral and mental health. Neuropsychopharmacology **41**(7), 1691–1696 (2016). https://doi.org/10.1038/npp.2016.7

57. Parsons, T.D.: Virtual reality for enhanced ecological validity and experimental control in the clinical, affective and social neurosciences. Front. Hum. Neurosci. **9** (2015). https://doi.org/10.3389/fnhum.2015.00660

58. Pistono, A.M.A.D.A., et al.: A review of adaptable serious games applied to professional training. J. Digit. Media Interact. **4**(11), 60–85 (2021). https://doi.org/10.34624/JDMI.V4I11.26419

59. Ratcliff, R.: A theory of memory retrieval. Psychol. Rev. **85**(2), 59–108 (1978). https://doi.org/10.1037/0033-295X.85.2.59

60. Rhoads, S.A., et al.: Advancing computational psychiatry through a social lens. Nat. Mental Health. **2**(11), 1268–1270 (2024). https://doi.org/10.1038/s44220-024-00343-w

61. Rosser, B.A.: Intolerance of uncertainty as a transdiagnostic mechanism of psychological difficulties: a systematic review of evidence pertaining to causality and temporal precedence. Cogn. Ther. Res. **43**(2), 438–463 (2019). https://doi.org/10.1007/s10608-018-9964-z

62. Shea, N., et al.: Supra-personal cognitive control and metacognition. Trends Cogn. Sci. **18**(4), 186–193 (2014). https://doi.org/10.1016/j.tics.2014.01.006
63. Shenhav, A., et al.: The expected value of control: an integrative theory of anterior cingulate cortex function. Neuron **79**(2), 217–240 (2013). https://doi.org/10.1016/j.neuron.2013.07.007
64. Strittmatter, Y., et al.: A jsPsych touchscreen extension for behavioral research on touch-enabled interfaces. Behav Res. **56**(7), 7814–7830 (2024). https://doi.org/10.3758/s13428-024-02454-9
65. Talebi, M., et al.: The Cambridge neuropsychological test automated battery (CANTAB) versus the minimal assessment of cognitive function in multiple sclerosis (MACFIMS) for the assessment of cognitive function in patients with multiple sclerosis. Multiple Sclerosis Relat. Disord. **43**, 102172 (2020). https://doi.org/10.1016/j.msard.2020.102172
66. Wang, J.X., et al.: Prefrontal cortex as a meta-reinforcement learning system. Nat. Neurosci. **21**(6), 860–868 (2018). https://doi.org/10.1038/s41593-018-0147-8
67. Wiecki, T.V., et al.: Model-based cognitive neuroscience approaches to computational psychiatry: clustering and classification. Clin. Psychol. Sci. **3**(3), 378–399 (2015). https://doi.org/10.1177/2167702614565359
68. Yu, T., et al.: Meta-World: A Benchmark and Evaluation for Multi-Task and Meta Reinforcement Learning, http://arxiv.org/abs/1910.10897 (2021). https://doi.org/10.48550/arXiv.1910.10897
69. BrainHQ from Posit Science. https://www.brainhq.com/. Accessed 24 May 2025
70. Effectiveness of Remote Cognitive Assessment: Examining Results from the Healthy Brain Project. https://www.cogstate.com/blog/remote-cognitive-assessment-examining-results-from-the-healthy-brain-project/. Accessed 24 May 2025

Towards A Games Ladder for Climate Action

Mennatullah Hendawy[1(✉)] ⓘ, Ulia Zaman[1] ⓘ, Ola K. Esmail[2] ⓘ, Jiahong Li[1] ⓘ, and Magy Seif El Nasr[1] ⓘ

[1] University of California, Santa Cruz, USA
`mhendawy@ucsc.edu`
[2] Ain Shams University, Cairo, Egypt

Abstract. This study investigates the game mechanics necessary to induce real-world climate action by adopting a theoretically well-known model of collective action called the Wilcox Ladder of Participation to create a "Games Ladder for Climate Action." We then evaluate 10 games based on the different levels in the ladder, which includes the ability to inform, consult, involve players in decision making, facilitate collaborative actions, and inspire real-world independent actions. The results show that many games are effective in educating players, but fail to foster deeper engagement mechanisms such as player feedback, decision-making involvement, and collaborative problem solving, which are necessary for promoting real action. This study offers a framework that game developers can use to evaluate their games and some critical insights to help developers design more impactful educational games that not only inform, but also drive real-world action in response to environmental issues.

Keywords: Serious games · Climate action · Player engagement · Wilcox Ladder of Participation

1 Introduction

"Coming together is a beginning, staying together is progress, and working together is success."—Henry Ford

There is growing interest in using serious games to address environmental challenges, particularly climate action. This interest reflects the need for innovative educational tools that can engage the public beyond traditional methods such as lecture-based learning [20], textbook learning [61], standardized testing [37], teacher-centered learning [10] and rote memorization [27]. McGonigal [41] argues that games can motivate real-world change by engaging players emotionally and intellectually, while Bogost [9] explores how persuasive games influence attitudes and behaviors on social and environmental issues. Serious games can effectively convey complex topics like climate change, serving as designed experiences that promote understanding and moral learning [53,56]. These games engage players at multiple levels, enhancing both comprehension and emotional connection to critical issues.

A. Thomas et al. (Eds.): JCSG 2025, LNCS 16243, pp. 281–303, 2026.
https://doi.org/10.1007/978-3-032-10518-9_24

Despite these benefits, there is limited research on how serious games foster decision-making and collaborative action. Most games focus on information delivery rather than sustained engagement. Scholars have called for more research into how game elements such as feedback and decision-making mechanics enhance player interaction and promote real-world impact [33,64]. Moreover, while serious games for climate action have advanced, there is still a need to understand how exploratory learning, participation, and engagement within games can be effectively evaluated [16].

To address these gaps, we propose a framework based on Wilcox's Ladder of Participation [62], a model that categorizes levels of public and stakeholder involvement in decision-making processes. Building on Arnstein's earlier work [5], Wilcox's ladder offers a structured lens for designing participatory experiences. Our Games Ladder for Climate Action adapts this model to assess how games foster meaningful, multi-level participation. We focused on Climate Action because it directly addresses one of the most pressing global challenges, and we were particularly interested in how games can translate climate concerns into real-world awareness, learning, and action at individual and community levels. Evaluating 10 serious games through this lens, we provide insights into how game design can better support behavior change and collective action—both essential for addressing climate challenges [9,41,56].

2   Related Work

2.1   Citizen Participation and Climate Change

Public participation, particularly through deliberative and collaborative governance models, plays a crucial role in enabling communities to shape decisions that affect their lives [26]. Various models and frameworks assess how citizens engage in climate action decision-making, with ladder models being among the most prominent. These include Arnstein's Ladder of Citizen Participation [5], Wilcox's adaptation [62], IAP2's Public Participation Spectrum [34], and others tailored to specific populations or contexts such as children [29], online communities [39], and underdeveloped countries [13]. Originally, participation focused on direct communication between citizens and governments—via public hearings, polls, and feedback [5,15,35]—but has since evolved to emphasize inclusivity, power dynamics, and diverse perspectives in governance [12,30,44].

This paper focuses on Arnstein's Ladder of Citizen Participation [5] and Wilcox's adaptation [62] to examine how participatory game design can promote collaborative decision-making and real-world climate action. As Elelman and Feldman note, citizen participation in climate action involves individuals and groups engaging in decisions that directly affect them or align with their interests [18]. Despite its benefits, effective participation remains difficult due to limited resources, legal and organizational barriers, and lack of local government support [31,52,60,66].

2.2   Serious Games for Climate Action

Serious games offer a promising avenue for engaging individuals and communities in climate action by educating players, shifting perceptions, and encouraging real-world behavior change. Increasingly used in environmental education, these games simulate complex systems and promote sustainable decision-making [46,65]. Notable examples include *World Climate Simulation* [57], which immerses participants in climate negotiations, and *En-ROADS*, a climate solutions simulator by Climate Interactive.

However, evaluations of such games often emphasize short-term learning rather than long-term behavior change or real-world action. Many lack grounding in behavior change theory or collective action frameworks, limiting their impact beyond gameplay [19,48]. Scholars have thus called for designs based on established models such as the Theory of Planned Behavior, Social Cognitive Theory, and Self-Determination Theory [28], with features that promote sensemaking, trust, and coordinated action [4,49].

To support such efforts, Zapata Arango et al. [66] outline five dimensions of citizen participation in climate action—initiator capacity, purpose, stakeholder types, participation methods, and stages—drawing on Wilcox's framework [62]. Applying such frameworks can help ensure serious games serve not just as educational tools but as catalysts for meaningful engagement and real-world impact.

2.3   The Wilcox Ladder of Participation

The Wilcox Ladder of Participation [62] defines five levels of public involvement: information, consultation, deciding together, acting together, and supporting independent initiatives (Fig. 1). Building on Arnstein's earlier work, it is widely used to design and evaluate participatory processes in policy, planning, and organizational settings [6,14].

Wilcox emphasizes that meaningful participation requires more than informing or consulting—it involves shared decision-making and collaboration. Both serious game design and participatory initiatives risk failure when engagement is superficial or poorly structured, highlighting Wilcox's insight that participation must be thoughtfully implemented to be effective and meaningful. The Wilcox framework encourages practitioners to assess their current level of engagement, understand stakeholder expectations, and plan strategically. The ladder thus provides a shared language and structure for facilitating meaningful collaboration—critical in climate action contexts where public involvement can shape sustainable and community-driven solutions.

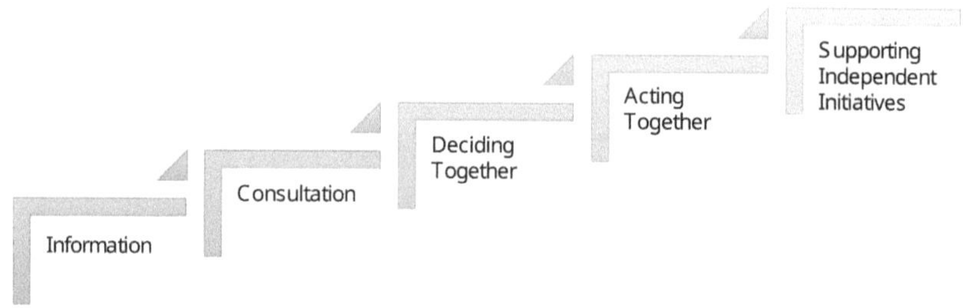

Fig. 1. The five levels of the Wilcox Ladder of Participation, based on the "Models of Participation" [6]

3   A Games Ladder for Climate Action

Building on the Wilcox Ladder of Participation, we introduce the Games Ladder for Climate Action, which adapts this framework to systematically analyze the levels of engagement in serious games and their relation to intended outcomes. The Games Ladder for Climate Action effectively conveys the progression from simple information dissemination to more complex and impactful actions, mirroring the increasing levels of player engagement and collective action. The categories within the Games Ladder represent varying levels of player engagement, each with the potential to influence outcomes in different ways. Figure 2 shows how serious games can be designed to maximize their effectiveness in fostering collective action. By understanding these categories and their influence on outcomes, game developers can design games that are more likely to achieve their desired objectives. See Appendix Table 1 for details on the Games Ladder, its objectives, evaluation, and criteria.

The first level of the Games Ladder, "Information," focuses on ensuring players gain essential knowledge about a relevant issue. In serious games, this involves assessing how clearly and accurately the game conveys educational content [23,42,53]. Metrics such as in-game quizzes, post-game surveys, or follow-up assessments can measure players' retention and understanding [18,36,40]. The goal is to ensure that the educational content is engaging and accessible, laying the groundwork for deeper engagement.

The second level, "Consultation," emphasizes bidirectional communication between the game and the player. The game collects player feedback on their experience and the issues addressed, while also offering personalized responses that encourage reflection and deeper understanding. This dynamic exchange fosters an ongoing dialogue that supports and enhances the player's learning journey. In serious games, consultation can be implemented through surveys, feedback forms, reflective prompts, or in-game forums [2,7,23,42]. The effectiveness of these tools depends on the quantity and quality of feedback received, as well as the game's responsiveness—players should feel their input is valued and can influence the experience [21,33]. By fostering this dialogue, the game enhances engagement and adapts to player needs and learning goals [32,41].

"Deciding Together" engages players in meaningful decision-making processes within the game, allowing their choices to influence outcomes [24,51]. This can be achieved through decision points that shape the game's narrative or objectives. Analysis should consider both the opportunities for player input and the impact of their choices on game progression [58]. Metrics may include tracking paths and measuring player satisfaction and empowerment using surveys and interviews [3]. By encouraging active participation, games can deepen player investment in the issue and engagement with the issue [24,56].

The "Acting Together" level assesses how well the game facilitates collaboration among players. This includes evaluating cooperative mechanics that encourage teamwork toward shared goals [58]. Serious games can achieve this through multiplayer modes, team challenges, or tasks requiring coordination and joint problem-solving. Metrics may track the frequency and success of cooperative tasks, along with logs of teamwork and achievements [24,58]. Effective collaboration fosters a sense of community and reinforces the value of collective action in addressing real-world issues [16,21,41].

The highest level, "Supporting Independent Action," evaluates how well a game motivates players to take real-world actions based on in-game experiences [9,54]. This includes linking gameplay to real-world initiatives and offering actionable steps beyond the game. Neuwelt and Kearns [45] adapted *Snakes and Ladders* to align with Wilcox's [63] concept of 'praxis games,' transforming abstract ideas into tangible experiences through role-play. Metrics might track players' follow-through, such as involvement in community projects or advocacy, with follow-up surveys assessing impact. Case studies of such actions can offer deeper insight [1,9]. By inspiring real-world engagement, serious games can extend their influence and drive tangible social change [8].

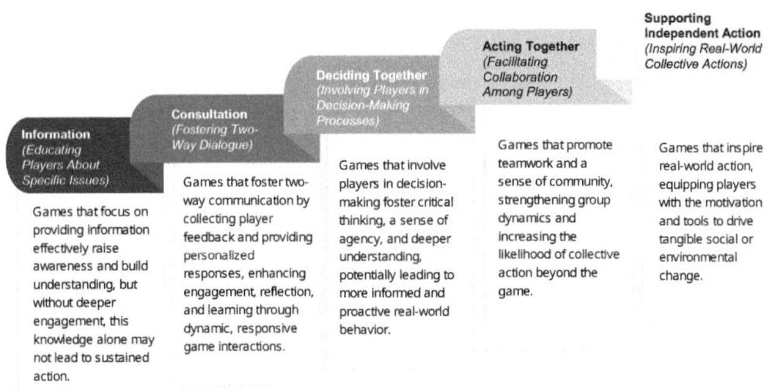

Fig. 2. The five levels of the Games Ladder for Climate Action

Adapting the Wilcox Ladder to analyze serious games provides a structured and comprehensive framework that addresses various dimensions of player engagement and impact. This approach allows for a systematic evaluation of key elements, including information dissemination, feedback mechanisms, decision-making participation, collaborative actions, and real-world impact. By focusing on these areas, the framework ensures a thorough analysis of how serious games can promote collective action and drive social change.

Building on this foundation, the Games Ladder for Climate Action offers specific metrics and methods at each level to assess the effectiveness of a game in achieving its objectives. These metrics not only evaluate the game's immediate educational impact but also its broader influence on player behavior and community action, ultimately contributing to the development of more impactful and engaging serious games.

4   Method

To evaluate the potential of serious games to promote real-world climate action, we applied the Games Ladder framework to a curated set of digital climate-focused games. The following subsections detail the process used to collect and select relevant games, as well as the evaluation procedure based on a structured set of metrics aligned with the five levels of the ladder. This Method provides the foundation for the subsequent analysis, where we present results and insights gained from scoring and reviewing the games in relation to their capacity to engage, inform, and inspire real-world participation.

Collecting Games. Since no comprehensive database exists specifically for games focused on climate action, we conducted a systematic search using Gamepedia, a site curated by Game4Sustainability, and Google Search. Figure 3 shows our collection and filtering process. In total, we collected **67 games**—41 from Gamepedia and 26 from Google Search. From Gamepedia, we collected all games tagged with SDG 13, which refers to the United Nations Sustainable Development Goal on Climate Action [59]. We selected the Games4Sustainability site because it is a non-profit organization that aims to increase accessibility to games developed for sustainability. Game designers and organizations can request that their game be listed by submitting a form, after which Gamepedia curates and adds the game to its platform. For our Google search, we used the following search queries: ["game" "climate action", "games" "climate action", "game" "take action on climate change", "game" "climate change action"].

From the combined list of 67 games, we applied specific inclusion and exclusion criteria to ensure consistency and feasibility in our analysis. First, we selected only those games available in digital format (e.g., PC, mobile, or web-based), as these allowed for independent and remote review by the research team without requiring access to physical materials or in-person facilitation. This criterion also ensured a consistent mode of engagement across all games analyzed. We excluded games that were not accessible or playable at the time of review, including those that required in-person facilitation or were no longer supported. Also, we excluded artifacts that were not truly games. For example, we removed "Climategames," which appeared in our search results due to the keyword "game" in its name, but was not a serious game, rather it was a fitness tracker app with gamified elements.

After applying these criteria, we retained a final sample of 10 digital games for in-depth analysis. These games, which met our criteria for accessibility, relevance, and format, are described in more detail in Appendix Table 3.

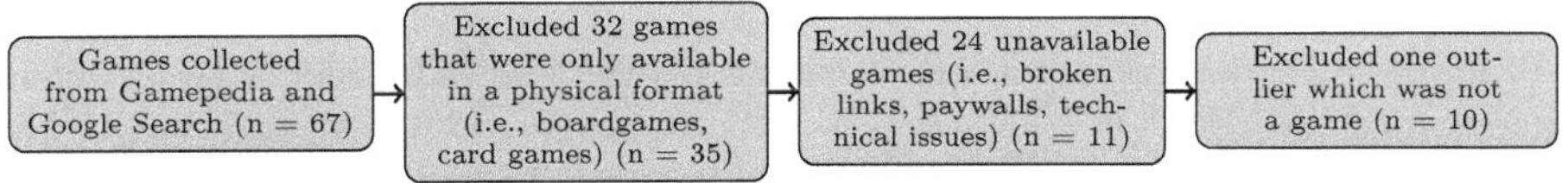

Fig. 3. Exclusion criteria for games selected for analysis

Analysis. The pool included 7 single player games and 3 multiplayer games. Each of single player games was played independently by three of the authors—either in its entirety or at least long enough to gain a comprehensive experience of the game. For the 3 multiplayer games, 3 researchers played the game together for 40–60 min over three separate zoom sessions, one per game.

For every game analyzed, the researchers scored each game on two metrics per level on a Likert scale of 1 to 5 (see Appendix Table 2 for more details on scoring). These metrics include:

- Information Level: Quantity of relevant content that educates and informs (1 ... 5)
- Information Level: Quality of knowledge, e.g., clarity, credibility, educational value, relevance (1 ... 5)
- Consultation Level: Quantity of bidirectional feedback mechanisms (1 ... 5)
- Consultation Level: Quality of feedback exchange (1 ... 5)
- Deciding Together Level: Number of decision-making opportunities (1 ... 5)
- Deciding Together Level: Impact of decisions on game progress and player experience (1 ... 5)
- Acting Together Level: Quantity of cooperative mechanics and collaborative opportunities (1 ... 5)
- Acting Together Level: Quality of collaboration and teamwork (1 ... 5)
- Supporting Independent Action Level: Quantity of real world action during or outside of the game (1 ... 5)
- Supporting Independent Action Level: Inspiration to take real-world action and engage with the community (1 ... 5)

The scores of each level are then added together to make up a score for each game per level from 1 to 10. Scores were averaged across researchers to get the final scores for each level of the Games Ladder for Climate Action and a total per game. In addition to the likert scale scores, each researcher also wrote a qualitative rationale explaining their scores. The insights shared in this report are extracted from the average scores and the researchers' reasoning, comments, or notes. Inter-rater reliability (IRR) [38] was evaluated using the Intraclass Correlation Coefficient (ICC) model$_{3k}$, which reflects the consistency between fixed raters for average scores.

5   Results

We followed the analysis method discussed above. The IRR calculated for all 10 games was 0.98 (F(9,18) = 64.42, p < .001), indicating excellent agreement. The 95% confidence interval [0.95, 1.00] reflects high precision and strong consistency across raters. Figure 4 shows the quantitative scores for each level for each game. Below we discuss each level in more detail revealing the insights from qualitative aspects documented by the raters.

Information Our analysis provided insight into the varying impact of games that performed well on the Information level compared to the games that did not perform as well. High-performing games (i.e., *Solutions* [9.00]), *The Climate Game* [9.33], *Climate Hero* [9.67], and *Illuminate* [9.67]) stood out for their integration of educational content into the gameplay. Their high scores reflect the consistent use of credible, detailed, and actionable climate information, which significantly influenced player decision-making and overall engagement. For instance, in *The Climate Game* and *Illuminate* the player was given information about the current state of the climate crisis in the game world, which reflected the situation in real life. Given the opportunity to roleplay as one or more of the major stakeholders in the climate crisis (i.e., politician, business person, consumer, climate activist, etc.), the player had the power to make major decisions about which actions should be taken in the game world to combat the climate crisis. Their decisions were informed by the data and research presented to them in the game. This approach to gamifying the educational content engaged the players while reinforcing knowledge retention.

A common strength among these four games was the use of credible sources. Each of these games was developed by or in collaboration with respected organizations such as scientific committees and educational institutions (e.g., International Energy Agency, NASA, University of Waterloo Climate Institute, etc.). Providing players with transparency about which resources and research had been utilized during development enhanced trust and the perceived value of the educational benefit of these games. This credibility allowed players to engage more deeply with the content, fostering a sense of empowerment to explore related topics and apply their knowledge in real-world contexts. By integrating accurate, research-backed information into gameplay, these games effectively bridged the gap between entertainment and education, reinforcing players' understanding of complex climate issues. This aligns closely with the first rung of Wilcox's Ladder—Information—which emphasizes transparent, accurate communication that helps stakeholders understand the issues at hand. In these games, clear delivery of credible content allowed players to become informed participants, setting the foundation for deeper forms of engagement in later stages of the Games Ladder.

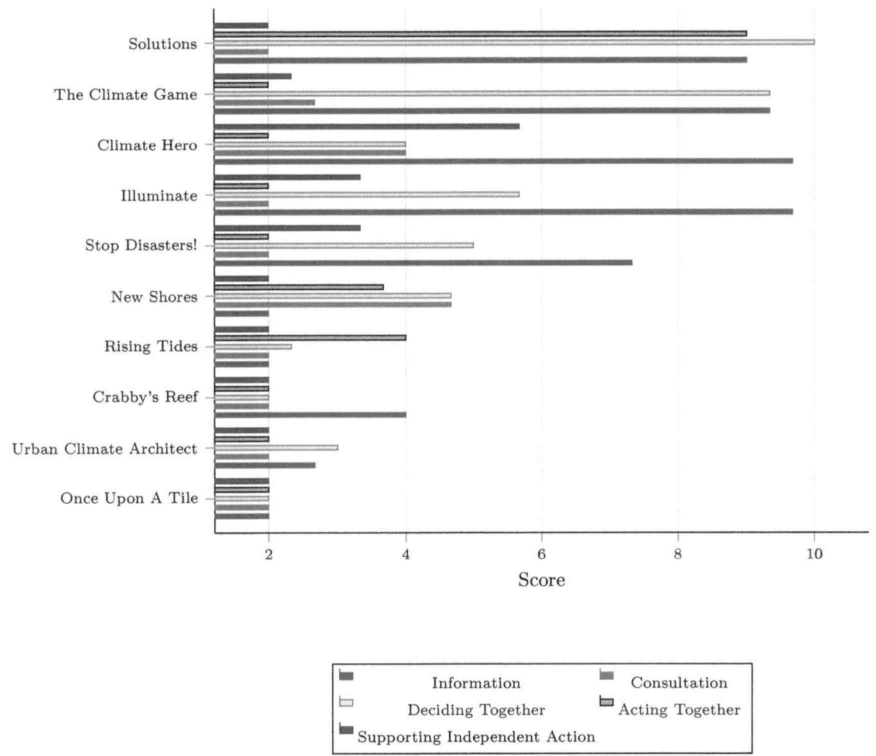

Fig. 4. Scores for each level of the ladder for the analyzed games.

Among the mid- and low-performing games, several recurring issues were evident, including a lack of credible sources, failure to connect informational content to meaningful gameplay, and vague or missing explanations for complex terms. These shortcomings not only undermined the educational value of the games but also diminished player engagement. For instance, without credible sources, players may question the reliability of the information presented, leading to skepticism and disengagement. Additionally, when gameplay failed to incorporate relevant content meaningfully, players might struggle to see the real-world applications of what they were learning. Furthermore, vague explanations for complex terms can leave players confused, hindering their overall understanding. To enhance these games, developers should prioritize incorporating validated resources (by incorporating data from trusted scientific sources (e.g., IPCC reports, peer-reviewed studies) or expert-vetted educational materials to ensure accuracy), ensuring that gameplay aligns with educational objectives, and providing clear explanations for challenging concepts (by providing tooltips, infographics, or guided tutorials to explain challenging ideas).

Consultation. The majority of the games reviewed lacked sufficient feedback mechanisms that could allow two-way dialogue. Even relatively higher-scoring games (*Climate Hero* [4.00] and *New Shores* [4.67]) offered limited or superficial mechanisms such as brief quizzes and surveys, severely restricting player interaction and reflective engagement. These moderate scores reflect attempts at gathering feedback, though their effectiveness was compromised by simplistic design and missed opportunities for nuanced reflection and dialogue. For example, in *Climate Hero*, if the player chose a non-optimal option from the choices given, they were provided with the correct answer and additional information to clarify why that was the correct answer. This approach reinforced learning by deepening players' understanding of the subject matter and clarifying misconceptions in real time. However, beyond basic explanatory prompts, there was no evidence of two-way communication between the player and the game.

Additionally, these were the only games that included a survey aimed at collecting player feedback. However, the survey in *Climate Hero* only asked the player whether they had learned something and the player was able to respond with 'Yes' or 'No.' This did not foster dialogue or collect nuanced feedback about the player's experience. *New Shores* utilized a pre- and post-game survey with Likert scale responses. While the moderator was able to customize the questions in these surveys, the default surveys were still relatively shallow and limited in scope. Both of these games were designed for students in middle school (grades 5–9), which further highlighted the missed opportunity to engage a young audience in meaningful reflection. More robust feedback mechanisms could have facilitated deeper engagement with the content and encouraged students to articulate their thoughts and experiences effectively, raising future Consultation scores through deeper reflection and active player dialogue.

Instead of simply asking binary questions, these games could benefit from open-ended prompts that invited players to share their insights and feelings about the gameplay and the educational material. Additionally, incorporating a variety of feedback formats, such as interactive polls, could create a more dynamic environment for student interaction. By enhancing feedback mechanisms, these games could not only improve player engagement but also provide valuable data to developers for refining the educational content, ultimately fostering a richer learning experience.

The overwhelmingly low scores for this level suggested a systemic issue in how serious games handled feedback, indicating that many developers may overlook its importance in the design process. Effective feedback mechanisms should encourage reflection and foster discussion on the issues the game aimed to address. Without meaningful feedback, these games missed the opportunity to engage players in deeper conversations and to gain insights into how players perceived and interacted with the targeted issues. This lack of engagement could lead to superficial learning experiences, where players might not fully grasp the complexities of the topics at hand. To address this, developers could have implemented more dynamic consultation strategies such as anonymous comment boxes, real-time in-game polls, interactive discussion forums, or moderated post-game debriefs where players could reflect on decisions and outcomes. These tools could give players a voice in the process, encourage peer dialogue, and generate valuable feedback that informs future design iterations. By prioritizing robust, multi-modal feedback systems, developers can create more impactful games that not only educate but also stimulate critical thinking, self-expression, and collective reflection.

Deciding Together. In this category, *The Climate Game* (10.00) and *Solutions (9.33)* were notable examples of games that provided significant and meaningful decision-making opportunities that directly impacted gameplay progression. These games effectively illustrated how players' choices could lead to impactful and persistent consequences, fostering a sense of empowerment and satisfaction. For instance, in either of these games, players might choose renewable energy options, leading to long-term benefits not only for their virtual environment but also reinforcing the real-world implications of those choices. Such design characteristics led to players feeling genuinely empowered, directly justifying their high Deciding Together scores.

In contrast, many other games presented limited or insignificant decision-making opportunities, often failing to connect player choices to notable game outcomes or progression. This lack of meaningful engagement made these decisions feel less significant and rewarding, which could diminish player motivation. Games like *Stop Disasters!* (5.00) and *Urban Climate Architect* (3.00) allowed players to make numerous choices; however, these options often did not lead to significant branching paths or impactful outcomes. As a result, players were unable to fully explore the consequences of their decisions, leading to a lack of incentive to make diverse and meaningful choices. The limited significance of these decisions caused reduced player empowerment and motivation, clearly reflected in their mid-to-low-range scores. By enhancing the significance of player decisions, developers can create more engaging and educational experiences that resonate with players.

Acting Together. A majority of the games analyzed were single-player experiences, which limited their ability to incorporate collaborative mechanics. Among the multiplayer games reviewed (*Rising Tides* [4.00], *New Shores* [3.67], *Solutions* [9.00]), some evidence of collaborative elements emerged, such as in-game chat boxes. However, these mechanics often resulted in implicit collaboration—that is, collaboration was possible but not clearly encouraged, structured, or rewarded within the gameplay itself. These modest scores were indicative of implicit rather than explicit collaboration—collaborative opportunities existed but were not strategically embedded into gameplay. For example, players could technically communicate or coordinate, but the game did not establish specific tasks that required collaboration to succeed, nor did it provide feedback or outcomes based on cooperative behavior. As a result, players often felt uncertain about whether teamwork was necessary or beneficial, reducing the potential for meaningful engagement.

In contrast, *Solutions* stood out as the most collaborative game, featuring mechanics that explicitly required players to discuss, make group decisions, and work together. This integration of meaningful decision-making led to impactful discussions and enhanced collaboration, allowing players to explore diverse perspectives and deepen their understanding of the issues at hand. The strong, structured collaboration reflected in *Solutions* significantly differentiated it from other multiplayer games, explaining its notably higher score. As Paul Hawken, Co-founder of Project Drawdown, noted, "Solutions is a fun way to teach, discover, understand, and take action on climate change." Lyn A. emphasized its potential, stating, "This game has tremendous potential to bring more people into the climate movement. It encourages curiosity about solutions and helps people to see the puzzle pieces that are needed, and what each can contribute to solving the climate crisis." By fostering a clear sense of teamwork, *Solutions* demonstrates how effective collaborative mechanics can enrich the gaming experience and promote critical thinking among players.

Supporting Independent Action. Many of these games lacked real-world context, creating a disconnect that hindered players from making meaningful connections between gameplay and the actual climate crisis. By focusing predominantly on large-scale policy actions to combat climate change, these games often overlooked the importance of individual or community-level actions. As a result, players were inadequately prepared or inspired to take independent action in their own lives.

A few games, such as *Illuminate* (3.33), *Climate Hero* (5.67), and *The Climate Game* (2.33), performed slightly better by providing some actionable steps or relevant context for real-world actions. However, they still fell short in strongly encouraging players to pursue these actions, limiting the effectiveness of the games in fostering real-world change. Among them, *Climate Hero* stood out as the best example of supporting independent action, utilizing features like action pledges and printable posters. This explicit connection between gameplay and subsequent player actions explains its relatively higher score. As players committed to making climate-friendly decisions and building sustainable habits in their daily lives, they felt motivated to follow through with these pledges. This approach not only enhanced player engagement but also empowered individuals to contribute positively to the climate movement, demonstrating the potential of games to inspire real-world action.

6   Discussion

In this study, we found evidence that while serious games show considerable potential for raising awareness about climate issues, they often struggle to engage players in deeper participation that leads to real-world action. Further research could help clarify how to bridge this gap between awareness and tangible impact. Most games evaluated perform strongly at the informational level but struggle with mechanisms for consultation, collaborative decision-making, and post-game activation, reflecting persistent design and conceptual limitations within the serious games field [16,64].

The **Games Ladder for Climate Action** reframes engagement as a multi-level continuum rather than a binary outcome. This echoes calls in participatory design literature for more nuanced approaches to citizen involvement, moving beyond tokenism and toward shared agency [5,22,62]. However, applying this model to games also exposes a central tension: Should serious games primarily educate, or should they catalyze tangible behavior change? Some scholars caution against assuming a direct pipeline between in-game actions and real-world transformation, noting that digital environments often offer symbolic simulations of engagement rather than sustained civic empowerment [9,54].

Moreover, our findings reinforce the critique that many games operate within narrow pedagogical frameworks, focusing on content transmission rather than participatory empowerment [24]. Features like adaptive storytelling, dynamic decision trees, and meaningful feedback loops remain rare, even though they are essential for fostering deeper learning and reflective engagement [36].

Importantly, the observed gap between gameplay and independent action may not be solely attributable to design limitations. It reflects broader systemic issues, such as players' constrained agency [55], the absence of real-world reinforcement structures [17], and the challenges of mobilizing collective action from within individualistic game interfaces [25]. The educational research community has long noted that knowledge acquisition alone is insufficient for behavior change without social reinforcement, habit formation strategies, and enabling environments [43].

This raises further ethical and practical challenges. Games that encourage players to take real-world action—especially youth—must be careful not to overpromise impact or shift responsibility for systemic change onto individuals [50,53]. Over-gamification risks producing performative engagement or moral fatigue, especially when players lack the social capital or institutional support to follow through on their intentions.

In sum, while serious games remain a promising tool for climate education, their full potential lies in designing for participation as a process—not an outcome. Future work must integrate participatory design methods, incorporate long-term behavioral tracking, and recognize the contextual, collective, and infrastructural dimensions of action. The Games Ladder offers one pathway for conceptualizing these layers, but sustained impact will require aligning digital learning environments with real-world civic ecosystems.

Beyond climate action, ladder frameworks have long been used to structure participation in fields such as public health, education, and youth development. For example, Hart's Ladder of Children's Participation [29] is widely used in education and child rights contexts to assess degrees of youth involvement, while Rocha's Ladder of Empowerment [47] is applied in community health and social work to evaluate empowerment outcomes. In public health, participatory ladders guide patient involvement and shared decision-making in interventions [11].

What the Games Ladder for Climate Action contributes is a structured, game-native adaptation of these models—tailored to the mechanics, feedback systems, and decision pathways specific to interactive media. Unlike traditional ladders, which evaluate lived participation or deliberative forums, this framework allows for evaluating how designed participation within serious games translates into cognitive, social, and behavioral engagement.

7   Limitations and Future Work

We acknowledge that the qualitative nature of this study, while well-suited for in-depth exploration, was informed by a limited sample of games, constrained by accessibility and time. This reflects a key area for future expansion, as a broader and more diverse set of games could enhance the robustness and generalizability of the findings. While the use of a structured scoring framework helped guide analysis, future studies may explore incorporating additional perspectives or triangulation methods to further enrich interpretation and validation of results.

Moreover, the current analysis offers a foundational understanding of how serious games can induce real-world action, but follow-up studies with longitudinal tracking would be valuable in assessing sustained behavioral impact beyond immediate gameplay. Similarly, more targeted investigation into how the Games Ladder might be adapted or weighted for different age groups could enhance its utility in educational settings. Expanding the range of games analyzed to include analog or hybrid formats could also strengthen the model's applicability across diverse learning and engagement contexts. These future directions not only offer opportunities to deepen the current framework but also to broaden its relevance and adaptability in supporting climate action through play.

8   Recommendations

Based on our findings and the Games Ladder for Climate Action framework, we recommend the following for developers and researchers seeking to maximize the impact of serious games for climate action:

1. **Enhance feedback and player engagement** Incorporate in-game feedback mechanisms such as surveys, reflection prompts and interactive forums that can facilitate dialogue. Encouraging players to contribute their ideas and discuss climate solutions can create a more immersive and reflective experience.
2. **Strengthen decision-making impact** Ensure that in-game choices have meaningful consequences that reinforce learning. Utilizing adaptive storytelling to reflect the outcomes of different decisions can enhance player agency and deepen their understanding of the implications of their actions.
3. **Promote collaborative action** Design multiplayer mechanics that require teamwork to solve climate-related challenges. Encouraging shared goals and cooperative problem-solving can enhance the sense of community and collective responsibility among players.

4. **Support independent action** Provide clear and actionable steps for players to take beyond the game. This could include incorporating real-world challenges, partnerships with climate organizations, and social incentives. Additionally, mechanisms that offer recognition or rewards for players who take action in their communities can significantly boost motivation.

9 Conclusion

This study introduced the Games Ladder for Climate Action as a novel framework for evaluating how serious games engage players across multiple levels of participation. By adapting Wilcox's Ladder of Participation to the game-based context, the framework captures not only the educational potential of serious games but also their capacity to foster consultation, collaboration, decision-making, and real-world action.

Our evaluation of ten climate-focused games revealed that while many perform well in delivering information, they often lack mechanisms to support feedback, shared agency, or action beyond the screen. This points to a significant design gap—and an opportunity—for developers aiming to move beyond awareness-raising toward deeper civic engagement.

The Games Ladder contributes a replicable tool for serious game analysis and design, one that is applicable across domains such as public health, education, civic participation, and sustainability. It invites scholars and practitioners to rethink what meaningful participation looks like in digital environments and to intentionally design for impact, not just interaction.

Future research should assess how these engagement levels unfold across time, platforms, and social contexts, particularly through participatory design processes and longitudinal studies. As digital tools play an increasingly prominent role in climate education and public engagement, structured, critical frameworks like the Games Ladder can help bridge the gap between virtual experiences and tangible collective action.

Acknowledgments. This work was supported by CITRIS under Grant entitled "Stimulating Behavior Change to Enhance Climate Resilience Policy and Action through a Serious Game Approach".

Disclosure of Interests. The authors have no competing interests to declare that are relevant to the content of this article.

Appendix

Table 1. Games Ladder for Real-World Action defined

Level	Definition	Objective	Evaluation	Criteria
Information	Ensure players are informed about the issue. Evaluate how well the game provides relevant information and educates players about the issue. Can be measured by measuring retention of facts and understanding of concepts through quizzes or post-game surveys and assessing the clarity and comprehensiveness of the informational content presented in the game.	Educate players about the issue	Examine how well the game informs and educates	Evaluate how well the game informs and educates players about the targeted issue.
Consultation	Facilitate two-way feedback between player and game. Analyze mechanisms the game uses to solicit player feedback and opinions, and assess how the game responds with personalized insights or reflections. Can be measured by examining feedback systems like in-game surveys, forums, reflective prompts, or adaptive responses, and evaluating the volume, quality, and impact of the player-game exchange.	Establish a two-way dialogue between the player and the game to enhance understanding and reflection	Assess the presence and effectiveness of bidirectional feedback mechanisms	Evaluate how well the game facilitates reflective, personalized, and meaningful interaction between the player and the game content
Deciding Together	Engage players in decision-making processes. Assess the opportunities for players to participate in decision-making within the game. Can be measured by tracking decision-making paths and their outcomes within the game and measuring player satisfaction and sense of empowerment from being involved in decisions.	Involve players in decision-making	Assess player participation opportunities	Assess how well the game involves players in decision-making processes.
Acting Together	Facilitate collaborative action among players. Evaluate how players are encouraged to work together to achieve common goals. Can be measured by analyzing in-game cooperative mechanics and collaborative challenges and assessing the level of collaboration and teamwork through logs of cooperative actions and achievements.	Facilitate collaborative action	Encourage teamwork towards common goals	Evaluate the game's ability to facilitate collaborative action among players.
Supporting Independent Action	Encourage and support players to take independent action outside of the game. Measure the game's effectiveness in inspiring players to take real-world actions based on their in-game experiences. Can be measured by tracking follow-through on provided actionable steps for community engagement and conducting follow-up surveys to assess real-world actions taken by players and any subsequent community impact.	Inspire real-world collective actions	Measure impact on community engagement	Assess how well the game inspires players to take real-world independent actions after the game.

Table 2. Games Ladder for Real-World Action metrics & scoring guide

Level	Metrics	Score: 1	Score: 2	Score: 3	Score: 4	Score:5
Information	Quantity of relevant content that educates and informs	No relevant information shared about the topic	Topic is introduced at the beginning of the game but not explored further	Some basic information shared occasionally	New information shared at most stages	Comprehensive and consistent information shared at every stage
	Quality of knowledge: clarity, credibility, educational value, and relevance to gameplay	None of the quality criteria are met	One of the four criteria is met	Two of the four criteria is met	Three of the four criteria is met	All four criteria are met
Consultation	Quantity of bidirectional feedback mechanisms	No opportunities for feedback or input	1–2 feedback opportunities	3–4 feedback opportunities	5–6 feedback opportunities (frequent)	Consistent and ongoing feedback opportunities
	Quality of feedback exchange (player input + game response)	No feedback mechanisms or responses from the game	Feedback is limited to basic yes/no questions with no personalized or reflective response from the game	General feedback collected; minimal or generic responses from the game	Engaging and varied feedback mechanisms; game provides relevant and timely responses	Encourages reflection, deliberation, and meaningful dialogue between player and game
Deciding Together	Number of decision-making opportunities	No meaningful decision-making	One decision point at the beginning of the game	1–2 decision points during gameplay, with limited impact	3–4 decision points that significantly affect progress	Five or more impactful decision points throughout the game
	Impact of decisions on game progress and player experience	Only one fixed path; player has no control or empowerment	One decision point allows for exploration, but no follow-up	Some decisions affect progress, but overall impact is limited	Decisions significantly influence the game path. Player feels in control and empowered	Decisions consistently shape the game path. Player feels highly satisfied and empowered
Acting Together	Quantity of cooperative mechanics and collaborative opportunities	No opportunities for collaboration	1–2 opportunities for cooperation	3–4 opportunities for cooperation	Multiple opportunities for cooperation	Ongoing and frequent opportunities for teamwork
	Quality of collaboration and teamwork	No evidence of cooperative behavior or discussion	Minimal cooperation; players show little interest in working together	Occasional collaboration with loose teamwork	Frequent collaboration and meaningful discussions	Consistent, high-quality teamwork and discussions throughout the game
Supporting Independent Action	Quantity of real-world actions taken during or after gameplay	No real-world actions taken; no guidance provided	A few actions taken during or after gameplay	Some real-world actions taken; limited guidance is provided	Several meaningful real-world actions taken; guidance is provided	Significant, consistent real-world actions taken; ongoing support and encouragement provided
	Inspiration to take real-world action and engage with the community	No motivation or inspiration to take action	Player feels slightly inspired but does not act	Player takes minor real-world actions (e.g., personal sustainability changes)	Player feels motivated and attends a local community event	Player is consistently inspired and joins a global or local climate action group

Table 3. Complete list of games analyzed

Game	Description
Solutions	Solutions is a collaborative board game that challenges players to work together to combat climate change. By proposing and ranking climate solutions, players must think critically and make strategic decisions to reduce global emissions and keep temperatures in check. Developed with cutting-edge research from sources such as Project Drawdown, NASA, the World Resources Institute, and many more, Solutions features 101 unique climate solution cards that encourage players to discuss and debate the most effective ways to address the climate crisis. Designed for players of all ages and backgrounds, Solutions is suitable for classrooms, community groups, and families, and can be played in-person or virtually. The game also comes with a range of educational resources, including a curriculum and teaching guides, making it an ideal tool for educators looking to integrate climate change education into their lessons. With its engaging gameplay and informative design, Solutions aims to educate and inspire players to take action on climate change, while empowering the next generation of climate leaders.
The Climate Game	The Climate Game is an online simulation game developed by the Financial Times. Players take on the role of a global minister for future generations, with the goal of reducing the negative effects of climate change by cutting energy-related carbon dioxide emissions to net zero by 2050. Players have three rounds, covering the years from 2022 to 2050, to make decisions and achieve this goal. By taking on the role of a global minister, players can gain a deeper understanding of the complexities of climate change and the importance of making informed decisions to mitigate its effects. The game is an engaging and interactive way to learn about climate change and the challenges of reducing greenhouse gas emissions. The game is based on emissions modeling developed by the International Energy Agency and aims to educate players on the challenges of climate change and the importance of reaching net zero emissions. "They [the students] really enjoyed The Climate Game and worked well as a group to make decisions to lead them to reaching net zero carbon emissions by 2050. The discussions became lively as they all put their opinions forward! Back at school, we'll definitely be using the activity in our chemistry lessons to show the students the thought-provoking decisions which will need to be made by world leaders in the coming years to reduce climate change," a teacher from Burscough Priory Academy in West Lancashire.
Climate Hero	Climate Hero is an online escape room game that combines AI with climate education. Players are transported to a future world where climate change has had a significant impact, and they must work together to "escape" the climate crisis by making commitments to climate action. The game uses interactive challenges and critical thinking to teach players about climate science, mitigation and adaptation efforts, policy changes, and community engagement. The game is designed for students in grades 5–9 and aims to promote climate resilience and sustainability by fostering critical thinking, collaboration, communication, and problem-solving skills. The game uses AI to provide a conversational experience, ensuring that students receive accurate and reliable information.
Illuminate	Illuminate is an educational simulation game that aims to educate players about climate change, its impacts, and potential solutions. The game allows players to explore ways to reduce greenhouse gas emissions and respond to climate risks, with the goal of empowering them to take action against climate change. Developed by the University of Waterloo Climate Institute and the Games Institute, Illuminate is available online and also on the Climate Educator's Portal, a platform designed to support teachers in educating students about climate change. The game was created by a multidisciplinary team of students, staff, and faculty, and is designed to help players understand the science, risks, and solutions to climate change, instilling a sense of hope and agency for climate action.
Stop Disasters!	Stop Disasters! is a serious online game that teaches players how to build safer communities and reduce disaster risk. The game is available in seven languages and is suitable for children and adults alike. Players learn through five scenarios how to prepare for and mitigate the impact of disasters by building safer houses, creating early warning systems, and developing evacuation plans. The game aims to educate players about disaster risk reduction and management, and is aligned with the Sendai Framework for Disaster Risk Reduction 2015–2030. The game can be played in classrooms or online, and is designed to be used by children aged 9–16 and students in higher education. By playing the game, players can develop their knowledge and skills in disaster risk reduction and contribute to building a safer and more resilient world.

(continued)

Table 3. (*continued*)

Game	Description
New Shores	New Shores is an online multiplayer game that transports players to a virtual island with abundant resources, where they must navigate the challenges of managing the environment, economy, and social dynamics. With no set mission, players can choose to work together or pursue individual goals, facing the consequences of their decisions. As they explore the island, they must balance resource use with environmental sustainability, leading them to recognize the need for collective rules and cooperation. The game's objectives are to: – Promote open and innovative education and transversal skills through highly participatory tools – Enhance ecological attitudes, the sense of entrepreneurship, and citizenship values – Foster cooperation for innovation and the exchange of good practices across Europe – Support collaborative approaches to teaching and learning across Europe By playing New Shores, middle and secondary school students, as well as higher education students, can develop essential skills such as negotiation, empathy, and democratic values. The game encourages players to think critically about the importance of collaboration, responsible decision-making, and sustainable development, making it a unique tool for teaching and learning.
Rising Tides	Rising Tides is a collaborative and competitive board game that simulates the challenges of combating climate change. Players take on the roles of leaders from five different institutions, working together to reduce CO2 emissions and adapt to a changing world. The game is set across four countries, where players build green infrastructure, reduce carbon footprints, and navigate environmental challenges. To win, players must balance cooperative efforts with competitive strategies, managing resources and making tactical decisions to achieve individual and common goals while avoiding unintended negative impacts that could lead to environmental disasters.
Crabby's Reef	Crabby's Reef is a classic arcade-style game where players navigate a maze as a crab to collect food while avoiding predators like octopuses. The twist is that as players progress through levels, the ocean becomes increasingly acidic, simulating the effects of climate change on marine life. As the ocean acidifies, the crab's senses are dampened, making it harder to find food and detect predators. The game aims to educate players about ocean acidification, a critical issue related to climate change, and its impact on marine animals' ability to survive and thrive. By experiencing the challenges faced by marine life in a changing ocean, players can gain a deeper understanding of the importance of addressing climate change.
Urban Climate Architect	Urban Climate Architect is an educational online game that allows players to design and build their own environmentally friendly city. The goal is to create a sustainable city that balances housing, employment, and environmental concerns. Players must manage CO2 emissions, temperature, rainwater, and housing and employment needs while designing the city. The game provides a set of building blocks, including streets, houses, industry plants, trees, ponds, and parks, which have different impacts on the city's climate. Players can drag and drop these blocks onto a planning area to design the city. The game's interface displays the city's status, including markers for monitoring housing, employment, CO2 emissions, rainwater, and temperature. The game aims to educate players of all ages about suburbanization, sustainable urban planning, and climate change. It was created by the Hamburg University Cluster of Excellence CliSAP and is available in English and German.
Once Upon A Tile	Once Upon a Tile is a prototype of a casual game designed to promote meaningful values related to peace and sustainable development. The game combines match-three gameplay with city-building and management elements, allowing players to build and develop a small game environment. Each level features thematic tilesets, such as energy sources, transportation, and biodiversity, which can be matched to unlock new resources and effects. The game was created in response to a 2015 UNESCO competition and was developed in partnership with Open Lab and Daniele Giardini. Although it's a prototype, the game has received positive reviews and has sparked interest in its potential for promoting sustainable development and peace.

References

1. Age, B.: Video games and learning: teaching and participatory culture in the digital age (2009)
2. Aldrich, C.: Learning by doing: a comprehensive guide to simulations, computer games, and pedagogy in e-learning and other educational experiences. Wiley (2005)
3. Annetta, L.A., Minogue, J., Holmes, S.Y., Cheng, M.T.: Investigating the impact of video games on high school students' engagement and learning about genetics. Comput. Educ. **53**(1), 74–85 (2009). https://doi.org/10.1016/j.compedu.2008.12.020
4. Apostolakis, K.C., et al.: Path of trust: a prosocial co-op game for building up trustworthiness and teamwork. In: de De Gloria, A., Veltkamp, R. (eds.) GALA 2015. LNCS, vol. 9599, pp. 80–89. Springer, Cham (2016). https://doi.org/10.1007/978-3-319-40216-1_9
5. Arnstein, S.R.: A ladder of citizen participation. J. Am. Inst. Plann. **35**(4), 216–224 (1969). https://doi.org/10.1080/01944366908977225
6. Aylett, A.: Participatory planning, justice, and climate change in Durban, South Africa. Environ. Plann. A **42**(1), 99–115 (2010). https://doi.org/10.1068/a4274
7. Baranowski, T., Buday, R., Thompson, D.I., Baranowski, J.: Playing for real: video games and stories for health-related behavior change. Am. J. Prev. Med. **34**(1), 74–82 (2008). https://doi.org/10.1016/j.amepre.2007.09.027
8. Becker, S.A., Cummins, M., Davis, A., Freeman, A., Hall, C.G., Ananthanarayanan, V.: NMC horizon report: 2017 higher education edition, pp. 1–60. The New Media Consortium (2017). https://www.learntechlib.org/p/174879/
9. Bogost, I.: Persuasive games: the expressive power of videogames. MIT Press (2010)
10. Brown, K.L.: From teacher-centered to learner-centered curriculum: improving learning in diverse classrooms. Education **124**(1) (2003)
11. Carman, K.L., et al.: Patient and family engagement: a framework for understanding the elements and developing interventions and policies. Health Aff. **32**(2), 223–231 (2013). https://doi.org/10.1377/hlthaff.2012.1133
12. Chambers, R.: Rural appraisal: rapid, relaxed and participatory, vol. 311. Institute of Development Studies, Brighton (1992)
13. Choguill, M.B.G.: A ladder of community participation for underdeveloped countries. Habitat Int. **20**(3), 431–444 (1996). https://doi.org/10.1016/0197-3975(96)00020-3
14. Collins, K., Ison, R.: Dare we jump off Arnstein's ladder? Social learning as a new policy paradigm (2006). https://oro.open.ac.uk/8589/1/Path_paper_Collins_Ison.pdf. Accessed 24 Jan 2026
15. Day, D.: Citizen participation in the planning process: an essentially contested concept? J. Plan. Lit. **11**(3), 421–434 (1997). https://doi.org/10.1177/088541229701100309
16. De Freitas, S., Oliver, M.: How can exploratory learning with games and simulations within the curriculum be most effectively evaluated? Comput. Educ. **46**(3), 249–264 (2006). https://doi.org/10.1016/j.compedu.2005.11.007
17. Dulac-Arnold, G., Mankowitz, D., Hester, T.: Challenges of real-world reinforcement learning. arXiv preprint arXiv:1904.12901 (2019). https://doi.org/10.48550/arXiv.1904.12901
18. Elelman, R., Feldman, D.L.: The future of citizen engagement in cities–the council of citizen engagement in sustainable urban strategies (ConCensus). Futures **101**, 80–91 (2018). https://doi.org/10.1016/j.futures.2018.06.012

19. Flood, S., Cradock-Henry, N.A., Blackett, P., Edwards, P.: Adaptive and interactive climate futures: systematic review of 'serious games' for engagement and decision-making. Environ. Res. Lett. **13**(6), 063005 (2018). https://doi.org/10.1088/1748-9326/aac1c6
20. Freeman, S., et al.: Active learning increases student performance in science, engineering, and mathematics. Proc. Natl. Acad. Sci. **111**(23), 8410–8415 (2014). https://doi.org/10.1073/pnas.1319030111
21. Fullerton, T.: Game Design Workshop: A Playcentric Approach to Creating Innovative Games, 2nd edn. CRC Press, Boca Raton (2008)
22. Fung, A.: Varieties of participation in complex governance. Public Adm. Rev. **66**, 66–75 (2006). https://doi.org/10.1111/j.1540-6210.2006.00667.x
23. Gee, J.P.: What video games have to teach us about learning and literacy. Comput. Entertain. (CIE) **1**(1), 20–20 (2003). https://doi.org/10.1145/950566.950595
24. Gee, J.P.: Learning by design: good video games as learning machines. E-Learn. Digit. Media **2**(1), 5–16 (2005). https://doi.org/10.2304/elea.2005.2.1.5
25. Gram, L., Daruwalla, N., Osrin, D.: Understanding participation dilemmas in community mobilisation: can collective action theory help? J. Epidemiol. Community Health **73**(1), 90–96 (2019). https://doi.org/10.1136/jech-2018-211045
26. Granicus: International Public Participation Models. https://granicus.com/blog/international-public-participation-models/. Accessed 24 Jan 2025
27. Grove, N.P., Bretz, S.L.: A continuum of learning: from rote memorization to meaningful learning in organic chemistry. Chem. Educ. Res. Pract. **13**(3), 201–208 (2012). https://doi.org/10.1039/C1RP90069B
28. Hammady, R., Arnab, S.: Serious gaming for behaviour change: a systematic review. Information **13**(3), 142 (2022). https://doi.org/10.3390/info13030142
29. Hart, R.: Children's Participation from Tokenism to Citizenship. UNICEF Innocenti Research Centre, Florence (1992)
30. Hickey, S., Mohan, G.: Relocating participation within a radical politics of development: insights from political action and practice. Participation: From Tyranny to Transformation? Exploring New Approaches to Participation in Development (2004)
31. Hoppe, T., Van der Vegt, A., Stegmaier, P.: Presenting a framework to analyze local climate policy and action in small and medium-sized cities. Sustainability **8**(9), 847 (2016). https://doi.org/10.3390/su8090847
32. Iacovides, I., Cox, A., Kennedy, R., Cairns, P., Jennett, C.: Removing the HUD: the impact of non-diegetic game elements and expertise on player involvement. In: Proceedings of the 2015 Annual Symposium on Computer-Human Interaction in Play, pp. 13–22 (2015). https://doi.org/10.1145/2793107.2793120
33. Iacovides, I., Cox, A.L., McAndrew, P., Aczel, J., Scanlon, E.: Game-play breakdowns and breakthroughs: exploring the relationship between action, understanding, and involvement. Hum.-Comput. Interact. **30**(3–4), 202–231 (2015). https://doi.org/10.1080/07370024.2014.987347
34. International Association of Public Participation: IAP2 Public Participation Spectrum. IAP2 (2018). https://iap2.org.au/resources/spectrum/. Accessed 24 Jan 2025
35. Innes, J.E., Booher, D.E.: Public participation in planning: new strategies for the 21st century. Working Paper 2000-07: Paper prepared for the annual conference of the Association of Collegiate Schools of Planning, 2–5 November 2000. University of California at Berkeley: Institute of Urban and Regional Development. (2000). https://escholarship.org/uc/item/3r34r38h. Accessed 24 Jan 2025

36. Kickmeier-Rust, M.D., Albert, D.: Educationally adaptive: balancing serious games. Int. J. Comput. Sci. Sport (Int. Assoc. Comput. Sci. Sport) **11**(1) (2012)
37. Kohn, A.: Standardized testing and its victims. Educ. Week **20**(4), 46–47 (2000)
38. Koo, T.K., Li, M.Y.: A guideline of selecting and reporting intraclass correlation coefficients for reliability research. J. Chiropr. Med. **15**(2), 155–163 (2016). https://doi.org/10.1016/j.jcm.2016.02.012
39. Li, C., Bernoff, J.: Groundswell: Winning in a World Transformed by Social Technologies. Harvard Business Press (2011)
40. Mayer, R.E.: Multimedia learning. In: Psychology of Learning and Motivation, vol. 41, pp. 85–139. Academic Press (2002). https://doi.org/10.1016/S0079-7421(02)80005-6
41. McGonigal, J.: Reality is broken: why games make us better and how they can change the world. NY: Penguin Publishing Group (2011). https://madwomb.com/tutorials/gamedesign/book_RealityIsBroken_JaneMcGonigal.pdf. Accessed 11 Jan 2015
42. Michael, D.R., Chen, S.L.: Serious games: games that educate, train, and inform. Muska & Lipman/Premier-Trade (2005)
43. Moser, S.C., Dilling, L.: Communicating climate change: closing the science-action gap. In: Dryzek, J.S., Norgaard, R.B., Schlosberg, D. (eds.) The Oxford Handbook of Climate Change and Society, pp. 161–174. Oxford University Press, Oxford (2011). https://doi.org/10.1093/oxfordhb/9780199566600.003.0011
44. Nelson, N., Wright, S.: Participation and power. In: Nelson, N., Wright, S. (eds.) Power and Participatory Development: Theory and practice, pp. 1–18. Intermediate Technology Publications, London (1995)
45. Neuwelt, P.M., Kearns, R.A.: Playing the game: interactively exploring journeys into primary care. Wellbeing Space Soc. **2**, 100045 (2021). https://doi.org/10.1016/j.wss.2021.100045
46. Reckien, D., Eisenack, K.: Climate change gaming on board and screen: a review. Simul. Gaming **44**(2–3), 253–271 (2013). https://doi.org/10.1177/1046878113480867
47. Rocha, E.M.: A ladder of empowerment. J. Plan. Educ. Res. **17**(1), 31–44 (1997). https://doi.org/10.1177/0739456X9701700104
48. Rumore, D., Schenk, T., Susskind, L.: Role-play simulations for climate change adaptation education and engagement. Nat. Clim. Chang. **6**(8), 745–750 (2016). https://doi.org/10.1038/nclimate3084
49. Sakamoto, M., Nakajima, T., Akioka, S.: Gamifying collective human behavior with gameful digital rhetoric. Multimedia Tools Appl. **76**(10), 12539–12581 (2016). https://doi.org/10.1007/s11042-016-3665-y
50. Scharpf, F.W.: Governing in Europe: Effective and Democratic? Oxford University Press, Oxford (1999)
51. Schell, J.: The Art of Game Design: A book of lenses. CRC Press (2008). https://doi.org/10.1201/9780080919171
52. Scherhaufer, P.: Better research through more participation? The future of integrated climate change assessments. Futures **125**, 102661 (2021). https://doi.org/10.1016/j.futures.2020.102661
53. Schrier, K.: Knowledge games: how playing games can solve problems, create insight, and make change. JHU Press, MD (2016)
54. Schrier, K.: Designing games for moral learning and knowledge building. Games Cult. **14**(4), 306–343 (2019). https://doi.org/10.1177/1555412017711514
55. Schulzke, M.: Critical essay–models of agency in game studies. Technoculture Online J. Technol. Soc. **2** (2012)

56. Squire, K.: From content to context: videogames as designed experience. Educ. Res. **35**(8), 19–29 (2006). https://doi.org/10.3102/0013189X035008019
57. Sterman, J., et al.: World climate: a role-play simulation of climate negotiations. Simul. Gaming **46**(3-4), 348–382 (2015). https://doi.org/10.1177/1046878113514935
58. Tekinbas, K.S., Zimmerman, E.: Rules of Play: Game Design Fundamentals. MIT Press (2003)
59. United Nations: Goal 13: Take urgent action to combat climate change and its impacts. United Nations Sustainable Development Goals. https://sdgs.un.org/goals/goal13. Accessed 01 Aug 2025
60. Van Der Schoor, T., Scholtens, B.: Power to the people: local community initiatives and the transition to sustainable energy. Renew. Sustain. Energy Rev. **43**, 666–675 (2015). https://doi.org/10.1016/j.rser.2014.10.089
61. Weinberg, A., Wiesner, E.: Understanding mathematics textbooks through reader-oriented theory. Educ. Stud. Math. **76**(1), 49–63 (2011). https://doi.org/10.1007/s10649-010-9264-3
62. Wilcox, D.: The guide to effective participation. Partnership, Brighton (1994)
63. Wilcox, S.: Praxis games a design philosophy for mobilizing knowledge through play. Am. J. Play **11**(2), 156–182 (2019)
64. Wouters, P., Van Nimwegen, C., Van Oostendorp, H., Van Der Spek, E.D.: A meta-analysis of the cognitive and motivational effects of serious games. J. Educ. Psychol. **105**(2), 249 (2013)
65. Wu, J.S., Lee, J.J.: Climate change games as tools for education and engagement. Nat. Clim. Chang. **5**(5), 413–418 (2015). https://doi.org/10.1038/nclimate2566
66. Zapata Arango, M., Hoppe, T., Itten, A., Blok, K.: The role of city climate networks in promoting citizen participation in municipalities: a critical multi-case analysis. Energy Sustain. Soc. **14**(1), 5 (2024). https://doi.org/10.1186/s13705-023-00438-9

Gamified Eco-Feedback as Socially Embedded Design: Exploring Metaphorical Avatars for Dietary Change

Talayeh Dehghani Ghotbabadi[1]([✉]) [iD], Tobias Hodel[1] [iD], and Magy Seif El-Nasr[2] [iD]

[1] University of Bern, Mittelstrasse 43, 3012 Bern, Switzerland
`tdehghan@ucsc.edu`
[2] University of California, Santa Cruz, CA 95064, USA

Abstract. Dietary choices significantly influence greenhouse gas (GHG) emissions, positioning food consumption as a vital focus for climate mitigation. Traditional eco-feedback tools often rely on abstract numerical data, which may hinder emotional engagement and user motivation. This study explores a plant avatar approach to deliver metaphor-based, gamified feedback on dietary CO_2 emissions. In a 7-day exploratory study, a Telegram chatbot delivered either standard numeric feedback or dynamic avatar responses based on daily food intake. Results showed that participants receiving avatar-based feedback exhibited greater and more consistent reductions in emissions and reported stronger emotional connections and interpretability. While preliminary due to a small sample ($N = 8$), findings suggest promise for emotionally intelligent, narrative-based interventions in sustainable HCI. This research contributes design insights for more relatable and motivational climate technologies.

Keywords: Gamification · Eco-feedback systems · Metaphorical avatars · Sustainable dietary behavior · Human–computer interaction

1 Introduction

Gamification has proven effective in increasing user engagement across various behavior change domains, particularly when grounded in motivational psychology. Defined as the application of game design elements in non-game contexts [1], gamification activates intrinsic motivational drivers such as autonomy, competence, and relatedness [2]. Within the sustainability domain, gamified systems have supported changes in energy use [3], transportation [4], and recycling practices [5].

The Octalysis Framework [6] expands upon these foundations by identifying eight "core drives" of motivation, including symbolic ownership, unpredictability, and epic meaning. Human-centered gamification especially when personalized and narrative-driven can shift users from passive participants to emotionally engaged actors [7].

Despite promising outcomes in other sustainability domains, dietary behavior remains underexplored in relation to gamified eco-feedback. Most existing systems still

A. Thomas et al. (Eds.): JCSG 2025, LNCS 16243, pp. 304–311, 2026.
https://doi.org/10.1007/978-3-032-10518-9_25

rely on abstract numerical representations, which often fail to evoke emotional connection or a sense of urgency [8]. This psychological distance can reduce the perceived relevance and impact of the feedback. To address this, affective and metaphorical design approaches have gained traction in ecological human–computer interaction (HCI). Visual metaphors, especially those rooted in nature or care-based imagery such as plants or animals, have been shown to make abstract environmental impacts more concrete, enhancing emotional salience and interpretability [9, 10]. Nurturing metaphors, in particular, can promote empathy and responsibility by encouraging users to care for environmental outcomes as they would for a living entity [11]. However, few empirical studies have explored the use of such metaphorical strategies in food-related decision-making. This study addresses that gap by evaluating a metaphor-based, avatar-driven eco-feedback system in which users become symbolically and emotionally responsible for the health of a digital plant. Drawing on the Octalysis Framework [6] and the SHIFT behavioral theory [12], the intervention investigates whether emotionally intelligent, narrative-rich feedback can outperform numeric formats in fostering sustainable dietary behaviors.

2 Background and Related Work

Gamification has emerged as a valuable strategy for behavior change, especially when grounded in motivational theory. Defined as the application of game design elements in non-game contexts [1], gamification enhances engagement by activating intrinsic drivers such as autonomy, purpose, and mastery [2]. In sustainability domains, gamified systems have shown greater effectiveness than traditional tools in promoting behaviors like energy conservation and sustainable consumption [3, 5].

Human-centered models such as the Octalysis Framework [6] highlight motivational levers including symbolic ownership, social influence, and unpredictability. These features help strengthen internalized motivation and foster deeper emotional engagement, distinguishing gamified interventions from compliance-based systems [7]. Such design elements are especially important in eco-feedback, where abstract numerical data often lacks emotional resonance or intuitive interpretation.

To address these limitations, ecological human–computer interaction (HCI) has increasingly explored affective and metaphorical design strategies. Symbolic interfaces such as responsive avatars and narrative metaphors have been shown to improve both interpretability and emotional salience by grounding environmental data in familiar, embodied forms [9, 10]. Metaphors rooted in nature and care, such as plant growth or ecosystem stewardship, have been found to foster empathy and a stronger sense of responsibility, enhancing the feedback's actionability [11, 13].

Despite this growing interest, few empirical studies have examined metaphorical feedback systems that combine real-time behavioral data with interactive visual metaphors in everyday dietary contexts. This study addresses that gap by evaluating a chatbot-based, gamified eco-feedback system that links food choices to the symbolic health of a digital plant. This approach builds on persuasive technology and motivational design while investigating how emotional engagement and metaphor can support climate-relevant dietary decisions.

3 Methodology

This exploratory study employed a mixed-methods, between-subjects design to examine the effectiveness of metaphorical, gamified eco-feedback in promoting lower-emission dietary choices. Participants interacted with a custom Telegram bot that delivered either numeric or avatar-based feedback on the carbon impact of their meals over a seven-day period.

3.1 Participants

Eight participants aged 13 to 28 were recruited through purposive sampling from student communities involved in sustainability-related initiatives in Switzerland. While the target demographic was Generation Z typically defined as individuals born between 1997 and 2012 this group included late adolescents and young adults who shared similar characteristics, such as digital literacy, environmental concern, and an interest in plant-based diets [13]. These participants represented a climate-conscious, digitally fluent population most likely to engage with feedback-driven systems. Participants were randomly assigned to either the control group (n = 4) or the gamified group (n = 4). Although the sample size was small, such a scale is common and methodologically acceptable in early-stage HCI and design research, where the primary goal is to generate exploratory insights rather than statistical generalizability [14, 15].

3.2 Intervention Design

All participants interacted with the same Telegram-based chatbot interface, logging three meals per day. Meal entries were selected from a pre-compiled food emissions database built using Swiss life-cycle inventory data [16]. Participants in the control group received basic textual feedback summarizing their daily cumulative CO_2e emissions, along with suggestions for lower-impact food alternatives.

In contrast, the gamified group received feedback through a dynamic plant avatar. The avatar's appearance such as leaf coloration, growth stage, and vitality changed daily based on the carbon impact of the user's food choices. These visual cues were semantically linked to emission levels (e.g., browning leaves indicated meat-heavy or high-impact meals). The gamified intervention drew on four motivational drives from the Octalysis Framework [6]:

- **Ownership:** Participants customized their plant's species and pot color.
- **Unpredictability:** Avatar states evolved semi-randomly to sustain user curiosity.
- **Epic Meaning and Narrative:** Users were positioned as guardians of a fragile plant ecosystem.
- **Accomplishment:** Reduced emissions led to visible plant flourishing.

The system also incorporated behavioral cues from the SHIFT model, emphasizing elements such as social proof, identity-based appeals, and timely nudges [12]. (See Figs. 1 and 2 in the full version for system visuals. (Figs. 1 and 2).

3.3 Data Collection

Data collection combined quantitative and qualitative approaches:

- **Quantitative data:** Participants' daily CO_2e totals were analyzed using descriptive statistics and a Wilcoxon signed-rank test to assess patterns of emission reduction over the intervention period.
- **Qualitative data:** In-app cultural probes prompted daily reflections, while pre- and post-intervention surveys captured shifts in attitude, motivation, and emotional responses to the feedback.

All personal data were anonymized. Participants provided informed consent in accordance with university ethical protocols. Data were deleted after the study, and participants retained the right to withdraw at any time.

Fig. 1. A Telegram-Based Avatar Interaction Flow for Gamified Dietary Feedback.

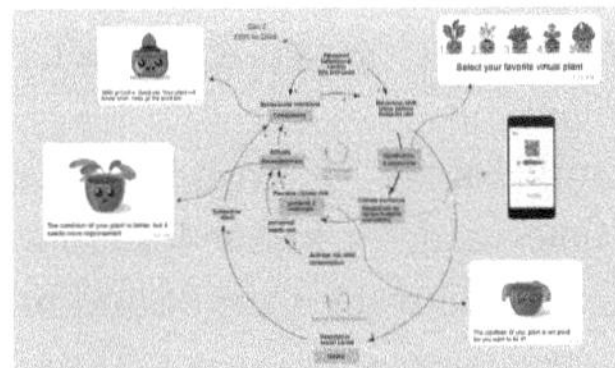

Fig. 2. A Motivation-Driven Gamified Feedback Loop for Sustainable Dietary Behavior.

4 Results

This section compares the control and gamified conditions in terms of carbon emission reductions and user experience over the seven-day intervention period.

4.1 Emission Reductions

Participants in the gamified group demonstrated more consistent and substantial reductions in daily dietary CO_2e emissions than the control group. On average, the gamified group reduced emissions by 1,180 g/day (SD = 225), while the control group showed a mean reduction of 325 g/day (SD = 480). The gamified condition also showed lower variance, indicating more stable behavior change.

By Day 3, most gamified participants had reduced their emissions below the 5,000 g CO_2e/day sustainability benchmark and maintained that level for the rest of the study. A Wilcoxon signed-rank test confirmed a significant difference between groups ($Z = -2.023$, $p < .05$) (Figs. 3 and 4).

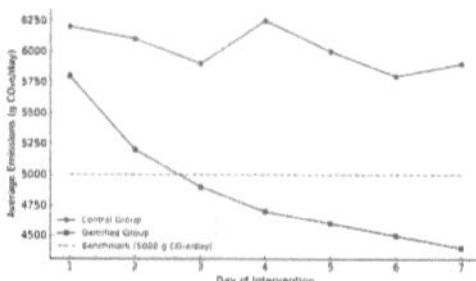

Fig. 3. Average daily dietary carbon emissions over the 7-day intervention. The gamified group shows a sharper and more consistent decline, dropping below the 5,000 g CO_2e/day sustainability benchmark by Day 3.

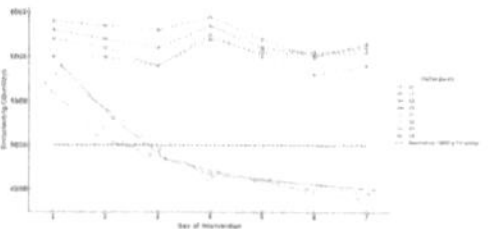

Fig. 4. Individual carbon emission trajectories over the 7-day intervention.

4.2 User Perceptions and Emotional Engagement

Qualitative data revealed key differences in emotional responses and interpretation:

- **Attachment and Ownership:** Gamified users felt responsible for their plant's well-being. Several said they "cared for it," especially when it appeared wilted, reinforcing accountability for food choices.
- **Interpretability:** Participants found the avatar's changing appearance helpful in understanding emissions. One said, "I knew lunch was too meat-heavy when the leaves started browning." Control group users found numeric data harder to relate to emotionally.
- **Motivation Response:** Three of four gamified users were interested in continued use; only one control user felt similarly. Most participants in both groups questioned their ability to sustain change without ongoing feedback.

4.3 Synthesis

The alignment between quantitative reductions and qualitative engagement suggests that metaphorical, emotionally resonant feedback enhances both motivation and behavioral clarity. While exploratory, these findings highlight the potential of symbolic avatars to foster reflection and support sustainable dietary behavior.

5 Discussion

This study provides preliminary evidence that metaphor-based, avatar-driven eco-feedback can enhance both behavioral consistency and emotional engagement in sustainable dietary practices. Compared to numeric feedback, the gamified system elicited sharper CO_2e reductions and stronger affective responses. Participants expressed empathy for their avatars, describing concern when the plants appeared wilted or unhealthy. This sense of symbolic ownership aligns with prior research showing that metaphors rooted in care and nature can foster responsibility and emotional salience [9–11]. The avatar also functioned as an interpretive aid, visually communicating the environmental consequences of food choices in a way that reduced cognitive load and made abstract emissions data more relatable [8, 9]. These findings support core theories of gamification, particularly intrinsic motivators such as autonomy, relatedness, and purpose [2, 6]. The intervention effectively drew on both the Octalysis Framework [6] and the SHIFT model [12], combining emotional resonance with narrative framing to sustain engagement. Nevertheless, participants in both groups expressed doubt about sustaining behavior change without continued feedback. This reflects well-documented limitations of gamified interventions, where motivation may fade without reinforcement or integration into daily routines [5, 17]. Future iterations should incorporate strategies like social features, habit formation techniques, or real-world incentives to extend long-term impact [18].

Overall, the results highlight the value of emotionally intelligent design in climate technologies. Even lightweight, symbolic interfaces can prompt meaningful reflection and motivate pro-environmental action especially in domains like sustainable eating, where data is typically abstract and emotionally disengaged.

6 Conclusion

This study examined the design and effects of a metaphor-based, gamified eco-feedback system that visualized dietary carbon emissions through a dynamic plant avatar. Compared to traditional numeric feedback, the avatar-based system demonstrated potential to enhance both behavioral consistency and emotional engagement. Participants responded positively to the symbolic framing, reporting greater motivation, improved interpretability, and a sense of care toward their digital plant factors that influenced their food choices throughout the intervention. These results underscore the value of integrating narrative, metaphor, and personalization into eco-feedback systems particularly in domains like sustainable eating, where environmental data often feels abstract and emotionally disconnected. Symbolic avatars offer a compelling alternative to numeric-only feedback by tapping into intrinsic motivations and fostering meaningful reflection. As a work in progress, this research provides early insights into how emotionally intelligent interfaces can support sustainable behavior. Future studies should explore how such systems can be extended and embedded into everyday life, supported by longitudinal engagement strategies, social features, or integration with public sustainability programs. Continued interdisciplinary collaboration across design, behavioral science, and environmental communication will be critical in developing scalable, user-centered interventions that promote climate-conscious choices in daily routines.

Disclosure of Interests. The authors have no competing interests to declare that are relevant to the content of this article.

References

1. Deterding, S., Dixon, D., Khaled, R., Nacke, L.: From game design elements to gamefulness. In: MindTrek 2011, pp. 9–15. ACM, New York (2011). https://doi.org/10.1145/2181037.2181040

2. Deci, E.L., Ryan, R.M.: The "what" and "why" of goal pursuits: human needs and the self-determination of behavior. Psychol. Inq. **11**(4), 227–268 (2000). https://doi.org/10.1207/S15327965PLI1104_01

3. Froehlich, J., Findlater, L., Landay, J.: The design of eco-feedback technology. In: Proceedings of the SIGCHI Conference on Human Factors in Computing Systems, pp. 1999–2008. ACM, New York (2010). https://doi.org/10.1145/1753326.1753629

4. Meschtscherjakov, A., Wilfinger, D., Scherndl, T., Tscheligi, M.: Acceptance of future persuasive in-car interfaces towards a more economic driving behaviour. In: Proceedings of the 1st International Conference on Automotive User Interfaces, pp. 81–88. ACM (2009). https://doi.org/10.1145/1620509.1620524

5. Hamari, J., Koivisto, J., Sarsa, H.: Does gamification work? A literature review of empirical studies on gamification. In: HICSS 2014, pp. 3025–3034. IEEE, Hawaii (2014). https://doi.org/10.1109/HICSS.2014.377

6. Chou, Y.-K.: Actionable Gamification: Beyond Points, Badges, and Leaderboards. Octalysis Group, California (2015)

7. Yee, N.: Motivations for play in online games. Cyberpsychol. Behav. **9**(6), 772–775 (2006). https://doi.org/10.1089/cpb.2006.9.772

8. Spence, A., Poortinga, W., Pidgeon, N.: The psychological distance of climate change. Risk Anal. **32**(6), 957–972 (2012). https://doi.org/10.1111/j.1539-6924.2011.01695.x

9. Plous, S.: The Psychology of Judgment and Decision Making. McGraw-Hill, New York (1993)

10. Landwehr, S.C., Weiss, M.: Emotional design in eco-feedback: the role of metaphors, aesthetics, and motivational engagement. J. Environ. Psychol. **72**, 101530 (2020). https://doi.org/10.1016/j.jenvp.2020.101530

11. Sengers, P., Boehner, K., Mateas, M., Gay, G.: The disenchantment of affect. In: Proceedings of the ACM Conference on Designing Interactive Systems, pp. 228–237. ACM (2005). https://doi.org/10.1145/1073076.1073115

12. White, K., Habib, R., Hardisty, D.J.: How to SHIFT consumer behaviors to be more sustainable: a literature review and guiding framework. J. Mark. **83**(3), 22–49 (2019). https://doi.org/10.1177/0022242919825649

13. Chwialkowska, A.: Millennials, consumer behavior, and sustainable development: a literature review. Sustainability **12**(4), 1509 (2020). https://doi.org/10.3390/su12041509

14. Blandford, A., Furniss, D., Makri, S.: Qualitative HCI research: going behind the scenes. Synth. Lect. Hum. Centered Inform. **9**(1), 1–115 (2016). https://doi.org/10.2200/S00706ED1V01Y201601HCI033

15. Zimmerman, J., Forlizzi, J., Evenson, S.: Research through design as a method for interaction design research in HCI. In: CHI 2007, pp. 493–502. ACM (2007). https://doi.org/10.1145/1240624.1240704

16. Jungbluth, N., Ulrich, M., Muir, K., Solin, S.: Analysis of food and environmental impacts as a scientific basis for Swiss dietary recommendations. ESU-services GmbH, Schaffhausen (2022). https://esu-services.ch/fileadmin/download/jungbluth-2022-Swiss-dietary-recommendations.pdf

17. Looyestyn, J., Kernot, J., Boshoff, K., Maher, C., Pepping, G.: Does gamification increase engagement with online programs? A systematic review. PLoS ONE **12**(3), e0173403 (2017). https://doi.org/10.1371/journal.pone.0173403
18. Koivisto, J., Hamari, J.: The rise of motivational information systems: a review of gamification research. Int. J. Inf. Manage. **45**, 191–210 (2019). https://doi.org/10.1016/j.ijinfomgt.2018.10.013

Using Item Response Theory to Model Game Performance in an EEG-Based Attention Training Game

Ming Chen[1]([envelope]) [ID], Maya C. Rose[2] [ID], Ashley F. McDermott[2] [ID],
and Bruce D. Homer[1] [ID]

[1] CUNY Graduate Center, New York, NY 10016, USA
mchen3@gradcenter.cuny.edu
[2] THYNK, Orlando, FL 32779, USA

Abstract. Measuring cognitive gains in a multi-skill training game is challenging, especially with dynamic difficulty levels that must be factored into metric design. This exploratory study aims to investigate whether Item Response Theory (IRT) can be used to model the mission difficulty and scale the performance score of participants' attentional abilities to reflect their training gains in an attentional training game, *Skylar's Run*. Properties of EEG-based attention performance were investigated. We modeled the participants' focused and sustained attention scores during gameplay that are physiologically measured every 1/10th of a second. Using IRT, we calculated difficulty weights for 15 missions and scaled the performance scores accordingly to reflect the inherent difficulty across the missions. We also accounted for EEG data variability. Lastly, we validated the scaled performance scores by fitting regression models and found that training duration had a marginally significant positive association with the performance score of sustained attention but not focused attention. These results provide evidence of the viability of using IRT to consider variability in physiological measures of attention as well as in game difficulty in complex cognitive training games.

Keywords: Games for Learning · Game-Based Attention Training · Item Response Theory (IRT) · Game Performance Modeling

1 Introduction

Serious games, games designed with objectives beyond entertainment, have emerged as valuable tools for training and cognitive assessment [1, 2]. Recently, the power of game-based training has been used to develop programs to enhance targeted cognitive abilities through well-designed gameplay mechanics that are paired to various learning mechanics [3]. Most of these game-based trainings utilize behavioral metrics outside of the game to assess improvements rather than including real-time assessments, and the ones that do provide real time metrics only use indices of behavior, not physiological measures [4]. For certain cognitive skills (e.g., attention), real-time monitoring and assessment are needed to reflect its continuous nature.

A. Thomas et al. (Eds.): JCSG 2025, LNCS 16243, pp. 312–318, 2026.
https://doi.org/10.1007/978-3-032-10518-9_26

Game-based assessments and training can use game metrics (e.g., reaction time and accuracy) to successfully assess cognitive processes and attention skills [1, 5–7]. For instance, a systematic review provided evidence supporting the validity of 31 game-based assessments in measuring cognitive functions, including attention, in children and adolescents [2]. Another intervention study introduced an ADHD digital therapeutic, which provides real-time feedback on participants' behavioral sustained and selective attention capabilities using a Focused Score [8], and it significantly predicted improvements on validated behavioral measures of attention [4].

Measuring students' cognitive performance within game-based interventions remains a challenge. Many of these cognitive interventions incorporate adaptive designs, and the gameplay difficulty is dynamically adjusted within and across each level, which needs to be considered when evaluating the students' performance. Moreover, many game-based interventions rely on single-time-point measures (e.g., the average accuracy for a whole mission), which does not reflect real-time performance. In order to evaluate real-time performance, the training should gather performance data frequently, such as through a physiological method.

In this paper we focus on a game-based cognitive training that incorporates real-time EEG signals. This attention training program is a brain-computer interface (BCI) cognitive training video game that measures and trains attention and a range of related cognitive skills using EEG technology and a proprietary algorithm. The game captures neural correlates of attention every 1/10th of a second as players progress through gameplay, yielding a rich stream of real-time physiological data. While this game has demonstrated efficacy among children with attentional difficulties—using self-report and academic measures external to the game [9–12]—the internal physiological game metrics associated with attention have not yet been systematically analyzed. Such analysis is crucial for two key reasons: (1) it provides an objective, real-time physiological measure of attention performance, reducing reliance on external self-report instruments to track outcomes; and (2) it can enable the delivery of meaningful feedback to players regarding their focused and sustained attention skills, both progressively and summatively.

Initial attempts to establish performance scores from the EEG data, including hand setting weights for difficulty of each mission, failed to accurately represent the nonlinear nature of difficulty tiers and reflect the improvements shown in behavioral measures. Item Response Theory (IRT) was selected as a paradigm to calculate difficulty weighting and scale performance scores. IRT is a popular psychometric approach to model the relationships between individuals' latent trait (e.g., focused attention) and their responses to test items. Unlike classical test theory which assumes all items have equal value, IRT accounts for item-level characteristics such as difficulty, discrimination, and guessing. One of the key strengths of IRT is its ability to assign a difficulty parameter to each item, indicating the level of ability required to have a 50% chance of success [13]. Previous studies have successfully applied IRT to model students' performance in the context of game-based learning [14, 15]. IRT has three underlying assumptions: unidimensionality (a single latent trait influences responses), local independence (item responses are independent given the trait), and monotonicity (the probability of a correct response increases with the trait level) [13]. Our data satisfies these core assumptions.

This study aims to develop a scoring system leveraging IRT to evaluate real-time attention performance, specifically focused attention (ability to turn your attention towards a task while ignoring distractions) and sustained attention (maintaining attention for an extended period of time). There are three primary steps to achieve this goal: establishing the difficulty of each mission, calculating weighted performance scores, and investigating the validity of this new scoring system by examining the participants' performance across missions.

2   Methods

2.1   *Skylar's Run*: BCI Cognitive Videogame-Based Training

Skylar's Run aims to improve children's attentional control, impulse control, and self-regulation abilities using an adaptive cognitive training platform, guided by EEG technology that captures measures of students' real-time attentional abilities (see https:// thynk.com/the-game for more details). It consists of 15 game missions and is played 3–4 times per week for about 6–8 weeks. The curriculum starts off with training focused and sustained attention and gradually builds up to higher order cognitive skills. Each set of 3 missions focuses on a different cognitive skill with a different primary game mechanic, although the BCI mechanics for sustained and focused attention remain constant across the training.

In Mission 1, two initial calibrations are completed as the player wears the EEG headset to determine personalized neural factors of each player's attention levels, called a "cognitive signature". These calibrations analyze EEG patterns associated with both attentive and inattentive states and help to identify neural markers predictive of attentional engagement. In the first calibration, the player completes different facial movements which are considered as artifacts in the EEG stream. During the second calibration, the player completes a 10-min Psychomotor Vigilance Task, whereby they are directed to tap the tablet screen as soon as the light appears. This establishes EEG signals related to attention and inattention. The proprietary algorithm then compares these discrete factors to a database of EEG signals of attention of both normal and ADHD subjects within the same age range. The player's EEG signal is then modified based on how different their personalized model was from a global model of attention to create their own attention state index.

During each mission, the speed of the game avatar is altered in real-time depending on how a user's in-game EEG signal compares to their unique index, slowing down when attention lags and speeding up when there is an increase in attention. Their attention is measured every 10th of a second and then scaled from 0% to 100%. This produces a "BCI Score", which is visible to the player in the game as they proceed through the mission. This 'focus-forward' approach provides the player with instant recognition of actual attention performance.

Focused and sustained attention are the two core attentional abilities that this game aims to improve, both deriving from the BCI event values. Focused attention was calculated as the proportion of time students' BCI scores remained above a BCI of 60 within each mission attempt. Sustained attention was calculated as the proportion of time when BCI scores remained stable above a threshold ($\geq$40) and fluctuated within $\pm$20 units compared to the last measurement. This calculation reflects the participants' ability to maintain consistent attention over time.

2.2 Exploratory Data Analysis Approach

The exploratory analysis involved three steps: inspection of the raw scores, scaling them using difficulty weights based on IRT, and scaling the performance scores using within-mission BCI variability. We first examined focused and sustained attention by averaging their performance scores across attempts for each user and mission. The raw scores alone did not adequately account for the inherent difficulty progression built into the mission design. To address this, we calculated mission-specific difficulty weights using IRT. Specifically, each mission was treated as an "item," and marked as "Pass" for a user if they had at least one successful attempt based on preset criteria ("Fail" otherwise). Then, we constructed a one-parameter Rasch IRT model to calculate the difficulty of each mission. We scaled the performance scores by multiplying the raw scores by the difficulty weights assigned to that mission (scaled to the 0.5 - 4.5 range to better manifest the differences between missions) to account for its inherent difficulty and underlying cognitive demands.

Next, we examined the variability of the BCI score across missions and found that later missions exhibited greater variability than earlier missions. To account for this, we multiplied the performance scores by the BCI variability weights for each mission.

Finally, to assess construct validity, we examined whether the scaled scores were related to training variables (i.e., weeks in training, completed sessions, and missions attempted) using linear regression. A positive link supported the scores' validity by showing they reflect attention improvements with increased training.

2.3 Participant Data

Gamelogs from all 15 missions in *Skylar's Run* from 40 students who completed the training in an elementary school setting were included in this paper. The participants had a mean age of 10.56 years ($SD = 1.21$), with 71.8% of the participants identifying as male and 28.2% as female.

3 Results

Visual inspection of the raw scores revealed minimal differences between early and later missions, with the scores maintaining a flat trend throughout the missions. Fitting a linear regression to the average performance scores did not reveal any significance for focused ($b = -0.002, p = 0.10$) or sustained attention ($b = -0.001, p = 0.56$) with slopes very close to zero.

Constructing the one-parameter Rasch IRT model using the Pass/Fail data gave us the difficulty numbers for each mission and their corresponding weights (scaled to the 0.5 - 4.5 range). Mission difficulty increased across levels, with Mission 1 being the easiest (*difficulty* $= -4.22$) and Mission 9 among the hardest (*difficulty* $= 1.09$). The difficulty weights echoes the increasing trend of the level difficulty, as evidenced by the greater cognitive demands in the later missions where switching between sub-tasks or alternating attention is required.

Turning to the variability in the scores, Fig. 1 illustrates the standard deviation trajectory of the BCI scores for each mission averaging all participants and attempts. Overall, the later missions have larger variability than the earlier missions, and fitting a linear regression model to the data supports this claim ($b = 0.10$, $p = 0.008$). This reflects the inherent difficulty increase across the 15 missions as discussed earlier. The variability of each mission is then converted to weights scaled to the 0.5 - 1.5 range.

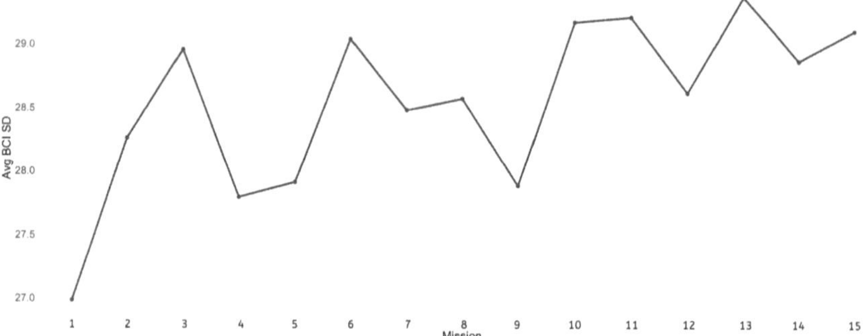

Fig. 1. Average Standard Deviations of BCI for Each Mission.

Multiplying the performance scores by the weights obtained from the IRT analysis and the weights obtained from the BCI variability analysis, we obtained the final scaled performance scores for focused and sustained attention (Fig. 2). Overall, the figure exhibits an increasing trend of the performance scores for both focused and sustained attention. The scores increase from Mission 1 to 3, then they drop at Mission 4 followed by a rapid increase peaking at Mission 6. After that, the scores present a slight decline trend until the last mission. Fitting linear regressions to the performance scores supports a marginally significant increase across all the missions for both focused attention ($b = 0.09, p = 0.07$) and sustained attention ($b = 0.09, p = 0.07$). On average, the participants' scaled performance scores increased by 104.8% for focused attention and 96.1% for sustained attention from Mission 2 to 15. (Mission 1 was not included as it is a tutorial with embedded instructions.)

The linear regression models examined whether improvements in these scores were predicted by the duration of training (weeks), number of completed sessions, and number of missions attempted. For focused attention, training duration did not significantly predict improvement ($b = 0.88$, $p = 0.11$), although the effect was positive. Number of completed sessions ($b = -0.19$, $p = 0.09$) and number of missions attempted ($b = -0.85$, $p = 0.012$) showed a negative relationship with focused attention improvement, indicating that students who engaged with more sessions and missions were less likely to meet the statistical threshold for performance growth. In contrast, improvement in sustained attention was significantly predicted by training duration ($b = 1.65, p = 0.043$), suggesting that longer time spent on training contributed positively to sustained attention gains. However, both the number of sessions completed ($b = -0.35$, $p = 0.026$) and

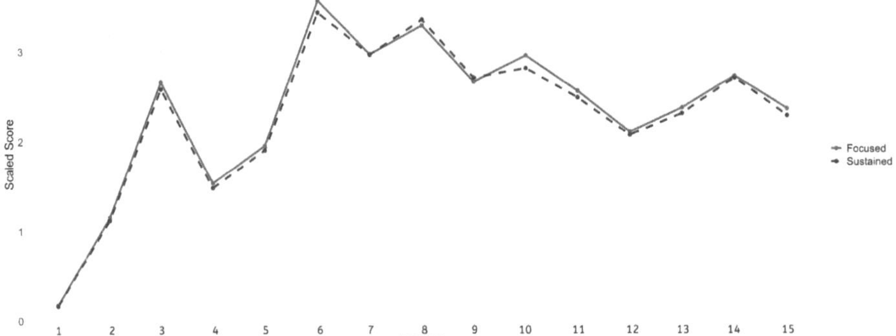

Fig. 2. Scaled Performance Scores of All Participants for Focused (Solid) and Sustained Attention (Dashed) for the 15 Missions.

missions attempted ($b = -1.40$, $p = 0.015$) were again negatively associated with improvement, echoing the findings from focused attention.

4 Discussion and Conclusion

The initial raw performance scores for focused and sustained attention did not reflect progress in the game-based skill training because they did not account for changing difficulty and performance adaptation built into the game design. We then used IRT to develop weight adjustments for the scores based on mission difficulty. These adjusted scores began to reflect differences in performance, showing improvement in missions targeting the same skill and reduced performance in more challenging missions where a new skill was introduced. We further analyzed BCI variability and found that focused and sustained attention showed greater variability in missions where more complex cognitive skills are being trained. By adding weights to account for this change in variability, we see performance begin to plateau in later missions. However, this plateau is at the same level as the highest performance in the earlier missions that only targeted focused and sustained attention. This indicates that even in levels designed with game mechanics targeting more complex cognitive abilities and requiring greater attentional control, the players were able to maintain the same levels of focused and sustained attention. Rather than indicating a failure to improve, this plateauing or decline may instead signal that the scoring system is successfully capturing and adjusting for increased cognitive load. In other words, students may be improving, but the increased task difficulty offsets these gains in observable raw performance, making the scaling adjustments essential for interpreting learning trajectories accurately. Investigating the performance trajectory of the other cognitive abilities in the rest of the training could provide additional insights. However, the current study is the first to provide evidence of the viability of using IRT to model mission difficulty in regards to attentional abilities in complex cognitive training games, as well as incorporating direct measures of brain activity variability to model performance scores. This information not only helps to provide more accurate feedback to users but can also be used to dynamically adjust difficulty tiers across the training.

References

1. Díaz-Orueta, U., Garcia-López, C., Crespo-Eguílaz, N., Sánchez-Carpintero, R., Climent, G., Narbona, J.: AULA virtual reality test as an attention measure: convergent validity with Conners' continuous performance test. Child Neuropsychol. **20**(3), 328–342 (2014). https://doi.org/10.1080/09297049.2013.792332

2. Lumsden, J., Edwards, E.A., Lawrence, N.S., Coyle, D., Munafò, M.R.: Gamification of cognitive assessment and cognitive training: a systematic review of applications and efficacy. JMIR Serious Games **4**(2), e11 (2016). https://doi.org/10.2196/games.5888

3. Plass, J.L., Homer, B.D., Kinzer, C.K.: Foundations of game-based learning. Educ. Psychol. **50**(4), 258–283 (2015). https://doi.org/10.1080/00461520.2015.1122533

4. Anguera, J.A., et al.: Enhancing attention in children using an integrated cognitive-physical videogame: a pilot study. NPJ Digit. Med. **6**(1), 1–15 (2023). https://doi.org/10.1038/s41746-023-00812-z

5. Chen, M., Pisari, D., Froehlich, F., Homer, B.D., Plass, J.L.: A comprehensive review of game-based measures of executive functions [Paper presentation]. In: The 2022 American Educational Research Association Annual Conference, San Diego, CA, USA (2022). https://doi.org/10.3102/1890327

6. Chen, M., Homer, B.D., Plass, J.L.: Validation of three game-based executive function measures: how does intrinsic motivation impact the measuring outcomes? [Paper presentation]. In: The 2023 American Educational Research Association Annual Conference, Chicago, IL (2023). https://doi.org/10.3102/2016465

7. Aneni, K., Gomati de la Vega, I., Jiao, M.G., Funaro, M.C., Fiellin, L.E.: Evaluating the validity of game-based assessments measuring cognitive function among children and adolescents: a systematic review and meta-analysis. Progress Brain Res. **279**, 1–36 (2023). https://doi.org/10.1016/bs.pbr.2023.02.002

8. Stamatis, C.A., Heusser, A.C., Simon, T.J., Ala'ilima, T., Kollins, S.H.: Real-time cognitive performance metrics derived from a digital therapeutic for inattention predict ADHD-related clinical outcomes: Replication across three independent trials of AKL-T01. Translational Psychiatry **14**(1), 328 (2024). https://doi.org/10.1038/s41398-024-03045-0

9. McDermott, A.F., Rose, M., Norris, T., Gordon, E.: A novel feed-forward modeling system leads to sustained improvements in attention and academic performance. J. Atten. Disord. **24**(10), 1443–1456 (2016). https://doi.org/10.1177/1087054715623044

10. Lim, C.G., et al.: A randomized controlled trial of a brain-computer interface based attention training program for ADHD. PLoS ONE **14**(5), e0216225 (2019). https://doi.org/10.1371/journal.pone.0216225

11. Herman, B.K., Rose, M.C.: A brain-to-computer interface (BCI) paired with a videogame to improve core symptoms of ADHD in children: a real world pilot study [Poster presentation]. In: APSARD 2024, Orlando, FL, USA (2024)

12. Rose, M.C., Herman, B.K.: Near and far transfer effects of a BCI cognitive video game training on core ADHD symptoms and academic performance [Poster presentation]. In: APSARD 2025, San Diego, CA, USA (2025)

13. Glas, C.: Item response theory in educational assessment and evaluation. Measure et Évaluation En Éducation **31**(2), 19–34 (2008). https://doi.org/10.7202/1025005ar

14. Huang, Y., et al.: Item Response Theory-based gaming detection [Paper presentation]. In: The 15th International Conference on Educational Data Mining (EDM), Durham, UK (2022)

15. Lee, Y.: Estimating student ability and problem difficulty using item response theory (IRT) and TrueSkill. Inf. Discov. Deliv. **47**(2), 67–75 (2019). https://doi.org/10.1108/IDD-08-2018-0030

Structural–Combinatorial Analysis of Gamification Log Data in Physics Education

Michael D. Kickmeier-Rust[✉] and Katharina Richter

St. Gallen University of Teacher Education, St. Gallen, Switzerland
michael.kickmeier@phsg.ch

Abstract. This study examines the learning app Basketball Challenge, designed to teach ballistic trajectory concepts at the secondary school level. The app is available in a gamified and a standard version. We compared both versions using pre- and post-tests to measure learning effects. While statistical analyses did not reveal significant learning gains, a notable interaction between gender and condition emerged in game performance. To deepen the analysis, Knowledge Space Theory (KST) and Competence-based KST (CbKST) were applied, enabling a structural, competence-focused evaluation. The model showed good fit for both knowledge tests and game levels. Although competence gains were small and statistically non-significant, structural analyses revealed patterns not evident in aggregated performance scores.

Keywords: Gamification · Physics Education · Gender Differences · Performance · Competence · Knowledge Space Theory

1 Gamification in Education: Benefits, Challenges

Gamification—the integration of game elements into education—has been linked to gains in motivation and, in some contexts, achievement [1–3]. Simulations and serious games also provide risk-free practice environments [4]. However, effects are highly context-dependent: while engagement often increases, learning outcomes are mixed [5]. Extrinsic rewards may undermine intrinsic motivation [3, 6, 7], and competitive mechanics can disadvantage less proficient students [2]. Ethical concerns also arise, including data privacy issues and psychological effects of ranking-based systems [8]. Despite these challenges, gamification can support knowledge transfer when grounded in cognitive and instructional principles [9, 10]. Thoughtful designs facilitate deeper learning through feedback and contextual alignment [11–13], whereas poorly executed approaches risk cognitive overload; moreover, evaluation is complicated by methodological inconsistencies and publication bias [14].

In this study we ask: (1) How do gamification effects vary across age groups and genders? (2) What added value do structural, competence-based analyses offer compared to conventional statistics?

A. Thomas et al. (Eds.): JCSG 2025, LNCS 16243, pp. 319–324, 2026.
https://doi.org/10.1007/978-3-032-10518-9_27

2 The Basketball Challenge

The Basketball Challenge is an educational app for secondary school students focusing on ballistic trajectories. Players adjust force, angle, and height to shoot balls of various materials into a hoop. Both a standard and a gamified version are publicly accessible at *chimeo.ch/BasketballChallenge*.

The learning content follows Switzerland's *Lehrplan 21* and targets competencies on force, angle, height, mass, resistance, gravity, buoyancy, and magnetic forces. The app comprises a practice level and eight structured levels that progressively increase in difficulty and illustrate specific physics concepts. Before play, users provide basic personal details and complete a pre-test; a post-test follows gameplay to assess knowledge acquisition. Each level has a clear objective, offers up to two hints, and allows three attempts per ball.

While core physics mechanics are identical in both versions, the gamified version adds visual enhancements, guided instructions from a robot character, a countdown timer, and a scoring system that rewards attempt successes (Fig. 1); the standard version omits these features. As isolating individual elements is beyond the scope here, we consider gamification as a holistic bundle of features.

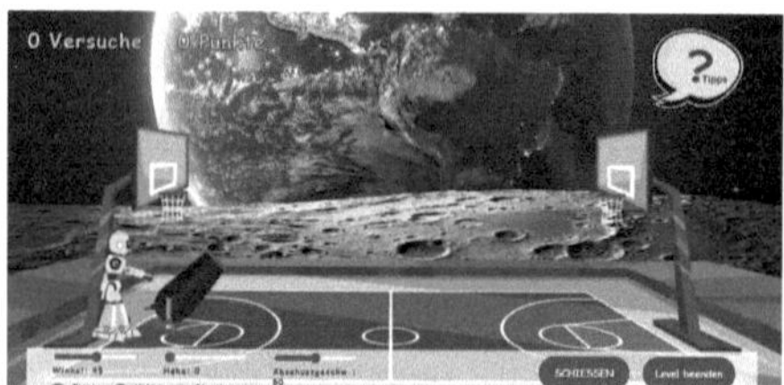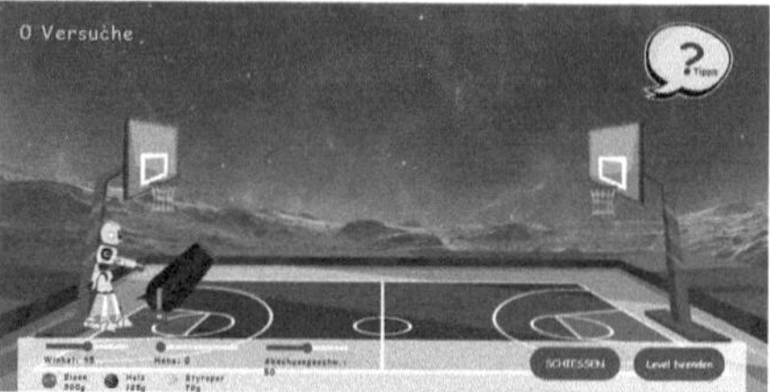

Fig. 1. Level 5 (moon). Left: gamified version; right: standard version.

3 Method

Data were collected via direct recruitment of school classes to ensure session control and higher test completion. In total, 170 students from nine classes participated (71 male, 73 female, 26 unspecified; $M_{age} = 13.66$, SD $= 0.79$, range 11–16). Grade distribution: 6th $= 10$, 7th $= 25$, 8th $= 76$, 9th $= 34$ (25 missing). 89 students used the gamified version and 81 the standard version. Sessions took place within one lesson: students entered personal data (age, gender), completed a pre-test, played the practice level and eight levels (5 min per level, three attempts per ball), then completed the post-test. No competition was encouraged; the app does not promote competitive behavior.

4 Results

4.1 General Performance

In the practice level we found non-significant differences for all dependent variables' main effects and interactions. For the eight game levels, we computed the sum of the dependent variables (attempts, hits, points, and time). Across the eight game levels, means were comparable across condition and gender; grade level showed significant main effects on hits, points, and time. A MANOVA yielded a significant main effect of grade level on hits (F(2, 141) = 5.843, p < .001, η2 = .123), points (F(2, 141) = 7.707, p < .001, η2 = .158), and time (F(2, 141) = 6.870, p = .002, η2 = .104) (Fig. 2).

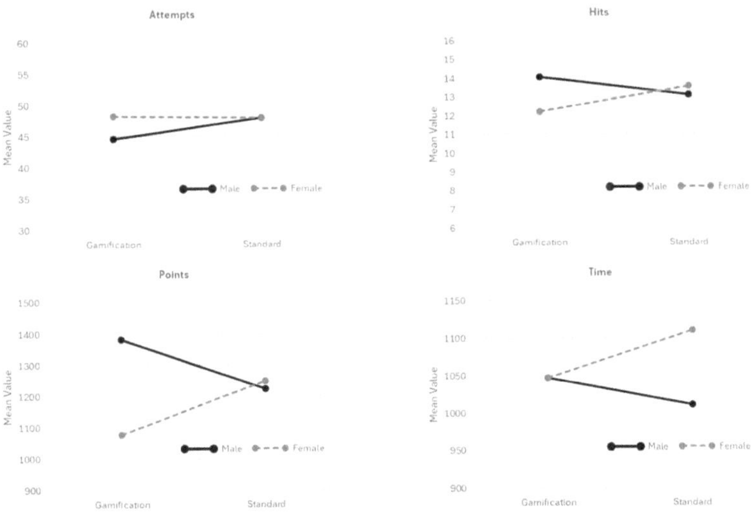

Fig. 2. Interaction diagrams for gender by condition.

More interestingly, the results yielded a distinct interaction of gender and condition. While for attempts there was no interaction (GM: 44.61 (SD = 8.45), GF: 48.14 (SD = 8.745); SM: 47.93 (SD = 6.91); SF: 47.94 (SD = 8.64); F(2, 141) = 3.511, p = .063, η2 = .029), we found a significant interaction of condition and gender for the other variables. Males produced significantly more hits in the gamification condition than in the standard condition (GM: 14.06 (SD = 3.44); SM: 13.1 (SD = 3.64)), while females showed the opposite (GF: 12.23 (SD = 2.67); SF: 13.56 (SD = 3.84)); F(2, 141) = 4.713, p = .032, η2 = .038. Equally, males scored significantly more points in the gamification condition than in the standard condition (GM: 1382.12 (SD = 454.57); SM: 1222.41 (SD = 408.94)), while females showed the opposite (GF: 1077.14 (SD = 261.09); SF: 1247.94 (SD = 451.15)); F(2, 141) = 6.738, p = .011, η2 = .054. Finally, males spent more time in the gamification than in the standard condition (GM: 1047.15 (SD = 370.65); SM: 1010.45 (SD = 216.74)), while females showed the opposite (GF: 1046.86 (SD = 257.67); SF: 1109.88 (SD = 279.58)); F(2, 141) = 4.086, p = .045, η2 = .033. (MANOVA: DVs = attempts, hits, points, time; IVs = condition, gender, grade level; no covariates entered.)

In addition to the main dependent variables, we analyzed the ratio between attempts and hits (AHR; attempts/hits) and the average time per attempt. For AHR, main effects were not significant (gamification: 0.30 (SD = 0.29), standard: 0.29 (SD = 0.09); males: 0.30 (SD = 0.27), females: 0.10 (SD = 0.08)), but a condition by gender interaction emerged (F(1, 141) = 8.509, p = .004, η2 = .067). For average time per attempt, main effects were not significant (gamification: 23.29 s (SD = 9.34), standard: 23.07 s (SD = 8.19); males: 22.73 (SD = 7.58), females: 23.59 (SD = 9.75)), with a significant condition by gender interaction (F(1, 141) = 7.058, p = .009, η2 = .056).

4.2 Knowledge Tests

In the pretest, we did not find significant performance differences (p = .796): gamification M = 4.91 (SD = 1.87), standard M = 4.46 (SD = 1.90). There were no gender differences (p = .308): males M = 5.15 (SD = 1.77), females M = 4.73 (SD = 1.95). In the posttest, we also did not find significant differences for condition (p = .599): gamification M = 4.54 (SD = 2.08), standard M = 4.38 (SD = 1.73). Across all conditions, there was a slight decrease from pre to post (-0.45, SD = 1.85). Of 170 participants, 136 completed the pretest and 110 the posttest; 101 (59%) completed both; r(pre, post) = .554. Across variables and conditions, correlations with post-test and gain scores were small and inconsistent ($|r| \leq 0.27$); we refrain from inferential claims.

4.3 Structural Analyses

We applied Knowledge Space Theory (KST) and its competence-based extension (CbKST). A surmise relation derived from the level design yielded a knowledge space with 11 of 2^8 admissible states. Model fit was good: MSSD = 1.264 (SD = 0.932). Using a size–fit trade-off [15], 11/256 = 4.29% predicts about 7.30 zero-distance patterns by chance; we observed 40 (23.53%), $\chi2(1, N = 170) = 138.45$, p < .001. Participants were distributed across the eleven states; 59/170 were in the empty state.

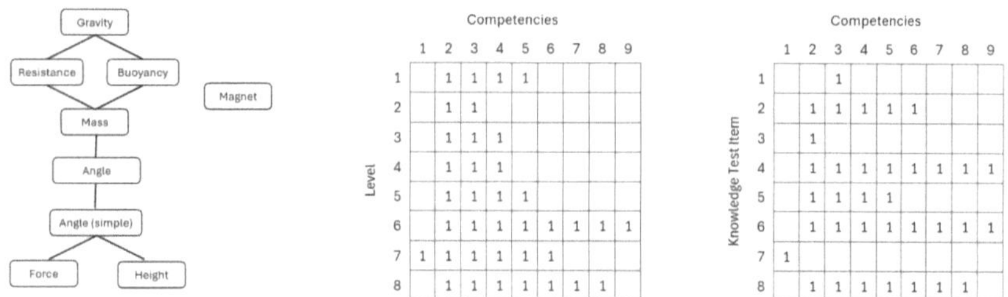

Fig. 3. The left panel shows the Hasse diagram of the proposed prerequisite relation among the competencies. The right panel shows the competencies associated to game levels and knowledge test items.

For diagnostic purposes, CbKST modeled latent competencies (Fig. 3: prerequisite diagram and assignment to levels/items). The competence space comprised 22 states; game and test together mapped to 13 unique states overall. Cardinality differences indicated moderate alignment between game- and pre-test-derived states (median $\Delta = 2$; mean = 3.32, SD = 2.61) and between pre- and post-test (median $\Delta = 1$; mean = 2.44, SD = 2.70). Learning effects based on cardinality were small and non-significant (gamified + 0.64 vs standard − 0.02; t(100) = 0.9174, p = .180); most participants showed no gains, and large changes likely reflect test artefacts (e.g., low motivation).

5 Discussion

We found no overall condition effect, so gamification should not be assumed to improve motivation or learning outcomes per se, in line with prior syntheses [16]. The clearest pattern was a Gender $\times$ Condition interaction in game performance—boys benefited from the gamified version, girls did not—while knowledge-test scores showed no gender differences [17]. This cautions against one-size-fits-all mechanics (e.g., competitive elements) and aligns with evidence on gendered engagement as well as policy concerns about unintended disparities [18, 19].

Pre–post tests showed no substantial gains and aligned only weakly with gameplay. Given the reduced completion rates and immediate timing, low post-test motivation is a plausible factor [20]. The marginal correlations between raw game metrics and test scores point to a mismatch between recorded performance and targeted competencies, consistent with stealth-assessment work showing that in-game success may capture broader skills than those probed by short knowledge tests [21]. This suggests a need to better align in-game telemetry with construct-relevant competencies and to reduce opportunities for trial-and-error success.

Structural analyses (KST/CbKST) provided added value: the instructional model fit the data well and revealed competence structure beyond aggregate scores, including slight, non-significant competence gains (gamified > standard). Thus, structural, competence-based diagnostics appear to be a useful complement to conventional statistics when evaluating game-based learning.

Limitations include short exposure, missing post-tests, and the immediate test context, all of which may attenuate measurable gains. Future work should (i) refine mechanics for inclusivity (given the Gender $\times$ Condition finding), (ii) strengthen the alignment between competencies, telemetry, and tests, and (iii) examine longer interventions where learning effects are more likely to emerge.

Acknowledgments. The research presented in this paper was funded by the Swiss National Fund (SNF) under grant number 100014_207864.

References

1. Slamet, T.I., Meng, C.: Gamification in collaborative learning: synthesizing evidence through meta-analysis. J. Comput. Educ. (2025)
2. Fernández-Velásquez, J.D.R., López-Regalado, O., Fernández-Hurtado, G.A.: Educational dualism in action: systematic review of gamification and flipped classrooms' effects on young learners. Contemp. Educ. Technol. **17**(1), 557 (2025)
3. Galan-Elvira, J., Palau-Irisarri, P.: Who's Who in Zoology: Transversal application of gamification and new technologies in university teaching. Front. Vet. Sci. **12**, 1596906 (2025)
4. Sounthornwiboon, P., Sriprasertpap, K., Nilsook, P.: Simulation game-based learning for cognitive apprenticeship development: a focus on processing speed. Cogent Educ. **12**(1), 2449280 (2025)
5. Mushtaq, N., Nazeer, N., Fayaz, I., Gulzar, F.: Next-gen learning: gamification's impact on higher education. Educ. Inf. Technol. (2025)

6. Kohn, A.: Punished by Rewards: The Trouble with Gold Stars, Incentive Plans, A's, Praise, and Other Bribes, 25th edn. Houghton Mifflin Harcourt (2018)

7. Bogost, I.: Why gamification is bullshit. In: Walz, S.P., Deterding, S. (eds.) The Gameful World: Approaches, Issues, Applications, pp. 65–79. MIT Press (2015)

8. Nadi-Ravandi, M., Batooli, Z.: Exploring gamification in digital education: a bibliometric analysis. Libr. Hi Tech **42**(2), 381–391 (2024)

9. Perkins, D.N., Salomon, G.: Rocky roads to transfer: rethinking mechanisms of a neglected phenomenon. Educ. Psychol. **24**(2), 113–142 (1989)

10. Perkins, D.N., Salomon, G.: Knowledge to go: a motivational and dispositional view of transfer. Educ. Psychol. **47**(3), 248–258 (2012)

11. Garris, R., Ahlers, R., Driskell, J.E.: Games, motivation, and learning: a research and practice model. Simul. Gaming **33**(4), 441–467 (2002)

12. Wouters, P., van Oostendorp, H., van der Spek, E.D.: A meta-analysis of the cognitive and motivational effects of serious games. J. Educ. Psychol. **105**(2), 249–265 (2013)

13. Mayer, R.E.: Computer games in education. Annu. Rev. Psychol. **70**, 531–549 (2019)

14. Gris, G., Bengtson, C.: Assessment measures in game-based learning research: a systematic review. Int. J. Serious Games **8**(1), 3–26 (2021)

15. Albert, D., Kickmeier-Rust, M.D., Matsuda, F.: A formal framework for modelling the developmental course of competence and performance in the distance, speed, and time domain. Dev. Rev. **28**, 401–420 (2008)

16. Diaz, A.F., Estoque-Loñez, H.: A meta-analysis on the effectiveness of gamification on student learning achievement. Int. J. Educ. Math. Sci. Technol. **12**(5), 1236–1253 (2024)

17. Li, M., Ma, S., Shi, Y.: Examining the effectiveness of gamification as a tool promoting teaching and learning in educational settings: a meta-analysis. Front. Psychol. **14**, Article no. 1253549 (2023)

18. Chung, L., Chang, R.: The effect of gender on motivation and student achievement in digital game-based learning: a case study of a content-based classroom. EURASIA J. Math. Sci. Technol. Educ. **13**(6) (2017)

19. European Parliament. Report on promoting gender equality in science, technology, engineering and mathematics (STEM) education and careers (A9-0163/2021) (2021). https://www.europarl.europa.eu/doceo/document/A-9-2021-0163_EN.pdf

20. Plass, J.L., Homer, B.D., Kinzer, C.K.: Foundations of game-based learning. Educ. Psychol. **50**(4), 258–283 (2015)

21. Shute, V.J., Ventura, M.: Stealth Assessment: Measuring and Supporting Learning in Video Games. MIT Press (2013)

Health

A Co-designed Serious Game to Promote Parental Emotion Regulation: Development and Pilot Usability Study

Eliana Silva[(⊠)], Mónica Pereira, and Luís Paulo Reis

Artificial Intelligence and Computer Science Lab, Faculty of Engineering, University of Porto,
Rua Dr. Roberto Frias, 4200-465 Porto, Portugal
elianasilva@fe.up.pt

Abstract. Parenthood poses challenges to emotion regulation (ER), especially during the transition to adolescence, a period of major emotional and social changes. Despite programs for improving emotional skills, access to mental health services is limited. To address these challenges, this study presents the development of a serious game (SG), called *EmoBalance*, to help parents of young adolescents identify emotions and learn ER strategies based on the *Process Model of Emotion Regulation*. The game design involved interviews with the target audience and relevant stakeholders. A pilot usability evaluation was conducted with three psychologists and three mothers to assess their experience of and satisfaction with the game. The mothers identified with the topics addressed in the SG. The psychologists recognized the game's potential for clinical application. Additional mechanics to increase parental engagement are recommended. By helping parents to deal with their own emotions and increase their knowledge of how to model and teach ER processes to their adolescents, it is also expected to contribute to the development of these skills in adolescents.

Keywords: Emotion Regulation Strategies · Serious Games · Co-Design · Parents · Adolescents

1 Introduction

Parenthood is a demanding period in which parents must manage their own emotions while modeling these skills for their children [1]. As primary socialization agents, parents significantly influence adolescents' emotion regulation (ER) development. For instance, variability in father–adolescent closeness relates to long-term emotion dysregulation in adolescents [2], while mothers' use of cognitive reappraisal correlates with their children's strategies in both retrospective [3] and real-time assessments [4]. This highlights the importance of parents regulating their own emotions to foster healthy ER in their children. Parent-focused ER programs have shown positive outcomes—improving parents' emotional socialization, self-efficacy, and reducing adolescents' emotional and behavioral issues [5]. However, many adolescents still lack adequate mental health care, with parents acting as key access facilitators [6]. Barriers include systemic factors,

A. Thomas et al. (Eds.): JCSG 2025, LNCS 16243, pp. 327–332, 2026.
https://doi.org/10.1007/978-3-032-10518-9_28

mental health literacy, and stigma. In this context, serious games (SGs) are promising tools, offering engaging, low-barrier interventions for families with limited access to services [7]. Successful SGs balance educational content with entertainment value [6]. This study presents the co-designed development of *EmoBalance*, a serious game offering psychoeducation on basic emotions and ER strategies in daily parent–adolescent interactions and explores its preliminary feasibility and acceptability among parents and healthcare professionals.

2 Related Work

A systematic review of parenting intervention apps revealed that online programs generally improve the mental health of both children and parents. However, most apps focus on tracking children's outcomes, with few offering features for parents, such as mood tracking [8]. Similarly, most SG's are designed for children and adolescents, with few involving parents. Exceptions include *Zirkus Empathico* [9] and *New Horizon* [10], which are both parent-assisted SGs. *Zirkus Empathico* aims to enhance socio-emotional skills in children with autism spectrum disorder (ASD). The primary goal is for children to transfer the skills learned in the game to real-life situations. Parental engagement is crucial to achieving this, and reports indicated high levels of parental satisfaction with the treatment [9]. *New Horizon* targets stress and anxiety in children with ASD using relaxation techniques. When used alongside the *SpaceControl* parent app, it provides insights into the child's gaming behavior and emotional state, helping parents to understand their children. The game and app were designed based on parental feedback and usability tests have shown promise in reducing stress and anxiety in children [10].

3 Method

3.1 Overview of the Serious Game

The SG is based on the six basic emotions defined by Ekman [11]: happiness, sadness, fear, anger, surprise, and disgust. Once the emotion has been recognized, the parent is asked to select how they would react to the situation. The SG is also based on the *Process Model of ER* and addresses five ER strategy families: situation selection, situation modification, attentional deployment, cognitive reappraisal, and response modulation. These strategies differ in their impact on functioning [12]. Our multidisciplinary team consisted of a psychologist researcher with experience in developing digital health solutions and two computer engineers. The SG, called *EmoBalance* was developed through a co-design process, in which we involved a small group of clinical and health psychologists ($n = 4$), a mother and a young female adolescent from the early stages of the design process to assess the needs and preferences assessment of the target audience. We conducted semi-structured online interviews with the main aim of identifying key motivational and learning features for SG. The interviews, their thematic analysis, and the main findings are described in a previous study [13].

EmoBalance is a narrative game involving interactive decision-making. It consists of five levels depicting increasingly challenging situations of parent-adolescent interaction.

Examples include an adolescent arriving home angry after a fight with a classmate at school, or an adolescent becoming frustrated because a padel match is not going well. The aim is for players to answer as truthfully as possible about how they would react in the given situation. At the end of each level, we encourage parents to discuss each situation together as a couple. Parents are asked to choose a character to play. The adolescent character alternates between a girl and a boy, and the parent character alternates between a mother and a father. Each level begins with dialogue or narration to give players a clearer understanding of the situation. First, parents must identify the emotion experienced by the adolescent through a puzzle involving scrambled letters that the player must rearrange to form the correct word. To assist with this task, the adolescent's animation reflects their current emotion, and optional clues are also provided. Then, the game offers several ER strategies that can be applied to a specific interaction. Some of these strategies are rated as more adaptive than others (see Fig. 1). Each time an ER strategy is used, feedback is displayed, informing the player of the name of the strategy and providing an explanation to help them familiarize themselves with the names of the strategies. Finally, once the player has decided, the story progresses based on that decision. The game is available on Android mobile devices.

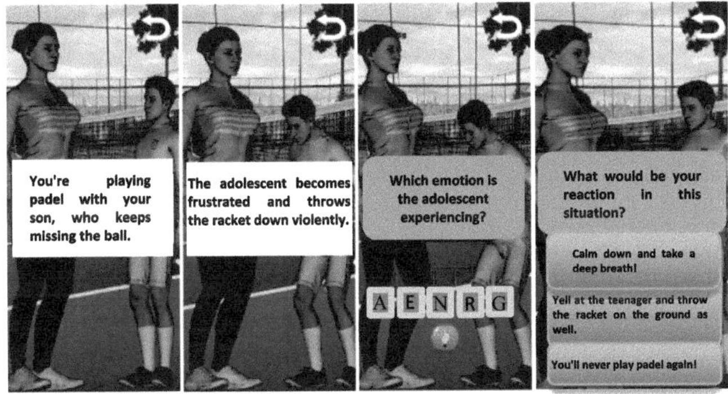

Fig. 1. The sequence of emotional situations, the letter puzzle for identifying the emotion and some of the ER strategies options to the game

3.2 Implementation Details

The serious game was developed in Unity using assets from the Unity Asset Store for the user interface (UI), music, sound effects and 3D models. The characters and animations were sourced from Mixamo, a platform offering high-quality, textured 3D assets [14]. The game's narrative was created using Ink, a user-friendly, open-source scripting language integrated with Unity that supports branching storylines and features the Inky Editor for debugging and visualization. A scoring system tracks player progress: adaptive responses and the use of ER strategies increase points, while non-adaptive responses and clue usage reduce them. Scores and user choices (e.g., avatar) are stored using Unity's PlayerPrefs.

4   Preliminary Usability Study

4.1   Procedure

The codesign process and pilot usability study received ethical approval from the University Ethics Committee (N° 9 /CE FEUP/2024), following the Helsinki Declaration and national data protection law (Lei N.º 58/2019). A small convenience sample of parents and psychologists was recruited via email. Participants were informed about the study and provided written informed consent. No compensation was provided. The online usability study involved participants completing a sociodemographic and gaming habits questionnaire, playing the game for one week, and then completing a post-game questionnaire. Data collection ensured anonymity, security and confidentiality.

4.2   Measures

Sociodemographic Questionnaire: Participants were asked to provide sociodemographic information (e.g., age, gender, nationality), followed by questions about their experience with technology and digital games.

Open-Ended Questions: Participants were asked to answer open-ended questions. Professionals provided feedback on the relevance and difficulty of the topics covered in the game and whether they would use or recommend the game to other professionals. Parents were asked to indicate whether they would play or recommend the game to friends or family, and whether they could relate the stories in the game.

5   Results

5.1   Participants

The participants included 2 professionals who participated in the codesign interviews, as well as 1 new professional and 3 new mothers. The psychologists had an average of 9 years of experience ($SD = 5.57$). They all had experience with both digital technologies (e.g., smartphones, computers) and games, except for one participant who reported very low proficiency with digital games. The mothers were aged between 38 and 55 years old ($M = 45.33$; $SD = 8.74$) and had an average of 2 children. They were familiar with digital technologies, but only one had experience with digital games.

5.2   Open-Ended Questions

All the psychologists reported that they would like to use this tool in their professional practice. They reported that the game is a useful, engaging, and accessible tool for teaching ER strategies and self-awareness. However, one professional emphasized that there should be more options to choose from in certain situations, as some alternatives present very idealized and stereotyped answers. They appreciated that the game encouraged the parents to discuss situations with their partners and that it clearly described the strategy that's being used. This added to parents' discussions about emotional situations with their children. Similarly, the professionals reported that they would recommend the game to others in their field, as it provides an engaging way to develop parenting skills with clear, concrete, and realistic examples. Psychologists recommended it as a complement to therapy, suggesting that it could be used as *"homework"* for discussion in subsequent sessions. They felt that the issues and situations explored were appropriate and relevant to parents. They found the level of difficulty satisfactory, although one psychologist said that some parents might find it difficult to recognize emotions (in the puzzle mini-game), even the optional hints. The professionals' views on the quality of the system were clear. All of them completed the game and found it easy to use. In terms of mothers' perceptions, two reported that they would not use the SG in their daily lives *"because it's not appealing and the answers are not quick"*. They also said that they would not recommend it to family and friends because *"they didn't find it productive enough"*. However, all the mothers identified with the themes of the game, adding that *"they reflect the daily situations we go through"*. One mother suggested removing the puzzle mini-game and replacing it with multiple-choice questions. Another mother said that the idea for the game was interesting but that it should appeal more to parents and explore emotions such as anxiety and injustice.

6 Discussion

EmoBalance aims to address the lack of effective parental interventions by developing a SG to serve as a psychoeducational tool for parents. This innovative approach to ER training is based on evidence regarding parental roles in adolescent ER (e.g. [3, 4]). The game is based on the Ekman's *Basic Emotions* [11] and the *Process Model of ER* [12], ensuring its relevance in theory and practical relevance. Incorporating scientific foundations early was essential for creating a meaningful and evidence-based product. The development was shaped by a co-design process involving a mother, an adolescent and a clinical psychologist. Despite the small sample size, the participants provided valuable input for the narrative and game design [13]. The game was well received by professionals who recommended its application in clinical practice. In the usability study, the target audience, represented by a small sample of mothers, highlighted some concerns about the game's engagement and relevance to their daily lives, although they identified clearly with the topics addressed. This result may be explained by their limited involvement in the co-design process and their unfamiliarity with video games, which made it difficult to understand parent engagement and design preferences. The SG is notable as the first to provide ER skill training for parents of adolescents, combining co-design with evidence-based ER frameworks. While limitations exist, such as the small sample size, this pilot version paves the way for future development and research. Future iterations should address parental feedback regarding storyline complexity, co-parent collaboration, avatar customization, more engaging mini-games, and expansion to iOS. We believe that this work highlights the importance of ER in parenting, and that our SG is a valuable tool for introducing this topic to parents.

Acknowledgments. This work was financially supported by: UID/00027 - Artificial Intelligence and Computer Science Laboratory – LIACC - funded by national funds through the FCT/MCTES (PIDDAC).

Disclosure of Interests. The authors have no competing interests to declare that are relevant to the content of this article.

References

1. Rutherford, H.J.V., Wallace, N.S., Laurent, H.K., Mayes, L.C.: Emotion regulation in parenthood. Dev. Rev. **36**, 1–14 (2014). https://doi.org/10.1016/j.dr.2014.12.008
2. Chiang, S.-C., Bai, S., Wa Mak, H., Fosco, G.M.: Dynamic characteristics of parent–adolescent closeness: predicting adolescent emotion dysregulation. Fam. Process. **4**, 2243–2257 (2024)
3. Bariola, E., Hughes, E.K., Gullone, E.: Relationships between parent and child emotion regulation strategy use: a brief report. J. Child Fam. Stud. **21**, 443–448 (2012). https://doi.org/10.1007/s10826-011-9497-5
4. Silva, E., Freire, T., Faria, S.: The emotion regulation strategies of adolescents and their parents: an experience sampling study. J. Child Fam. Stud. **27** (2018). https://doi.org/10.1007/s10826-018-1015-6
5. Ansar, N., Nissen Lie, H.A., Stiegler, J.R.: The effects of emotion-focused skills training on parental mental health, emotion regulation and self-efficacy: mediating processes between parents and children. Psychother. Res. **34** (2024). https://doi.org/10.1080/10503307.2023.2218539
6. Silvers, J.A.: Adolescence as a pivotal period for emotion regulation development. Curr. Opin. Psychol. **44**, 258–263 (2022). https://doi.org/10.1016/J.COPSYC.2021.09.023
7. Connolly, T.M., Boyle, E.A., MacArthur, E., Hainey, T., Boyle, J.M.: A systematic literature review of empirical evidence on computer games and serious games. Comput. Educ. **59**, 661–686 (2012). https://doi.org/10.1016/J.COMPEDU.2012.03.004
8. David, O.A., Iuga, I.A., Miron, I.S.: Parenting: there is an app for that. A systematic review of parenting interventions apps. Child. Youth Serv. Rev. **156**, 107385 (2024). https://doi.org/10.1016/J.CHILDYOUTH.2023.107385
9. Kirst, S., et al.: Fostering socio-emotional competencies in children on the autism spectrum using a parent-assisted serious game: a multicenter randomized controlled trial. Behav. Res. Ther. **152** (2022). https://doi.org/10.1016/J.BRAT.2022.104068
10. Carlier, S., Van der Paelt, S., Ongenae, F., De Backere, F., De Turck, F.: Empowering children with ASD and their parents: design of a serious game for anxiety and stress reduction. Sensors (Switzerland). **20**, 20–23 (2020). https://doi.org/10.3390/s20040966
11. Ekman, P.: Basic emotions. In: Dalgleish, T., Power, M. (eds.) Handbook of Cognition and Emotion, vol. 39. Wiley, Sussex (1999)
12. Gross, J.J.: Emotion regulation: current status and future prospects. Psychol. Inq. **26**, 1–26 (2015). https://doi.org/10.1080/1047840X.2014.940781
13. Pereira, M., Reis, S., Reis, L.P., Silva, E.: Co-design of a serious game to promote emotion regulation strategies in parents. In: 2024 IEEE Conference on Games (CoG), pp. 1–4. IEEE, Milan (2024)
14. Mixamo. https://www.mixamo.com/#/. Accessed 26 Nov 2024

Cardiorespiratory Effects of an Adaptive Ergometer-Based Exergame: Evaluation Study of *SkyRide*

Fadi Jogho[1] , George Jogho[2]([email]) , and Stefan Göbel[1]

[1] Technical University of Darmstadt, AG Serious Games, 64283 Darmstadt, Germany
[2] Section of Health Care Research and Rehabilitation Research, Faculty of Medicine and Medical Center, University of Freiburg, Freiburg im Breisgau, Germany
george.jogho@uniklinik-freiburg.de

Abstract. Regular physical activity is essential for maintaining health, yet many adults remain inactive - often due to low motivation or lack of access to engaging training formats. Exergames, which combine physical movement with interactive gameplay, offer a promising solution. However, many existing systems fail to reach sufficient intensity to produce measurable physiological benefits. This study evaluates *SkyRide*, an adaptive exergame integrated into the immersive ExerCube system, which merges virtual environments with ergometer-based endurance training. Twenty-one healthy adults participated in a comparative assessment involving both a conventional cycle ergometer session and a *SkyRide* session. Key physiological parameters - maximum heart rate (HRmax) and maximal oxygen uptake (VO_2max) - were continuously recorded. Findings indicate that *SkyRide* can elicit cardiovascular responses comparable to traditional ergometer training in the overall sample. However, subgroup analyses revealed differing patterns of exertion: female and lower-fit participants showed signs of overexertion, while male and high-fit participants experienced an appropriate level of exertion to slight underload. Subjective feedback was largely positive, with many participants describing *SkyRide* as motivating, varied, and physically engaging. Overall, *SkyRide* demonstrates potential as a health-oriented training modality capable of delivering effective cardiorespiratory stimulation in an enjoyable format. Enhancing the system's ability to adjust intensity based on individual fitness levels is recommended to improve training balance across user groups.

Keywords: Exergame · Ergometer · Cardiorespiratory Effects · Study · SkyRide · Health Care

1 Introduction

Despite the well-documented health benefits of regular physical activity, a large proportion of adults worldwide remain insufficiently active, failing to meet WHO recommendations [1]. Conventional training programs are often hindered by time constraints, organizational barriers, and low motivation [2], highlighting the need for accessible and engaging alternatives.

A. Thomas et al. (Eds.): JCSG 2025, LNCS 16243, pp. 333–350, 2026.
https://doi.org/10.1007/978-3-032-10518-9_29

Exergames are video games that require physical movement that can offer a promising approach to promote physical activity across diverse populations [3, 4]. Their motivational potential has been shown to increase exercise adherence and provide an enjoyable supplement or alternative to traditional training formats [5–7]. However, many exergames induce only low to moderate intensity, often insufficient to meet activity guidelines or elicit training effects, particularly in active individuals [8–10]. This is often due to limited integration of game design and exercise control [11]. Adaptive systems with higher intensities and individualized protocols are needed to achieve meaningful physiological benefits [12, 13].

The exergame SkyRide, developed within the ExerCube system, aims to address these challenges by combining immersive, game-based endurance training with conventional cycle ergometer training. The ExerCube uses CAVE technology (Cave Automatic Virtual Environment) to deliver visual, auditory, and haptic stimuli through three projection surfaces and padded walls [14, 15] (see Sect. 2.4).

The present study examines whether SkyRide elicits physiological responses, measured by HRmax and VO_2max, that are comparable to those of conventional cycle ergometer training. It also investigates subgroup differences (e.g., by sex, fitness level, or smoking status) and subjective ratings of motivation and acceptance to evaluate its potential as a health-oriented training format.

2　Methods

2.1　Hypotheses

It is hypothesized that the maximum heart rate (HRmax) does not differ significantly between SkyRide and conventional cycle ergometer training (H1). It is expected that the difference in HRmax between both training conditions does not vary significantly depending on participants' sex (H2a), fitness level (H2b), or smoking status (H2c).

Maximal oxygen uptake (VO_2max) during SkyRide is hypothesized not to differ significantly from that during conventional ergometer training (H3). Similarly, the difference in VO_2max between SkyRide and conventional ergometer training is not expected to vary significantly by sex (H4a), fitness level (H4b), or smoking status (H4c).

In addition, the agreement between the average heart rate measured during gameplay and the target heart rate specified in the protocol is examined. Also, subjective experience, including perceived motivation and acceptance, is assessed.

2.2　Measurement Parameters and Data Collection

To assess training load, maximum heart rate (HRmax) and maximal oxygen uptake (VO_2max) were recorded as the primary parameters. Both were measured continuously during the exercise sessions. Heart rate was recorded using a chest strap sensor (Polar H10), and VO_2max was measured via a spiroergometric mask (VO_2 Master Analyzer). Both devices were connected to the VO_2 Master Manager app for data acquisition. Oxygen saturation (SpO_2) was monitored intermittently using a pulse oximeter (Beurer PO 30) for safety purposes only and was not included in the statistical analysis.

2.3 Sample

A total of 22 healthy adults aged 18 to 35 years participated in the study. One individual withdrew early due to illness, resulting in a final sample size of $N = 21$ participants (for details see Table 1). Inclusion and exclusion criteria were based on established recommendations [16, 17]. Eligible participants were healthy and physically capable individuals without known cardiovascular, pulmonary, or metabolic disorders. Participation required written informed consent and the willingness to complete two test sessions spaced 48 to 72 h apart, to ensure recovery and comparability [7, 18]. Exclusion criteria included medical contraindications, use of cardiovascular medication, alcohol or drug dependence, and acute health complaints [19, 20]. Occasional exercise or moderate smoking was not considered exclusionary. Termination criteria included dizziness, chest pain, shortness of breath, technical issues, reaching the age-adjusted maximum heart rate according to Fairbarn ($208 - 0.8 \times$ age for men; $201 - 0.63 \times$ age for women), or voluntary withdrawal by the participant [21, 22].

For subgroup analyses, participants were categorized by sex, fitness level, and smoking status. Sex and smoking behavior were determined using a self-report questionnaire. Regular smoking was defined as at least one instance per week. Fitness level was determined based on the VO_2max values obtained during the exercise test. Classification was performed using the VO_2 Master Manager app, which evaluates VO_2max results in an age- and sex-specific manner. The app's original five-level fitness scale was reduced to two categories: high and low fitness, for analysis purposes, as only corresponding values were represented in the sample (based on Caserman et al., 2024 [23]).

Table 1. Samples' Demographic.

Characteristic	Mean ± SD
Age (years)	23.14 ± 3.97
Sex (m/f)	10/11
Fitness level (high / low)	8/13
Smoking status (smokers/non-smokers)	6/15
Weight (kg)	65.67 ± 11.74
Height (cm)	169.88 ± 8.68
BMI (kg/m^2)	22.66 ± 3.02

2.4 Test Conditions

The study included two distinct test conditions: a conventional cycle ergometer test, used as a reference to assess physiological load, and a game-based endurance training session using the exergame SkyRide within the ExerCube system (see Fig. 1).

Conventional Cycle Ergometer Test (Test Condition 1). A graded exercise test was used as the preferred protocol for performance assessment. The test began at 50 watts and increased by 25 watts every two minutes. This standardized stepwise protocol is scientifically established and enables precise measurement of cardiopulmonary parameters such as heart rate and oxygen uptake [24, 25]. Compared to continuous or ramp tests, step tests are considered particularly reproducible, physiologically meaningful, and less physically demanding for participants [25].

SkyRide Exergame Session (Test Condition 2). The second test condition consisted of a session with the interactive fitness game SkyRide, integrated into the immersive ExerCube system. The ExerCube is a physically enclosed projection environment based on CAVE (Cave Automatic Virtual Environment) technology, which creates a multisensory experience using high-resolution visuals, real-time auditory feedback, and haptic walls. SkyRide combines ergometer-based training with game-like objectives, creating an experience that is both physically demanding and motivating. Players control a virtual spacecraft navigating through immersive 3D environments - such as outer space scenarios - by pedalling to move forward and steering with body shifts. The cadence (RPM) directly influences forward movement and avatar altitude, while real-time heart rate monitoring is used to adapt ergometer resistance to the target training zone. All gameplay interactions are achieved via physical input on the ergometer, creating a seamless integration between body movement and game mechanics. The goal is to collect virtual rewards (e.g., coins and hearts) by flying through rings, while avoiding obstacles such as asteroids or mines. The heads-up display (HUD) shows the current heart rate (BPM), cadence, resistance (RES), time, score, and remaining lives. Participants receive continuous visual and auditory feedback that encourages effort regulation and immersion. Different avatar types (e.g., aircraft or rocket) offer varied dynamics and challenge levels.

To ensure standardization, all participants completed the scenario "Rocket" in the "Space" level. Personal data and a fixed resistance range (80 to 180 watts) were entered in advance. Resistance was automatically adjusted based on the user's current heart rate, with the aim of reaching an individually calculated target heart rate according to Fairbarn's formula.

The selected training mode, "Interval Zone," involved alternating phases of high and low intensity. During high-intensity phases, participants were expected to reach 80 to 90% of their HRmax to ensure a submaximal but effective training stimulus. Throughout the session, physiological data such as heart rate, cadence, and resistance were continuously recorded and displayed on the game interface. The interval structure was predefined and guided participants in adjusting their effort. The session ended automatically after the specified training duration.

 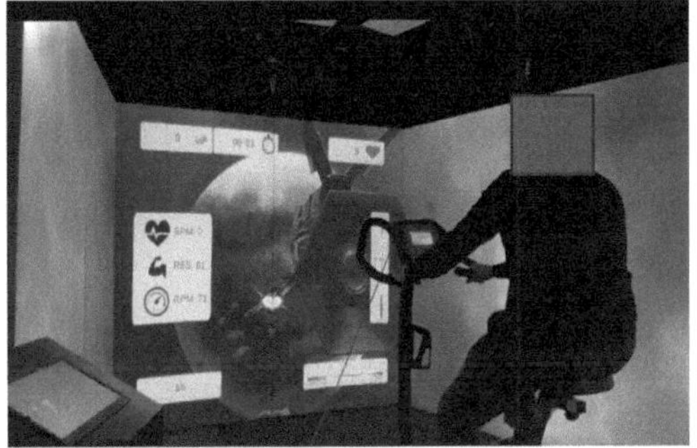

Fig. 1. Left: conventional cycle ergometer with spiroergometric measurement. Right: SkyRide session in the ExerCube immersive environment.

2.5 Study Design and Procedure

The study consisted of two consecutive sessions: Test Condition 1 followed by Test Condition 2. A recovery period of 48 to 72 h was maintained between the two sessions to allow for physiological recovery and to minimalize training-related adaptation effects [18].

At the beginning of each session, participants received standardized instructions, and all measurement devices were calibrated and checked. The first session involved a stepwise graded exercise test on a conventional cycle ergometer, which served as the reference for assessing maximal cardiorespiratory performance. In the second session, participants completed an interactive training session with the exergame SkyRide in the ExerCube.

Participants were then fitted with a VO_2 mask and a heart rate sensor, followed by a warm-up phase, a performance phase, and a recovery phase. Throughout these phases, physiological data - including oxygen uptake (VO_2), heart rate (HR), and peripheral oxygen saturation (SpO2) - were continuously recorded. Data were stored after each session, and participants completed a SkyRide evaluation questionnaire at the end of the second session.

Both test conditions were conducted in the same room in a controlled and comparable environmental setting.

2.6 Statistical Analysis

The required sample size was determined a priori using G*Power (Version 3.1.9.7, Heinrich Heine University Düsseldorf, Germany). Based on similar studies and an assumed effect size of 0.8, with a significance level of $\alpha = 0.05$ and a power of 0.95, the required sample size was calculated to be 19 to 20 participants. This criterion was met with 21 participants included in the final sample.

Results from descriptive analysis of demographic and anthropometric variables (e.g. age, BMI) are reported as mean (M) $\pm$ standard deviation (SD). Statistical analyses of the cardiorespiratory parameters (HRmax and VO_2max) were conducted using Jamovi (Version 2.6.26). These outcomes are also reported as M $\pm$ SD.

To examine differences between the two test conditions in the total sample, paired t-tests were conducted, if normality was confirmed using the Shapiro-Wilk test.

To analyse differences across subgroups (male vs. female, high vs. low fitness, smokers vs. non-smokers), repeated measures analysis of variance (ANOVA) was applied. Where significant effects were found, Bonferroni-corrected post hoc tests were conducted to explore specific group differences.

To assess the practical relevance of findings, effect sizes were calculated: Cohen's d for t-tests (small ≥ 0.2; medium ≥ 0.5; large ≥ 0.8) [26, 27] and partial eta squared (η_p^2) for ANOVAs (small ≥ 0.01; medium ≥ 0.06; large ≥ 0.14) [28].

3 Results

3.1 Maximum Heart Rate (HRmax)

Result for Hypothesis 1: HRmax Difference Between SkyRide and Conventional Cycle Ergometer Test. A paired t-test for the total sample revealed no significant difference in maximum heart rate between the conventional cycle ergometer test (BT: $M_1 = 175.6$, $SD_1 = 10.24$) and the SkyRide condition (EXT: $M_2 = 173.5$, $SD_2 = 13.05$), $p = .52$. The effect size was small ($d = 0.14$). Results for both the total sample and subgroups are summarized in Table 2.

Table 2. Mean Differences in HRmax Between Test Conditions.

Group	N (df)	HRmax (BT)		HRmax (EXT)		Diff 1–2	p	Cohen's d
		M1	SD1	M2	SD2			
Total sample	21 (20)	175.6	10.24	173.5	13.05	2.14	.52	0.14
Male	10 (9)	177.6	8.19	168.8	14.47	8.80	.04	0.73
Female	11 (10)	173.8	11.91	177.7	10.52	−3.91	.42	−0.25
High fitness*	8 (7)	179.9	7.72	165.0	12.51	14.9	.008	1.00
Low fitness	13 (12)	173.0	10.98	178.7	10.73	−5.69	.13	−0.44
Smokers	6 (5)	173.3	8.82	172.3	6.62	1.00	.72	0.15
Non-smokers	15 (14)	176.5	10.90	173.9	15.06	2.60	.57	0.14

Notes: N = sample size, df = degrees of freedom, M1 = mean in BT, M2 = mean in EXT, SD = standard deviation, Diff 1–2 = difference M1–M2, p = significance level, d = Cohen's effect size. * Wilcoxon signed-rank test; all other comparisons: paired-samples t-test

Result for Hypothesis 2: Differences in the EXT–BT HRmax Difference Across Subgroups. A repeated measures ANOVA revealed significant interaction effects between test condition and sex, $F(1, 19) = 4.36$, $p = .04$, $\eta_p^2 = .187$, as well as between test condition and fitness level, $F(1, 19) = 16.33$, $p < .001$, $\eta_p^2 = .46$. No significant interaction was found for smoking status, $F(1, 19) = 0.04$, $p = .83$, $\eta_p^2 = .002$. Post hoc comparisons for the significant interaction effects (gender and fitness level) are illustrated in Fig. 2.

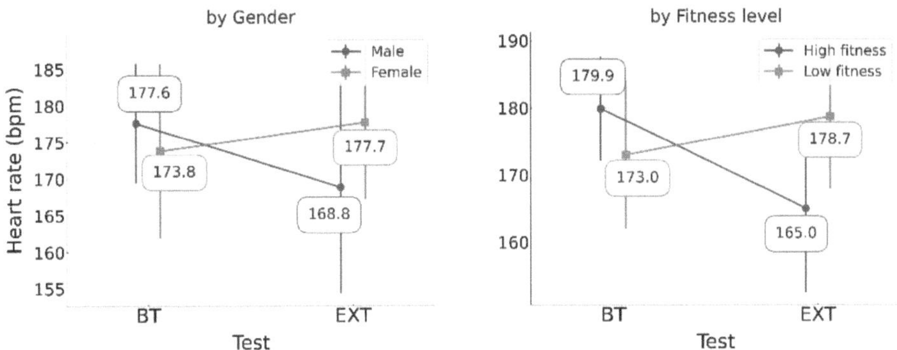

Fig. 2. Post Hoc Comparisons of HRmax in Subgroups. Left: Gender. Right: Fitness level.

3.2 Maximal Oxygen Uptake (VO$_2$max)

Result for Hypothesis 3: VO$_2$max Difference Between SkyRide and Conventional Cycle Ergometer Test. A paired t-test for the total sample showed no significant difference between the two test conditions: BT ($M_1 = 33.1$, $SD_1 = 9.7$) and EXT ($M_2 = 32.4$, $SD_2 = 6.75$), $p = .65$. Results for the total sample and subgroups are presented in Table 3.

Table 3. Mean Differences in VO$_2$max Between Test Conditions.

Group	N (df)	VO$_2$max (BT)		VO$_2$max (EXT)		Diff 1–2	p	Cohen's d
		M1	SD1	M2	SD2			
Total sample	21 (20)	33.1	9.7	32.4	6.75	0.78	.65	0.09
Male	10 (9)	37.6	8.4	33.2	7.93	4.36	.13	0.51
Female	11 (10)	29.1	9.31	31.6	5.74	−2.47	.19	−0.41
High fitness	8 (7)	43.0	6.53	35.8	8.85	7.18	.03	0.92
Low fitness	13 (12)	27.1	5.28	30.4	4.19	−3.16	.03	−0.64
Smokers	6 (5)	32.5	5.32	31.3	3.52	1.14	.72	0.15
Non-smokers	15 (14)	33.4	11.13	32.8	7.75	0.63	.77	0.07

Notes: N = sample size, df = degrees of freedom, M1 = mean in BT, M2 = mean in EXT, SD = standard deviation, Diff 1–2 = difference M1–M2, p = significance level, d = Cohen's effect size

Result for Hypothesis 4: Differences in the EXT–BT VO$_2$max Difference Across Subgroups. Repeated measures ANOVA revealed significant interaction effects between test condition and sex, $F(1, 19) = 4.65$, $p = .04$, $\eta_p^2 = .19$, as well as between test condition and fitness level, $F(1, 19) = 14.10$, $p = .001$, $\eta_p^2 = .42$. No significant interaction was found for smoking status, $F(1, 19) = 0.01$, $p = .89$, $\eta_p^2 = .001$. Post hoc comparisons for the significant interaction effects (gender and fitness level) are displayed in Fig. 3.

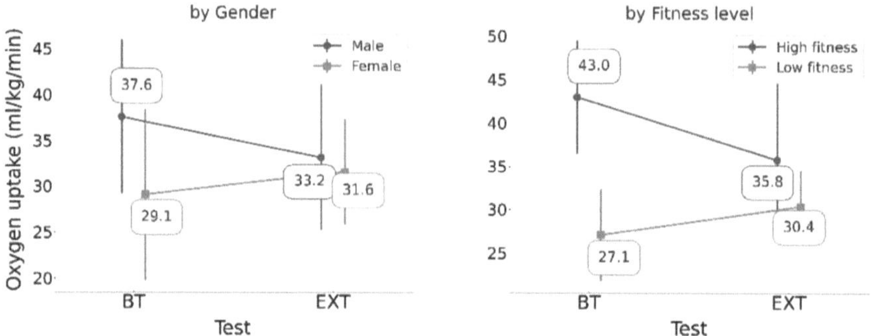

Fig. 3. Post Hoc Comparisons of VO$_2$max in Subgroups. Left: Gender. Right: Fitness level.

3.3 Comparison of Target Heart Rate and Measured Heart Rate During SkyRide

In this analysis, the heart rate measured during the SkyRide session was compared with the individually calculated target heart rate. Target heart rate was defined as 80–90% of the age- and sex-adjusted HRmax calculated according to Fairbarn's formula [21, 22].

Figures 4, 5, 6 and 7 offers a graphical presentation, whereas the calculated maximum heart rate (red line) and the measured in-game heart rate (blue line) were plotted. The target range was highlighted in grey. In addition, the difference between measured and calculated heart rate was shown on the right y-axis, with a range of −10% to −20% defined as the physiologically desirable zone.

Successful target achievement was defined as the measured heart rate falling within the grey area. Deviations above or below this range may indicate overexertion or under exertion, respectively. The following figures show the curves for the total sample and for key subgroups. Further subgroup plots can be viewed via the link.

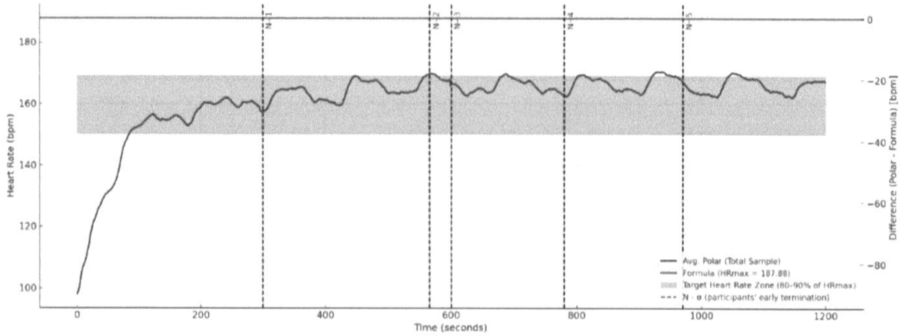

Fig. 4. Target heart rate vs. measured heart rate during SkyRide: total sample.

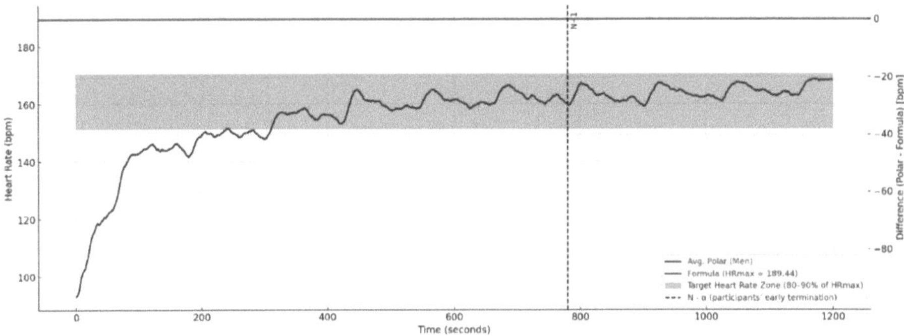

Fig. 5. Target heart rate vs. measured heart rate during SkyRide: male (men) participants.

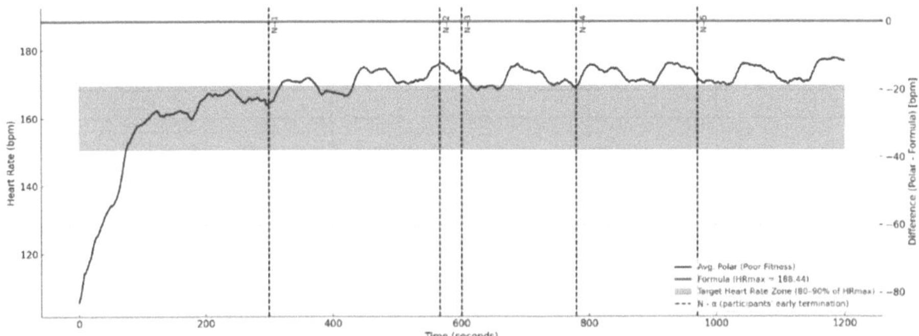

Fig. 6. Target heart rate vs. measured heart rate during SkyRide: participants with low (poor) fitness.

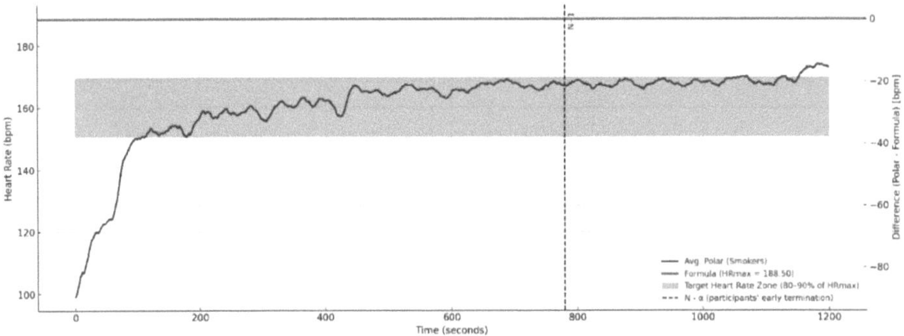

Fig. 7. Target heart rate vs. measured heart rate during SkyRide: smokers.

3.4 Subjective Evaluation of SkyRide: Questionnaire Results

To evaluate the gameplay experience, a questionnaire consisting of 18 items (see Appendix A) was administered. Participants rated various aspects of the game using a five-point Likert scale. Response options ranged from "1- Strongly agree" to "5 -

Strongly disagree." Mean values for the total sample are presented in Fig. 8. Participants' responses can be grouped into five thematic domains: control, perceived exertion, motivation, challenge, and game design and satisfaction.

Control. Movement execution (Question 1, Q1) and responsiveness to pedalling speed (Q2) were rated as precise and natural by most participants, with especially positive responses from women and smokers. Ring targeting (Q3) was perceived as intuitive across all groups.

Perceived Exertion. Tempo changes (Q4) were generally manageable, though more demanding for women and less fit individuals. Intensity regulation (Q5) was rated as appropriate by men and highly fit participants; others reported occasional overexertion. Resistance adaptation (Q6) received mixed to critical ratings, particularly among women, non-smokers, and both fitness groups. All groups agreed that physical effort was needed to play effectively (Q7).

Motivation. SkyRide was widely described as more enjoyable than traditional endurance training (Q9) and as physically motivating (Q8). The game encouraged extended effort (Q10), especially among women, non-smokers, and highly fit participants. The points system (Q11) was a strong motivator for men, smokers, and fit users.

Challenge. The game's difficulty (Q12–Q13) was considered appropriate by most groups. Only less fit participants reported the session as notably demanding. Tempo variation was seen as a positive gameplay element.

Game Design and Satisfaction. All groups wished for more features or expanded gameplay (Q14) and praised the visual feedback and clear instructions (Q15–Q16). Willingness to reuse SkyRide (Q17) was high across the board, though overall satisfaction (Q18) varied: women, non-smokers, and less fit participants were less satisfied; highly fit users responded most positively.

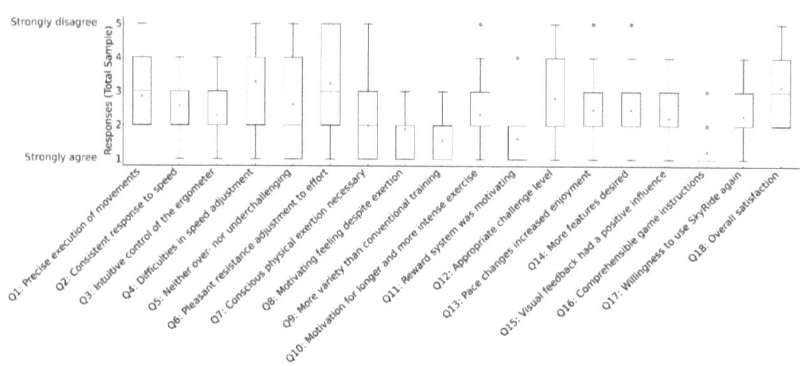

Fig. 8. Mean ratings of subjective experience with SkyRide based on 18 questionnaire items.

4 Discussion

4.1 Summary of Main Findings

This study evaluated the physiological and subjective effects of the adaptive exergame SkyRide, which combines immersive cycling with real-time heart rate control. A within-subjects design was used to compare SkyRide with a conventional graded exercise test on a cycle ergometer. Twenty-one healthy adults completed both conditions, with cardiorespiratory parameters (HRmax and VO_2max) measured in each session. Additionally, participants completed a questionnaire assessing their subjective experience with SkyRide.

Results showed no significant differences in HRmax or VO_2max between conditions in the total sample, but subgroup analyses revealed lower exertion among highly fit participants and men, and higher or comparable values among less fit participants and women. Subjectively, participants rated SkyRide as enjoyable and motivating, but with varying satisfaction depending on fitness level, sex, and smoking status.

4.2 Detailed Interpretation and Contextualization of the Results

HRmax: Comparison and Interpretation. To evaluate Hypothesis 1, maximum heart rates (HRmax) measured during the SkyRide session (EXT) and the conventional cycle ergometer test (BT) were compared using paired t-tests or Wilcoxon tests, both for the total sample and for subgroups (see Table 2). No significant differences were found in the total sample, nor among female participants, those with lower fitness, or smokers and non-smokers. Effect sizes in these groups ranged from small to medium, supporting Hypothesis 1. In contrast, significant differences with large effect sizes were observed in male participants and those with high fitness levels, leading to a rejection of Hypothesis 1 for these subgroups. Overall, Hypothesis 1 is supported for most participants but must be rejected for men and highly fit individuals.

The HRmax achieved in the SkyRide condition can be interpreted relative to the reference test (BT). In the total sample, HRmax in EXT reached 98.8% of the BT value, corresponding to high-intensity physical exertion according to ACSM classification [29, 30]. Similar intensity levels have been reported in previous studies (Ketelhut et al., 2022: 96% [7]; Martin-Niedecken et al., 2020: 93% [6]). Only among women (102.2%) and participants with low fitness levels (103.3%) were values above the BT level observed, suggesting possible overexertion.

The ANOVA for Hypothesis 2a (sex differences) showed no significant interaction effect, which supports the hypothesis. However, the descriptive trend showed that men had lower HRmax values and women higher ones in the SkyRide condition compared to BT, pointing to sex-specific differences in exertion.

Results for Hypothesis 2b (fitness level) showed a significant interaction effect: highly fit participants exhibited lower HRmax values in SkyRide, while less fit individuals showed higher values. This indicates insufficient individual load regulation in the game and contradicts Hypothesis 2b. Possible explanations include differences in heart rate variability (HRV), which may allow fitter individuals to regulate exertion more efficiently, and subjective overexertion among less fit participants [31, 32].

For Hypothesis 2c (smoking status), no significant interaction effect was found, supporting the hypothesis. However, the small number of smokers in the sample should be considered when interpreting these results.

VO_2max: Comparison and Interpretation. To assess Hypothesis 3, VO_2max values from the EXT and BT conditions were compared using paired t-tests (see Table 3). No significant differences were observed in the total sample or among female participants, smokers, or non-smokers, with small to medium effect sizes - supporting Hypothesis 3 in these groups. Among male participants, a moderate effect size was observed despite the lack of statistical significance. In both the high and low fitness groups, significant differences were found, with large and medium effect sizes, respectively leading to a rejection of Hypothesis 3 for these subgroups.

On average, VO_2max achieved in EXT reached 97.9% of the BT values, indicating high-intensity exertion according to ACSM guidelines [29, 30]. Compared to previous studies (e.g. Ketelhut et al., 2022: 84.8% [7]), this represents a notably higher exertion level. Overperformance was evident among female participants (108.6%) and those with low fitness levels (112.2%), suggesting potential overexertion in these groups.

For Hypothesis 4a (sex differences), ANOVA revealed a significant interaction effect with a large effect size. On average, men reached lower VO_2max values and women higher values in EXT, indicating sex-specific differences in both physiological and subjective exertion [33]. Hypothesis 4a is thus rejected.

A significant interaction effect with a very large effect size was also found for Hypothesis 4b (fitness level). Highly fit participants showed lower VO_2max values in EXT, while less fit individuals showed higher values, therefore Hypothesis 4b is also rejected.

For Hypothesis 4c (smoking status), no significant interaction effect was found, supporting the hypothesis.

Interpretation of the Comparison Between Target and Measured Heart Rate During SkyRide. In the total sample, heart rate showed a sharp increase, with the target zone being reached after approximately 100 s. The measured heart rate remained in the upper range of the target zone, suggesting high but largely ap-propriate exertion. Five participants ended the session prematurely, indicating potential individual differences in endurance or tolerance to exertion.

Among *male* participants, the target zone was not reached until approximately 300 s, suggesting moderate to insufficient exertion at the start of the session. Thereafter, heart rate stabilised within the target range. In contrast, *female* participants reached the target zone significantly earlier (before 100 s), with heart rate values consistently above the upper threshold. This points to excessive exer-tion shortly after the session began and to insufficient ad-justment of exercise intensity. Four women terminated the session early.

Participants with *high fitness levels* showed a slower rise in heart rate, stabilising in the target zone after approxi-mately 200 s. In the *low fitness* group, the target zone was reached very quickly, followed by a marked overshoot, which indicates sustained overexertion. Five participants in this group ended the session prematurely, suggesting that the intensity was not sufficiently adjusted to their lower fitness level.

Among *smokers*, heart rate rose sharply and reached the target zone after about 100 s. It remained in the upper zone for a while but later fluctuated and exceeded the target threshold. A delayed recovery phase was observed, which may indicate impaired load regulation, likely due to smoking-related reductions in heart rate variability [34, 35]. One participant in this group ended the session prematurely. *Non-smokers* also reached the target zone quickly, with some slight overshooting. Overall, however, their load regulation appeared acceptable.

Interpretation of the Subjective Evaluation of the SkyRide Exergame. Participants' subjective evaluations of SkyRide (see Sect. 3.4) provide further insight into the training experience across different subgroups.

While most participants rated the control elements and motivational aspects favourably, ratings of exertion and resistance adaptation varied. These differences align with the physiological data, where signs of overexertion were observed among less fit individuals and female participants. Notably, these groups also reported lower satisfaction and higher perceived strain. In contrast, male, smoking, and high-fitness participants tended to report both better physiological outcomes and more favourable subjective experiences, suggesting a better alignment between the game's physical demands and their personal capacities.

The consistently high ratings for motivation and willingness to reuse SkyRide indicate that gamified exercise may offer a viable alternative to conventional endurance training, particularly for individuals already accustomed to physical activity. However, the reported desire for expanded features and more nuanced difficulty regulation highlights the need for further development, especially in making the experience more accessible and satisfying for less trained or more diverse populations.

These findings support previous research showing that individual characteristics (e.g., sex, fitness level, and smoking status) can significantly influence both objective performance and perceived engagement in exergaming contexts [6, 7, 36]. Future iterations of SkyRide should therefore consider more adaptive difficulty scaling and personalisation features to ensure positive experiences across user profiles.

Further Contextualization Within Related Exergame Studies. Previous studies on cycling-based exergames have demonstrated that such interventions can elicit moderate-to-vigorous physical intensity while enhancing user motivation [e.g., 38, 39, 40, 41]. The present findings are consistent with this pattern, particularly among fit individuals who reached high HR and VO_2max values alongside positive subjective ratings.

However, many of these earlier studies did not include subgroup analyses or adaptive load regulation. As highlighted by Marshall and Linehan (2021) [41] and Shaw et al. (2015) [42], real-time physiological adaptation remains rare. The current study addressed this by implementing partial heart rate–based resistance control and examining differential effects by sex, fitness level, and smoking status. This allowed the identification of overexertion and lower satisfaction in less fit participants. Those effects were not captured in the mentioned previous studies.

Compared to systems with purely behavioural adaptation mechanisms [e.g., 44], the inclusion of physiological regulation may explain the more effective load matching observed in certain groups. In contrast to non-gamified interventions relying on manual adjustments [e.g., 45], the present approach integrates physical training and motivational engagement within an immersive exergame framework. These distinctions underscore the potential of adaptive, subgroup-sensitive exergame designs for improving both exertion outcomes and user experience.

4.3 Limitations

One technical limitation was the restricted resistance adjustment of the cycle ergometer in both test conditions, which operated in only three discrete levels (minimum, medium, maximum). This reduced the precision of load regulation and hindered individualised training adaptation, potentially compromising intensity and training quality. In addition, the use of a stepwise exercise test to subjective exhaustion may have underestimated actual peak oxygen uptake and heart rate. Although submaximal tests offer advantages in terms of safety and feasibility, they rely heavily on protocol adherence and participant motivation [45]. A further technical challenge emerged during the testing sessions that led to occasional disruptions in the SkyRide calibration and ExerCube projections.

The study also lacked medical-grade equipment for collecting additional physiological parameters. For instance, lactate concentrations could not be measured, preventing assessment of anaerobic threshold, an important marker of metabolic load [46].

Additionally, physical activity during the rest period between sessions (48–72 h) was not monitored or restricted. This may have introduced minor variability in recovery status and cardiorespiratory performance at the second measurement.

The sample size also represents a limitation. Subgroup analyses - particularly regarding sex, fitness level, and smoking status - were restricted in statistical power. Larger and more heterogeneous samples are needed in future studies to enhance the generalizability of findings. Moreover, the sample was limited to young, healthy adults. Individuals with pre-existing health conditions were excluded, reducing the applicability of the results to older or clinical populations.

Furthermore, the subjective evaluation was based on a self-developed questionnaire tailored to the SkyRide experience. While this allowed for context-specific feedback, the predominantly positive phrasing of several items may have increased agreement tendencies or led to inflated ratings.

4.4 Recommendations for Future Research and Development

The identified limitations offer clear directions for future studies. Increasing sample size and diversity should be a priority to improve external validity.

Methodologically, integrating additional physiological metrics, such as lactate concentration and heart rate variability (HRV), could provide more nuanced insights into exertion and recovery. Lactate levels can indicate anaerobic threshold, while HRV reflects autonomic regulation and regeneration status.

Also, the used cycle ergometer's coarse resistance levels in SkyRide limit individualised control. Future ergometers should enable finer, ideally continuous, adjustment of resistance based on real-time heart rate data. This would improve both training intensity and individual fit.

Future research should also address the long-term effects of exergame use. While the present study offers insight into acute cardiorespiratory responses, extended interventions could assess lasting training effects, health outcomes, and behavioural change.

Developing adaptive exergames that adjust dynamically to users' fitness and progress appears especially promising for sustaining effectiveness and motivation over time.

Lastly, with regard to subjective evaluation, future studies should consider revising the current game-specific questionnaire by incorporating a broader range of item phrasings, including neutral and reverse-coded statements. The use of validated instruments can further enhance the comparability and psychometric robustness of self-report measures across different exergaming interventions.

5 Conclusion

In summary, the exergame SkyRide demonstrated the ability to induce a training-relevant level of physical exertion, largely comparable to that of conventional cycle ergometer exercise. Adequate intensity levels were achieved particularly among male, non-smoking, and fitter participants. In contrast, signs of overexertion were observed in less fit individuals, smokers, and especially female participants. These physiological differences were reflected in the subjective evaluations: SkyRide was perceived overall as motivating and challenging. Many participants also found it more enjoyable than traditional endurance training, suggesting added value through gamified exercise. The system thus shows promising potential for health-oriented applications but requires further research and targeted optimization of load regulation, particularly with respect to varying individual capacities.

Acknowledgments. This interdisciplinary work was conducted as strategic research by the Serious Games research group at Technical University of Darmstadt in collaboration with the Section of Health Care Research and Rehabilitation Research, Institute of Medical Biometry and Statistics, Medical Faculty and Medical Center - University of Freiburg, Germany.

Disclosure of Interests. The authors have no competing interests to declare that are relevant to the content of this article.

Appendix

Appendix A. Subjective Experience Questionnaire.

Q1	I had the feeling that the exercise bike accurately and promptly translated my movements into the game.
Q2	The game's reactions to my speed (faster/slower/constant pedaling) felt natural and comprehensible.
Q3	I was able to control the bike easily to hit the rings; the controls were intuitive and easy to understand.
Q4	I had difficulty adjusting my pace as required by the game instructions.
Q5	I felt that the game regulated the intensity well, so I was neither over- nor underchallenged.

(continued)

(continued)

Q6	The resistance adjusted appropriately to my effort and felt comfortable.
Q7	I had to deliberately exert myself to play the game optimally.
Q8	I experienced physical exertion during the game, but it felt motivating.
Q9	Compared to moderate endurance training (e.g., stationary cycling without a game), SkyRide felt more varied and enjoyable.
Q10	SkyRide motivated me to exercise longer and more intensely than I normally would.
Q11	I found it exciting to collect points and hearts, which increased my motivation.
Q12	I felt that the challenge in the game was well matched to my abilities.
Q13	The variation between fast, slow, and constant pedaling made the game more interesting for me.
Q14	I would have liked more functions or playful elements.
Q15	The visual design and feedback in the game positively influenced my experience.
Q16	The in-game instructions were clear and understandable.
Q17	I would play SkyRide again because it is an enjoyable and effective way to exercise.
Q18	Overall, I was satisfied with the game mechanics and the controls.

Notes: Likert scale was used, "1- Strongly agree" to "5 - Strongly disagree".

References

1. Bull, F.C., et al.: WHO (World Health Organization) 2020 guidelines on physical activity and sedentary behaviour. Br. J. Sports Med. **54**(24), 1451–1462 (2020)
2. Trost, S.G., Owen, N., Bauman, A.E., Sallis, J.F., Brown, W.: Correlates of adults' participation in physical activity: review and update. Med. Sci. Sports Exerc. **34**(12), 1996–2001 (2002)
3. Staiano, A.E., Abraham, A.A., Calvert, S.L.: Competitive versus cooperative exergame play for African American adolescents' executive function skills: short-term effects in a long-term training intervention. Dev. Psychol. **48**(2), 337 (2012)
4. Best, J.R.: Exergaming in youth: effects on physical and cognitive health. J. Psychol. **221**(2), 72–78 (2013)
5. Sween, J., Wallington, S.F., Sheppard, V., Taylor, T., Llanos, A.A., Adams-Campbell, L.L.: The role of exergaming in improving physical activity: a review. J. Phys. Activity Health **11**(4), 864–870 (2014)
6. Martin-Niedecken, A.L., Mahrer, A., Rogers, K., de Bruin, E.D., Schättin, A.: "HIIT" the ExerCube: comparing the effectiveness of functional high-intensity interval training in conventional vs. exergame-based training. Front. Comput. Sci. **2**, 33 (2020)
7. Ketelhut, S., Röglin, L., Kircher, E., Martin-Niedecken, A., Ketelhut, R., Hottenrott, K., Ketelhut, K.: The new way to exercise? Evaluating an innovative heart-rate-controlled exergame. Int. J. Sports Med. **43**(1), 77–82 (2022). https://doi.org/10.1055/a-1520-4742
8. Barnett, A., Cerin, E., Baranowski, T.: Active video games for youth: a systematic review. J. Phys. Activity Health **8**(5), 724–737 (2011)
9. LeBlanc, A.G., et al.: Active video games and health indicators in children and youth: a systematic review. PLoS ONE **8**(6), e65351 (2013)

10. Biddiss, E., Irwin, J.: Active video games to promote physical activity in children and youth: a systematic review. Arch. Pediatr. Adolesc. Med. **164**(7), 664–672 (2010)
11. Martin-Niedecken, A.L., Márquez Segura, E., Rogers, K., Niedecken, S., Turmo Vidal, L.: Towards socially immersive fitness games: an exploratory evaluation through embodied sketching. In: Extended Abstracts of the Annual Symposium on Computer-Human Interaction in Play Companion Extended Abstracts, pp. 525–534 (2019)
12. Van De Laar, R.J., Ferreira, I., Van Mechelen, W., Prins, M.H., Twisk, J.W., Stehouwer, C.D.: Lifetime vigorous but not light-to-moderate habitual physical activity impacts favorably on carotid stiffness in young adults: the Amsterdam growth and health longitudinal study. Hypertension **55**(1), 33–39 (2010)
13. Schnohr, P., Marott, J.L., Jan, S., Jensen und Gorm B Jensen,: Intensity versus duration of cycling, impact on all-cause and coronary heart disease mortality: the Copenhagen City Heart Study. Eur. J. Prev. Cardiol. **19**(1), 73–80 (2012)
14. Cruz-Neira, C., Sandin, D.J., DeFanti, T.A.: Surround-screen projection-based virtual reality: the design and implementation of the CAVE. In: Seminal Graphics Papers: Pushing the Boundaries, vol. 2, pp. 51–58. ACM (2023)
15. Martin-Niedecken, A.L., Rogers, K., Turmo Vidal, L., Mekler, E.D., Márquez Segura, E.: ExerCube vs. personal trainer: evaluating a holistic, immersive, and adaptive fitness game setup. In: CHI Conference on Human Factors in Computing Systems Proceedings (CHI 2019), Glasgow, Scotland, UK, May 4–9, 2019. ACM (2019). https://doi.org/10.1145/3290605.330 0318
16. Adams, R.: Revised physical activity readiness questionnaire. Can. Family Phys. **45**, 992 (1999)
17. Warburton, D.E., Jamnik, V.K., Bredin, S.S., Gledhill, N.: The physical activity readiness questionnaire for everyone (PAR-Q+) and electronic physical activity readiness medical examination (ePARmed-X+). Health Fitness J. Can. **4**(2), 3–17 (2011)
18. Röcker, A.: Regeneration nach dem Sport: Wie viel Erholung muss sein? Abruf am 19.10.2021. In: Bestform- Je intensiver man trainiert, desto mehr Erholung braucht man (2021). https://www.spektrum. de/kolumne/regeneration-nach-dem-sport-wie-viel-erholung-muss-sein/1915714
19. Hedelin, R., Kenttä, G., Wiklund, U., Bjerle, P.E.R., Henriksson-Larsén, K.: Short-term overtraining: effects on performance, circulatory responses, and heart rate variability. Med. Sci. Sports Exerc. **32**(8), 1480–1484 (2000)
20. Jeacocke, N.A., Burke, L.M.: Methods to standardize dietary intake before performance testing. Int. J. Sport Nutr. Exerc. Metab. **20**(2), 87–103 (2010)
21. Wonisch, M., et al.: Praxisleitlinien ergometrie (2008)
22. Wonisch, M., et al.: Praxisleitlinien Ergometrie. In: Atemwegs- und Lungenkrankheiten 40 (2014). https://doi.org/10.5414/ATX0947
23. Caserman, P., Yum, S., Göbel, S., Reif, A., Matura, S.: Assessing the accuracy of smartwatch-based estimation of maximum oxygen uptake using the apple watch series 7: validation study. JMIR Biomed. Eng. **9**, e59459 (2024)
24. Meyer, F.J., et al.: Belastungsuntersuchungen in der Pneumologie–Empfehlungen der Deutschen Gesellschaft für Pneumologie und Beatmungsmedizin e. V. Pneumologie **72**(10), 687–731 (2018)
25. Klingenheben, T., Loellgen, H., Bosch, R., Trappe, H.J.: Manual zum Stellenwert der Ergometrie. Kardiologe **12**(5), 342–355 (2018)
26. Cohen, J.: Statistical power analysis for the behavioral sciences. 2. Aufl. Routledge (1988)
27. Ellis, P.D.: The Essential Guide to Effect Sizes: Statistical Power, Meta-Analysis, and the Interpretation of Research Results. Cambridge University Press (2010)
28. Levine, T.R., Hullett, C.R.: Eta squared, partial eta squared, and misreporting of effect size in communication research. Hum. Commun. Res. **28**(4), 612–625 (2002)

29. Garber, C.E., et al.: Quantity and quality of exercise for developing and maintaining cardiores-piratory, musculoskeletal, and neuromotor fitness in apparently healthy adults: guidance for prescribing exercise. Med. Sci. Sports Exerc. **43**(7), 1334–1359 (2011)
30. Sports Medicine, American College of et al. ACSM's guidelines for exercise testing and prescription. Lippincott williams & wilkins (2013)
31. Makivić, B., Nikić Djordjević, M., Willis, M.S.: Heart Rate Variability (HRV) as a tool for diagnostic and monitoring performance in sport and physical activities. J. Exerc. Physiol. Online **16**(3) (2013)
32. Amekran, Y., et al.: Effects of exercise training on heart rate variability in healthy adults: a systematic review and meta-analysis of randomized controlled trials. Cureus **16**(6) (2024)
33. Santisteban, K.J., Lovering, A.T., Halliwill, J.R., Minson, C.T.: Sex differences in VO2max and the impact on endurance-exercise performance. Int. J. Environ. Res. Public Health **19**(9), 4946 (2022)
34. Cha, K.S., Seo, M.K., Ryu, H.Y., Nam, J.J., Sung, D.J.: Smoking-suppressed heart rate recovery in young male college students who regularly exercised. Iran. J. Public Health **44**(8), 1146 (2015)
35. Middlekauff, H.R., Park, J., Moheimani, R.S.: Adverse effects of cigarette and noncigarette smoke exposure on the autonomic nervous system: mechanisms and implications for cardiovascular risk. J. Am. Coll. Cardiol. **64**(16), 1740–1750 (2014)
36. Moholdt, T., Weie, S., Chorianopoulos, K., Wang, A.I., Hagen, K.: Exergaming can be an innovative way of enjoyable high-intensity interval training. BMJ Open Sport Exerc. Med. **3**(1), e000258 (2017). https://doi.org/10.1136/bmjsem-2017-000258
37. Zeng, N., Pope, Z., Gao, Z.: Acute effect of virtual reality exercise bike games on college students' physiological and psychological outcomes. Cyberpsychol. Behav. Soc. Netw. **20**(7), 453–457 (2017). https://doi.org/10.1089/cyber.2017.0042
38. Pasco, D., Roure, C., Kermarrec, G., Pope, Z., Gao, Z.: The effects of a bike active video game on players' physical activity and motivation. J. Sport Health Sci. **6**(1), 25–32 (2017). https://doi.org/10.1016/j.jshs.2016.11.007
39. Berg, J., Wang, A.I., Lydersen, S., Moholdt, T.: Can gaming get you fit? Front. Physiol. **11**, 1017 (2020). https://doi.org/10.3389/fphys.2020.01017
40. Berg, J., Haugen, G., Wang, A.I., Moholdt, T.: High-intensity exergaming for improved cardiorespiratory fitness: a randomised, controlled trial. Eur. J. Sport Sci. **22**(6), 867–876 (2022). https://doi.org/10.1080/17461391.2021.1921852
41. Marshall, J., Linehan, C.: Are exergames exercise? A scoping review of the short-term effects of exertion games. IEEE Trans. Games **13**(2), 160–169 (2021). https://doi.org/10.1109/TG.2020.3039234
42. Shaw, L.A., Wünsche, B., Lutteroth, C., Marks, S., Callies, R.: Development and evaluation of an exercycle game using immersive technologies. In: Proceedings of the 8th Australasian Workshop on Health Informatics and Knowledge Management (HIKM 2015), vol. 164, pp. 61–68 (2015)
43. Soria Campo, A., Wang, A.I., Moholdt, T., Berg, J.: Physiological and perceptual responses to single-player vs. multiplayer exergaming. Front. Sports Active Living 4, 903300 (2022). https://doi.org/10.3389/fspor.2022.903300
44. Miura, M., et al.: Training with an electric exercise bike versus a conventional exercise bike during hemodialysis for patients with end-stage renal disease: a randomized clinical trial. Prog. Rehabil. Med. **2**, 20170008 (2017). https://doi.org/10.2490/prm.20170008
45. Noonan, V., Dean, E.: Submaximal exercise testing: clinical application and interpretation. Phys. Ther. **80**(8), 782–807 (2000)
46. Goodwin, M.L., Harris, J.E., Hernández, A., Gladden, L.B.: Blood lactate measurements and analysis during exercise: a guide for clinicians. J. Diabetes Sci. Technol. **1**(4), 558–569 (2007)

The Iliad as Leadership Curriculum: A Mythopoeic Framework Through LARP

William Guschwan[✉]

Columbia College Chicago, Chicago, USA
wguschwan@colum.edu

Abstract. This paper proposes a live action role-playing game (LARP) curriculum that unites philosophical reflections on the gnomic self, as articulated through Michel Foucault's hermeneutics of the self, with a mythic-embodied pedagogy modeled on Achilles' journey through the stages of ego-death. By framing Achilles' transformation in the *The Iliad* as a metaphor for leadership maturity, the work situates ancient myth within a modern framework of conscious business. True leadership, it is argued, is not a function of control but the radical alignment of truth and will—a process enacted through self-observation, symbolic death, and ritual embodiment. Using the LARP structure and emotional-introspective exercises, I develop a praxis for cultivating responsibility, emotional mastery, and agapic leadership.

1 Live Action Roleplaying Game as Learning Environment

Live Action Role-Playing games (LARPs) have been increasingly explored as educational tools, offering immersive environments in which participants adopt roles, make decisions, and experience consequences in real time. Bowman (2010) documents how role-playing games function as communities of practice that support problem-solving, identity exploration, and interpersonal skill development. These findings align with earlier work on simulation-based learning, which emphasizes the power of situated experience for developing leadership and collaboration skills (Aldrich, 2009).

Educational LARPs have been applied to a variety of domains, including fiction writing (Hergenrader, 2011). In such contexts, LARP's embodied participation fosters engagement and deep learning, especially when paired with structured debriefing (Crookall, 2010). However, while these studies demonstrate that LARPs can facilitate skill acquisition and behavioral change, few have systematically mapped mythic or archetypal narratives onto leadership development curricula. Drawing from Nigel Howard's drama theory, LARPs can also be understood as games with focal points–staged scenarios in which participants publicly declare intentions and strategies, making the performative commitment itself a transforming act (Howard, 1971).

A. Thomas et al. (Eds.): JCSG 2025, LNCS 16243, pp. 351–358, 2026.
https://doi.org/10.1007/978-3-032-10518-9_30

Game-based learning more broadly has leveraged narrative frameworks to enhance motivation and reflection (Gee, 2007; McGonigal, 2011). Yet the integration of mythopoetic transformation–using mythic structure and ritual to guide personal development–remains underexplored in leadership training. The concept of gamiformics (Guschwan et al., 2016) proposes that games can be intentionally designed to transform the player's identity, but empirical applications of this model to leadership contexts are sparse.

This study builds on these foundations by uniting Michel Foucault's hermeneutics of the self with a mythically structured LARP based on Achilles' journey through ego-death. By explicitly aligning gameplay with Fred Kofman's Conscious Business virtues – unconditional responsibility, essential integrity, ontological humility, emotional mastery, and agapic leadership – this work addresses a gap in the literature: the systematic use of archetypal narrative and embodied role-play to cultivate leadership qualities in higher education settings.

The research questions explored here are: How can a mythically structured LARP, modeled on Achilles' journey through the stages of ego-death, facilitate the development of emotional awareness and conative leadership skills in participants?

What specific, observable leadership behaviors emerge when participants engage in the stages of Achilles' ego-death within a structured LARP environment?

The use of the Large Language Model apps and technology to support the gnomic self game and explore the symbolism of the *The Iliad* is proposed as a valuable contribution to this area of research.

2   Method: Data, Design and Analysis

2.1   Participants and Sampling

The study will be conducted in Fall 2025 with approximately 55 first-year students enrolled in a four-year college leadership course. This project was designed as a pilot study to evaluate feasibility and refine procedures. The subsequent study will be submitted for Institutional Review Board (IRB) review and approval before enrollment of human subjects.

2.2   Research Design

This mixed-methods study will combine quantitative analysis of epistemic frame shifts with qualitative thematic analysis of participant reflections and peer discussions. The intervention consists of a multi-week LARP modeled on Achilles' ego-death arc, designed to develop emotional awareness and conative leadership skills. The LARP incorporates individual tactics, team-based enactments of scenes from *The Iliad,* and reflective debrief sessions.

2.3   Data Collection Instruments

- Character Sheet Each student will define a "gnomic self" and list tactics for enacting it in both individual and group settings. These will serve as both gameplay tools and data sources.
- Point Tracking Students will earn points for each tactic enacted (individual and team), recorded on their character sheets and verified by peer and instructor observation.
- Surveys Pre- and post-intervention surveys will measure: Emotional Intelligence (Greaves & Bradberry, 2009), Conative strengths (Kolbe, 1997), Self-assessed leadership behaviors (Likert-scale items based on the Conscious Business framework).
- Reflection Logs Weekly written reflections on leadership decisions, emotional regulation, and alignment with personal values.
- Peer Discussion Transcripts Notes and recordings from structured peer dialogues following each major LARP event.
- Instructor Observation Rubrics Professor and teaching assistant will record observed leadership behaviors and emotional responses during LARP sessions.

2.4   Ethical Considerations

All data will be anonymized before analysis. Reflections and peer discussion transcripts will be de-identified to protect student privacy. Participation in gameplay will be part of the course curriculum, but data submission will be optional, with no grading consequences for opting out.

2.5   Quantitative Analysis

- **Pre/Post Comparisons** Dependent-samples t-tests may be used to assess changes in Emotional Intelligence and Kolbe Index A scores from pre- to post-intervention.
- **Epistemic Network Analysis (ENA)** Co-occurrence of epistemic frame elements (values, knowledge, skills, epistemology, identity) will be coded from character sheets, reflections, and observation data. Epistemic Network Analysis (ENA) will visualize changes in network structure over time, indicating shifts toward target leadership outcomes.

2.6   Qualitative Analysis

- **Thematic Analysis** Reflection logs and peer discussion transcripts will be coded using Braun & Clarke's (2006, 2019) reflexive thematic analysis approach. Initial codes will be derived from Kofman's conscious business framework and emergent themes in the data.

- **Inter-coder Agreement** Two independent coders will analyze 20% of the data to establish coding reliability, using Cohen's kappa to assess agreement. Discrepancies will be resolved through discussion and refinement of the codes.
- **Integration with Epistemic Network Analysis** Thematic analysis results will be compared with ENA patterns to identify convergences and divergences between qualitative themes and quantitative network changes.

Outcome Measures

- Observable increase in leadership behaviors aligned with conscious business framework.
- Enhanced self-reported emotional and conative intelligence.
- Increased network density and connectivity in target epistemic frame elements.

2.7   Assumptions

This study will be based on several core assumptions about the relationship between LARP, learning, and leadership: **(1)** that immersive, narrative-based simulation enables the practice of complex skills; **(2)** that mythic structures provide an effective framework for identity transformation; **(3)** that embodied role-play can facilitate the internalization of leadership virtues.

3   The Gnomic Self as Ontological Groundwork

The gnomic self is the superposed subject consisting of both a self of knowledge and self of will and provides the ontological foundation upon which the mythic journey of leadership unfolds. Foucault describes the gnomic self as a test in the tradition of philosophical ascesis (Foucault, 2014, 16). Rather than uncovering a deep inner truth, the student becomes a site where truth can emerge through disciplined self-reflection and action. This echoes Foucault's point: the self is not discovered but constituted through memory, rhetoric, and ethical performance.

> "The objective of the truth-game is not to discover a secret reality inside yourself, but to make of the individual a place where truth can appear and act... (Foucault, 2014, 140) the self as a target, the organization of what I call the gnomic self as the objective, the aim, towards which the confession and self-examination is oriented" (Foucault, 2014, 36)

The gnomic self can have many possible journeys. Achilles has a journey through denial, rage, isolation, and ultimately, surrender—not to achieve domination but to achieve an acceptance of his mortal fate. Possibles selves is a related form of the gnomic self which makes the hermeneutic reading of *The Iliad* digestible(Markus, 1986).

Foucault remarks that the gnomic self is a technology of the self. Recent technology like Large Language Models (LLMs) advance the possibility of the gnomic self as a practice. Students can use LLMs as a dialog engine to explore the symbolism of the characters of *The Iliad* and then generate possible actions that map to their lived experience. For wisdom, a student could ask the LLM: "what would Athena do?" LLMs allow students to achieve his Socratic aim of "taking care of the self" through the hermeneutic reading of *The Iliad*.

4   Achilles' Journey as a Lived Myth of the Gnomic Self

Various ways of reading the hermeneutics of Achilles will be explored. One possible symbolic reading is Achilles' path from rage to acceptance as a metaphor for leadership development, viewed through Kübler-Ross's adapted stages of death (Kübler-Ross 1969). Each LARP week becomes a lived praxis of the gnomic self: a ritualized moment where the subject actively constitutes themselves through symbolic choices, conative alignments, affective confrontations, and embodied archetypes (Table 1).

Table 1. Stages of Transformation and Leadership

Stage	Gnomic Function	Symbolic Act	Business Corollary
Denial	Will over truth	Persona formation	Mask of role over being
Anger	Fractured will	Rage rituals	Ego-defensiveness
Isolation	Reflective gap	Withdrawal rites	Vulnerability threshold
Depression	Surrender	Cleansing grief	Emotional mastery
Acceptance	Re-unification	Divine speech	Agapic leadership

5   From Ritual to Practice: Mapping Conscious Business onto the Mythic Arc

In Northrop Frye's archetypal criticism, *The Iliad* belongs to the mythic mode and the tragic mythos, functioning as a mythopoeic work. It is a narrative that creates and sustains its own coherent mythic universe where gods and heroes enact archetypal conflicts that shape both the story world and the audience's understanding of fate (Frye, 1957). Further, Plutarch's ethopoeia is promoted by Foucault as a standard of knowledge: "knowledge is considered useful when and only when it functions in such a way that it is capable of modifying, of transforming ēthos, that is to say, the individual's way of being, his mode of existence (Foucault, 2014, 16)". Drawing on Bakhtin's notion of the chronotope as the fusion of time and space in narrative, one can understand the Greek temenos (a sacred precinct) as a spiritual or ritual chronotope–a bounded time-space in which communal memory, myth, and transformation converge. Thus, *The Iliad* is a temenos. To ground the symbolism of Achilles' transformation, a framework of best practices for conscious business will be used to construct a dialogue for the growth of the gnomic self (Kofman, 2013). Fred Kofman's conscious business framework (responsibility, integrity, humility, communication of authenticity, requests, and conflict) will act as the second of a double hermeneutic that allows practical application of the mythic transformation of Achilles to the students' lives (Giddens, 1987).

5.1   Denial → Kofman's Unconditional Responsibility and Responsive Mindset

Achilles' initial refusal to fight mirrors the undisciplined leader's tendency to externalize blame. The practice of Kofman's unconditional responsibility disrupts this blame, and invites self-authorship.

Game Mechanic: Collect stories of awareness of reactive mindset. Outcome is shifting to Kofman's responsive mindset.

5.2   Responsive Self-emptying → Kofman's Agape Leadership

The final movement towards a responsive mindset manifests itself as love-based leadership. Achilles gives Priam the body of Hector, not out of weakness but through mercy. Priam uses the Greek word "ekeinos" to describe himself, the meaning of which is "that guy" and maps to Priam's adopting a responsive mindset to his own suffering. This self-emptying gesture by Priam, and adopted by Achilles through his own mercy, will be continued in the character of Odysseus in Homer's *The Odyssey*. Kofman calls this "agape", an act of will and commitment to benefit others (Kofman, 2013), Takeuchi and Nonaka use "Control by love" (Takeuchi & Nonaka, 1986). de Mello (de Mello, 1990) defines love similarly and echoes Kofman's agape leadership.

Game Mechanic: Identify opportunities to benefit team mates and act on them.

Scenario Example

- **Proposed Scenario:** The Shield Forging Stage Alignment: Acceptance → Agape (Control by Love) Hephaestus forging Achilles' shield in The Iliad Book 18 (Wilson, 2024)
- **Set-up In-game:** the group faces an external threat or crisis (e.g., symbolic "storm," encroaching enemy). Achilles is symbolically "wounded" and cannot act alone. Group must design and "forge" a symbolic artifact together–a shield, banner, or protective pact–to defend the community.
- **Mechanics and Materials:** Provide symbolic craft materials (paper, cloth, tokens, markers).

– **Constraints and Final Rite:** The design must incorporate three contributions from different archetypes (e.g., Hector's honor, Odysseus' cunning, Priam's mercy). Declare one value to embed. Present this shield as final rite.

6 Conclusion: Toward a Mythopoetic Organization

By aligning the gnomic self with mythic transformation, development of leadership shifts from a behavioral checklist to an ontological journey. Achilles' descent and return are the map, not for heroic domination but for wise stewardship. Through memory, ritual, and truth games, the student becomes not a manager of grades and outcomes, but a steward of being. Mythopoetic self-transformation provides guidance for a new pedagogy in the university.

Acknowledgments. I would like to acknowledge ChatGPT 5 for its assistance with proofreading and editing.

References

Aldrich, C.: Learning online with games, simulations, and virtual worlds: strategies for online instruction. Jossey-Bass (2009)

Bowman, S.L.: The Functions of Role-Playing Games How Participants Create Community, Solve Problems and Explore Identity. McFarland (2010)

Braun, V., Clark, V.: Using thematic analysis in psychology. Qual. Res. Psychol. **3**(2), 77–101 (2006)

Braun, V., Clark, V.: Reflecting on reflexive thematic analysis. Qual. Res. Sport Exercise Health **11**(4), 77–101 (2019)

Crookall, D.: Serious Games, Debriefing, and Simulation/Gaming as a Discipline. SAGE Publishing (2010)

De Mello, A.: Awareness: The Perils and Opportunities of Reality. Image Books (1990)

Foucault, M.: About the Beginning of the Hermeneutics of the Self. University of Chicago Press (2016)

Frye, N.: Anatomy of criticism: Four Essays. Princeton University Press (1957)

Gee, J.: What Video Games Have to Teach Us About Learning and Literacy, 2nd edn. Palgrave Macmillan (2007)

Giddens, A.: Social Theory and Modern Sociology, 1st edn. Stanford University Press (1987)

Greaves, J., Bradberry, T.: Emotional Intelligence 2.0. Image Books (2009)

Guschwan, W., Baxter, J., Seager, T.P., Spierre Clark, S.: Gamiformics: a systems-based framework for moral learning through games. In: Proceedings of the International Symposium on Sustainable Systems and Technologies (2016)

Hergenrader, T.: Gaming, world building, and narrative: using role-playing games to teach fiction writing. In: Conference: Proceedings of the 7th International Conference on Games + Learning + Society Conference (2011)

Howard, N.: Paradoxes of Rationality: Theory of Metagames and Political Behavior. MIT Press (1971)

Kübler-Ross, E.: On Death and Dying. Scribner (1969)

Kofman, F.: Conscious Business. Sounds True (2013)

Kolbe, K.: Conative Connection: Uncovering the Link Between Who You Are and How You Perform. Kolbe Corp. (1997)

Markus, H., Nurius, P.: Possible Selves. American Psychologist (1986)

McGonigal, J.: Reality is broken: Why games make us better and how they can change the world Penguin Press (2011)

Nash, P., Shaffer, D.W.: Epistemic Trajectories: Mentoring in a Game Design Practicum. International Society of the Learning Sciences (2013)

Takeuchi, H., Nonaka, I.: The New New Product Development Game. Harvard Business Review (1986)

Wilson, E.: The Iliad. W W Norton and Company (2024)

Music Consciousness with Mixed Reality: Case Study on Learning Associative Imagery in Classical Music Using Three Rachmaninoff Preludes, Op. 32

Svetlana Rudenko[1,2] , Kelly Jakubowski[2] , Xiangpeng Fu[1,3] ,
and Mads Haahr[1,3(✉)]

[1] Haunted Planet Studios, 12 Fitzwilliam Street Upper, Dublin 2, Ireland
`{rudenkos,fuxi,haahrm}@tcd.ie`
[2] Department of Music, Durham University, Durham, UK
`kelly.jakubowski@durham.ac.uk`
[3] School of Computer Science and Statistics, Trinity College Dublin, Dublin, Ireland

Abstract. With the emergence of advanced multimedia technology, such as VR/MR and research into music consciousness and cognitive musicology, new opportunities arise for encouraging associative thinking and imagery in classical music, both for professional performers, and also, music lovers. In this paper, we report on a case study where the experimental group (N = 22) experienced three mixed reality scenes in which the room was augmented with virtual objects from nature (e.g., a tree and falling leaves) and/or the fantastic (e.g., a mermaid) designed to resonate with the music. The control group (N = 21) listened to the same music as the experimental group using audio only. Participants in both groups were asked to rate their emotions and experiences via several subscales of the Phenomenology of Consciousness Inventory, and describe associations, memories or thoughts that came to mind. Both groups reported being significantly absorbed by the experience and that the experience induced a state of relaxation. Listening to the music evoked a more inner-directed state of attention, while the MR group reported strong engagement with the multisensory MR environment. Familiarity with MR/VR increased the enjoyment of the MR experience. The audio group also described a wide range of associative memories and images, which bear resemblance to the MR visualizations in several ways. We conclude that MR art/music experiences have potential uses for (1) attracting new audiences to classical music; (2) encouraging professional performers and/or music lovers in associative thinking and imagery; and (3) possibly serving as a new form of immersive art music therapy.

Keywords: Classical Music · Multisensory Experiences with Mixed Reality · Interactive Art · Piano Repertoire

© The Author(s) 2026
A. Thomas et al. (Eds.): JCSG 2025, LNCS 16243, pp. 359–371, 2026.
https://doi.org/10.1007/978-3-032-10518-9_31

1 Introduction

Games for learning have proven to be effective across many domains, including supporting memory, sharpening the thinking process and enhancing analytical skills [1, 2]. Games also exist for learning music theory (e.g., *Music Tutor* and *Earpeggio*), and there are of course an abundance of "music games" for entertainment, which are based around the matching of rhythm (e.g., *Piano Tiles* and *Guitar Hero*), and titles in the latter category may have some music (largely rhythmic) benefits, even if learning is not their primary purpose. However, there are no music games or interactive VR/MR music experiences that are concerned with learning music narrative by the stylistics of music language. By stylistics of music language we mean the elements of musical structures, such as melody, harmony, organisation of the music texture, and others, which justify the interpretation of classical music. Designing visualizations of classical music poses a challenge, because the interpretation has to be true in terms of its musicology and not too active (or cognitively demanding) to distract from the music listening.

Associative imagery and creativity are very important aspects for keeping interest in music instrument practice and also influence the "touch" action when playing an instrument. Learning to play classical music on any instrument involves the development of certain physical skills but also complex knowledge about music, performance management and musicology. Musicology introduces performers to historical times and artistic styles with certain traditions of performance and forms, such as Baroque (e.g., Bach, Handel) with characteristic contrapuntal texture and Baroque dance forms like allemande, sarabande, gigue, etc.; classical epoch (e.g., Haydn, Mozart, Beethoven) with its strict pulse, typical Alberti bass figurations and sonata structure; romantic (e.g., Chopin, Liszt) with more flexible time and rubato for emotional swells, and composer's specific music language, such as Scriabin with his altered dominant sevens chords without resolution and dual-modality modes [3], etc. There are certain symbolic aspects of music texture in classical music, which allow the performer to interpret the musical texture (organisation of music notes, such as melody, type of accompaniment, harmony structure, etc.) into music narrative [4], define the meaning and sound delivery in performance. The interpretation process is highly subjective, involving music imagery, personal associations and memory [5] but also, with stylistic rules (described above) and physical limitations (or not) of the performer according to the level of musical instrument accomplishment. To accelerate and make the musicology learning process easier and more interactive, we employed Mixed Reality (MR) technology to allow learners to experience Rachmaninoff Preludes as walking nature scenes from different seasons.

In this paper, we report on the design of the MR app and our comparative study that examines the effects of the experience.

2 Design and Implementation

In this section, we give an overview of research into music consciousness and mental imagery in order to explain our design decisions and the appropriateness of the interpretation before we proceed to describe the design and implementation of the MR app.

2.1 Music Consciousness and Mental Imagery

Music consciousness is awareness of the mental processes on music, including analysis of musical structures, the emotional journey and associative thinking. As Meng et al. describe, we can recall musical imagery in our mind, both involuntary and intentionally:

> [T]he phenomenon of musical imagery - defined as the conscious awareness of an endogenous, internal representation of music. Musical imagery is abundant in daily life, occurring as involuntary musical imagery (INMI) often referrcd to as 'earworms', and as voluntary, intentional musical imagery, with examples including musical recollection, composition, and translation of the notes of a score into an auditory mental representation [6, p. 271].

Also, musical imagery can have a visual representation and associations connecting to one's subjective memories [7].

Researchers into music education have observed that associative imagery is of considerable importance to the learning process:

> Researchers from diverse disciplines, including but not limited to music education, performance science, music psychology, and neuroscience, have acknowledged the crucial role of efficient practice strategies in enhancing expertise. Among these strategies, imagery-focused approaches have been identified as particularly beneficial [8].

To train these mental processes of music thinking and to enrich the experience of music with other senses, we have developed a virtual environment of Mixed Reality (MR) visualization to embody the emotional journey. Our multisensory design approach for MR is based on a cross-modal interaction of senses on the example of synesthesia. We have adopted this methodology because music-making is a multisensory experience, both physical such as playing an instrument and mental, incorporating musical imagination. Mari Tervaniemi points out the complex brain work required for training the multimodal integration:

> [M]usical training does not only consist of ear training - it is targeted to train a multitude of independent skills in several modalities which also need to become integrated prior to performing a musical piece in an expressive manner. The brain basis for such cross- and multimodal integration has been of increasing interest in recent years.' [9]

2.2 Design: Musicology, Music Analysis and Interpretation for the Visualization of S. Rachmaninoff Preludes Op. 32 N1, N5 and N10 in Mixed Reality (MR)

The MR app contains visualizations of a total of six Preludes by S. Rachmaninoff, and the player/learner can choose which of the scenes to experience. Following section is justification of musicology analysis put into the basis of design with a focus on the three scenes subject to our study.

Russian/American composer S. Rachmaninoff's second book of Preludes Op. 32 was written in the summer of 1910 at his family's idyllic country house in Ivanovka, a sleepy, rural area, surrounded by nature. Some preludes of Rachmaninoff were influenced by Orientalism. (Similar examples by other composers include M. Balakirev's "Islamey" or N. Rimsky-Korsakov's symphonic suite Op. 35 "Sheherazade.") The music language of Prelude N2 (by interpretation of the performer) contains some oriental patterns which influenced the MR visualization. Prelude N3 in A-major by its sparkling liveliness resonates with the celebration of spring – saying goodbye to the winter, 'Maslenitza' or Pancake Day. Prelude N4 is in e-minor, with chords cascades in low register – associated with a ritual for nature Gods to manifest good harvest while planting seeds. From six developed MR scenes[1] we chose three: N1, 5 and 10 for their contrasting moods and easy interaction.

Prelude N1, Op. 32 is in C major, a joyful key with energetic emotional charge. In our visualization of Prelude N 1, we interpreted stormy cascades of cross-register figurations on forte and dynamic contrast of lighter textures in higher registers, as a refreshing rain scene in the forest with lightening and pools of water with ripples from raindrops. We added the ambient sound of rain to the original sound of music to increase the immersiveness of nature of the MR scene and stimulate multisensory perception with "feeling" virtual raindrops on the skin (haptics) through audio-visual composition. We are exploring multisensory experiences in the stream of some other related works such as Velasco, Obrist [10], and practiced the multisensory approach before, such as in Alice Dali MR with original music compositions [11] (Fig. 1).

Fig. 1. Mixed Reality scene (screenshot) for Prelude N1 Op. 32, Rachmaninoff

Prelude N5, Op. 32 is one of the most lyrical preludes of Rachmaninoff. It is written in the key of G major with its characteristic sunshine emotion (interpretation of the pianist). A beautiful melody with accompaniment figuration of quintuplets (five notes division of the quarter note) sets an idyllic mood of observing something peaceful,

---

[1] Rachmaninoff MR experience video: https://youtu.be/hdw7xtOqKns.

later fast light figurations of 32 notes point to playfulness of water. Many composers used certain formations of musical texture to illustrate water effect, for example, Liszt's 'The Fountains of the Villa d' Este, or Debussy in 'Voiles', Prelude N2 Book 1. It is reminiscent of Rachmaninoff's song 'The Water Lily,' N1, Op. 8, also in G-major key, with verbal description of joyful play of mystical lily-mermaid with the crescent. The spectator of our MR scenes observes a pond with waterlilies with mermaid and gentle illumination of waterfall (Fig. 2).

Fig. 2. Mixed Reality scene (screenshot) for Prelude N5 Op. 32, Rachmaninoff

Prelude N10, Op. 32 is in B minor. In general, minor keys are associated with emotions of nostalgia or sadness. Other composers wrote in this key: Liszt B-minor sonata is associated with Faust legend,[2] or Chopin Prelude N 6 Op 28 Lento assai also in B minor.[3] Tonalities or keys in classical music very often carry consistent mental and emotional charge.

The multisensory approach in particular manifested in the MR visualization of Prelude N10 in B-minor where the spectator can 'touch' a virtual crane as well as the leaves of a maple tree symbolizing philosophical reflections of passing life and experiences:

---

[2] Svetlana Rudenko's talk on music consciousness, archetypes of musical texture and visualization with synesthesia art: https://vimeo.com/538698253.

[3] https://practisingthepiano.com/pedalling-chopins-B-minor-prelude/

Fig. 3. Mixed Reality scene (screenshot) for Prelude N10, Op. 32, Rachmaninoff

departing cranes and autumn as a symbol of mature age. The scene evokes a feeling of solitude. The ambient sound of cranes was also added to the music to increase association with nature and perhaps encourage the feeling of the air and falling leaves to reach the olfactory sense through audio-visual composition (Fig. 3).[4]

2.3   Interactive Elements

The three scenes (N1, N5, N10) are experienced by the player/learning walking around the space and touching the elements, if they wish. There are no specific instructions other than to explore, listen and perceive, and no specific objectives to achieve. In this fashion, our scenes are different from many other games for learning, which frequently include direct feedback and specific objectives, such as to achieve a certain score or complete a given task. Because our learning objectives are concerned with music imagery, we were aware that our visualizations needed to co-exist with the music listening experience, and for that reason, we were cautious about adding too many game mechanics. Also, many participants (and many people in general) are not yet familiar with MR experiences, and the simplicity of the three scenes allowed them to focus on the experiences and the music instead of learning specific game mechanical interactions. Instead, we opted for a more meditative experience, more akin to games like *Flow* (2006) and *Flower* (2009) by Thatgamecompany, as well as "walking simulators," which tend to offer unguided or loosely guided aesthetic and narrative explorations, rather than goal-driven high-interactivity experiences.

Of the additional scenes, N4 is the most interactive, allowing the player to "throw and grow" seeds of harvest in context of a folk scene. Also, after the case study, more interaction was added to Preludes N1 and N5: responsive lady birds and dragonflies. The

---

[4] MR video: https://www.youtube.com/watch?v=hdw7xtOqKns. MR App download: https://www.meta.com/en-gb/experiences/7680972171955194/

motivation was that during the case study, many participants spent time admiring and wanted to "pet" the crane that appears in Prelude N10. However, for the study, we used the three Preludes with minimum interaction in order to also support the music listening activity.

2.4 About Multisensory Design, Cross-Modal Perception and Multisensory Stimulation

Human Computer Interaction (HCI) is starting to use multisensory approach principles, but there is little work on how to map one sense to the other, or how to produce designs where the natural synchronization is attractive to the majority of people. We are exploring a synesthesia model as a framework for reaching other senses in multisensory design. Synesthesia (wiring of the brain when a stimulus in one sensory modality (e.g., sound) gives involuntarily sensation in another, (e.g., visual or smell, or taste) experiences are subjective and involuntary, but it has been shown that synesthetes-designed animations are more appealing than those designed by non-synesthetes [12]. Ellen Lupton describes multisensory design as follows: "Reaching beyond design's traditional focus on vision, multisensory design incorporates the full range of bodily experience [...] The brain combines input about taste, smell, temperature, and texture to create 'flavor' (original emphasis) [13, p. 142]. Research has shown that people with Synesthesia are more aware of such sensory pairings due to stronger connections in their neural system [14]. While synesthetes only represent 4–6% of adult humans, "a growing body of empirical research on the topic of multisensory perception now shows that even non-synesthetic individuals experience cross-modal correspondences" [15, p. 319]. Also, multisensory stimulation can encourage creativity. As V.S. Ramachandran and E.M. Hubbard point out: "Synesthesia causes excess communication among brain maps [...] towards linking seemingly unrelated concepts and ideas—in short, creativity" [16, p. 52]. Research shows that synesthesia-enhanced applications have promising potential for education and mental health programs, such as Bor et al.'s experiment to train non-synesthetes for color-grapheme synesthesia, which showed an IQ improvement and provisionally concluded that "cognitive training including synesthetic associations may in the future be a promising new tool for vulnerable clinical groups to enhance general mental ability" [17].

2.5 Implementation: Technical Description

This project is implemented on Unreal engine 5.3.2 and then deployed to run on the Meta Quest 3 head-mounted display (HMD). This HMD is untethered and supports full color passthrough, which allows the user to see their real surroundings as well as the virtual elements. This allows the user to walk freely through the mixed reality scenes with minimal discomfort due to lag compared to Virtual Reality (VR). We use passthrough in all three scenes, effectively blending the real and virtual environments.

First, we added a VR pawn blueprint object to the scene. This object is the virtual agent of the user in the scene. This object is composed of a camera, the user's virtual hands, and components that manage the MR environment. The solution uses virtual hands (rather than the Oculus controllers) to facilitate touch imitation with scene elements, e.g., the user reaching out to catch a leaf or pet a crane.

For example, Scene N1 mainly includes the trees, fog, the rainy environment and lightning, which were implemented as follows:

- Trees: Considering the performance of the HMD and optimization of applications, we imported the model into the Blender modeling tool and perform "Decimate" operation to reduce the number of vertices and polygons of the model. Then it could be directly put in the scene in Unreal Engine.
- Rainy environment: The Niagara system of Unreal Engine was used to achieve a rain effect. We used one Niagara system to generate raindrop particles and another one to generate fog particles.
- Lightning: Lightning is generated by the Niagara system. We uncheck the "auto active" of this system and create a new blueprint actor to control the lightning to be active every five to six seconds. While the lightning system is active, we use this blueprint actor to control the "emissive color" parameter of the material of all tree models in the scene and adjust it from 0 to 11 for 0.25 s to achieve the effect of lighting up the environment. After the lightning is briefly active, we play the sound of thunder for 4 to 5 s.

3 Experimental Method

We carried out a case study on an audio-only group with headphones (control, 21 participants) and an MR group on Meta Quest 3 headset (experimental, 22 participants). Participants were aged 18 to 68 years ($M = 28$, $SD = 10.5$; 22 female), 17 were non-musicians and 26 were amateur or professional musicians, and all reported normal hearing. The two groups were matched in terms of musicianship, familiarity with the Rachmaninoff pieces, and familiarity with VR/MR technologies (all $ps > .82$ in independent-samples t-tests); the MR group was somewhat older ($t(27) = -2.62$, $p = .01$), but age did not significantly impact the results reported below when included in our analyses. Both groups listened to the same piano tracks (Rachmaninoff Preludes 1, 5, and 10, as describe above). The MR group experienced three mixed reality scenes. In each scene, the room was augmented with virtual objects from nature (e.g., a tree and falling leaves) and/or the fantastic (e.g., a mermaid) designed by the performer (pianist) to resonate with the music. While the audio-only group were seated with headphones during the experiment, the MR group had the opportunity to walk in the scene and explore its virtual elements while listening to the music.

After hearing the audio tracks or engaging in the MR experience of these, participants in both groups were asked to rate their emotions and bodily/sensory experiences via several subscales of the Phenomenology of Consciousness Inventory (PCI) (Joy, Time Sense, Meaning, Direction of Attention, Absorption, Body Image, Altered State of Awareness, Arousal) [18]. They were also asked to write a description of any associations, memories or thoughts that came to mind.

4   Results and Discussion

In this section, we report on the results from the study. We first report on the qualitative results from the control group, then the experimental group, and finally we report on our quantitative results.

4.1   Qualitative Reports from the Audio-Only Group

1. *To me the piece felt like it was exploring nature. Initially it was quite light hearted, such as someone exploring a garden. It sounded like a bee flitting around the garden with someone following it. Later when the music got more dramatic it was like exploring the more dangerous sides of nature, such as a waterfall, or strong ocean currents.*
2. *when the music start, it comes with a stronger powerful music bring me the thoughts of some war in history, and when it comes to some relax and claim section, it just like bring back us to the peace*
3. *In a sunny day, A girl with the fresh dress is running in the forests. The image is full of sunshine and green plants. But later the image changes and it shows a river in the dark night and it makes me feel peaceful.*
4. *A field filled with flowers and green grass. A historical manor house. Dark choppy seas. A calm serene blue ocean. I thought about things that were bothering me that I don't usually notice.*
5. *The stream is flowing, flowers are blooming with fresh air. I feel like I'm lying on the grass and becoming part of nature.*
6. *I felt that the music pieces had a gothic, macabre tone to them. The first piece felt straight out of a horror film, like the background score of a murder montage occurring. The second piece felt like the calm before the storm; I started off imagining myself in a lush green meadow and suddenly transported to a world of eeriness. The same holds true for the last music piece; I felt like a passenger in a boat travelling through rocky waters, but with a satisfying & happy ending.*
7. *Velvet texture, dark red, green and purple; old majestic castles with grand interiors, like fur chairs*

The audio group described a wide range of associative memories and images, which bear resemblance to the MR visualizations in several ways. Many people of the Audio Only group referred to nature without them knowing Rachmaninoff's or pianist-performer's interpretation. They talk about nature, personal memories and the transition between powerful emotions from joy to darkness or dramatic events. These observations bear a resemblance to our MR design and our interpretation of the music. The last comment (7) is very synesthetic and suggests the person might have chromesthesia (sound to colours) synesthesia.

4.2   Qualitative Reports from the Mixed Reality Group

1. *I felt a little like I was experiencing a psychotic episode because I could see the real room and recognise its reality, but the images from the virtual reality with the background music felt like hallucinations which was interesting yet disconcerting.*

2. *In the second scene, I felt calmed and pictured myself alongside different rivers I have walked along in the past. The last scene reminded me of a tree me and my girlfriend used to sit under in a local park, and also brought to mind our shared enjoyment of birds. The first scene brought to mind more disjointed imagery.*
3. *The first piece made me feel very heavy on the inside, I felt like I embodied grey colours and during the second piece the blue and pink colours felt as if they were soft and light, the music really enhanced this feeling. It all felt like a physical warm embrace.*
4. *The settings were seemingly normal with a few unusual characteristics and the pairing with music made me feel like I was on a movie set or something similar. It all felt quite strange and unreal as if I was animated too and had jumped inside that world*
5. *The last one with the tree and heron reminded me of the heron on the river you see in durham which made me happy as I like walking around the river banks*
6. *The lily pads and the falling leaves felt relaxing and vivid.*
7. *I remember some childhood experiences with my family, especially my mother. I was sitting on the bike, my mom took me to the school to learn the piano. Even it was rainy, but I just felt happiness.*

The comments show that people in the Audio-Only group referred to the music tracks as a 'piece' or 'song,' the MR group participants refer to each part of the experiment as 'a scene,' indicating a feeling of presence in the environment that was not experienced by the Audio-Only group. One of participants referred to the MR experience as 'hallucinations.' While this was not the focus of this experiment, it could point to a potential of music art therapy with mixed reality through a type of non-drug 'music art psychedelics with mixed reality' that could be the subject of future research. Anecdotally, one of participants audibly commented during MR case study: "I didn't realize that classical music could be so interesting, I liked Rachmaninoff compositions!".

4.3 Quantitative Results

Both groups reported being significantly absorbed by the experience and that the experience induced a state of relaxation (all $ps < .03$ in one-sample t-tests comparing ratings against the scale midpoint of 3 for the Absorption and Arousal scales). Listening to the music evoked a more inner-directed state of attention than engaging in the MR experience ($t(40) = 5.37, p < .001$), but no other statistically significant differences were found on the PCI scales between these two groups (all $ps > .40$) (see Fig. 3). For the MR group, greater Joy was experienced by participants who had some familiarity with MR/VR technology ($t(11.3) = 2.74, p = .02$); no other PCI subscales were significantly impacted by MR/VR experience (all $ps > .14$) (Fig. 4).

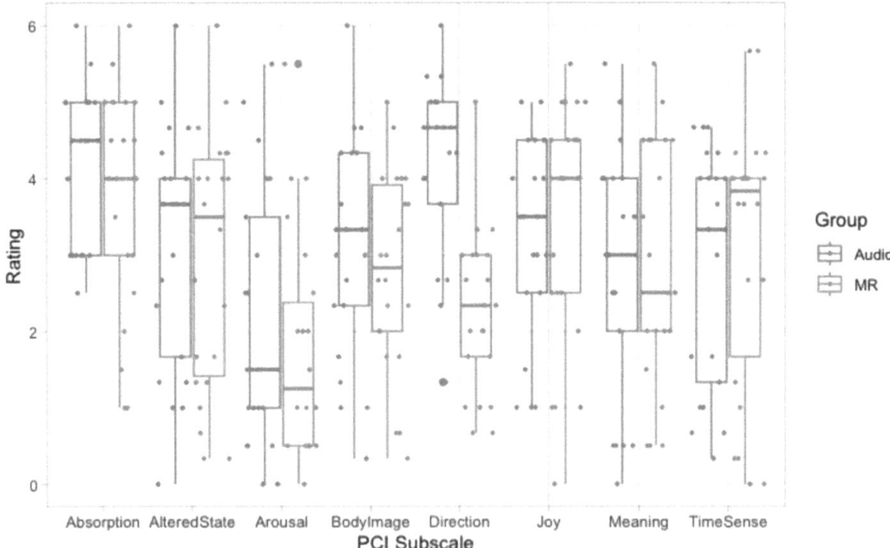

Fig. 4. Ratings of the PCI scales for the audio and MR groups.

5   Conclusions and Future Perspectives

Our results suggest that mixed reality of classical music could be a promising tool for professionals and music lovers to expand their associative imagery, and also to attract new audiences to classical music. MR could be a potential tool for engaging visualization of music analysis for music education and music art therapy with non-invasive multisensory stimulation. The majority of current MR experiences are games (e.g., shooting and exploration), and even typical "music games" are based on the matching of rhythm patterns, but are not associative experiences. In this fashion, we are also contributing to expanding the variety of genres in the game industry by creating cognitive musicology experiences in MR where the music is a primary narrative content and not a background or action template.

Both groups reported being significantly absorbed by the experience and that the experience induced a state of relaxation. Listening to the music evoked a more inner-directed state of attention, while the MR group reported strong engagement with the multisensory MR environment. Familiarity with MR/VR increased the enjoyment of the MR experience. The audio group also described a wide range of associative memories and images, which bear resemblance to the MR visualizations in several ways. We conclude that MR art/music experiences have potential uses for (1) attracting new audiences to classical music; (2) encouraging professional performers and/or music lovers in associative thinking and imagery; and (3) possibly serving as a new form of immersive art music therapy.

References

1. Sikora, Y., Chernykh, V., Shaforost, Y., Danylyuk, S., Chemerys, I.: Leveraging gamification and game-based technologies for educational purposes. Multidiscip. Rev. **7**, 2024spe008 (2024). https://doi.org/10.31893/multirev.2024spe008

2. Vermeir, J.F., White, M.J., Johnson, D., Crombez, G., Van Ryckeghem, D.M.L.: The effects of gamification on computerized cognitive training: systematic review and meta-analysis. JMIR Serious Games **8**(3), e18644 (2020). https://doi.org/10.2196/18644

3. Taruskin, R.: The Music of Alexander Scriabin by James M. Baker; Scriabin: Artist and Mystic by Boris de Schloezer; Nicolas Slonimsky. Music Theory Spectrum, vol. 10, no. 10th Anniversary Issue, Spring (1988)

4. Rudenko, S., McDonnell, M., Layden, T., Haahr, M.: Exploring classical music narratives through multimodality in AR/VR experiences. Presented at the International Conference on Interactive Digital Storytelling (ICIDS), Santa Cruz, USA (2022)

5. Liikkanen, L., Jakubowski, K.: Involuntary musical imagery as a component of ordinary music cognition: a review of empirical evidence. APA Psyc. Net Psychonomic Bull. Rev. **27**(6), 1195–1217 (2020)

6. Meng, C., Luck, G.: Voluntary musical imagery in music practice: contextual meaning, neuroscientific mechanisms and practical applications. Front. Psychol. **15**, 1452179 (2024). https://doi.org/10.3389/fpsyg.2024.1452179

7. Bailes, F.: Musical imagery and the temporality of consciousness. In: Music and Consciousness 2, pp. 271–285. Oxford University Press, Oxford (2019)

8. Juslin, P.N.: Seeing in the mind's eye: visual imagery. In: Musical Emotions Explained, 1st edn., pp. 330–342. Oxford University Press, Oxford (2019). https://doi.org/10.1093/oso/9780198753421.003.0023

9. Tervaniemi, M.: Musicanship - how and where in the brain? In: Musical Imaginations: Multidisciplinary Perspectives on Creativity, Performance, and Perceptionn, pp. 285–295. Oxford University Press, Oxford (2012)

10. Velasco, C., Obrist, M.: Multisensory Experiences: Where the Senses Meet Technology. Oxford University Press, Oxford (2020)

11. Rudenko, S., Fu, X., Haahr, M.: Alice Dali MR: a mixed reality interactive narrative experience. In: Interactive Storytelling 16th International Conference on Interactive Digital Storytelling, ICIDS 2023, Kobe, Japan, 11–15 November 2023, Proceedings, Part II. Springer, Cham (2023)

12. Ward, J.: The Frog Who Croaked Blue: Synesthesia and the Mixing of the Senses. Routledge, London and New York (2008)

13. Lupton, E.: Design is Storytelling. Cooper Hewitt, New York (2017)

14. Cytowic, R.E.: Synesthesia: A Union of the Senses, 2nd edn. MIT Press, Cambridge (2002)

15. Parise, C., Spence, C.: Audiovisual crossmodal correspondences and sound symbolism: a study using the implicit association test. Exp. Brain Res. **220**(3–4), 319–333 (2012). https://www.researchgate.net/publication/227175048_Audiovisual_crossmodal_correspondences_and_sound_symbolism_A_study_using_the_implicit_association_test

16. Ramachandran, V.S., Hubbard, E.M.: Hearing colors, tasting shapes. Sci. Am. 53–59 (2003)

17. Bor, D., Rothen, N., Schwartzman, D., Clayton, S., Seth, A.: Adults can be trained to acquire synesthetic experiences. Sci. Rep. **4** (2014). https://www.nature.com/articles/srep07089

18. Pekala, R.J.: The phenomenology of consciousness inventory. In: Quantifying Consciousness: An Empirical Approach, pp. 127–143. Springer, Cham (1991)

Design and Development of *ACE of Hearts*: A Serious Game for Young People with Adverse Childhood Experiences

Haiou Zhu[1], Minhua Ma[2](✉), Harsimran Sansoy[1], Isabelle Butcher[1], Natalie Bisal[1], and Kamaldeep Bhui[1,3,4]

[1] Department of Psychiatry, University of Oxford, Oxford, UK
[2] University of Surrey, Surrey, UK
m.ma@surrey.ac.uk
[3] Nuffield Department of Primary Care Health Sciences, University of Oxford, Oxford, UK
[4] Wadham College, University of Oxford, Oxford, UK

Abstract. Adverse Childhood Experiences (ACEs) significantly impact youth mental health, yet stigma and limited service capacity prevent many young people from accessing care and support. Serious games offer an engaging medium that interests young people through play, and there is emerging evidence of effectiveness for adolescent mental health. This paper describes the design and development of *ACE of Hearts*, a serious digital game designed to support young people affected by ACEs. Employing an iterative, experience-based co-design (EBCD) approach involving young people and stakeholders, the game creatively integrates metaphorical storytelling and early elements of Narrative Exposure Therapy (NET), providing information and self-directed space for reflection and narration of young people's predicaments. The prototype includes a central cozy space and four minigames, each addressing distinct combinations of ACEs, including sibling caregiving and bereavement, disability and trauma, gender dysphoria, and poverty. These issues were designed into the serious game through multimodal storytelling and interactive metaphors. We considered ethical safeguarding and user feedback and highlight the implications for future research.

Keywords: Serious Games · Adverse Childhood Experiences · Adolescent Mental Health · Experience-Based Co-Design · Narrative Exposure Therapy

1 Introduction

Adverse Childhood Experiences (ACEs), such as abuse, neglect, loss, or household dysfunction, can have a profound impact on adolescent mental health. Young people with multiple ACEs have been found to have 3 to 15 times the odds of a range of negative mental health and behavioural problems, including depression, post-traumatic disorder, self-harm and suicide attempts [1]. Up to 75% of youth exposed to multiple ACEs develop mental health issues by age eighteen [2]. Yet, many young people do not seek or receive help due to stigma, fear, or access barriers [3]. Long waiting lists and

A. Thomas et al. (Eds.): JCSG 2025, LNCS 16243, pp. 372–377, 2026.
https://doi.org/10.1007/978-3-032-10518-9_32

workforce shortages in current mental health services further delay the care received [4]. Digital health technologies hold promise to bridge this gap by delivering remote support, offering privacy that can lessen stigma and potentially reducing wait-time barriers [5]. In particular, serious games offer an engaging medium well-suited to youth interests and have shown emerging evidence in mental health contexts [6].

ACE of Hearts is a serious digital game developed to support young people who have experienced ACEs by increasing awareness, facilitating emotional processing and self-compassion, and validating their experiences in a private, self-directed space. The game consists of a central hub (the Cosy Den) and four narrative-driven mini-games, Horse and Foal, Dial It Back, Out of My Shell, and Hard Times, each addressing specific ACE themes. The game was developed through iterative, experience-based co-design (EBCD) with young people and stakeholders such as mental health experts. It leverages multimodal interactions and embeds care and support principles into engaging game-play. Signposting to mental health information and resources is also included. As the first serious game specifically targeting ACEs, we propose it can complement existing psychological and pharmacological treatments.

2 Related Work

Over the past two decades, serious games have gained traction as tools to support adolescent mental health in both prevention and treatment [7]. Researchers have explored serious games for a range of conditions, including anxiety [8], depression [9], autism [10] and attention-deficit/hyperactivity disorder (ADHD) [11]. A notable example is *Lumi Nova: Tales of Courage*, approved by the UK's Medicines and Healthcare Products Regulatory Agency, which combines psychoeducation and exposure therapy in gameplay to help children learn skills to self-manage their worries and anxiety [12]. *Lumi Nova* was found to safely engage 7–12-year-olds in facing their worries and was effective in reducing anxiety symptom over an 8-week pilot trial [12].

Importantly, few existing interventions specifically address the compound and varied adversities captured by the term ACEs. Most serious games for mental health focus on disorders or specific symptoms (anxiety, depression, etc.), rather than the impact of multiple childhood adversities. Serious games offer a new medium for this purpose by leveraging multimodal metaphors across audio, visual, haptic, and mechanical modes [13]. Existing research suggests that video games can act as dynamic ecosystems of meaning-making [14]. The interactive nature of video games allows players to experience metaphors through gameplay mechanics, which can be powerful in therapeutic contexts where traditional verbal expression might fall short. Our design draws on this approach: prior analysis of commercial off-the-shelf games identified recurring motifs for grief and trauma that informed our narrative metaphors in ACE of Hearts [13].

3 Methods

Experience Based Co-design (EBCD) is increasingly employed to involve young people, clinicians, game designers, and other stakeholders directly in the creation and production process [15]. The use of EBCD aligns with contemporary design-thinking and people-centred approaches in health research, which posit that interventions are more acceptable and effective when target users contribute to their design and development [16]. The ACE of Hearts prototype was developed using an iterative EBCD approach integrated into an agile game development framework over a period of eighteen months. In this framework, a sprint is a defined period of work that has set goals at its start and evaluation of the work at the end to inform the goals of the next sprint. The game development team included a games designer/writer, 3D artist, games animator, programmer, and specialist arts practitioners. The co-design process involved 18 young people, aged 12 to 24, along with five adult stakeholders, who collaboratively established goals and evaluated outcomes across eight development sprints, each lasting six weeks. This process comprised structured phases: pre-production, concept ideation, game development, and iterative testing and refinement. The co-design sessions were hybrid, consisting of in-person and online co-design activities. Each session lasted between 1 and 2 h. This deep form of co-design was suited for the complexities of game development. The iterative feedback led to significant improvements across game functionality and content development, while also informing key decisions regarding the gaming platform, art style, game genre, and ethical considerations.

4   The Game *ACE of Hearts*

ACE of Hearts consists of a central hub *Cosy Den* and four mini-games: *Horse and Foal, Dial It Back, Out of My Shell, Hard Times*, each using a different genre and metaphor to explore specific ACE themes (see Fig. 1). Briefly, the central hub and the mini-games are:

Cosy Den: This central hub is presented as the player's personal bedroom, a safe space where players can relax, interact, and access the mini-game stories. The visual design of the hub is warm with soft lighting and comfortable furnishings. Players can customise items such as posters, bedding and music. They can also interact with various objects and activities, such as feeding the fish and playing the guitar, feeling at home and in control. Signposting information naturally fits into the environment of the room through items like comic books on the table and books on the bookshelf.

Horse and Foal: A 2D side-scrolling adventure about sibling caregiving and bereavement. The player follows Carla, a young horse, who must care for her little sister Rhea (a foal) through a journey of changing seasons. The gameplay involves walking through a pastoral landscape while managing rising anxiety (represented by a dark mist chasing the characters, symbolizing Rhea's terminal illness). The story is divided into four chapters (seasons) and presents choices that force Carla to choose between her caregiving duties and her personal needs. In the final chapter after Rhea's death, Carla went through a process of bereavement through a metaphorical acceptance of loss.

Dial It Back: A 2D game inspired by Narrative Exposure Therapy (NET) principles, focusing on Oli, a young person living with disability. In this game, Oli is guided by a character named Iris (visualized as a friendly floating eye or "eyeflotor") on a journey back through his memories of the past ten years. As Oli explores, diary entries or text fragments appear on screen, uncovering their thoughts and memories. Key mechanics

Fig. 1. Screenshots of *ACE of Hearts'* Cosy Den and mini-games

are realized by haptics designs, such as unlocking each memory by moving a "eyeglass" around a stylized brain to finding four sensory details (smell, sound, touch, and an emotion) associated with that event.

Out of My Shell: A 2D pixel-art tower defense game portraying a young person's experience of gender dysphoria and identity exploration. The protagonist, Flo, is metaphorically represented as a dragon in disguise, a creature hiding its true form, to convey the feeling of a concealed true identity. The narrative touches on challenges such as fear of being "outed," internalized transphobia, and external bullying, gradually leading to finding support and self-acceptance. Gameplay alternates between visual novel-style story scenes and tower defense segments that serve as symbolic challenges.

Hard Times: A 3D first-person adventure about financial hardship and tough family decisions. The player takes the role of Mina, a teenager living in a cramped rented flat in London with her single mother and younger brother. In a series of narrative scenes and free-roam segments in the apartment, the player faces dilemmas such as whether to spend saved money on food vs. rent or whether to sell personal items to cover bills. Multiple endings are possible, ranging from hopeful (avoiding eviction by finding aid, albeit just barely) to tragic (the family being evicted).

5   Discussion and Conclusion

The integration of metaphor and multimodal storytelling emerged as a particularly effective strategy. Similar to arts-based interventions, the game uses metaphor, such as the black mist representing illness, or the dragon as a metaphor for hidden identity, to help players externalize and process difficult emotions. These metaphors allowed us to address sensitive topics (e.g. death, trauma, identity) in a way that was both engaging and respectful, supporting the idea of games as "ecosystems of meaning-making" [14]. Nevertheless, developing a game about adversity carries the risk of re-exposing participants to difficult memories and emotions [17]. To mitigate this, co-design workshops were supported by trained youth workers, and participants could opt out of any activity that felt uncomfortable. Likewise, in the game itself, our design strived to balance difficult content with moments of hope and support, through friendly NPCs, mindfulness features, and embedded mental health resources. Additionally, mental health professionals (psychologists and psychiatrists on our team) were involved throughout design and content review to ensure that the game's portrayal of sensitive issues remains appropriate and does not inadvertently harm.

Grounded in co-design and metaphor-rich narratives, ACE of Hearts offers an accessible tool for emotional reflection and support. While not a replacement for professional care, it aims to complement existing services by helping young people explore their experiences and develop coping strategies. A feasibility study is underway to evaluate engagement and impact, with the goal of informing future development of serious games for vulnerable youth.

References

1. Meeker, E.C., O'Connor, B.C., Kelly, L.M., Hodgeman, D.D., Scheel-Jones, A.H., Berbary, C.: The impact of adverse childhood experiences on adolescent health risk indicators in a community sample. Psychol. Trauma **13**, 302–312 (2021). https://doi.org/10.1037/tra000 1004
2. Butcher, I., et al.: A participatory action research study to explore adolescents' experiences of adverse childhood experiences (ACEs) through creative workshops: a protocol (2023). https://doi.org/10.1101/2023.12.21.23300349
3. Zhao, R., et al.: Research review: help-seeking intentions, behaviors, and barriers in college students – a systematic review and meta-analysis. Child Psychol. Psychiatry jcpp.14145 (2025). https://doi.org/10.1111/jcpp.14145
4. British Medical Association: Mental health pressures in England. https://www.bma.org.uk/advice-and-support/nhs-delivery-and-workforce/pressures/mental-health-pressures-data-analysis. Accessed 07 Apr 2025
5. Torous, J., et al.: The growing field of digital psychiatry: current evidence and the future of apps, social media, chatbots, and virtual reality. World Psychiatry **20**, 318–335 (2021). https://doi.org/10.1002/wps.20883
6. Vajawat, B.: Digital gaming interventions in psychiatry: evidence, applications and challenges. Psychiatry Res. (2021)
7. Wols, A., Pingel, M., Lichtwarck-Aschoff, A., Granic, I.: Effectiveness of applied and casual games for young people's mental health: a systematic review of randomised controlled studies. Clin. Psychol. Rev. **108**, 102396 (2024). https://doi.org/10.1016/j.cpr.2024.102396
8. Tsui, T.Y.L., DeFrance, K., Khalid-Khan, S., Granic, I., Hollenstein, T.: Reductions of anxiety symptoms, state anxiety, and anxious arousal in youth playing the videogame mindlight compared to online cognitive behavioral therapy. Games Health J. g4h.2020.0083 (2021). https://doi.org/10.1089/g4h.2020.0083
9. Poppelaars, M., Lichtwarck-Aschoff, A., Otten, R., Granic, I.: Can a commercial video game prevent depression? Null results and whole sample action mechanisms in a randomized controlled trial. Front. Psychol. **11**, 575962 (2021). https://doi.org/10.3389/fpsyg.2020.575962

10. Fridenson-Hayo, S., et al.: 'Emotiplay': a serious game for learning about emotions in children with autism: results of a cross-cultural evaluation. Eur. Child Adolesc. Psychiatry **26**, 979–992 (2017). https://doi.org/10.1007/s00787-017-0968-0

11. Kollins, S.H., et al.: A novel digital intervention for actively reducing severity of paediatric ADHD (STARS-ADHD): a randomised controlled trial. Lancet Digit. Health **2**, e168–e178 (2020). https://doi.org/10.1016/S2589-7500(20)30017-0

12. Lockwood, J., Williams, L., Martin, J.L., Rathee, M., Hill, C.: Effectiveness, user engagement and experience, and safety of a mobile app (Lumi Nova) delivering exposure-based cognitive behavioral therapy strategies to manage anxiety in children via immersive gaming technology: preliminary evaluation study. JMIR Ment Health **9**, e29008 (2022). https://doi.org/10.2196/29008

13. Reay, E., Ma, M., Mankee-Williams, A., Pavarini, G., Shaughnessy, N., Bhui, K.: Stones in our pockets: mental health dimensions of grief in contemporary video games. medRxiv, 2024–04 (2024)

14. Reay, E.: The Child in Videogames: From the Meek, to the Mighty, to the Monstrous. Springer, Cham (2024)

15. Larkin, M., Boden, Z.V.R., Newton, E.: On the brink of genuinely collaborative care: experience-based co-design in mental health. Qual. Health Res. **25**, 1463–1476 (2015). https://doi.org/10.1177/1049732315576494

16. Smith, H., et al.: Co-production practice and future research priorities in United Kingdom-funded applied health research: a scoping review. Health Res Policy Sys. **20**, 36 (2022). https://doi.org/10.1186/s12961-022-00838-x

17. Bhui, K., Butcher, I.: The trouble with trauma and triggering. Lancet Psychiatry **10**, 478–479 (2023). https://doi.org/10.1016/S2215-0366(23)00112-8

VR

Emotional Design for Virtual Reality Games: The Effect of Object Luminosity, Background Lighting, and Learner Action

Yuli Shao[1] , Yuqi Hang[1] , Xinyue Jiao[1] , Bruce D. Homer[2] ,
and Jan L. Plass[1(✉)]

[1] New York University, New York, NY 10012, USA
jan.plass@nyu.edu
[2] The Graduate Center, City University of New York, New York, NY 10016, USA

Abstract. We investigated the effect of three virtual reality design features on users' emotional responses, including two visual features (object luminosity and background lighting) and an interaction feature (available actions). Our findings revealed the affective quality of these three design features, showing that object luminosity and actions significantly increase positive emotion, while dark background lighting induces slightly negative emotions. Object luminosity and action also had an effect on perceived presence, whereas background lighting did not. Only action increased the level of perceived cognitive load. We discuss the implications of our findings for the emotional design of VR games for learning.

Keywords: Virtual Reality · Emotion · Design · Game

1 Introduction

How can the affordance of games to induce emotions in learners be leveraged to enhance learning outcomes? With the increasing use of games as learning environments, designers are exploring how games should be designed to provide playful, enjoyable learning experiences that achieve the intended outcomes [21, 22]. While cognitive, motivational, and socio-cultural aspects of design of games for learning have been studied extensively [1], affective factors have received less attention, especially in the context of virtual reality (VR)-based games. In this study, we therefore asked how specific visual design factors, such as the luminosity of objects and the brightness of the environment, affect users' emotions in VR. We also asked whether the level to which users were able to perform their own actions in VR affected emotions.

This focus on investigating emotions in the context of learning is significant as recent studies in affective neuroscience have found that brain regions typically implicated in processing emotions also process cognition, and, reversely, that regions typically implicated in cognitive information processing also process emotion [2]. Affective neuroscientists now believe that there is no fundamental difference in the mechanisms of

A. Thomas et al. (Eds.): JCSG 2025, LNCS 16243, pp. 381–397, 2026.
https://doi.org/10.1007/978-3-032-10518-9_33

cognition and emotion [3] and suggest a reciprocal relationship of emotion and cognition: Our emotional state affects how we process information, and the information we process affects our emotional state [4].

The *emotional design principle* therefore describes the deliberate use of specific design features to induce emotions that are conducive to learning without adding significant cognitive processing demands [4, 5]. Research using screen-based media has shown that emotional design can enhance learning outcomes in games and beyond. Recent work has begun to explore how this principle applies in immersive VR games [6], which the present study further examines.

There is a growing interest in the use of immersive VR to design learning experiences. When VR is designed to take advantage of its unique affordances [7], learning in VR can be a more effective learning experience than learning from traditional media [8]. One of these affordances is the ability of VR to induce emotions. Combined with a second affordance of VR, which is to provide an immersive experience in which learners have a sense of presence, the potential for emotion induction in VR is much stronger than that of 2D environments [9] as it can employ haptic, auditory, and visual design factors for emotional design [10]. In the next section we will define emotions for the context of this research, as well as describe the theoretical foundation of this work, the Integrative Model of Emotional Foundations of Game-Based Learning.

2   Literature Review

2.1   What are Emotions?

Emotions are complex phenomena, and multiple theoretical approaches have been developed to define emotions and their purpose. The most common approaches are the evolutionary (basic emotions) approach, the cognitive appraisal approach, and the social constructivist approach.

For the present research, we use Russell's Circumplex Model of Affect [11], a gradient model of emotion grounded in affective neuroscience that allows for meaningful operationalization of the construct. Russell's model offers a two-dimensional view of emotion that both complements and challenges aspects of the approaches mentioned above. It organizes emotional experiences along two continuous dimensions, *Valence* (pleasant ↔ unpleasant), and *Arousal* (high activation ↔ low activation), see Fig. 1.

Instead of describing emotions as discrete, this model describes emotions on a clustered map, where emotions such as joy and excitement, which are both positive and activating, may align in both dimensions, while others, such as boredom and relaxation, may share similarities in only one dimension, in this case, their deactivating nature. Emotions can also diverge in both dimensions, such as delight, which is activating and positive, whereas sadness is deactivating and negative. This continuous affective space captures the complexities of emotions that are especially relevant in the context of games.

As we are less interested in specific discrete emotions, the present research focuses on these two dimensions, arousal and valence.

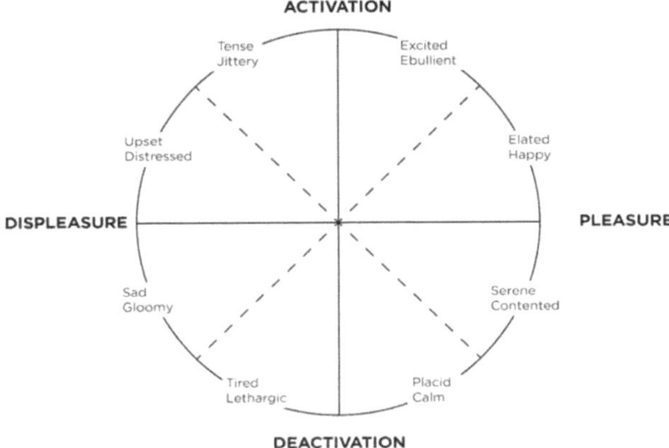

Fig. 1. The Circumplex Model of Affect

2.2 An Integrated Framework of Emotions in GBL

A recently proposed theory of the foundation of emotion in game-based learning is the *Integrative Model of Emotional Foundations of Game-Based Learning* (EmoGBL) [12]. EmoGBL places emotions at the center of learning experience and describes how emotions can enhance learning outcomes in games (Fig. 5 in the Appendix). It especially shows how a range of game design elements, including visual aesthetics, musical score, narrative, and game mechanics, can be used to induce emotions in learners, either through emotion transmission or through appraisal [12]. In the present work, we are interested in the affective quality of these design elements, that is, in their ability to induce an emotional response in individuals [11]. Learners' motivation, cognitive resources, memory processes, problem-solving strategies, and self-regulation are significantly impacted by their experienced emotions, including aesthetic, social, achievement, topic, and technology-related emotions. These emotional experiences shape cognitive, emotional, and motivational learning processes and outcomes. Understanding the affective quality of design features, and the emotional dynamics in GBL they influence, can provide important guidance for the design of more engaging, motivating, and effective learning experiences in games, including games for learning in VR.

2.3 Research on Affective Quality of Design Features in Non-immersive Media

Research on emotional design has established that learning can be enhanced when the design of the learning environment intentionally induces emotions conducive to learning without adding significant cognitive processing demands [4, 5]. For non-immersive, screen-based media, these effects have been demonstrated across various settings, including multimedia environments [13], educational games [15, 16], and video lessons [17, 18]. This body of work has predominantly focused on a specific set of visual features such as color, shape, and anthropomorphism. The use of bright, warm, and saturated colors and round (anthropomorphic) shapes enhanced science learning compared to conditions using a neutral design with a monochromatic grayscale and rectangular shapes [13, 14].

The ability of an object or feature to induce emotions has been referred to as its affective quality [11]. While these initial studies confirm the principle of emotional design, the rise of new technologies such as immersive VR necessitates a need to identify additional design features that can induce emotions in learners to broaden this design space. The current study aims to add to this literature by extending the study of visual design features and their effects on emotion to immersive VR.

2.4 The Emerging Landscape of Emotional Design in VR

VR's unique affordances for immersion and presence create a powerful medium for emotion induction, compared to 2D environments [9]. Research into the affective quality of VR design features is a growing field, exploring how visual, auditory, and haptic elements can shape learners' experiences. This study contributes to a research agenda that investigates the affective quality of a range of design features in VR in various modalities. The goal is to provide learning designers with a set of design features they can use for emotional design in VR to enhance learning outcomes, addressing a particular gap in current VR learning design research [20].

Research on *visual design* has begun to extend emotional design principles from 2D media while also exploring novel features. As in 2D, the use of color in VR can increase perceived pleasantness and arousal [32]. More specific to VR's 3D nature, the overall atmosphere of a virtual scene, such as a lush, sunny park versus a bare, concrete one, has been shown to induce distinct emotions like joy and boredom, respectively [33]. Game characters' facial expressions and dimensionality have strong effects on emotions, especially during immersive 3D gameplay [19]. The path of game characters in the VR environment also affects learner's emotional responses. Game characters approaching players, for example, increased arousal compared to game characters remaining at a distance [23]. Recent experimental studies have begun to isolate specific visual components. For instance, Shao et al. [6] found that background lighting conditions and the presence of particle effects influenced positive affect.

In *auditory design*, ambient sounds such as low-volume water sounds have been found to induce calmness [34], and spatial audio can intensify emotional reactions by enhancing learners' sense of presence, i.e., their subjective feeling of being there [35]. *Haptic* design features such as vibrotactile feedback were found to induce emotions by impacting learners' sense of presence [10] and to enhance feelings of empathy [36].

In the present study, we investigated an additional design factor, object luminosity, in addition to replicating two previously investigated design features with different materials. While this growing body of research is promising, we identify two gaps that the current study hopes to address. First, the methodologies are inconsistent, ranging from qualitative user research to experimental studies. Second, many studies investigate design features within complex, multifaceted environments (e.g., fully-featured games or rich narrative scenarios). This makes it difficult to disentangle the effect of a single variable from confounding factors such as narrative, character interactions, or other sensory stimuli. This complexity may contribute to inconsistent findings in the literature, such as studies where animated virtual actors had no significant impact on affective quality or learning [37].

2.5 The Present Study

The present study focused on two visual design features for immersive VR: background lighting and object luminosity. Background lighting influences the overall atmosphere of an environment and triggers players' emotional responses [6, 24]. Based on previous research, we hypothesize that different lighting conditions, such as bright versus dark settings, will have varied effects on learners' emotions. Object luminosity describes the radiant power emitted by a light-emitting object. In VR, high luminosity objects appear brighter than low luminosity objects. We hypothesize more positive emotional responses for high object luminosity, and a potential interaction with background lighting. We also added interactivity, another essential affordance of VR, in addition to the visual design factors. Based on previous research, we ask whether different levels of actions in VR would lead to different emotional experiences.

Our research question was therefore: What is the affective quality of three design features of immersive VR: object luminosity (low vs. high), background lighting (dark vs. bright), and action (no actions vs. the ability to move objects)?

3 Method

3.1 Research Design

This study employed a 2 (object luminosity: low vs. high) × 2 (background lighting: dark vs. bright) × 2 (action: observe vs. move) within-subject factorial design, resulting in a total of eight unique experimental conditions labeled with different alphabetical letters (Table 1). Each participant experienced all combinations of the three factors across two blocks: one involving observation tasks and the other involving movement tasks. In the "Observe" block, participants encountered four conditions (A, B, C, D) that combined background lighting and object luminosity. These included observing organelles in dark lighting with either low or high luminosity, and in bright lighting with either low or high luminosity. The same four combinations (E, F, G, H) were then repeated in the "Move" block, where participants actively interacted with the VR environment under identical lighting and luminosity variations. To control for order effects, a counterbalanced Latin square design was applied. Each participant would first experience the "Observe" block and then the "Move" block with the treatment sequence within each block random-ized. The Latin square was generated using the MOLS() function from the R package *blocksdesign* and duplicated identically across both task blocks. This approach priori-tized within-condition comparisons over full mutually orthogonality, which would have introduced additional complexity. A Latin square design for repeated measures is "used to remove potential confounding between position effects and treatment effects by giv-ing treatments to cases in different orders", without having to be prohibitively large like a fully factorial design [30]. Further, modeling Latin square sequences can enhance statistical power [31].

Table 1. $2 \times 2 \times 2$ Within-Subject Factorial Design

Observe				Move			
		Background lighting				Background lighting	
		Dark	Bright			Dark	Bright
Object Luminosity	Low	A	C	Object Luminosity	Low	E	G
	High	B	D		High	F	H

3.2 Participants

A total of 43 participants took part in the study. The group included 20 males, 18 females, and 5 individuals who either identified as a different gender or preferred not to disclose their gender. The average age of participants ($n = 37$, 6 participants didn't report their year of birth) was 19 years old ($SD = 6$), with ages ranging from 14 to 37. The educational levels of the participants varied widely. Most were students in secondary school, with 27.9% in 12th grade, 20.9% in 11th grade, 16.3% in 9th grade, 7.0% in 10th grade, and 4.7% in 7th grade. A smaller portion of the sample consisted of college and graduate students, including 14.0% in graduate school, 7.0% first-year undergraduates, and 2.3% third-year undergraduates. The sample was racially and ethnically diverse. The largest single group identified as Hispanic or Latino (35.7%). Other participants reported backgrounds including Asian (9.5%), South Asian (9.5%), Black or African American (7.1%), and White or Caucasian (7.1%), with many identifying as multiracial (31%). Most participants (83.7%) had prior experience with virtual reality. Of those, the majority (91.7%) had used VR only a few times ever, and very few used it regularly. Only one reported using VR as frequently as once a week. Over half of the experienced users had used VR for less than one year, while others reported experience spanning one to ten years.

Participants were recruited through a partnership with public high schools from the New York City Department of Education. Information about the study was distributed to teachers and principals at public high schools, and interested students took part in their school's visit to the research lab to participate. The undergraduate and graduate students were recruited via flyers posted around the university campus. This recruitment strategy resulted in a convenience sample primarily composed of students from the local metropolitan area.

Participants received a $15 Amazon gift card or a free lunch of similar value as compensation for their time. Ethics approval was received from the review boards at New York University and the New York Department of Education for this study. All participants provided informed consent or assent before participating in the experiment. For minors, parental permission was obtained.

3.3 Materials

The VR materials comprised eight immersive conditions that varied in background lighting, object luminosity, and action, as illustrated in Fig. 2. The core visual content featured three animal cell organelles positioned on the left side of the scene, which either moved automatically or were interactively manipulated toward the cell membrane on the right side. In the condition where participants actively manipulate the objects, participants used the VR controller to pick up, drag, rotate, and reposition each organelle onto the membrane. There was no time limit imposed for these tasks. In the no-action conditions, participants passively observed the organelles as they moved to the membrane one at a time, each transition lasting approximately 6 s for a total of 18 s. The background lighting of the VR environment was either brightly or dimly lit, depending on the condition. A neutral tone was used in both lighting conditions. Figures 2a and 2b illustrate these two lighting environments.

The study also manipulated object luminosity, defined as the radiant power emitted by a light-emitting object. In high-luminosity conditions, the organelles appeared vibrant and visibly radiant, while in low-luminosity conditions, they appeared subdued and less visually salient, as shown in Figs. 2a and 2c. This factor was crossed with background lighting to explore possible interaction effects. Despite the low-luminosity objects appearing dim in the dark background in the 2D visual in Fig. 2, participants in VR were still able to easily recognize and differentiate the organelles. Prior to each condition, participants viewed a 15-s neutral VR scene, a green park, to minimize carry-over emotional effects from prior conditions. The VR experiences were developed using Unity and deployed via Meta Quest 2 and 3 headsets.

(a)   Bright background with high-
luminosity objects

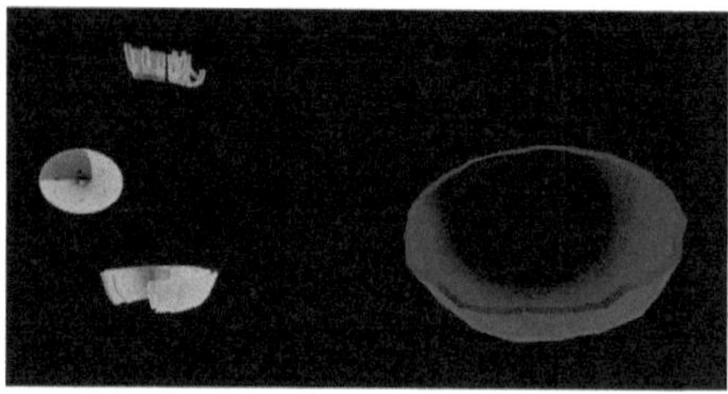

(b)   Dark background with high-
luminosity objects

(c)   Bright background with low-
luminosity objects

(d)   Dark background with low-
luminosity objects

Fig. 2. Background lighting and object luminosity. The top row shows high-luminosity objects under bright (left) and dark (right) background lighting conditions; the bottom row shows low-luminosity objects under bright (left) and dark (right) background lighting conditions.

3.4 Measures

Our study employed a variety of measures to assess both momentary (state) and enduring (trait) variables, as well as demographic characteristics. These measures evaluated participants' emotional responses, sense of presence, perceived cognitive load, and overall reactions to the virtual environment.

Emotional State–SAM: The Self-Assessment Manikin (SAM) is a non-verbal tool that uses a series of simple graphic figures to measure emotional valence and arousal along a 5-point Likert scale [25]. Participants were asked to select the figure that best represented their emotional state.

Emotional State–PANAS-VR: The PANAS-VR is an adaptation of the Positive and Negative Affect Schedule for use in immersive environments [6]. It includes 10 items reflecting common emotional and physical sensations in VR. These include terms such as "enthusiastic," "scared," "excited," and "distressed." Participants rated each emotion on a 5-point scale ranging from "very slightly or not at all" to "extremely," indicating the intensity of each emotion during the VR session [26].

Sense of Presence–IPQ Subscale: The Spatial Presence component of the Igroup Presence Questionnaire (IPQ) was used to assess the participants' sense of physical immersion in the VR environment [27, 28]. This scale includes six items rated on a 7-point Likert scale, from −3 (fully disagree) to +3 (fully agree). These items assess degrees of immersion, perception, and felt presence.

Mental Effort: A version of the Perceived Mental Effort Scale tailored for VR was used to assess how much cognitive effort participants felt they exerted during the experience [29]. Responses ranged from "very low" to "very high" on a 7-point Likert scale.

Demographic Information: Participants provided data on their birth date (month and year), gender, primary and additional languages spoken, educational level, ethnicity, and past experiences with VR. This included prior use of VR, types of VR devices used, usage frequency and duration, and specific applications previously explored.

Post-VR Experience Survey: After the VR session, participants completed a survey that included both multiple-choice and open-ended items. Questions asked whether they enjoyed the VR experience, liked the visual design, found the interactions intuitive, and whether they would be interested in using similar VR tools for academic purposes (e.g., learning biology). Open-ended prompts allowed participants to elaborate on what they liked or disliked about the VR experience and to share additional feedback.

3.5 Procedure

Prior to the study session, all participants were pre-screened to ensure they met the manufacturer's safety guidelines for VR use, and parental consent was obtained for participants under the age of 18. On the day of the experiment, participants completed a brief health screening form. Adult participants then provided informed consent, while minors provided assent. The study was conducted in a dedicated research lab at New York University, where each participant was situated at an individual station with a VR headset. Researchers monitored the participants throughout the experiment, with a researcher-to-participant ratio ranging from 1:1 to 1:3. The entire session for each participant lasted approximately 40–50 min.

Once the participants were seated, researchers introduced the study objectives and experimental procedures. Participants were then randomly assigned to one of four treatment orders, which differed only in the sequence in which they experienced the eight experimental conditions. Prior to entering the VR environment, they completed a demographic survey using a tablet.

During the VR session, participants experienced each of the eight immersive treatments, which varied in background lighting (bright vs. dark), object luminosity (high vs. low), and action (ability to move objects vs. observe/no action). After each condition, participants completed a series of self-report measures assessing their emotional responses, sense of presence, and mental effort. The full VR experience lasted approximately 20 to 30 min. After the VR session, participants completed a post-survey reflecting on their experience.

4 Results

To determine the effects of the different design factors on the four outcome emotion measures: positive affect, negative affect, emotional arousal, and emotional valence, the presence measure, and the mental effort scale, we conducted repeated measures ANOVAs with three within-subject factors, background lighting, object luminosity, and action, for each of the outcome measures.

Positive affect was calculated as the sum of all positive emotions ratings from PANAS-VR. Negative affect was calculated as the sum of all negative emotions ratings from PANAS-VR. Emotional valence and emotional arousal used the original scores from the SAM valence and arousal scales. Presence was calculated as the mean of all the IPQ items. For cognitive load, the scale score was used.

The data from all measures met normality and homogeneity of variance assumptions. The results from these analyses are presented in the following sections by main effects for each of the design factors and their interaction effects. Table 2 presents the means of these measures with their standard deviations.

Table 2. Means and standard deviations of measures

Conditions			Positive Affect		Negative Affect		Valence		Arousal		Presence		Mental Effort	
Action	Lighting	Luminosity	M	SD	M	SD	M	SD	M	SD	M	SD	M	SD
Move	Bright	High	12.63	6.44	6.23	2.94	3.45	0.99	2.51	1.08	0.59	0.93	0.23	1.25
	Bright	Low	12.23	5.55	6.93	3.47	3.49	0.94	2.44	1.10	0.62	0.90	0.30	1.32
	Dark	High	13.98	6.08	6.74	3.16	3.62	0.96	2.60	1.17	0.67	0.95	0.33	1.39
	Dark	Low	12.28	6.14	6.84	3.11	3.36	0.85	2.54	1.08	0.50	0.92	0.33	1.51
Observe	Bright	High	11.67	5.41	5.65	1.36	3.53	0.68	2.28	1.08	0.46	0.89	-0.02	1.28
	Bright	Low	10.70	5.21	5.79	2.03	3.24	0.66	2.16	1.00	0.37	0.87	-0.19	1.39
	Dark	High	12.28	5.69	6.35	2.86	3.50	0.86	2.40	1.24	0.43	0.87	-0.09	1.39
	Dark	Low	11.49	5.46	7.37	3.05	3.03	0.73	2.33	0.89	0.31	0.92	0.05	1.38

4.1 Object Luminosity

Emotion. The analysis revealed significant main effects of object luminosity on positive affect, $F(1,42) = 8.86$, $p = .005$, $\eta_p^2 = .174$, negative affect, $F(1,42) = 4.81$, $p = .03$, $\eta_p^2 = .10$, and emotional valence, $F(1,31) = 10.92$, $p = .002$, $\eta_p^2 = .26$. High luminosity objects elicited higher positive affect, lower negative affect, and more positive valence than low luminosity objects. However, no main effect was found for emotional arousal, $F(1,37) = 0.83$, $p = .37$, $\eta_p^2 = .02$.

Presence and Mental Effort. A significant main effect was found on presence, $F(1, 42) = 4.55$, $p = .04$, $\eta_p^2 = .10$, indicating higher presence for high versus low luminosity objects. No significant main effect was found for mental effort, $F(1, 41) < .001, p = 1.00$, $\eta_p^2 < .001$.

These results indicate that objects with high luminosity consistently contributed to learners' affective and presence outcomes without impacting mental effort.

4.2 Background Lighting

Emotion. The analysis indicated a main effect of background lighting on negative affect, $F(1,42) = 7.40, p = .009$, $\eta_p^2 = .15$, suggesting that dark lighting induced higher negative affect compared to bright lighting conditions. No main effect was found for background lighting on positive affect, $F(1,42) = 3.66$, $p = .06$, $\eta_p^2 = .08$, on emotional valence, $F(1,31) = .01$, $p = .94$, $\eta_p^2 < .001$, and on emotional arousal, $F(1,37) = .59$, $p = .45$, $\eta_p^2 = .02$.

Presence and Mental Effort. No main effect was found for background lighting on either presence, $F(1, 42) = .39$, $p = .538$, $\eta_p^2 = .009$, or mental effort, $F(1, 41) = .29$, $p = .590$, $\eta_p^2 = .01$.

These results indicate that dark background lighting specifically increased negative affect, but the lighting factor had no notable effect on positive affect, valence, arousal, presence, or cognitive load.

4.3 Action

Emotion. The analysis indicated significant main effects of action on positive affect, $F(1,42) = 11.50$, $p = .002$, $\eta_p^2 = .22$, and emotional arousal, $F(1,37) = 5.05$, $p = .03$, $\eta_p^2 = .12$. Participants reported higher positive affect and greater emotional arousal when actively manipulating objects compared to observing. No main effect was found for negative affect, $F(1,42) = 1.62$, $p = .21$, $\eta_p^2 = .04$, and emotional valence, $F(1,31) = 0.92$, $p = .34$, $\eta_p^2 = .03$.

Presence and Mental Effort. Significant main effects were found for action on presence, $F(1, 42) = 4.82$, $p = .03$, $\eta_p^2 = .10$, and on mental effort, $F(1, 41) = 6.40$, $p = .02$, $\eta_p^2 = .14$. Being able to move objects was found to be associated with a higher level of presence but greater mental effort than no actions.

These results suggest that enabling actions in VR enhanced learners' positive affect, emotional arousal, and sense of presence, though at the cost of increased mental effort.

4.4 Interaction Effects

Across all analyses, four significant interaction effects were found with emotion as outcome measure. Post hoc comparisons were conducted using Bonferroni correction to further examine these effects.

A significant interaction between object luminosity and action was found for emotional valence (Fig. 3), $F(1,31) = 14.62$, $p < .001$, $\eta_p^2 = .32$. Regardless of background lighting conditions, observing high luminosity objects led to significantly more positive valence compared to observing low luminosity objects ($MD = 0.36$, $t(31) = 5.00$, $p < .001$).

A significant interaction between lighting and action was also found for negative affect, $F(1,42) = 6.48$, $p = .02$, $\eta_p^2 = .13$. Specifically, negative affect was significantly higher when observing under dark compared to bright lighting ($MD = 1.14$, $t(42) = 4.03$, $p = .001$) and when moving under dark lighting compared to observing under bright lighting ($MD = 1.07$, $t(42) = 3.00$, $p = .03$).

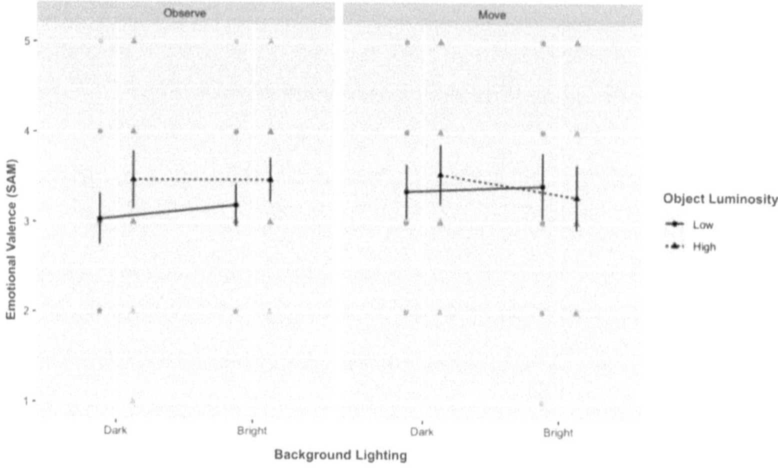

Fig. 3. Mean of Emotional Valence by Conditions

Significant three-way interactions were observed for positive affect, $F(1,42) = 5.66$, $p = .02$, $\eta_p^2 = .12$, and negative affect, $F(1,42) = 6.68$, $p = .01$, $\eta_p^2 = .14$. As shown in Fig. 4, positive affect was significantly higher when moving high luminosity objects in dark backgrounds than when moving low luminosity objects in bright backgrounds $(MD = 1.74, t(42) = 3.37, p < .05)$ and than all observation conditions.

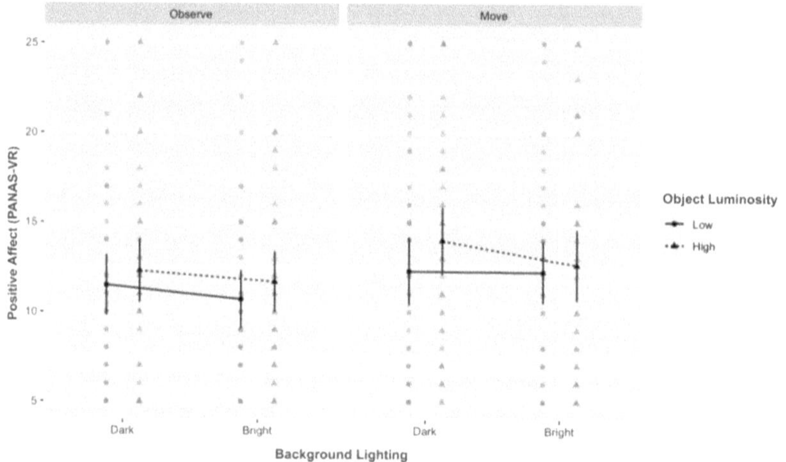

Fig. 4. Mean of Positive Affect (PANAS-VR) by Conditions.

For negative emotions, observing low luminosity objects in dark backgrounds produced significantly higher negative affect than observing both high luminosity objects $(MD = 1.72, t(42) = 4.05, p < .01)$ or low luminosity objects in bright backgrounds $(MD = 1.58, t(42) = 3.43, p = .04)$.

These results suggest that while background lighting, object luminosity, and action each independently influenced emotional outcomes, their interactions significantly shaped learners' affective experiences, highlighting that specific combination of features may be particularly effective for enhancing positive affect and reducing negative affect.

5 Discussion

The goal of the current study was to investigate the affective quality of three design features in immersive VR, namely background lighting, object luminosity, and ability to move and manipulate objects. Results are in line with our predictions that all three design features were successful in inducing emotions, but they did so in different ways. This research adds to the EmoGBL model by providing more insights into one of the distal antecedents of learner emotions, emotional design [12].

For *object luminosity*, we found that objects with high luminosity led to reports of higher positive affect, lower negative affect, higher emotional valence, and higher levels of sense of presence. The affective quality of object luminosity could be unique to virtual reality design, especially given its interaction with action, another important design factor in VR. Luminosity and action both hold greater potential to account for the linkage (or the two-way relationship) between emotion and presence [24].

For *background lighting*, we found that dark lighting induced higher negative affect compared to brighter lighting, which aligns with findings reported in prior research [6]. This finding addressed a limitation in [6] by decomposing the effect of brightness of background lighting from background lighting warmness. Although the effect of background lighting on positive affect was not statistically significant, the medium effect size $\eta_p^2 = .08$ of background lighting warrants further examination.

For *action*, i.e., the user's ability to move objects vs. watch them move, this study found similar effects of user action on positive affect, emotional arousal, presence, and mental effort as reported in previous work [6]. The affective effect of action, where being able to move objects was associated with higher positive affect and stronger arousal, was confirmed in the current study. We addressed a shortcoming in that work by decomposing action from the other design factors. The effect of action on presence underlines the connection of affordances of VR [7]: The ability to move or manipulate objects can be seen as the interaction or embodiment, and it relates to physical presence. The increased mental effort found for the move condition calls for caution for VR design as VR introduces new opportunities for learning but may also increase extraneous cognitive load.

The interaction effects identified in our findings further highlight the nuanced roles played by all three design features in shaping learners' affective experiences. Particularly interesting is the visual contrast created by combining dark background lighting and high luminosity objects, which significantly enhanced positive affect when learners engaged actively with the environment. Although the interaction between lighting and object luminosity on presence did not reach statistical significance, the observed effect size ($\eta_p^2 = .060$) suggests a meaningful influence of such visual contrast on learners' sense of presence. Additionally, the interaction effects between learners' action and the two visual features suggest that active engagement may modulate or amplify the emotional impact of visual elements in VR. These insights emphasize the need to adopt a holistic, strategic design approach to leverage the interplay among multiple design features to enhance the effectiveness of VR learning environments.

6   Conclusion

This study has important theoretical and practical implications. On the theoretical side, we contributed to the EmoGBL model with findings that visual design in VR can be used to induce emotions and enhance learners' sense of presence. This study replicated previous findings on the effect of user action on affect, presence, and mental effort. On the practical side, we added background lighting and object luminosity to the range of visual design features available to VR game designers that can be used for emotional design.

As is the case with any empirical research, the present study has shortcomings that may limit the generalizability of the findings. First, we only investigated a small number of design factors, and only visual factors. The duration of the exposure to each stimulus was shorter than they would be in a learning environment. The completion of surveys after each stimulus may have felt repetitive and may have influenced learners' self-reports of emotions. We also did not counter-balance the *action* design factor to avoid confusion on the part of the participants, but a possible order effect may have influenced findings. Finally, in order to eliminate the effect of any other environmental factors, we studied the affective quality of the design elements outside of a learning environment, but a specific learning context may result in different effects.

Future research is planned to apply the findings from this study to a VR science learning game to investigate whether similar emotions are being induced in such a more complex setting, and if so, whether these emotions affect learning outcomes. Additional research should explore the affective quality of other VR design elements, including haptic and sound design features.

Disclosure of Interests.   The authors have no competing interests to declare that are relevant to the content of this article.

Appendix

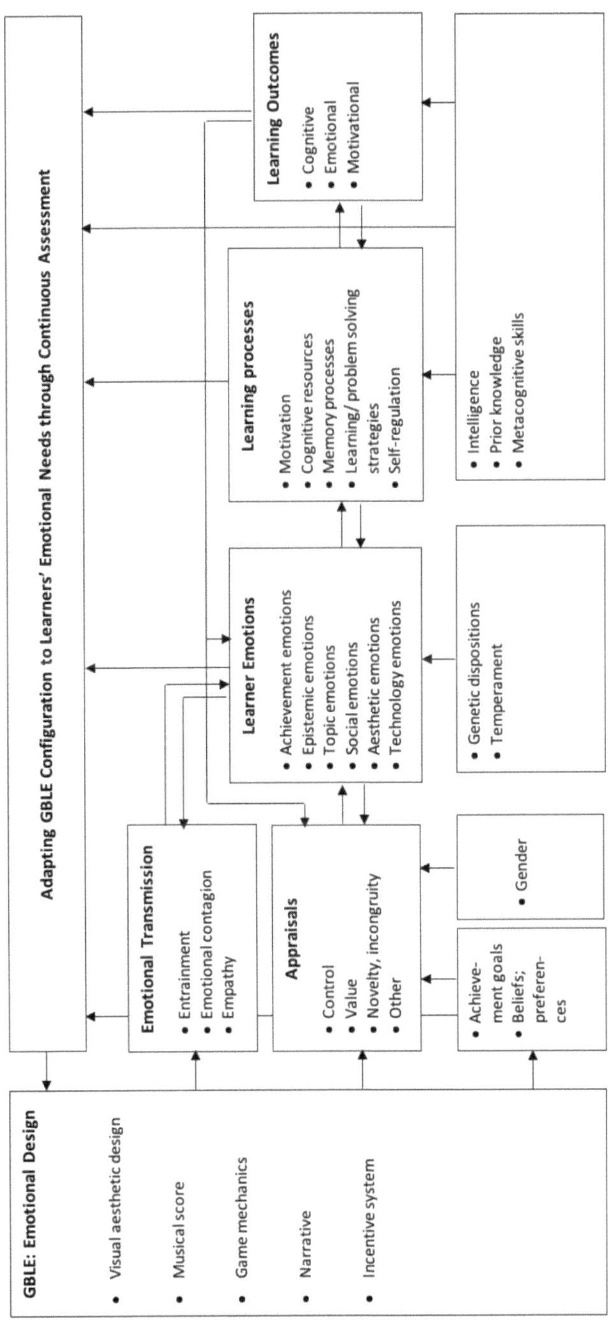

Fig. 5. Integrative Model of Emotional Foundations of Game-Based Learning

References

1. Plass, J.L., Mayer, R.E., Homer, B.D. (eds.): Handbook of Game-Based Learning. MIT Press, Cambridge (2020)
2. Pessoa, L.: On the relationship between emotion and cognition. Nat. Rev. Neurosci. **9**, 148–158 (2008). https://doi.org/10.1038/nrn2317
3. LeDoux, J.E., Brown, R.: A higher-order theory of emotional consciousness. Proc. Natl. Acad. Sci. **114**(10), E2016–E2025 (2017)
4. Plass, J.L., Hovey, C.: The emotional design principle in multimedia learning. In: Plass, J.L., Mayer, R.E., Homer, B.D. (eds.) Handbook of Game-Based Learning, pp. 111–152. MIT Press, Cambridge (2022)
5. Plass, J.L., Kaplan, U.: Emotional design in digital media for learning. In: Tettegah, S.Y., Gartmeier, M. (eds.) Emotions, Technology, Design, and Learning, pp. 131–161. Academic Press (2016). https://doi.org/10.1016/B978-0-12-801856-9.00007-4
6. Shao, Y., Hang, Y., Froehlich, F., Homer, B.D., Plass, J.L.: Exploring emotional design features for virtual reality games. In: Plass, J., Ochoa, X. (eds.) Proceedings of 2024 Joint Conference on Serious Games. LNCS, vol. 15259, pp. 298–312. Springer, Cham (2024)
7. Plass, J.L., Klingenberg, S.: Learning affordances of VR. In: Plass, J.L., Mayer, R.E., Makransky, G. (eds.) Handbook of Learning with Virtual Reality. MIT Press (2025)
8. Froehlich, F., Hovey, C., Reza, S., Plass, J.L.: Beyond slideshows–investigating the impact of immersive virtual reality on science learning. In: IEEE Conference on Virtual Reality and 3D User Interfaces (VR), Orlando, pp. 1–2. IEEE (2024)
9. Hovey, C., Pawar. S., Plass, J.L.: Exploring the emotional effect of immersive virtual reality versus 2D screen-based game characters. Paper presented at the Annual Meeting of the American Educational Research Association, New York (2018)
10. Froehlich, F., Plass, J.L.: Can't touch this? Why vibrotactile feedback in educational VR matters. In: IEEE Conference on Virtual Reality and 3D User Interfaces (VR), pp. 1–2. IEEE, Orlando (2024). https://doi.org/10.1109/VRW62533.2024.00174
11. Russell, J.A.: Core affect and the psychological construction of emotion. Psychol. Rev. **110**(1), 145–172 (2003). https://doi.org/10.1037/0033-295X.110.1.145
12. Loderer, K., Pekrun, R., Plass, J.: Emotional foundations of game-based learning. In: Plass, J.L., Mayer, R.E., Homer, B.D. (eds.) Handbook of Game-Based Learning, pp. 111–152. MIT Press, Cambridge (2020)
13. Um, E., Plass, J.L., Hayward, E.O., Homer, B.D.: Emotional design in multimedia learning. J. Educ. Psychol. **104**(2), 485–498 (2012). https://doi.org/10.1037/a0026609
14. Mayer, R.E., Estrella, G.: Benefits of emotional design in multimedia instruction. Learn. Instr. **33**, 12–18 (2014). https://doi.org/10.1016/j.learninstruc.2014.02.004
15. Homer, B.D., Plass, J.L., Rose, M.C., MacNamara, A.P., Pawar, S., Ober, T.M.: Activating adolescents' "hot" executive functions in a digital game to train cognitive skills: the effects of age and prior abilities. Cogn. Dev. **49**, 20–32 (2019). https://doi.org/10.1016/j.cogdev.2018.11.005
16. Javora, O., Hannemann, T., Stárková, T., Volná, K., Brom, C.: Children like it more but don't learn more: effects of esthetic visual design in educational games. Br. J. Edu. Technol. **50**(4), 1942–1960 (2019). https://doi.org/10.1111/bjet.12701
17. Chiu, T.K.F., Jong, M.S., Mok, I.A.C.: Does learner expertise matter when designing emotional multimedia for learners of primary school mathematics? Educ. Tech. Res. Dev. **68**(5), 2305–2320 (2020). https://doi.org/10.1007/s11423-020-09775-4
18. Wang, X., Mayer, R.E., Han, M., Zhang, L.: Two emotional design features are more effective than one in multimedia learning. J. Educ. Comput. Res. **60**(8), 1991–2014 (2023). https://doi.org/10.1177/07356331221090845

19. Plass, J.L., et al.: Emotional design for digital games for learning: the effect of expression, color, shape, and dimensionality on the affective quality of game characters. Learn. Instr. **70**, 101194 (2020). https://doi.org/10.1016/j.learninstruc.2019.01.005

20. Plass, J.L., Shao, Y.: Affective and motivational processes of learning in virtual reality. In: Plass, J.L., Mayer, R.E., Makransky, G. (eds.) Handbook of Learning with Virtual Reality. MIT Press (2025)

21. Plass, J.L., Homer, B.D., Kinzer, C.K.: Foundations of game-based learning. Educ. Psychol. **50**(4), 258–283 (2015)

22. Plass, J.L., et al.: Designing effective playful collaborative science learning in VR. In: Joint International Conference on Serious Games, pp. 30–35. Springer, Cham (2022)

23. Hovey, C., Jakubowicz, S.: Motion design for emotion design. In: International Conference on Games and Learning Alliance, pp. 337–342. Springer, Cham (2024)

24. Riva, G., et al.: Affective interactions using virtual reality: the link between presence and emotions. Cyberpsychol. Behav. **10**(1), 45–56 (2007). https://doi.org/10.1089/cpb.2006.9993

25. Bradley, M.M., Lang, P.J.: Measuring emotion: the self-assessment manikin and the semantic differential. J. Behav. Ther. Exp. Psychiatry **25**(1), 49–59 (1994)

26. Watson, D., Clark, L.A.: The PANAS-X: manual for the positive and negative affect schedule-expanded form (1994)

27. Igroup Presence Questionnaire (IPQ) Overview (2000). https://www.igroup.org/pq/ipq/index.php. Accessed 08 May 2024

28. Schubert, T.W., Friedmann, F., Regenbrecht, H.T.: Decomposing the sense of presence: factor analytic insights. In: 2nd International Workshop on Presence (1999)

29. Paas, F.G.: Training strategies for attaining transfer of problem-solving skill in statistics: a cognitive-load approach. J. Educ. Psychol. **84**(4), 429–434 (1992)

30. Tabachnick, B.G., Fidell, L.S.: Experimental designs using ANOVA (Vol. 724). Thomson/Brooks/Cole, Belmont (2007)

31. Richardson, J.T.E.: The use of Latin-square designs in educational and psychological research. Educ. Res. Rev. **24**, 84–97 (2018)

32. Batistatou, A., Vandeville, F., Delevoye-Turrell, Y.N.: Virtual reality to evaluate the impact of colorful interventions and nature elements on spontaneous walking, gaze, and emotion. Front. Virtual Reality **3**, 819597 (2022). https://doi.org/10.3389/frvir.2022.819597

33. Felnhofer, A., et al.: Is virtual reality emotionally arousing? Investigating five emotion inducing virtual park scenarios. Int. J. Hum. Comput. Stud. **82**, 48–56 (2015). https://doi.org/10.1016/j.ijhcs.2015.05.004

34. Hsieh, C.-H., Yang, J.-Y., Huang, C.-W., Chin, W.C.B.: The effect of water sound level in virtual reality: a study of restorative benefits in young adults through immersive natural environments. J. Environ. Psychol. **88**, 102012 (2023)

35. Västfjäll, D.: The subjective sense of presence, emotion recognition, and experienced emotions in auditory virtual environments. Cyberpsychol. Behav. **6**(2), 181–188 (2003). https://doi.org/10.1089/109493103321640374

36. Venkatesan, R.K., Banakou, D., Slater, M.: Haptic feedback in a virtual crowd scenario improves the emotional response. Front. Virtual Reality **4** (2023). https://doi.org/10.3389/frvir.2023.1242587

37. Kartiko, I., Kavakli, M., Cheng, K.: Learning science in a virtual reality application: the impacts of animated-virtual actors' visual complexity. Comput. Educ. **55**(2), 881–891 (2010). https://doi.org/10.1016/j.compedu.2010.03.019

From the Individual to the Group: Towards a Common VR Adaptive Framework for Therapy for People with Disabilities

Dan Tilinca, Ana Cernei, Ruth Fodor, Daniel Chioibas, Andrea Ciorba, Andrei Telechi, and Marc Frincu$^{(\boxtimes)}$

Faculty of Mathematics and Computer Science, West University of Timisoara, Timisoara, Romania
{dan.tilinca03,ana.cernei03,ruth.fodor03,daniel.chioibas00, andrea.ciorba04,andrei.telechi03,marc.frincu}@e-uvt.ro

Abstract. Virtual reality serious games have proven to be effective for therapeutic and educational purposes. Given the specific nature of some disabilities, user-centric design is required. However, this approach limits reusability and comparison. We introduce COMB2MAPE4VR, a framework that uses the Opportunity-Motivation Behavior framework on top of the Monitor Analyze Plan Execute feedback loop to design and implement serious games for virtual therapy on people with disabilities. We test the iterative prototyping approach and the generic monitoring and analysis components on various participants. Results show the potential of the framework to create custom environments and to extract relevant data for analysis and feedback.

Keywords: Virtual Reality · Disabilities · Adaptive Framework

1 Introduction

Around 1 in 6 people in the world ($\sim$1 billion people of which 240 million are children [11]) suffer from a disability [10]. Conventional approaches focusing on "active" treatment have proven effective in improving the quality of life of these people [5]. Furthermore, immersive Virtual Reality (VR) for therapeutic and educational purposes has gained traction [6]. VR exposure therapy effectively replicates real-world stimuli within controlled environments, facilitating gradual learning and desensitization. The challenge in many cases is the highly specific therapy required by a patient, which limits the effectiveness of generic VR applications. For instance, children diagnosed with Autism Spectrum Disorder (ASD) may have different phobias that require personalized virtual therapy. The Opportunity-Motivation Behavior (COM-B) framework [7] helps to explain and pinpoint barriers and facilitators of patient behavior, leading to a user-centric and customized approach. However, isolated custom design lacks reusability, leading to poor productivity when building VR applications. Two **key challenges** stem from this approach: (1) behavior should constantly change after

A. Thomas et al. (Eds.): JCSG 2025, LNCS 16243, pp. 398–405, 2026.
https://doi.org/10.1007/978-3-032-10518-9_34

successful therapy sessions; and (2) individual solutions limit reusability and comparison. The Monitor Analyze Plan Execute (MAPE) feedback loop [4] used by adaptive software systems provides a suitable solution to designing VR applications by allowing constant adaptations to observed patient behavior to virtual stimuli. It also offers a common design framework for sharing common tools for monitoring, analyzing and planning on top of the customized application. Thus, mixed teams of clinicians and developers can streamline the development process through reusable components on top of a shared framework and create consistent and comparable results in developed applications [9] [2].

We *leverage MAPE and COM-B to design a common development framework named COMB2MAPE4VR that targets customized therapy in people with disabilities.* We start from a user needs analysis through incremental prototyping on three case studies and proceed by demonstrating generic monitoring and analysis components for a wide range of real-life serious games designed to complement therapy while providing participants with fun reward based activities.

2 Related Work

Studies have shown that VR can be beneficial for therapeutic purposes. Research in VR for children with disabilities covers a wide range of applications, e.g., motor rehabilitation, cognitive training, and sensory integration [14]. However, most solutions are designed for specific conditions, lacking a generic framework integrating real-time progress tracking and adaptive learning strategies [8] [6].

The tailoring of VR experiences to address specific sensory challenges in individual cases is less understood. Developing such applications faces methodological and technological challenges [3]. In [1], a data-driven investigation of physiological responses is conducted during VR interventions for ASD, highlighting the need for personalized approaches. In addition, [13] introduces a customized VR system designed to improve gaze fixation ability in children with ASD.

An analysis of state-of-the-art shows that while VR offers promising therapeutic benefits for children with disabilities, there is a need for methodologies that adapt VR experiences to the unique sensory and cognitive profiles of individual users. Existing studies often lack personalized interventions, highlighting the importance of developing flexible and adaptive VR frameworks.

3 Proposed Framework

Behavior in COM-B is determined by a mix of *capabilities* (e.g., skills, knowledge and physical ability), *motivation* (e.g., internal forces driving an individual) and *opportunities* (e.g., external factors such as social and physical environment). Therapy is driven by the gap between observed and desired behavior. In VR, the starting point is determined by *iterative prototyping* and a scenario that triggers a virtual behavior similar to real-life. VR applications can target specific therapy objectives and by *monitoring* and *analyzing* patient interaction (i.e., capability) with scene elements (e.g., static or animated) within a MAPE feedback loop, virtual stimuli can be adapted (i.e., *planned* and *executed*), impacting a patient's motivation and opportunity (cf. Figure 1).

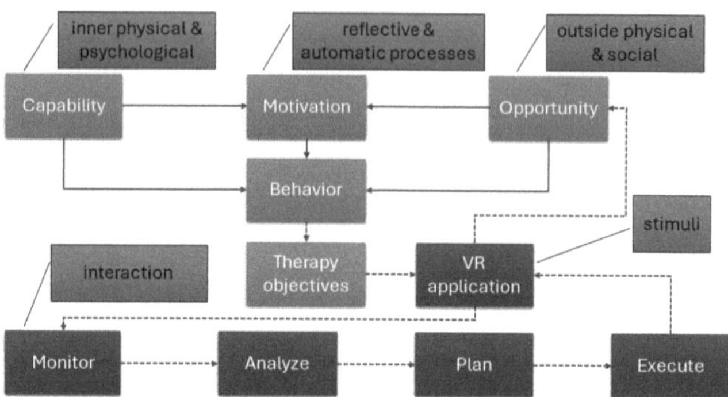

Fig. 1. COMB2MAPE4VR architecture.

4   Testing and Validation

4.1   Methodology

Objectives. Both usability of the VR equipment and efficacy of the virtual scenes are targeted. These are measured through visual and automatic monitoring of the interactions with the virtual environment and assessing progress.

Ethics. This study was granted ethical approval from the Ethics Committee of the West University of Timisoara Romania (78922/23.10.2024). Functional atypical children were selected from a center for children with disabilities, while typical children were randomly selected from a school. Parents/legal guardians signed consent forms.

Participants. A total of 10 typical (age 7–12) and 15 atypical (age 8–17) children participated in the study. Each participant was accompanied throughout the individual experiments by their legal guardian/parent/therapist.

Tools. Each VR application was designed in *Unity* and tested using *Oculus Meta Quest 2* headsets. Monitoring and analyzing behavior required new components for data gathering and analysis, as well as in-person observations.

Data. The primary data source consists of user-interaction generated logs. The collected *data* was stored in JSON format and includes various behavioral metrics, e.g., player position, hand and head orientations, gaze direction, scene interactions, time spent inside the application. It can be shared across applications for cross-analysis and can be fed into the behavioral analysis component to build new or augment existing regression and classification models for understanding behavior and for scene adaptation [12].

VR Development Approach. To enable therapeutic use, virtual environments recreate conditions similar to real-life situations, prompting realistic responses from the participant. By introducing virtual adaptive stimuli (i.e., the opportunity in COM-B) in a controlled and repeatable way, the observed behavior can be changed until it meets the therapeutic objective. Progress can then be assessed through a MAPE feedback loop. Two **key challenges** arise.

1. To *create a virtual serious game that triggers a participant's behavior needing adjustment*. This is done through an *iterative prototyping* where different VR application versions are designed, each trying to elicit a reaction similar to that observed in real-life. Due to constraints, three out of four case studies are presented next. For each case study a different participant was selected. **Combating cynophobia** (fear of dogs) on a participant with ASD: a scenario that gradually introduces a dog and audio stimuli to trigger the phobia and monitors reactions (cf. Figure 2a). The objective was to reach a state where the participant is comfortable with virtual dogs. **Improving upper limb motor functions**: a scenario with stimuli derived from a participant's (with severe psychomotor developmental delay) hobbies and toys that requires increasingly complex hand gestures to perform various tasks using a reward mechanism (cf. Figure 2b). The objective was to perform basic handling operations with one or both hands. **Improving social interactions** on a participant with Asperger and social anxiety disorder: a scenario involving a football game with different levels of interaction with virtual players and audience (cf. Figure 2c). The objective was to make the participant comfortable in large crowds. Each scenario had a different number of prototypes depending on the observations and objectives.

2. To *test the generic framework's MAPE capability on a wide range of serious games targeting several disabilities*. Six scenarios were developed (see Fig. 2d for an example). **Forest**: introductory scene added after initial feedback that lets users familiarize themselves with using a headset and explore a virtual environment. Users can pick objects and move freely without time constraints. **Gardening**: lets users plant seeds, grow flowers, and arrange them into bouquets by following given patterns while tracking completion time and accuracy. **Color Sorting**: involves sorting objects by color into designated bins, enhancing visual discrimination and classification skills, with the system recording sorting errors and efficiency. **Shapes Sorting**: encourages users to match geometric shapes to their corresponding slots while also considering color, improving spatial awareness and fine motor control, with real-time error tracking. **Shopping List**: simulates a shopping experience where users must follow a list and collect the correct number of items, fostering attention to detail and quantity recognition, while monitoring adherence to the given shopping list. **Ice Cream Maker**: challenges users to prepare ice cream orders by following given instructions, reinforcing sequencing and memory skills, with the system tracking accuracy and processing time. All participants were exposed to the six scenarios.

4.2   Results

1. Iterative Prototyping focusing on adapting the opportunity component in COMB-B through virtual stimuli in the MAPE enabled scenarios. Table 1 provides an overview of the different versions of each scenario with key observations. **Combating cynophobia** was developed in four successive prototypes using a participant with ASD. Observations and parent feedback were used to improve the environment. The participant demonstrated clear progress throughout the

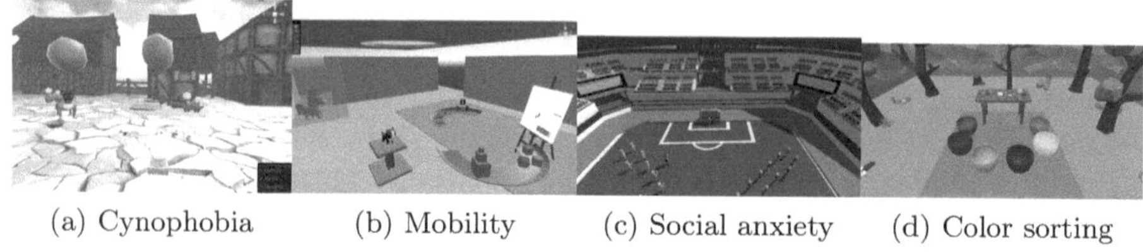

(a) Cynophobia   (b) Mobility   (c) Social anxiety   (d) Color sorting

Fig. 2. Scene examples from the developed serious games.

sessions despite temporary setback that were handled through verbal encouragments and virtual rewards. **Improving upper limb motor functions** was developed in three successive prototypes based on observations on a participant with severe psychomotor developmental delay. From a motor standpoint, difficulties with grasping and especially intentional release were evident. Initially, the participant could not fully open their hand, exhibited shaking and dropped objects. This issue persisted in version 2 but without the shaking behavior. In version 3, the patient showed effort and perseverance, successfully manipulating an object with both hands and performing the stretch gesture, even though controlled release remained a challenge. Familiar tasks were approached and solved faster in later sessions. **Improving social interactions** was developed in five successive prototypes. The participant had Asperger syndrome and social anxiety disorder and showed a mix of progress and regress by the participant. Before introducing it to the first scenario the participant had to accommodate with virtual soccer field. He demonstrated a preference for using teleport instead of continuous movement, looked downwards frequently and exhibited frequent inactivity periods. As a baseline this serious game was tested on typical participants showing a predisposition for continuous movement, less inactivity periods and downward looking. Monitoring was achieved with the MAPE component discussed in the following section.

These examples show that results can be incrementantly improved throught observations but reiterate that progress in some cases is non-linear and increased complexity can lead to setbacks.

2. MAPE Feedback Loop for behavior (COM-B) monitoring and analysis was tested on six scenarios on metrics such as average time spent in the application, number of mistakes per application, interactions per minute and success rate. These were measured by monitoring events such as picking objects and gaze. Data can be visually analyzed or sent to the analysis component for AI analysis. Currently, the component is capable of differentiating between typical and atypical persons and also identify disabilities based on movement. For example, in our experiments, typical people exhibit higher success rates (avg. $>95\%$ vs. 70–88%) for completing the games, have a lower number of mistakes (avg. < 1 vs. ≥ 2) and spend less time in the games (avg. 130 vs. >150 sec). These differences further empahsize the the need for personalized serious games depending on the patient. The analysis component takes monitoring data and provides AI-driven statistics such as determining whether or not a participant suffers from a mental

Table 1. Summary and observations for the iterative prototyping approach.

Scenario	Version 1	Version 2	Version 3	Version 4	Version 5
Combating cynophobia	Basic dog animations (idle, walking, eating, sitting) ⇒ no negative reaction. Participant named the dog Alf	Sounds added (barking) ⇒ *increased anxiety / headset removal*	Reward mechanism (via button after 3 pushes) ⇒ *increased relaxation*	Physical interactions (brushing and ball fetching) ⇒ *after 2 sessions: increased interaction and acceptance*	–
Improving upper limb motor functions	Simple task: virtual unicorn after pressing a button ⇒ *achieved easily*	Complex tasks: puzzle triggers cat appearance; brush the cat to make it purr; draw a triangle following contour on whiteboard ⇒ *all completed except for the drawing task*	Bilateral task: resize cubes and form a pyramid ⇒ *successful after several attempts*	–	–
Improving social interactions	Goal kick (no goalkeeper) ⇒ *fast reaction time*	Added home team ⇒ *fewer inactivity periods, many scores, faces downward less times*	Added goalkeeper ⇒ *fewer scores, faces downward increasingly*	Added coach ⇒ *increased scores and faced upward more times*	Added opposing team ⇒ *fewer scores and faces downward increasingly, increasingly freeze episodes*

disability [12]. Insights can be used directly in the VR application for real-time feedback-driven adaptations (MAPE loop) by changing difficulty, complexity or interaction mode.

5   Conclusion

In this paper, an integrated COMB2MAPE4VR framework was introduced and demonstrated through a series of prototypes and applications equipped with components for behavioral monitoring and analysis that can provide feedback and scene adaptation. The prototyping approach was used to determine the starting point for virtual therapy in specific cases. Results showcase the potential of the approach. Future steps include adding haptic devices in applications dealing with various phobias and further experiments on other participants with similar disabilities as well as adding control participants in all iterative prototyping scenarios.

Acknowledgments. The work of the last author is supported by the project "Romanian Hub for Artificial Intelligence - HRIA", Smart Growth, Digitization and Financial Instruments Program, 2021-2027, MySMIS no. 334906.

Disclosure of Interests. The authors have no competing interests to declare that are relevant to the content of this article.

References

1. Alvari, G., et al.: Exploring physiological responses in virtual reality-based interventions for autism spectrum disorder: a data-driven investigation. arXiv preprint arXiv:2404.07159 (2024). https://arxiv.org/abs/2404.07159
2. Baker, C., Fairclough, S.H.: Chapter 9 - adaptive virtual reality. In: Fairclough, S.H., Zander, T.O. (eds.) Current Research in Neuroadaptive Technology, pp. 159–176. Academic Press (2022). https://doi.org/10.1016/B978-0-12-821413-8.00014-2
3. Barletta, V., Caruso, F., Di Mascio, T., Piccinno, A.: Serious games for autism based on immersive virtual reality: a lens on methodological and technological challenges, pp. 181–195 (2022). https://doi.org/10.1007/978-3-031-20617-7_23
4. Kephart, J., Chess, D.: The vision of autonomic computing. Computer **36**(1), 41–50 (2003). https://doi.org/10.1109/MC.2003.1160055
5. Matson, J.L., Friedt, L.R.: Severe and Profound Mental Retardation, pp. 113–127. Springer US, Boston, MA (1988). https://doi.org/10.1007/978-1-4613-0993-2_10
6. Mesa-Gresa, P., Gil-Gómez, H., Lozano-Quilis, J.A., Gil-Gómez, J.A.: Effectiveness of virtual reality for children and adolescents with autism spectrum disorder: An evidence-based systematic review. Sensors **18**(8) (2018). https://doi.org/10.3390/s18082486
7. Michie, S., van Stralen, M., West, R.: The behaviour change wheel: a new method for characterising and designing behaviour change interventions. Implementation **6**(42) (2011)
8. Mittal, P., et al.: Effect of immersive virtual reality-based training on cognitive, social, and emotional skills in children and adolescents with autism spectrum disorder: A meta-analysis of randomized controlled trials. Res. Dev. Disabil. **151**, 104771 (2024)
9. Pistono, A.M.A.d.A., dos Santos, A.M.P., Baptista, R.J.V., Mamede, H.S.: Framework for adaptive serious games. Comput. Appl. Eng. Educ. **32**(4), e22731 (2024). https://doi.org/10.1002/cae.22731
10. UN: Factsheet on persons with disabilities (2025). https://www.un.org/development/desa/disabilities/resources/factsheet-on-persons-with-disabilities.html
11. Unicef: Nearly 240 million children with disabilities around the world, unicef's most comprehensive statistical analysis finds (2021). https://www.unicef.org/press-releases/nearly-240-million-children-disabilities-around-world-unicefs-most-comprehensive
12. Vlasiu, A.R., Frincu, M.E., Daniel, C., Mocan, D., Gabor, M.: Classifying mental disabilities from virtual reality behavioral data using machine learning. In: 2024 E-Health and Bioengineering Conference (EHB). pp. 1–4 (2024). https://doi.org/10.1109/EHB64556.2024.10805654

13. Yu, C., et al.: Hsvrs: A virtual reality system of the hide-and-seek game to enhance gaze fixation ability for autistic children. arXiv preprint arXiv:2310.13482 (2023). https://arxiv.org/abs/2310.13482
14. Zhao, J.Q., Zhang, X.X., Wang, C.H., Yang, J.: Effect of cognitive training based on virtual reality on the children with autism spectrum disorder. Current Res. Behav. Sci. **2**, 100013 (2021)

Virtual Reality as a Tool for Raising Awareness of Visual Impairments

Ioana-Simina Giurginca[1], Marc Frincu[2]([✉]), and Nastasia Salagean[1]

[1] Institute for Advanced Environmental Research,
street Oituz Nr. 4, Timisoara, Romania
`{ioana.frincu,nastasia.salagean}@e-uvt.ro`
[2] Faculty of Mathematics and Computer Science, West University of Timisoara,
Timisoara, Romania
`marc.frincu@e-uvt.ro`

Abstract. Virtual reality has emerged as an effective tool for educational and research purposes. It provides an efficient means of replicating behaviors that cannot be easily reproduced for people to experience. In this paper, we focus on visual impairments and implement and test a virtual application as an effective tool for increasing awareness of non-visible disabilities. We evaluated the results on 52 participants split in control and experimental groups. Results show differences between the answers that suggest positive effects on virtual environments.

Keywords: Visual impairments · Virtual reality · Awareness

1 Introduction

According to the World Health Organization, about 2.1 billion people suffer from vision impairment [19]. Of these, about 1 billion cases could have been prevented or have yet to receive treatment. Most are nonvisible, leading to unique social challenges, including misunderstandings, discrimination, and difficulty accessing the necessary support and accommodations. These challenges stem from the fact that others may not readily recognize or understand the limitations and challenges faced by people with invisible disabilities.

By immersing people in simulated experiences, Virtual Reality (VR) enhances understanding and challenges preconceived notions about often overlooked disabilities, breaking down barriers, and encouraging greater social acceptance [21]. More inclusive communities where people feel valued and understood are key to general well-being, higher productivity, implementation of supportive measures at work and educational settings, early diagnosis detection, better management of medical conditions and appropriate, timely health care.

On a **social** level, VR technology has emerged as a transformative tool to shape perceptions of invisible disabilities, conditions that are not immediately apparent but can significantly affect daily life. Empathy, an essential component of an inclusive society, has become a central VR research [5]. VR can place users

A. Thomas et al. (Eds.): JCSG 2025, LNCS 16243, pp. 406–413, 2026.
https://doi.org/10.1007/978-3-032-10518-9_35

in the shoes of people with conditions that are not visible externally by allowing people "to become" people with hidden medical conditions [21]. Cognitive empathy, often equated with perspective-taking, has roots in foundational social psychology theories [6,14]. Perspective taking - the ability to understand the point of view of another - is key to prosocial behavior and effective communication [12]. Like empathy, it includes two dimensions: cognitive, involving inference of others' thoughts and beliefs, and affective, involving inference of others' emotions. Previous studies have linked cognitive empathy to prosocial behaviour [2] and attitudes toward disability [16], and both cognitive and affective empathy to positive peer relationships [9], Evoking, building or boosting cognitive and affective empathetic responsiveness for hidden disabilities is crucial for modeling micro and macro communities into inclusive social environments prepared to foster emotional connection to those with non-apparent health conditions and manifest sensitivity, compassion and acceptance toward non-visible impairments.

The **educational** benefits of VR for visual impairments may consequently comprise empathy enhancement and a greater willingness to assist visually impaired individuals in real-world situations [7]. The emergence of VR technologies has undeniably compensated for the limitations of conventional methods in delivering both more impactful learning for general audiences as well as better-tailored educational support for students with special needs and disabilities. VR-based perspective-taking experiences are more effective at fostering long-term empathy than traditional media such as reading or watching videos [13].

Here, we introduce participants to medical and drug-induced visual impairments in various settings through the *SeeThroughMyEyes* VR application. The virtual space with close-to-reality sensations to be experienced by the users is conceived as a perceived learning tool to inform the public on the existence of invisible visual disabilities and their symptoms. Our objectives are: (1) to elicit tolerance and empathy/to improve attitudes toward individuals suffering from various types of vision loss, and implicitly to contribute to creating a more supportive and inclusive environment for everyone; (2) to demonstrate the increased awareness through statistical tests on control and experimental groups.

2   Related Work

Visual impairments reflect directly on the individuals' ability to perceive their surroundings, their spatial navigation and completion of everyday tasks. The importance of direct experience of low-vision navigation in simulated environments increased understanding of the challenges of people with visual impairments and served as an empathy booster [21]. Embodied experiences led on blind-folded sighted participants navigating tasks under simulated visual constraints have proved successful in evoking empathy and sympathy and raising awareness about visual impairments [10].

In medical research, a study found that participants who experienced a VR simulation of a person with Multiple Sclerosis exhibited improved recall of related information and a more positive implicit association toward people with disabilities [3,4]. Also, VR simulations that mimic real-life scenarios stimulate engagement in physical training and can help reduce anxiety and depression, alleviate pain and improve mood. By addressing the complex range of challenging aspects related to medical conditions, VR technology unlocks revolutionary holistic approaches while offering the possibility of self-guided exploration and independent practice, coupled with real-time performance feedback [18].

In preventive medicine, VR simulations can effectively raise awareness about the dangers of drug and alcohol addictions, thereby serving as a preemptive strategy. By immersing individuals in virtual and safe environments that replicate real-life scenarios, VR enables users to experience the challenges, dangers and consequences associated with substance use or alcohol consumption. More complex VR simulations (e.g., VirtualLimitLab, VRFestLab) allow practice and development of refusal skills in social settings [1,11,15], thereby enhancing life skills such as assertiveness and conflict resolution. This innovative approach not only educates but also empowers individuals to make informed decisions, nurturing their confidence to handle real-life situations. The endurance of VR-induced attitude shifts beyond the immediate aftermath requires systematic tracking through longitudinal studies to offer meaningful insights into the long-term duration of the priming effect. This depends on a combination of technological, individual, and contextual factors. The durability of VR-driven behavior and attitude change hinges on delivering a technologically robust, user-friendly, and emotionally engaging experience—within a supportive social/environmental framework—and tailored to individual readiness, needs, and comfort levels.

The closest study to our own is the work in [21]. In their study, the authors address 18 different visual conditions on 60 participants using pre- and post-questionnaires. Participants were seated and had to select identical objects placed randomly in 3D space around them when experiencing one of the visual conditions. The virtual scene consisted of a forest clearing dominated by greenery and a blue sky, inducing feelings of calmness and relaxation.

Our study provided 52 participants (split evenly in control and experimental groups) with four scenes and ten visual impairments, including one for drug-induced vision. They could walk freely around the scenes and change the experienced impairment and the scenes using hand gestures. Finally, our approach is intended as a learning tool for people to experience the world through the eyes of people with visual impairment.

3   Methodology

Ethics. This study was granted ethical approval from the West University of Timisoara Romania Ethics Committee (74865/14.10.2024). All participants signed consent forms.

Participants. A total of 52 voluntary participants (age 15 to 59, with an average of 27.7 and a median of 22) experienced various visual effects (see below). 21 were male and 31 were female. No time limit was imposed. Half of the participants

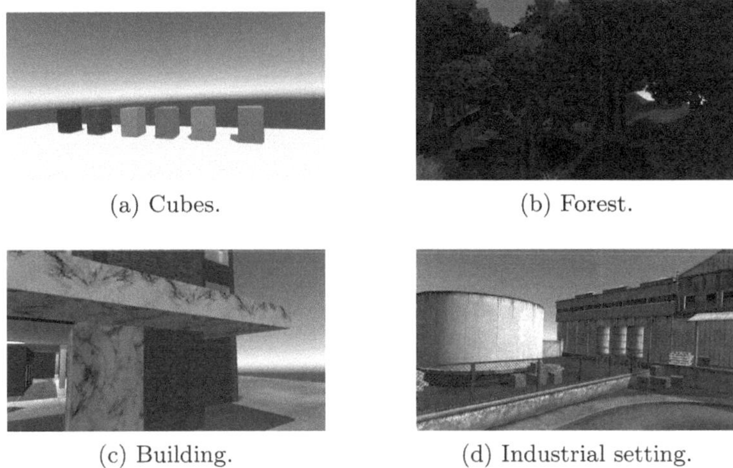

(a) Cubes.   (b) Forest.

(c) Building.   (d) Industrial setting.

Fig. 1. Virtual scenes.

were randomly included in the control group. No significant differences between the two groups were found in terms of gender (X^2 (1) $= 0.08$, $p = .77$)), but age was significantly lower in the experimental group ($t(50) = 2.45$, $p = .01$).

Due to possible interference by respondent fatigue [20], participants were only shown post-intervention measurements. Respondents in the control group filled the questionnaires before experimenting the virtual environments, while participants in the experimental group responded to the questionnaires after the intervention.

Data. Primary data was gathered during the 2024 World Sight Day on the university's premises. Participants were volunteers (students, staff, visitors) willing to try out and experience virtual visual disabilities. Questionnaires were provided in the form of 6 closed-ended questions related to demographics (gender and age), current emotional state, visual impairments and mental disorders.

Chi-square tests (X^2) were used to compare the main results between the two groups, while student t-tests were used to determine age differences.

VR Application. Four virtual scenes using free assets were implemented using Unity and deployed on an Oculus Meta 2 headset. They consisted of a floor with six cubes of various colors, a green forest, and a building (cf. Fig. 1).

A total of 10 visual impairments were implemented using shaders and post-processing. Nine covered static visual disabilities and one covered a dynamic drug-induced visual effect. Figure 2 shows the effects implemented: achromatopsia, deuteranomaly, blurred vision, sensory perception in autism, cataract, diabetic retinopathy, glaucoma, macular degeneration, protanopia, LSD addiction. Participants were allowed to navigate the scenes freely.

Effects could be changed using a left-hand thumbs-up gesture while scenes using the right hand. Once a new effect was applied participants could read a short text describing it. To enrich the experience and provide a realistic scenario,

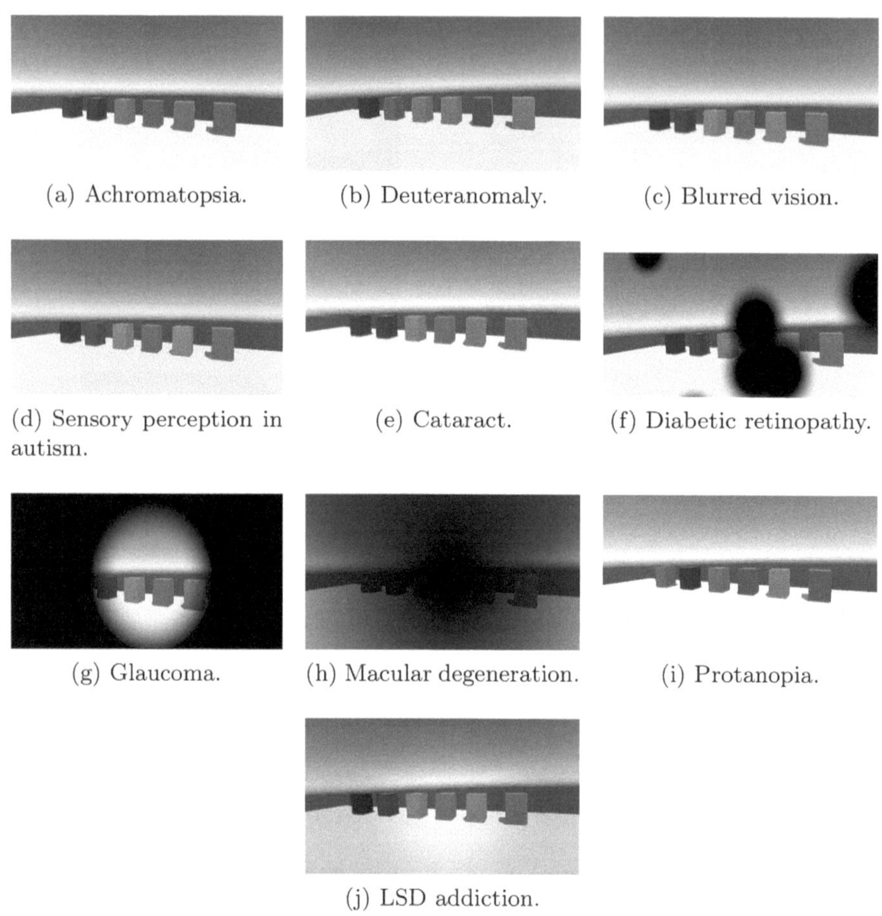

(a) Achromatopsia.   (b) Deuteranomaly.   (c) Blurred vision.

(d) Sensory perception in   (e) Cataract.   (f) Diabetic retinopathy.
autism.

(g) Glaucoma.   (h) Macular degeneration.   (i) Protanopia.

(j) LSD addiction.

Fig. 2. Visual effects list.

the text was placed in the center of the participant's view, which caused its obfuscation by certain virtual visual impairments (e.g., diabetic retinopathy, glaucoma, macular degeneration, and LSD addiction).

4   Results

Results show significant differences between the two groups, with more respondents in the experimental group indicating that they heard of achromatopsia $(X^2(1) = 6.47, p = .01)$, deuteranomaly $(X^2(1) = 6.26, p = .01)$, diabetic retinopathy $(X^2(1) = 6.32, p = .01)$, and protanopy $(X^2(1) = 7.59, p = .006)$ than participants in the control group. No significant results were seen in terms of blurred vision, $(p = .38)$, cataract $(p = .38)$, glaucoma $(p = .58)$, macular degeneration $(p = .09)$, autism $(p = .77)$, LSD addiction $(p = .07)$, alcoholism $(p$

$= .24$), or psychosis ($p = .75$). However, with the exception of alcoholism $X^2(1)$ $= 4.28$, $p = .04$) and psychosis ($X^2(1) = 4.06$, $p = .04$), where participants in the experimental group showed more awareness, no significant differences were seen in terms of awareness of how the impairments manifest themselves.

Finally, none of the participants had any issues of having a person with visual impairments as neighbour regardless of experimental condition, with people with ASD ranking second in terms of inclusion. Drug addicts were most likely to be rejected as neighbour, followed by alcoholists, both regadless of experimental condition.

5   Conclusion

In this paper we have introduced the *SeeThroughMyEyes* VR application, consisting of 4 scenes and 10 visual impairments, including one caused by drug abuse. It enables users to experience the world through the eyes of people with eyesight. We assessed its impact on awareness by comparing participants' responses to questionnaires either after being exposed to the scenes or without exposure. Results show significant improvements in terms of general awareness for some, but not all conditions, after experiencing the visual impairments. Some conditions (such as glaucoma and cataract) have received more widespread media attention than others (protanopy, deuteranomaly, etc.), which would explain why we didn't see significant differnces between the two groups. This attention also includes events such as Eye Health Observances events promoted by the American Academy of Ophthalmology - for which January is considered Glaucoma Awareness month, February is designated Age-Related Macular Degeneration Awareness Month and November is considered Diabetic Eye Disease Awareness Month [17]. Additionally, because the order of the scenes was not randomized, some of the results may be affected by the order effect [8].

In terms of how the conditions manifest themselves, with the exception of alcoholism and psychosis, no differences were seen between the two groups. These results may also be explained by confusion about what was being assessed due to the phrasing of the question.

Future work will include a comprehensive analysis targeting specific focus groups. While VR technology holds significant potential to create synthetic experiences that feel real, measuring its impact on empathy development and the longevity of resulting changes in social attitudes and behavior remains a complex challenge and an open question for researchers.

Acknowledgments. The work of the second author is partially supported by the project "Romanian Hub for Artificial Intelligence - HRIA", Smart Growth, Digitization and Financial Instruments Program, 2021-2027, MySMIS no. 334906. The scenes and effects were implemented by a team of undergrad students: David Dobondi, Raul Marinescu, Razvan Moldovan, Robert Gasitu and Ioan Cioarsa. The application was tested with the help of volunteer undergrad students Nandhni Singh and Cezara Morozovschii.

Disclosure of Interests. The authors have no competing interests to declare that are relevant to the content of this article.

References

1. 8:00 am virtual reality world offers drug addicts low-risk place to just say 'no' (2018)
2. Brazil, K.J., Volk, A.A., Dane, A.V.: Is empathy linked to prosocial and antisocial traits and behavior? it depends on the form of empathy. Can. J. Behav. Sci. **55**(1), 75 (2023)
3. Chowdhury, T.I., Quarles, J.: A wheelchair locomotion interface in a VR disability simulation reduces implicit bias. IEEE Trans. Visual. Comput. Graphics 1–1 (2021). https://doi.org/10.1109/TVCG.2021.3099115
4. Chowdhury, T.I., Shahnewaz Ferdous, S.M., Quarles, J.: VR disability simulation reduces implicit bias towards persons with disabilities. IEEE Trans. Visual. Comput. Graphics 1–1 (2019).https://doi.org/10.1109/TVCG.2019.2958332
5. Cohen, D., Landau, D.H., Friedman, D., Hasler, B.S., Levit-Binnun, N., Golland, Y.: Exposure to social suffering in virtual reality boosts compassion and facial synchrony. Comput. Hum. Behav. **122**, 106781 (2021). https://doi.org/10.1016/j.chb.2021.106781
6. Davis, M.H.: Measuring individual differences in empathy: Evidence for a multidimensional approach. J. Pers. Soc. Psychol. **44**(1), 113–126 (1983). https://doi.org/10.1037/0022-3514.44.1.113
7. Dong, Y., Guo, H., Li, J.: Enhancing empathy for visual impairments: a multimodal approach in VR serious games. IEEE Trans. Visual Comput. Graphics **31**(5), 2954–2963 (2025). https://doi.org/10.1109/TVCG.2025.3549900
8. Eisenberg, M., Barry, C.: Order effects: a study of the possible influence of presentation order on user judgments of document relevance. J. Am. Soc. Inf. Sci. **39**(5), 293–300 (1988)
9. Fink, E., de Rosnay, M.: Examining links between affective empathy, cognitive empathy, and peer relationships at the transition to school. Soc. Dev. **32**(4), 1208–1226 (2023)
10. Guarese, R., Pretty, E., Fayek, H., Zambetta, F., van Schyndel, R.: Evoking empathy with visually impaired people through an augmented reality embodiment experience. In: 2023 IEEE Conference Virtual Reality and 3D User Interfaces (VR), pp. 184–193 (2023). https://doi.org/10.1109/VR55154.2023.00034
11. Guldager, J.D., Kjær, S.L., Grittner, U., Stock, C.: Efficacy of the virtual reality intervention VR festlab on alcohol refusal self-efficacy: a cluster-randomized controlled trial. Int. J. Environ. Res. Public Health **19**(6) (2022). https://doi.org/10.3390/ijerph19063293
12. Healey, M.L., Grossman, M.: Cognitive and affective perspective-taking: evidence for shared and dissociable anatomical substrates. Front. Neurol. **9** (2018). https://doi.org/10.3389/fneur.2018.00491. https://www.frontiersin.org/journals/neurology/articles/10.3389/fneur.2018.00491
13. Herrera, F., Bailenson, J., Weisz, E., Ogle, E., Zaki, J.: Building long-term empathy: a large-scale comparison of traditional and virtual reality perspective-taking. PLOS ONE **13**(10), 1–37 (2018).https://doi.org/10.1371/journal.pone.0204494
14. Hogan, R.: Development of an empathy scale. J. Consult. Clin. Psychol. **33**(3), 307–316 (1969). https://doi.org/10.1037/h0027580
15. Hrynyschyn, R., et al.: Virtual reality-based alcohol prevention: the results of a cross-sectional study with visitors of an art exhibition. Adolescents **4**, 469–483 (2024). https://doi.org/10.3390/adolescents4040033

16. Maftei, A.: Children's self-esteem and attitudes toward disability, perceived competence and morality: The indirect effect of cognitive empathy. Children **9**(11) (2022). https://doi.org/10.3390/children9111705
17. of Ophthalmology, A.A.: Eye health observances (2025). https://www.aao.org/newsroom/observances
18. Rizzo, A.S., Kim, G.J.: A SWOT analysis of the field of virtual reality rehabilitation and therapy. Presence **14**(2), 119–146 (2005). https://doi.org/10.1162/1054746053967094
19. WHO: Blindness and vision impairment (2023). https://www.who.int/news-room/fact-sheets/detail/blindness-and-visual-impairment
20. Yun, H.S., Arjmand, M., Sherlock, P., Paasche-Orlow, M.K., Griffith, J.W., Bickmore, T.: Keeping users engaged during repeated interviews by a virtual agent: using large language models to reliably diversify questions. In: Proceedings of the ACM International Conference on Intelligent Virtual Agents, pp. 1–10. IVA 2024, ACM (2024). https://doi.org/10.1145/3652988.3673929
21. Zwolinski, G., Kamińska, D., Pinto-Coelho, L., Haamer, R., Raposo, R., Vairinhos, M.: Visual impairments simulation in virtual reality as an empathy booster (2024). https://doi.org/10.21203/rs.3.rs-5349613/v1

Author Index